UNDERSTANDING SEXUAL INTERACTION

UNDERSTANDING SEXUAL INTERACTION

Second Edition

Joann S. DeLora

San Diego State University

Carol A. B. Warren

University of Southern California

Carol Rinkleib Ellison

University of California, San Francisco

With contributions by Douglas Kirby

Houghton Mifflin Company   **Boston**

Dallas   Geneva, Illinois   Hopewell, New Jersey   Palo Alto   London

Illustrations for the cover and for the part and chapter opening pages by Dorothea Sierra.

Position drawings by Jan Palmer.

Anatomical drawings by Jennifer Giancarlo.

Printed in the U.S.A.
Library of Congress Catalogue Card Number: 80–82895
ISBN: 0–395–29724–9

Contents

xi

Chapter Eighteen / *Current Trends and Alternative Futures* 541

Appendix / *Methods and Methodological Problems of Sex Research* 563

Preface

The central aim of this book is to provide an overview of the current scientific knowledge concerning human sexuality. It is designed for use in any human sexuality course, regardless of the specific discipline within which the course is taught.

The study of human sexuality is necessarily interdisciplinary. In order to fully understand sexual interaction, information must be brought together from a wide variety of disciplines and specialities. This text surveys research findings from all the various specialties touching upon sexuality, and integrates these findings within three broad perspectives: the social, the psychological, and the physiological-medical.

Understanding Sexual Interaction is specifically designed for students enrolled in undergraduate courses concerned with human sexuality. However, it also should be an invaluable aid to anyone in a helping profession who needs to understand the sexual functioning of other persons. The book will also have an appeal to any person who wishes to better understand her or his own sexual nature, as well as the sexuality of friends, lovers, and family members. There are no prerequisites for reading and understanding this book. Its language is deliberately lacking in jargon and technical terms, and any words that are potentially unfamiliar to a high school graduate are explained in the glossary.

The emphasis of the book is on understanding sexuality as a form of interaction between two or more persons, and between these persons and the specific cultural milieu in which they are located. Examples of sexual patterns in other cultures are often used to highlight the manner in which culture affects the sexual functioning of individuals within it.

The common sexual patterns found in the United States for persons of all ages—from infancy to old age—are examined. Patterns less common to our society as well as the persons participating in these less common patterns are described. We make few judgments as to the "health" or "sickness" or "normality" or "abnormality" of typical or less typical sexual patterns.

Understanding Sexual Interaction is unique in the quantity, quality, and variety of empirical data brought to the subject matter. The breadth of the most recent data from national surveys is complemented by the data obtained from controlled laboratory studies. A fuller understanding of survey and laboratory data is provided by liberal use of field research and case study materials, some of which are the outcome of previously unpublished interviews conducted by the authors.

The entire Second Edition has been totally updated by a complete review of the research literature that has appeared since the publication of the First Edition. This review has resulted in the inclusion of 198 new studies, published from 1977 through 1980. The contents of these studies have been covered throughout the text, with reference information given in the bibliography.

Many new topics and sections are included in this edition. There are new sections on the effects of hormones on sexuality, sexuality among the disabled, and recent progress in contraceptive research. Other new topics now included are multiple orgasms in males, latest figures on the rising incidence of venereal disease, sexual and affectional relations during pregnancy, menstrual cycles in relation to mood cycles, selecting the sex of your baby, the latest research by Masters and Johnson on same-sex versus opposite-sex love-making patterns, fetal differentiation in relation to biological differences between males and females, genetic engineering, endorphins for improved sexuality, cohabitation without marriage, asexual parenting, the latest research on gays as role models and parents, the "coming out" process, and gay lifestyles.

This book is designed to provide the professor with maximum flexibility in adapting it to the requirements of a specific course. Part 1, Perspectives on Human Sexuality, discusses basic physiology and provides an overview of the various perspectives important to an understanding of human sexuality, information that is basic for any student of human sexuality. Part 2, Sexuality and Reproduction: Medical and Social Aspects, is most applicable to courses that stress an understanding of the physiological issues related to sexual functioning. Part 3, Sexuality and the Life Cycle: Typical Patterns, may be emphasized in courses that are more concerned with typical sexual patterns. Part 4, Alternative Sexual Patterns, can be emphasized in courses dealing with less typical, or alternative, sexual patterns. Part 5, Sexuality in Society: Dimensions of Change, is important for most sexuality courses in that it relates individual sexual functioning to social functioning and projects possible future patterns. Chapter 18 on future trends has been largely rewritten and updated to include the latest research developments, as well as possible scenarios for sexual relations in the immediate future in connection with current social and economic trends. The Appendix covers methods and methodological problems of sex research; it may be emphasized in courses where students are concerned with these issues or omitted when methodology is outside the scope of the course. Parts 2, 3, 4, and 5 and the Appendix are

each independent and complete units, any one of which may be emphasized, de-emphasized, or omitted without affecting the understanding of
other portions of the book.

We would like to acknowledge the help of Douglas Kirby who wrote
the appendix on methods and methodological problems in sex research.

We would also like to acknowledge the help of several persons who
read and made comments on earlier versions of our manuscript. These
persons are John H. Curtis, Valdosta State College; H. D. Heath, California State University, Hayward; Laud Humphreys, Pitzer College; Thomas
S. Jandebeur, Athens State College; Janice Litwack, Kent State University;
Wayne C. Seelbach, Lamar University; Kenneth J. Smith, University of
Miami; and F. Donald Yutzler, The George Washington University.

Joann S. DeLora Sandlin
Carol A. B. Warren
Carol Rinkleib Ellison

UNDERSTANDING SEXUAL INTERACTION

Part I / *Perspectives on Human Sexuality*

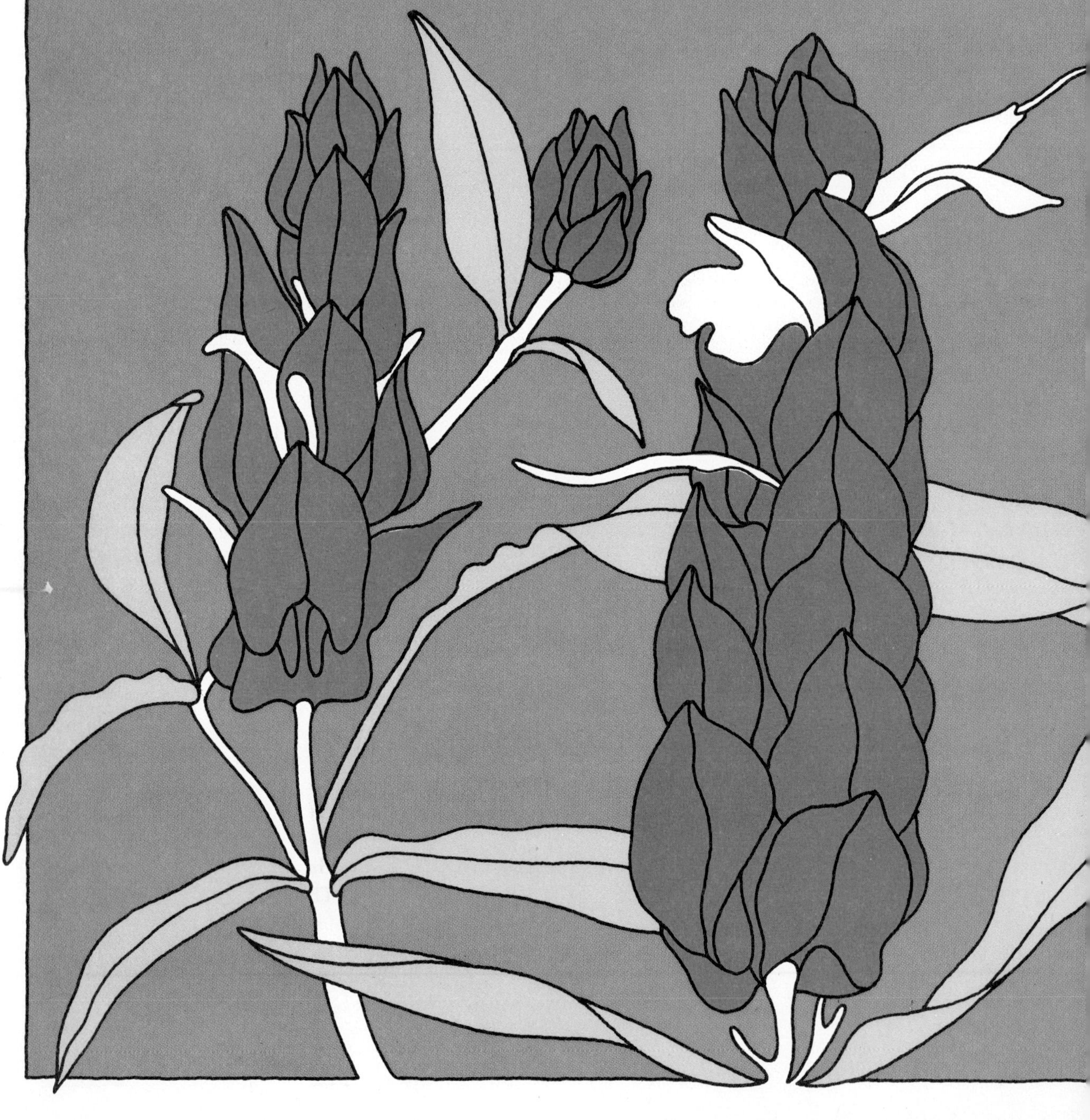

His hands were groping her breasts, fumbling for the buttons on her blouse. She hoped he didn't break them.... When was she going to feel something? She tried to respond....

"Relax, little baby," David whispered as his head went to her breasts. He began licking each one gently and she felt her nipples harden ... and the odd sensation in her pelvic area.... He took off her bra. She was standing in her boots and stocking pants. He lifted her up and carried her into the bedroom.... She tried not to think of her long silk skirt lying in a heap on the living room floor.... He tossed her on the bed. Then he pulled off her boots and her panty hose.

And then she was lying there completely nude and he was telling her she was beautiful.

Susann, 1974, pp. 166–167

This sexual scenario comes from Jacqueline Susann's popular novel *Once Is Not Enough*. The casual reader of such a passage takes it for granted; however, for the sex researcher, it reflects important assumptions about sexuality and sex roles in society.

Susann's sexual scenario is profoundly social, anchored in Western contemporary society. The clothing the characters are wearing are those of Western society — panty hose, bra, blouse, and skirt, clothes that typically interfere with smooth, romantic seduction scenes. As is common in Western society, it is the man who seduces the woman. *He* admires *her* nudity, and *he* tells *her* she is beautiful, removing her clothes and guiding her actions.

The passage also reveals the social influences on emotions as well as events. The woman wonders why she is not feeling what she is supposed to, and when she will begin doing so. She attempts to follow the patterns of activity that she perceives as correct in the situation: "She tried to respond."

At the same time, January "felt her nipples harden" in a physiological response that to a great degree is independent of social learning. David "licked" her nipples in a fairly common Western sexual technique. In any sexual interaction, the participants are influenced not only by the social expectations related to sex roles, sex actions, and appropriate emotions, but also by the physiology of sexual arousal and response. The two are not independent of one another, but are reflexive, each profoundly influencing the other in a given sexual interaction and during sexual development.

In the novel, January is portrayed as emotionally and sexually driven by a sexual attraction to her father, Mike. This deeply motivating attraction is not reflected directly in her sexual actions and her thoughts while engaged with David because it is unconscious, clear to the reader or observer, but not to the woman herself. In addition to the social and physiological influence of sexuality, then, there is a psychological influence based on the individual's emotional relationship to parents and other significant, intimate persons.

Three Perspectives on Sexuality

This book approaches sexuality from three academic perspectives: the physiological or medical, the psychological, and the social or sociological. In Part 1, the three perspectives are described in detail: the social perspective in Chapter 1, the psychological perspective in Chapter 2, and the physiological perspective in Chapters 3 and 4. However, the reader must be aware that this separation is for analytical purposes only; as in David and January's encounter, the three aspects of sexuality are reflexive, each modifying and interacting with one another to produce the experience of sexuality.

Plan of the Book

Chapter 1 gives a general overview of the relationship among sexuality, the individual, and society in the context of the development of sex   4 research from the eighteenth to the twentieth century. The theme of the relationship among sex, society, and the individual is again focused on in Part 5, with analyses of current and future sex and sex-related trends, and changing dimensions of the relationships between individuals in such areas as love and other emotions, and sexual ethics and values.

Part 2 analyzes the medical and social aspects of sexuality and reproduction: venereal disease, childbirth, contraception, and sex therapy. Parts 3 and 4, respectively, give descriptive and analytic overviews of typical and atypical sexual adaptations in contemporary society. Part 3 focuses on the development of sexuality during the five major phases of the life cycle: childhood, puberty and adolescence, young adulthood, middle age, and old age.

Part 4 covers common and less common variations on the typical themes outlined in Part 3, such as variations in gender, age, and relationship of sex partners, and variations in sexual activity that depart from conventional monogamous heterosexual coitus. Part 5 analyzes the interdependence of people and society as they affect social change.

Finally, the appendix discusses the methodology of the major scientific studies of sexuality used in this book. Scientific knowledge of sexuality is increasing, but at the moment it is hampered by considerable methodological problems and constraints. At the same time, even some limited empirical or factual basis for sexual knowledge is better than the myths and mysteries that are the only alternatives.

In the following chapters, our focus is descriptive rather than explanatory or predictive, although we deal with explanation and prediction where they seem most relevant. The focus is theoretical in that we discuss sexuality within the context of the physiological, psychological, and sociological perspectives and their interaction. Religious and moral perspectives are used as background material, but, wherever possible, we have attempted to present the most up-to-date research data, and it has been our aim to present data rather than make a case for a particular moral or religious point of view.

Today knowledge of human sexual interaction is still incomplete, uneven, and in the nature of a beginning statement rather than an ending. The reader must approach *Understanding Sexual Interaction* with this in mind: we have attempted to draw together present information into a coherent whole, not as a definitive statement but as one of many steps toward knowledge.

5

Sexuality in Historical Perspective

Tracing historically the transition from agrarian to industrial society gives us important clues to understanding changes in sexual attitudes and behavior that have occurred in our recent past. In the United States and other Western nations, the shift from agrarian to industrial took place from about the middle of the eighteenth century to the beginning of the twentieth century, with a transitional period, the Victorian era, in the nineteenth century. This change affected all aspects of society, including sexuality and the family.

Agrarian Society

In an agrarian economy there are basically two occupations and two social classes: the aristocracy who own the land and the peasant farmers who work the land. In such an economy, children are a valuable asset for both social classes. They are important to the aristocracy as heirs, so that titles and property can be retained within the family. They are an economic asset to the peasant class because in an agricultural economy children produce more than they consume. Furthermore, because agrarian societies of the past and present do not have social security programs, children are needed to take care of aged parents (Cipolla, 1970).

The Procreative Function of Sex   In such a society the birthrate is high, and the peasant woman's function, besides working as a field laborer, is primarily producing and rearing children. Sexuality in a society with a focus on childbirth tends to be seen primarily or exclusively in terms of procreation, especially for women. Particularly in the Judeo-Christian tradition, the use of any sexual position or activity for the purpose of only enjoyment and not procreation is taboo. Masturbation (the biblical "sin of Onan"), oral-genital or anal sex (biblical "sodomy"), and the use of birth control devices are condemned because they are not directed toward the production of children.

Because the death rates in agrarian societies are high, aristocratic women also must bear many children to insure at least one male heir to lands, titles, and fortunes. The chastity of aristocratic women is protected carefully to insure the legitimacy of the heir. In societies such as that of Europe in the Middle Ages, where inheritance is patrilineal (through the male line), the paternity of a child is carefully guarded. This means, in effect, that women are carefully guarded, because whereas maternity can be proved by observation, paternity is never actually provable. The economic arrangements of an agrarian society, then, form the basis of the

double standard of sexual interaction: women must not give birth to children of uncertain paternity, but men can father all the children they like.

Sexuality and Religion In Western agrarian nations, religion has had a significant influence on sexuality and the family since the beginning of the Judeo-Christian era. The Christian religion, in particular, reinforced the sexual, moral, and familial standards of agricultural Europe in the Middle Ages (Tripp, 1975). Although the chastity of the priesthood was not the rule until about six hundred years after the death of Christ, biblical tradition — particularly in the New Testament — praises chastity as the height of religious morality, although at the same time it praises fertility as much as any other agrarian religion does. The chastity of unmarried females and their sexual fidelity after marriage were enforced by ecclesiastical law. The sexual variations of sodomy, homosexuality, and the like were forbidden by a variety of statutes. Until the Victorian era — when "good" women came to be defined as sex hating — women were regarded as highly sexed beings set to lure men from chastity, fidelity, and religion. Women were persecuted and burned as witches by the Christian church-state more often than men were, because witchcraft was regarded as a sexual condition of women: a demonic possession by satanic libido. The

In agrarian society, sex was primarily for the purpose of conceiving children who could help farm the land.
Soloman D. Butcher Collection/Nebraska State Historical Society.

8

Judeo-Christian tradition supported the patriarchal family, in which the male was the head, and the female and children the inferior subordinates.

Divorce and artificial methods of birth control were condemned morally and even legally by religious authorities until the separation of church and state during the Industrial Revolution (and still are today in countries like Italy). Birth control practices were forbidden by most Protestant denominations, as well as by the Roman Catholic church, well into the twentieth century, as was divorce. Again, this meant that sexuality was closely connected with the family, with procreation, and with state and supernatural or religious authority.

Sexuality and Sex Roles Little is known directly about sexuality in preindustrial society, because surveys of sexual practices and attitudes were not made until the 1940s. However, we do have historical data on sex roles, the general behaviors and attitudes seen as appropriate to men and women, and some evidence about sexuality may be inferred from these roles. The agrarian family was patriarchal: in law, the male of the family unit had the power to prescribe the fate of the family, from decisions about where to live to the disposal of any money or property the wife might have. The woman passed from the legal guardianship of her father to that of her husband, socially symbolized by having first the father's and then the husband's surname.

Both males and females had sex roles that varied according to the placement of the family in the social class hierarchy. In the peasant or serf family, the woman worked in the fields alongside the man and was expected to be as strong as he was, or stronger, because she also had the biological responsibility of childbearing and the socially defined responsibility of child rearing. The male, although he was nominally powerful within his own family, was tied to the land belonging to his feudal lord, and so was virtually powerless. Some historians speculate that rural peasant families in England and other countries were in fact considerably more egalitarian than they might appear to be from their legally patriarchal structure (Laslett, 1975).

The Aristocratic Family The aristocratic family of agrarian and Victorian times was not at all egalitarian. The highest-class males and females were not expected to work, but they had different spheres of interest and involvement: the males with their estates, hunting, and male companionship, and the females with female relatives, friends, household help, and their children and domestic duties. Upper-class males were literate and often highly educated, but upper-class women, particularly before the Victorian era, were often illiterate. Even literate women were fre-

9

quently versed in little more than religious readings, needlework, and music, because intellectual pursuits were considered unfit for a female.

The upper classes enforced a strict double standard of sexuality related to the paternity and childbearing roles of males and females. Males of the upper class controlled female sexuality both by guarding the female body — literally, and symbolically through voluminous clothing — and by defining away the existence of an autonomous female sexuality.

Standards of Purity   Although there is some evidence that even upper-class females were defined as sexual beings prior to the reign of Queen Victoria, the emerging middle classes during the nineteenth century set the standards of purity for both males and females. Ideally both the male and the female were sexually pure, but in fact males frequently visited prostitutes, bringing venereal diseases into their households. The purity

During the nineteenth century, there were ideal standards of purity for both men and women.

From Collection of Charles G. Whitchurch, Wilmette, Illinois.

10

of women was enforced much more rigidly, to the point of denying that women who were not prostitutes had any sexual feelings. (See Selection 1.1) From the limited scientific literature on sexuality in Victorian times, it is clear that female sexuality was defined solely by males, and in terms of what males demanded sexually — a passive wife who would accede to a man's demands, bear children, and never assert sexual or any other type of independence. It is also clear, however, that there was some awareness of the power of femal sexuality: a few Victorian doctors performed clitoridectomies on young girls and women in order to exorcise the demon of active sexuality from their bodies.

Sexual Attitudes in the Victorian Era

Selection 1.1

Female and Male Sexuality

With rare exceptions, both of person and of instances, in married life all the sexual aggressiveness is with the male. Wives seldom seek the closer embraces of their husbands. They are generally indifferent; often absolutely averse. With the husband, while in perfect health, the conditions are quite the opposite; and the wisdom of the Creator is manifest in the fact that were the wife equally quickened by the same amative tendencies, the male nature would be called into such frequent and continuous exercise that the power of reproduction would be either totally destroyed or so impaired that the race would degenerate into moral, intellectual and physical pigmies. God has made the passivity of the wife the protection of her husband and a source of manifold blessing to their children (p. 49).

Sylvanus Stall, *What a Young Husband Ought to Know*, Philadelphia, VIR Publishing Co., 1897

Perhaps of the great majority of women it would be true to say that they are largely devoid of sexual pleasure (p. 124).

Sexual Frequency

Some physicians are inclined to limit the relation to once a month; upon the other hand, all who have given attention to this subject have learned of instances of excess which do not fall at all short of conjugal debauchery. It might be said that no man of average health, physical power and intellectual acumen can exceed the bounds of once a week without at least being in danger of having entered upon a life of excess both for himself and for his wife (p. 95).

Sexual Knowledge

In the first place a young husband should know that many women, even at the time of their marriage, are totally ignorant of all questions relating to sex. There are some women who do not so much as know that there are any physical differences between men and women. There are others who may know there is some difference, but into whose minds the thought of coition has never once entered. While this may not be true in a majority of cases, yet it is true in a large number of instances. We have even known of young wives who have approached the period of their first confinement who did not know the cause of their increasing bodily size; and we recently learned of an instance where the physician was already in the room to attend the expectant mother, who thought that she was to be delivered of her child by a surgical operation. She thought that the doctor was to make an incision in the abdomen, and remove her child in that way (pp. 132–133).

Contraception

The only safe and sure way is for husband and wife to remain strictly apart. There are methods which are sometimes suggested, by even well-meaning physicians, to those who desire to escape the results of the marital relation, but when pressed for the expression of a candid and honest conviction these same physicians are always compelled to admit that for absolute safety there is but one provision.

These various methods are not only unsatisfactory and unavailing, but are ruinous in their effects upon the individuals who practice them. In some instances nature does not visit her penalties immediately, but eventually the old declaration proves true that although justice travels with a sore foot it is sure to overtake the transgressor (p. 186).

Industrialization

With the onset of the Industrial Revolution, the economic viability of childbirth was set in reverse. In an industrial economy children tend to consume more than they produce. In the nineteenth century this meant that peasant parents who migrated to urban areas sent their children to work in the factories as they had once worked on the farms. But the children's wages did not cover even the cost of their own survival, let alone add to the well-being of the family. Gradually the death rate in modern industrial societies dropped because of the conquering of malnutrition, famine, and disease. Somewhat later, also gradually, the birthrate fell (Cipolla, 1970).

The lessening economic need for children brought about an unchaining of sexuality from its ancient function of socially obligatory procreation. Today, birth control has been sanctioned by most of the Judeo-Christian denominations (except Roman Catholics) that once thundered against it. General prosperity and increased leisure have made the pursuit of pleasure more respectable, and sexuality has become a leisure-time option rather than a procreative necessity.

12

Despite considerable changes, sex roles and sexuality today are still affected by the agrarian and Victorian procreative and sex-role standards. The typical female in United States society is still financially dependent first upon her father and then upon her husband; this dependence is still symbolized by her having first one and then the other male surname. In law, although there have been great strides against sex discrimination in the social institutions during the past five or six years, women still have vestiges of legally dependent status. For example, a divorced woman earning the same salary as her divorced husband will not be able to obtain credit as easily, and is more likely than a man to be protected by alimony payments.

Although the definitions of appropriate female sexuality have changed, they still seem to reflect the fluctuation in male demands upon the female rather than the flowering of female sexuality. For example, whereas males once expected females to submit to sex with fear and trembling — but to submit — today many males expect females to enjoy sex with gusto and fervor — but they had better like it, or they are likely to be labeled "frigid" or "hung up."

The Women's Movement   A challenge to the male sexual domination of females and the traditional structure of both male and female sex roles has arisen in recent years in what is generally known as the women's liberation or feminist movement. From one perspective, the feminist movement is indeed one movement — a changing of consciousness, however slight, in many of the women in our society. From another perspective, however, there are many different movements among women, such as disinterest, hostility, or involvement in any of a range of feminist groups, from relatively conservative organizations, such as NOW, to the more radical feminist organizations.

Today's feminism differs from the Victorian suffragette movement in that it is focused less on economic and social discrimination and more on cultural aspects of sex roles. The nineteenth- and early twentieth-century suffragettes fought for the right of women to vote, hold employment in certain occupations, and get equal pay. Rarely did they attempt to change the cultural definitions or symbolic apparatus attached to the female role. Today, however, feminists have branched out from issues of equality and discrimination, which are still salient, to a wider inquiry into the female sex role, female sexuality, and the relationships between men and women and between women and women.

The degree to which these issues are relevant to groups within the movement varies with the ideological nature of the group. The more conservative organizations, such as NOW, are generally more preoccupied with matters related to discrimination and equality, like the passage   13

Many women's groups today are focusing their efforts on combating sex discrimination in pay and employment.
Thomas Levy/ICON

of the Equal Rights Amendment or enforcement of the civil rights provisions against sex discrimination in pay and employment. The more radical the organization, however, the more involved its membership tends to be with an attempt to restructure the female sex role.

As feminists see it, the main problems of the female sex role arise from the economic and social dependence of females on males. Under the pressures of marriage and child rearing, women are financially dependent

14

for a large portion of their lives on men, who generally earn more, and at the same time they often lack the self-fulfillment that men gain from their higher-prestige occupations. Socially, the female is still often seen mainly or only as an appendage of the male, without whom she lacks social identity or a place in the status hierachy. Feminists attack both the roots and the symbols of female dependence on males, including what women wear or do to entice males to support them for the rest of their lives, such as wearing cosmetics or feigning stupidity.

Most particularly, many feminists are concerned with the control of female sexuality that males have traditionally exercised, and still do exercise in many ways. This control is both direct and indirect. Direct control is exemplified by the fact that until recently most writing about female sexuality has been done by males; indirect control includes defining female sexuality in terms of what the male wants for his own pleasure — the penis in the vagina — or in terms of female role satisfaction through childbirth. In the first instance, feminists have attacked the male propensity to label as frigid women whose sexual pleasure comes mainly from clitoral and not from vaginal contact; in the second instance they have attacked the concept that female identity is fulfilled mainly through childbirth and that female sexuality is only a means to this end. Most feminists remain hopeful for male companionship and sexual learning, but others have turned entirely or partly away from males. Some, like Shulamith Firestone, have chosen chastity, reasoning that men today cannot possibly have a high enough consciousness to engage in a mature relationship with a woman. Others, like Ti-Grace Atkinson, have turned away from the concept of romantic love as yet another type of enslavement of women. Still others, though not defining themselves as born lesbians, have become "politicalesbians," learning to enjoy sexual interaction with other women because they despair of finding an equal sexual relationship with males.

Although the women's liberation movement has changed the consciousness of many women who do not overtly identify with it, it does not appeal to all segments of society. Besides the anti–women's liberation writers, who oppose the movement directly, there are some lower-class and ethnic groups with cultural patterns that militate against the development of a feminist consciousness.

The Contemporary Versus the Victorian Woman   The typical woman's life today, then, is not like the typical Victorian woman's. In some ways, though, it retains similarities. A woman still may be symbolically though not legally under her husband's control. For example, she usually takes his surname, lives where he wants to live, and subordinates her "job" to his "career" when necessary. Whether she likes sex or not, she is expected   15 to be responsive to her husband's sexual needs. Rarely is it acceptable for her to be sexually aggressive. Although many women are now aware of their sexual potential and desire orgasmic satisfaction, they are sometimes left frustrated by men who quickly take care of their own needs and remain insensitive to women's. Males are often still the arbiters of what is considered proper sexual response and timing, and what is feminine and sexy for a female.

The Contemporary Versus the Victorian Man   Like the woman, the man of today faces a different situation than the Victorian did. In the agrarian society, when he was head of a household composed of a wife (often pregnant or nursing) and several small children, the man's presence was important to their physical survival. He provided part of the family's protection as well as their livelihood. Now protection is provided largely by the legal and police system rather than by the man of the house, and the wife may be economically capable of supporting her family alone. As the necessity for having a man as head of a family has lessened, traditional male dominance in family is being challenged.

In the sexual area men also face new challenges. The woman who realizes her sexual potential and wants her sexual rights demands much more from a man than swift penetration and ejaculation. His sexual masculinity is no longer measured only in terms of his ability to reproduce or conquer. Now he must be able to satisfy a woman whose sexual needs may equal or exceed his own.

The Religious Perspective

Inquiry into sexuality prior to the twentieth century was restrained by religious taboos. Any human interaction related to the concept of deity was fraught with moral and religious connotations, and almost all areas of human life were seen as having religious significance. Thus, not only was inquiry into sexuality discouraged, but also inquiry into other areas that were perceived as the province of God, such as whether the planet Earth was at the center of the universe.

The religious and moral heritage of sexuality remains highly significant today because it has been modified, not eliminated, by the development of scientific perspectives. The physiological perspective on sexuality was built upon a previous foundation of moral rules, and the psychological and sociological perspectives upon that double foundation.

The religious and moral perspective on sexuality and the scientific perspective are also intertwined: the religious heritage affects the scien-   16 tific perspective, and the scientific perspective has implications for the religious posture. For example, the Lutheran Church in the United States in 1970 adopted a resolution that stated: "Sex, marriage and family are gifts of God in which to rejoice. Their essential goodness cannot be obscured by any crisis of our time" (Smith, 1975, p. 1). This statement illustrates both the tenacity of the religious heritage and its responsiveness to social and scientific change. As religious leaders have insisted for centuries, sexuality is linked inextricably with marriage and the family. However, sexuality is recognized as an independent force in the sex-marriage-family equation, and as something good — not to be overlooked, eliminated, or reduced to a necessary duty for reproduction as it was in earlier religious perspectives.

The sex roles of today have both an agrarian and a religious heritage: they echo the patriarchal family of the past and its biblical justification. In all social classes, sexual behavior, sexual attitudes, and sex roles may still be strongly influenced by religious factors. In fact, it is only within the past few decades, in the Western industrial nations, that religion has released some of its monopoly on the enforcement and preservation of sexual morality. Even today, however, some religious groups attempt with some success to control their adherents' marital and reproductive behavior by setting up moral standards.

For both males and females the frequency of attendance at religious services is related to sexual behavior. Religiously inactive men and women engage in more kinds of sexual activity resulting in orgasm than do more devout men and women, regardless of whether their religious affiliation is Protestant, Catholic, or Jewish. Religiously inactive women are more likely to masturbate both before and after marriage, to engage in petting to orgasm, to have sexual relations before marriage, to engage in homosexual activities to orgasm, and to have extramarital sexual relations. The frequency of attendance at religious services is not related to the frequency with which women engage in sexual relations with their husband and is not related to the frequency with which they are able to achieve orgasm in their marital sexual relations (Kinsey et al., 1953).

Men who attend religious services less frequently are more likely to engage in masturbation, premarital sexual intercourse, marital sexual intercourse, and homosexual activities. The frequency of male and female petting and of nocturnal emissions is not related to frequency of religious observance (Kinsey et al., 1948, pp. 465–496).

For both men and women the degree of religious devotion is related to the kinds and frequency of sexual activity. The incidence of nearly all types of sexual activity, except marital coitus, is lower among persons who attend religious functions more often and higher among those who attend less often. Among religiously active males who do eventually participate in religiously disapproved activities such as masturbation or pre-marital sex, their frequencies are lower than for the less devout males. But among religiously active females who engage in disapproved activities, their frequencies are the same as those of their less devout peers (Kinsey et al., 1948; Kinsey et al., 1953).

Research on Human Sexuality

The development of sex research has closely paralled the development of scientific research in general since its flowering in seventeenth- and eighteenth-century medicine. During the eighteenth century the focus of scientific research on the human being was predominantly medical; during the nineteenth century the psychological perspective was added and developed; the sociological perspective was developed most fully in the twentieth century.

The extension of new physiological, psychological, and sociological techniques and understandings into the subject of sex was highly tentative during each of these three centuries. Furthermore, the research of people who dared investigate human sexuality was often subjected to extreme criticism by the majority, though equally often welcomed and praised by an intellectual minority.

The Eighteenth Century: The Physiological Perspective

During the eighteenth century the pioneering medical doctors interested in the physiology of sexuality often tended to look upon even heterosexual coitus as a type of illness. Masturbation and other forms of sexual expression were considered "sick" as well as "sinful." As Bullough comments:

The key transition figure seems to be Hermann Boerhaave (1668–1738) who attempted to build a new system of medicine. In his *Institutiones medicae* Boerhaave (1728) wrote that the "rash expenditure of semen" brought on a "lassitude, a feebleness, a weakening of motion, fits, wasting, dryness, fevers, aching of the cerebral membranes," obscuring of the sense, a decay of the spinal cord, "a fatuity, and other like evils. . . ."

Boerhaave was not alone in this respect and other system builders of the eighteenth century such as Georg Ernest Stahl (1660–1734), Frederick Hoffman (1660–1742) and John Brown (1735–1788) all managed to equate sexuality with illness.

Bullough, 1975, p. 292

18

Medical researchers of the eighteenth century were interested in the physiology of the human body in general, and in the relationship of bodily "inputs" such as food, to bodily outputs, such as blood, excrement, and semen. They defined the sexual act for both males and females in terms of a loss of bodily fluids that would have to be replaced by bodily intake. Excessive sexual indulgence would drain the body of energy; the results included tuberculosis, jaundice, cancer, the birth of "perverted" offspring, and even death (Bullough, 1975, pp. 293–295). Even today some persons feel that sexual abstinence the night before a big game is advisable for athletes in order to conserve their energy.

Despite their condemnation of most forms of sexual activity — even marital coitus if practiced "excessively" — the eighteenth-century sex researchers were sometimes censured for even daring to inquire into the subject. The nineteenth-century sex researchers continued to emphasize the physiology of sexuality and the concept of sex as a sickness, but also expanded into new areas.

The Nineteenth Century: The Psychological Perspective

The nineteenth century saw the development of psychological research on sexuality, and the beginnings of a closer inquiry into the relationship between sexuality and society. Discussions of sexuality were no longer confined to the physiology of reproduction. Magnus Hirschfeld in Germany (1868–1935), for example, investigated the effects of war on sexuality and also wrote about homosexuality; he coined the term *third sex* and argued that homosexuality should be legalized (Ruitenbeek, 1974). Richard von Krafft-Ebing (1840–1920), also from Germany, published during the same period his famous *Psychopathia Sexualis*, in which he investigated the psychology of the most far-fetched types of sexuality along with much commoner variations such as oral sexuality and homosexuality (Ruitenbeek, 1974, pp. 25–27).

The psychology of sex was, however, most completely developed by Sigmund Freud, as we discuss at length in Chapter 2. Freudian psychological interpretations of sexuality indelibly marked the work of later nineteenth-century sex researchers such as Havelock Ellis, and remain today the main focus of the psychological perspective on sexuality.

The Twentieth Century: The Sociological Perspective

Freud, Hirschfeld, and Krafft-Ebing were interested in the relationship between sexuality and society, but their focus was on the psychological dynamics of the neurotic, or sexually "different" person. Freud and Havelock Ellis were also interested in sexuality as the expression of a basic,   19 and thus essentially normal, human drive. Kinsey and his research associates in the 1940s and 1950s expanded the psychological discussion of normal and variant sexuality into the sociological arena.

The Kinsey Reports   Like most of the sex research that preceded them, the Kinsey reports on the human male and female stirred up considerable controversy, backlash, and anger, as well as praise and acclaim. Tripp summarizes the climate of the times:

By the spring of 1950, the Kinsey Report . . . had been out for two years. It had received the highest honors, with nearly unanimous acclaim from reviewers, including scientists in a dozen fields. And it had been recognized as the most extensive effort ever made to gather and present data on what people do sexually . . . Although Kinsey was very modest in his claims of accomplishment and leaned over backward to avoid drawing sweeping sociologic conclusions, the enormous prestige of his work drove his critics into a kind of hysteria. Dr. Harold Dodds, president of Princeton University, wrote a critique of the Kinsey Report for the *Readers Digest* in which he compared the work to "toilet-wall inscriptions". . . . Clare Boothe Luce came before the National Council of Catholic women to say "the Kinsey Report, like all cheap thrillers, would fall into obscurity if so much attention was not paid to it."

Tripp, 1975, pp. 232–233

Today the Kinsey reports are generally recognized as a monumental and brilliant, if not methodologically perfect, attempt to examine the sexual practices of large numbers of men and women in American society (see the appendix).

Contemporary surveys of sexual behavior stir little controversy as legitimate sociological approaches today, although their methodology is still questioned (see the appendix). Other methods of studying sexuality continue to be developed, however, and continue to provoke reactions.

Masters and Johnson   The Masters and Johnson approach to the study of sexuality is geared more to physiological and psychological than to sociological generalizations, but it has stirred considerable controversy both because of the methods used and because of the social implications of the findings.

Masters and Johnson have been criticized for violating the "essentially private" nature of sexual response by monitoring it with measuring equipment and observational devices. Their findings, particularly in the area of the controversial clitoral-vaginal orgasm debate (see Chapters 2 and 3), are challenging both to traditional psychological concepts of maleness and femaleness and to traditional sex-role stereotypes in Western society.

20

The seventeenth, eighteenth, and nineteenth centuries, then, saw two parallel developments in sex research: the orienting of sex research in the direction of general scientific research and the extreme reactions provoked by each new attempt to apply scientific understanding to sexuality. The history of sex research can be helpful in illuminating the general relationship of sexuality to society, for people's reaction to sex research can provide a monitor of the sexual climate.

Sexuality and Society

The relationship of sexuality and society involves defining the meaning of sexuality itself. In this book, in an attempt to reflect the complexity of the social definitions involved, we use the term *sexuality* to refer not only to sexual behavior but also to sexual attitudes, because behavior and attitude are both significant, although they are conceptually and empirically distinguishable.

Sexual attitudes and behavior are not always consistent in today's changing society.
Arthur Grace/Stock, Boston

21

Behavior and Attitudes

Sexual behavior itself is not easy to define. In their studies of the human male and female, the Kinsey group used the criterion of activity that culminates in orgasm to define sexual behavior. However, as indicated in later chapters, people — particularly women — do not always reach orgasm in coitus even though coitus seems an obvious example of sexual behavior. Similarly, the eating of dirt may seem peculiar and asexual to the observer, yet may be fraught with sexual meaning to those who engage in it. In addition, although behavior can be described as romantic, erotic, or sensual to differentiate it from the sexual, the distinctions may not always be clear. The stroking of a person's back might be interpreted as sexual in one culture or by one person, but as erotic, sensual, or just friendly by another. Similarly, a mouth-kiss can be seen as a form of romantic, erotic, sensual, or sexual behavior.

Without engaging in the debate concerning the existence and nature of attitudes, we will define the term *attitudes* according to its usage in surveys: the opinions given concerning sexual matters. An individual may say one thing about sexuality and yet do another. For example, in his book *Tearoom Trade*, Humphreys reports his observations of men engaging in sex with other men in "tearooms," or public rest rooms (see Chapter 16, page 495. When later he disguised himself and asked the same men their views of vice squad activity in places like the tearooms, a number of his "closet queen" respondents — men who concealed their homosexual behavior — said they thought vice squad activities were not strict enough and should be stepped up.

The minister . . . felt that the police should not give as much regard as they do to the rights of citizens. Vice squad activity, he insisted, should be increased: "This moral corruption must be stopped!" One young closet queen had this to say about vice squad activity: "They should be more strict. I can think of a lot of places they ought to raid."   Humphreys, 1975, p. 141

Ira Reiss (1967) has investigated the reported sexual behavior and attitudes of the same individuals. He has found that in the area of premarital intercourse, there is a high correspondence between the sexual attitudes and reported sexual behavior of adolescents. Reiss concludes that the basic socialization by parents and by peers during the first ten years of life manifest themselves in this interaction of behavior and standards; as the adolescent ages there is some tendency toward increased permissiveness in both attitudes and behavior, which is regulated by the potential for permissiveness in his or her basic socialization (Reiss, 1967, pp. 105–128).

Neither Reiss nor Humphreys claims knowledge of what their respondents really thought; they report only verbalized attitudes. Moreover,   22

Reiss's data include only reports, not actual observations of behavior; these reports may not be accurate reflections of past sexual activity, because the very taboos surrounding sexual activity could induce respondents to forget or falsify responses in accordance with their self-image. For example, a young woman who conceives of herself as virtuous might be reluctant to admit her premarital sexual experience even to an anonymous questionnaire, and a would-be Don Juan with no sexual experience might be reluctant to admit to his lack of premarital coitus.

A female in her early thirties recalls: When I was in high school we all filled out a questionnaire about our sexual behavior. I was so up tight that I did not put down even that my boy friend had touched my breast or that we had done heavy petting, and certainly not that we had had sex. I just put that night in the drive-in out of my mind. It was not part of me; it was as if someone else had been there.

From the authors' files

Humphrey's data, on the other hand, like those of Masters and Johnson, are based on direct observation of sexual activity. His research, too, has provoked considerable controversy.

Undoubtedly public reaction to *Tearoom Trade* will be strongly affected by the subject matter and the way in which the findings are presented. Many readers, finding the whole topic revolting, will channel their distaste against the author and sociology in general. Indeed, Humphreys invites this reaction by lacing the text with graphic detail that does not seem to be called for by his scientific goals.

Warwick, 1973, pp. 27–38

The relationship between sexual behavior and sexual attitudes is complex, and research into this relationship is clouded by the difficulties involved in measuring attitudes directly and observing behavior directly. Because most research relies on individuals' reports of their own attitudes and behavior, it is not surprising that there is similarity between the two. Research in the future, as better indicators of sexual attitudes and behaviors are perfected, may discover a more complex relationship.

Sexuality and Social Class

In agrarian society there were two major classes: a landowning aristocracy and a peasant working class. During the Victorian era of industrialization, the small middle class of clergy and merchants grew and diversified into what is today's large and varied middle class. Today, as we use them here, the terms *upper class*, *middle class*, and *lower class* refer to socioeconomic class, and each is associated with a particular definition of what constitutes the proper attitudes and behavior for that group in many areas of

life, including sexuality. Social scientists today have extensive empirical data on the premarital sexuality, marital sexuality, extramarital sexuality, and sex roles of the different classes.

Premarital Sexuality　Attitudes toward sexual relations before marriage are not strongly related to social class alone, regardless of how one measures social class — by income, education, occupation, or a combination of these factors. In contrast to sexual attitudes, sexual behavior, particularly for males, is definitely related to social class.

Lower-class males are more likely to have intercourse before marriage with girl friends and with prostitutes, and after marriage to have extramarital sexual intercourse. Men of lower-status occupations are also more likely to have had some type of homosexual contact. In contrast, men of a higher class are more likely to engage in masturbation both before and after marriage, petting to climax, nudity in intercourse, oral and manual stimulation of sex partners, and varied positions for sexual intercourse. There are also social class differences in reported frequencies of nocturnal emissions ("wet dreams"), which are supposedly an involuntary sexual outlet. Between puberty and age fifteen, males of higher classes report nocturnal emissions nearly seven times as often as lower-class males (Kinsey et al., 1948, p. 343). No totally satisfactory explanation can be

24

offered for this finding, which could be explained either as *actual* differing rates of nocturnal emissions or as differential willingness to *report* them. (For a discussion of Kinsey's research methods, see the appendix.)

The relationship between sexual behavior and social class is somewhat different for females. Women who have more formal education are more likely to report masturbation to orgasm and homosexual activities than are women with less education. Women with more education and women from higher-status occupational backgrounds are somewhat more likely to report experiencing orgasm in marital sexual relations and to have extramarital sexual relations. Premarital petting and premarital sexual intercourse are related to age at marriage, with women of all social levels usually engaging in these activities only in the year or two prior to marriage. For women social class is not related to nocturnal sex dreams or frequency of marital sex (Kinsey, 1953).

The Meaning of Sexual Experience   In the lower classes premarital sexual experiences have a different meaning for males and females. Males seek sexual conquests because of the physical pleasure they get from intercourse and because of the prestige male friends accord them when they have many conquests. Lower-class females are less likely than middle-class females to get physical pleasure or orgasm from premarital relations, and their status among their friends may be lowered by promiscuity. When lower-class females accede to a male's demands, it is often in an effort to secure more attention or affection from him, to obtain a declaration of love or proposal of marriage, or just to keep from losing him to a more sexually accessible female (Ruppel, 1973).

In the middle and upper classes there is more emphasis on sex as an extension of a love relationship, and less of a double standard for male and female behavior. Because of the greater likelihood of mutual commitment, there is often less guilt and more pleasure in premarital relations among the higher classes than among the lower. Emotional commitment tends to be important for the female, because it distinguishes her from the "easy lay" stigmatized by our society (Ruppel, 1973).

Marital Sexual Behavior   Patterns of sexual behavior in marriage are also related to social class. In the lower-class marriage there is often less emphasis than in the upper and middle classes on togetherness and shared activities in all aspects of the relationship. Where there are few shared activities and a high degree of segregation in the role relationships of husbands and wives, the couples do not usually develop a mutually satisfactory sexual relationship. The lower-class male's exploitative attitude toward the opposite sex does not necessarily improve much with marriage, and his concern remains primarily with securing his own satisfaction in sexual relations. He uses less varied sexual techniques and less

25

elaborate foreplay than men in higher classes. It is not surprising to find that lower-class women are less likely to reach orgasm in their marital relationships and report less interest and enjoyment in marital sex than women of middle and upper classes (Rainwater, 1965, pp. 61–117). Other structural factors contributing to this lesser enjoyment include larger families, longer working hours, and cultural attitudes that deemphasize female sexual satisfaction.

Permissiveness   Each social group tends to view its own sexual patterns as proper and normal, and to view those of everyone else as immoral and unnatural. Social scientists, however, find it more interesting to determine which social class is more sexually liberal or permissive than to condemn the practices and attitudes of any class. First, however, it is necessary to define liberal or permissive, and to differentiate attitudes and behavior.

If permissive sexual behavior is defined in terms of premarital sexual intercourse, then lower-class males are more liberal or sexually permissive in their behavior — but not necessarily in their attitudes. Even though lower-class males rarely view casual sex as morally right, they feel it is natural for them to seek it. On the other hand, upper- and middle-class males are more likely to view premarital sex as morally wrong unless it is legitimated by a love relationship, and are less likely to engage in it.

If liberal sexual behavior is defined in terms of practicing a variety of techniques for stimulating one's partner and a variety of methods for achieving orgasm, then higher-class males are more liberal in their behavior than lower-class ones. For example, middle- or upper-class people are more likely to practice oral or manual breast stimulation, and are more likely to give and expect oral and manual genital stimulation. In their dating relationships higher-class males are more likely to engage in deep kissing and petting to orgasm. They are also more likely to use masturbation as a supplement to their other sexual outlets. Whereas lower-class males view many of these practices as perversions, higher-class males see them as acceptable and important for adding to their partner's pleasure and for sexual outlets when intercourse is not possible or advisable. The patterns of sexual activity are different for the social classes, and each class has its own version of morality. The lower-class male is doing what he feels is proper because of his "nature." The higher-class male thinks it is morally incorrect to exploit women sexually, although he may actually do so.

Macho and Martyr Roles   In the lower-class community, male and female roles are characterized by anthropologist Oscar Lewis (1966) as "macho" and "martyr." Like their agrarian and Victorian counterparts, today's lower-class men and women have different spheres of interest and involvement, the men with work and drinking buddies, and the women

26

with female relatives and child rearing. The men stress "macho" values: the sexual exploitation and conquest of women, drinking and sometimes violence, and the display of material goods. The women, who are expected to be faithful to their husbands and to overlook any violence and disruption in the home caused by drinking and chasing women, have a martyred air about them; they complain constantly to female relatives, yet feel they can do nothing to change their man's "nature." Sex and childbearing are, by and large, regarded as duty rather than as pleasure or fulfillment. In the lower-class household, then, the sex roles tend to be extremely separate, unequal, and largely unaffected by the changes in sex roles noted earlier.

Sex Roles Sex roles and sexuality in the United States have a common historical heritage in agrarian and Victorian society; they also contain a considerable element of class-linked and ethnic diversity. Sex roles, sexual attitudes, and sexual behavior and response are also interdependent.

Sexuality and sexual response are influenced by sex roles to the extent that the equality or inequality inherent in such roles is extended to the arena of sexual interaction in such concepts as active and passive sexual response. In addition, the economic and household tasks allocated by sex roles can have a profound influence on the timing, location, and desire for sexual interaction.

Sex roles often define what is regarded as the appropriate sexual response for each gender, and they also provide a generalized atmosphere of trust or hurt, care or impersonality, which is the emotional background to human sexual interaction. If a man really respects and likes a woman and cares about her pleasure, he is likely to attempt to satisfy her sexually according to her own standards of satisfaction. If he has been taught that women are to be used and brutalized, he is likely to have sex speedily and leave the female as quickly and scornfully as possible.

Conversely, if a woman has been brought up with strong religious taboos against sexuality and views it as an unpleasant necessity for the production of children, she is unlikely to experience great sexual satisfaction. On the other hand, if she has been taught that she is required to be sexy and turned on at all times, she runs the risk of developing a negative self-image when she does not feel like being sexually active.

Culture and Ethnicity

The way in which sexuality is expressed in a given society is learned through culture. Individuals are born and raised in a particular cultural context that includes sexual and other norms, values, and ideals, as well as   27 a material technology that may include sexual items such as contraceptives. The material and nonmaterial sexual culture of different societies is a topic for sociological and anthropological analysis in both Western industrial and nonwestern agrarian societies.

Cultural Norms

Norms, in general, are culturally learned rules that guide behavior. The distinction between sexual attitudes and sexual behavior closely parallels the distinction between ideal cultural norms and real cultural norms.

The ideal norms of a culture may be inferred from what its members say about their sexuality; for example, one of the ideal norms of our culture is the proscription of premarital intercourse. Real norms, on the other hand, may be inferred from people's behavior; premarital intercourse is a real norm for many individuals and groups in our culture.

Ideal cultural norms in the area of sexuality as well as other areas consist of both proscriptions and prescriptions. A proscription is a negative norm that specifies what types of conduct should be avoided; a prescription, on the other hand, defines the course of action considered culturally appropriate. Homosexual behavior and incestuous behavior are proscribed by ideal sexual norms; marriage to a member of one's own ethnic group and general class is prescribed.

The Anthropological Perspective

Throughout the chapters that follow we use anthropological data to indicate ways in which the sexuality of other cultures differs from the sexuality of the culture in the United States. The anthropological perspective provides a necessary corrective to an exclusive focus upon one's own society. The realization that many cultures permit premarital and extramarital intercourse (Murdock, 1949) and that many cultures do not teach fear of homosexuality (Tripp, 1975) adds to an understanding of human sexuality.

Ethnicity is the sociological term used to designate both racial and cultural differences between peoples: an ethnic group is one that shares a common heritage, subjective feelings of indentification, and, sometimes, a common language or dialect. The main ethnic groups in the United States are the so-called white ethnic groups; blacks; Chicanos, Puerto Ricans, and other Hispanics; Asians; and native Americans. For the purpose of relating sexuality and ethnicity, this chapter will deal mainly with whites and blacks because the most complete data exist for these two groups.

The Heritage of Slavery

The history of black sexuality and the family in the United States has two dimensions in addition to those of agrarianism and Victorianism: slavery, 28

Differences in sex roles and relationships between blacks and whites are due in part to the black heritage of slavery. This photograph was made in 1862 of blacks who were technically still in slavery.
The New York Historical Society, New York City

and a prior heritage in African culture. These two added elements have resulted in considerable differences between blacks and whites in family structure and sex roles and relationships, which have ramifications in the area of sexual response. The effects of slavery and prior African culture on black society today, however, are the subject of considerable debate. We present first the conventional depiction of the effects of slavery on black men and women, then the alternative perspectives of *Time on the Cross* — a book that discusses the economics of black slavery in the United States (Fogel and Engerman, 1974) — and African cultural resilience.

The Conventional Perspective With the uprooting of blacks from their culture and kin in the nations of Africa, blacks of many ethnic groups, languages, and customs were cast together as slaves in the new continent. Whatever they made of family and sexual relationships was a composite of enforced Southern white patterns, fragmented memories of past culture, and adaptations brought about by the condition of slavery itself. With regard to sexuality, the pivotal factor was the dismantling of any definite, stable family structure and the encouragement of promiscuity so that new slaves could be produced in as great a number as possible.

Use to be they was always tellin' us — "Have a lotsa babies, have a lotsa babies!" — cause they wants a lotta work done on the land. Now they tellin' us — "Don't have no mo' babies" — cause they don't want so many colored peoples goin' up to vote!

Carson, 1969, p. 210

Since the time of slavery, many black women have had to raise their families and fend for themselves in the absence of husbands or other

Female-Headed Households, in Percentages   Table 1.1

Lowest Social-Class Level		Middle Social-Class Level		Highest Social-Class Level	
White	Negro	White	Negro	White	Negro
15.4	43.9	10.3	27.9	0.0	13.7

Source: Daniel P. Moynihan, "The Negro Family" (Washington, D.C.: U.S. Department of Labor, March, 1965), p. 36.

stable relationships with males. To a large degree this is still true. A disproportionate number of the households headed by females in the United States are headed by black females. (See Table 1.1) In contrast, black males have been virtually without any important role in the black family other than a sexual one. During slavery they were not even able to protect their wives and daughters from the sexual advances of the white men.

Black wives assume that they are basically responsible for the family; they know they can head their households if they must, and their culture provides techniques and support for doing this. The men take for granted that they can ignore family responsibilities without serious repercussions. The black male's marginal economic status means he is often unable to fulfill the role of provider. In addition, the black male peer group gives high marks for masculinity to those who do not become too thoroughly domesticated after marriage (Liebow, 1967). In the black lower-class community, getting married is seen not so much as the contracting of a long-term relationship but more as a rite that everyone should go through to signify coming of age or adult maturity. The result is a pattern of marital instability (Rainwater, 1970, pp. 155–187).

It's the man's fault because he doesn't want to settle down. He's not willing to accept responsibility. He doesn't know how to be a husband. . . . It's not a strong marriage to begin with. They're either too young or there's a lack of income. Usually it's the man, sometimes the woman, who causes it. Steady income is the main problem. If the husband is working she would not have to seek aid, and you can't get aid with a man around the house.

Rainwater, 1970, p. 169

Time on the Cross   The vast difference between the conventional depiction and that of *Time on the Cross* (Fogel and Engerman, 1974) is summarized by Jane Cassels Record as she first quotes from Alvin Poussaint, a black psychiatrist, and then summarizes *Time on the Cross's* argument:

"Families were broken: black men were emasculated and black women were systematically exploited sexually and otherwise vilely degraded."

Record, 1975, p. 361

It will certainly be news to many sociologists and historians that slave owners were highly sensitive to and desirous of maintaining the integrity of the slave family; that violations of slave women were rare, that male slaves held most of the traditional rights of husbands and fathers, and that when slaves had to be sold, every effort was made to keep the slave family intact.

Record, 1975, p. 363

Time on the Cross attempts to re-evaluate the effects of slavery on blacks, using a newly popular methodological approach called cliometrics. Cliometricians use quantifiable historical records as data; in the case of slavery, these include the quantity and type of food reserved for slaves, birth and death records, and records of slave sales. In addition to asserting that slaves were often better off and better fed than free white workers at the same level, Fogel and Engerman (1974a) give a completely new picture of the slave family and black and white sexuality.

Fogel and Engerman note that the slave family was rarely fragmented. Records from slave transactions in New Orleans show that more than 84 percent of all slaves over the age of fourteen who were sold were unmarried, and that of those who had been married 6 percent were sold with their mates and about 25 percent were probably voluntarily separated. Statutes forbade the sale of children under eleven with the exception of orphans, and only 9.3 percent of the sales were of children under thirteen.

Further, the authors of *Time on the Cross* argue that slaves contracted informal marriages, which were sanctioned and enforced by slaveowners to the extent of punishing slaves who committed adultery. The slave family was male dominated and patriarchal, just like the Southern white family of which it was the echo.

Fogel and Engerman do not argue that interracial sex between black males and white females was strongly proscribed. They do imply that black female slaves were much more rarely sexually abused by masters than has been assumed in the conventional argument.

Fogel and Engerman have been accused of overidealizing slave life and of ignoring the qualitatively debased aspect of slavery in favor of dry quantification (Record, 1975; Bryce-Laporte, 1975). However, although they have been criticized methodologically their findings do challenge the conventional portrayal of the black family's cultural heritage as unremittingly disadvantaged.

The African Heritage   Yet another less dismal alternative portrayal of black sexuality and the family stresses the African heritage of blacks in the United States and their "cultural resilience" (Herskovitz, 1944). The black-heritage perspective interprets the black family with a female as its head differently from the conventional depiction and implicity challenges Fogel and Engerman's depiction of the patriarchal slave family.

31

As Table 1.1 shows, there is a greater percentage of households headed by females among blacks than among whites, especially in the lower classes. The conventional argument suggests that this is because of the family-shattering heritage of slavery. An individual who believes that the black family is basically patriarchal might argue that these families are only nominally matriarchal; the mother must hide her male companion from prying welfare workers in order to obtain Aid to Families of Dependent Children or other aid. Both these views of the household headed by a female have a hidden value bias: this type of household is a bad thing.

Those who favor the African-heritage explanation, however, might point out that *matrilocality*, or residence with or near the mother, is a common cultural pattern in many African societies. To imply that such a pattern is "bad" is to denigrate all but the agrarian patriarchal family model (here feminists might agree with black culturalists). Further, to insist on the conventional portrait of the emasculated black man is simply a way of reinforcing prejudices about blacks while symbolically castrating the sexually feared black man.

More empirical research is needed to understand the historical background of blacks in the United States and the significance of such phenomena as the female headed household. Until such research is completed, the empirical data on black sex roles and sexuality exist in a vacuum of theoretical interpretation.

Sexual Behavior and Attitudes Among Blacks

There are some studies of the differences between blacks and whites in sexual behavior and attitudes. Blacks, for example, are generally more inclined than whites to express acceptance of premarital sexual intercourse. But there are important differences in attitudes within the black community. For example, the differences between black men's and black women's sexual attitudes are similar to the differences in attitude between white men and white women. Specifically, black men are more accepting of premarital sexuality than black women are, although the difference in attitude is not as large as that between white men and white women. Black women are more likely than black men to be influenced in their attitudes toward premarital sex by the affectionate or love quality of the relationship (Staples, 1972; Christensen and Johnson, 1978).

Black Men and Women   In the general black subculture there is less of a double standard of sexual behavior for men and women than there is among whites. The experience of intercourse is often a symbol of status or of passing into womanhood for the lower-class black woman. Black women tend to be freer from the stigma of being considered an "easy lay"   32 when they participate in sexual relations than their white counterparts are. Unlike white women, who often view sex as a necessary duty with the purpose of giving a man pleasure, black women expect their sexual partners to try to satisfy them sexually. In contrast to most white women, black women talk with other women about female sexual experiences.

The sexual attitudes and behavior of middle-class blacks today are closer to those of middle-class whites than to those of lower-class blacks.
Joel Gordon

33

Because of this greater openness regarding women's sexual needs and activities, it is not surprising to find that a greater proportion of black lower-class women than white lower-class women reach orgasm in their premarital sexual activities (Staples, 1972; Staples, 1978a; Staples, 1978b).

Social Class Factors   Attitudes and sexual practices of blacks also differ depending on social class. Among middle-class blacks sexual attitudes and behavior are closer to those of middle-class whites than to those of lower-class blacks. For example, virginity at marriage as well as erection difficulties among males and inability to reach orgasm among females are more common in the black middle class than in the black lower class.

Because the concentration of blacks in the lower class is relatively greater than that of whites, it is not surprising to find that there is considerably more reported premarital intercourse among blacks than among whites in the teenage years, particularly for females. A black adolescent girl is about three times more likely to report premarital sex than a white adolescent girl. But this difference between black and white females disappears when social class or age at marriage is held constant. Among males, blacks have a slightly higher incidence of premarital intercourse than whites, but this difference also disappears when social class is held constant (Staples, 1972; Roebuck and McGee, 1977).

Black lower-class sex roles and sexuality patterns are similar to lower-class patterns in general. Black lower-class males, like other lower-class males, prove their macho potency by the sexual exploitation of women. The women, though more sexually open and economically independent than lower-class women in general, nevertheless may be sexually subservient to the men. One black woman comments:

If she's a young woman she has to have sex and if she don't have a husband she goes from one man to another. She misses the care that her husband gives her and also the rest because she has to work hard because he is not there to give it to her. Women make it so bad on themselves. They go from one man to another, and this just runs them down.

Rainwater, 1970, p. 178

Interracial Sex

Interracial sexual interaction and procreation during the time of slavery were permitted between white men and black women, but not between white women and black men under any conditions. Although sexual relations between the white men and black women were not sanctioned legally or by the church, they were quite common in the South. Sexual relationships between white women and black men were not completely unknown, but they were labeled as so morally reprehensible in the South that they were extremely rare. Some blacks felt that white males were

34

afraid of the rumored sexual superiority of black men, and therefore white men tried to prevent sexual interaction between white women and black men because they feared white women might come to prefer blacks (Davis and Cross, 1979).

One young black man proudly asserts: The sexual ideal for the black man is to be considered a super stud by his peers, both male and female. Therefore I feel that the idea of the black male possessing super sexual virility is for the most part true. Not because I am black, but rather because I feel that so much pressure and emphasis is put on the black male during sexual relations that he becomes defensive, and in his defense becomes more conscious of his performance causing him to reach out to his partner stronger than a nonblack ... Regardless of what anthropologists think, I see a well-defined difference between black and white men of equal size and height ... One is that black males are more tailored through the waist, buttocks and thighs. Secondly, I honestly believe that the black male has a bigger penis.

From the authors' files

Interestingly, at the present time the pattern of interracial relationships may be quite different. We say "may be" because the only empirical evidence for such patterns comes from studies of college students. The frequency of sexual contacts between black men and white women is probably greater than sexual contacts between white men and black women. One study of college students reported that 90 percent of the black men reported experiences in interracial dating, but only 12 percent of the white men had such experiences. None of the white men had ever had more than a casual dating relationship with a black woman, but almost half the black males had "gone steady" with a white female (Staples, 1972, p. 14).

If one accepts the conventional perspective on the effects of slavery, the current relationship between white men and black women can be partially explained. In the past, the black woman was treated as nothing more than a sex object by the white man. She was virtually unprotected from unwanted sexual advances, and served as a concubine or prostitute for him. Although she was an acceptable sex object, she was considered too inferior to be his wife. Even today black women are sometimes the object of annoying or obscene approaches by white men. Today, when a white man wants to date a black woman, she may assume that he is interested in nothing but sex. She is likely to feel insulted and to reject his advances. At the same time the white man feels that he gains no status from dating a black woman because he defines her by cultural stereotypes such as "inferior" and an "easy lay" (Staples, 1972).

In contrast, it may be considered a status symbol for a black man when he can date a white woman in a culture that has traditionally considered blacks unsuitable even to attend the same schools as whites. White

35

women may find in black men an acceptance in sexual relationships that they do not always find among white men.

One white woman comments: I always did feel attracted to black men because they don't mind big women and I am sensitive about my weight. Besides, they like to be with white women so I feel instantly accepted. . . . My sister married a black, but she always was the rebel of the family and I think that is why she did it. But there is such a difference in class between them that I don't think they can make a go of it. Like one time when I was at their house for dinner I was eating with my left hand in my lap and he said, "Why don't you put your arms on the table and relax and enjoy the food instead of sitting there so fucking prissy like that." It's just a difference in the way we were all brought up.

From the authors' files

Some black men will pursue interracial sex in order to enhance their male peer status, with an enthusiasm that often angers black women (Day, 1972). With the development of black pride in their ethnic identity, this status may no longer be forthcoming, and interracial sexual activity may be stripped of its great social and psychological significance.

It is clear that there are some differences in the sexual attitudes and behavior of whites and blacks. Many of these differences are related to the educational, occupational, or status differences between most segments of the two groups, and others are related to the historical experience of black slavery. As the barriers to black and white parity slowly fall, blacks may merge with the white majority in their cultural ideals and behavior. On the other hand, institutional parity between blacks and whites may not mean integration and the melting pot, but rather cultural pluralism. In this case, black culture hopefully will take what is best for the development of human sexual potential from both the white and black cultures, and leave what is least fulfilling.

Social Institutions and Sexual Interaction

Sociologists and sex researchers are interested not only in cultural norms but also in social structural factors that affect sexuality. Sexuality in our society does not stand alone; it is embedded in a context of social institutions (the horizontal dimension of social structure) and social strata (the vertical dimension).

Social Institutions

Sexuality in all societies is embedded in a series of other institutional contexts: economics, the family, law, religion, politics, and so on. Fur-

36

thermore, it is affected by the historical developments occurring in all these related institutions, and in society in general.

Traditionally, sexuality has not been institutionalized as a sphere distinct from the family and other institutions, although this may be changing today. Even the sociological and anthropological definition of the family locates sexuality within it: among its other functions, the family is said to regulate and organize sexual behavior.

On the other hand, there is a gap between the study of the family and the study of sexuality. Experts on family structures tend to come from the sociological tradition, whereas sex researchers have an eclectic variety of backgrounds in psychology, sociology, anthropology, medicine, and other disciplines. Family sociologists frequently take little cognizance of sexual activity within the family, and sex researchers fail to appreciate the significance of sexuality within the family. As a result, although sexuality is linked with the family, little is known empirically about the way they overlap; for example, the way in which spouses organize their sexual contact around the demands of household and child care has never been analyzed.

The influence of the Judeo-Christian heritage on the family and sexuality is still felt in contemporary society, as in this Jewish wedding ceremony.
Joel Gordon

Law and religion have had a great influence on human sexuality in Western society. This influence tends to be mutually reinforcing because the Judeo-Christian heritage combines religious and legal authority. The sexual norms and laws of our culture, whether real or ideal, are strongly influenced by the patriarchal authority of Jewish and Christian religious leaders since the period of Jewish exile in Babylon in about 550 B.C. (Tripp, 1975, p. 6).

Politics and formal education are two institutions whose relation to sexuality has come into sharp focus only in recent years. Sex education in the schools, a still controversial subject, has in many school districts come to supplement sex education gleaned from parents and peers.

The school has been given by society a clear-cut role to play, to be a primary and trustworthy source of truth and factual knowledge for every child. Every right-thinking parent should welcome the honest efforts of educators to present the true facts about human sexual behavior at those moments in the child's evolution when such facts are most necessary to him for his protection and orderly development. Never, under any circumstances, can the school be considered as trying to replace the parents — its aim is rather to supplement and complement their efforts so that all of us may share the same knowledge and live in mutual respect of it.

Calderone, 1968, p. vi

The Political Perspective

The political perspective on human sexuality involves a new interpretation of the fact that sexuality in our society includes not only sex behavior and sexual attitudes but also sex roles. Feminist writers such as Kate Millett (1969), Caroline Bird (1971), and Shulamith Firestone (1970) have been instrumental in developing the political perspective in sexuality, and the definition of sex roles and sexuality as political matters. From the political perspective, sex roles are neither biologically determined nor chance developments of history but occur as a result of the domination of one sex over the other.

A disinterested examination of our system of sexual relationships must point out that the situation between the sexes now, and throughout history, is a case of . . . a relationship of dominance and subordinance . . . the birthright priority whereby males rule females. . . . Sexual dominion obtains as perhaps the most pervasive ideology of our culture and provides its most fundamental concept of power.

Millett, 1969, p. 25

Sexual Interaction

Culture and social structure form the background for the sexual scenario: sexual interaction in our society. An individual engaging in solitary mas-

38

turbation, two individuals engaging in homosexual or heterosexual activity, or a group of individuals at an "orgy" come equipped with both a cultural background and a specific social class, ethnicity, age, and sex. At the same time, the scenario is guided by its own dynamic: people begin lines of action, develop them, and modify them in interaction with what others are doing in the social situation. Actual incidents of sexual interaction are as important in the study of sexuality as general cultural and behavioral trends are, although they have only very recently been the subject of direct observation and analysis (Humphreys, 1970). Furthermore, incidents of sexual interaction provide a link between the social and individual levels of analysis.

Human sexuality is profoundly social and at the same time profoundly human and profoundly individual. Every human society must institutionalize sexuality in a way that takes account of the biological shaping, sexual arousal and release, birth, death, and maturation of human organisms: the physiology of humanity and sexuality. At the individual level, individual psychology is instrumental in motivating people to choose among the alternative patterns of sexuality (however culturally limited this range might be) that are available in all societies.

Sexual Motivation

Individual sexual motivation is a complex concept, with both psychological and sociological aspects. Psychologically, motivation refers to drives, needs, or energy sources; sociologically, motivation refers to the symbolic linking of people with their actions.

The Psychology of Motivation Psychiatrists and psychologists have taken as their province of research the often unconscious needs, forces, and drives that direct individuals to one source of satisfaction rather than another. Psychologists and psychiatrists vary in their views on which particular need or needs are the most fundamental motivation for sexual and other conduct: the sexual drive itself (Freud), the will to power (Adler), or sexual and spiritual needs (Jung). All agree, however, that needs motivate behavior and that behavior can be the result of unconcious forces.

We are all creatures of need. We are born needing, and the vast majority of us die after a lifetime of struggle with many of our needs unfulfilled. These needs are not excessive — to be fed, kept warm and dry, to grow and develop at our own pace, to be held and caressed, and to be stimulated. . . . A loved child does not grow up into an adult with an insatiable craving for sex. He has been held and caressed by his parents and does not need to use sex to satisfy that early need.

Janov, 1970, p. 20

39

The Sociology of Motivation   From the sociological perspective, motives are the symbolic links between people and actions (Mills, 1940). Sexual motives are the ways in which individuals in society interpret their own sexual behavior and that of others, to make it meaningful. Kando, for example, cites the motives given by a transsexual for having undergone a sex-change operation:

I did it for the psychological thing. . . . I need the reassurance that I am a woman. I don't have a man to make love to me and I don't care. . . . I wanted to be a woman, whether the sex part was successful or not. I wanted to be of one sex, dress like one, act like one. . . . Well, mentally I always thought of myself as a woman. I don't even remember thinking of myself as a man.

Kando, 1973, p. 96

The physiology, psychology, and sociology of sexuality interact to produce a particular culture and particular sexual interactions among individuals. In turn, sexuality, the individual, and society influence one another; a change in one area has profound ramifications for each of the others. This interdependence is essential in all aspects of the human condition.

Chapter 2 / *The Psychology of Sexual Interaction*

Sexuality is seen from the physiological perspective in terms of the functioning of the body, from the sociological perspective in terms of social interaction, and from the psychological perspective as an aspect of individual personality development. From the psychological perspective, human sexuality is interpreted as a product of universal psychological processes rather than of extensive cultural shaping.

The Freudian Heritage

Although contemporary psychology has a variety of subperspectives, the contributions of Sigmund Freud in the early 1900s remain central to the discipline. Controversial as many of Freud's theories were and still are, their importance to the study of sexuality cannot be overlooked. At the most general level, his major contributions were the redefinition of sexuality as an acceptable topic of research and analysis, and his conception of psychological determinism.

In several decades of reflection and observation of medical cases, Freud, a physician, became convinced that the presumed asexuality of children,

Freud considered the asexuality of children to be in reality a repression of sexual desires.
Jean-Claude Lejeune/Stock, Boston

"good" women, and others was in reality a repression of universal sexual desires — desires that negated the traditional separation of body and spirit, male and female, and child and adult. Freud began to study scientifically the sexual life and sexual repression, the result of which he called *neurosis.* One of the major findings of his life's work was that human beings are sexual beings and that sexuality is normal. Freud's second contribution was *psychological determinism,* or the theory that the causes of human behavior are located in psychological processes that are universal and cross-cultural.

Eros and Libido

The most fundamental human drives, for Freud, were *eros,* the life instinct, and *thanatos,* the destructive drive toward death. Freud conceptualized eros as the source of the instinct for survival. Part of the survival instinct involves the intake of food, the drive toward which is labeled *hunger.* Another part of the survival instinct is sexuality, the drive toward which Freud labeled *libido.* Libido is a sexual energy that involves the whole being rather than simply the genitals, and is a major determinant of life activities.

According to Freud, libido energy follows a pattern of developmental stages corresponding to the physical growth of the individual. For the child the whole libido is centered in the self — an *ego libido.* In this stage the child is totally egoistic and self-absorbed. The next stage is the *narcissistic libido,* when the libido takes on erotic associations. As the child develops further, the libido is transferred to outside objects; this is *object libido.*

In Freud's psychoanalytic conception of neurosis, abnormality is often related to the inability to transfer libido energy to outside objects. The individual should be able to transfer libido to others and in turn receive the libido of others in sexual and affectional exchanges. Otherwise, a variety of neuroses may develop.

Id, ego, and superego　In his later writings, Freud altered his main focus from the libido to a three-part division of the human psyche, which he called the id, the ego, and the superego. The *id* is the home of the unconscious mind, that realm of childhood sexual experiences that has been repressed out of easy conscious recall. Freud distinguished between the unconscious and the preconscious, which contains experiences that have been forgotten but are not repressed.

The *ego* is the rational part of the human personality and operates in the unconscious, preconscious, and conscious mind. The ego develops during the socialization process by which a child becomes an adult; the ego acts as a mediator between biological instincts and cultural rules.　43

Even prior to Freud's time, sexual energy was often equated with life energy, as indicated by this Peruvian pottery from the Mochica culture, about 600–700 A.D.

Courtesy of William Dellenback, Institute for Sex Research, Inc.

The *superego* is the conscience; in sociological terminology it represents the internalization of society within the individual; for the psychologist it represents the internalized parent. The superego is a moral monitor, the judge of what is wrong and the self-punisher. The *ego ideal,* on the other hand, is an internalized sense of what is right and ought to be rewarded.

Repression   Repression is a major factor in the inability to transfer libido to outside forces, and occurs when experiences from the conscious or preconscious are forced into the unconcious. Most likely to be repressed are early-childhood experiences, often of a sexual nature, that cause trauma or extreme emotional disturbance. Much of what is repressed in childhood consists of sexual experiences and thoughts, particularly sexual thoughts concerned with parents.

44

Repression involves the inability to transfer libido to outside forces.
Frank Siteman/Picture Cube

The repressed material remains in the unconscious as unresolved emotional conflicts, causing later emotional problems. The focus of Freud's life's work was psychoanalysis, by which method he hoped to cure people of the emotional problems caused by repressed material. Although Freud's concern was to define sexuality as normal, most of what he wrote about was what he perceived as pathological sexuality. This emphasis occurred mainly because he developed his theories from working with patients who had emotional troubles.

Sublimation Whereas repression is potentially harmful emotionally, sublimation is a necessary aspect of human life in society. All societies require the sublimation of a great deal of libido or sexual energy, which is why, for Freud, culture was the enemy of the individual human being. *Sublimation* is the blocking and rechanneling of sexual energies by the demands of the culture. These blocked sexual energies are then transferred to other areas, such as art and science. Freud pointed out the irony that in those cultures with the most sublimation, the people may be the

45

most creative and advanced technologically — yet people tend to be happier and more fulfilled sexually in less advanced civilizations

Stages of Sexual Development

Freud proposed a theory of stages of sexual development, universal in all cultures, which culminate in mature, adult sexuality. He explained what he called sexual "aberrations" or "perversions" as cases of sexual development arrested at one of the immature stages.

The Pregenital Stage   The first stage of sexual development, from birth until three to five years of age, Freud referred to as *pregenital,* or *infantile,* sexuality. Infantile sexuality is both autoerotic and polymorphously perverse. In its *autoerotic aspect,* the libido is centered upon the self in ego libido. The *polymorphous perverse aspect* refers to the fact that childhood sexuality is not focused on the genitals as a source of pleasure, but can in fact attach itself to any part of the body found pleasurable by manual exploration.

Freud called the parts of the body that the child stimulates to pleasure *erogenous zones,* and noted that the mucous membranes of the mouth, genitals, or anus are frequently the chosen sources of libidinous pleasure. Freud subdivided infantile pregenital sexuality into two subphases related to the mucous membranes: the oral, or cannibalistic, stage and the anal-sadistic stage.

The *oral stage* of pregenital sexuality begins with the experience of feeding, from nipple or bottle. The child who suckles the mother is, in fact, a little cannibal who seeks to devour and incorporate the source of food during feeding.

The *anal-sadistic stage* of sexual development occurs as the child is toilet trained. The pushing, active action of the bowel in expelling feces is, according to Freud, the prototype of masculine activity that in its extreme form becomes sadism. At the same time, the pleasure that the child obtains from the passage of feces through the mucous membrane of the bowel signifies the feminine, passive principle that in its extreme form becomes masochism. According to Freud, the individual's basic sexuality and personality are determined by experiences during the oral and anal pregenital stages.

The Latency Phase   Between the ages of three and five, the child passes into the latency phase of childhood in which early-childhood sexuality and traumatic experiences are sublimated and repressed. During the period from the inception of latency to puberty, sexual impulses that do arise are quickly stifled by the counterforces of sublimation. The psychic   46 counterforce of sublimation produces controls over sexual impulses in the form of morality, shame, and guilt.

Puberty   The transition to adult sexuality occurs at the period of physiological change known as puberty. The sexual directions of adulthood, according to Freud, are determined by the directions taken at puberty; but the sexual choices of puberty are determined by repressed infantile sexuality. Thus, adult sexuality (and in the logic of Freudian psychology, the entire personality) is dependent upon early-childhood sexuality. At the time of puberty, male sexuality and female sexuality begin to take different directions: males pay more direct attention to their enhanced libido, and females experience a new repression of theirs.

Adult Genital Sexuality   Adult sexuality is centered on the genitals rather than diffused throughout the body, and is directed toward another individual rather than being autoerotic. In Freud's terms, the libido of adulthood is object libido rather than narcissistic or ego libido.

Freud distinguished between the sexual object and the sexual aim. The sexual object is the person — or thing — toward which the individual is sexually attracted, whereas the sexual aim is the type of fulfillment sought, whether in intercourse, oral contact, or something else. For Freud, the only normal sexuality is that which has as its aim genital sexual intercourse and as its object a nonrelative of the opposite sex.

Sexual activity other than intercourse with a member of the opposite sex was normal for Freud only if it was confined to what he called *fore-pleasure.* He distinguished between fore-pleasure and the orgasm, or *end-*

According to Freud, adult sexuality is directed toward another individual rather than being autoerotic and is centered on the genitals rather than diffused throughout the body.
Peter Menzel/Stock, Boston

pleasure. For Freud, the only sexual act that qualified as mature adult sexuality was sexual intercourse between a man and a woman culminating in orgasm. Freud regarded any other form of sexuality as, at least to some extent, an aberration.

Clitoral Versus Vaginal Orgasm

Freud wrote little on the male orgasm but much on the female orgasm, and what he wrote has stirred controversy that continues even today. The controversy about female sexuality concerns the clitoral versus the vaginal orgasm. (See Selection 2.1.) The early genital sexuality of the female, according to Freud, is focused on the clitoris as a source of pleasure. The girl learns to masturbate by manipulating her clitoris just as the boy learns to stimulate his penis. The sign of mature female sexuality is the transfer of sexual pleasure and orgasm from the clitoris to the vagina. This transference signals the end of penis envy and the acceptance of the role of the female as passive receptacle in the sexual act. According to Freud, for the male there is only one type of orgasm, but for the female there are two: the immature clitoral orgasm and the mature vaginal one.

The Clitoral-Vaginal Orgasm Controversy   Selection 2.1

The controversy initiated by Freud concerning the female orgasm involves one of two issues: the existence of some difference between the clitoral and the vaginal orgasm, and the superiority of one type of orgasm over the other.

   In the following statements, Freud argues both that a differentiation exists and that the vaginal orgasm is more mature than the clitoral. Masters and Johnson present evidence that there is no difference. Anne Koedt, a contemporary feminist, asserts that there is only one type of orgasm; therefore, there can be no controversy regarding superiority or inferiority. Finally, Jill Johnson, a radical lesbian feminist, stresses that she has experienced a subjective difference between clitoral and vaginal orgasms and that the vaginal type is more mature.

Freud / The Vaginal Orgasm

   All that I have been able to discover about masturbation in little girls refers to the clitoris, and not to the other external genitals which are so important for the future sexual functions. . . .

   If the woman finally submits to the sexual act, the clitoris becomes stimulated and its role is to conduct the excitement to the adjacent genital parts; it acts

Freud, 1938, pp. 613–614

here like a chip of pinewood, which is utilized to set fire to harder wood. It often takes some time before this transference is accomplished, and during this transition the young wife remains anesthetic. This anesthesia may become permanent if the clitoric zone refuses to give up its excitability; a condition brought on by profuse sexual activities in infantile life. It is known that anesthesia in women is often only apparent and local. They are anesthetic at the vaginal entrance, but not at all unexcitable through the clitoris or even through other zones. Besides these erogenous causes of anesthesia, there are also psychic causes, likewise determined by the repression.

If the transference of the erogenous excitability from the clitoris to the vaginal entrance succeeds, the woman then changes her leading zone for the future sexual activity.

Masters and Johnson / Human Sexual Response

Finally, a brief consideration of the fifth and last of the questions raised about the role of the clitoris in female sexuality: Are clitoral and vaginal orgasms truly separate anatomic entities? From a biologic point of view, the answer to this question is an unequivocal No. The literature abounds with descriptions and discussions of vaginal as opposed to clitoral orgasms. ... From an anatomic point of view, there is absolutely no difference in the responses of the pelvic viscera to effective sexual stimulation, regardless of whether the stimulation occurs as a result of clitoral-body or mons area manipulation, natural or artificial coition, or, for that matter, specific stimulation of any other erogenous area of the female body.

Masters and Johnson, 1966, p. 66

Anne Koedt / The Myth of the Vaginal Orgasm

Whenever female orgasm and frigidity are discussed, a false distinction is made between the vaginal and the clitoral orgasm. Frigidity has generally been defined by men as the failure of women to have vaginal orgasms. Actually the vagina is not a highly sensitive area and is not constructed to achieve orgasm. It is the clitoris which is the center of sexual sensitivity and which is the female equivalent of the penis.

... the orgasm necessarily takes place in the sexual organ equipped for sexual climax — the clitoris. The orgasm experience may also differ in degree of intensity — some more localized, and some more diffuse and sensitive. But they are all clitoral orgasms. All this leads to some interesting questions about conventional sex and our role in it. Men have orgasms essentially by friction with the vagina, not the clitoral area, which is external and not able to cause friction the way penetration does. Women have thus been defined sexually in terms of what pleases men; our own biology has not been properly analyzed. Instead, we are fed the myth of the liberated woman and her vaginal orgasm — an orgasm which in fact does not exist.

Koedt, 1971, pp. 308–309

49

Jill Johnson / The Myth of the Myth of the Vaginal Orgasm

I always agreed with one half of Freud's equation. That a woman moves from clitoral to vaginal orgasm. And that the latter *is* more mature in the sense that the activation of the inner walls brings about a more profound intensification of orgasm. I would add that this shift occurs in two kinds of time — over a period of months or years as a "discovery" of the orgastic potential of the internal walls, and as a transition in every sexual encounter, moving from initial stimulation of clitoris (as the seat of sensation, the *origin* of satisfaction) to full orgasm experienced in the total organ which includes the "deep" vaginal wall. I take issue like the feminists with Freud's postulation of "heterosexual maturity." Since a woman can achieve vaginal orgasm herself or with another woman clearly his case for maturity was in the interests of the continuation of phallic imperialism.

Johnson, 1973, pp. 169–170

It is clear from an examination of women's accounts of orgasm that the subjective perception of the location and intensity of orgasm varies considerably. The arguments about the existence and inferiority or superiority of different types of orgasm are, in a sense, pointless. Ample evidence is available from empirical studies and subjective accounts to make it clear that the female orgasm is variable subjectively.

The Jungian Perspective

Jung carried Freud's identification to perhaps an even greater extreme. Jung differentiated between the *personal unconscious,* a concept of the unconscious similar to Freud's, and the collective unconscious. According to Jung, the *collective unconscious,* from which consciousness itself emerges, was shaped in the remote past of human experience; it is located in the physiological contours of the brain. The collective unconscious contains the animus and anima.

The *anima* is the masculine element contained in the collective unconscious of the female; the *animus* is the female element present in the male. Animus and anima enable male and female to comprehend the experience of the other sex. Animus and anima are the mirror image of each other and have roughly the same dichotomous qualities Freud associated with masculine and feminine, such as active/passive, weak/strong, and dominant/nurturing.

According to Jung, human life is motivated by a fundamental "general life instinct," which he also called *psychic energy* or *libido.* Unlike Freud, however, he believed that libido was not solely a sexual energy, but was the total of a variety of drives, including spiritual and intellectual drives (1972, pp. 29-30).

50

Like Freud, Jung saw neurosis as the product of repression and a divided self: "Neurosis is self division" (1972a, p.20). However, an individual could repress spiritual needs and be consciously sexual just as she or he could repress sexual needs and be consciously spiritual.

Havelock Ellis's Perspective

Havelock Ellis was critical of Freud for many of the reasons Freud is criticized by contemporary psychologists. He pointed out, for example, that Freud overgeneralizes in his conceptualization of psychological forces as universal, because different cultures have different family structures and different sexual norms and values. Ellis also criticized Freud for not taking into account the subjectiveness of human beings, which monitors incoming experience and assigns meaning to it. In particular, he felt, it was not possible to assign to the mind of the child such adult meanings as *homosexual, incestuous,* or even *sexual.* In these criticisms, Ellis questioned both the nonsociocultural approach of Freud and his thoroughgoing psychological determinism.

Havelock Ellis himself studied and wrote about what he perceived as both normal and abnormal sexuality. His concept of sexuality was similar

51

to Freud's: normal sex is that which has the potential for procreation; therefore, normal sex is heterosexual intercourse between an adult man and woman. At the same time, Ellis was careful to point out that by labeling all other forms of sexuality as "abnormal" or "deviations" he was not making the negative value judgment implicit in Freud's term *perversion*. In fact, throughout Ellis's writings there is a studied attempt to avoid value judgments relating to sexual behavior, an attempt that is sometimes successful and sometimes not.

Ellis criticized Freud's conceptualization of male and female sexuality, particularly the concept of the transfer of the orgasm from clitoris to vagina. Ellis was aware of the continuing significance of the clitoris for the adult female orgasm, although unlike some later theorists he did not claim that the vagina lacked sensation. At the same time, Ellis was almost as adamant as Freud in linking biological maleness and femaleness with sociopsychological masculinity and femininity. Furthermore, he emphasized the role of procreation in sexuality even more heavily than Freud, and regarded the childless marital sexual union as something of a tragedy.

Behaviorist Psychology

Behaviorist psychology is as far removed from Freudian influences as it is possible to move, given the vast influence of Freudian thinking on all theories of sexuality today. In relation to sex, the only apparent Freudian influence on the behaviorists is in the concepts that sex is normal and that it is pleasurable, both of which are implicit rather than explicit in behaviorist psychology. The major distinction between Freud and the behaviorists is that whereas Freud was concerned almost exclusively with internal psychic processes, the behavioral psychologists focus only on observable, measurable human and animal behavior.

Human and Animal Behavior

Behaviorists are interested in animal behavior because animals may be easily observed and their behavior measured in laboratory settings. As a result of their laboratory observations, behaviorists conceptualize three levels of human and animal behavior: imprinted, instinctive, and learned.

Imprinting   Although the term *imprinting* was not in use during the nineteenth century, what Freud explained as fetishism is similar to the process psychologists now call imprinting. *Fetishism* is sexual arousal by some object or body part, such as a handkerchief, fur wrap, or foot. Freud   52 believed that fetishism arises as a result of some incident during the critical period of a child's development, at two or three years of age. Brecher summarizes:

The object of the imprinting may vary widely; anything from fur or velvet to a particular kind of hairdo may function as a fetish. Once a man adopts a fetish, he does not adopt a second fetish. The imprinting occurs at a particular moment and is complete without repetition. Neither its initiation nor its survival depends on extrinsic rewards or punishments.

Brecher, 1969, p. 269

   Imprinting differs from ordinary learning because it occurs during a single brief experience rather than over an entire lifespan, and requires neither reinforcement, repetition, nor reward and punishment. In one brief instant the object becomes imprinted on the child, and it is never superseded by another fetish object (Brecher, 1969, p. 269).

Instinctive Behavior   In the area of sexuality, the behavior of many lower animals is predominantly instinctive and oriented toward the reproduction of the species. Behaviorist researchers have described the sexual behavior of the stickleback fish as an example of instinctive behavior.

The stickleback's mating behavior occurs in a very definite and unalterable sequence in which the completion of one phase is necessary to provide the sign stimuli for eliciting the next phase. The stickleback does not begin to build his nest until he has defended the territory for a while. As the first step in nest building, the stickleback digs a small hole. If someone fills up the hole, the stickleback will dig again. Only after many failures will he proceed to build the superstructure without a pit or depression under it. The next phase (courting) normally will not occur until the nest-building phase is completed. If a female enters the territory before the nest is complete, she will be driven away or at best greeted with a few abortive zigzags, which are the beginnings of the courting behavior. . . .

Walker, 1969, pp. 6–7

   When all is ready, the appearance of a female with an egg-swollen belly elicits in the male a characteristic zigzag dance. The dance elicits courting behavior on the part of the female, which in turn causes him to lead her to the nest. He indicates the entrance to the nest and she enters. The male quivers as he nudges the female near her tail. This induces her to spawn. The presence of eggs induces the male to fertilize them.

Learned Behavior   Behavior in human beings is learned through a complex association of stimulus with response. In the human psyche, stimulus and response are associated by symbolic as well as neurological sequences. Even nonhuman primates may, to a degree, exhibit learned

53

behavior. In the following example, Lucy — a chimpanzee reared since infancy in a human family — masturbates using a vacuum cleaner:

Lucy masturbates unexpectedly and with a most imaginative range of objects. One afternoon we watched her leave the living room, take a glass from a kitchen cabinet, get a bottle of gin from the cupboard and pour herself two or three fingers. Then she came back to the living room with her drink, picked up a copy of *National Geographic* and sipped her drink while leafing through the magazine.

Temerlin, 1975, p.61

Suddenly she stopped, as though an idea had hit her. She jumped up and went to the utility closet at the far end of the hall. She opened the door, took out the vacuum cleaner, brought it back to the living room and plugged it in. She removed the end brush from the long aluminum tube to which it was attached, turned on the machine, and applied the pipe to her genitals. She continued to masturbate with the suction from the machine until she had what I inferred to be an orgasm. Then she turned off the machine, picked up her glass of gin and her magazine, lay back on the couch and continued to drink and contemplate the pictures.

The Behaviorist Tradition

Behaviorist learning theory has traditionally been associated with the pioneering work done between the 1900s and the 1930s by Ivan Pavlov, John B. Watson, and Edward L. Thorndike. Today, behaviorism is principally associated with B. F. Skinner, whose *operant reinforcement theory* stresses "the study of responses that are not necessarily elicited by any stimulus (operants) but are strongly under the influence of the consequences of the responses (reinforcement)" (Hall and Lindzey, 1970, p. 477). Skinner distinguishes his concept of operant reinforcement from classic behaviorist psychology, which focuses on the relationship of stimulus to response rather than on the consequences of the response.

Stimulus Response

For the classic behaviorists the basic learning equation is $S \rightarrow R$. S is the observed, measurable stimulus to behavior, R is the observed measured response; between them is the (at least potentially) observable and measurable change or learning in the nervous system that produces the response R. Behavior is learned through a series of stimulus-response situations in which some stimuli are associated with pleasurable and rewarding nervous system changes, and the response is reinforced, and other stimuli are associated with pain and punishment, and the response is extinguished.

54

For the behaviorists the only legitimate data for understanding sexual interaction are the overt, observable responses to overt, observable stimuli. Sexual interaction is not, as it was for Freud, the culmination in action of intricate psychological processes that are symbolic of some early-childhood experiences. Instead, sexuality is a measurable physiological response to a measurable stimulus. Of all the psychological subperspectives, the behaviorist view is closest to the physiological perspective on sexual interaction.

Existential and Humanistic Psychology

Existential psychology and humanistic psychology are both different from Freudian psychology and are considerably distant from the behaviorist emphasis on overt and measurable behavior. Like Freud, humanistic and existentialist psychologists, such as Rollo May, Abraham Maslow, and Erich Fromm, emphasize sexuality as part of the total personality. However, they reverse the causality proposed by Freud: sexuality is no longer the *cause* of human personality development, but instead one *result* of it. Furthermore, sex is only one facet of personality development; like Jung, the humanists do not view sexuality as the primary causal agent in human behavior. Sexuality may be a cause of human behavior, but not the only one. Humanistic psychologists seek cause in the experience of the individual. Like the behaviorists, they seek empirical evidence. Unlike the behaviorists, however, they consider the realm of the empirical to include the subjective, internal experience of the human actor.

Existential Psychology

Existential psychology has its roots in the existential and phenomenological philosophy of Edmund Husserl, Martin Heidegger, Sören Kierkegaard, Jean-Paul Sartre, Albert Camus, and others. The central concept of existentialist psychology is the idea of *being-in-the-world*, or the style of being that a person adopts, as her or his essential, central approach to life. Every individual, according to existential psychologists, has a particular mode of being-in-the-world; those who seek psychotherapy are not medically ill, but simply wish to change their mode of being-in-the-world with the help of the psychotherapist.

Rollo May, an existential psychologist and psychiatrist, is concerned with the ways in which contemporary sexuality can block self-actualization. Contemporary sexuality, he says, is mechanized, banalized, and 55

Existential and humanistic psychologists view sexual love as an affirmation of the self.
Joel Gordon

alienated from the experience of passion. He comments that the Victorians sought love without sex; the moderns are sexy but repress passion.

People today, according to May, are often preoccupied with the technical aspects of sex as performance, which engenders a good deal of anxiety and guilt about inadequate performance. At the same time, people seek their identities in the sex roles they play, so that their sexual failure generalizes to a feeling of failure as a whole person.

Like Freud, Rollo May has a definition of "good" (mature adult) sexuality, which he says can legitimately provide a meaningful sense of personal identity. One value in what he calls *sexual love* is an affirmation of the self; another is the expansion of one's awareness by the experience of commingling. The experiences of tenderness and togetherness and the loss of aloneness are also values inherent in sexual love. Finally, the sexual climax unites the pair in a transcendent consciousness that makes them one with nature. In Rollo May it is possible to find the mysticism of Jung and the psychoanalytic expertise of Freud, combined with a knowledge of existential philosophy.

Humanistic Psychology

Humanistic psychology is similar in many ways to existential psychology, but it has a different heritage, in the work of William James, G. H. Mead, and other nineteenth- and twentieth-century thinkers concerned with the philosophical nature of the self (Hall and Lindzey, 1970, pp. 515–543). The central concepts of humanistic psychology and psychotherapy are self-actualization and nondirective therapy. Contemporary practitioners include Carl Rogers, Abraham Maslow, and Erich Fromm.

Carl Rogers   Carl Rogers is a well-known psychotherapist identified with the concept of *nondirective,* or *client-centered, therapy.* In *client-centered therapy,* the client outlines her or his own goals, and the therapist's role is to help actualize them. In *Becoming Partners* (1972), Rogers relates the experiences of several married couples who came to him to find new ways to arrange their sexual and marital relationships; he acted as guide through their exploration of the possibilities for change rather than as judge of the clients' sickness or health.

The nondirective therapist such as Rogers is concerned with the human being as a complete person; this generalization extends not only to the client but to the therapist. In client-centered therapy, the therapist relates to the client, and the client to the therapist, as a full self, within their entire range of experience and emotion (Hall and Lindzey, 1970, p. 554).   57

Abraham Maslow Another client-centered therapist, the late Abraham Maslow, stressed self-actualization. He interpreted love and sexuality as basic elements in the search for self-actualization. Love is "the expansion of the self, the person, the identity" through identification with the loved one (1971, p. 209).

Maslow, like Erich Fromm, idealized loving sexuality as the basis of mature, self-actualizing intimacy. He asserted that many people come to therapy troubled by the overlap between dominance/submission themes and sexuality; they learn in therapy that

taking orders from a superior is not equivalent to being raped; that stronger people need not be made a sexual oblation to in order to avert their anger. It is hoped for the woman that her sexual surrender becomes *not* a giving up of her ego or self-respect; it is *not* a conquest in which by surrendering she concedes her slavish status thereafter.

Maslow, 1971, p. 335

The male must learn that by penetrating his wife he has neither conquered nor asserted mastery nor committed a sadistic act. Nor has she thereby conceded submission in other areas of life.

Erich Fromm Like Abraham Maslow and Rollo May, Erich Fromm interprets sexuality as a product rather than a cause of the entire personality. Fromm criticizes Freud for his focus on genital eroticism as the definition of mature love, and denies also that the love of friends and family is simply a sublimation of sexual desire and an inhibition of a fundamentally genital sexual aim.

Fromm, unlike Freud, claims that sexual problems are caused by the inability to love, rather than that the inability to love is caused by sexual blockages, and that psychoanalytic data support his interpretation rather than Freud's. Like Rollo May, Fromm believes that the best type of mature adult sexuality is that between persons who share intimacy and caring in addition to purely erotic attraction.

For Erich Fromm, the major self-actualizing function of sex is in mitigating the essential feelings of aloneness that accompany being human. For both, the sexual interaction of two close, caring people is both highly symbolic and expressive of the transcendence of existential aloneness. Anonymous, impersonal sex, they insist, is alienating — an attitude that is persistent even in today's relatively permissive sexual climate.

The Human Potential Movement Rollo May and Erich Fromm both use psychoanalysis as their major method of treatment. Their version of psychoanalysis is informed by the humanistic notion of a relationship between two people rather than a one-sided catharsis of repressed feelings.   58

Other humanistic psychologists, such as Carl Rogers and Abraham Maslow, advocate self-actualization through an assortment of methods loosely labeled the human potential movement. Whereas most traditional psychoanalytic and behavior-modification techniques of treating neuroses and sexual malfunctions are individual, the human potential movement includes group therapy and the concept that growth rather than treatment or cure is the goal of therapy.

The group therapy that takes place in the context of the human potential movement is known as an *encounter group, T, or Training, group,* or *sensitivity group.* The aim of such groups is to enhance the awareness of feelings, both the feelings one has about others and the feelings others have about oneself. The purpose of such awareness is twofold: to generate intensity in short-term relationships and to enable people to relate to one another and themselves more honestly, openly, and sensitively.

The human potential movement relates to sexuality at several levels. In the first instance, since many of the feelings people have about one another are sexual or at least sensual, the encounter group ideally provides a nonthreatening context for the expression of such feelings without punishment. Second, many of the encounter groups stress nudity, touching,

Many encounter groups stress touching as a means of increasing awareness of body and feelings.
Hap Stewart/Jeroboam

59

or both, either to increase sexual awareness or to increase sensuousness and become more in touch with the body and the feeling level of the self.

Forer (1972) notes that touching and cuddling are childhood needs that are repressed in adulthood or perhaps were never met in childhood. As a result of unmet needs, people confuse sexuality with the need to touch: "Many people indulge in intercourse when the need for cuddling is suppressed out of fear or anxiety or shame" (1972, p.199). He cites examples of how encounter group participation enables people to learn to touch.

A homosexual woman had established relationships in which she touched women both warmly and sexually in order to maintain control over them. She, herself, was afraid of being touched. She enacted simultaneous roles of mother and child in her relationships but could not tolerate the cuddling she knew she needed. After a time in group she was able to ask women to sit by her and gradually invited them to touch various parts of her body. Whenever her anxiety became pronounced, she stopped the contact. . . . She gradually lost all anxiety about being touched in group and began to enjoy the sensuality without fear of being taken over. She began to experiment with touching a male homosexual in the group who himself had been terrified of contact with a woman. Later she permitted him to touch her. Her wishes for childlike mutual body exploration with this man emerged along with feelings of trust. They planned to spend an evening together and had occasional dinners to share their fears and to set limits on themselves. Both feared intercourse, and the therapist cautioned them that intercourse was not the appropriate goal at this time, that the underpinnings of sexuality such as trust and reassuring body experience were the crucial issues.

Forer, 1972, p. 207

Gestalt Therapy

Gestalt therapy was named and initiated in the 1950s by Fritz Perls, who had been influenced by earlier gestalt psychology of the German school. The basis of *gestalt psychology* is a view of the individual personality as a single unit rather than as a sum of its parts, such as the intellectual aspect and the sexual aspect, with a concomitant emphasis on the problems of total functioning and wholeness. Gestalt group therapy is similar to encounter-group therapy, with an emphasis also on sensual experience; a favorite saying of Perls was "Lose your mind and come to your senses" (Levitsky and Simkin, 1972).

Encounter Groups and Sex Roles

There are many specialized encounter groups for women, men, and couples to work on problems of growth related to sex roles and sexuality. Meador et al. found, for example, that women in all-female encounter groups "are questioning what they have been taught they should be in three areas: sexuality, motherhood and childrearing" (1972, p. 343). Encounter groups for men may be homosexual or heterosexual in orientation with a focus on sexuality or sex-role problems related to masculine stereotypes. Finally, encounter groups for couples generally have as goals the development of understanding about the underlying dynamics of their relationship and the development and acceptance of a broader range of feeling and experience within the relationship (Pilder, 1972).

Psychology has been linked to sexuality since the early explorations of Freud postulated the sexual energy of the libido as the basic life force. Today, much of psychology, psychiatry, and psychotherapy is still heavily influenced by the Freudian model of libido, family constellations, and individual development. At the same time, contemporary directions in psychology such as behaviorist psychology and the human potential movement have somewhat different perspectives on the relationship of sexuality to the self than Freud had. For the behaviorists, sexual arousal can be elicited or extinguished by the manipulation of a variety of reward or punishment stimuli. For the existential and humanistic psychologists, sexuality is but one aspect of the enormous range of human potentialities and aspirations, to be explored in relation to all else that is human.

Chapter 3 / *Sexual Physiology and Response*

The development of the physiological perspective on human sexuality from the 1700s until very recently might best be described as medical, for the doctors who formulated the perspective viewed sexuality as a type of illness (Bullough, 1975). Today that perspective has become more physiological and is concerned with sexuality as a normal physical response rather than as a bodily aberration.

The physiological perspective on sex focuses on the nature of female and male sexual response and on the structure of the sexual and reproductive organs. Detailed knowledge of male and female sexual response was not acquired until the 1960s, with the first observations of male and female arousal and orgasm in the laboratory. However, physiological knowledge of the male and female organs was fairly advanced by the mid-twentieth century and is fairly complete today.

The Female Genitals

The external female genitals (Figure 3.1) are collectively called the *vulva* (Latin: wrapping, covering) and are comprised of the mons veneris, labia majora, labia minora, clitoris, and the outer portion of the vagina. Robert Rimmer observed in his novel *Thursday, My Love* that, like human faces, no two vulvas are identical, and described the vulva as "the other lovely face of the female" (1972, p. 177). The sexual ambivalence of our culture is reflected in another term for vulva: *pudendum,* a Latin word meaning "something to be ashamed of" *(Webster's New World Dictionary).*

Mons Veneris

The *mons veneris* (Latin: mountain of Venus, after the goddess of love) is the rounded, hair-covered, fatty cushion over the pubic bone. One of the functions of the pubic hair covering, present from puberty onward, is to trap scent-gland secretions that occur during sexual excitement and that have a characteristic erotically stimulating odor (Hassett, 1978). At least this is nature's design; cultural conditioning may have negatively labeled these odors for some people. Nerve endings concentrated in the mons area can produce pleasurable sensations when stimulated by touch and pressure.

Labia

The folds of fatty tissue on either side of the vaginal openings that are also covered with pubic hair are labeled the *labia majora* (Latin: major lips). For women who have never borne children, the labia majora may meet in the   63

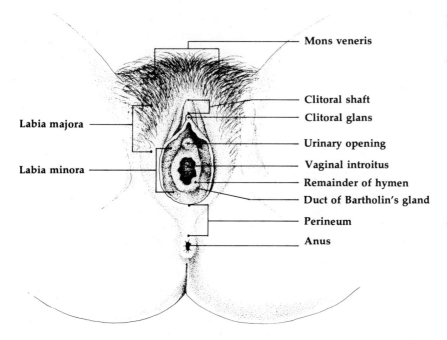

Figure 3.1

External female genitals

Mons veneris

Clitoral shaft

Clitoral glans

Urinary opening

Labia majora

Vaginal introitus

Labia minora

Remainder of hymen

Duct of Bartholin's gland

Perineum

Anus

middle. In women who have borne children, and some who have not, these lips remain apart. The *labia minora* (Latin: minor lips) are the small lips, composed partially of erectile tissue, that frame the sides of the vaginal opening. In some mature women the labia minora protrude beyond the labia majora. They are pink or reddish in color and meet just below the mons to form the *prepuce* or *hood* for the clitoris.

Clitoris

The *clitoris* (Greek: to hide) is apparently the only human organ with the single function of producing pleasure. The clitoris ranges in size from woman to woman from less than one-quarter inch to one inch or more in length and is located below the mons and above the urinary meatus, the external opening of the urethra. The clitoris is composed of a *shaft,* the inner segment, and a *glans* (Latin: acorn), the tip of which is like a small bump beneath the prepuce. The erectile tissue of the clitoris fills with blood during sexual arousal, and the organ becomes stiff or erect.

Small glands secrete smegma, a white material resembling a cheesy or waxy material that collects around the glans of the clitoris underneath the prepuce. Retraction of the prepuce or hood and daily washing can easily remove this smegma. A build-up of smegma can develop a strong odor, become irritating, and serve as a breeding ground for infection. Sometimes the irritation from smegma collection will cause the prepuce to adhere to the glans, making retraction impossible. Smegma build-up may cause discomfort during sexual stimulation; this discomfort may be relieved by simple cleansing. Adhesion of the prepuce to the glans may or may not interfere with sexual functioning. If it causes discomfort it can be corrected by a very simple surgical procedure (Graber and Kline-Graber, 1979, pp. 205–212).

Vestibule and Perineum

The area that includes the vaginal opening and the urinary meatus and is surrounded by the labia minora is called the *vestibule* (Latin: entrance hall). The external area below the vestibule, between the vagina and the anus, is called the *perineum*. The vestibule, clitoris, and labia minora are all rich in nerve endings and blood vessels and are highly sensitive to stimulation. The urinary *meatus* (Latin: a passage), the opening through which urine is released from the body, lies between the clitoris and the vaginal opening.

Bartholin's Glands

The *Bartholin's glands* are small, mucus-producing glands located in the groove between the hymen and the labia minora, about one-third of the way up from the lower boundary of the orifice (Netter, p. 90). These contribute moisture to the vaginal entrance and were once thought to be responsible for female lubrication during sexual arousal. It is now known that this lubrication comes primarily from the vaginal walls. Usually neither seen nor felt, the Bartholin's glands are occasionally sites of cysts or infection (Lanson, 1975, p. 30).

Hymen

The *hymen* (Greek: the god of marriage) is a stretchable membrane across the lower portion of the vaginal entrance. Slang terms for the hymen include "cherry" and "maidenhead." An intact hymen has traditionally been regarded as a sign of virginity. In reality, there are many means not involving sexual activity by which the hymenal membrane can be stretched or torn before first intercourse. The type, shape, and thickness of hymens varies greatly among women. (See Figure 3.2.) Occasionally a female is born with very little hymenal tissue and may appear not to have a hymen. In rare instances the entire vaginal opening is covered by hymenal membrane, a condition called *imperforate hymen*. Because no menstrual blood can pass through, this condition is usually discovered when medical attention is sought because a girl seems mature but has not yet   65

Figure 3.2

Types of hymens

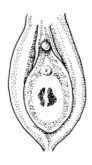

Imperforate hymen   Septate hymen

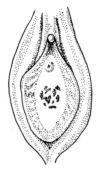

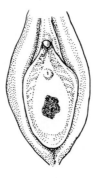

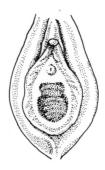

Cribriform hymen   Annular hymen   Parous introitus

begun to menstruate or because trapped menstrual blood is causing discomfort. Some women choose to stretch their vaginal opening before their first act of intercourse so that their first experience of intercourse can be pleasurable and unaccompanied by the discomfort or pain that could come from rupturing an unstretched hymen. (See Selection 3.1.)

The Virginal Hymen   Selection 3.1

In her book *From Woman to Woman — A Gynecologist Answers Questions About You and Your Body*, Lucienne Lanson, M.D., recommends that women do the following dilating exercise for about five minutes a day for two or three weeks before first intercourse. She suggests doing the exercises in a warm bath, because the added heat may make the tissues stretch more easily.

66

The middle finger, covered with a lubricant like a nonprescription surgical jelly, is inserted about halfway into the vagina and gently pressed downward toward the rectum until the vaginal opening is felt to be stretching. At the point of mild discomfort, the finger is held for a few moments and then released, the vagina being allowed to relax. Pressure is alternately applied and released for three or four seconds at a time, stopping before the stretching becomes painful.

When the vagina can accommodate both the index and middle fingers, the stretching sensation can be created by spreading the fingers apart intermittently. If the tips of the middle and index fingers can be inserted into the vagina and separated a quarter of an inch or more, the vaginal opening is probably adequate for intercourse without discomfort from stretching of the hymenal membrane.

A woman in her mid-twenties describes her first coital experience as painful: Anyhow, when I was nineteen and living in a coed dorm at college I finally decided to get rid of my virginity 'cause it was a pain. I wanted to know what everyone was talking about when they talked about sex — like was it *really* that great. I didn't think it would be all waves crashing on the shores and the earth shaking, but I figured it had to be pretty good. One night when I was quite stoned on sopas [a downer] and feeling very uninhibited, I encouraged my boy friend — he was seventeen years old and also very stoned on sopas and wine — to give it a try. I wasn't really worked up, but I was wet enough so that when he put his penis in, it hurt some but not too much. . . . The next night we decided to try again, but this time we used Vaseline on his penis and my vagina so it would be easier to insert. It wasn't much easier, just greasier, and it still hurt. I didn't really enjoy sex at all and would have been satisfied just to have kept on petting and kissing.

From the authors' files

Vagina

The *vagina* (Latin: sheath) is positioned between the bladder at the front and the rectum behind. Most of the time it is a potential rather than an actual space, since its walls are usually touching. In the unaroused state, the vagina is three to five inches long; during sexual excitement it may extend up to two more inches in length and to a diameter of two inches. During childbirth the vagina may dilate to five inches across. Internally, the vagina is moist, the type and amount of moisture varying with the age of the woman and, in women of menstrual age, with the phase in the menstrual cycle. Vaginal lubrication occurs in a biorhythmic cycle of approximately ninety minutes (Lowry, 1973, personal communication). In childhood and after menopause, when levels of circulating estrogen are low, the vaginal mucous membrane is thin, fragile, and less stretchable than during the childbearing years, when the vagina is a "succulent, stretchable passageway" (Lanson, 1975, p. 12). Vaginal muscle tone varies

67

individually with age; some women use exercises to improve vaginal muscle tone (see Selection 3.2).

Vaginal Muscle Tone

The *pubococcygeal* muscle system surrounds the vagina, anus, and urethra. When this muscle is not firmly toned, the vagina is loose and may gap open. When it is well conditioned, the vagina is long and narrow. Vaginal exercises to tone the pubococcygeal *(P-C)* muscle were introduced into the medical literature by the late Arnold H. Kegel, M.D., who taught them to his patients in treatment of urinary-stress incontinence. Since that time, reported benefits of vaginal exercises have included increased vasocongestion during sexual arousal, which in turn causes increased vaginal lubrication and sensation, improvement in bladder control, relief of constipation, filling in of separations in the vaginal wall caused by childbirth, improvement of conditions of vaginal fibrosity that cause *dyspareunia* (painful intercourse), softening and flattening of old episiotomy scars that cause discomfort during intercourse, increase in vaginal control for giving pleasure to one's partner, and increased personal pleasure as the tightened vagina increases movement of the foreskin over the clitoral shaft (Hartman and Fithian, pp. 83–93).

It has been found that pubococcygeal muscle exercises by men will improve their sexual pleasure also (Zilbergeld, 1978).

The P-C muscle is used by women to start and stop the flow of urine. Hartman and Fithian, southern California sex therapists, recommend four exercises to their clients:

1. Contract the P-C muscle, hold for three seconds, relax. Do this 25 times per day if the muscle is well-toned, 50 if the muscle needs conditioning. The recommendation of Dr. Kegel was three twenty-minute sessions per day. These are exercises that can be done practically anywhere: standing in line at the grocery store, sitting in class, or even during sexual intercourse.

2. Flick the muscle, i.e. contract and relax very rapidly, 25 to 50 times per day. This is much like what this muscle does during orgasm, although no research subject has ever been able voluntarily to flick the muscle as rapidly as the involuntary contractions flow during orgasm.

3. Tighten the genital muscles, pulling up from the vagina as a deep breath is taken in. Exhale and relax the pelvic region. Do this ten times per day.

4. Bear down as though expelling something from the vagina, as during childbirth. Release. Then contract the muscle as in Exercise 1 and release. This exercise is especially valuable in increasing vasocongestion and vaginal lubrication.

Cervix

The *cervix* (Latin: neck), the neck of the uterus, blocks the vagina at its upper end. The cervical *os* (Latin: mouth, opening) is the opening in the center of the cervix, about the size of a small drinking straw in the non-pregnant woman. Through the os sperm travel upward to the Fallopian tubes in search of a fertilizable ovum, the contents of the uterus are discharged during menstrual flow, and the baby passes during childbirth, when the os is dilated by muscle contractions.

Uterus

The *uterus,* also called the womb, is the reproductive organ in which a baby develops; in some women it gives sexual pleasure as well. This stretchable, pear-shaped organ is about three inches long and two inches across at its widest point in the *nulliparous* (never pregnant) woman. Almost 90 percent of its volume is the thick, muscled layer of the uterine wall called the *myometrium.* (See Figure 3.3.) The *perimetrium,* or outer wall, consists of elastic fibrous tissue. The inner layer of the uterus, the *endometrium,* consists of tissue that thickens in preparation for pregnancy, most of which sloughs off during menstruation when pregnancy does not occur.

During pregnancy the uterus stretches until, at full term, it contains infant, placenta, and amniotic fluid. A few weeks after delivery it is only

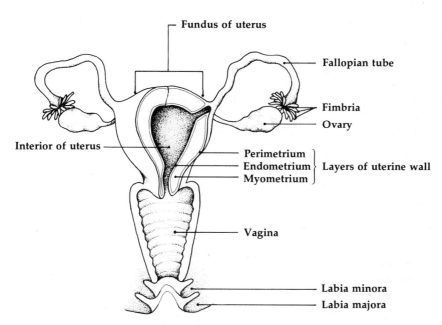

Figure 3.3

Front view of internal female reproductive organs

69

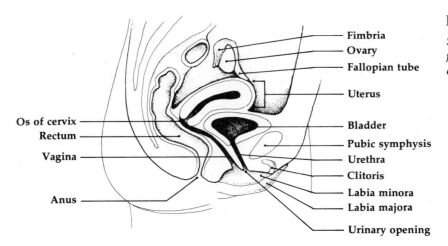

Figure 3.4

Side view of internal female reproductive organs

Fimbria
Ovary
Fallopian tube

Uterus

Os of cervix
Rectum
Vagina

Bladder
Pubic symphysis
Urethra
Clitoris
Labia minora
Labia majora

Anus

Urinary opening

slightly larger than it was in the nonpregnant state. The top of the normally positioned uterus bends slightly forward, and the lower portion points down and back toward the spine. (See Figure 3.4.) The uterus is attached to ligaments and is mobile. Hormonal influences on the uterus and the menstrual function are discussed in Chapter 6.

Fallopian Tubes

It is through one of the pair of *Fallopian tubes,* named after their discoverer, Italian anatomist Gabriel Fallopio (1523–1562), that an ovum passes each month on its way to the uterus of the menstrual-age woman. Each of these tubes, attached to the uterus at its upper end, is about four or five inches long and about the thickness of a drinking straw. Each tube is composed mostly of muscular, elastic walls. The actual passageway, which is lined with hairlike cilia, is little larger than the bristle of a hairbrush (Lanson, 1975, p. 19). At the outer ends of the tubes are fringes of fingerlike fimbria, which apparently draw the ova to the tube. Fertilization, the union of sperm and egg, normally occurs in one of the tubes, usually in the upper one-third. The fertilized ovum, moved on its way by the muscle contractions of the tube and the movement of the cilia, then takes two or three days to reach the uterus.

Ovaries

The *ovaries* (Latin: egg containers), one on each side of and somewhat behind the uterus, have the dual function of producing the female sex hormones, *estrogen* and *progesterone,* and of producing the female *gametes*

70

(reproductive cells), the *ova* (Latin: eggs). Each ovary is about the size and shape of a shelled almond (Kogan, 1973, p. 39) and is attached to the uterus by ligaments. At birth each ovary contains forty thousand to four hundred thousand microscopic follicles, saclike structures consisting of a ring of cells in which a primordial sex cell (*oogonium*: premature ovum) is contained. At birth each female has all the primitive sex cells she will ever have. These are incapable of being fertilized until they ripen into mature ova after puberty. Estimates of the exact number vary tremendously in the scientific literature (Kogan, p. 39).

Related to the female reproductive organs is the menstrual cycle, which is an important aspect of conception and pregnancy. (See Chapter 6 for a discussion of menstruation, conception, and pregnancy.) Like the male genitals, the female genitals may function both as organs of sexual pleasure and as organs of reproduction.

The Male Genitals

The male and female genitals appear quite different, but they have developed from tissue that is sexually undifferentiated during the first weeks of embryonic life. Many of the male and female reproductive and sexual organs are homologous — developed from the same embryonic tissue — and/or analogous — similar in function. The ovaries of the female and the testes of the male are both homologous and analogous: both produce hormones that affect sex characteristics and both produce gametes capable of developing into an embryo. The clitoris of the female and the penis of the male both develop from the same embryonic tissue, and both function as organs of sexual pleasure.

The male sexual organs (see Figure 3.5) fulfill two essential reproductive functions: the production of sperm and the depositing of viable sperm into the female reproductive tract.

Scrotum

Spermatogenesis (Latin: formation of sperm) occurs in the testes, which are suspended loosely within the *scrotum*, the external sac that lies between the upper thighs. The scrotum is a functional organ that regulates the temperature of the testes (Campbell and Harrison, 1970, p. 161). In order for sperm production to occur, the testes must be maintained at a temperature slightly lower than normal internal body temperature. Temperature regulation is accomplished through contraction and relaxation of the *cremasteric muscle,* which increases or decreases the surface area of the 71

Figure 3.5

External male genitals

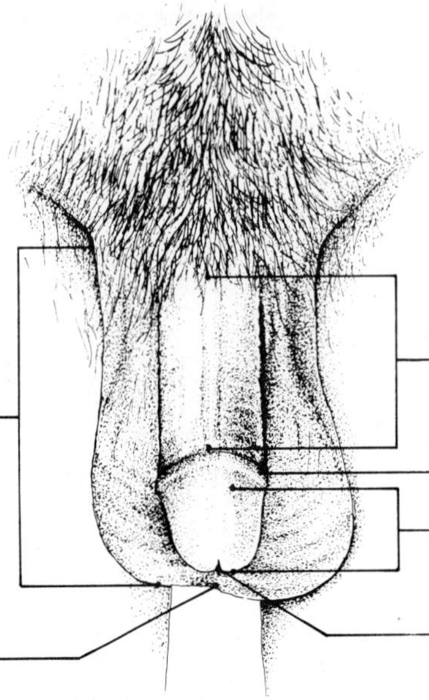

Shaft of penis

Scrotum
(containing testes)

Corona

Exposed
glans of
circumcised penis

Urinary opening

Raphe

scrotum; through sweating of the scrotum; and through alterations in the vascular system that can cool blood by about three degrees centigrade on its way to the testes (Campbell and Harrison, p. 173). The deeply pigmented skin of the human scrotum is extremely thin and contains hair follicles and *sebaceous* (oily sweat-producing) glands. The scrotum is divided into halves along its surface by a median ridge called the *raphe.* The *dartos,* a second layer beneath the skin, forms a complete sac for each of the two testes. The dartos, together with the cremasteric muscle, governs the changes in scrotal size that occur with changes in temperature, sexual arousal, exercise, and emotion (Campbell and Harrison, pp. 31–32).

Testicles

The *testicles* (Latin: witness; from the ancient custom of placing the hand on the genitals when testifying) are the basic elements of the male reproductive system (Campbell and Harrison, 1970, p. 161). Within the testes the primary male hormone, testosterone, is manufactured and the male sex cells, the *spermatozoa* (Greek: seed), are produced. Each testis is ovoid in shape, about one and a half to two inches long, one inch wide, and weighs about half an ounce; it lies loosely in the scrotum and has only one scrotal attachment, a scrotal ligament. The left testicle usually hangs slightly lower than the right.

72

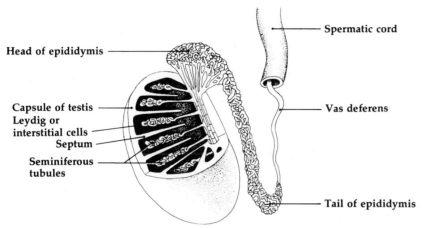

Figure 3.6

Cross section of male testis

Head of epididymis

Spermatic cord

Capsule of testis
Leydig or
interstitial cells
Septum
Seminiferous
tubules

Vas deferens

Tail of epididymis

An extremely dense fibrous membrane surrounds each testis, and the interior of the membrane forms a fibrous framework for the *seminiferous tubules,* where sperm production occurs. In each testis between six hundred and twelve hundred tubules, each of them one to three feet in length, unite with themselves and each other to form coiled canals with a combined total length in both testes of up to a mile or more (Campbell and Harrison, 1970, pp. 32–33). (See Figure 3.6.)

Sperm Production   The outer layer of a seminiferous tubule cell is formed of *spermatogonia,* undifferentiated germ cells that migrate away from the tubule lining, enlarge, and pass through a complex transformation to become mature sperm called *spermatozoa.* The head region of a mature spermatozoon contains enzymes that enable the sperm to penetrate the outer covering of an egg; the tail portion nearest the head contains energy-generating units important for viability and movement; and the whiplike portion of the tail contributes to the movement that may enable a sperm to travel three to ten inches within one minute (Avers, 1974, p. 95).

Approximately half of all the sperm produced by a male contain an X or female chromosome and half contain a Y or male chromosome. Some researchers have found differences in the shape and mobility of X and Y sperm. The Y sperm reportedly have a smaller head and a longer tail, enabling them to travel faster when moving from the vagina to the Fallopian tube in search of an ovum. It is assumed that the larger-headed X sperm will travel more slowly but retain their fertilizing capacity for a longer time (Shettles, 1972). For couples who wish to select the sex of their child, it is possible to use this knowledge of the differences between X and Y sperm to increase the likelihood of conceiving either a boy or a girl. (See Selection 3.3.)

73

An adult human male usually produces several hundred million sperm per day. Production of a mature sperm takes an average of sixty to seventy-two days, and sperm in the seminiferous tubules are found at all stages of development (Avers, 1974, pp. 95–96). After the onset of puberty, spermatogenesis is a continuous function terminated only at death unless extraneous factors such as poor general health, malnutrition, or endocrine disorders intervene. A mathematician computing the number of sperm produced by a typical male between the ages of twenty-five and thirty-five came up with the figure 339,385,500,000 (Campbell and Harrison, 1970, p. 168).

Selecting the Sex of Your Baby

Selection 3.3

Based on Shettles, 1972, and Harlap, 1979

To increase the chances of conceiving a girl:

1. The couple should have intercourse regularly except for two or three days after ovulation.

2. There should be shallow penetration at the time of ejaculation.

3. The woman should not experience orgasm.

4. The woman should douche before intercourse with a solution of two tablespoons of vinegar in a quart of water.

To increase the chances of conceiving a boy:

1. The couple should abstain from intercourse for a week before ovulation and have intercourse the day or two after the woman ovulates.

2. There should be deep penetration at the time of ejaculation.

3. The woman should experience orgasm.

4. The woman should douche before intercourse with a solution of two tablespoons of baking soda dissolved in a quart of water.

Hormone Production   The intertubular connective tissue of the testes contains blood vessels and the *Leydig* (or *interstitial*) *cells,* where hormone production occurs. The cells produce *testosterone,* the major male hormone upon which the secretions and functioning of the other reproductive organs depend. Additional hormones, both estrogens and androgens, are   74 also produced in these testicular cells. Luteinizing hormone *(LH)* released from the pituitary controls secretion of the testicular hormones by the Leydig cells. LH probably also acts with follicle-stimulating hormone *(FSH)* when the latter hormone stimulates spermatogenesis. This stimulation for release of the LH and FSH comes from the hypothalamus in the brain. LH and FSH are the same hormones that cause estrogen and progesterone production in the ovary of the female. In the male, however, LH is produced continuously rather than cyclically, and FSH release is phased to the rhythm of spermatogenesis rather than that of ovum development (Kogan, 1973, pp. 94–95; Campbell and Harrison, 1970, p. 176).

Testicular Development and Descent   The testes usually descend from the abdomen, through the inguinal canal, and into the scrotum about two months before birth. Occasionally this does not happen, and at birth one or both of the testes remain undescended, a condition known as *cryptorchidism* (Greek: hidden testicle). If the testis is not brought down out of the abdomen before puberty, permanent sterility results for that testis, although hormone production still occurs (Avers, 1974, p. 95). Under the influence of maternal hormones an abundance of Leydig cells are present from the fifth fetal month until birth. After withdrawal of maternal hormones at birth, Leydig cells are not found again in the interstitial spaces until maturity. The maturing process may begin any time between nine and nineteen years of age, and takes an average of three years for completion. Development of the seminiferous tubules precedes Leydig cell activity. The stages of spermatogenesis begin and finally culminate in production of mature sperm. When a male is about sixteen years of age, Leydig cells appear and, coincident with testosterone production, so do signs of maturity: enlargement of the penis, pubic and underarm hair, enlargement of the prostate and seminal vesicles, deepening of the voice, and often some acne (Campbell and Harrison, 1970, pp. 167–168).

Sperm Pathway

After production in the seminiferous tubules of the testes, mature spermatozoa pass through the epididymis, vas deferens, ejaculatory duct, and urethra before ejaculation through the external opening, the urethral meatus. Secretions are added by the accessory organs: the seminal vesicles, prostate, and Cowper's, or bulbourethral, glands. The prostate and urethra are single organs. All others are paired. (See Figures 3.7 and 3.8.)

The network of seminiferous tubules unite at the back of each testis in about a dozen ducts that form the first part of the *epididymis* (Greek: upon testicle), a sausage-shaped tube that might extend about twenty feet if unwound, but which is coiled into little more than two inches in length.   75

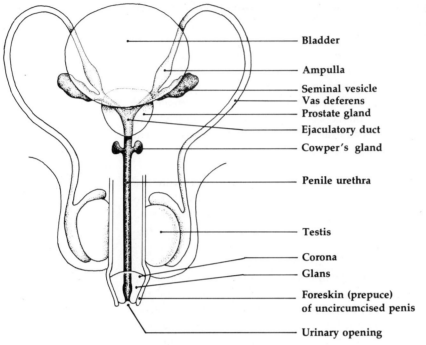

Figure 3.7

Front view of internal male reproductive organs

Bladder

Ampulla

Seminal vesicle
Vas deferens
Prostate gland
Ejaculatory duct
Cowper's gland

Penile urethra

Testis

Corona

Glans

Foreskin (prepuce) of uncircumcised penis

Urinary opening

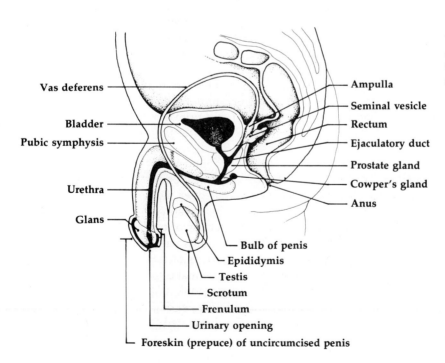

Figure 3.8

Side view of internal male reproductive organs

Vas deferens

Bladder

Pubic symphysis

Urethra

Glans

Ampulla

Seminal vesicle

Rectum

Ejaculatory duct

Prostate gland

Cowper's gland

Anus

Bulb of penis

Epididymis

Testis

Scrotum

Frenulum

Urinary opening

Foreskin (prepuce) of uncircumcised penis

76

The function of the epididymis is twofold: to remove damaged sperm and cells, and to serve as a ripening organ for increasing the fertilizing capacity of the sperm (Campbell and Harrison, 1970, p. 186).

The coiled duct of the epididymis leads into the *vas deferens,* a firm, cylindrical tube about fourteen inches long that extends from the tail of the epididymis to the prostate. The vas and the nerves, lymphatics, and blood vessels within its sheath make up the spermatic cord by which the testicle is suspended in the scrotum. The vas deferens is composed of smooth muscle capable of powerful peristaltic contractions that force the sperm upward. The upper end of the vas is a four-inch-long enlargement called the *ampulla.* The ampulla serves as a pre-ejaculatory reservoir from which the sperm are discharged into the *ejaculatory duct.* The ejaculatory ducts carry the sperm through the prostate and into the posterior urethra. The ejaculatory ducts result from the fusion of each seminal vesicle with the ampulla of its respective vas deferens (Campbell and Harrison, 1970, p. 37).

Seminal Vesicles The paired *seminal vesicles,* each about two inches long, are actually glands. They received the name *vesicles* because of an old, erroneous notion that they were reservoirs for semen rather than secretory organs (Campbell and Harrison, 1970, p. 145). They provide a portion of the ejaculate that contributes to the nutrition and reactivation of the sperm (Campbell and Harrison, p. 39) and probably contains fructose, ascorbic acid, and prostaglandins. *Prostaglandins* are recently discovered fatty-acid chemical derivatives that are thought to aid sperm movement in the female reproductive tract by inducing contractions of the smooth muscles lining the uterus (Avers, 1974, p. 99). The seminal vesicles and prostate are the male's largest accessory sex organs. Their only known function, to secrete the seminal plasma, is dependent on a continuing supply of testicular hormones. Their combined secretions serve primarily to dilute and carry the sperm (Campbell and Harrison, 1970, p. 137).

Prostate The *prostate* is the only accessory male sex organ found in all orders of mammals (Campbell and Harrison, p. 139). The normal adult prostate, a firm, elastic organ, serves as the pedestal for the bladder. The ejaculatory ducts and a portion of the urethra pass through this chestnut-size organ (Campbell and Harrison, pp. 19 and 142). In this section of the urethra the prostatic secretions unite with the sperm and nutrients passing into the urethra through the ejaculatory ducts. The secretions of the prostate that are released only seconds before ejaculation occurs make up most of the seminal fluid (semen) and give it its characteristic odor. The prostate also secretes small amounts of fluid, up to two milliliters per day, that are discharged into the urethra at frequent intervals and eliminated in the urine (Campbell and Harrison, p. 145).

77

The prostate, composed of glandular and muscle tissue, usually shrinks during the aging process (see Chapter 11). In some males, however, it becomes enlarged and/or hardened and produces discomfort or interferes with urination, thus necessitating surgical removal. A sphincter muscle at the neck of the bladder closes the bladder off during sexual arousal to prevent release of urine during sexual activity. A frequent complication of prostate surgery is interference with this sphincter muscle. When this happens the ejaculate may go into the bladder instead of out through the urethra. Orgasm and ejaculation are still experienced, but the ejaculate does not leave the body until it flows out later during urination. Because the prostate is a frequent site of cancer in men over the age of fifty, rectal examination of the prostate is an important part of the routine physical exam for men over forty. By inserting a gloved finger into the rectum, a physician can check the prostate's size and consistency.

Bulbourethral Glands   The tiny pea-shaped *bulbourethral,* or *Cowper's, glands,* located below the prostate on either side of the penile urethra, secrete the shiny alkaline lubricating fluid that appears at the tip of the penis soon after sexual arousal. The alkalinity of this substance serves to neutralize the acidity of the urethra and thereby enhance the suitability of that environment for the safe passage of sperm. This fluid sometimes contains sperm that can initiate pregnancy.

Semen   Human *semen* (Latin: seed) is composed of fluids from the prostate, seminal vesicles, ampullae, vas deferens, Cowper's (bulbourethral) glands, and the epididymides. The spermatozoa are semidormant until they encounter the seminal vesicle and prostatic secretions immediately prior to ejaculation. Contact with these secretions enhances the fertilizing capacity of the sperm and is necessary for their maximum motility (capacity for spontaneous movement). Human semen immediately coagulates upon emission and then reliquefies. The relation of this process to fertilization is unclear, but sperm motility does not reach its maximum until the reliquefication is completed (Campbell and Harrison, 1970, pp. 187–188).

Researchers in India and West Germany have recently discovered a startling property of semen: it contains a substance that is apparently an antibiotic at least as potent as penicillin. One West German researcher even speculates that regular intercourse protects women from the microorganisms that often cause vaginal infections (*Newsweek,* October 1, 1979, p. 40). Although no authorities have yet recommended semen as a first-aid cream, this would seem a logical use of its antibiotic properties. Although it is not always instantly available in emergencies, it does have the advantage of being easily transported in its natural container and therefore of being potentially available in even the most remote regions.

Urethra   The male *urethra* conducts both urine and semen. It extends from the bladder neck to the external urinary meatus, a distance of about nine inches. The urethra is divided into two major sections; the anterior and posterior urethras. The urethra terminates at the external urethral *meatus,* or opening. The lips of the meatus are formed by the spongy tissue of the glans.

Penis

The functions of the penis are dual: the penis is the primary male sexual organ, and it also serves as the passageway for urine. The skin of the penis is extremely loose, so that erection can occur, and it is hairless. The penis is composed of three elongated spongy cavernous masses. The two cylindrical masses along either side of the penile shaft are the *corpora cavernosa* (Latin: cavernous bodies). The third, which stands out as a distinct ridge when the penis is erect, runs along the bottom of the shaft and is called the *corpus spongiosum* (Latin: spongy body). The two large cavernous bodies separate at the root of the penis and are attached to the bones of the pelvis. The spongy body enlarges at its base to form the bulb of the penis and expands at its outer end to become the smooth, rounded head of the penis, the *glans.* The glans is the male counterpart of the glans of the female clitoris. Because of its rich supply of nerve endings, the glans is very sensitive to tactile stimulation. Most sensitive of all is the *frenulum* (also called frenum; from the Latin: bridle), the thin fold of skin on the lower surface of the glans where the glans connects to the *prepuce* or *foreskin,* the portion of the penile skin covering that overhangs the glans. The *corona* (Latin: crown), the ridge at the junction of the shaft of the penis and the glans, is also highly sensitive.

Smegma   In the angle formed between the frenulum and the corona are located the glands of Tyson. These secrete a fatty lubricant material that together with cells shed from the glans forms the cheesy substance called *smegma.* Smegma build-up can develop a strong odor, become grainy and irritating, and occasionally serve as a breeding ground for infection. Daily cleansing is a simple, routine hygienic practice that prevents smegma accumulation.

Circumcision   Surgical removal of the foreskin is called *circumcision* and is common during the first few days of life, and sometimes in adulthood, for religious or hygienic reasons. In most uncircumcised males the foreskin is easily retracted and the glans exposed. Retraction occurs automatically during intercourse. In rare instances the foreskin is too tight to be retracted and circumcision must be performed. Masters and Johnson determined experimentally that there is no difference between the excitability of the circumcised and uncircumcised penis:

The 35 uncircumcised males were matched at random with circumcised study subjects of similar ages. Routine neurologic testing for both exteroceptive and light tactile discrimination were conducted on the ventral and dorsal surfaces of the penile body, with particular attention directed toward the glans. No clinically significant difference could be established between the circumcised and uncircumcised glans during these examinations.

Masters and Johnson, 1966, p. 190

Ritual circumcision of males dates to prehistoric times and is required by Jewish religious law. Today, the United States is the only developed country except Israel that continues to circumcise a large majority (over 80 percent) of infant males (*Newsweek,* October 1, 1979, p. 40). Ten or twenty years ago studies suggested that women were less likely to develop cancer of the cervix if their sexual partners were circumcised. Recent studies have shown this is not true. Cleansing under the foreskin is important in preventing cancer of the penis, but this can be accomplished by men who have not been circumcised if they merely retract the foreskin while washing. Many authorities now conclude that "circumcision is not indicated on grounds of cancer prevention," and "neonatal circumcision should not be considered a routine procedure" (Klauber, 1973, pp. 446–447).

Penis Erection   When the corpora fill with blood, the penis becomes erect. The erective firmness is produced entirely by the blood trapped in the erectile tissues. The slang term "boner" for the erect penis is a misnomer for the human penis. Although there is a bone in the penis of most carnivorous mammals and a cartilaginous rod in the penis of many of the primate species, this is not true of the human male (Avers, 1974, p. 100).

The erective process functions at birth. Mothers frequently find their infant sons with erections at diaper-changing time. During sleep there is an approximately ninety-minute biorhythm of penile erection that correlates with the periods of rapid eye movement (REM), or dreaming, sleep. Penile tumescence (swelling) during REM sleep has been observed in both newborns and adults. Fisher et al. (1965, p. 44) hypothesize that the early-morning erections with which many men awake may actually result from the last period of REM sleep before waking rather than from the irritation of a full bladder, as has usually been supposed. (Erection is further discussed in the section on sexual response.)

There are a number of pathological conditions that interfere with the erective process. Among these are diabetes and alcoholism. Routine use of certain drugs, such as tranquilizers and some of the drugs prescribed for hypertension, may also cause problems with erection. In a rare condition known as priapism, erections become painful and prolonged. Such erections are usually unaccompanied by sexual desire and may damage the penis so that the final result is a penis that is permanently flaccid and incapable of further erection (Amelar, 1971, p. 164). Priapism sometimes occurs with sickle-cell disease among blacks and with leukemia (Amelar, 1971, p. 164).

Penis Size   Masters and Johnson label as myth the concept that the larger the penis, the more effective a male is as a partner in intercourse (1966, p. 191–193). In general, smaller flaccid penises will increase proportionately more in size through erection than larger flaccid ones. In fact, there is evidence that the vagina adjusts to fit penis size, whether large or small (Masters and Johnson, 1966, pp. 193–195). The normal range of flaccid penile length varies from 8.5 to 10.5 centimeters (3.5 to 4 inches); the average is about 9.5 centimeters (3.75 inches) (Masters and Johnson, 1966, p. 191). In one sample of eighty men Masters and Johnson found that the length of the smaller penises (7.5 to 9 centimeters — 3 to 3.5 inches — in the flaccid state) increased upon erection by an average of 7.5 to 8 centimeters (2.95 to 3.15 inches). In contrast, penises that measured 10 to 11.5 centimeters (4 to 4.5 inches) in the flaccid state increased upon erection by an average of 7 to 7.5 centimeters (2.75 to 2.95 inches) (Masters and Johnson, 1966, pp. 191–192).

Men tend to be extremely concerned about the size of their penises, whether erect or nonerect.

A thirty-eight-year-old male recalls: We were all bathing in the pool naked. I hated to do it, because my peter looked so small — men's get so small in the cold water. So when I got out, I quickly wrapped a towel around me.

From the authors' files

Some men are afraid their partners will be dissatisfied with their small penises, even though there is a predominance of evidence that many females do not regard a large penis as an important qualification for a partner. On the other hand, many male homosexuals do regard a large penis as important in a sexual partner.

A great degree of male sensitivity about penis size is probably related more to symbolic factors than to partner satisfaction. In Western society the penis is a symbol of male supremacy and power; like the biggest car or the largest house on the block, a large penis symbolizes great masculine power.

Physiology of Sexual Response

Within a context of awareness that sexual response is an interaction of mind, body, and emotions, the focus of this section is on the physiological responses of the body.

81

When one is presented with a model such as that of Masters and Johnson, there is danger of measuring one's own responses against the model and of assigning an implicit value of "better" or "worse," "right" or "wrong," according to how closely they match those in the model. Such a model, however, is merely a composite description of observed subjects, not of how all people either do react or should react. Judging one's own sexual experiences by externally imposed criteria can be frustrating and can deflate one's self-esteem. Focusing on internal awareness of what is personally enjoyed or not enjoyed can be liberating.

A sexual experience is a continuum of experience that may flow and ebb in intensity of physiological response. For descriptive purposes arousal levels and certain behaviors have been labeled so that we can speak of phases or stages of the cycle of sexual response. Since Masters and Johnson published their *Human Sexual Response* in 1966, their descriptive language has been adopted by most sexologists. Masters and Johnson break the continuum of sexual response into four stages: excitement, plateau, orgasm, and resolution. Earlier writers used other terms. For Van de Velde (1926 [1968 edition], pp. 131–132), sexual intercourse or "communion" comprised "the prelude, the loveplay, the sexual union, and the afterplay or epilogue (postlude)."

It is easy to lose sight of the tremendous variety in individual responses within the outline of the model when the pattern of responses reported by Masters and Johnson is reduced to oversimplified diagrams like those in Figures 3.9 and 3.10. Masters and Johnson, for example, devote an entire twenty-three-page chapter of their book to the clitoris alone and go into

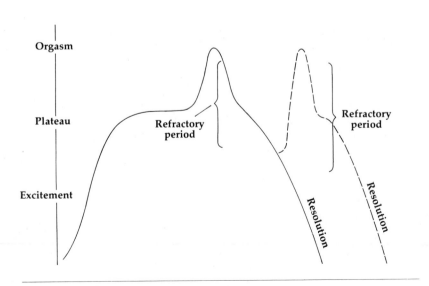

Figure 3.9

A typical male sexual response pattern

Source: *William H. Masters and Virginia E. Johnson,* Human Sexual Response *(Boston: Little, Brown, 1966), p. 5*

82

detail about individual variation. Kinsey states: "There is nothing more characteristic of sexual response than the fact that it is not the same in any two individuals" (Kinsey et al., 1953, p. 594). Even though physiological response to arousal and orgasm may assume a more or less predictable pattern in males and females, the subjective experience of sexual response varies greatly from person to person.

A teacher in her mid-thirties reports her sensations: Just before orgasm there is a moment of certainty that "it's coming." Sensation seems to suspend itself for a little bit; time seems to stop. If I have a cold or don't feel too well, I am suddenly not aware of it. All sensation gathers and forms in my genital area — a great warmth like fire in the clitoral area, a lesser warmth all around and inside the vulva and vagina. Then a contraction happens in my clitoris and spreads at once to my vagina; the feeling is basically indescribably pleasurable. I lose some sense of time and space, but not all as some people do. I can feel my face contracting, my legs stiffening, and what sounds to me like distant moans are sometimes — my partner tells me — loud screams! . . . The orgasms are of different depths and quality, seeming to come from my skin or my bowels, and every variation in between.

From the authors' files

In contrast, a dentist in his late thirties describes his sensation of orgasm: Just before it starts there is a kind of a welling-up urgency in the groin that almost feels like the whole area is engorged. This welling-up feeling — that's the best way I can describe it — is when it all becomes involuntary and the house could

From the authors' files

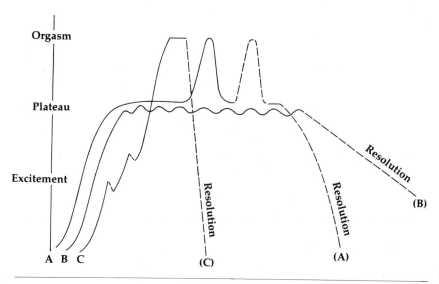

Figure 3.10

Some typical female sexual response patterns

Source: William H. Masters and Virginia E. Johnson, Human Sexual Response *(Boston: Little, Brown, 1966), p. 5*

83

burn down and I wouldn't know it because it's a totally consuming sensation and I'm not aware of anything else. . . . Once it starts, there is a combination feeling of contraction and of something coming out of the penis. This combination is just exquisite in sensation. During urination you have some awareness of something coming out, but it doesn't even approach feeling good like this. . . . All the feeling is centered in the genitals and the most enjoyable sensation is in the urethra — more at the base than at the tip of the penis — this sensation of something passing through. It is a very deep sensation, but definitely centered in the genitals regardless of the other stimulation going on at the time.

But Kinsey also emphasized that although "variations are striking and sometimes very prominent, the basic physiologic patterns of response are remarkably uniform among all the mammals" and "essentially the same among females and males, at least in the human species" (Kinsey et al., 1953, p. 594). (See Selections 3.4 and 3.5 and Figures 3.11 and 3.12)

Four Phases of Female Sexual Response — Selection 3.4

Excitement Phase

Vagina — Lubrication within ten to thirty seconds of effective stimulation. Barrel lengthens, inner two-thirds distends. Irregular expansive movements of walls late in phase; wall color changes to darker, purplish hue.

Developed from Masters and Johnson, Human Sexual Response, 1966

Labia majora — Thin and flatten against perineum in nulliparous women; become markedly distended with blood in multiparous women.

Labia minora — Expand markedly in diameter.

Clitoris — Shaft increases in diameter through vasocongestion, elongates in some women (less rapidly than vaginal lubrication occurs; vaginal lubrication, not clitoral erection, is the "neurophysiological parallel" to male penile erection) (p. 181). Vasocongestion of glans varies from barely discernible to twofold expansion of glans, depending on whether stimulation is direct or indirect and on individual variations in anatomy.

Uterus — Pulled slowly up and back if initially in normal anterior position.

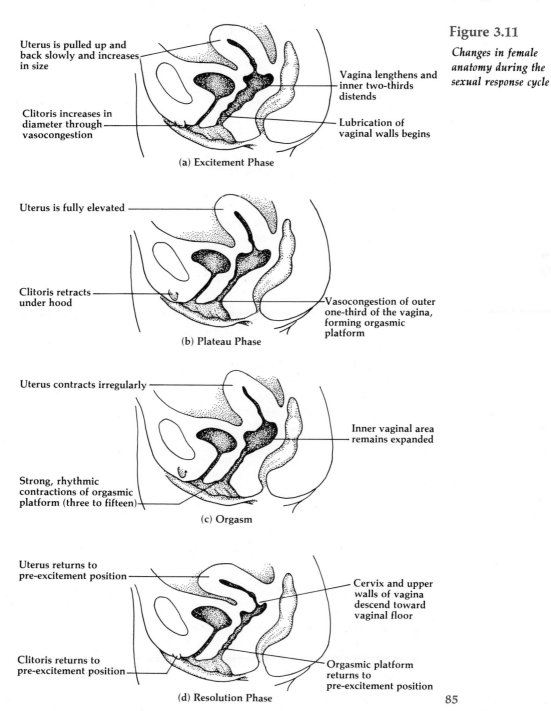

Figure 3.11

Changes in female anatomy during the sexual response cycle

Uterus is pulled up and back slowly and increases in size

Vagina lengthens and inner two-thirds distends

Clitoris increases in diameter through vasocongestion

Lubrication of vaginal walls begins

(a) Excitement Phase

Uterus is fully elevated

Clitoris retracts under hood

Vasocongestion of outer one-third of the vagina, forming orgasmic platform

(b) Plateau Phase

Uterus contracts irregularly

Inner vaginal area remains expanded

Strong, rhythmic contractions of orgasmic platform (three to fifteen)

(c) Orgasm

Uterus returns to pre-excitement position

Cervix and upper walls of vagina descend toward vaginal floor

Clitoris returns to pre-excitement position

Orgasmic platform returns to pre-excitement position

(d) Resolution Phase

85

Breasts	Nipple erection due to involuntary contracting of nipple muscle fibers. Vein patterns in breast extend and stand out. Actual breast size increases and areolae markedly engorge toward end of phase.
Sex flush	In some women a rash appears between the breast-bone and navel late in this phase or early in the plateau phase.
Myotonia	Initial total-body responses include increasing restlessness, irritability, and rapidity of voluntary and involuntary movement. Myotonia (muscular rigidity) increases in long muscles of arms and legs; abdominal muscles involuntarily tense; involuntary contractile rate of muscles between ribs increases, increasing respiratory rate.
Other	Heart rate and blood pressure increase.

Plateau Phase

Vagina	Marked vasocongestion further reduces central opening of the outer third by at least one-third. Base of vasocongestion encompassing outer third of vagina and engorged labia minora, called the *orgasmic platform*, "provides the anatomic foundation for the vagina's physiological expression of the orgasmic experience," and is regarded as a sign that plateau stage has been reached (p. 76).

Further increase in inner width and depth of vagina during this phase is negligible. Production of lubrication slows, especially if phase is prolonged. |
Labia majora	No further changes.
Labia minora	Vivid color changes; nulliparous from pink to bright red; multiparous from bright red to deep wine. Orgasm invariably follows if stimulation continues once this "sex skin" color change occurs.
Clitoris	Retracts from normal position late in phase; withdraws; at least 50 percent overall reduction in length of total clitoral body by immediate preorgasmic period.
Uterus	Full elevation is reached.

86

Breasts	Markedly increased areolar engorgement. Unsuckled breast increases one-fifth to one-fourth over unstimulated size by end of phase; little or no increase in breast that has been suckled.
Sex flush	Spreads over breasts in some women; may have widespread body distribution by late plateau stage on those affected.
Myotonia	Overall increase. Involuntary facial contractions, grimaces, clutching movements; involuntary pelvic thrusts late in phase near orgasm.
Other	Hyperventilation develops late in phase. Further increase in heart rate and blood pressure.

Orgasm Phase

Vagina	Strong, rhythmic contractions of orgasmic platform (three to fifteen), beginning at intervals of eight-tenths of a second and gradually diminishing in strength and duration; may be preceded by spastic contraction lasting two to four seconds. Inner vaginal area remains essentially expanded.
Labia	No changes.
Clitoris	Retracted and not observed.
Uterus	Contracts irregularly.
Breasts	No specific reaction.
Sex flush	Peaks.
Myotonia	Muscle spasms and involuntary contraction throughout the body. Loss of voluntary control.
Other	Hyperventilation, heart rate, and blood pressure peak. Urinary meatus will occasionally slightly dilate, returning to usual state before orgasmic platform contractions have ceased. Rectal sphincter sometimes rhythmically contracts involuntarily.

Resolution

| Vagina | Central opening of orgasmic platform rapidly increases in diameter by one-third. Cervix and upper walls of vagina descend toward vaginal floor in |

87

minimum of three to four minutes. Vaginal color returns to pre-excitement state, usually in about ten to fifteen minutes. Occasionally production of lubrication continues into resolution phase; suggests remaining or renewed sexual tension.

Labia majora	Rapidly back to pre-excitement levels if orgasm; slowly if only plateau levels were reached.
Labia minora	Sex-skin color returns to light pink within five to fifteen seconds after orgasm. Further color loss is rapid.
Clitoris	Returned to pre-excitement position within five to fifteen seconds after cessation of orgasmic platform contractions. Vasocongestion of glans and shaft usually disappears five to ten minutes after orgasm, ten to thirty minutes in some women; may take several hours if there was no orgasm.
Uterus	Cervical os dilates early in phase; observable in nulliparous women.
Breasts	Rapid detumescence of areolae. Nonsuckled breasts lose size increase in about five to ten minutes. Superficial vein patterns may last longer.
Sex flush	Rapidly disappears from body sites in almost opposite sequence of appearance.
Myotonia	Obvious muscle tension usually disappears within five minutes of orgasm. Overall myotonia resolves less rapidly than superficial or deep vasocongestion.
Other	Heart rate and blood pressure return to normal. Hyperventilation ends early in stage. A sheen of perspiration appears over the bodies of some women.

Four Phases of Male Sexual Response

Selection 3.5

Excitement Phase

Penis	First physiologic response to effective stimulation is erection, within three to eight seconds; erection may wax and wane throughout excitement phase.

Developed from Masters and Johnson. *Human Sexual Response*, 1966.

88

Figure 3.12

Changes in male anatomy during the sexual response cycle

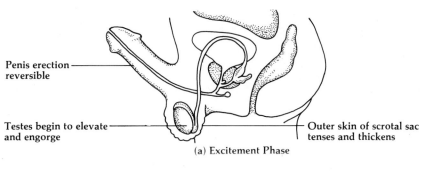

Penis erection reversible

Testes begin to elevate and engorge

Outer skin of scrotal sac tenses and thickens

(a) Excitement Phase

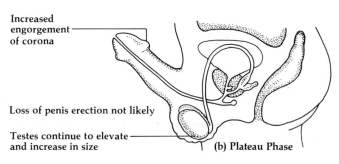

Increased engorgement of corona

Loss of penis erection not likely

Testes continue to elevate and increase in size

(b) Plateau Phase

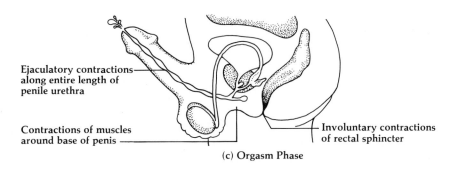

Ejaculatory contractions along entire length of penile urethra

Contractions of muscles around base of penis

Involuntary contractions of rectal sphincter

(c) Orgasm Phase

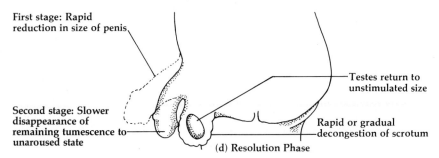

First stage: Rapid reduction in size of penis

Second stage: Slower disappearance of remaining tumescence to unaroused state

Testes return to unstimulated size

Rapid or gradual decongestion of scrotum

(d) Resolution Phase

Scrotal sac	Decreases in internal diameter; outer skin tenses and thickens; dartos-layer muscle fibers contract. Localized vasocongestion.
Testes	Elevate toward perineum; if phase is prolonged, may redescend and re-elevate several times. Spermatic cord shortens.
Breasts	Nipple erection and tumescence develop in some men late in phase; remain throughout rest of sex cycle.
Sex flush	Sometimes appears late in phase. Occurs or fails to occur with wide variation in same individual and between individuals.
Myotonia	Observed late in phase. Similar to female pattern. Both voluntary muscle tension and some involuntary.
Other	Heart rate, blood pressure, and respiration increase as sexual tension increases. Rectal sphincter contracts irregularly after direct stimulation.

Plateau Phase

Penis	Increase in coronal area of glans due to increased vasocongestion. Glans deepens in color in some men.
Scrotum	No further reactions.
Testes	Continue to increase in size until about 50 percent larger than in unstimulated state. Further elevate until in pre-ejaculatory position against perineum.
Sex flush	First appears late in plateau more frequently than in excitement phase. Indicates high levels of sexual tension.
Myotonia	Voluntary and involuntary tensions increase. Pelvic thrusting becomes involuntary late in phase. Total body reactions of male and female quite similar.
Other	Further increases in heart rate and blood pressure. Hyperventilation appears late in phase.

90

Orgasmic (Ejaculatory) Phase

Penis	Ejaculatory contractions along entire length of penile urethra. Expulsive contractions start at intervals of eight-tenths of a second and after three or four reduce in frequency and expulsive force. Final contractions are several seconds apart.
Scrotum	No specific reactions.
Testes	No reactions observed.
Myotonia	Loss of voluntary control. Involuntary contractions and spasms.
Other	Heart rate, blood pressure, and hyperventilation peak. Degree of sexual tension is frequently indicated by physiological intensity and duration of hyperventilation. Involuntary contractions of rectal sphincter.

Resolution Phase

Penis	Two stages: Rapid reduction in size to about 50 percent larger than in unstimulated state; less rapid if excitement or plateau stages have been intentionally prolonged. Slower disappearance of remaining tumescence, especially if sexual stimulation continues to take place.
Scrotum	One of two patterns: Rapid decongestion, or decongestion occurring over one or two hours. Typically, but not always, individuals consistently follow one pattern or the other. In general, within the individual pattern, the more the prior stimulation, the longer the resolution process.
Testes	Rapid or slow resolution relative to scrotal pattern.
Breasts	Loss of nipple erection if present; may occur slowly.
Sex flush	Disappears rapidly in reverse order of appearance.
Myotonia	As in female, rarely lasts more than five minutes, but not lost as rapidly as many of the signs of vasocongestion.

91

Other   Heart rate and blood pressure return to normal.
                          Perspiration sometimes appears on soles of feet and
                          palms of hands. Hyperventilation resolves during
                          refractory period. Ejaculation cannot again occur
                          until this refractory period has passed.

Male Responsiveness

Erection occurs when arterial blood rushes into the cavernous and spongy
bodies of the penis and venous outflow is cut off. The erection declines
and disappears when this process is reversed and the blood leaves the
chambers. The process of erection can be rapid, taking as few as five to ten
seconds to complete. Thoughts, emotions, and reflexes from the highly
sensitive nerve endings in the tip of the penis interact in the erectile
process. Because higher brain centers exert control over nerve cell activity,
thoughts and emotions can cause erection in the complete absence of
mechanical stimulation. Conversely, thoughts and emotions can also interfere with the usually automatic nervous and vascular sexual responses
(based on Avers, 1974, p. 101).

Psychic and Reflex Erections   Erections are of two types: psychic and reflex. Psychic erections are those stimulated by erotic fantasies, reading
stimulating literature, seeing a potential partner, and the like. The impulse originates in the brain and travels via the spinal cord to the penis.
Reflex erections are stimulated by effective tactile stimulation of the penis
or genital area. Nerve impulses travel only from the site of touch, through
the sacral area, the lowest section of the spinal cord, and back to the
muscular walls of the blood vessels that act in the erective process. Men
with spinal cord injuries usually no longer experience psychic erections
but still have reflexive ones. Reflex erections can be stimulated nonsex-
ually by a full bladder or irritation of the glans.

Orgasm   Orgasm and ejaculation are two separate events in the male and
one can occur without the other. Very few men are nonorgasmic; however, Rush (1973, p. 217) suggests that many more men may be nonorgasmic than is statistically reported in that they may ejaculate and yet
experience little emotional or physical release throughout their bodies.
    Masters and Johnson have formulated a composite description of the
male orgasm based on interviews of 417 men ranging in age from eighteen
to eighty-nine. As the plateau phase ends, "a sensation of ejaculatory
inevitability" develops an instant prior to, and then accompanies, the
accessory organ contractions that initiate the ejaculatory process. The   92

man can no longer delay or control the process once this stage is reached and ejaculation occurs within two or three seconds (Masters and Johnson, 1966, p. 215). At least two different contractile sensations are perceived during the ejaculatory phase. "Two or three expulsive contractions of the penile urethra" are followed by "slowed, almost tensionless, final contractions of the ejaculatory process" (p. 215).

Refractory Period   Masters and Johnson found that there is a *refractory period* immediately following orgasm during which most men find additional penile stimulation not sexually arousing or possibly even painful. The length of the refractory period varies greatly and depends on many factors, such as the male's age, the erotic potential of the total sexual situation, and the type of sexual stimulation. In a young man in a situation he finds very exciting, the refractory period may last for only a minute or so, during which he loses only part of his erection. After this time he may have another full erection and orgasm.

Multiple Orgasms   Males who have not reached puberty, and who therefore do not ejaculate with orgasm, apparently do not have a refractory period. They may enjoy continued stimulation after orgasm and may have a series of orgasms in rapid succession.

After reaching puberty most males ejaculate with each orgasm. But orgasm and ejaculation in the male are separate events and do not always occur together. Some men who have difficulty achieving erection and sexual arousal may ejaculate without the sensation of orgasm, and some men with spinal cord injury report a sensation of orgasm without ejaculation (Robbins and Jensen, 1976, p. 323).

Some men are able consciously to control their ejaculation and thereby have a series of orgasms in rapid succession without losing their erection, delaying ejaculation until the final orgasm. This final orgasm with ejaculation is described as the most intense. Afterward they lose their erection and have a typical refractory period (Petersen, 1977).

Results of laboratory monitoring of males during multiple orgasm episodes confirm subjective experience of a series of orgasms. Polygraph tracings indicate that anal contractions accompanied by peaks in heart rate and respiration coincide with the subjects' orgasms (Robbins and Jensen, 1976, pp. 323–327).

Female Responsiveness

Masters and Johnson present a composite description of female orgasm based on interviews with 487 women. They picture the onset as a "sensa-   93 tion of suspension or stoppage" that lasts only an instant and is "accompanied or followed immediately by an isolated thrust of intense sensual awareness, clitorally oriented, but radiating upward into the pelvis" (Masters and Johnson, 1966, p. 135). Often there is a "sense of bearing down or expelling" (p. 135). In the second stage a sensation of warmth pervades the pelvic area and spreads throughout the body. The third stage of subjective awareness is a perception of "involuntary contraction" focused in the vagina or lower pelvis and frequently described as "pelvic throbbing" (p. 136).

Josephine and Irving Singer believe that some women attain satisfaction and complete relaxation without involuntary vulval contractions, and that Masters and Johnson have described only one of the orgasmic responses that women can experience. The Singers describe three types of subjective female orgastic experience. The type of orgasm characterized by "involuntary, rhythmic contractions of the orgasmic platform" and by the other physiological changes described by Masters and Johnson is called a *vulval orgasm* by the Singers. These vulval contractions are absent in the uterine orgasm, but it, too, involves measurable changes. The *uterine orgasm* is characterized by "a gasping cumulative type of breathing" that culminates in an "involuntary breath-holding response, which occurs only after considerable diaphragmatic tension has been achieved." The breath is "explosively exhaled" at orgasm and "immediately succeeded by a feeling of relaxation and sexual satiation" (Singer and Singer, 1972, p. 260). This kind of response seems to be dependent upon repeated deep stimulation involving penis-cervix contact that displaces the uterus and causes stimulation of the *peritoneum,* the membrane lining the abdominal cavity. The *blended orgasm* combines elements of the other two types. The blended orgasm is regarded subjectively as deeper than a vulval orgasm and is characterized by both the breath-holding response and by contractions of the orgasmic platform. According to the Singers, different patterns of stimulation lead to different patterns of orgasmic response. The length of time involved in stimulation and the parts of the body that are directly stimulated are influencing factors. Singer and Singer conclude that "different kinds of orgasm provide different kinds of satisfaction" and no one "is necessarily preferable to any other" (1972, p. 264).

The Vaginal-Clitoral Orgasm Controversy Sigmund Freud implied in 1927 (p. 139) that vaginal orgasms are more mature than clitoral orgasms. This concept was incorporated into marriage manuals and gynecology textbooks and was coupled with the heavily laden value implication that a woman who did not have vaginal orgasms was frigid. Over the last fifty years many women who did not define themselves as having vaginal orgasms, and many men whose partners did not experience vaginal or- 94 gasms, have accepted this value judgment and felt sexually inadequate as a result. The controversy has centered on the questions of whether vaginal and clitoral orgasms are separate entities and, if they are, whether one is more mature or "better" than the other.

A recent study of a random sample of 100 undergraduate women at the State University of New York at Stony Brook asked if these women believed there is a distinction between a clitoral and vaginal orgasm. Fifty said yes, 26 said no, and 24 were unsure. Those who said yes were unable to agree on which was preferable. Some claimed greater intensity of the clitoral orgasm; others experienced greater intensity of the vaginal orgasm (Clifford, 1978, p. 189).

The Singers' approach, which regards orgasmic experiences as different rather than "better," invalidates the heavy value judgments that led to these questions. Women and men can learn to avoid some of the negative influences of external judgments and opinions on their sexual experiences by valuing their own inner sensations and feelings of enjoyment and by trusting in their own self-knowledge and awareness.

Multiple Orgasms   Masters and Johnson concluded that women do not have a refractory period and may have multiple orgasms if effective stimulation is continued. Not all women do have multiple orgasms, however, and some report that additional clitoral stimulation immediately following orgasm is uncomfortable or painful.

A woman in her late thirties reports: Maybe it sounds funny the way I like to do it, but usually I want both kinds of orgasms with the clitoral one first. After that, if it's a good one, I don't want it touched anymore, but I have a terrible need for several really deep, deep, inside orgasms. . . . If he can keep it up, I can have at least six more that way with really deep hard banging. It takes that kind to make me feel really satisfied all over my insides.

From the authors' files

Additional research is needed on multiple orgasms and the conditions under which they are possible and not possible for both men and women. It appears now that Masters and Johnson were premature in concluding that men have a refractory period but women do not, and that women may have multiple orgasms but men may not.

Female Ejaculation   A few women report that they gush fluid or ejaculate with orgasm. This fluid is thinner in consistency than male ejaculate or female vaginal lubricant and is usually colorless with little aroma. All the women who experience this ejaculation report that orgasms with ejaculation are more satisfying for them than orgasms without ejaculation (*Sexuality Today*, February 25, 1980).

Clitoral Retraction   Unaware partners are sometimes confused by the retraction of the clitoris that occurs when plateau phase levels of tension are reached. A man stimulating his female partner manually may note the disappearance of the clitoris, equate this with loss of male erection, and think his partner is "turned off" when in fact she has become more aroused. He may withdraw or interrupt stimulation at the very moment she feels an intense need for it to continue. Movement and pressure in the mons area will put tension on the clitoral hood and usually provide continuing effective stimulation without direct clitoral contact. There is a fine line between pleasurable stimulation and irritation of especially sensitive areas like the clitoris, the nipples of the breasts, and the glans of the penis. What is pleasurable at one moment may only a few moments later be perceived as irritating — and vice versa — as levels of tension or relaxation change. Generally, areas are more sensitive in early stages of arousal, and as tension builds, tolerance for intensity of stimulation builds also.

Hormones and Sexuality

Testosterone, the primary androgenic hormone, often known as "the male hormone," is produced principally by the male testes. Estrogen and progesterone, known as "the female hormones," are produced principally by the female ovaries. However, males also have some female hormones and females have some male hormones because the adrenals in both sexes secrete these hormones. The relative concentrations of the androgenic and estrogenic hormones in a person's body play an important part in her or his sexuality.

The presence or absence of androgenic hormones in the bloodstream of a fetus affects the development of its external genitalia. In the absence of androgen a fetus will develop female genitals. Androgen also exerts an organizing influence on the brain of the developing fetus. Hormones and their relationship to fetal development will be discussed in more detail in Chapter 6.

Androgen also has an effect on adult sexual behavior: it increases the sex drive in both males and females. For example, men who are deprived of their main source of testosterone by castration gradually lose a great deal of their sexual desire and ability. After removal of their adrenals, their principal source of testosterone, women also experience loss of sexual interest. On the other hand, both men and women who are given testosterone for medical purposes experience an increased sex drive, particularly when the androgen-estrogen ratio has been low. Apparently testosterone activates the brain to increase sexual desires, and at the same time provides the chemical environment that is required for the proper   96 functioning of the sexual organs. Testosterone is occasionally given to both men and women as treatment for low sex drive. Its use in women is limited by its tendency to cause masculinizing side effects (Kaplan, 1974, pp. 50–51).

Studies of male humans and lower primates indicate that psychological states can influence testosterone levels. Sexually attractive opportunities and positively stimulating experiences tend to be associated with an increase in the blood testosterone level. Depression, defeat, humiliation, and chronic stress are associated with a measurably lowered androgen level (Kaplan, 1974, p. 52).

Estrogen apparently does not increase the sex drive of human females. There is some evidence that progesterone inhibits female sexual response, possibly because it antagonizes the actions of androgen. A drop in the level of the female sex hormones may even increase sexual response by unmasking the action of testosterone, manufactured by the woman's adrenal glands (Kaplan, 1974, p. 53).

Conclusion

Knowledge of female and male sexual response has increased immensely during the past decade, along with the development of a more varied contraceptive technology (see Chapter 7). Today, mainly as a result of the pioneering work of Masters and Johnson, we have considerable knowledge not only of reproductive and sexual systems but also how they react during actual sexual interaction.

The physiological perspective has been criticized for its lack of attention to emotional and other psychological variables. However, the physiological perspective is only one of several perspectives. The psychological and sociological perspectives on sexual interaction covered in the following chapters do not supersede the physiological perspective; they build upon it, adding the internal psychological processes related to sexuality, and then the social context in which sexual arousal and response takes place.

Chapter 4 / *Sexual Arousal and Intercourse*

Knowledge of the physiology of the genitals and the way the human body reacts during arousal and orgasm is important as a basis for understanding how one may induce sexual pleasure in oneself and one's sexual partner or partners. With this basic knowledge of physiology one is prepared to understand the various techniques by which people can be aroused and brought to orgasm. Throughout the discussion of these techniques in this chapter, however, it should be kept in mind that people differ greatly with respect to what brings them the most sexual pleasure and also that, for most people, sexual pleasure is closely bound up with emotions, so that what is effective with one partner or in one situation may not be effective in another.

Human relationships can range from very intimate to very impersonal. The type of relationship one has with one's sex partner — intimate, impersonal, or somewhere in between — may greatly influence one's potential for sexual arousal. Some people are in the frame of mind most conducive to sexual arousal when they are with someone with whom they have a very intimate human relationship. Others may find that love or interpersonal intimacy in a sexual relationship inhibits their capacity for sexual response. These people may express their sexuality to the fullest only when they are with virtual strangers.

One nineteen-year-old man reports: If I really want to have a ball — I mean really get it off — then I just pick up one on the street. . . . All that kissing and love stuff is nice, but it sure messes up a good fuck.

From the authors' files

The major means for inducing sexual arousal in our society are whole-body eroticism, masturbation, sexual fantasy, use of the hand or tongue, mood setting, coitus, and more rarely, anal intercourse. Some kinds of arousal are autoerotic, whereas others are appropriate with a partner or partners of the same or opposite sex. Coitus refers only to intercourse with a partner of the opposite sex.

Body and Self

Humans are born with a body that has the potential for eroticism, as a whole or in part. Any part of the body — even a foot or an ear — can become the primary source of sexual pleasure for oneself or for a partner. (See the section on fetishism in Chapter 14.) At the same time, the body as a whole, covered as it is with nerve-sensitive skin, has a potential for sensual arousal that can contribute immensely to genital sexual pleasure. Intermediate between whole-body eroticism and sexual focus on nonsexual zones are the erogenous zones.

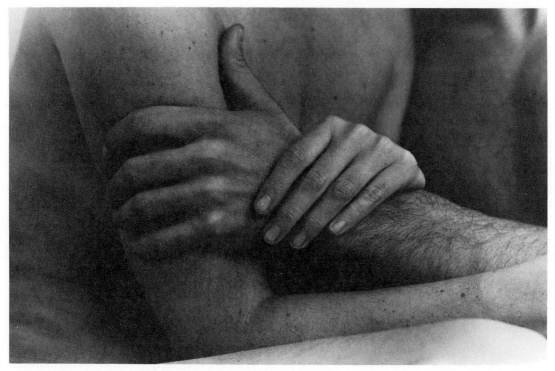

The entire body, not just the genitals, can serve as a source of sensual and sexual pleasure.
Frank Siteman/Stock, Boston

Body Sensuality

The entire body can serve as a source of sensual and sexual pleasure. However, many people in our society are unaware of their bodies and bodily feelings, and are thus unable to deepen sexual pleasure through general bodily sensations.

Comfort, 1972, p. 10

The starting point of all lovemaking is close bodily contact. Love has been defined as the harmony of two souls and the contact of two epidermes. It is also, from our infancy, the starting point of human relationships and needs. Our culture ("Anglo-Saxon"), after several centuries of intense taboos on many such contacts — between friends, between males — which are used by other cultures, has cut down "intimacy" based on bodily contact to parent-child and lover-lover situations. We're getting over this taboo, or at least the part which has spilled over into baby-raising and explicit lovemaking, but coupled with our other cultural reservation, which says that play and fantasy are only safe for children, it has dealt us a bad hand for really full and personal sex. Our idea of sex wouldn't be recognizable to some other cultures, though our range of choice is the widest ever. For a start it's over-genital: "sex" for our culture means putting the penis in the vagina. Man's whole skin is a genital organ.

100

Sexual behavior in humans is highly variable and is subject to both conditioning and reconditioning. Even though most of us have learned from our culture that sex means a penis in a vagina, we are capable of expanding our concept of sex to include a vast array of sensual pleasures — pleasures that we may extend beyond our sexual relationships to add joy to many other acts, such as running along a foggy beach or touching the face of a friend. Sometimes having one's body rubbed with scented lotion or oil (often called sensual massage) can help one become aware of the pleasure that can come from the whole body and not just from the body's erogenous zones. Sensual massage is sometimes used as one technique in sex therapy (see Chapter 5) to facilitate physical communication between couples, and in so doing develop their ability to enjoy giving and receiving bodily pleasure.

Masturbation

Masturbation is derived from the Latin word *manus,* which means hand. Sometimes it is used to refer to any type of hand stimulation during sex play, such as mutual masturbation by two or more people exploring and manipulating one another's genitals. In this book, however, we restrict the meaning of the term to self-stimulation (often to orgasm) by the hands, sexual fantasies, vibrators, or other devices. (See the section on devices in Chapter 14.)

Masturbation, like all types of sexuality other than coitus, is even today condemned by some religious leaders; in January 1976 the Pope proclaimed that masturbation is a "grave moral disorder" (*Newsweek,* January 26, 1976, pp. 46–47). Such attitudes are a reminder of earlier times in which all sexual activities except marital, procreative sex were condemned.

Female Masturbation   The most common technique for female masturbation is stimulation of the clitoral shaft, clitoral area, or vulval area with the hand. This method is used by about 79 percent of the 3,019 women questioned in one study (Hite, 1976, p. 19).

At the onset of masturbation, women usually stimulate their breasts, abdomen, inner thighs, or labia before touching the clitoris. At the onset of clitoral stimulation they may manipulate the glans for a time, but usually move from stimulation of the glans to stimulation of the clitoral shaft or to the general vulval area (Masters and Johnson, 1979, p. 63). Some women rub up and down along one or the other side of the shaft of the clitoris; some use a circular motion around the clitoral shaft and glans. Others rub from the shaft down across the glans and the urinary opening, to the vaginal opening and minor lips, and then back up to the shaft again. A few tug on the minor lips, thereby causing the loose skin covering the glans of the clitoris to slide back and forth.

101

Occasionally women will not use direct or indirect clitoral stimulation, but will concentrate on in-and-out movements of their fingers in the vagina, stimulating the vaginal opening and orgasmic platform or jostling the uterus.

A woman in her early forties states: I can't do it just by rubbing on the clitoris like the books say and I don't know why I can't. But I just have to have something moving inside me. I like to move my middle finger in and out slowly, pushing it up against the ridged area at the top part of the vagina just under the bone in front. Then when I get going good, I stick it in deep enough to hit the end of the womb again and again. That's the really good part because I can feel the warm feelings flowing all through the lower part of my body.

From the authors' files

In manual masturbation women may use the top of one finger, several fingers at once, the palm of the hand, the whole hand, or a combination of these. Nonmanual techniques include inserting objects such as candles, hairbrush handles, or vibrators into the vagina (vibrators may also be applied directly to the clitoral area). Much less commonly, a washing machine may be used for vibration or pillows may be rubbed against the genitals. Some women enjoy directing onto the genitals a stream of warm water from a shower or bathtub faucet or the jet in a whirlpool bath. Female orgasm may also be reached by crossing the legs and moving them across the genital area or exerting rhythmic thigh pressure. Some women can reach orgasm through fondling their breasts or fantasizing (Masters and Johnson, 1966, p. 67). Of course, combinations of any of these methods may be used.

I wet my clitoral area and use an electric vibrator, the kind with attachments. I like to use my other hand with the fingers against the vibrator, so I get the sensation from both the vibrator and my hand. I like to have something (smooth bottom end of a candle, or a bottle) move in and out of my vagina at the same time the vibrator is rubbing the clitoral area. I keep my legs apart. Sometimes I hold the vibrator still and move against it, sometimes I move very little and let the vibrator move. Lately I've pulled the skin under my pubic hair up toward my stomach so I can see my clitoris as I'm masturbating. Super exciting! Occasionally I use a mirror so I can see myself.

Reprinted with permission of Macmillan Publishing Co., Inc. from *The Hite Report* by Shere Hite. Copyright © 1976 by Shere Hite.

Women are more likely than men to vary the rate and pressure of genital stroking deliberately, sometimes stopping and starting clitoral stimulation in a self-teasing manner. Unlike most men, women usually continue their self-manipulative activity during orgasm, although sometimes at a slowed rate (Masters and Johnson, 1979, pp. 63–64).

Male Masturbation   Males show less variety than females in their masturbatory techniques. They usually begin masturbation by directly stimulating the penis rather than other parts of the body. Until the penis becomes erect, the manipulation may be casual and relatively slow. In early stages the genital play usually includes both shaft and glans. As full erection develops, the force and speed of the stroking pattern increase, and manipulation usually focuses on the shaft (Masters and Johnson, 1979, pp. 62–63). The degree of pressure, the speed of movement, and the extent of contact with the glans vary greatly with individual preference.

A male in his early twenties states: I do it different at different times. Mostly I like to be looking at a sexy book and just barely touching my thing at first — sliding my finger along the bottom just below the head, but really lightly. Then when I can't stand it anymore, I grab it really, really hard, and then just a few good jerks does it.

From the authors' files

Unlike women, at orgasm most men slow their movements or stop them altogether because further stimulation would be uncomfortable or painful.

Other methods of male masturbation involve lightly touching or tugging at the skin around the frenulum, the fold of skin on the lower surface of the glans, or lightly flicking the penis with the fingers or other objects. Some men masturbate by lying face down and thrusting against the bedding; some use alternating thigh pressure with the erect penis between the thighs (Masters and Johnson, 1979, p. 63). A few men use vibrators or artificial vaginas to masturbate. A vibrator may be rubbed along the shaft and on the glans of the penis, rubbed on the testicles, or inserted in the anus. (See Chapter 14 for further discussion of sexual devices.)

Although most men require some penile stimulation to reach orgasm, many supplement this during masturbation by fantasizing or by such techniques as gently massaging the testicles, rubbing the area between the anus and the testicles, running warm water over the genitals, massaging the nipples, inserting fingers or objects in the anus, or rubbing the genitals with a soft or furry object.

Sexual Fantasies and Masturbation   Many people, especially males, fantasize during masturbation. Kinsey found that 72 percent of men and 50 percent of women reported that they almost always fantasized while masturbating (Kinsey et al., 1953, p. 438). In a study of adolescents, Sorensen found that 57 percent of boys and 46 percent of girls reported that most of the time they fantasized during masturbation (Sorensen, 1973, pp. 130–139). (For a discussion of the methodology of Kinsey and of Sorensen, see the appendix.)

103

Although sexual fantasies are highly personal and individualized, their content is apparently influenced by social factors (Biblarz and Biblarz, 1976; Goleman and Bush, 1977). There is some evidence that ethnicity influences the content of sexual fantasies. For example, one study of elderly mental patients found that Jewish women often imagined that they were being accused of adultery, while black women imagined that they heard voices accusing them of lesbianism (Schimel, 1972).

Differences in the content of male and female fantasies have been found in several studies (Biblarz and Biblarz, 1976; Friday, 1980). Male sexual fantasies are likely to involve the male in a situation where he is powerful and aggressive in getting sex in a relatively impersonal encounter.

A male college student reports: My fantasy includes having several females of different races and ages actively pursuing me and my being able to sample from any, some, or all as I desired. This way I would sometimes be the aggressor and other times the one sought after but in either case the women would be active, sensual, and eagerly interested. All types of activity would be enjoyed with little excluded. Of course the women would all be very attractive.

From the authors' files

In contrast, female fantasies usually are either highly romantic (Shope, 1975, pp. 215–216) or involve the woman's being forced to submit in a sexual situation (Barclay, 1973; Friday, 1980).

A female college student reports her favorite fantasy: I'm walking at sunset out in the country through a field of flowers with horses running around freely and the wind blowing softly. I've gone by myself to just think and dream when suddenly a beautiful man rides up on a horse. He asks me if I would like to join him and the two of us ride off together and make love with a beautiful full moon and millions of bright shiny stars illuminating the sky. And in the morning we go skinny dipping in a clear rushing stream and just hug and kiss and enjoy each other's bodies all over again.

From the authors' files

Some writers suggest that both males and females are aroused by fantasies in which their self-worth is enhanced (Biblarz and Biblarz, 1976). Males tend to imagine themselves as powerful and aggressive with great power to satisfy women. Females establish their worth by imagining themselves as highly valuable either as love objects or as sex objects, stressing more the tender, emotional aspects of sexuality (Hessellund, 1976). The content of male and female sexual fantasies in our culture is apparently greatly influenced by the cultural stereotypes of appropriate masculine and feminine behavior.

104

Sexual Interaction

Many of the fantasies and masturbatory techniques of autoerotic sexual activity can be brought into sexual encounters with a partner or partners.

Fantasy and Sexual Interaction

Fantasy is common during sexual interaction as well as during masturbation. A recent study of 421 college students at a midwestern university found that nearly 60 percent of males and females reported fantasizing at least sometimes during intercourse (Sue, 1979). Females were more likely than males to fantasize about being forced into a sexual relationship or about someone of the same sex. Male fantasies were more likely to have themes involving an imaginary lover or forcing others to have sex. (See Table 4.1.)

Among married persons or those in long-term relationships, one partner may fantasize that she or he is engaged in sexual activities with another person, either someone he or she knows or a fantasized stranger.

Fantasies During Intercourse, in Percentages   Table 4.1

Theme	Males	Females
A former lover	42.9	41.0
An imaginary lover	44.3	24.3
Oral-genital sex	61.2	51.4
Group sex	19.3	14.1
Being forced or overpowered into a sexual relationship	21.0	36.4
Others observing you engage in sexual intercourse	15.4	20.0
Others finding you sexually irresistible	55.2	52.8
Being rejected or sexually abused	10.5	13.2
Forcing others to have sexual relations with you	23.5	15.8
Others giving in to you after resisting at first	36.8	24.3
Observing others engaging in sex	17.9	13.2
A member of the same sex	2.8	9.4
Animals	0.9	3.7

Note: For comparison, the responses of "frequently" and "sometimes" were combined for both males and females to obtain the percentages in [Table 4.1]. The number of respondents answering for a specific fantasy ranged from 103–106 for males and from 105–107 for females.

Source: "The Erotic Fantasies of College Students During Coitus" by David Sue reprinted by permission from the *Journal of Sex Research,* 1979, 15, p. 303.

Sexual fantasies are often used with a familiar partner to relieve the monotony of the sexual relationship.

A woman in her late forties says: I really care about my husband, but most of the time when we have sex I imagine that I'm with someone else. I'd never want to really be unfaithful or anything like that, and I never think about anyone I know now — it's always someone I dated in college or high school. Except of course I never really had sex with any of them — just necking and some petting and that sort of thing. But it really is exciting to remember the things I used to do on dates and to imagine that we are doing all those things I never dared to do then. . . . Dates and sex were so exciting then.

From the authors' files

Apparently the use of erotic imagery is developed in proportion to an individual's awareness of sexuality and its pleasures. Persons with full and diversified sex lives are the ones most likely to fantasize when they engage in sex. Women who easily achieve orgasm are those who usually entertain the most erotic fantasies during their sexual activities (Crépault, et al., 1976).

Learning Effective Arousal Techniques

The techniques of arousal learned during masturbation provide some clues for oneself and one's partner concerning what is stimulating during sexual encounters, although sexual encounters with other people often include an element of surprise in learning of new things that "turn one on."

Many people, including most of those who prefer sexual relations with partners of the same sex, maintain that people of the same sex are better sex partners than people of the opposite sex because each person understands the special sensitivities of her or his own sexual organs — an understanding that can easily be generalized to other persons of one's own sex. Laboratory comparison of the love-making approach of same-sex and opposite-sex couples lends some support to this assumption. For example, in same-sex couples the males often concentrated stimulation on the frenulum of the partner's penis. In opposite-sex couples, the females were apparently unaware of the particular sensitivity of this area when they stimulated their male partners. In same-sex couples, women were careful to stimulate their partner's breasts gently but lavishly, resulting in high levels of sexual excitement or sometimes orgasm for the woman being stimulated. Males were observed to be more rushed and rough in breast stimulation of women (Masters and Johnson, 1979, pp. 66–77).

106

This presumed lack of knowledge of the sensitivities of the genitals and other parts of the body of the opposite sex can be overcome if heterosexual partners are willing to learn the other's special preferences and are free to communicate their own unique needs for stimulation. Willingness to learn and freedom to communicate are important for all couples. Women are to some degree different from men in their sexual responses, but it is also true that every individual is different in some way from every other individual. A new sex partner always represents a new learning situation, regardless of the gender of the partner.

Erogenous Zones: Arousal Techniques

Sex play can focus on stimulation of the erogenous zones of the body or sensual arousal through mood-setting techniques. *Erogenous zones* are parts of the body that produce sexual arousal when stroked. The more typical erogenous zones are the genitals, breasts, lips, and thighs; but the back, chest, ears, neck, palm of the hand, or stomach — in fact any area of the body — may be erogenous zones for a given individual. The breasts and the genitals have an easily understood neural relationship to sexual arousal; the erotic potential of other parts of the body is apparently dependent upon previous conditioning or fantasized association with sexuality.

Kissing   The lips and the tongue are a very common part of sex play in the United States, as well as in many other cultures (Opler, 1969). Kissing may involve simply the gentle touching of the lips to the lips of another. With the use of teeth and tongue as well as the lips, kissing may assume uncounted forms. Sex partners may alternate tiny caresses with the tongue around the lips with deep thrusts of the tongue in and out of the other person's mouth. Gentle (and sometimes not so gentle) nibbling of the partner's lips and tongue may also be a stimulating variation of kissing. Mouth-to-mouth kissing may not only be a prelude to intercourse, but may also continue throughout intercourse.

Kissing need not be confined to the mouth, but may be effectively used on any part of the body for erotic stimulation — the eyelids, cheeks, or earlobes, for example, as well as the breasts, genitals, and other parts of the body, including occasionally the anal area. Often an imaginative sex partner will vary kissing techniques from gentle to hard, from teasing to passionate, moving tongue and lips over the entire body and covering unexpected places like shoulders, fingertips, navel, and toes (Comfort, 1972, p. 121).   107

Kissing may be effectively used on any part of the body for erotic stimulation.
Joel Gordon

Breast Stimulation Many women find that breast stimulation is one of the more sexually arousing forms of sex play, and, as noted above, a few women can reach orgasm by breast stimulation alone (Masters and Johnson, 1966, p. 67). Many men also become sexually excited from breast stimulation, although other men find it annoying (Kinsey et al, 1953, p. 308). For most people the most sensitive part of the breasts is the nipples, although most women also enjoy stimulation of the entire breast. Breast sensitivity varies from person to person, and the size of the breasts is in no way related to their degree of sensitivity (Comfort, 1972, p. 100).

Breasts may be stimulated by almost any part of the partner's body or by inanimate objects. Usually a person will touch her or his partner's breasts with hands or mouth. A woman's breast may be gently massaged or kneaded with the hands — the degree of gentleness or roughness depending on the woman's preferences. The nipple may be sucked, flicked with the tongue, gently nibbled with the teeth, pinched with the fingers, or tugged at with fingers or mouth (Ellis, 1963). A sex partner may use many other means for breast stimulation besides hands and mouth. For example, the toes, the penis, a lock of hair, the nose, an ear, a feather, or a piece of furry material may be sexually exciting when rubbed over the breasts.

As well as being an arousal technique in sex play (or possibly a source of orgasm), breast stimulation can be combined with intercourse or with other forms of genital stimulation to produce more intense pleasure than might be obtained by genital stimulation alone.

108

Many women enjoy hand stimulation of their breasts and genitals.
Joel Gordon

Genital Stimulation

Many methods of stimulating the genitals can produce sexual arousal. They can be used as preparation for intercourse by a heterosexual couple, or to induce orgasm as well as arousal by a couple of the same sex, a heterosexual couple, or a group of people. The most common methods of genital stimulation prior to, or as an alternative to, intercourse are hand stimulation and mouth stimulation.

109

Using the Hands   The hands are sensitive, versatile instruments in sex play. They may be used to express affection and to give sensual pleasure, as well as to produce erotic stimulation. Often men and women learn the experience of hand pleasure through masturbation, an experience that they can then communicate and teach to sexual partners (Comfort, 1973, p. 66). Watching one's partner masturbate is a very helpful means of learning some of the techniques effective for stimulating her or his genitals. Unfortunately, some people are shy about or ashamed of prior masturbation and may thus be unable or unwilling to show their partners techniques that please them.

Hand Stimulation of the Female Genitals   Methods of hand caressing of a woman's genitals depend both on how aroused she is and on her individual preferences. Before a woman is sufficiently aroused to become lubricated, pressure on the clitoris or the insertion of fingers into the vagina may be uncomfortable or painful. At a later, more excited state of sex play, heavier stimulation of these areas may be welcomed.

Hands and fingers can be used to penetrate, to stroke the outer vaginal areas, and to manipulate the clitoris, clitoral area, and mons veneris. Many women are highly sensitive to direct touching on the glans of the clitoris and prefer stimulation of the mons veneris, the clitoral shaft, the general clitoral area, or the external genital area.

Movements of the hand on the female genitals may be rapid or slow, gentle or firm, concentrated in one area or quickly shifting from place to place, according to the wishes of the woman. The ideal stimulative technique may vary from time to time, even for the same woman. A woman may be relatively more or less aroused by up-and-down movements along the clitoral shaft, by touching of the right or left side of the clitoral shaft, or by side-to-side or circular motions.

As was noted in the section above on female masturbation, some women enjoy stimulation primarily in the clitoral area, others primarily in the vagina, and some in both areas at once (Fisher, 1973). Some enjoy simultaneous stimulation of the genitals along with nearby areas such as the urinary opening, the anus, or the area between the anus and the vagina (the *perineum*). Alex Comfort (1972) recommends that the best method for manually stimulating a woman's genitals is with "the flat of the hand on the vulva with the middle finger between the lips, and its tip moving in and out of the vagina, while the ball of the palm presses hard just above the pubis . . ." (Comfort, 1972, p. 118).

Hand Stimulation of the Male Genitals   Manual stimulation of the male genitals can combine any or all of the techniques described above that men use when they masturbate. This stimulation can be used either to induce an erection prior to intercourse or to give the man pleasure, with or without orgasm and with or without intercourse.

110

Gentle tugging on the penis or massaging the penis or testicles may be sufficient to produce an erection. Rolling the penis between the palms of both hands or applying pressure at the midpoint between the penis and the anus can also induce an erection (Comfort, 1972, p. 118). When the penis is erect, hand stimulation usually involves gripping the shaft of the penis with the thumb and forefinger encircling the shaft just below the corona, and moving the hand up and down, causing the foreskin (if the man is uncircumcised) to slide back and forth over the glans. The other hand can provide additional stimulation by a variety of means, such as gripping the base of the penis, fondling the testicles, massaging the perineum, tweaking the nipples, or stimulating the anus.

Many men find direct rubbing of the unlubricated glans uncomfortable. The amount of pressure, the speed of movement, and the timing of changing speed — slowing down or stopping to lower tension or speeding up to raise it — can be varied most effectively by an empathetic partner responding to feedback from the man being stimulated (Comfort, 1972, p. 118).

A man may find that it adds to his pleasure if he can fondle the genitals of his partner, as long as he is not distracted from concentrating on his own pleasure. It also may add to his degree of arousal if his partner appears truly to enjoy this form of giving sexual pleasure (Eichenlaub, 1961).

Using the Mouth   The mouth can be used on any part of the body, but is most frequently used in mouth kissing, stimulation of the genitals, stimulation of the other erogenous zones, and — more rarely — stimulation of the anus and perineum. Oral-genital stimulation, like hand stimulation of the genitals, may be the sole means used to reach orgasm, or may be combined with other methods as a technique to heighten sexual tensions. Many persons assume that only the person receiving oral-genital stimulation would become aroused or have orgasm. However, many men develop erections while orally stimulating their partners, and some women reach orgasm while becoming involved in the orgasmic experience of the person they are stimulating (Masters and Johnson, 1979, p. 76).

Some partners prefer to take turns in oral sex, with oral-genital contact being performed first by one partner and then by the other. Oral-genital contact also can be performed simultaneously (see pp. 112–113).

Cunnilingus   The term *cunnilingus*, literally translated from the Latin, means "he who licks the vulva." Cunnilingus is stimulation of the clitoris, labia, vulva, and the opening to the vagina by the partner's tongue and lips. Although cunnilingus is against the law in many states, many women report that they have experienced it. Hunt found that both fellatio and cunnilingus are now used within marriage by a majority of high-school-educated people and by a large majority of those with some college education (Hunt, 1974, pp. 166–200). (For a discussion of Hunt's research methods, see the appendix.)

In cunnilingus the focus is most often the clitoral area, interspersed with general exploration of the entire genital area with tongue and lips. As in hand stimulation, a woman may prefer contact with the clitoral hood or shaft, or she may want her partner or herself to expose the glans for direct stimulation. Some women prefer having the tongue thrust in and out of the vaginal opening or having the minor lips sucked and licked. As in hand manipulation, a woman may like rapid or slow motions or side-to-side, up-and-down, or circular motions, or different methods at different times. Some women enjoy a finger, vibrator, or some other object stimulating their vagina or anus during cunnilingus.

With oral sex, as with other methods, open communication and a spirit of mutual cooperation and experimentation between sexual partners are helpful to discovering the most pleasurable modes of stimulation.

Cunnilingus is highly stimulating and sexually exciting for many women, and for some may be the chosen or sole method to attain orgasm.

One thirty-one-year-old woman reports: The only way I can reach orgasm is by hand or by oral sex. Sometimes when I am extremely sexually excited I can reach orgasm with my partner's hand manipulations alone, very forcefully and rhythmically without stopping. In general, I can attain orgasm consistently with hand manipulation followed by cunnilingus, and with fingers inserted and moving inside my vagina. The orgasm I attain that way is the best of all.

From the authors' files

The preference of some women for orgasm reached through manual or oral stimulation rather than penile-vaginal intercourse does not imply that these women are failures or are inferior, immature, or abnormal. Some women cannot attain orgasm by means of coitus alone, but need additional breast or clitoral stimulation. This does not present a problem unless a woman or her partner is concerned about it; it is simply one variation within the range of sexual response found in women (Kaplan, 1974, pp. 388–408). (See also Chapter 3.)

Fellatio The term *fellatio* comes from the Latin word *fellare,* which means "to suck" (McCary, 1973, p. 169). It refers to oral stimulation of the male's genitals by his partner. Like cunnilingus, fellatio is illegal in most states, although the majority of people in the United States with more than a grade-school education have engaged in oral-genital stimulation.

Techniques in fellatio are varied, the most common being sucking on the glans of the penis and licking the glans and frenulum. Some variations include very gentle nibbling along the shaft of the penis with the teeth, sucking on the testicles, or placing the entire shaft of the penis and also

the testicles into the mouth. The latter technique is possible only if the penis is flaccid (not erect) or smaller than typical, or if the person performing fellatio has learned to relax the throat muscles so that the penis can be taken deep into the throat. Sucking motions can alternate with blowing ones, and the tongue can be flicked over the frenulum and around the glans while the penis is being sucked.

113

Fellatio may be combined with any other technique that the man finds enjoyable, such as caressing parts of the penis not being sucked, or stimulating the testicles, anus, perineum, or breasts.

Fellatio is a highly stimulating sexual experience for most men. An intense enjoyment of, or a strong preference for, fellatio is typical of many men and should not be construed as a sign of a lack of masculinity or as an indication of homosexual tendencies (unless perhaps the man also primarily prefers partners of the same sex) or any kind of sexual or personal abnormality. Both fellatio and cunnilingus are common forms of sex play in our culture in spite of the moral and legal sanctions against them. Sometimes a man who enjoys fellatio will seek the services of a prostitute if his partner is unwilling to stimulate him orally.

A young woman who manages a massage parlor reports: Most of the men who come to my place just want a good blow job [fellatio]. Usually they're married and they get sex at home, but their wives won't give them a blow job because they think it's beneath them or something.

Mutual Oral-Genital Stimulation Fellatio and/or cunnilingus may be performed simultaneously. This can be accomplished in one of several positions. One common position is with the partners lying abdomen to abdomen, but with their heads in opposite directions. This is sometimes called "sixty-nine" or "soixante-neuf," because the number 69 resembles the juxtaposition of the two bodies. (See Figure 4.1). Another possible position for mutual oral-genital stimulation is with one person lying on her or his back, perhaps with buttocks or head supported on a pillow, while the partner kneels astride with head toward the other's feet.

From the authors' files

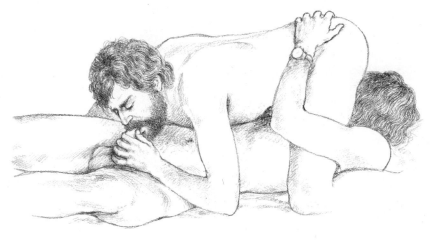

Figure 4.1

Mutual oral-genital stimulation in a "69" position

114

Mutual oral-genital stimulation may be a prelude to coitus or a substitute for coitus with one or both partners reaching orgasm. Mutual orgasm through mutual oral-genital stimulation is difficult for most couples, however (Comfort, 1972, p. 129). Effective oral stimulation of one's partner requires some concentration on technique, which distracts one from concentration on his or her own pleasure. Also the abandon some people experience at orgasm may need to be controlled, so that one does not get too carried away with passion and suck painfully hard or bite the partner's genitals.

Oral Sex and Cleanliness   Oral sex can be very satisfying to both men and women, and can be enjoyed by both the recipient and the giver. Unfortunately, our society teaches that sex in general and genitals in particular are dirty and shameful. Therefore, some individuals are afraid to allow themselves to be stimulated orally for fear they will turn off or repulse their partners. Similarly, certain people are willing to be orally stimulated but unwilling to reciprocate, since they have been taught that the smell and sight of even healthy, clean genitals are disgusting.

A thirty-eight-year-old woman describes her concern with genital cleanliness: I love to be orally stimulated to orgasm — although I must say I am always very concerned about if I am clean down there and if my partner really likes doing it. However, I have never done it to a man. I can't get over the idea that the man pees with it so it must be dirty, and the idea that he might come in my mouth — that seems quite frightful to me.

From the authors' files

Some persons are willing to perform fellatio on their partners as a means of giving pleasure or increasing sexual arousal, as long as the partner does not reach orgasm and ejaculate during oral stimulation. Although semen is free of germs and completely harmless, some persons are afraid to swallow it, or feel repulsed at the thought of having it in their mouth.

Arousal Through Mood Setting

Sexual arousal is the result of what happens within one's mind as well as what is done to one's body. Effects of mood on sexual arousal vary; mood or mental state may make arousal virtually impossible regardless of the physical techniques used, or the appropriate mood may induce arousal even in the absence of physical stimulation.

Privacy   Most people enjoy sexual activities in an environment where they have privacy and are free from distractions such as ringing phones and workaday worries. Occasionally, however, a person will enjoy sex with others watching, as might occur at a swinging party or orgy. (See Chapter 12.)

Some persons find an outdoor setting most enjoyable for sex play and sexual arousal.
Joel Gordon

Setting The type of physical setting can be a factor in enhancing the sexual mood. A very luxurious setting such as an expensive resort hotel is appealing to some. A natural setting like a hayloft, a field of daisies, or an isolated cabin high in the woods may be more exciting to others.

Décor Couples who live in the same house, as well as people who live alone, may spend considerable time, thought, and money in decorating their bedroom (or their entire home) in a manner that they find conducive to enhancing sexuality. Mirrors on the walls and ceiling, fur rugs and

116

bedspreads, candlelit alcoves, erotic art, burning incense, and soft music are a few of the things that are sometimes part of a "sexy" décor.

Variety   Often the introduction of some bit of novelty into the usual atmosphere will prove to be an aphrodisiac, particularly in an enduring relationship. Shifting the sexual encounter from the bedroom to some other part of the house — such as the bathtub, the living room floor, or the kitchen counter — may serve as a delightful sexual stimulus. New perfumes, strobe lights, or some new and frankly sensual underwear are but a few of the means sometimes used to add a bit of variety.

One woman reports her way of enlivening a monogamous marriage: My husband had always kidded me about how he liked blondes, so this one time I was in this department store I saw one of those little curly blonde wigs sitting on the counter and I thought, "Boy, that's for me!" I didn't tell him about it, though. I just waited until he got in bed and then I came out wearing that blonde wig and nothing else. Boy oh boy, did he go for that! . . . He said it was just like having a blonde chick that was just as good as me —'cause he knows nobody is as good for him as me. Now anytime I really want to get him going, I just come out in that wig.

From the authors' files

For many people a vacation or a break from the usual day-by-day routine can provide the variety that serves as a stimulus for more enjoyable or more frequent sex play.

Games   Some couples act out fantasies to enhance their sexual activities. One couple may like to pretend that they are children playing "doctor" and inspect each other's bodies. Another couple may enjoy acting out a rape scene in which one partner pretends to force the other to take part in sex. A few couples find sex exciting if one person is tied down (often called bondage) or spanked (often called discipline) in a gamelike atmosphere as part of their sex play.

Learning to Set the Mood   Most people can anticipate the parts of the body that generally produce sexual responses when stimulated, but it is much more difficult to anticipate ways to create a *mental* state in an individual that is most likely to make him or her sexually aroused. In addition, mental stimulation, like physical stimulation, is variable, not only from person to person, but possibly within the same individual from time to time. As a result, setting the appropriate mood to enhance sex play in another individual is a challenge to a person's ingenuity and sensitivity. We have described here only a few of the more common variables that may affect a person's receptivity to sexual arousal.

117

Coitus

Coitus comes from the Latin word *coitio*, which literally means "a coming together" (Goldstein, 1976, p. 142). Coitus generally refers to penetration of the woman's vagina by the man's penis, although it is occasionally used with an adjective to signify an act other than penile-vaginal intercourse. For example, the term *oral coitus* may be used to refer to oral-genital stimulation, and *femoral coitus* refers to the male inserting his penis between the thighs of his partner.

Frequently used synonyms for coitus are *copulation* or *sexual intercourse*, although the latter term may be used in a more general sense to refer to a variety of sexual acts; *penile-vaginal intercourse* is a more precise term than *sexual intercourse*. As we use the term, *coitus* is the sexual act that can be performed only by two persons of the opposite sex.

Variations in Positions Coitus, or penile-vaginal intercourse, can be performed in a wide variety of positions. Although no one position is more normal than others, each society typically has a position in which intercourse is most commonly practiced by members of that society (Beigel, 1953); in turn, the society's members consider that position to be the normal one for all humans. In the United States many people think that the only proper position for coitus is with the woman lying on her back and the man above and facing her. Younger people and more educated people use a greater variety of positions, and acceptance of other positions

Figure 4.2

Penile-vaginal intercourse in a face-to-face, man-above position

is becoming more common in this country (Hunt, 1974, pp. 202–204). (See also Chapter 11.)

It would be impossible to describe here all the possible variations in position for penile-vaginal intercourse; instead we will describe some of the positions more commonly used in this society. We are not implying that these are the "best" positions. Each couple, through experimentation, can discover which of the almost countless positions is the most pleasurable for them. Preferences here, as in other areas of sexual functioning, are a highly individual matter.

Face-to-Face, Man-above Positions   As was pointed out above, the face-to-face, man-above position is the most commonly used and accepted position in the United States. (See Figure 4.2) It has the advantage of allowing the couple to face each other, permitting during intercourse other sex play such as kissing and breast stimulation. It has a disadvantage in that the woman may be unable to move freely if the man rests much of his weight on her body, and it may be somewhat tiring for him if he supports most of his weight with his arms and legs.

This position may be varied in several ways. For example, the woman may place her legs together, between those of the man, allowing less vaginal penetration, or she may draw her knees up toward her chest with

Figure 4.3

A variation of the man-above, face-to-face coital position

119

the man between her legs, thus facilitating deeper penetration. (See Figure 4.3.) The man may lie with his body resting on the woman's, with much body contact, or he may use his arms and legs to keep his weight off her body, permitting her to move freely and be a more active partner. Also he may sit back on his heels and lift her buttocks to rest on his thighs, allowing either of them to stimulate her clitoris manually if she desires it.

Face-to-Face, Woman-above Positions   In the face-to-face position with the woman above the man, she may rest most of her body against his with his legs between hers (see Figure 4.4) for more penetration, or her legs between his for less penetration. She may sit astride his body facing him, with her torso upright, allowing her considerable freedom of movement as well as an opportunity for either of them to stimulate her clitoris manually. Or she may sit astride his body while facing toward his feet. In any of the variations of this position, the woman has more freedom of movement than the man, and the position is more tiring for her than for him. However, most males have more ejaculatory control in this position than in some others where they must take a more active role.

Figure 4.4

Penile-vaginal intercourse in a face-to-face, woman-above position

120

Figure 4.5

Penile-vaginal intercourse in a face-to-face side-by-side position

Face-to-Face, Side-by-Side Positions   Probably the least tiring position for both partners is facing each other and lying side by side. (See Figure 4.5). This, like most other face-to-face positions, allows for freedom in sex play and displays of affection. Both partners have considerable freedom of movement, and there is not very deep penetration. It may be varied by the relative positions of the legs of the couple.

Rear-Entry Positions   Penile-vaginal intercourse may take place with the man facing the woman's back and entering her vagina from behind. This can be done in several different postures. For example, she may rest on her knees and elbows while he stands on his knees behind her, leaning over her body and grasping her waist. (See Figure 4.6.) Rear entry may also be accomplished with the couple lying side by side with the man facing the woman's back, or with the woman sitting in the man's lap with her back toward him. Most of the rear-entry positions (except when the woman lies flat on her stomach) allow deep penetration as well as provide opportunity for manual clitoral stimulation.

Other Possibilities   Most of the positions described above assume that the couple is using a flat horizontal surface such as a bed. However, sexual intercourse may be enjoyed with the couple standing, sitting in a chair, or with one person resting partially on a surface such as a bed or table while the other stands on the floor.

There are almost endless possibilities, some of which may be found in popular sex manuals and some of which may be seen depicted in ancient or contemporary works of art. For a given couple some positions may appear unduly strenuous or even somewhat silly; others may suggest exciting variations to enliven their sexual relationship.

Figure 4.6
Penile-vaginal inter-course in a rear-entry position

Anal Intercourse

Anal intercourse refers to the man placing his penis in the anus of another person. It is not a very common sexual practice in the United States. Of married couples under age thirty-five, less than half have tried it even once. Older persons and unmarried persons are even less likely to have engaged in it (Hunt, 1974, pp. 202–204). Although it is not common among heterosexual couples and is completely absent from sexual encounters between females, anal intercourse occurs often in sexual relations between two males. (See Chapter 13 for additional discussion of male homosexual activities.)

Pleasure in Anal Intercourse   Some heterosexual couples find the thought of anal intercourse repulsive, but others derive great pleasure from it. Some women report orgasm during anal intercourse, even in the absence of additional stimulation. During anal intercourse, either partner may provide the woman with manual stimulation of her breasts, clitoris, or vagina to enhance her response. In anal intercourse between two men, the man receiving anal penetration may have his penis stimulated manually by his partner or may stimulate himself so he may also reach orgasm   122

Many men find anal intercourse more exciting than penile-vaginal intercourse because the anal opening is usually smaller and tighter than the vagina. Probably the forbidden aspect of anal intercourse also makes it more exciting for some people.

Problems in Anal Intercourse   The sphincter muscles surrounding the anal opening are usually quite tight, and sometimes practice is required before they can be sufficiently relaxed to permit the penis to enter without considerable pain for the recipient. The anal sphincter responds to the initial penetrative effort with a strong spastic contraction. This involuntary spasm may last for a minute or longer in persons who do not often experience anal penetration. In persons who receive anal intercourse more frequently, the involuntary relaxation usually begins in a few seconds (Masters and Johnson, 1979, p. 85). In addition, the anus is not naturally provided with the lubrication found in the stimulated vagina, so a lubricant such as surgical jelly must usually be used to avoid pain.

Bacteria found in the anus are often infectious to the vagina. Even though the man washes his penis after anal intercourse, some bacteria may be transferred to the vagina. For this reason the use of a condom during anal intercourse is recommended for persons who also engage in penile-vaginal intercourse. Continued and very frequent anal intercourse may cause fissures in the anal opening, particularly if insufficient lubricant is used.

Other Anal Stimulation   Some persons enjoy having objects such as fingers, tongue, vibrators, or even a fist inserted in their anus. Oral-anal contact (often called "rimming") carries some risk because fecal matter contains bacteria and parasites that can be quite harmful to the person who consumes it (Shilts, 1976). Insertion of large objects such as dildoes or fists into the anus can be very dangerous if the rectum is torn. Additionally, this form of stimulation may eventually damage the anal sphincter muscles so that fecal incontinence results (Swerdlow, 1976).

Sexuality and Disability

There is a popular myth in our culture, perpetuated by the mass media, that sex must always be perfect. The myth involves two hearts beating in unison with perfect love, and two bodies vibrating simultaneously with mutual passion. According to this myth the individuals live happily forever after, with their perfect bodies joined in continuing, perfect sexual ecstasy.

Although this myth may describe some people some of the time, it does not apply to most of us most of the time. Almost all of us will experience some degree of physical disability or lack of physical perfection sometime in our life. The body that is physically beautiful at age twenty may fall far short of perfection by age seventy. The passion that seems unquenchable may cool to nearly zero when a body is drained by illness, overwork, financial setbacks, a death in the family, or other problems that come with living. Sometimes the most attractive and healthy body may respond eagerly to certain forms of stimulation not mentioned by the marriage manuals and fail to respond to other forms that are reputed to guarantee success for everyone. Finally, an accident or illness can leave an individual with a permanent disability with serious consequences for sexual functioning.

Although only a small percentage of the population suffers from serious disabilities, it is instructive for all persons to understand the sexuality of the severely disabled. It makes it easier to accept our own lack of physical perfection and to function sexually with creativity and compassion in a variety of circumstances.

Disability and Sexual Needs

Until recent years any expression of sexuality or sexual needs by disabled persons was seen as inappropriate or bizarre. More recent thinking accepts the sexuality of those with physical limitations. Disabled persons need to see themselves as lovable and loving, and they desire physical intimacy, although sometimes the acquisition of a physical handicap may disrupt their self-concept and sexual feelings (Romano and O'Connor, 1978).

J, a 45-year-old married woman, underwent radical mastectomy for breast carcinoma and, postoperatively, begged the hospital staff to prevent her husband from visiting her. When the staff refused to comply with her wishes, she hid beneath the bedclothes, avoiding her husband's visits, totally rebuffing his efforts to approach her even on the most superficial level. . . . As she worked through her grief over her loss and integrated a positive self-image, her withdrawal from her husband decreased, and within six months after surgery she and her husband were again engaging in sexual relations with one another as they had done prior to surgery.

Romano and O'Connor, 1978, p. 89

Disability and Adaptation

The adaptations a disabled person needs to make depend on the nature and severity of the illness, injury, surgical trauma, or birth defect that caused the disability. The loss of an arm or leg, for example, does not alter

124

the functioning of the sexual organs but may interfere with feelings of sexual attractiveness. On the other hand, an injury to the spinal cord may cause loss of most or all feeling and function in the sexual organs. Disabled persons need straightforward information from their doctor or rehabilitation personnel regarding their particular sexual capabilities and limitations. They also need a partner who can accept their limitations and explore with them some of the wide variety of means of giving and receiving sexual-sensual pleasure.

Conclusion

There are many ways of giving and receiving sexual pleasure, both autoerotically and with a partner or partners. The range of techniques is limited basically only by biology and by culture. Biology limits the number of positions and ways of access to the human body; for example, very few men and no women can perform autoerotic oral sex. Culture further limits the range of options for sexual arousal by norms and laws that specify what is dirty and what is clean, and, as indicated in Part 4, what is normal and abnormal, legal and illegal, stigmatizing and not stigmatizing. The key to sexual pleasure is individual and interpersonal. Experimenting with and communicating sexual techniques that do not harm or offend a partner can provide maximum gratification and self-fulfillment as a sexual and human being.

Equally important as the freedom to communicate and experiment with sexual techniques is the quality of the human relationship between sexual partners. Many men and most women stress the intimacy of the total relationship as the most important factor contributing to the joy of the sexual relationship. One woman summarized it very well:

I like the intimateness of lovemaking almost as much as the sex itself. Hugging and kissing and caressing someone is more loving than sex, and is very important. I also love the way people talk and smile and giggle when they make love. People after sex tend to become very silly, and sharing that is really important to feel loved. If you want a good orgasm, you can masturbate. The whole reason you make love with someone is to share the closeness and warmth of making love, of giving pleasure, of appreciating each other's bodies, of saying things you would never say elsewhere, of being very loving without feeling silly or foolish — anything is okay to say in bed.

Part II / *Sexuality and Reproduction: Medical and Social Aspects*

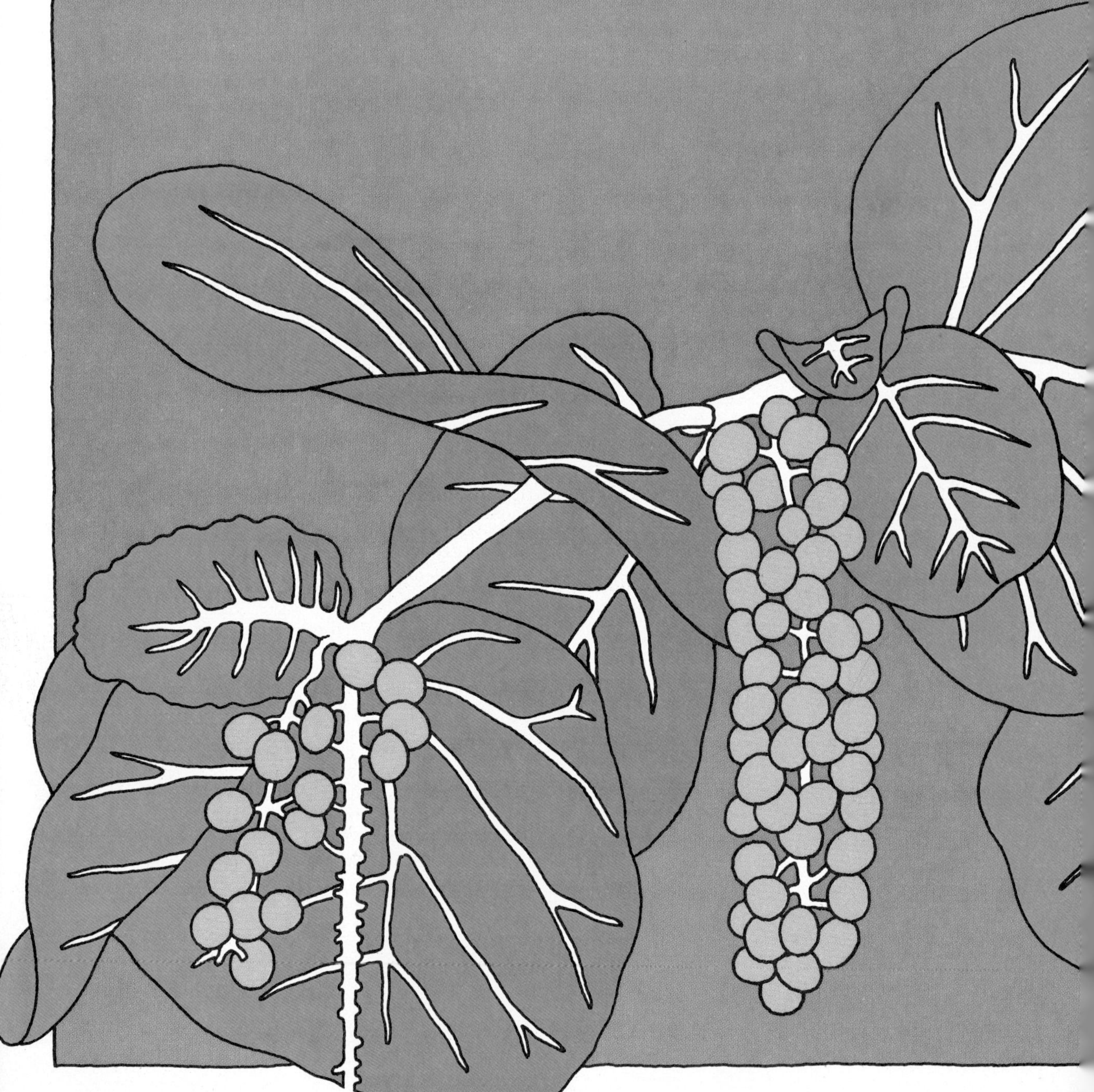

Birth, growth, conception, and death seem, at first glance, to be quintessentially physiological or biological events. As both research and common sense quickly make clear, however, all these processes are both profoundly biological and profoundly psychosocial. The medical and psychosocial aspects of human biological events are inextricably interwoven.

Medical Aspects

The medical perspective on sexuality and reproduction must, first of all, be accepted by society as a legitimate one. Before the Reformation, the religious perspective on sexuality and reproduction held sway, and alternative perspectives were not permitted. For example, medical researchers were not allowed to dissect corpses, since bodies and their operations were sacred mysteries belonging to God. Szasz comments on the ways in which the medical perspective has supplanted the religious perspective on sexuality; "temptation" is redefined as "impulse" and "wrongdoing" as "sickness": "Temptation — resisted or indulged — has been supplanted by drives, instincts and impulses — satisfied or frustrated. Virtue and vice have been tranformed into health and illness" (Szasz, 1974, p. 149).

Institutionalization of the Medical Perspective

Contemporary society has not only facilitated the use of the medical perspective in examining sexual, reproductive, or other phenomena; it has also institutionalized the medical perspective. As we will see in Part 4, for example, deviations from the monogamous, heterosexual norm of sexuality are defined as "sickness," with discoverable causes and proposed cures. As indicated in Part 1 — particularly in Chapters 3 and 4 — the nature and manipulation of the physiological equipment with which people enter sexual encounters are regarded as vital aspects of the sexual interaction that takes place.

Medical Knowledge

The institutionalization and pervasiveness of the medical perspective on sexuality and reproduction has given rise to a current increase in the quantity and quality of medical knowledge of these topics. As indicated in Part 1, medical knowledge concerning human anatomy, menstruation, conception, and pregnancy has been advancing rapidly for several decades longer than the knowledge about sexual arousal and response covered in Chapters 3 and 4. Similarly, knowledge about those diseases associated with sexuality and reproduction, such as venereal disease and menstrual difficulties, is currently greater than knowledge about the various types of sexual difficulties, such as anorgasmia (the inability of a woman to achieve orgasm) or premature ejaculation, which contemporary women and men may define as problems. However, current research is now closing some of these gaps in knowledge.

The Medical and the Social

In Part 2, knowledge about medical aspects of sexuality is combined with a consideration of the social context within which they occur.

Sex therapy today is both a medical and a social matter, as Chapter 5 indicates. As Szasz points out, where once sexuality itself was seen as a sort of sickness — especially in women — today asexuality may be seen as medically unsound. He contrasts contemporary medical presumptions with earlier religious perspectives on sex as "temptation":

A man not tempted by a woman, especially his wife, or who resisted her sexual charms, was now said to be "impotent," and this condition was considered to be a form of mental disease. Similarly, the woman who was not tempted by the man or who resisted his charms, especially if he was her husband, was now said

Szasz, 1975, p. 151

128

to be "frigid," and this condition too was considered to be a form of mental disease. In this a whole host of new "diseases" came into being, all of which had in common the fact that the person said to have been sick was not tempted, when, according to psychiatric standards, he should have been tempted; or if he was tempted, he refused to yield to it, when, according to psychiatric standards, he should have yielded.

Chapter 5, therefore, deals with sex therapy both as a medical and as a sociocultural phenomenon, since the need for such services relates to the presence of physiological conditions, social definitions of the goodness or badness of these conditions, and psychological discomfort with the experience of such conditions.

Menstruation, conception, and pregnancy are examined in Chapter 6, both as measurable and universal physiological processes and as subjects for cultural definition. Similarly, modes of birth control are analyzed in Chapter 7, both with respect to medical aspects of technology, use, and success and to psychological and social aspects of the motivation and desire to use contraceptives and to limit childbirth.

Clearly, physiologically measured diseases relating to sexuality and reproduction carry social meanings linked with the taboos attached to sexuality itself. Venereal diseases, for example, although they have clear-cut medical symptoms and treatments, are also clearly "social diseases." Chapter 8, therefore, deals with venereal disease as a medical phenomenon, but sets it within the context of society.

Chapter 5 / *Sex Therapy*

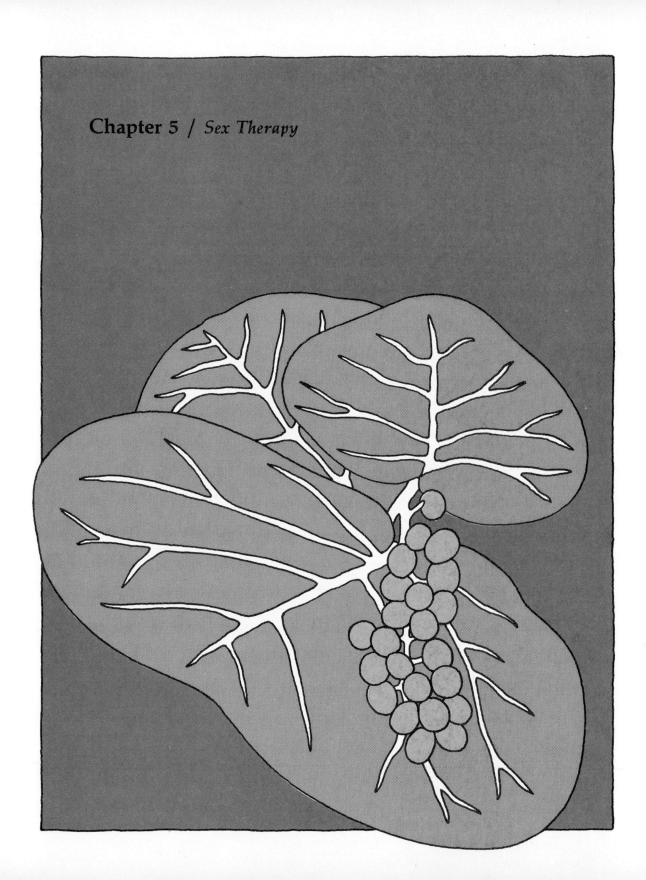

Sex therapy in its current form is a relatively new development, especially if it is defined as treatment directed specifically toward changing only sexual behaviors without attempting to treat the total personality.

Of course, there have always been those who treated and theorized about sexual problems. In the mid-1700s the English physician John Hunter advised an "impotent" patient to go to bed with his partner but avoid intercourse for six nights. The ban had its effect, and the patient was soon cured.

In Chapter 2, we saw that Freud defined the life force itself in the context of sexuality and the libido, and located the source of individual personality and growth within the sexual and family sphere. Directly influenced by Freud, psychoanalysts treated many sexual complaints with methods relying primarily on verbal exchange and insight.

In the 1940s, 1950s, and 1960s a number of practitioners, including physician James Semans, hypnotherapist Milton Erickson, and behavioralists such as Joseph Wolpe, Arnold Lazarus, and Albert Ellis, treated sexual problems with many methods that are now familiar. These included changing negative attitudes about sex, reducing anxiety, enhancing communication, and providing information about sexual functioning (Zilbergeld and Evans, 1980).

The development of contemporary sex therapy resulted from the pioneering work of William Masters and Virginia Johnson at the Reproductive Biology Foundation in St. Louis, Missouri, now called the Masters and Johnson Institute. Sex therapy as we now know it was born with their publication of *Human Sexual Inadequacy* in 1970; their work rapidly became the standard for the field. They developed a treatment program that, though borrowing liberally from older sources, was different in many ways from traditional approaches. They trained a number of sex therapists and, through their publications, public appearances, and workshops, influenced a great many more. Most sex therapy programs in the United States today use some of the treatment techniques they developed or modifications of those techniques.

Causes of Sexual Difficulties

To define themselves as having sexual difficulties, people must have some feeling of dissatisfaction with their sexual functioning. The source of this dissatisfaction may involve social, relationship, or personal factors, or any combination of these. For example, a woman may be unhappy because she does not experience orgasm and her partner also may feel this is a sexual problem for them. In other cases only one person may feel dissat- 131

The quality of the relationship between two persons usually affects the quality of their sexual interaction.
Cary S. Wolinsky/Stock Boston

isfied about the sexual relationship. For example, a man may be quite proud of his ability to ejaculate rapidly, whereas his female partner sees it as a problem of premature ejaculation that leaves her very frustrated.

Among individuals with sexual difficulties there are many different pathways to any given dysfunction. For example, one woman who is not orgasmic may never have learned to respond orgasmically, another may be angry with her partner, and a third may be taking a medication that interferes with her sexual functioning. Other women may be nonorgasmic for other reasons.

Moreover, any one of the factors that lead to sexual problems may have different effects on different people; factors that lead to sexual dysfunction in some people seem to have no observable effect on others. For example, one man may react to anxiety by not getting an erection, another by ejaculating too quickly, and a third by experiencing no sexual difficulty.

At best we can say that the factors to be discussed in this chapter will lead to sexual difficulties for some people. The factors are assigned here to four categories — physiological, psychological, cultural, and relationship — for the purpose of organizing the discussion; in any given case, there will be interaction of factors from all four categories.

Physiological Factors

Illnesses, drugs, and various physical conditions, even those that seem unrelated to sexuality, can affect sexual functioning. Effects may be reduced energy levels, changes in mood, pain or discomfort during sexual interaction, absence or decrease of sexual interest, and absence or slowing of specific physiological responses.

Rare physical anomalies that may lead to impaired sexual functioning in the male include an excessively tight foreskin, congenital absence of gonads, and Peyronie's disease, a curvature of the penis caused by build-up of plaques. Among the physiological conditions that may lead to sexual difficulties in the female are an imperforate or thick hymen, a constrictive clitoral hood or clitoral adhesions, and pubococcygeal muscle weakness or fibrosis.

Some diseases that may lead to impaired sexual functioning in the female are vaginal infections, endometriosis, and ovarian and uterine tumors and cysts. Obstetrical or surgical trauma of the sex organs, such as poor *episiotomy* (incision of the area between the vagina and anus during childbirth), can lead to female sexual dysfunctions. Diseases that may impair sexual functioning in either males or females include diabetes, prostatitis, arthritis, diffuse arteriosclerosis, and multiple sclerosis. Treatment for these conditions may lead to improvement in sexual functioning.

Accidental or surgical trauma involving the brain, spinal cord, or perineal nerves may interfere with sexual functioning in both sexes, as may chronic use of alcohol, heroin, methadone, and many prescribed medications, such as tranquilizers or sympathetic blocking agents used in treatment of high blood pressure. Hormonal changes associated with   133

aging (see Chapter 11), poor nutrition, fatigue, stress, and depression may also have adverse effects on the sexual functioning of both sexes. Again, in some instances there can be improvement with treatment of the underlying condition (Amelar, 1971; Kaufman, 1967; Story, 1974; Kaplan, 1974). Other organic conditions, such as anemia, congestive heart failure, and pulmonary disease, may interfere with sexual desire and functioning.

The pioneering therapy program developed by Virginia Johnson and William Masters focuses on physiological and behavioral causes of sexual difficulties.
Photo by Scott F. Johnson. Courtesy of the Reproductive Biology Research Foundation.

Psychological Factors

Only a small percentage of sexual difficulties are the result of physiological problems; the great majority result from personal and relationship problems. Consequently, while many sex therapy approaches provide for testing to see if physiological problems exist, most sex therapy focuses on dealing with these psychological and interpersonal factors.

134

Fear or Anxiety There are a variety of fears and states of anxiety, some rational and some irrational, that can lead to sexual difficulties. Fear or anxiety may prevent an individual from being receptive to a partner's advances and lead to unsatisfying sexual interaction, impaired sexual functioning, or avoidance of sex altogether.

A common cause of anxiety in sexual situations is a performance orientation toward sexual activity. Given the high value placed on achievement in most segments of our society, it is not surprising that many people experience performance pressure in the bedroom. *Performance anxiety,* fear that one will not be able to perform sexually according to some preconceived notion of adequacy, can inhibit much or all of sexual response and result in the self-defined "failure" that was feared. This can start a vicious circle, in which the next sexual encounter is anticipated with increased anxiety because of the past "failure," with another "failure" occurring as a result (Masters and Johnson, 1970). Performance anxiety can be directed at living up to a partner's expectations as well as to one's own. Some people are so concerned about a partner's pleasure that they will concentrate on pleasing their partner at the expense of personal pleasure.

Spectatoring is a frequent symptom of a performance orientation toward sexual interaction. In spectatoring, individuals remain "outside themselves," observing their sexual reactions rather than suspending distracting thoughts and losing themselves in erotic experiences. Typical intrusive thoughts indicative of spectatoring are: How am I doing? Am I going to make it? I'm not turning on fast enough, what can I do? Am I going to lose my erection? Can I last long enough? Acting as spectator and critical judge of one's lovemaking can produce anxiety and interfere with both sexual functioning and pleasure.

There are also other causes of sexual anxiety. Some people fear they will appear foolish or lose control if they allow themselves free sexual expression with the cries, sounds, and facial expressions that passion can bring. Some may fear hurting their partner, being hurt, or imminent desertion by their partner. Others fear they may lose consciousness or bladder or bowel control. In still other cases anxiety may be traced to other causes (Fink, 1974).

Anger or Hostility Regardless of its source, and even when it is unconscious, anger or resentment can be destructive. Like anxiety, anger may inhibit openness to a partner's advances or interfere with sexual interaction when it is indirectly expressed. Also like anxiety, anger or hostility can lead to avoidance of sex or to sexual interaction that is dysfunctional or, at the least, unsatisfying.

135

Avoidance of Sex   People can find many ways to avoid sex. Some make sexual invitations under circumstances in which their partner is very tired, very busy, or in some other way obviously unavailable. Yet when their partner seems to be in the mood, they will have a headache, remember an important golf game, have to deal with a messy kitchen or work from the office, or have some other apparently reasonable excuse. Some people start quarrels, criticize, or bring up worrisome problems just before initiating sexual interaction. Others will avoid sex by becoming generally unattractive to their partner in some way, such as by gaining weight, becoming careless about appearance and grooming, or becoming verbally abusive.

Cultural Factors

Because all cultures regulate sexuality in some way, it is to be expected that all people who have been effectively socialized will have learned something of their culture's rules with respect to sex and sexual functioning. Among cultural factors that may lead to sexual difficulties are the sexual values and scripts for sex roles and sexual behavior that an individual has learned.

Traditional Sex Roles   Sexual behavior is learned, much of it from popular novels, movies, TV, dirty jokes, pornography, and other media. In his book *Male Sexuality,* Zilbergeld calls the predominant model of sexuality that we learn from these sources the "fantasy model." It is a model of performance and superhuman expectations. Anyone who takes it too seriously is more likely to experience performance anxiety or sexual dysfunction than to have sexual experiences that are rewarding and lead to feelings of intimacy. Yet the fantasy model provides the basis for the scripts for sexual interaction that most people learn in our culture.

In the exaggerated fantasy model, a man believes that sex is the primary way he can prove his masculinity; that the man is responsible for sex and, consequently, ultimately responsible for its outcome; that he must pursue, initiate, run the show, and know everything there is to know about sex; and that he must always be interested in sex and turn on, no matter what.

His partner believes that a good woman is chaste and virtuous; that a woman should repress her sexual feelings because such feelings are dirty, sinful, or not nice; that if she maintains her purity, some day her prince will come, sweep her off her feet, and turn her on in spite of herself. Of course, she will protect his fragile male ego, even if that means faking orgasms — or multiple orgasms. Many women who take the model too literally learn to turn off their sexual feelings and be nonorgasmic rather than sexually responsive.

Repressive Learning   A large proportion of adults in our society report they did not receive positive messages about sex from their parents while they were growing up. Not all of these people were receiving negative messages, but many were. However, many people survive a sexually restrictive upbringing without becoming entirely alienated from their own sexuality. Many learn to feel fear and guilt only when they violate a strong social taboo, such as public exhibition of the genitals. Others develop learned prohibitions that inhibit their sexual response to some degree even in socially acceptable situations, such as marital intercourse.

It has not been uncommon in our culture for persons, particularly those reared in very religious households, to feel that sexual expression is sinful or evil. Labeling all premarital sexual acts as sinful may be an effective way of preventing premarital sex in some cases. Often, however, such labeling does not discourage youthful sexual experimentation. Instead, it may interfere not only with premarital sexual pleasure but also with all sexual pleasure, even when it is socially legitimized by marriage.

Another prohibition often taught in our culture is that the sex organs and the secretions naturally involved in the sex act are dirty, smelly, or untouchable. It is easy to understand how this feeling can develop from

137

the reaction of parents to a child's natural curiosity about his or her body
and its functions. Children who are frequently assailed by tense repri-
mands such as "Nasty," "Don't touch," "That has germs," "Go wash your
hands" when they look at or touch their genital area may generalize the
feeling of dirtiness they learn to include even clean healthy genitals,
normal vaginal secretions, and seminal or preseminal fluids. Some will
reach adulthood with a sense of revulsion toward touching their own or
another's body.

Traumatic Sex   Sometimes accident or circumstance causes a trauma that
can interfere with sexual functioning. The young person who is just beginning to experiment with sex is particularly vulnerable to long-lasting
negative consequences of an unsuccessful sexual experience or an unkind
response from a sexual partner (Kaplan, 1974). For example, during the
furtive fumblings of the first attempts at sexual lovemaking the female
will probably not experience orgasm and the male is likely to ejaculate
prematurely. Add a derisive response from a partner thrown in the face of
a "failure," particularly for an inexperienced person who has no backlog
of successes against which to evaluate what seems to be a sexual disaster,
and the potential for escalating sexual difficulties is increased.

    Sometimes later sexual experiences are more positive and can correct
the negative learning that took place in a few bad experiences. But if more
fortunate circumstances do not intervene, counseling or reassuring information is rarely available to a young person to reduce the anxiety likely to
accompany future sexual interaction (Kaplan, 1974).

Relationship Factors

Even a physically and psychologically healthy person depends to some
degree upon the cooperation of at least one other person for sexual release, unless she or he chooses to have no sexual life beyond masturbation. The quality of the relationship between sexual partners usually
affects, to some degree, the quality of their sexual interaction. Some couples have a varied, freely expressive, and very satisfying sexual relationship even though every other aspect of their interaction is fraught with
rejection, hostility, tension, and mistrust. But they are the exception. Sex
therapy is rarely as successful for couples who are obviously incompatible
or frankly hostile to each other as for those without these characteristics.

Power Struggles   Interaction in some relationships is characterized by
perpetual struggles for power. Although often unaware of the dynamics
of their relationship, some couples constantly spar while each tries to   138

dominate the other and at the same time avoid being dominated. Because of the power struggle, an individual who desires lovemaking may refuse his or her partner's advances rather than feel dominated by the other's sexual schedule. Or more seriously, a woman may remain nonresponsive or nonorgasmic and a man not attain an erection or ejaculate because of not wanting to give in to what the partner desires. Unconsciously, each prefers to relinquish his or her own orgasmic pleasure rather than give satisfaction to the partner-adversary (Kaplan, 1974).

Sexual Ignorance and Poor Communication Ignorance or lack of communication about sexual matters can result in sexual difficulties in a physically and emotionally stable couple with a loving and mutually supportive relationship. For example, ignorance of sexual anatomy or a failure to communicate preferences can result in a couple continuing for years to use ineffective techniques of sexual stimulation.

Types of Sexual Difficulty

Most of the sexual problems for which people seek sex therapy fall within several basic categories. Males typically report erectile dysfunction, premature ejaculation, or retarded ejaculation. Females report anorgasmia and vaginismus (Kaplan, 1974). Both males and females may report problems with sexual arousal and excitation, lack of desire, or discrepancies in desire.

Erectile Dysfunction

In *erectile dysfunction,* commonly called *impotence,* the male is unable to produce or maintain an erection. Erectile difficulty occurs in men of all ages, races, and socioeconomic groupings; in its milder forms it is quite common. Even though erectile difficulties are not unusual, they are often traumatic.

When I was overseas I was having problems with my wife — but a lot of the guys were having problems with their wives. As soon as I got back to the states I called her and first thing she said she wanted a divorce. . . . The next week I met a girl at a pool party, and it did not take much before we were in bed together. She was really a doll and really built. But when I got ready to go in her, I lost my hard. I tried again later in a little while, but the same thing happened. It happened about three more times after that. It really shook me

From the authors' files

139

up. I don't know how to describe it. Like I had been through Vietnam and everything over there and people were getting killed all around me and I was never afraid of death. But this was something else, and it shook me up more than anything I had been through. Maybe it was the stress of Vietnam and getting out, or maybe it was guilt because I knew I was still married then, or maybe it was just everything all at once like the divorce and my brother on drugs and finding out my best friend was a homosexual. But it really cracked me up when it happened.

The complex physiological mechanisms that control erection are vulnerable to both physical and psychological factors that can impair the erectile reflex. If the vascular reflex mechanism fails to pump sufficient blood into the penis, or if the blood that is pumped in does not remain there, the penis will not become firm and erect.

Erectile function may be impaired when a man experiences anxiety. Anxiety affects people in different ways. Some may have an erection during foreplay but lose it when they attempt penetration; others may experience difficulties only in specific situations, such as with a lover but not with their wife (or vice versa); a few may never have an erection under any circumstances; and some have no erection problems at all.

Premature Ejaculation

Premature ejaculation occurs when the male lacks control over his progress toward orgasm. When very high levels of sexual excitement are reached, orgasm and ejaculation are involuntary reflex actions. But a man can learn to control his excitement before he reaches this point of no return, and can thereby maintain a fairly high level of sexual tension for prolonged periods before reaching orgasm.

Premature ejaculation is often cited as the most common of the male sexual difficulties. Some premature ejaculators are unaware that the condition hampers their own and their partner's sexual pleasure. They consider their rapid orgasm as normal or even desirable. More often, inability to control orgasm results in feelings of inadequacy and guilt because the pleasure of the female partner is severely limited. Sometimes these negative feelings over premature ejaculation cause men to avoid intercourse altogether or to have difficulty getting an erection.

I am twenty-five years old and have been married eighteen months. I have a problem which is turning me into a nervous wreck, has caused tremendous unhappiness and frustration and might destroy my marriage. I'm referring to my problem of premature ejaculation. I've had this problem ever since my first sexual experience at the age of eighteen. Because of my disability, I seldom

Greenwald and Greenwald, 1973, p. 427

indulged in sex until my marriage. I thought perhaps that with a steady partner, I would be cured. But such has not been the case. In fact, it has become somewhat a vicious circle. The more tense and insecure I become, the less I am able to control my ejaculation.

Premature ejaculation is most often the result of a faulty learning process. Either the man has not learned to recognize the sensations associated with increasing levels of sexual tension in himself, or has not learned the mechanisms by which he can voluntarily lower his level of excitement while it is still controllable. Anger, anxiety, or other strong emotion may also be a factor in premature ejaculation, especially if a man has previously had adequate ejaculatory control.

Retarded Ejaculation

A man who experiences *retarded ejaculation* responds to sexual stimuli with erotic feelings and a firm erection but is unable to achieve orgasm even though he desires to do so. The severity of retarded ejaculation varies considerably, ranging from occasional instances of inhibition of orgasm, to cases in which a man can reach climax only under special circumstances (such as solitary masturbation), to cases in which the man has never experienced orgasm.

Retarded ejaculation due to organic causes is quite rare, although neuropathy or some drugs can cause the condition. More often a specific traumatic event precedes onset of the difficulty and triggers an involuntary and unconsciously conditioned inhibition (Kaplan, 1974, pp. 320–328). In some cases, lack of arousal prevents the orgasmic response.

Female Orgasmic Difficulty

Orgasmic difficulty, or *anorgasmia* (Greek: lack of orgasm), is inability of a woman to reach orgasm. Orgasmic difficulties are probably the most frequent sexual complaints of women.

The severity of orgasmic difficulty varies, from women who have never experienced orgasm by any means to women who have occasional anorgasmia in intercourse. Some women may be accepting of occasional absence of orgasm. Consistent anorgasmia may be the source of great distress for some women and a matter of no concern to others, just as some men may be very concerned with premature ejaculation and others may not. An occasional woman may not even know that women are capable of orgasm, and thus may not be concerned over anorgasmia.

The great majority of cases of female orgasmic difficulty are interpersonal or psychological in origin. Some psychological factors that can lead

141

to inhibition of orgasm are guilt about sexuality, fear of letting go of emotions, and hostility toward the sexual partner. Interpersonally, the important factor in orgasmic difficulty may be inadequate stimulation because of ignorance in the woman and her partner or poor communication (Fisher, 1973; Fink, 1974; Kaplan, 1974, p. 384). Sometimes a skilled and sympathetic partner can help a previously nonorgasmic woman reach her first orgasm without any professional intervention.

Annette was getting migraines and going to the doctor for them, but I told her the doctor couldn't do any good because her trouble was she was not having any orgasms because her husband just got his and got off and left her lying there. Then she wanted to go to bed with me right away to see if she could have one with me. But I said let's talk first. We petted for maybe forty-five minutes until she was really excited. I talked to her a lot and made her laugh because I knew that would relax her. I can hold back pretty good so I talked to her while I was inside her — like I would ask her if it felt good and told her to concentrate on her feelings and not worry about pleasing me because I enjoyed just being with her. I tried to get her to feel confident in herself and I let her take the dominant role and do what she liked, and I would pretend she was really turning me on so it would encourage her. She finally had one and afterwards I cuddled and kissed her a lot to make her feel really good about it. It gave me great satisfaction that I could make her feel like a human again. I think that is why I could do it — because I made her feel like I cared enough to take time and to want to give her something and listen to her feelings and care about how she felt about it all.

From the authors' files

Vaginismus

Vaginismus is a relatively uncommon disorder in which there is an involuntary spasm of the muscles surrounding the vaginal entrance whenever an attempt is made to introduce an object into the vagina. The spasm closes the vaginal opening so tightly that intercourse is impossible or quite painful. Vaginismus is a response that usually has resulted from pain or fear associated with vaginal penetration. Early brutal sexual experiences, painful pelvic examination, fear of men, and ignorance about sex and childbirth are some of the factors that may lead to the development of this difficulty. Treatment involves dealing with both the fear and the pain.

I don't know why it hurts me so I can't have sex, but I know it does. . . . Bill says he should have known better than to marry me because he could hear me yelling way out in the waiting room when the doctor tried to fix me up with a diaphragm right before we got married. But that was the first time a doctor or

From the authors' files

anyone had tried to stick something inside me and I knew it would break something the first time and really hurt. . . . I'm OK if Bill will just neck and stuff like when we were courting, but then he gets excited and wants to stick it in me and then I get scared and he gets mad and we wind up fighting about it. So I had just as soon not do anything at all now and I guess he would too.

Vaginismus is not always associated with inhibition of sexual arousal or of orgasm. Some women afflicted with the disorder may enjoy aspects of lovemaking other than intercourse, and some are orgasmic through clitoral or other stimulation.

Problems of Arousal and Excitation

General sexual nonresponse refers to an inhibition of the arousal aspect of the sexual response. There is generally both a lack of erotic feelings and an impairment of physical excitation, that is, of genital vasocongestion and vaginal lubrication or erection (Kaplan, 1974). Zilbergeld and Ellison

Sometimes a woman may not become sexually aroused in a sexual situation.
Arthur Sirdofsky/Editorial Photocolor Archives, Inc.

143

(1980) have found it diagnostically useful to distinguish between arousal (erotic feelings) and physical excitation, because in some cases one will be present without the other.

Physical excitation is expressed as genital vasocongestion, a process under the control of the autonomic nervous system. Physical excitation is evidenced by erection in the male and vaginal swelling and lubrication in the female. Any strong emotion, such as rage or fear, can override the autonomic reflex and may impair excitation. Among the origins of these emotions may be an unconscious unresolved conflict, an immediate anxiety such as fear of failure, or a reaction to a partner's lack of sensitivity (Kaplan, 1974; Zilbergeld and Ellison, 1980).

In women the severity of general sexual nonresponse varies from women who respond sexually only in particular situations to women who have never responded in any situation. In men, general sexual nonresponse is frequently diagnosed as erectile dysfunction. However, some therapists distinguish between cases of erectile dysfunction, in which lack of arousal is the primary cause, and cases in which other causes are primary.

Discrepancies in Desire

A common complaint of couples is that one person wants sex more often than the other. With some couples, it is the man who wants sex more often.

> The biggest [problem] is wanting more sex than she is always able to give. Frequency seems to be the problem. . . . My spouse many times just refuses sex if she doesn't feel good, or if something is bothering her. At times she gives in to my desires and it becomes mechanical.

Pietropinto and Simenauer, 1979, p. 96

With other couples, the woman has more sexual desire than the man.

> My spouse's biggest sexual difficulty is his need of sex isn't as often as I would like. He is terrific when we are making love but I would like quantity with quality.

Pietropinto and Simenauer, 1979, p. 101

Sometimes a difference in desire is due to one person's sexual problem, such as a lack of orgasm by the woman or premature ejaculation by the man. In these cases the apparent difference in desire can be treated best by treating the sexual problem. But in other cases both persons are free of problems that can be treated by Masters and Johnson's approach to sex therapy, yet one has less sex drive than the other. These cases must be treated by other approaches.

144

Treatment Methods of Sex Therapy

Couples or individuals who feel they have sexual problems can find several ways of getting help. They can choose among therapies that focus on changing the way people think and feel about themselves, that focus on changing the way they relate to others, or that focus on changing specific sexual behaviors. Most forms of sex therapy focus on techniques for changing sexual behavior, but many also deal to some degree with relationship and psychological processes.

The choice of a particular sex therapy depends on many factors such as cost, presence of a cooperative sex partner, availability of therapists, degree of other emotional problems (which may or may not be related to the sexual problem), and goals of the person seeking therapy as well as his or her intelligence, education, and social sophistication. The following types of sex therapy indicate the range of choices available in many metropolitan areas of the United States. Not all these choices may be found in every area. Furthermore, two or more approaches may be used in any given therapeutic situation.

Masters and Johnson's Approach

In *Human Sexual Inadequacy* Masters and Johnson present a treatment model they call *co-marital* therapy, in which a male-female team of therapists works with a couple who have a sex problem. Masters and Johnson believe the dual-sex therapy team facilitates communication and rapport between therapists and patients because each patient has an ally of the same sex to interpret his or her feelings (Masters and Johnson, 1970, pp. 4–5).

A basic premise of the approach developed by Masters and Johnson is that there is no such thing as an uninvolved partner in a marriage in which there is some form of sexual difficulty. They believe that treating both sexual partners recognizes that sexual functioning is a form of interaction between two persons. Sexual trouble is treated as a couple problem and not as the concern of only the husband or only the wife (Masters and Johnson, 1970, pp. 2–3).

At the Masters and Johnson Institute in St. Louis, couples are seen daily, seven days a week, in an intensive two-week program. According to Masters and Johnson, an advantage of this approach is that couples are isolated from the usual demands of their everyday world, leaving them the time and energy to focus on the resolution of their difficulties. Because couples are seen daily, the problems they encounter in carrying out their assignments may be dealt with immediately and resolved before they engender more fears of failure (Masters and Johnson, 1970, pp. 17–20). 145

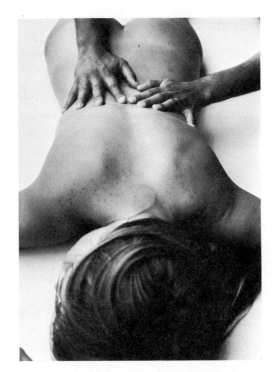

In sensate focus the couple take turns touching each other in ways that give sensual pleasure.
Paul Fusco/Magnum Photos, Inc.

General Therapy Format   After a brief introductory session, the sessions on the first two days are devoted to taking a sex history. Until the round-table discussion on the third day, patients refrain from overt sexual activity and from discussing the questions or answers of the history taking (Masters and Johnson, 1970, pp. 30–56).

On the third day the couple have an intensive physical examination, including a medical history, before they join the therapists in a round-table discussion. In this discussion the therapists summarize the material acquired during the history taking and allow for questions and discussion. Unless the round-table discussion has been overwhelmingly intense, the couple are encouraged to continue the discussion later in the privacy of their own quarters. They are also given instructions for performing their first exercise, called *sensate focus.* In the privacy of their living quarters they are to remove their clothing; one of them (designated by the therapists) is to touch the other in a way intended to give sensual pleasure. Sexual caresses are not allowed. After a period of time the roles are reversed and the receiving partner becomes the giver. In this exercise each partner is to focus on his or her physical and psychological reaction to the giving and receiving process (Masters and Johnson, 1970, pp. 67–75).

146

On each remaining day of therapy, part of the therapy session is devoted to discussion of the couple's experiences in following the instructions given during the previous session. The basic instruction on day four and on subsequent days is to repeat the sensate focus session before following any other directions. It is intended that in this way the couple will learn that an expression of an innate desire to touch is not necessarily a sexual invitation. Additional instruction given on day four is that the recipient place his or her hand lightly on that of the partner who is doing the touching to indicate preferences for pressure, rate of stroking, or area to be touched. Also, touch is to include breasts and genitals, but without the intention to produce orgasm.

On the fourth day the therapists also instruct the patients in the basics of male and female sexual anatomy, utilizing diagrams of internal and external structures (Masters and Johnson, 1970, pp. 85–91). After day four in the basic treatment program, which to this point is uniform for all couples, therapeutic efforts are directed toward treating the specific difficulties of the couple.

Treatment of Premature Ejaculation   Treatment of premature ejaculation begins with instructions for the *squeeze technique.* The woman is instructed to stimulate the male to a full erection and then immediately squeeze the head of the penis with her thumb and first two fingers for three to four seconds. (See Figure 5.1.) The man will lose his urge to ejaculate and will usually also lose 10 to 30 percent of his full erection. After fifteen to thirty seconds the woman again stimulates the penis to full erection and applies the squeeze to stop the urge to ejaculate. It is intended that in this manner the couple will be able to engage in a long period of sex play without the man reaching orgasm (Masters and Johnson, 1970, pp. 101–105).

Figure 5.1

Method of gripping penis for application of squeeze technique

Figure 5.2

A woman-above, face-to-face position for developing male ejaculatory control

If no other transitory problems (such as erection difficulties) develop, a man will usually develop sufficient control, after several days of practice sessions combining the manual stimulation and the squeeze, to permit progression to nondemanding intercourse. The man lies on his back and the woman kneels astride his body, facing him (the *female-above position;* see Figure 5.2). After bringing the man to full erection two or three times, she inserts the penis in her vagina and then remains motionless in order to

Figure 5.3

A side-by-side, face-to-face coital position

provide no further stimulation. When the man's level of excitement threatens to escape his still shaky control, he is to communicate this to the woman, so that she can rise from the penis and apply the squeeze technique again (Masters and Johnson, 1970, pp. 106–107).

In subsequent days the man is instructed to provide just enough pelvic thrusting to maintain his erection, but not enough to bring about orgasm. In the final phase the couple can move into the lateral (side-by-side) coital position (see Figure 5.3) in which Masters and Johnson believe there is maximum opportunity for male orgasmic control (Masters and Johnson, 1970, pp. 107–110).

Treatment of Retarded Ejaculation During treatment of retarded ejaculation, the woman is encouraged to manipulate her partner's penis, and to ask for specific verbal and physical direction in techniques that are particularly appealing to him. Masters and Johnson believe that once a man has reached orgasm in response to the woman's stimulation, he can identify with her as a pleasure-giving partner. They also believe it is important that the man feel stimulated not only by the woman's approach but also by her responses to his sexual approaches. During treatment the man is encouraged to approach his partner sexually in order to provide her with orgasm and relief from sexual tensions.

149

If the man becomes able to reach orgasm through manual stimulation by his partner, the therapists instruct the couple in developing ejaculation within the vagina. The woman is to stimulate the man manually to a high level of sexual excitement and then, kneeling astride his body, rapidly insert his penis into her vagina. (See Figure 5.2). Immediately after insertion the woman is to begin hard pelvic thrusting against her partner's penis. If the man does not reach orgasm very soon, the woman is to remove his penis from her vagina and return to manual stimulation. If the man gets to a point where he is regularly ejaculating within the woman's vagina, the couple is instructed to continue manual stimulation before intercourse, but to insert the penis into the vagina at lower levels of excitement for the man so that progressively longer periods of penile-vaginal thrusting can be used to produce ejaculation. If the couple have difficulties at any step, the therapists provide specific instructions for dealing with them.

Treatment of Erectile Dysfunction   One of the primary goals in treating erectile dysfunctions is to remove the man's anxiety concerning his sexual performance and thus alter his spectator role. Some performance fears are neutralized by the instructions prohibiting sexual intercourse during the first days at the clinic (Masters and Johnson, 1970, pp. 195–201).

First steps toward treating erectile difficulties are taken when the couple is instructed in the technique of sensate focus during day four. It is intended that quiet, nondemanding body stroking will provide an opportunity to think and feel sexually without any demand for sexual performance. Often the couple find that a partial or complete erection develops when they are engaged in sensual pleasuring, even without any direct physical contact with the genital areas (Masters and Johnson, 1970, pp. 201–202).

On day five the therapists instruct the couple to continue sensate focus, this time including the breast and genital areas. They emphasize that the purpose is not to produce penile erection or vaginal lubrication, but to discover what is most pleasurable to each (Masters and Johnson, 1970, pp. 203–204).

If the couple reach a point where an erection occurs without the male trying to force it or the female demanding it, the woman is instructed to stimulate the male to erection, cease stimulation until the erection subsides, and return to sexual play to induce another erection. This teasing exercise is to be repeated for a half hour in a slow, nondemanding fashion. If this exercise is enjoyable and stimulating to both partners, it helps establish confidence that the erection will return even when it is temporarily lost during sex play (Masters and Johnson, 1970, p. 206).

As a next step the woman is told to kneel astride the man's body before beginning sex play. When a full erection develops, she is to insert the penis into her vagina in a slow, nondemanding manner while continuing active manual stimulation of the penis. After insertion she is to move slowly up and down on the penis. Then she remains quiet and the man is encouraged to thrust slowly, concentrating on the sensual pleasures derived but with no concern for bringing about orgasm either for himself or his partner.

On subsequent days the couple continue the slow pelvic movements with no pressure to achieve orgasm. Many couples who follow this pattern reach a point where orgasm occurs during coitus.

Treatment of Vaginismus   The initial step in Masters and Johnson's treatment of vaginismus is physical demonstration of the involuntary vaginal spasm experienced by the woman. First the therapists use diagrams to illustrate the specific anatomical involvement. Then the woman is placed in the typical position for gynecological examination, so that the therapists may demonstrate to both her and her partner the presence of involuntary vaginal spasm when an attempt is made to insert an examining finger in the vagina (Masters and Johnson, 1970, pp. 262).

Once the clinical existence of vaginismus has been demonstrated and both partners understand that the condition results from an involuntary muscle spasm, the therapists instruct the couple in the use of Hegar dilators in graduated sizes. The man dilates the vaginal opening under the woman's direction in the privacy of their quarters. At first she manually controls his insertion of the smallest dilator; later he can insert larger dilators with her verbal instructions. If the larger dilators are successfully inserted, she is encouraged to retain a dilator for several hours each night (Masters and Johnson, 1970, p. 263).

In addition to physical relief from the spastic constriction of the vaginal opening, therapy is directed toward contending with the fears that led to the onset of symptoms. The therapists explain the psychophysiology of the dysfunction, what it is, how it developed, and how it can be treated (Masters and Johnson, 1970, pp. 263–264).

Treatment of General Female Nonresponse and Orgasmic Difficulty   Masters and Johnson's treatment for general female nonresponse and orgasmic difficulties is instituted after the initial sensate focus exercises are judged successful by the therapists and the couple. The therapists instruct the couple to focus on the man's stimulating the woman's erogenous zones. The couple is shown a diagram of the nondemand position for female stimulation. (See Figure 5.4.) This position is intended to provide a feeling of warm security for the woman and allow freedom for the man to engage

151

Figure 5.4

A position for sensual and sexual stimulation of the female

in exploration of the woman's body. The woman places her hand lightly on her partner's hand to indicate her preferences for stimulative contact. A technique that is usually effective is a light, teasing touch, moving from breasts to abdomen to thighs to vaginal lips and back again to breasts, without concentrating on genital manipulation in the early stages. The therapists make it clear to the couple that orgasm is not the focus of this interaction; instead it is to provide the woman with an opportunity to express freely her sexual response without any demand for performance, while permitting her and her partner to learn her erotic preferences (Masters and Johnson, 1970, pp. 295–305).

If the genital manipulation exercises produce a high level of sexual excitement in the woman, the therapists instruct the couple in use of the female-above coital position. When both partners are sexually aroused, the wife inserts the penis into her vagina and remains still, allowing

152

herself time to experience awareness of the penis inside her. After a time she begins slow pelvic thrusting. She has been instructed to think of the penis as hers to play with and enjoy. If vaginal sensation develops into a pleasurable or demanding sensation, she signals the man to begin slow pelvic thrusting. This slow, exploratory coitus is to continue as long as it is pleasurable for both. At appropriate intervals the couple separate and simply lie together in each other's arms (Masters and Johnson, 1970, pp. 306–309).

Once the woman confidently enjoys the pleasure of pelvic play with the penis inside the vagina, the therapists instruct the couple in use of the lateral coital position. (See Figure 5.3.) This position provides flexibility for free sexual expression by both partners and is particularly effective for the woman because she can move in a manner that is stimulating for her (Masters and Johnson, 1970, pp. 310–314).

The therapists' directions in this treatment of the nonresponsive or nonorgasmic woman are designed to allow the woman to discover, accept, and share knowledge of the things she finds sexually stimulating.

Kaplan's Approach

Helen Singer Kaplan developed and directs the program for brief treatment of sexual disorders at the Payne Whitney Clinic of New York Hospital. Among her contributions to the sex therapy literature are *The New Sex Therapy* (1974) and *Disorders of Sexual Desire* (1979). Her training in psychoanalysis is frequently reflected in her treatment style. She also uses behavioral techniques like the following one prescribed for female orgasmic dysfunction.

Kaplan treats general female sexual dysfunction and female orgasmic dysfunction as two distinct disorders, with different procedures for each. Her treatment program for the sexually nonresponsive woman is similar to that developed by Masters and Johnson to treat both nonresponse and anorgasmia.

Kaplan's first behavioral instructions for the woman who has never been able to reach orgasm is to masturbate in privacy, using manual stimulation or a vibrator in order to induce her first orgasm. Once she can stimulate herself to orgasm regularly, her sexual partner is included in the treatment program. They are instructed to make love in the usual way until the man reaches orgasm. After the man is orgasmic, he is to use the vibrator or manual stimulation to bring the woman to orgasm, following her directions for the techniques she finds stimulating (Kaplan, 1974, pp. 388–400).

When a woman can reach orgasm through solitary masturbation and through direct clitoral stimulation by her male partner, the couple are   153 instructed in techniques to aid her in reaching orgasm during penile-vaginal intercourse. To heighten the woman's arousal, the couple are instructed to use teasing, nondemanding lovemaking techniques and a stop-start form of intercourse. In stop-start intercourse the man is to stop thrusting when he feels his orgasm approaching and to stimulate the woman's clitoris manually until his urge to ejaculate subsides (Kaplan, 1974, pp. 400–402).

To enhance the woman's vaginal sensations, her partner is instructed to use nondemanding thrusting motions that she indicates give her pleasure, while she concentrates on the sensations produced by the slow movement of the penis inside her vagina. Also the therapist advises the woman alternately to contract and relax the pubococcygeal muscles during intercourse (Kaplan, 1974, pp. 402-403).

One way to reach orgasm during intercourse is to stimulate the clitoris manually while the penis is in the vagina. The therapist instructs the couple to assume a coital position in which either of them can comfortably stimulate the clitoris during coital thrusting. (See Figures 5.5 and 5.6.) When the woman is near orgasm, manual stimulation is to cease, and she is to begin very active thrusting. If this does not produce orgasm for her, active thrusting is interrupted, and the clitoris is manually stimulated until orgasm is imminent. Again manual stimulation is stopped, and she resumes active thrusting. Sometimes the couple may use a vibrator rather

Figure 5.5

A coital position permitting manual coital stimulation

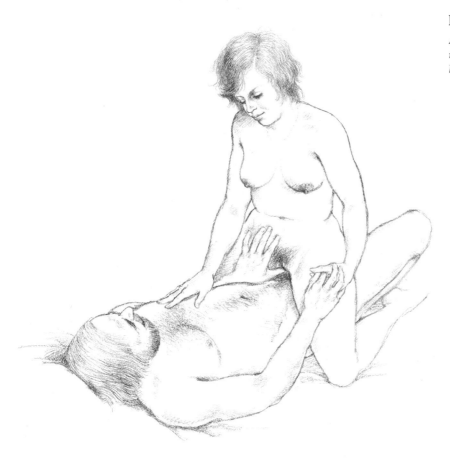

Figure 5.6
A coital position permitting manual stimulation

than manual stimulation. After practicing this procedure for several weeks, some women can reach orgasm by coital thrusting alone (Kaplan, 1974, pp. 403–408).

Approaches of Other Behavioral Therapists

Behaviorally oriented sex therapy exercises are often based on small steps that allow a couple or individual to become comfortable with one skill before moving on to other, more complex ones. The building of basic pleasuring, communication, and sexual skills is usually emphasized before the therapy focuses on a specific dysfunction. A woman or man who feels anxious or uncomfortable with her or his nudity, genitals, or sexual responses may be assigned a masturbation program based on the work of LoPiccolo and Lobitz (1972), in which reading assignments on the ratio-

155

nale for self-exploration exercises are followed by a series of body exploration exercises and then masturbation (McCarthy, 1977). Bibliotherapy assignments may be made in such books as Barbach's *For Yourself* (1975) or Zilbergeld's *Male Sexuality* (1978). Some sex therapy programs use audiovisual materials, such as the film *Reaching Orgasm*, in which sexual techniques or therapy exercises are modeled.

Clients are often guided to work through feelings of anxiety they experience while doing therapy assignments, so that anxious feelings will no longer be strong cues for feeling out of control or for avoiding sexual situations. A client may be instructed to stay with a sexual exercise, relax, and continue less anxiety-provoking touching and stroking until a sense of comfort is gained or regained. Individuals who are tense may be taught deep muscle relaxation; frequently their partner, even though less tense, will be included in those exercises. Exercises incorporating fantasy or guided imagery while in a relaxed state may also be assigned (McCarthy, 1977).

Clients are frequently taught sexual assertiveness, that is, to make clear, specific requests for the type of sexual stimulation they want or need. A therapist may role play, making assertive statements with a client, or direct a couple in role play during a therapy session (McCarthy, 1977).

Most behavioral therapists do not follow the co-marital format used by Masters and Johnson. Usually an individual therapist treats a client or couple. Also, one therapy session a week is more typical than the intensive two weeks of daily sessions used by Masters and Johnson.

Typically clients without partners are treated individually or in a group. However, in cases in which it seems appropriate, some therapists will match an individual client with a surrogate partner or body-work therapist who will participate in the therapy assignments and exercises with the client. It is much more common for a male client to work with a female surrogate or body-work therapist than for a female client to be provided with a partner.

Some sex therapists have found group treatment effective for those who come for therapy without a partner as well as for some who do have partners. For example, nonorgasmic women have been treated in group therapy, where the supportive and permission-giving nature of the group encourages development of orgasmic response in "homeplay" exercises. During early meetings the women discuss feelings about sex and early sexual traumas. At home the women follow a masturbation program designed to develop orgasmic response, and discuss their experiences with this program in subsequent group sessions (Barbach, 1974). Men experiencing sexual difficulties also have been successfully treated in group therapy similar to that of the women's group, with several hours of homework each week and group discussion of feelings (Zilbergeld, 1975).   156

Social-Skills Training

Many single men and women with sex problems lack the skills or confidence to meet potential partners and develop relationships. Either they have an inadequate repertoire of social skills, or they experience so much anxiety in social situations that they are unable to use the skills they do have. Social-skills training is frequently provided for such individuals as a part of their group or individual therapy or in workshops.

Social-skills training deals with such issues as fears of rejection and acceptance, where and how to meet people, initiating and maintaining conversations, getting to know others through a step-by-step approach, setting limits in dating, and getting into sex with a new partner. The therapy or workshop sessions provide opportunities for learning and practicing new techniques through didactic presentations by the therapist(s), role play, and small group exercises and discussions (Zilbergeld and Ellison, 1979).

A typical homework exercise might be to engage in coffee dates with a number of different people. A *coffee date* is an encounter lasting no longer than one hour, during which time no physical contact other than a handshake or a hug is permitted. A coffee date need have nothing to do with coffee, but could be a walk, a ride, or the sharing of a drink or a meal. The date partner is informed of the time limit when the date is made. The structuring of coffee dates gives individuals time to get to know other people better, but not so much time that they feel uncomfortable, at a loss for what to say, or start wondering if they should do something sexual. Individuals are encouraged to proceed slowly in developing relationships and not to rush into situations that may be anxiety provoking or difficult to handle (Zilbergeld, 1978).

In working with their clients on getting into sex with a new partner, therapists may model such statements as "I like you and am very turned on to you, but I don't feel ready to have sex yet," or "This is going way too fast for me; I want to spend more time touching and caressing before getting to intercourse." Clients are then given opportunities to role play typical situations (Zilbergeld and Ellison, 1979).

Sex Therapy for Disabled Clients

There are now a number of centers around the country, such as the Sex and Disability Program at the University of California Medical School in San Francisco, where special sex therapy programs are being developed to meet the needs of disabled individuals.

In some ways sex therapy with disabled individuals is similar to therapy with those who are able-bodied. Although it is frequently assumed, even by some physicians and therapists, that sexual dysfunction in a   157 disabled person is caused by the disability, this assumption is often erroneous. A disability produces no immunity to the negative influences on sexual functioning of anxiety, anger, uncomfortable situations, or similar factors, and these can frequently be dealt with through traditional sex therapy methods. One man who had had polio as a child and spent most of his time in a wheelchair said:

I had known Mary a long time and I liked her very much. But the first time we tried to have sex, I was trying very hard to please her, and I couldn't get an erection. I was lucky, because after we were intimate a few times and I relaxed a little, I did get erections. I'm glad my doctor didn't tell me my impotence was due to my disability and I should learn to live with it. I've had a wonderful sex life and two children.

From the authors' files

Cultural stereotyping has resulted in many negative myths about the handicapped that must be dealt with as issues in sex therapy with disabled individuals. Among these are:

1. Handicapped people are incompetent, not only professionally and in other aspects of their lives, but sexually as well.

2. Handicapped people are inferior and discredit their partners. A young, able-bodied man planning marriage to a disabled woman may be told by his parents: "Why would you want to marry her? You could do better than that."

3. Handicapped people are asexual, neither male nor female, and thus incapable of sexual encounters. Those disabled from childhood are often explicitly told by parents and teachers that they are not capable of getting a partner, having a primary relationship, or having children.

4. The handicapped should be kept from intercourse or sterilized. (Topp, 1975)

A person believing these myths to be true about herself or himself is not likely to be ready to become involved in a fulfilling intimate relationship. In becoming sexually expressive, a man or woman — disabled or able-bodied — must acknowledge himself or herself as a sexual being with needs for touching and intimacy and, more fully, as a human being capable of filling some of those needs for someone else (Ellison, 1977).

Individuals who are physically disabled frequently need social-skills training. By the time they reach adulthood, those who have grown up with physical disabilities are typically five to ten years behind the cultural norm in psychosocial development. Many men and women with congenital or childhood-acquired disabilities have few opportunities to develop personal relationships while growing up and reach adulthood believing they could not be regarded as potential partners. Many individuals with noncongenital handicaps feel undesirable after their illness or injury, even though they may once have been socially adept (Zilbergeld and Ellison, 1979).

Negative myths that get in the way of full acceptance of sexual options for the able-bodied are particularly discouraging to the physically disabled. One of the most negative of these myths is that sex equals intercourse. Those for whom intercourse is impossible or, at the least, impractical, may still be capable of engaging in snuggling, massage, orgasms, and loving intensely (Ellison, 1977).

In recent years there has been increasing awareness that people with physical disabilities and with medical conditions that affect sexual functioning need sexual information specifically related to their situations. Books, pamphlets, and sexual information are now available for those with ostomies, spinal cord injuries, mastectomies, heart disease, cerebral palsy, multiple sclerosis, and many other conditions.

Criticisms of Sex Therapy

Recently developed behavioral techniques are an important contribution to the treatment of sexual difficulties. Undesirable behaviors can be changed and more effective ones substituted. These changes can take place even when the cause of the problem is not understood by the patient or the therapist. Behavioral techniques make it possible to treat many sexual problems in a short time and at a relatively low cost. On the other hand, behavioral techniques in sex therapy have been criticized both generally and specifically.

Specific Criticisms of Technique

There are as many techniques of sex therapy as there are sex therapists. Some of the widely used approaches have been summarized here, but they cannot be accepted uncritically. Sex therapy is relatively new, and the various approaches and techniques still need further study. Consequently, many therapists have reservations about some of the more widely used techniques, and they are trying other therapeutic forms that also appear to be effective.

The Intensive Program Some therapists feel an intensive two-week program may not be ideal for all couples. It restricts sex therapy to those who have the social and financial resources to leave their usual responsibilities   159 and (usually) travel to another city for a two-week stay. Also it takes a couple out of their usual environment and away from their sources of stress and support. Some therapists feel that the long-range outlook for improvement is better when a couple work out their sexual dysfunctions while still coping with their everyday problems of work and family.

Some therapists also question the wisdom of a very intensive program with all treatment compressed into two weeks of daily sessions and exercises. Changes made so rapidly may be more difficult for the couple to integrate into their total personalities and relationship than changes spread over a longer period, with therapeutic sessions only once or twice weekly.

The Squeeze Technique   Some therapists (and patients) feel the squeeze technique is an unnecessarily complicated method of treating premature ejaculation; many recommend a stop-start method instead. This method is much the same as the squeeze technique except that stimulation of the penis is stopped when the man signals that he is reaching high levels of excitement. Once his sexual tension drops to a lower level, stimulation can be resumed.

Mechanized Treatment   Masters and Johnson's preference for the use of dilators in the treatment of vaginismus is too mechanical for some therapists. Others prefer to put more emphasis on helping the woman accept her body and her sexuality and less emphasis on physical treatment with dilators.

General Criticisms

Many of the general criticisms compare behaviorally oriented sex therapy unfavorably with the insight-oriented types of psychotherapy. Sex therapists, however, vary considerably in the emphasis they give to psychotherapeutic techniques relative to behavioral exercises. Most who call themselves sex therapists use a combination of the two. The brief description given here of the behavioral exercises developed for treatment of sexual dysfunctions does not adequately convey the quality and quantity of personal and interpersonal therapy that often go into the total process of sex therapy. For example, a couple's attempts to follow an exercise assigned by a therapist may result in anxieties, hostilities, and other emotions that must be dealt with in the next therapy session before other exercises can be attempted. The skill of the therapist in dealing with the emotions, communication barriers, or ignorance of the patient is much more important than the therapist's skill in describing the sex exercises.   160

In these psychobehavioral therapies there is constant interplay among therapist, technique, and patient.

Questioning the Effectiveness of Sex Therapy

One of the main reasons for the acceptance and popularity of sex therapy is its presumed effectiveness. Masters and Johnson, for example, claimed to have failed with only 20 percent of their clients. Recently, however, psychologists Bernie Zilbergeld and Michael Evans have questioned the validity and generalizability of these claims. They point out that Masters and Johnson did not clearly indicate the characteristics of their patient population, and the criteria and measures used to assess treatment effects initially and on follow-up. Zilbergeld and Evans say that other therapists have not been able to duplicate Masters and Johnson's results. Whether this is because other investigators are working with different client populations, are using different standards of success, or simply are not as good therapists as Masters and Johnson is impossible to determine. The authors conclude:

Masters and Johnson's research is so flawed by methodological errors and slipshod reporting that it fails to meet customary standards — and their own — for evaluation research. . . . From reading what they write it is impossible to tell what the results were. Because of this, the effectiveness of sex therapy — widely assumed to be high since the advent of Masters and Johnson — is thrown into question.

Zilbergeld and Evans, 1980, pp. 29–30

Zilbergeld and Evans are not suggesting that sex therapy is useless. They believe it has been and is helpful to many sexually troubled people. But they think we do not know exactly how successful sex therapy is, and they doubt it is as effective as Masters and Johnson have claimed. They suggest there is an urgent need for more accurate information:

There are many sexually troubled people who want help, and both they and those who treat them should have as good an understanding as possible of what can reasonably be expected from treatment, how long it might take, the chances of relapse, and the dangers. If the field of sex therapy is to continue to progress and to merit the respect and popularity it now enjoys, its practitioners will have to work toward giving more accurate and more specific answers to the questions of just what they can and cannot do.

Zilbergeld and Evans, 1980, p. 43

Conclusion

Sex therapy today has the advantage over psychotherapy of less cost of money and time. On the other hand, sex therapy remains something of an 161

unknown quantity. Not enough is yet known about the long-range benefits of sex therapy, nor about possible short- and long-range harm. However, as different types of sex therapy are developed, it is hoped that
careful and independent research will shed some light on these unanswered questions. Effective sex therapy can help large numbers of dis-
tressed individuals and couples who want to express themselves sexually
but do not know how. For people who want to make changes in their
sexual functioning, the development of effective sex therapies can be of
tremendous value.

Like n
invested
attention
other soc
out hum
tive ager
in claims
ception,
neither c

Pregna
tached to
regarded
motherho
people w

A thirty-o
until she l
and childr

The co
nitions. P
condition,
States tod
not gener
forty-one-
early twen

I was so pr
I noticed e
say, "Oh, y
nant yet." l
and frankly
me and tha

Pregnan
and biolog
defined eve
on the biol
mind that
ration. Fem
both of the
ifications.

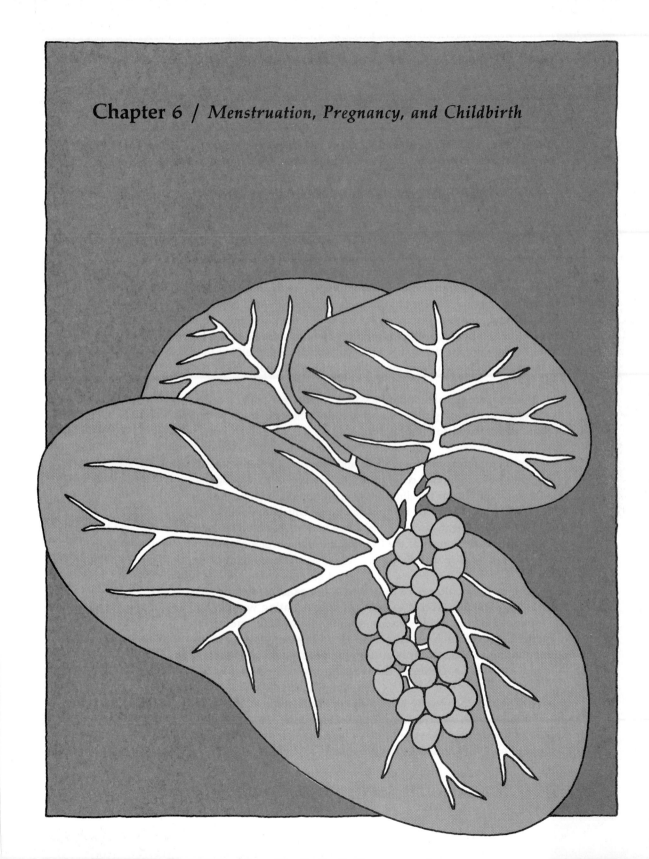

Menstr
aspects
time th
attachec
cal pher
compar
villagers
menstru
elima a
Among

Blood of
sickness
rious and
herself i
clan in d
and care
protectec

In contr
a gift, w
friends f

There is
news. . . .
standing
young be
another, f
replying
piest, mo

Menst
been reg
others, o
tion is r
cursed, c
Europea

A thirty-t
it "the cu
that this
curse Go

Menstruation

Menstruation is the monthly process by which blood that would otherwise nourish a fertilized ovum is flushed from the body of a woman who is not pregnant. Therefore, the onset of menstruation in a young female is the first sign that she may be capable of conceiving.

Between puberty and the menopause, human females experience recurring biorhythmic menstrual cycles of approximately twenty-eight days, but varying from woman to woman within a normal range of twenty-one to thirty-five days. This is a reproductive cycle of preparation for pregnancy, release of an ovum, and discharge of the prepared "nest" if conception does not occur. In the event of conception, the cycles are interrupted until the end of pregnancy.

Menarche

The first menstrual flow, called *menarche,* usually occurs between ages ten and seventeen, at the midpoint of the approximately five years it takes for the complete process of physical change from girlhood to adulthood. (Dalton, 1969, p. 84). At the age of seven or eight for most girls (later for the late bloomers) the pituitary gland, located in the brain, begins sending follicle-stimulating hormone *(FSH)* to the ovaries. Under the influence of the FSH some of the ovarian follicles begin to enlarge, mature, and produce *estrogen* (the hormone that produces female sex characteristics and controls the menstrual cycle), which is released into the blood stream. Gradually, under the influence of the estrogen, there is a marked increase in the size of the uterus, build-up of the uterine lining begins, the body contour begins to feminize, a growth spurt occurs, breasts start to bud and develop, and through the influence of both estrogen and other hormones called *androgens,* pubic and underarm hair appear (Lanson, 1975, pp. 48–49). As a rule, some breast development precedes menarche. It is not uncommon for one breast to begin to develop slightly earlier than the other.

The Message System

The *hypothalamus gland* is the basic brain control center for the menstrual cycle. The hypothalamus interprets blood levels of hormones involved in the process and sends this information on to the pituitary gland, the control center for the endocrine (hormonal gland) system. The pituitary sends out hormones that in turn facilitate release of additional hormones from other organs throughout the body. The organs of particular importance in the menstrual system are the adrenals and the ovaries. However, the entire endocrine system is interrelated and optimally is also in balance. A disturbance in the thyroid or pancreas, for example, or excessive stress would require adaptive adjustment throughout the entire system and could cause disturbances in the menstrual cycle. It has been estimated that about 80 percent of menstrual problems result from endocrine disturbances, the remaining 20 percent from nutritional disorders, congenital anomalies, emotional disturbances, organic brain disease, and chronic diseases such as tuberculosis (Jones, 1968, p. 46). Women imprisoned in concentration camps have reported cessation of menstrual periods as their bodies' survival needs in dealing with malnutrition and stress took precedence over reproductive functioning (Keith, 1947).

The Menstrual Cycle

The menstrual cycles of most women range from twenty-one to thirty-five days, counted from the first day of bleeding to the onset of the next bleeding period. Variation of from one to nine days in cycle length from one cycle to the next is not uncommon. Most women flow four or five days, but a regular pattern of from two to seven days can be considered normal. However, any dramatic change from a previously established pattern, even if the change does not exceed the aforementioned bounds of normalcy, should receive medical investigation (Jones, 1968, p. 45).

The cyclic model presented here outlines the intervals in a twenty-eight-day cycle (see Figure 6.1). In cycles of other than twenty-eight days, the postovulatory phase is still usually about fourteen days. Variations from woman to woman are generally in the length of the preovulatory portion of the cycle.

Days One to Five: The Menstrual Phase   These are the days of the menstrual flow, during which the developed *endometrium,* the inner lining of the uterus, is shed. The menstrual discharge is composed of blood, cervical and vaginal mucus, and degenerated endometrial particles. Color and consistency vary from woman to woman and in the same woman from day to day of her menstrual flow. Shreds or whole pieces of membrane may be seen. Small clots are not uncommon, but clots larger than a grape or accompanied by pain should be regarded as abnormal. Most menstrual blood forms clots in the endometrial cavity and then is reliquefied by enzymes before it becomes the menstrual outflow. The reliquefied blood is called *serum,* and this serum cannot clot again. When bleeding is heavy, some blood may flow into the vagina before it clots in the uterus and then clot in the upper vagina, or clots may be passed from the uterus before having a chance to reliquefy.

167

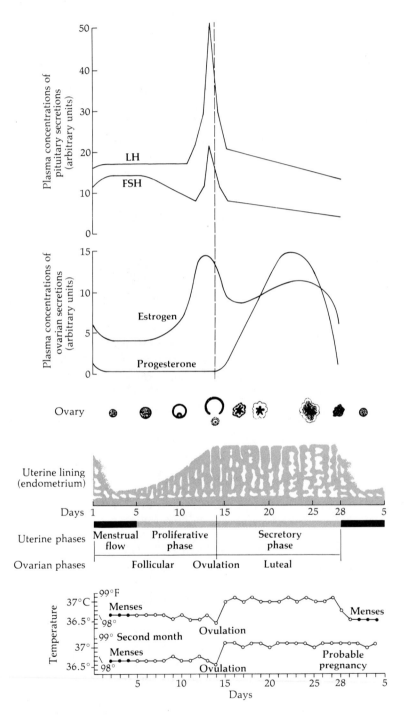

168

Contrary to old wives' tales, scanty blood loss does not indicate that blood is accumulating somewhere inside to poison the woman someday or to be expelled in a huge gushing hemorrhage. And heavy menstrual bleeding is not immediately life-threatening. Minute capillaries are exposed when the endometrium disintegrates, and it is from these that menstrual bleeding occurs. Total blood loss during a period is usually four to six tablespoons (Boston Women's Health Book Collective, 1973, p. 19).

When menstrual flow begins, the amounts of the hormones estrogen and *progesterone* (Latin. for bearing young) in the blood stream are low, and releasing factors from the hypothalamus stimulate the pituitary to release FSH into the venous blood stream. The FSH activates the ovaries and several (usually from two to thirty-two) immature ovarian follicles begin to ripen. Not all follicles are at the same stage of development nor do they mature at the same rate during this phase and the next. As the follicles develop they release estrogen into the blood stream. The estrogen causes renewing growth of the uterine lining and inhibits shedding at the point where the whole lining has been shed except for the bottom layer of cells. These serve as the foundation for the new lining.

Days Six to Thirteen: The Proliferative Phase During this phase the endometrium is reconstructed. The cells in the ripening follicles multiply greatly and continue to produce estrogen. There are at least three forms of estrogen secreted: estradiol, estrone, and estriol.

Days Ten to Thirteen: The Transition Stage A critical peaking of estrogen serves as a signal to the pituitary to decrease FSH production and begin releasing *LH* (luteinizing hormone.) For a short time FSH and LH together stimulate increased estrogen production until the high levels of estrogen further inhibit FSH production and LH becomes dominant.

Around the tenth day one of the follicles undergoes a sudden spurt of growth. In the following three or four days the ovum in this follicle matures and moves toward the surface of the ovary. The other follicles and their ova gradually regress, die, and are replaced by small scars. The endometrium grows, thickens, and forms glands that will secrete embryo-nourishing substances in the event of fertilization. Occasionally two or more ova may ripen and their fertilization result in a multiple birth.

Day Fourteen: Ovulation About the fourteenth day a spurt of LH causes the follicle containing the ovum to rupture, and the ovum is sent on its way toward the fimbria of one Fallopian tube. An ovum that is not fertilized will usually survive from twenty-four to thirty-six hours after its release.

Some women are aware of changes in their bodies that signify ovulation and can pinpoint fairly closely when the event occurs. Some experience *mittelschmerz* (German: middle pain), a cramp on the left or right side of the lower abdomen, possibly due to slight ovarian bleeding at ovulation or to changes in hormonal levels.

Days Fifteen to Twenty-eight: The Secretory Phase   Under the influence of LH the ovum-releasing follicle that remains behind on the ovary grows to the size of a lima bean, becomes yellowish in color, and begins to produce the hormone progesterone. The follicle at this point becomes the *corpus luteum* (Latin: yellow body). Under the continuing influence of LH, the corpus luteum produces progesterone, which together with estrogen stimulates the endometrium to become a rich bed of blood vessels and tissues ready to accept a fertilized egg. If pregnancy occurs, the life span of the corpus luteum extends to twelve weeks. If fertilization does not occur, the follicles and corpus luteum begin to disintegrate and are reabsorbed until only small depressed scars remain. By the twenty-sixth to twenty-eighth day the quantities of estrogen and progesterone in the blood stream have reached their lowest levels of the cycle. The low hormone levels cause the endometrium to begin sloughing off in menstrual flow and signal the need for release of FSH. A new cycle begins.

Superstition and Menstruation

Throughout history superstition has endowed menstrual blood with both valuable protective properties such as being able to extinguish fires, temper metals, protect men against wounds in battle, and treat headache, and harmful ones such as ruining crops and causing the strings of harps to break and clocks to stop. One old belief held that if a menstruating woman walked between two men, one of the men would be certain to die; thus, she should call out and warn the men of her presence. During the Middle Ages menstruating women were forbidden to attend church or take communion because the presence of a menstruating woman was believed to sour the wine (Dalton, 1969, p. 28). Menstruation was believed to demonstrate the essential sinfulness and inferiority of women. In the Bible, 15 Leviticus gives full instructions for the ritualistic cleansing to follow menstruation. (Also regarded as unclean in Leviticus are a man with a discharge and both the man and woman who have recently had intercourse.)

In contrast, among some families today first menstruation is regarded as a time for celebration of the advent of womanhood: 170

A thirty-two-year-old woman recalls: When I got my first period — at the age of ten, no less! — my mother bought me a lipstick and a pair of high-heeled shoes. I had been begging and begging her for these two things, but she had consistently told me I was too young. The shoes and the lipstick made the first period into something special.

From the authors' files

Premenstrual Syndrome and Dysmenorrhea

A syndrome is a group of symptoms that occur together. Each month during the last week or so of their menstrual cycles, some women experience a recurring group of symptoms that have been labeled *premenstrual syndrome.* The particular symptoms vary from woman to woman, but the most common are premenstrual tension (which includes the triad of depression, irritability, and a sense of tiredness), headache, breast pain, joint pain, backache, acne, hay fever, and asthma (Dalton, 1969, p. 43). Many women may have other recurring premenstrual symptoms.

Dalton (1969, pp. 62–63) believes that the *adrenal glands* play an important part in premenstrual syndrome. These small glands, one situated above each kidney, produce *adrenaline,* which is a part of the personal defense mechanism for fight, flight, and fear; and *corticosteroids,* which control the body's water and salt regulation, sugar metabolism, and natural defense mechanisms against disease, injury, and stress. Corticosteroids are also partially responsible for the secondary sex characteristics. It is significant that progesterone is the base from which all the other adrenal corticosteroids are formed. In instances of premenstrual syndrome it may be that the ovary produces insufficient progesterone for the requirements of the uterus during the menstrual flow and some progesterone is taken from the other source, the adrenals, leaving them short for corticosteroid production. The temporary imbalance of corticosteroids may result in water retention, imbalance of sodium, potassium, and other body salts, failure to control allergic reactions, changes in blood-sugar levels, and lowered resistance to infection.

Dysmenorrhea (Greek: difficult monthly flowing) is the term given to painful menstruation. Dysmenorrhea can be of at least two distinct types: congestive and spasmodic. *Congestive dysmenorrhea* is an intensification of the premenstrual syndrome and builds up in the last few days or week before menstruation begins. It typically includes increasing heaviness and a dull aching pain in the lower abdomen, and in some cases nausea, headache, breast pain, backache, change in appetite, constipation, and other symptoms. The physical symptoms are usually accompanied by premenstrual tension.

171

One thirty-year-old woman reports: A few days before my period, I become a From the authors' files mess! I get very hungry and eat everything in sight. I put on weight — probably because of water retention as well as eating. My belly sticks out. I sometimes get nausea and diarrhea. I also sometimes feel depressed and sorry for myself.

Spasmodic dysmenorrhea commences on the first day of menstruation and may continue for two or three days. The pain is usually perceived as cramps in the lower abdomen and is limited to the parts of the body controlled by uterine or ovarian nerves: the back, inner sides of the thighs, and lower abdomen. Because ovulation seems to be a prerequisite to spasmodic dysmenorrhea, first menstruations at puberty, when ovulation has not yet begun, are rarely accompanied by this type of pain (Dalton, pp. 40–42).

Both types of dysmenorrhea can be relieved with hormone treatment, but the treatments are different and the wrong hormone can increase or create symptoms rather than relieve them. Spasmodic dysmenorrhea is treated with estrogen therapy. For women wishing not to conceive, the contraceptive pills are often used. Congestive dysmenorrhea, on the other hand, responds to progesterone therapy. Progesterone therapy, or sometimes *progestin* (artificial progesterone) therapy, also often relieves disturbing symptoms of the premenstrual syndrome. For women who are prone to migraine, acne, epilepsy, hay fever, and asthma, predominantly during the premenstrual segment of their cycles, hormonal treatment often produces dramatic results.

Women with premenstrual tension or congestive dysmenorrhea may find it useful to decrease fluid and salt intake in the postovulatory two weeks of their cycles. Coffee or diuretic pills remove excess water from the body and may prove helpful, but do affect the body's sodium-potassium balance and should be used with a source of potassium such as bananas, figs, or oranges to be most effective. Calcium, vitamin C, and water-soluble B vitamins have also been recommended to prevent premenstrual syndrome (LeGare, 1974).

Menstrual Cycles and Mood Cycles

The menstrual cycle is accompanied in a substantial number of women by significant shifts in mood and behavior. During menstruation and the four days immediately preceding the beginning of the menstrual flow, women are much more likely to experience mood changes such as depression, irritability, and anxiety; behavioral disturbances, such as alcohol and drug abuse, crimes of violence, accidents, and suicides; and illness related to mood change, such as migraine headaches, gastrointestinal disturbances,   172 and schizophrenic episodes (Kaplan, 1974, pp. 54–55). There is an obvious relationship between hormone levels and mood changes: the highest incidence of these emotional disturbances is at the time of the cycle when estrogen and progesterone levels are at their lowest (Dalton, 1979).

When a woman experiencing any of these symptoms realizes their hormonal basis, she may find it easier to adapt to them, knowing they will go away in a few days. One study on college women has shown that academic performance does not fluctuate with their menstrual cycle. Presumably they are motivated enough to exert extra effort on the days of their cycle when they do not feel up to par (Bernstein, 1977).

Pregnancy

A menstrual period that does not occur when expected is often the most obvious first indication of pregnancy. However, only one-third of women whose menstrual periods are five days late and only about two-thirds of those with a period two weeks overdue are pregnant. An occasional woman will have one or two periods after conception. These will almost always be brief in duration and scant in amount. Although menstrual bleeding would not be cause for alarm, vaginal bleeding at any time during pregnancy should be regarded as abnormal and be medically investigated.

Conception

Conception occurs when a sperm unites with an ovum. Because the life span of an ovum after ovulation is not long, usually about twenty-four hours, and the passage of the ovum through the Fallopian tube usually takes at least two days, conception most often occurs in the upper third of a Fallopian tube. (See Figure 6.2.) Of the several hundred million sperm ejaculated by a male, only about one hundred to one thousand ultimately reach a Fallopian tube after ejaculation occurs in the vagina. To be fertile a man must ejaculate a minimum of thirty-five million functional sperm at one time, even though only one of these sperm will initiate the pregnancy by penetrating and fertilizing the egg cell. Sperm have been found in the female Fallopian tubes as early as five minutes after intravaginal semen application (Kremer, 1977, p. 680). An ejaculated sperm can survive about forty-eight hours.

During its two- or three-day passage through the tube to the uterus, a fertilized egg undergoes a series of cell divisions and becomes a hollow   173

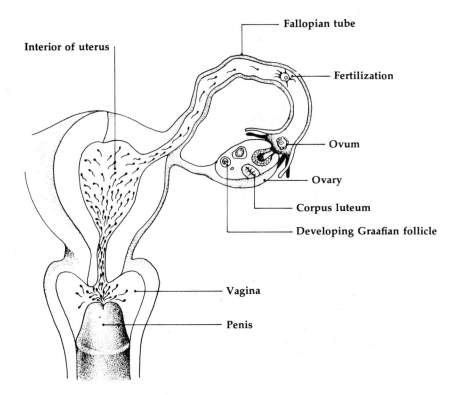

Figure 6.2

Cross section of female reproductive organs showing fertilization

Fallopian tube

Interior of uterus

Fertilization

Ovum

Ovary

Corpus luteum

Developing Graafian follicle

Vagina

Penis

ball of cells called a *blastocyst.* This blastocyst floats free in the uterine fluid for several days undergoing further cell divisions and development. About six or seven days after fertilization it begins to implant itself in the uterine lining.

Breast Changes   The earliest breast symptoms of pregnancy are exaggerations of the slight temporary enlargement and sensations of weight and fullness noted by many women prior to menstruation. The breasts become larger, firmer, and more tender. Veins become more prominent as blood supply increases. As time passes, the *areolae* (the dark circles of tissues surrounding the nipple) become darker in color, puffy, and increase in diameter. About the eighth week tiny milk glands develop within the areolae. Breast changes are more obvious and useful as indicators of pregnancy in women who have never been pregnant than in those who have already borne children (Eastman, 1957, pp. 5 and 6).

Frequency of Urination   A need to urinate more frequently may be one of the earliest symptoms of pregnancy. This is probably because the growing

174

uterus stretches the bladder, creating a sensation like that felt when the bladder wall is stretched with urine. In addition, hormonal changes may affect the body's water balance. The frequent need for urination soon subsides as the pregnancy continues and the uterus rises out of the pelvis. Although a frequent need to urinate is annoying, it is important for health that fluid intake not be less than six to eight glasses a day.

Nausea Many women never experience nausea during pregnancy. For those who do, it can range from slight queasiness upon arising in the morning to actual vomiting. When morning sickness does occur it usually begins about two weeks after the first missed menstrual period and lasts no longer than four to six weeks.

Fatigue Some women experience a strong urge to nap and sleep more than usual during the early weeks of pregnancy.

Laboratory Tests By the third or fourth week of pregnancy the developing embryo is secreting the hormone *human chorionic gonadotropin (HCG)* in sufficient amounts to be detected in the urine of the pregnant woman. Detection of this hormone is the basis of most laboratory tests. A procedure often used in the past took several days. Urine was injected into a laboratory animal, usually a rat, mouse, rabbit, or frog. If HCG was present in the urine, changes would occur in the reproductive system of the animal. A newer immunological test procedure takes only a few minutes. A few drops of urine are mixed on a slide with a substance that will appear smooth if no HCG is present, coagulated if the hormone is there. Accuracy of these tests is about 95 to 98 percent. Sometimes a test is made before there is enough hormone in the urine, and sometimes a test is performed or interpreted improperly. In rare instances a test will give a false positive reading (Boston Woman's Health Book Collective, 1973, p. 166).

A recently developed procedure can diagnose pregnancy before a menstrual period is missed, about three weeks earlier than any of the other available means. This test uses small quantities of a radioactive tracer that attaches to an antibody in a blood sample. This method can also be used to distinguish between a normal uterine pregnancy and an *ectopic pregnancy,* a pregnancy in which the embryo is implanted outside the uterus (Frishauf, 1974, p. 6). The procedure requires more sophisticated equipment than the other methods.

In-Home Tests Several brands of in-home early pregnancy tests are now commercially available. These are accurate as early as nine days after the first missed menstrual period when used exactly according to directions. 175

In the hands of someone who is nervous and not very careful, however, their accuracy cannot be guaranteed. Even when a pregnancy is carefully diagnosed at home, early consultation with a doctor is important. Continuing medical care is necessary during pregnancy.

Pelvic Exam   Once pregnancy has been established for about six weeks, a pelvic exam will reveal that the tip of the cervix has become softened and, because of increased venous blood circulation, darkened in color. The uterus will feel softer and may bulge where the embryo is attached.

Stages of Pregnancy

A normal pregnancy can last between 240 and 300 days, with about 266 days the average length. Most literature divides pregnancy into three-month periods called *trimesters*.

First Trimester   During the first trimester the signs and symptoms mentioned previously are the most noticeable physical changes. Psychologically this is a time of acknowledging and "owning" the pregnancy. During this time most women experience both negative and positive feelings about being pregnant.

Second Trimester   During the second trimester the pregnancy begins to show. The weight of the uterus increases about twenty times during pregnancy, with most of this increase occurring before the twentieth week as the fetus rapidly increases in size. (See Figure 6.4.) During the fourth or fifth month fetal heartbeats become audible through a stethoscope. Fetal heartbeats are much more rapid than those of the mother, about 120 to 140 beats per minute compared to her 70 to 80. The movements of the fetus become perceptible during the second trimester and by late in the trimester become visible as momentary protrusions and movements of the mother's abdomen. Any nausea or strong needs to nap that were present during the first trimester usually diminish and disappear during the second. By mid-pregnancy a woman's breasts, stimulated by hormones, have become functionally complete for nursing.

Third Trimester   The uterus becomes increasingly large during the third trimester, and a woman may become increasingly uncomfortable. The stomach and other internal organs become crowded. Pressure on the bladder may again cause frequent urination. Feelings of wanting to nap may return. The baby will frequently be felt moving, kicking, sometimes even hiccupping.

176

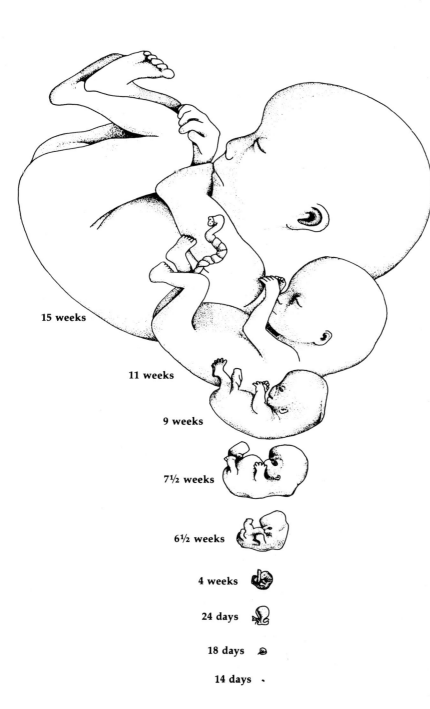

Figure 6.3

Size of embryo and fetus at early stages of intra-uterine development

15 weeks

11 weeks

9 weeks

7½ weeks

6½ weeks

4 weeks

24 days

18 days

14 days

Figure 6.4
Uterine size and position during pregnancy

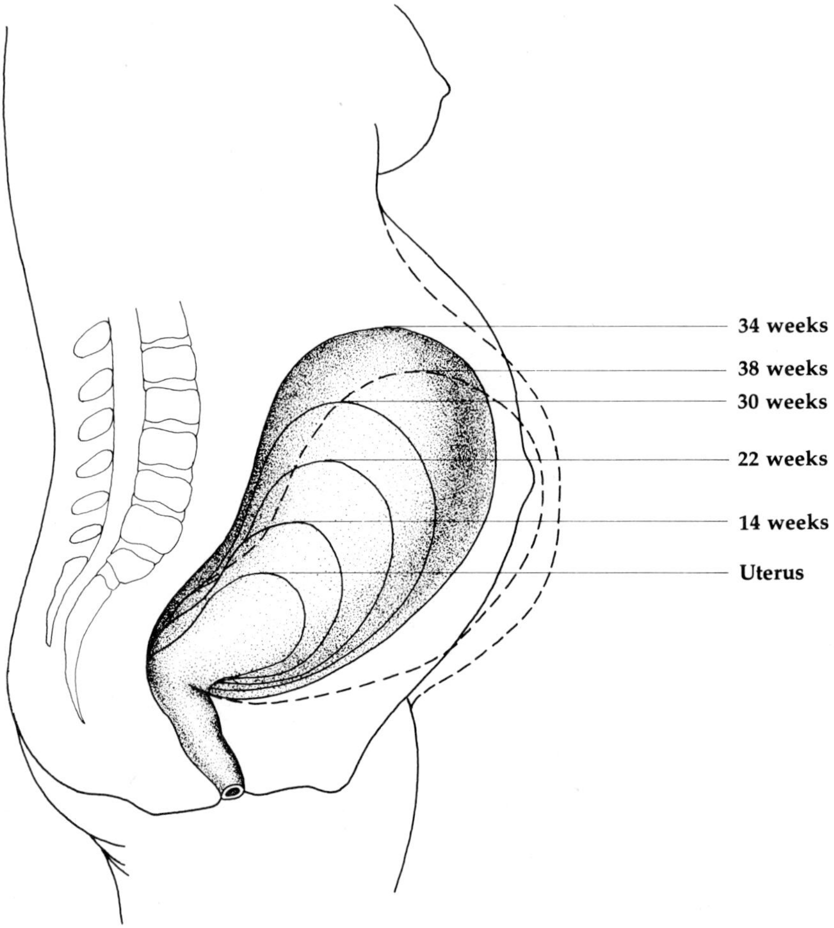

34 weeks

38 weeks

30 weeks

22 weeks

14 weeks

Uterus

One thirty-year-old mother of two children describes her third trimester: Boy, right at the last things really got crowded in there! I couldn't sit or stand or do anything like a normal person—I had to keep my back real straight and not lean forward because the baby was taking up so much space. And when I ate I could almost feel that the food was just sitting way high up in my chest because there was no room in my stomach for it. . . . My last one was a real kicker, and he perfected a bladder kick and a liver kick that were just real killers — at least I think it was my liver that got it — but I know the bladder did! I thought he might really injure me sometimes.

From the authors' files

Some relief usually comes about two to four weeks before the birth, sometimes earlier, when the baby's head settles down into the pelvis. This is called "dropping" or "lightening" and, because it takes some pressure off the stomach and diaphragm, can make the remainder of the pregnancy more comfortable than the preceding month or so.

Pregnancy and the Marital Relationship

Pregnancy and childbirth add a new dimension to the sexual life of a couple. Some changes in their sexual relationship may take place even before conception, as soon as the couple stop using contraceptive methods and try to conceive. The sexual relationship can be more deeply

A couple with positive feelings about pregnancy may find it enhances their relationship.
Mimi Forsyth/Monkmeyer
Press Photo Service

179

satisfying when the couple know that each coital act may result in a child they both want, assuming they share the same enthusiasm for parenthood. If they do not want children, the knowledge that they are not using some form of contraception may have a strong adverse effect on their sexual relationship. One married woman in her mid-thirties with very positive feelings about pregnancy describes it as an extension of a sexual experience:

For me pregnancy is like the ultimate completion of sex. It is one step more beyond orgasm. Even though orgasm is very satisfying, there is always some twinge of disappointment when he withdraws and I am left empty. But when I am pregnant it is as though he has stayed inside and the part that is inside grows and grows until I am completely filled. It is like wearing a symbol that says to the world that I am loved and filled.

From the authors' files

Physical Changes in Pregnancy   Pregnancy, even when it is desired, may have some disrupting effect on a couple's sexual relationship. Some of the normal physical changes of pregnancy may cause either partner to desire intercourse less often or to enjoy it less (Tolor and DiGrazia, 1976). The nausea and exhaustion that are typical for many women in the first three months of pregnancy may result in decreased sexual desire. Distention of the abdomen or increased vaginal secretions that often occur in the last trimester may make intercourse seem less desirable. In spite of some of the physical discomforts that often accompany pregnancy, many women experience an increase in sexual desire, particularly during the second trimester. This increased ardor may be due to a variety of sociocultural factors, such as a feeling of greater femininity. It may also be due to higher levels of progesterone or greater vasocongestion in the pelvic area (Sherfey, 1972).

Changes in Sexual Attitudes   There is a wide range of individual responses to sex during pregnancy. Some women choose to abstain from intercourse completely, even when their physician has not given them a medical reason for doing so. Other women experience decreased or increased sexual desires. But regardless of their desire for intercourse, virtually all women report a definite need for body contact and to be held close. The need for closeness during pregnancy appears to be a very powerful one for many women (Brenner and Greenberg, 1977).

A recent study of 200 expectant fathers found that many of them experienced a steady decrease in sex drive throughout their spouse's pregnancy. They lost their sexual interest for a number of different reasons, such as ambivalent feelings about fatherhood, a fear that intercourse might damage the fetus, the feeling that pregnant women are "madonnas"

180

Sexual and physical closeness are an important part of the emotional relationship of a couple during pregnancy.
Joel Gordon

181

who are above sex, and the feeling that sex with a pregnant woman is evil. Sometimes these men became angry at their wife because they saw her and her pregnancy as the cause of their declining sexual ability. These men usually suffered in silence because they did not realize other men have similar fears. Consequently their wives felt rejected because they did not understand the cause of their husband's apparent coldness. Because women often have a greater need for affection at this time, the man's withdrawal can place a great strain on the marriage (Zalk, 1979).

Intercourse During Pregnancy   Most physicians advise against intercourse during the last six weeks of a normal pregnancy. The prohibition is based on one of several beliefs: that penile thrusts against the cervix will rupture the membranes or induce labor, that the uterine contractions of orgasm will induce labor, or that intercourse will cause infection. There is some evidence that the contractions of orgasm at or near term may induce labor, but definitive data are lacking (Masters and Johnson, 1966). However, there seems to be little reason for concern about labor that occurs at or near term since it would presumably occur then anyway.

A twenty-nine-year-old woman comments: We always enjoyed sex together, even when I was pregnant — all the way through the pregnancy, even when the doctor said not to do it. In fact that started labor for my son because we were having real good sex and the contractions started. But it was OK because I was ten days overdue anyway.   From the authors' files

Potential Hazards   It is not true that intercourse will never be hazardous for any pregnant woman, neither is it inevitably dangerous. During pregnancy sexual intercourse should be avoided if it causes vaginal or abdominal pain or if any type of uterine bleeding is present. Once the membranes have ruptured, introduction of anything into the vagina increases the chance of intrauterine infection, which could be threatening to the health of both the mother and baby. A recent study of 26,886 pregnancies found evidence that intercourse one or more times a week in the month before delivery was associated with a higher incidence of infections of the amniotic fluid than that found among women who abstained during that time (Naeye, 1979). However, neither the editor of the journal that published the article describing this study nor the author of the article was prepared to recommend abstinence during pregnancy except for those who have had previous reproductive problems or who have premature thinning and opening of the cervix (*San Diego Union*, November 29, 1979).

When intercourse is forbidden by a physician because of a threat of miscarriage or premature labor, other sexual activity leading to orgasm should also be avoided because of the uterine contractions that occur during orgasm. If a couple engage in oral-genital activity during pregnancy, care should be taken that no air is blown into the vagina. In rare instances fatal air embolisms have resulted from this practice because the air passed through the cervix, into the placenta, and into the mother's or baby's blood stream.

Sexual Techniques As pregnancy advances, some positions for sexual intercourse previously used by a couple may become uncomfortable. Many couples find this a time to experiment with new positions and methods of mutual pleasuring, and may substitute side and rear-entry positions for positions ruled out by the woman's protruding abdomen. It is important that positions be avoided in which the partner's weight is on the woman's abdomen.

Uterine Contractions Sexual activity is not the only cause of uterine contractions during pregnancy. Throughout the pregnancy the uterus of a pregnant woman undergoes frequent involuntary contractions that

Regular medical checkups are important during pregnancy.
Paul Conklin/Monkmeyer Press
Photo Service

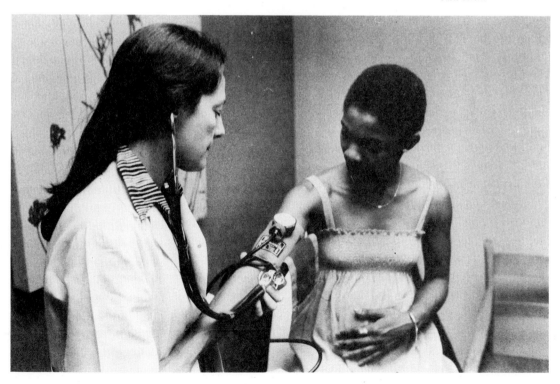

strengthen and prepare the uterine muscle for childbirth. Sometimes these contractions are mistaken for the beginning of labor.

Ectopic Pregnancy

Ectopic pregnancies are those in which the fertilized egg implants somewhere other than in the uterus, most frequently in a Fallopian tube. Usually this occurs because the fertilized ovum is blocked in its passage down the tube by malformation, malfunction, or scarring caused by earlier gonorrhea or other pelvic inflammatory disease. Conception with an intrauterine device *(IUD)* in place increases the likelihood of ectopic pregnancy.

Early signs of an ectopic pregnancy can be the same as those of a normal intrauterine pregnancy: absence of menstruation, breast tenderness, nausea, fatigue. The uterus may even enlarge slightly because of hormonal influences. However, sometime between the eighth and twelfth weeks the embryo will become so large that it can no longer be contained in the Fallopian tube and the tube will burst. Just before this happens the woman may perceive a sharp stabbing pain, cramps, or a constant dull pain. The rupture will cause internal bleeding, sometimes slow, sometimes heavy. Sometimes this will lead to shock. A ruptured ectopic pregnancy is a medical emergency and immediate medical help is needed. Sometimes, before or after the rupture, menstrual-like bleeding will occur because of hormonal changes. This can be mistaken for a spontaneous abortion. In cases of ruptured tubal pregnancy it is necessary for the involved Fallopian tube to be removed. (Boston Women's Health Book Collective, 1973, p. 178).

Rarely, an ectopic pregnancy is carried to term, resulting in a normal, healthy child. Occasionally the embryo will attach itself to a blood supply outside the uterus, possibly the exterior uterine wall or a part of the bowel. Sometimes this kind of ectopic pregnancy will proceed to term and not be definitively diagnosed as ectopic until the surgical cut is made to deliver the child by Caesarean section. Most of the live births of extrauterine fetuses are premature and 85 percent of these die shortly after birth (*San Diego Union*, December 1, 1979).

Tubal pregnancies are rare, but there are even rarer kinds. In one extremely rare incident an embryo developed not in a Fallopian tube but in a woman's abdomen. Ultimately, after at least eight months of pregnancy, the fetus died. Sophisticated medical facilities were unavailable in the small town in Spain where the woman lived, and the fetus was left in place. There it calcified and still remained forty years later when the woman was seventy-six years old ("Woman believed pregnant 40 years," UPI article, August 1, 1975).

184

Rh Blood Factor

A woman who has an Rh-negative blood type should learn about the implications of having this blood factor. If she should carry an Rh-positive child, she will need to receive a substance called Rhogam within seventy-two hours after delivery to prevent the build-up of antibodies in her body that could affect future pregnancies. She should also receive Rhogam if she carries an Rh-positive fetus that is aborted.

Childbirth

Entire books are devoted to pregnancy, fetal development, and childbirth. A detailed discussion is not within the scope of this text, and childbirth will be covered only briefly here. Emphasis is currently being placed on pregnancy and childbirth as important life experiences for all concerned: father, mother, infant, and other family members. There is a trend toward personalization and humanization of the childbirth experience. This has led to emphasis on preparation for childbirth.

Childbirth preparation means educating ourselves about what is likely to happen to our bodies, our minds, and our lives during the childbirth experience. It also means finding someone — husband, friend, or relative — to share this period with us. It is certainly not impossible to go through pregnancy, childbirth, and motherhood alone and unprepared, but it is difficult and unnecessary.

Boston Women's Health Book Collective, 1973, p. 182

Home Birth and Hospital Birth

In recent years increasing numbers of couples have questioned the idea that a hospital is the ideal place for the birth of a baby. These couples want to avoid restrictive hospital procedures, such as those that forbid the fathers, siblings, and friends from accompanying the woman during the birthing process; restrict visits to the mother during her hospital stay; and restrict the time mother and infant can be together. These couples often argue that birth is a natural process, not a medical problem, and therefore it does not ordinarily require medical intervention.

One study of 1,146 home deliveries found that home birth can be at least as safe as hospital birth for women with low-risk pregnancies who have received regular medical care throughout the pregnancy and are assisted by a well-trained midwife (*Medical World News*, April 19, 1976). However, 136 of these women had to be hospitalized because of complications that occurred during or after the birth; there were eleven infant deaths.

Confronted with the home-birth movement, more and more hospitals are revising their regulations and providing homelike birthing rooms. Many of these hospitals will permit fathers and sometimes other family members to accompany women during the birth process, permit parents and babies to stay together during recovery, and allow unrestricted sibling visits to mother and baby. One Chicago hospital found that, given the choice, 85 percent of women choose birthing rooms, which look like bedrooms, instead of traditional delivery rooms. Even pediatricians at that hospital who had been antagonistic to the new approach came to appreciate the quality of closeness felt by the parents with their newborn babies (*Medical World News*, October 3, 1977).

Labor

Women usually become aware of the onset of childbirth when they experience rhythmic uterine contractions commonly referred to as *labor*. Through a series of these repeated rhythmic contractions, the lengthwise muscles of the uterus involuntary work to pull open the circular muscles around the cervix, so that the baby can be moved through the birth canal and out into the world.

During the early stages of childbirth a woman feels rhythmic contractions of the uterus commonly called labor.
Steve Wall/Black Star

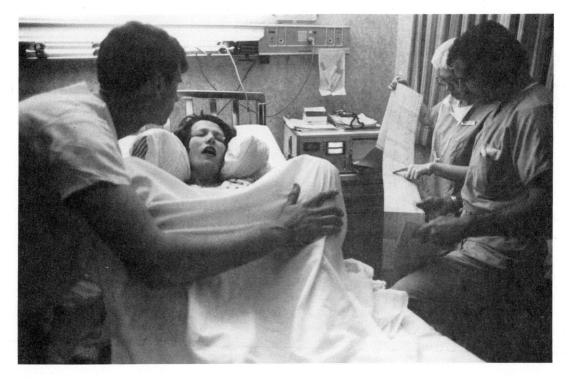

First Stage   The first stage of labor is further divided into three segments: early, late, and transition. Length of labor varies tremendously from woman to woman, but the average length of the first stage of labor for a woman having her first baby is twelve hours. Subsequent births tend to be quicker and easier. During the early first stage of labor a woman is usually aware of the contractions but does not experience discomfort. The contractions usually begin at far-apart intervals of fifteen to twenty minutes or more, and gradually increase in intensity and frequency as labor progresses.

A thirty-seven-year-old teacher comments on the birth of her second child: At first I wasn't sure it was real labor because I had felt contractions off and on all through the pregnancy. So I just walked around the house picking up things and getting ready, just in case it was the real thing. . . . Even when I got to the hospital I told them I wasn't sure if it was real labor. But they [the contractions] were five minutes apart then. . . . Since I wasn't moaning or carrying on or anything, they just left me alone and I kept walking around talking to people because it was more comfortable than lying down — particularly when I had a hard one. I would hold on to a door or something and swing one leg back and forth because it seemed to make it easier to stay relaxed when the hard ones came.

From the authors' files

The late part of the first stage is reached when the cervical opening has stretched to five to eight centimeters. The late first stage is usually shorter but more intense than the earlier segment. The transition stage, during which the final stretching of the cervix from eight to ten centimeters occurs, is usually the shortest segment of the first stage but is also the most intense and is often painful (Boston Women's Health Book Collective, p. 186).

Second Stage   When the cervix is fully dilated and the baby's head moves into the birth canal, the second stage of labor begins. (See Figure 6.5.) This is the stage of actual birth, during which the baby passes through the birth canal and out of the mother's body. During this second stage the mother can actively participate in pushing her baby out.

A twenty-six-year-old college student describes the birth of her first child: I had wondered how I would know when it was the right time to stop the relaxing-thing and start the pushing-thing. But all of a sudden I just *had* to push and nothing could stop me! Nothing! . . . I grabbed for the handles to hold onto, but there weren't any, so I grabbed my legs behind my knees so I could push harder. I must have looked pretty weird that way, but I couldn't have cared less. I was the center of the whole universe at that moment and nothing else was important to me. I can't describe what a wonderful feeling it was! I was producing another human being and it was just mind-blowing!

From the authors' files

187

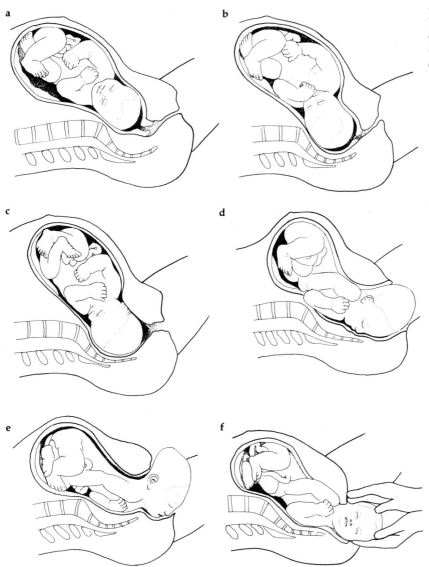

Figure 6.5

Movement of infant through birth canal during birth process

The second stage of labor may last anywhere from one half hour or less to two hours or more.

Often the doctor will make a small incision, called an *episiotomy,* in the vaginal opening to make it easier for the baby to emerge without tearing the perineum.

Third Stage   The third stage of labor is delivery of the placenta, "the life-supplying organ that has kept the baby healthy and comfortable during the first nine months of life" (Boston Women's Health Book Collective, 1973, p. 187). This stage may last from a few minutes to a half hour.

Postpartum

It takes about six weeks after birth for the uterus to return to its non-pregnant size and position. Breast-feeding speeds up the process by stimulating contractions of the uterus.

   During the first couple of weeks of the postpartum period the woman will have a bloody vaginal discharge similar to but often lighter in color than a menstrual period.

   Following delivery, estrogen and progesterone levels, which were elevated during pregnancy, drop rapidly, reaching almost zero about seventy-two hours after birth. This hormonal drop is often associated with feelings of depression in otherwise stable women. One study of thirty-nine pregnant women found that weeping increased significantly in almost 70 percent of the patients within ten days after delivery (*Medical World News,* June 28, 1976, p. 29).

A twenty-seven-year-old, college-educated woman comments on the period following the birth of her first child: I was so happy about the baby! She was the precious dream I had always wanted. So I couldn't understand why I cried at everything that happened. I could even read a sad story in the newspaper and burst into tears, and I had never done anything like that in my life! But I got back to being my old self after a couple of months.

From the authors' files

Intercourse After Childbirth   Most physicians tell their patients to refrain from intercourse for at least six weeks following childbirth. Many women ignore this advice and resume intercourse within a period of three weeks, or as soon as the vagina has healed sufficiently to permit intercourse without discomfort. Once vaginal bleeding has stopped and any incisions or tears in the vagina have healed, there is usually no physiological reason to prohibit intercourse following normal childbirth (Masters and Johnson, 1966).

A twenty-nine-year-old woman comments: And about two weeks after the baby was born we started [sex] again. I was nursing the baby but it did not stop our sex life or anything. In fact, he enjoyed tasting the milk at first.

From the authors' files

Not all women, however, are psychologically ready to resume intercourse soon after childbirth. Several factors may influence a woman's readiness to resume sexual relations. One is the quality of her experience with labor and childbirth. Individual experiences in delivery vary widely. For some women it is painful and traumatic, accompanied by medical complications. For others it is a joyful and even erotic experience (Newton, 1971). A woman who had a difficult birth or physical problems in pregnancy or postpartum may feel that her sexual organs are more a source of medical concern and less a source of erotic pleasure. It can take a long time for the woman with complications to redefine her healed vagina in terms of its erotic potential and forget that it was a source of considerable discomfort.

Sexuality and Breast-Feeding   It is surprising to most women that breast feeding their infant is sexually stimulating (Masters and Johnson, 1966). Some women can accept this as a pleasurable aspect of their relationship with their baby; others are quite disturbed or guilty about it.

A twenty-seven-year-old graduate student states: Nursing was sometimes erotic but only at night when I would fall asleep while I was nursing. If I was awake it was never erotic — or maybe I just never could admit it to myself when I was awake. But I really did enjoy it. . . .

From the authors' files

Some husbands find sensual pleasure in watching breast-feeding, but others feel extreme jealousy. Attitudes of both husband and wife toward

Some men experience sensual pleasure in watching breast-feeding.
Jim Harrison/Stock, Boston

190

breast-feeding may influence their sexual relationship during the nursing period. It is interesting to note that women who breast-feed their infants are more likely to resume intercourse as soon as possible and report a higher level of sexual interest than mothers who prefer bottle feeding (Masters and Johnson, 1966). But this does not mean that the breast-feeding itself causes a higher level of sexual interest or activity. It is equally plausible that women who are more sexually responsive and tolerant more readily accept both breast-feeding and intercourse as pleasurable experiences (Newton, 1971).

Children and Marital Sexuality

Data on the relationship between number of children in a family and the sexual satisfaction of the parents are scanty and somewhat contradictory. One study using a representative national sample of five thousand married women interviewed in 1965 (James, 1974) reported that couples with no children had coitus considerably more often than did those with children. Couples with only one child had coitus least often; those with two or three children had coitus more often than all others except the childless couples.

A study of 731 Detroit wives and 178 Michigan farm wives in the late 1950s (Blood and Wolfe, 1960) yielded somewhat different findings relating to the effect of children on a marital relationship. This study revealed that wives were the most satisfied with the love and affection they received from their husbands when they were mothers of preschool children. Young childless wives and honeymooners also had very high love satisfaction scores. The feeling of being loved was especially high when the first child was an infant. When the degree of satisfaction with love and affection was analyzed, taking into account the number of children in the home, wives with three children were the most satisfied. Blood and Wolfe conclude that "although children may depress the standard of living and the ability of the couple to find companionship outside the home, they increase the emotional bonds of understanding and love between the partners" (Blood and Wolfe, 1960, p. 232). This study considers three children the ideal number for marital happiness: "beyond this ideal number, the impact of more children on the husband-wife relationship seems to be deleterious" (p. 233).

Interviews with a national random sample of 2,164 adults in the United States in the early 1970s (Campbell, 1975) found that general life satisfaction was highest for women when they were young, married, and without children; men were most satisfied when they were over thirty, married, and without children. (See Figure 6.6) Couples with older children were more satisfied with life than were those with younger children. With or without children, married couples were overwhelmingly more

191

Most couples adjust to the demands of parenting and report that having children strengthened their marriage. Joel Gordon

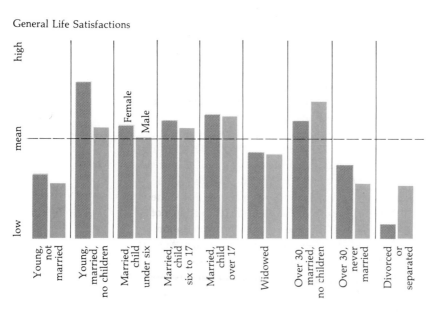

General Life Satisfactions

Figure 6.6

Life satisfactions of males and females at different life stages

satisfied with life than were people who had never married or who were widowed or divorced.

The addition of another person to the household necessarily affects the relationship between husband and wife. This is particularly true of an infant, who takes a considerable investment of time, money and emotional energy. A young mother may be stunned when she discovers that the baby she wanted so much is causing her to work sixteen hours a day, seven days a week, and remain on duty all night every night. A new father may be equally surprised to find that a household once organized to a large degree for his convenience is now almost totally dominated by the requirements of an infant, who cannot even say please or thank you. Time, energy, and privacy for husband and wife to enjoy lovemaking, as well as other shared activities, are often quite scarce with a new baby. One woman describes how small children both detract from and enhance her relationship with her husband:

Sometimes as I sit watching the children I suddenly think of Paul, of the smell and feel of him. . . . Paul's sleeping now on our bed, breathing heavily, his hair wet across his forehead. Not tonight, tonight I'll be too tired, he won't be well enough, but certainly tomorrow or perhaps in the early morning he'll reach over and touch my breasts and I'll roll toward him and for a while nothing else will matter, not his cold, not our children, not the book on revolutions — it will all wait for us to finish, to separate again. . . . Even though it's only a few short years, I seem to have always listened for the sound of a child's crying or calling.

Roiphe, 1970, pp. 247–248

Even most new parents who rate their marriage as successful and report that their child was planned describe adjusting to the first child as a severe crisis (LeMasters, 1957). Subsequent children may not constitute such a major crisis, but they are undeniably a drain on time, money, and energy — scarce resources in most families. Many of the issues involved in the contemporary decision of whether or not to have children are described in the essay by one young wife presented in Selection 6.1.

Making Babies Anne Taylor Fleming

Four years ago, when I was 21 and newly school-sprung, many of the women I knew — myself included — were agonizing about whether to marry. Most of us finally did. Now a lot of my friends and other women of my generation are agonizing about whether to get pregnant. Many of us haven't so far. And the troubling thought has crept into our souls or our wombs (presuming they are separate places, and sometimes I'm not so sure they are) that we just might never make babies, that we might enter middle age alone — perhaps divorced or

Selection 6.1

193

widowed — childless, womb-tight and woebegone. Why, if women face this almost certain aloneness later on, are so many of us so strangely steeled against pregnancy?

Some non-baby-making women explain it by saying something like: "The world's in a hell of a mess and I don't want to bring a baby into it"; or, "There are too many babies around already." I myself give lip service to answers like those; but I don't really buy them. After all, the world has always seemed a treacherous place to a prospective mother. As for overpopulation, it is a serious concern to serious-minded young women but I just don't believe it ever stopped one specific woman from having one specific baby.

Full Heads, Empty Wombs

The other most oft-given answer, and one I give more credence to, is: "Well, I have a career to pursue and I can't risk dividing my energies and loyalties between work and a baby." How stern and unlovely and downright corny that sounds. Yet I myself have said it many a time and will undoubtedly say it many more. I believe it. I believe that I am not put together enough right now to cope with dishes and diapers and postpartum depressions while trying to carry on what I imagine to be a life's work.

A baby was never going to fill my me-need, my what-am-I-going-to-do-when-I-grow-up-need. I always knew that. And then the women's movement came along and firmed up my resolve to work and the resolves of women like me. Also, many of us had watched our mothers try, at 40, to pick up the pieces of some long-abandoned life and work when our fathers had left them. Their example was not lost on us. I have many times said to myself and heard other women say: "That won't happen to me. I'll always have my work. Nobody — but nobody — can take that away from me."

And so, rather fiercely, we cling to our work as to a life raft, hoping that it will keep us afloat in good times and bad. Though we might in private moments yearn sometimes to trade back in our full heads and empty wombs for empty heads and full wombs, we cannot now. Having committed ourselves so early and so firmly to our so-called careers, we are afraid to commit also to a baby. We're afraid to risk failing twice. It is, in fact, precisely because we take motherhood so seriously — as, God help us, we seem to take everything these days — that we're staying away from it, at least for the moment.

An Obvious Irony

There is something, though, deeper than our work that is keeping many of us from making babies, something to do with sex. What has happened to many young women, I think, is that effective contraceptives — which we have used faithfully for a decade — are now so much a part of our bodies, and of our consciousnesses, that we are scared to set them aside, scared to get pregnant, not physically scared, some other kind of scared, a bigger kind. Before the recent

194

arrival of fail-safe contraceptives, lovemaking for women was always baby-making, pure and simple. But these new contraceptives put women on an equal footing — rather, on an equal bedding — with men, so that for us, sexual pleasure is now no longer an accidental by-product of procreation, just as a baby is now no longer the by-product of accidental afternoon lust. The very urges themselves, the lovemaking urge and the baby-making urge, have become separated in women. Now we can, like men, bed at will, without being physically or psychologically penalized, without having the moment complicated, or dignified, by the possibility of procreation. What a relief! What a joy!

So we are very reluctant to set aside the contraceptives, and are unwilling to have sex become so serious again so soon, and are afraid to have one moment of pleasure become something so tangible and so permanent as a baby. We are ready to be true sex objects at last!

But — and the irony is obvious — many men I listen to these days don't seem quite ready for women's newly liberated libidos. They are already greatly scared and greatly weary of our fierce wakefulness. In the marriages I know, in fact, it is the men, not the women, who nowadays want to make babies, perhaps as a way of holding on to us, just as women were forever having babies to try to hold on to men. And when women refuse to get pregnant, men have in their eyes a hint of what for so long they saw in ours: that fear of being left or, worse, of being cuckolded.

A Holding Pattern

This kind of fear is not pretty to me. Like many women, I have had too much of that kind of sexual fear myself all too recently. When the women's movement was in first bloom a few years ago, women, in their exhilaration, could not resist gloating a bit over male sexual insecurities. But now the movement is in its revisionist stage and men and women seem to want to be tender with one another again and to honor each other's needs, old and new. In that spirit, many of the women I know long to tumble easily and hopefully into pregnancy, like their mothers and grandmothers before them, with no agony aforethought, long to pledge allegiance with their wombs to the men they love. But they can't. They're stuck in a holding pattern. So am I. I'm feeling willful and wobbly and — oh, why do we women feel the need to soft-peddle it? — I'm competitive and ambitious and confused a lot and I don't think any baby ought to be subjected to me right now. At least no baby of mine.

Conclusion

The birth of a child is only the beginning. The woman with a husband must learn to adjust to being a parent as well as a spouse; both parents must work out together the details of this new, three-person relationship.   195

The couple with other children often have to help the older children to cope with feelings of jealousy. The unmarried woman must sometimes decide: Shall I keep my baby? Shall I give her or him up for adoption?

Not all couples, of course, want children, and most couples want to limit the number of children they have. Contraception, dealt with in the next chapter, is as important an aspect of the physiology of sexuality and of family relations as is the bearing of children.

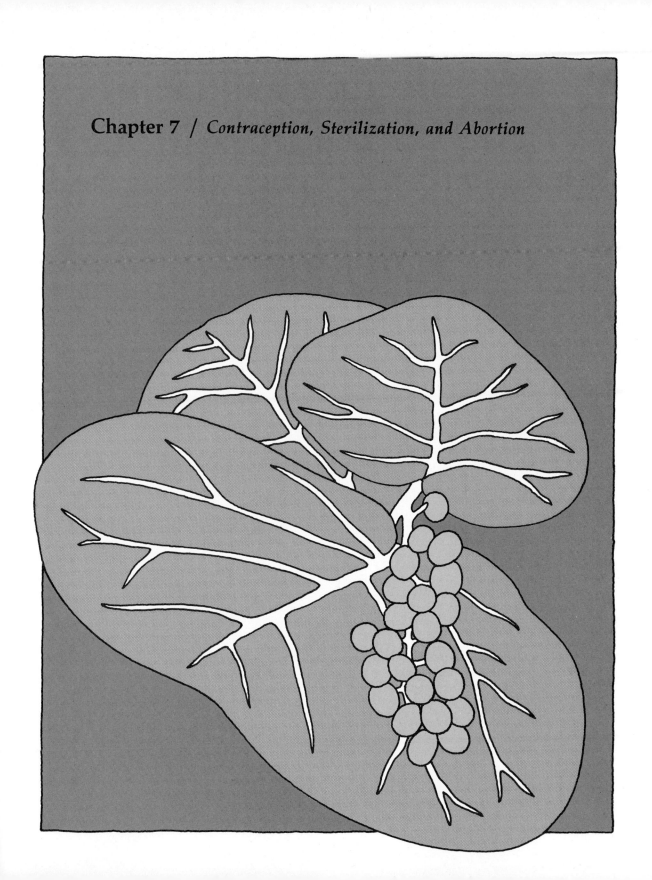

Contraception, sterilization, and abortion are all ways of preventing childbirth. Contraception and sterilization are used to prevent conception; abortion is used after conception to remove a fetus from a woman's body. All three processes can occur naturally. For example, if a male regularly takes prolonged hot baths, the heat on the testicles may decrease sperm production and act as a contraceptive measure. Sterility can occur in both women and men for a variety of reasons. Spontaneous abortion can occur, as well as abortion induced by medical measures.

All three methods of childbirth prevention have a long history, and all have taxed the inventiveness of people in a wide range of cultures. Similarly, societies have varied in the degree to which various methods of preventing excess population — including infanticide — have been seen as acceptable, desirable, moral, immoral, or even illegal. In the majority of Western agrarian societies, childbirth has traditionally been a welcome and necessary event; the major social institutions of the society, such as the church and the law, have generally condemned any attempt to interfere with birth.

The question of how many children to plan for is one with different repercussions at the social and at the personal levels. A couple might decide, for example, that a large family might be extremely functional or beneficial for their relationship and for their own happiness. But from the perspective of society as a whole — whether national or international — it is clear that in most areas having large families now threatens the survival of societies — or even human beings — on earth. In the United States, law and morality both reflect religious perspectives on contraception and abortion.

Contraception

Only during the last ten to fifteen years has contraception become well established as a right for women in the United States. For centuries both contraception and abortion were classified by the Christian church as homicide. In the late nineteenth century the Comstock Laws and various state laws were enacted that made the dissemination of birth control information illegal. At the turn of the century, for example, advertising or selling means for contraception or abortion was a felony in California. In that era there was general social agreement, "reflected in church pronouncements and state laws, that sexual intercourse was sinful except for legitimate reproduction" (Willis, 1975b, p. 1). The word *legitimate* implied that a woman was married to a man who could support her and her offspring. The early birth control pioneers, who espoused the value that "a woman should have only the offspring she could love and care for," encountered strong resistance. Their opponents feared birth control would lead to an ideological revolution that would overthrow the concept of sex as sin and thus "remove a powerful source of social control over women" (Willis, 1975b, p. 1). These opponents argued that birth control would "remove any reason for sexual restraint. It would threaten all the values of marriage, monogamy, self-discipline, and women's fidelity.... Contraception could mean sex without babies, sex without punishment," women enjoying sex for pleasure just as men did, and women free "from biology as destiny" (Willis, 1975b, p. 1).

As indicated above and in Chapter 1, contraception by any means other than abstinence from sexual intercourse was considered sinful by most medical, legal, and religious leaders throughout the history of early Christianity and into the early twentieth century. Today, Roman Catholic religious leaders and those of a few fundamentalist Christian sects regard contraceptives as interference with the will of God. Religious leaders from most other denominations, however, are in agreement with marriage experts that the use of contraceptives is a positive value in the marital and family relationship.

Most of the contraceptive methods available today, from condoms to oral contraceptives, have a long history. (See Selection 7.1.) However, contraceptives are more highly developed and more widely available in the industrialized nations of today than in earlier, nonindustrialized societies. Of concern to all people interested in the problem of overpopulation today are the responsibility for contraception as it varies by nationality, social class, age, sex, and other factors; the cost and distribution of contraceptives; and the effectiveness of the various devices.

Responsibility for Contraception

Taking responsibility for contraception involves many factors, perhaps the most important of which are the desire to limit childbirth and the willingness to plan and link sexual intercourse with contraceptive techniques.

History of Oral Contraceptives

Selection 7.1

The earliest observations relevant to hormonal control of fertility were probably made by farmers and veterinarians concerned with fertility and infertility in animal herds. As early as 1850, for example, *estrus*, the period of sexual desire and fertility, was initiated in sterile cows by crushing persistent corpora lutea. In the academic sphere, John Beard, anatomist at the University of Edinburgh, suggested in 1897 the role of the corpus luteum in inhibiting ovulation. By 1927

Goldzieher and Rudel, 1974.

Ludwig Haberlandt, an Austrian physiologist, was producing temporary sterility in mice by giving them ovarian extracts orally. In 1931 he prophetically visualized "hormonal sterilization" as the ideal method for future birth control. However, he died in 1932 before technology had advanced to the degree necessary to make his dream reality (Goldzieher and Rudel, 1974, pp. 421–422).

The active component of the corpus luteum was identified in 1928 by two physicians, George W. Corner and Willard M. Allen, and called *progesterone* (Latin: *pro*, in favor of; *gestare*, to bear). The hormore *estrogen* (Greek: *oistros*, mad desire; *gennein*, to beget) was named after it was isolated in 1929 by Dr. Edward Doisy, who demonstrated that the Graafian follicle of the rat ovary produced the hormone responsible for estrus (Pott et al., 1975, p. A-31). Since natural progesterone has minimal activity when taken orally, an important technological event was Carl Djerassi's synthesis of progestational compounds (called *progestins* or *progestogens*) in the early 1950s.

The political climate in the 1950s was not very conducive to contraceptive research. Drug companies were interested in hormonal research, but the management of several of the large companies regarded contraceptives as potentially unpopular and likely to have a detrimental effect on their business. As ovarian hormones became therapeutically available at reasonable cost, gynecologists prescribed them for amenorrhea, menstrual irregularities, dysmenorrhea, infertility, and other gynecological conditions (Goldzieher and Rudel, 1974, p. 423), but the concept of hormonal contraception, while occasionally mentioned, was generally ignored.

It was Margaret Sanger, founder of the Planned Parenthood Federation of America, and her wealthy friend, Katherine Dexter McCormack, holder of a master's degree in biology from MIT, who encouraged and financed the search of Gregory Pincus and his team of investigators for a new, more effective birth-control method. Feminists Sanger and McCormack wanted women to be free from reliance on male contraception and able to control their own fertility. Rock, Pincus, and Garcia tested two hundred progestins and found three to be powerful ovulation inhibitors. The first trials of a progestin on women were reported in 1955. Field trials of Enovid R, produced by G. D. Searle and Company, were sponsored by McCormack and initiated in San Juan, Puerto Rico, early in 1956. In 1960 oral contraceptives were licensed for general use in the United States and by 1965 were the most popular birth control method in the country (Guttmacher, 1969). By April, 1974, fifty million women around the world were reported to be using oral contraceptives, and in the United States approximately 20 percent of all women aged fifteen to forty-four were regularly purchasing oral contraceptives from pharamacies or receiving supplies from family-planning programs.

The estrogen and progestin in the birth-control pills replace estrogen and progesterone ordinarily produced by the ovary and prevent the pituitary gland from obeying a message from the brain to secrete the two gonadotrophic hormones, FSH and LH, which trigger monthly ovulation. As long as estrogen and progestin are present in sufficient amounts in the blood, ovulation will not occur. The trend since 1960 has been toward lower doses of both estrogen and progestin. By 1974 one formulation contained only twenty micrograms estradiol (an estrogen) combined with submilligram amounts of progestational agent (p. 425).

Childbirth Limitation   The motivation to limit the number of children may vary by nation, social class, and other factors. Compared to the Western industrialized nations, the developing nations that are still basically agrarian find considerable difficulty in motivating their citizens to use contraceptives. Like all agrarian peoples, African, Asian, and Latin-American peasants desire children to farm their lands and take care of them in their old age.

Within a single nation, such as the United States, birthrates vary with the degree of urbanization and with other factors, such as social class and ethnicity. As might be expected, the more urbanized the area, the lower the birthrate. Blacks and other nonwhite ethnic groups have, in general, higher birthrates than whites, and poor people have higher birthrates than wealthier people. This difference has often been explained by a phenomenon called *culture lag*, which means that social changes tend to occur earlier among the most advantaged groups of society, and filter downward to the less advantaged. Furthermore, the cost of contraceptives, sterilization, or abortion may discourage their use among poorer groups.

Female and Male Responsibility   A second aspect of the desire to limit childbirth relates to sex. Throughout history, in many societies motivation for limiting childbirth was confined mainly to women: the unmarried woman who might be able to conceal the illicit activities of premarital sexual intercourse, but who would be stigmatized by the birth of an illegitimate child, and the married woman who wished to have a rest from incessant childbirth or who feared that more children would mean poverty and disaster for the entire family.

Men in general have been less motivated to take the responsibility for contraception. Unwed fathers are less stigmatized than unwed mothers; they may in fact be undetectable. For many men — particularly in poorer nations and groups — the fathering of children, especially male children, has generally been a symbol of masculine potency. However, there have also been a certain number of men willing to bear the responsibility for contraception or for the arranging of abortions.

Before the introduction of the pill in the early 1960s, the most common contraceptives were condoms, used by the male. Modern availability of a number of highly effective methods for use by the female has reversed this trend, and responsibility for preventing conception now is most often placed upon the female.

201

Assigning contraceptive responsibility to the female brings with it a problem: acceptance of *premeditated* sexual intercourse. Traditionally, it has been the male who has initiated sexual encounters and the female — particularly the unmarried female — who has coyly resisted. In a situation in which the woman takes more and more responsibility for birth control, it is not surprising that illegitimacy rates are rising relative to the population.

Young People   It is estimated that six out of ten teenagers have their first sexual intercourse without any form of contraception (*Medical World News*, July 24, 1978). Many continue to be sexually active for several years without practicing contraception; others use birth control inconsistently or use relatively ineffective methods. As a result, many become pregnant; more than 1.3 million ten- to nineteen-year-olds in 1977. It is estimated that over one-third of today's fourteen-year-olds will have at least one pregnancy by the age of twenty (Scales and Gordon, 1979, p. 3).

Some of the primary reasons given by teens for not using birth control are fear of lessening the pleasure of intercourse and lack of access to contraception (Reichelt, 1979). However, even the availability of effective and nonintrusive methods of contraception does not guarantee their use by a teenager. There are stages of sexual awareness that influence readiness to use contraception. The self-concept of many adolescents at first intercourse does not include the possibility of pregnancy and giving birth. At this early stage of sexual awareness sexual activity tends to be unpredictable, and its spontaneity is valued. Contraception is viewed as evidence of premeditation that would spoil spontaneity (Lindemann, 1976).

As the frequency of sexual activity increases, awareness of oneself as a sexual being increases. Acceptance that one is going to be sexually active is usually a necessary condition to planning for birth control. A young girl describes her reluctance to make this commitment:

I've been thinking about it, the pill, that is. I've been persuaded by my boyfriend that I ought to get it. Haven't made up my mind yet. . . . If I get the pill I'm open. Then I can screw around when I want. I like the idea of having drawbacks. | Lindemann, 1976, p. 402

A relatively recent study of 222 college students at a southeastern university found that use of effective contraception was more likely among sexually experienced persons than among those trying intercourse for the first time. Seventy-six percent reported using either no birth control or an unreliable method, such as withdrawal or douche, at first intercourse. Only 21 percent were using unreliable or no birth control at their most recent intercourse. The likelihood of using reliable contraception increased when there was a high level of emotional involvement with the partner and when intercourse was planned, although involvement and planning were less important than sexual experience in determining contraceptive use (Maxwell et al., 1977).

In addition to sexual experience, sexual attitudes are an important determinant of contraceptive behavior of young single persons. Persons who are relatively negative toward sex, and especially premarital sex, are the ones least likely to use contraception in their sexual experiences. Individuals who are most accepting of their own sexuality are the most likely to practice effective birth control (Byrne, 1977).

Contraceptive Effectiveness

Whether adolescent or adult, heterosexually active people must make decisions about which contraceptive to use, as well as whether to use any at all. The *theoretical effectiveness* of a contraceptive method is the maximum effectiveness of that method: its effectiveness when used perfectly, without error, exactly according to instructions. *Use effectiveness* takes all users of the method into consideration: those who use the method according to instructions and those who are careless (Hatcher et al., 1974, p. 10). Effectiveness rates are often calculated in units of pregnancies per hundred woman-years or couple-years of use, that is, pregnancies per hundred women or couples using the method for one year.

[Table 7.1] gives the failure rate, in pregnancies/100 woman years, of the various methods of contraception. The Pearl formula (pregnancies/women years = 1300 × Total number of failures/Total number of cycles) was used in most instances to calculate and standardize the contraceptive failure rates found below.

Contraceptive Technology, p. 10

Because theoretical effectiveness rates are so close to 100 percent for all mechanical and chemical methods, the best contraceptive method for a couple is usually the most highly effective one they want to use and make work — the most effective of the ones that feel natural, usable, and comfortably acceptable to them.

Douching

Flushing out the vagina with water, Coke, or any other solution is *not* a birth control method. The very process of douching can force some semen up through the opening of the cervix. Even if all the sperm could be flushed out, douching would require leaping out of bed with not a moment taken to bask in an afterglow of pleasure. Some sperm can be in the

203

Approximate Failure Rate (Pregnancies per 100 Woman Years)   Table 7.1

	Theoretical Effectiveness	Actual Use Effectiveness
Abortion	0	0+
Abstinence	0	?
Hysterectomy	0.0001	0.0001
Tubal Ligation	0.04	0.04
Vasectomy	0.15	0.15+
Oral Contraceptive (combined)	0.34	4[a]–10[b]
I.M. Long-Acting Progestin	0.25	5–10
Condom + Spermicidal Agent	Less than 1[c]	5
Low Dose Oral Progestin	1–1.5	5–10[b]
IUD	1–3	5[a]
Condom	3	10[a]
Diaphragm (with spermicide)	3	17[a]
Spermicidal Foam	3	22[a]
Spermicidal Suppository	3	20–25
Coitus Interruptus	9	20–25
Fertility Awareness[f] (natural family planning)		
Calendar Only	13	21[a]
BB Temperature Only	7	20
BBT-no intercourse before ovulation	1	—
Cervical mucus only[g]	2	25
Lactation for 12 months[d]	15	40
Chance (sexually active)	90[c]	90[c]
Douche	?	40[a]

a. Ryder, Norman B., "Contraceptive Failure in the United States, *Family Planning Perspectives* 5:133–142, 1973. **b.** Oral contraceptive failure rates may be far higher than this, if one considers women who become pregnant after discontinuing oral contraceptives, but prior to initiating another method. Oral contraceptive discontinuation rates as high as 50–60% in the first year of use are not uncommon in family planning programs. **c.** Data are normally presented as Pearl indices. For conversion to the form used here, the Pearl index was divided by 1300 to give the average monthly failure rate n. The proportion of women who would fail within one year is then $1-(1-n)$. **d.** Most women supplement breast feedings, significantly decreasing the contraceptive effectiveness of lactation. In Rwanda 50% of non-lactating women were found to conceive by just over 4 months postpartum. It might be noted that in this community sexual intercourse is culturally permitted from about 5 days postpartum on (Bonte, M., and van Balen, H., *J. BioSoc. Sci* 1:97, 1969). **c.** This figure is higher in younger couples having intercourse frequently, lower in women over 35 having intercourse infrequently. For example, MacLeod found that within 6 months 94.6% of wives of men under 25 having intercourse four or more times per week conceived. Only 16.0% of wives of men 35 and over having intercourse less than twice a week conceived (MacLeod, *Fertility and Sterility* 4:10–33, 1953). **f.** *Periodic Abstinence*. Population Report, Series I, Number 1, June 1974. Johns Hopkins University, Population Information Program, Hampton House, 624 North Broadway, Baltimore, MD 21205. **g.** Klaus et al. *Fertility and Sterility* 28:1038–1043, 1977.

Source: R. A. Hatcher et. al., *Contraceptive Technology, 1980–81* (New York: Irvington Publishers, 1980).

uterus within moments after ejaculation. Frequent douching can remove the normal population of beneficial bacteria that live in a healthy vagina and can create an environment conducive to multiplication of other organisms that can cause *vaginitis*, infection of the vagina (see Chapter 8). Irritation from commercial douche preparations may cause vaginitis.   204

Coitus Interruptus

Also known as "being careful," "withdrawal," and "the French method," *coitus interruptus* is withdrawing the penis so that ejaculation takes place outside the vagina and away from the vulva. This method has been used since humans first realized that semen ejaculated into the vagina had something to do with conception. It is free and available to every couple in which the male has a reasonable degree of ejaculatory control. The method is not foolproof, however. Pre-ejaculatory fluid, the shiny lubricant from the Cowper's gland, sometimes contains sperm and can cause pregnancy; presence of sperm in this secretion is especially likely if there has recently been a previous ejaculation. Some men have leakage of semen in small amounts both before and after orgasm, and these men are usually not aware of when the semen first begins to be released. Any sperm reaching the vulva, especially areas that are moist with the vaginal lubricating secretions, can move up into the vagina and be on their way in search of a fertilizable ovum.

Although some critics of coitus interruptus claim that it will leave the couple, and especially the woman, frustrated and unsatisfied, many couples who focus their lovemaking on giving mutual pleasure develop techniques that let both receive full satisfaction. For example, the woman can reach orgasm through manual or oral techniques before the man's build-up toward ejaculation occurs.

Constant users of coitus interruptus have a failure rate of fifteen pregnancies per hundred couple-years. For occasional users, the use effectiveness is twenty to twenty-five per hundred couple-years. Coitus interruptus is not recommended as a regular method of birth control because of its low rate of effectiveness. However, when nothing else is available, it is far more effective than no birth control at all.

The Rhythm Method

The *rhythm method* refers to abstinence from intercourse during the fertile period of a woman's menstrual cycle. This method is also free and available to every couple. The major difficulties with the method are in accurately calculating when a woman is fertile and, for some couples, the frustrations of periodic abstinence.

The Fertile Period Calculation of the fertile period is based on the assumptions that sperm are capable of fertilization for seventy-two hours after intercourse; that the ovum survives for twenty-four hours after ovulation; and that ovulation occurs fourteen days, plus or minus two days,   205 before the beginning of a menstrual period. (Some formulas use slightly different survival periods for the ovum or sperm.) Educated use of this method involves pinpointing as nearly as possible the time of ovulation. Rhythm would become much more precise and usable if a sure, simple method of predicting ovulation about seventy-two hours in advance could be found.

Temperature A rise in basal body temperature follows ovulation as a result of a rise in progesterone level. Immediately preceding ovulation there is a slight drop in temperature. Charting the temperature (which is ideally taken each morning after at least five hours of uninterrupted sleep and before eating, drinking, or conversation) can usually indicate when ovulation has occurred but is not useful in indicating the unsafe preovulation period. Other factors can affect basal body temperature and interfere with the accuracy of this method. These include changes in health and sleep patterns, emotional tension, and medications. Special thermometers with widely spaced markings within the normal range are designed for use by women who want to use the rhythm method or want to determine their period of highest fertility in planning for conception. These thermometers are available at most pharmacies.

Cervical Mucus Method (Billings Method) Changes that occur in the cervical mucus are other clues that can be used to pinpoint the time of ovulation. The distinctiveness of the changes varies from woman to woman, but a woman can follow her own cycle and pay attention to what is normal for her. Immediately following menstruation, estrogen and secretion levels are low and the vagina is somewhat dry. As estrogen levels rise there is a cloudy yellow or white discharge of sticky consistency. Immediately before and after ovulation, during the fertile period, discharge from the cervix increases in volume, becomes clear, and is highly lubricative, with a consistency like egg white. This type of secretion is most noticeable at the time of ovulation and will usually last from one to three days afterward. Then the mucus level decreases sharply and the mucus becomes cloudy and sticky. In some women the mucus becomes clear and watery again before menstruation begins (Ross and Piotrow, 1974, p. I-7).

A machine for accurately measuring the viscosity of cervical mucus has been developed and is now being tested. The physician's model is effective in predicting the time of ovulation to within a few hours. A smaller, simpler version of the tackmeter is being developed for home use, but cannot be guaranteed for contraceptive use until further research assures its reliability when used by the public (*Medical World News*, June 13, 1977, p. 40).

Calendar Measurement   A *calendar method* involves keeping menstrual records over a period of eight months to a year. The earliest probable date of ovulation is calculated from the length of the shortest cycle and the latest day from the length of the longest cycle. The range of the fertile period can be calculated by subtracting eighteen days from the earliest and eleven days from the latest likely day of menstruation. Some women use the calendar method to calculate the first days of preovulatory abstinence and such clues to ovulation as temperature or cervical mucus to pinpoint the occurrence of ovulation so that intercourse can be resumed as soon as possible.

Physiological Difficulties   The fact that less than 10 percent of women have strictly regular menstrual cycles is a drawback to the rhythm method. In many women the cycle varies as much as one to two weeks in length over a year. In teenagers and women approaching menopause the menstrual cycle may vary much more.

Failure Rates   Constant users of the rhythm method experience about fifteen pregnancies per hundred woman-years. Use-effectiveness rates of up to twenty-five to forty pregnancies per hundred woman-years have been reported (*Contraceptive Technology*, p. 68).

Psychological Difficulties   Many couples find that prolonged periods of abstinence create psychosexual stress between them and interfere with their sexual spontaneity. For some there is a constant nagging fear of pregnancy even during the supposedly safe period. A relationship is likely to be threatened by use of the rhythm method if there is not a strong commitment to it by both partners.

The rhythm method is not recommended unless no other contraceptive method is acceptable, for example, because of religious beliefs. There are many, more effective methods that do not require the careful timing of sex required by the rhythm method. Some couples do not avoid sex altogether during the woman's fertile period, but instead develop noncoital methods of sharing pleasure and satisfaction. Even so, for many people periodic abstinence interferes with the natural spontaneous flow of sexual intimacy, especially for women whose sexual desires are strongest during their fertile period.

Nonprescription Mechanical and Chemical Methods

The condom, used by the male, and aerosol vaginal foam, used by the female, are the most effective of the nonprescription mechanical and chemical methods. Theoretical pregnancy rates are very low for both — in   207 the range of two to three per hundred woman-years for foam and less than five per hundred couple-years with the condom. Some family-planning clinics recommend that the two be used together. This combination has a theoretical pregnancy rate of less than one per hundred couple-years. The condom and foam are useful for individuals who have intercourse infrequently, and both work when used properly. Actual use-failure rates are higher than with other methods, but the higher failure rates are usually attributable to inconsistent use rather than to failure of the methods themselves. These are effective methods for individuals highly motivated to prevent pregnancy.

Condom

The *condom*, a sheath worn on the erect penis during intercourse, is the oldest reliable method of male contraception. Condoms are also called *"rubbers," "safes," "prophylactics,"* and *"French letters."* The name may come from Dr. Condom, physician to Charles II of England, who provided this method for the king in hopes of preventing illegitimate offspring. Or it may be from the Latin word *condus* (receptacle) or the Persian *kendu* or *kondu* (grain storage vessels made from animal intestines). Egyptian men wore decorative covers on their penises as early as 1350 B.C. (Hatcher et al., 1974, p. 14). In 1564 the Italian anatomist Fallopio wrote that a linen sheath worn on the penis during intercourse would prevent the spread of venereal disease. Condoms were probably used for that purpose earlier than for contraception. It is known that condoms were used in houses of prostitution in the eighteenth century and were mentioned in the memoirs of Casanova (1725–1798).

Types   Most condoms were made from sheep, calf, or goat intestinal membranes until the development of vulcanization for rubber in the mid-nineteenth century led to mass production from that material. Introduction of latex in the 1930s contributed to improved strength and durability. Most condoms are prerolled when purchased, but those that are not need to be rolled up in preparation for use. If the condom does not have a reservoir tip, about a half inch of space should be left at the closed end to receive the semen. To prevent air from being trapped in the closed end, the condom should be held closed while it is unrolled over the erect penis.

Method of Usage   Because of the possibility of release of some semen before ejaculation, it is important that a condom be in place before the penis approaches the vulva. If a condom is not prelubricated, it should be lubricated with the woman's vaginal secretions, saliva, surgical jelly, or   208

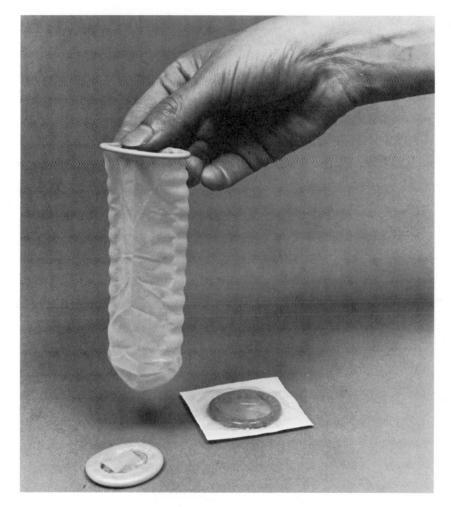

A condom
Michael Malyszko

contraceptive cream, jelly, or foam before it is inserted into the vagina. Vaseline (petroleum jelly) is not water soluble, is desensitizing, and causes rubber deterioration — all reasons to avoid this product as an artificial lubricant for intercourse.

Once ejaculation occurs, caution becomes necessary. As the erection diminishes, a condom may no longer fit snugly and semen can leak out of the open end. Or the condom can slip off and remain in the vagina when the penis is removed. As the erection wanes, the upper part of the condom should be held tightly against the base of the penis and the penis and condom withdrawn from the vagina. The condom should be checked upon removal for leakage, although leakage is highly unlikely and, with present-day quality control, rupture or tearing rarely occurs. Rubber does deteriorate, however, especially when exposed to heat and light in the presence of oxygen. Neither a wallet constantly exposed to body heat nor the glove compartment of a car is a suitable environment for condom storage. However, condoms can be stored away from heat and moisture for up to five years (Cherniak and Feingold, 1973, p. 33).

Use of condoms has increased in the past several years partly because of a re-emphasis on the man's role in family-planning responsibility and a decrease in the number of women using birth control pills (Seymour Mallis, M.D., personal communication). Carefully and consistently used, the condom can be highly effective. A recent study found only one pregnancy in 10,000 occasions of proper use (*Consumer Reports*, October, 1979, p. 583).

Disadvantages   Condoms require some preparation and planning. They must be purchased and readily available at the time of intercourse. Some couples feel that use of a condom interrupts the spontaneous flow of lovemaking. Some males feel that the condom reduces their pleasure, because the feeling of contact is decreased by this covering over the penis.

Advantages   Condoms are sold at all pharmacies and drugstores, at many discount stores, and by mail order. They do not require a prescription or any kind of fitting by a doctor. In many states they can be purchased by minors. In addition to their contraceptive function, they provide protection against venereal disease.

Vaginal Contraceptives

The only chemical methods used by women that do not require a doctor's prescription and do not produce systemic effects are the contraceptive creams, jellies, and foams that are inserted in the vagina. Recent clinical studies have indicated that some of the modern preparations, particularly the aerosol foams, can provide a high level of protection when used regularly and correctly. Pregnancy rates lower than five per hundred woman-years have been reported in recent studies in the United States. However, to be totally effective, foam *must* be used with every act of intercourse before the penis is inserted into the vagina.

The practice of inserting something into the vagina either to block or destroy sperm is an ancient one. Modern preparations have come a long way since 1900 B.C., when a combination of honey, natron (sodium carbonate), and crocodile dung was used as a vaginal contraceptive paste (*Population Reports H,* No. 3, p. H-38).

Composition Vaginal chemical contraceptives are composed of an inert base material that physically blocks sperm from entering the cervical opening and active spermicidal agents that chemically immobilize or destroy the sperm. The jellies, foam tablets, and suppositories are generally not as effective as the aerosol foams. Instructions for use of the vaginal methods vary from product to product, especially with respect to the length of time before intercourse the product must be inserted. All are packaged with instructions for use.

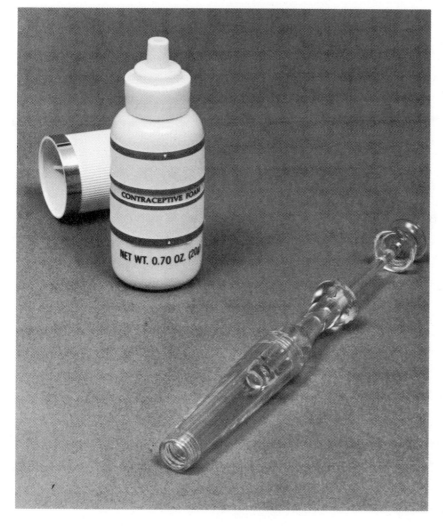

Spermicidal vaginal foam and applicator
Michael Malyszko

211

Failure Rates   For conscientious users who insert foam with every act of intercourse, the failure rate is in the vicinity of two to three pregnancies per hundred woman-years. Actual use effectiveness is between thirty and forty pregnancies per hundred. Common causes of failure are use of too little foam, having intercourse without using the foam each time, and douching or washing the foam out of the vagina less than six to eight hours after intercourse. Foam is a useful method for women who have intercourse infrequently. Couples who use another method sometimes use foam as a temporary-substitute method, such as when a woman has forgotten to take a pill or has a new IUD, or when a man has recently had a vasectomy and the vas deferens is not yet cleared of sperm. All the vaginal contraceptives, including foam, afford some, but not total, protection against venereal disease organisms.

Disadvantages   Some couples do not like foam because they feel it is messy or because it must be inserted at the time of intercourse. Others view these features as advantages, take pleasure in shared insertion of the foam, and welcome the additional vaginal lubrication provided.

Advantages   Vaginal methods have the advantage of being available in most drugstores, where they are usually clearly displayed in the feminine hygiene section. It is necessary to choose carefully from the products displayed, for some of the products on the shelf are designed for use only in conjunction with a diaphragm and others are douche preparations or vaginal-deodorant suppositories without contraceptive effect.

Prescription Contraceptives

Three methods — the diaphragm, intrauterine device (IUD), and oral contraceptives — are available in the United States only through medical prescription. The diaphragm must be individually fitted. The IUD must be individually fitted and also inserted. Oral contraceptives have powerful systemic effects, and the appropriate type for an individual woman must be selected from the many available. Two other methods, abortion and sterilization, are medical procedures.

The International Planned Parenthood Federation Central Medical Committee urges responsible, simple, nonmedical distribution of oral contraceptives. In some countries women are already purchasing oral contraceptives through commercial outlets without medical supervision. The committee suggested in a statement made in April 1973 that nurses, midwives, pharmacists, and storekeepers may be appropriate individuals to distribute oral contraceptives and that control of possible side effects can be carried out independently of distribution (Piotrow and Lee, 1974,   **212**

p. 22). In many family-planning clinics in the United States, much of the routine of contraceptive prescription is carried out by family nurse-practitioners and paraprofessionals under the supervision of physicians.

Diaphragm

The *diaphragm* is a dome of soft rubber or plastic sealed over a circular steel spring. It is worn inside the vagina during intercourse and serves as a container for a spermicidal cream or jelly, which it holds against the cervical opening. It also provides some mechanical blockage of the cervix.

The diaphragm was invented in the nineteenth century, and prior to the introduction of the pill and IUD in the early 1960s it was the most popular birth control method used by women in the United States.

Fitting Diaphragms range from fifty-five to one hundred millimeters in diameter and must be individually fitted so that the dome covers the cervix, with the front part of the rim fitting snugly behind the pubic bone and the back part of the rim fitting behind the cervix. The fit of a diaphragm should be checked every two years and after any weight gain or

Diaphragm with spermicidal jelly
Michael Malyszko

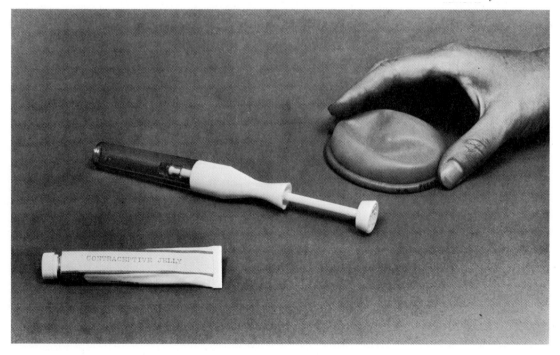

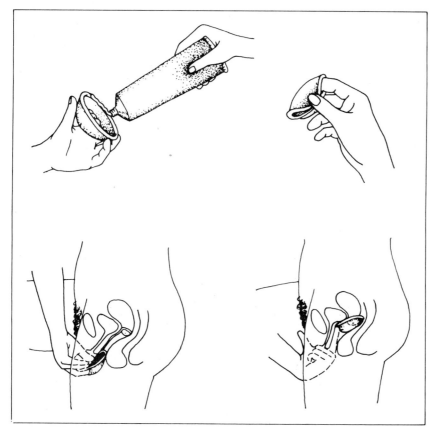

Figure 7.1

Insertion of diaphragm with spermicidal jelly

loss of ten or more pounds, childbirth, miscarriage, abortion, or gynecological procedure that might lead to changes in vaginal dimensions. Women who are fitted as virgins should have their diaphragm size rechecked a few weeks after beginning to have intercourse.

Spermicides A diaphragm should always be used with a spermicidal (sperm killing) cream or jelly. The jelly is the more lubricating of the two. A diaphragm is *not* an effective contraceptive when used alone. At least a teaspoon of spermicide is put inside the diaphragm, and a little is spread around the rim. With one hand the rim is pinched together to form an arc, the lips of the vagina are spread with the other hand, and the diaphragm is inserted into the vagina down and back as far as it will go. The front rim is tucked behind the ridge of the pubic bone. Proper positioning is then checked by feeling with a finger for the cervix under the dome of the diaphragm, a sensation something like that of touching the tip of the nose. (See Figure 7.1.) Inserting a diaphragm may seem complicated at first but   214 becomes simple and routine with a little practice. Squatting or standing with one leg propped up can facilitate insertion.

It is important that the diaphragm and spermicide be left in place for at least six to eight hours after intercourse for the spermicide to do its job. If there are one or more subsequent acts of intercourse during that time, the diaphragm should not be removed. Some clinics recommend that additional spermicide be inserted for each act with an applicator that can be purchased with the spermicide. Others believe that the original application of spermicide will be effective for up to twenty-four hours even though there are repeated ejaculations, so that no additional spermicide is necessary (Weideger, 1975, p. 103).

The diaphragm is removed by hooking a finger under the rim and pulling down and out. Care should be taken not to poke a hole in it with a fingernail. A diaphragm can be checked for holes either by filling it with water and looking for leaks or by looking through it toward a light source. A diaphragm is cared for by washing with soap and water, drying and dusting with cornstarch (not talcum powder), and storing it in its container.

Failure Rates   When used properly the diaphragm has a failure rate of about three pregnancies per hundred woman-years of use. Actual use-effectiveness rates are about twenty pregnancies per hundred woman-years, primarily because a diaphragm does not work while in a dresser drawer.

Disadvantages   The major disadvantage of the diaphragm is that attention must be paid to contraception as a part of each act of intercourse. As with foam, some couples make this disadvantage an advantage, incorporate insertion of the diaphragm into their loveplay, and may welcome the additional lubrication of the spermicide. An occasional woman or her partner may be allergic to rubber or to one of the spermicides, but this can usually be dealt with by changing to a plastic diaphragm or to a different brand of spermicide. A diaphragm may occasionally become dislodged during lovemaking in positions with the female on top, slightly decreasing its effectiveness. The few contraindications to use of the diaphragm are gynecological abnormalities, such as a greatly displaced uterus.

Advantages   The diaphragm is a highly effective method when used regularly and conscientiously. A diaphragm has no systemic effects and no effects on future fertility. During menstruation it can be used during intercourse to hold back the flow. A properly fitting diaphragm is not felt by either partner during intercourse. Family planners note that this contraceptive method is making a comeback in popularity and are predicting it will be the method of choice for many women not using the pill or IUD.   215

Intrauterine Devices (IUDs)

Intrauterine devices are foreign bodies placed within the uterus. Intrauterine pessaries were first mentioned in the Hippocratic writings on "Diseases of Women" and have been used for over two thousand years for many purposes, including population control. They have been made from wool, ivory, wood, glass, silver and gold, ebony, pewter, and even platinum studded with diamonds. For centuries Arabian and Turkish camel owners placed stones in the uteri of their saddle animals to prevent pregnancy (Southam, 1964, p. 3). Most of the nineteenth-century literature on intrauterine devices referred to their use in the correction of uterine displacement. However, in 1878 the Obstetrical Section of the British Medical Society was informed that women of high social standing were permanently wearing the *stem pessaries* (intravaginal devices with a stem that fits into the uterine canal) to prevent conception, a practice the speaker abhorred as "a way to sin without detection." Some listeners must have used that information for a purpose opposite to that intended by the speaker, because by the end of the century there was increased popular demand for the pessaries and they were prominently featured in surgical catalogues. A major problem with these devices was that the stem acted as a vehicle for infection of the uterus. It was when one of the stem pessaries accidentally broke and left a terminal ring in a uterus that the contraceptive efficacy of a completely intrauterine device was discovered (Peel and Potts, 1969, p. 128).

A report by Grafenberg in 1929 on a series of over two thousand insertions of silk and silver rings in Germany and another report from Britain by Norman Haire at about the same time further focused attention on the use of IUDs for contraception (Peel and Potts, p. 129). Grafenberg claimed a high success rate, but reports by others of numerous infections and other complications caused by the devices led to their being either condemned or ignored in medical texts in the United States. By the mid-1930s most American physicians would have nothing to do with them (Gilmore, 1969, p. 6). IUDs continued to be used in Israel and Japan on an experimental basis, and reports received in the United States from those countries in 1959 rekindled interest. Between 1959 and 1962 the Population Council, an organization that fosters population research and training, sponsored IUD development, and the outcome was a collection of plastic devices of various shapes and designs and a modified Grafenberg ring constructed of inert stainless steel (Peel and Potts, 1969, p. 130).

Types There are many types of IUDs in use today, and new types are constantly being developed and tested in an effort to overcome problems of those on the market. Some of the more popular IUDs now available in the United States are the Lippes Loop, the Saf-T-Coil, the Copper 7, the Copper T, and the Progestasert.

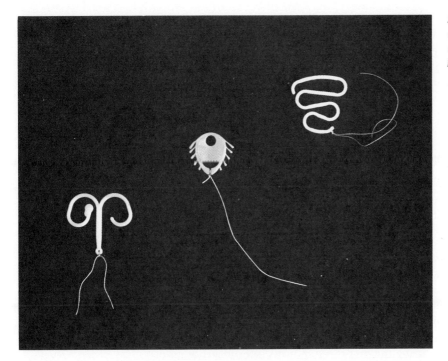

Function How IUDs work is not definitely known. Mechanisms of action vary among the various designs, and it is difficult, sometimes impossible, to extrapolate results of animal experiments to humans. Viable sperm and both fertilized and unfertilized ova have been recovered from the Fallopian tubes of women with IUDs, so the devices apparently do not suppress ovulation, interfere with the *corpus luteum* (progesterone-producing body that develops in the ruptured ovarian follicle), or completely inhibit sperm transport or fertilization. They do seem to interfere in some way with the implantation of the fertilized ovum in the lining of the uterus. It is believed that the IUD makes the uterine fluid inhospitable to a fertilized ovum and causes the uterine lining and ovum to become out of phase. "Colossal numbers of macrophages" have been found devouring intact spermatozoa in the postintercourse uterine fluid of women with IUDs (Huber et al., *Pop Reports,* 1975, p. B-25). The *macrophages* are a defensive cell reaction activated by the foreign body in the uterus. Several investigators have observed abnormal uterine contractility in the presence of IUDs at the time in the menstrual cycle when implantation would normally occur and have suggested this effect may be due to increased intrauterine *prostaglandin* (substances that stimulate the uterus to contract) levels (Huber et al., 1975, p. 25).

217

Insertion   Insertion of an IUD is in most instances a simple, rapid procedure. A uterine sounding device is inserted to measure the size of the uterus and discover the direction and tone of the cervical canal. An IUD is then loaded into an introducer, a narrow, hollow tube; the introducer is inserted into the uterus, and the device is released after being properly positioned. For many women this is painless. Others, especially women whose uterus has not been stretched by childbearing, may experience discomfort. With the Copper 7, reportedly the easiest of all IUDs to insert, the majority (in one study, about 83 percent of women who have never given birth and 94 percent of those who have borne children) experience no pain at all during insertion (Huber et al., 1975, p. 30). Uterine cramping for several days after insertion is not uncommon, but continued cramping may indicate an improperly positioned IUD. Many physicians prefer that IUD insertion be performed during a woman's menstrual period, thereby assuring against insertion into a pregnant uterus, taking advantage of a somewhat dilated cervix, and letting the menstrual flow mask the harmless bleeding that may occur.

Expulsion   On the average, 8 to 10 percent of IUDs inserted are spontaneously expelled, less by women who have been pregnant, more by those who have not (Boston Women's Health Book Collective, 1973, p. 123). Most expulsions occur during the first three months after insertion; most occur during menstruation. However, a spontaneous expulsion could occur at any time. It is important for a woman or her partner to check that the IUD strings that protrude through the cervix can be felt immediately after menstruation and once each week thereafter. If the strings cannot be felt or if the IUD can be felt protruding through the cervix, the woman should return to her doctor and should use another contraceptive method until she can ascertain whether or not she is still protected by the IUD.

Failure Rate   Theoretical effectiveness of most IUDs is in the range of one to five pregnancies per hundred woman-years of use. Use effectiveness is close to theoretical effectiveness. Use effectiveness is increased when a second method of birth control is used for the first month an IUD is in place.

Disadvantages   Some women experience heavy cramping during their first few periods following IUD insertion. Menstrual bleeding also becomes heavier for most women, more so with the plastic type than with the newer and smaller Copper T or Copper 7. Younger women who have never given birth tend to expel the devices more frequently, have heavier bleeding and cramping, and have higher pregnancy rates than do women over thirty who have borne children. Statistics available in 1970 indicated that almost 23 percent of women fitted with IUDs in the six previous years   **218** had discontinued use before the end of the first year after insertion, mostly because of bleeding, pain, or pelvic inflammatory disease (Huber et al., 1975, p. 35). A rare complication of IUD use, perforation of the uterus, usually occurs, or at least begins, at the time the IUD is inserted. One source estimates that an IUD perforates the uterine wall in about one out of every two thousand five hundred insertions (Cherniak and Feingold, 1973, p. 30). Pain is not always a symptom; not being able to find the tail strings may be the first sign that perforation has occurred. The IUD can usually be located by X ray and then surgically removed.

Advantages   The biggest advantage of the IUD is that it involves no manipulation, forethought, or action beyond initial insertion. The act of contraception is unrelated to the act of coitus. An IUD will not interfere with lactation. Difficulties with IUD use are significant, but they do not affect all women. Many women with IUDs have experienced a brief period of adaptation and then worn them comfortably for years.

Pregnancy   When a pregnancy does occur, most physicians will remove the IUD if the tail is visible and the woman desires the pregnancy to continue. The spontaneous abortion rate after removal of a Lippes Loop has been shown to be lower (about 25 percent) if the device is removed than if the loop is left in the uterus (about 50 percent). In the event the threads are not available, the device is not removed, because attempted removal would increase risk of spontaneous abortion (Hatcher et al., 1974, p. 50). Babies born to mothers with an IUD in place, including IUDs of the copper type, have no more congenital defects than those in the general population. Although the rate of spontaneous abortion is significantly higher, there is no increase in the incidence of fetal death in the uterus when an IUD is present. About one in twenty of IUD pregnancies are ectopic.

The Pill

The pill, as oral contraceptives are popularly called, can be any one of more than twenty pills manufactured throughout the world and prescribed to prevent ovulation. The common function of the most popular combination types is inhibition of ovulation at the hypothalamic-pituitary level. Secondarily, at the uterine level, the progestin thickens the cervical mucus, making it nonreceptive or hostile to the penetration of sperm, and changes the uterine lining so that it is unreceptive to implantation. These mechanisms are not activated uniformly by all oral contraceptives. Pills vary in size, relative dosages of estrogen and progestin, chemical structures, and systemic effects. Not all women can use the pill.

Health Restrictions on Use   The pill should not be used by women with thrombophlebitis, thromboembolic disorders, cerebrovascular accident, or a history of markedly impaired liver function or breast or reproductive-system malignancy; or by women who are pregnant or have had a pregnancy of twenty weeks or more terminated within the previous month. Migraine headaches, hypertension, prediabetes or diabetes, and undiagnosed abnormal vaginal bleeding are also conditions that preclude a woman's taking the pill. Other conditions that may make use of the pill undesirable include varicose veins, asthma, cardiac or renal disease, mental retardation, chloasma (pregnancy mask), family history of diabetes, uterine fibroids, epilepsy, depression, and late onset of menses or very irregular menses (which may indicate a tendency for subsequent fertility problems). Oral contraceptives may decrease milk supply and so should not be used during lactation.

Hormone Synthesis   Women differ in the amounts of hormones they synthesize and are able to tolerate. Hormone levels and relationships are probably as personal as fingerprints. Because the various oral contraceptives differ in the amount and type of hormones they contain, any one oral contraceptive can exceed the natural hormone requirements in some women and not meet them in others. Differences in the hormonal agents themselves are another important factor. Of mestranol and ethinyl estradiol, the two estrogens currently available in pills in the United States, mestranol is probably weaker in estrogenic potency. However, the progestins in some pills have some estrogenic effect and in other pills are antiestrogenic.

Many of the symptoms of estrogen excess and progestin deficiency decrease with successive cycles of taking the pill. Symptoms of progestin excess and estrogen deficiency tend to increase with successive months of use. Symptoms of estrogen deficiency may first occur after many months of continuous use of the pill (Dickey and Dorr, 1969, pp. 279–280).

Estrogen Excess   The symptoms of estrogen excess are similar to those of early pregnancy. They include nausea, leg cramps and swelling, dizziness, *leukorrhea* (vaginal discharge), uterine cramps, and *chloasma* (yellowish brown patches or spots on the skin, sometimes called *liver spots*). Contact lenses may fail to fit because of fluid retention. Breasts may feel tender and full and there may be cyclic weight gain. Headaches during the three weeks the pills are taken or constant anxiety, fatigue, and depression may also be symptoms of estrogen excess (Dickey and Dorr, 1969, p. 278; Hatcher et al., 1974, pp. 30–31).

220

Progestin Imbalances A deficiency in progestin results in late breakthrough bleeding and spotting with combination pills. Menstrual flow may be heavy, prolonged, and accompanied by clots and cramping. Symptoms of excess progestin include the increased appetite, weight gain, and tiredness common to pregnancy; decrease in the amount and duration of menstrual flow; and, in rare instances, increased facial or body hair, loss of scalp hair, acne, or jaundice. Headaches during the week the pills are not taken can be a symptom of progestin excess that may become worse over time (Dickey and Dorr, 1969, pp. 279–280; *Contraceptive Technology*, pp. 30–31).

Estrogen Deficiency Symptoms of estrogen deficiency are those common to menopause, the immediate premenstrual period, and late pregnancy. They include irritability, nervousness, hot flashes, decreased estrogenic effects on breast and vaginal tissues, and monilia vaginitis. (Progestin excess may be another factor in *monilia,* also called yeast infection). Estrogen deficiency is involved in early and midcycle bleeding and decreased amount of menstrual flow (Dickey and Dorr, 1969, p. 279).

Symptoms Headache, breast pain, spotting and breakthrough bleeding, decreased flow, and missed menstruation can have multiple causes. The time in the cycle they occur can often indicate which hormone is causing the problem. In one study 87.5 percent of 152 women with estrogen-related symptoms and 94.5 percent of 176 women with progestin-related symptoms were found to improve when they were changed to a pill that seemed closer to their individual natural hormone requirements (Dickey and Dorr, 1968, p. 92).

Advantages Oral contraceptives of the combination type offer virtually 100 percent protection against pregnancy if taken regularly. Use of the pill is associated with many beneficial side effects; oral contraceptives are sometimes prescribed for relief of spasmodic dysmenorrhea, irregular menstruation, pelvic endometriosis, acne, ovulation pain, premenstrual tension, treatment of ovarian cysts, and for postponement of menstrual periods for social occasions or religious ceremonies (Greenhill, 1968, pp. 312, 314–315). Women on birth control pills are reported to have raised hemoglobin levels, partly as a result of a decrease in number of days of menstrual flow and amount of blood lost (Peel and Potts, 1969, p. 103). Some couples feel that use of the pill results in more pleasurable, more spontaneous, and more frequent sexual relations because the contraceptive method is not used at the time of intercourse (Cohen, 1976). Some women experience an increase in breast size while using oral contraceptives and perceive that as a beneficial side effect.

221

Disadvantages About 40 percent of women on the pill have some minor side effects, at least initially. Many of these side effects, such as nausea, fluid retention, and many of the other estrogen-excess symptoms decrease or disappear after two or three pill cycles or may be eliminated by changing the brand of pill.

The most threatening disadvantage of pill use is the increased risk of blood-clotting disorders. The *British Medical Journal* attracted worldwide attention in April 1968, when it published reports on the relationship of use of the pill to thromboembolic disease and deaths from pulmonary, coronary, and cerebral thrombosis and embolism. A strong correlation was found between the use of oral contraceptives and death from pulmonary embolism or cerebral thrombosis in the absence of predisposing conditions (Inman and Vessey, 1968, p. 199; Vessey and Doll, 1968, p. 205). Estrogen was the hormone implicated. More recent studies have indicated that risk of fatal thromboembolism is lower with the low-dose brands of the pill than with the higher-dose pills available at the time of the original studies. However, one source estimates that about one pill user in 2,000 is hospitalized each year for blood-clotting disorders (Hatcher et al., 1974) and another source that the pill causes the death of about 1.5 per 100,000 users among young women (Cherniak and Feingold, 1973, p. 25). The complications of pregnancy and childbirth in this same age group have a mortality rate of about 23 per 100,000 pregnant women.

Recent studies have indicated that risks of stroke, clotting disorders, and heart attack are considerably greater for women over thirty-five than for younger women, and recommendations have been made that women of that age group use other contraceptive methods (*Family Planning Digest*, July-August, 1975, p. 145). In February 1976 the Population Council reported that for women over forty the pill carries a greater risk of death than does childbirth. Cigarette smoking increases the risk of serious effects on the heart and blood vessels of users of oral contraceptives. Women who smoke and those over age thirty-five should not use the pill (*Population Reports*, January, 1979). Most clotting disorders give forewarning signs that warrant immediate medical attention. These include severe headaches, sudden blurring or loss of vision, a sensation of flashing lights, severe leg pains, and chest pain or shortness of breath (*Contraceptive Technology*, p. 28). Data in a recent study indicate that women who use birth control pills for more than four years are almost twice as likely to develop skin cancer and three to five times as likely to develop cervical cancer when compared to nonpill users (*Sexuality Today*, November 27, 1978).

Effect on Growth Patterns Birth control pills and pregnancy can interfere with completion of normal growth patterns. Females who have not reached physical maturity should not use oral contraceptives (Cherniak and Feingold, p. 20). Signs of physical maturity include physical growth in height and weight, regular menstruation, breast development, and the growth of pubic and underarm hair. Physical maturity is usually reached between the ages of thirteen and eighteen; most females are physically mature by about age sixteen.

Method of Use   Birth control pills are taken in a pattern designed to mimic the regular menstrual cycle. Most brands are packaged in series of twenty or twenty-one pills. One pill is taken daily for three weeks, and then no pills are taken for one week. Some packages include seven placebo pills to be taken on the seven days when no contraceptive pills are taken. Many physicians and clinics recommend beginning the first pill on the fifth day of a menstrual cycle. Beginning no later than the sixth day is important if there is to be no chance of ovulation. One clinic recommends starting the first pack on the first Sunday after a period begins, because

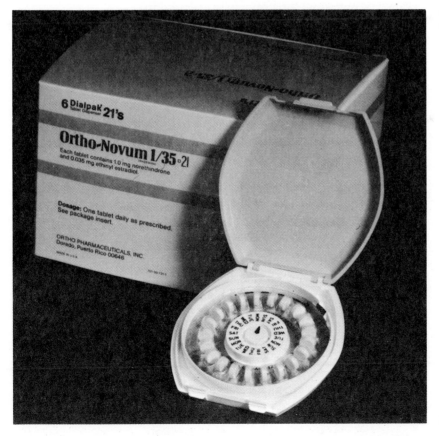

The contraceptive pill
Ortho Pharmaceutical
Corporation

223

Sunday is an easy day to remember and this pattern usually means that a woman won't be menstruating on a weekend. During the first two weeks of the first cycle of pills, a second method of birth control such as foam or condoms should be used.

One to three days after a series of pills is ended, menstrual-like bleeding brought about by withdrawal of the hormones usually begins. This period is usually briefer, scantier, and freer from discomfort than the regular menses. It is not medically necessary to cease taking the pill for several days each month, and some researchers have investigated other patterns of prescription. Flowers (1963, reported in Mears, 1965, p. 70) gave pills continuously until breakthrough bleeding occurred, stopped the pills for a week, and began a new series on the fifth day of the flow. With that method, cycles averaged forty-five to sixty days. Most women who wish to postpone a period can take pills for several extra days to extend a cycle without cause for concern. To prevent ovulation, it is important that pill taking be resumed on the fifth day of the period that follows or within a week of stopping the pills if no flow occurs. Because individual circumstances vary, it is important for a woman to check with a physician or family-planning clinic before modifying the mode of pill taking that has been prescribed for her.

Oral contraceptives need to be taken daily to be effective because they are metabolized in about twenty-four hours. If a tablet is missed, natural production of hormones may increase and cause an egg to mature and be released. If a pill is forgotten, it should be taken as soon as it is remembered, even if that means taking two pills in the same day. If more than twenty-four hours elapse after a combination pill is forgotten, the pill should be taken when remembered, but another birth control method should also be used for the remainder of that cycle. If two or more pills are forgotten in succession, a medical advisor or family-planning clinic should be consulted as to the course of action to take.

Minipills

Minipills, which provide small doses of progestin alone, have been available since January 1973. Minipills are taken continuously, even during menstruation. They may or may not inhibit ovulation but do tend to make cervical mucus hostile to sperm, and they interfere with the enzymes that allow sperm to penetrate the egg for fertilization, with ovum transport through the Fallopian tubes, and with implantation in the event an egg is fertilized. The theoretical effectiveness of minipills is 96 to 99 percent, slightly less than that of the combination type. Pregnancy rates with the minipills seem to be highest during the first six months of use. Minipills are typically prescribed for women who have problems with the estrogen in combination pills (Hatcher, et al., 1974).

224

Morning-after Pills

Massive doses of a synthetic estrogen, diethystilbestrol *(DES)*, can be used as an emergency measure after unprotected intercourse at midcycle. This is *not* a method for regular use. The massive doses of DES, which are begun within seventy-two hours — preferably within twenty-four hours — after intercourse and continued for five days, frequently cause nausea and vomiting. If the method fails and pregnancy does occur, the fetus may have been harmed by the DES. There are other alternatives open to a woman considering the morning-after treatment: an IUD may be inserted; she may await menstruation and seek menstrual extraction if her period is late; or she may wait until a pregnancy test can be made and if pregnancy is confirmed, decide whether to have a therapeutic abortion or continue the pregnancy (Hatcher et al., 1974, p. 42).

New Developments in Hormonal Contraception

Currently under investigation are a pill to be taken only once a month, new patterns of taking existing oral contraceptives, long-acting injections and implants, hormone-impregnated cervical rings and IUDs, and hormonal contraceptives for use by the male.

Sterilization

Sterilization is a surgical procedure that permanently blocks reproductive functioning. Although surgical reconstruction is sometimes performed, there is no guarantee of success in restoring fertility, and results are often disappointing. Permanent infertility is the expected outcome of a sterilization procedure, but it sometimes does not occur (Himes, 1970, p. 111). Nearly 11 million Americans have chosen surgical sterilization. It is now the number one choice of methods of contraception for persons over the age of thirty. (*Sexuality Today,* February 11, 1980).

Female Sterilization

A woman can be sterilized by removal of the ovaries or uterus or by blocking or severing the Fallopian tubes. Of the three alternatives, interruption of the Fallopian tubes is the simplest. Removal of the hormone-producing ovaries is undesirable, and the uterus is a source of sexual pleasure for some women. In addition, hysterectomy — the removal of uterus — is a major surgical procedure.

225

Female sterilization was mentioned by Hippocrates long ago, and the first published description of a procedure for tying the tubes is dated 1834. Until the early 1960s, however, tying of the tubes was a major abdominal operation. In the 1960s development of a cold-light source, a light that could illuminate the internal organs without producing heat, simplified the procedure from the patient's point of view so that female sterilization can now be performed with local anesthesia and on an out-patient basis, with the patient able to be discharged on the same day as the surgery.

Three different surgical procedures are currently used to block the Fallopian tubes: abdominal tubal ligation, vaginal tubal ligation, and electrocoagulation of the tubes via laparoscopy (Lanson, 1975, p. 242).

Tubal Ligation   Abdominal tubal ligation is the most frequently used method, and is usually the most suitable method immediately following childbirth. Right after childbirth, when the uterus is still enlarged, the Fallopian tubes branch off from the top of the uterus in the abdominal area near the navel. A small incision is made just below the navel and through this incision a portion of each tube is removed. The two cut ends of each tube are pinched shut and individually tied or cauterized. (See

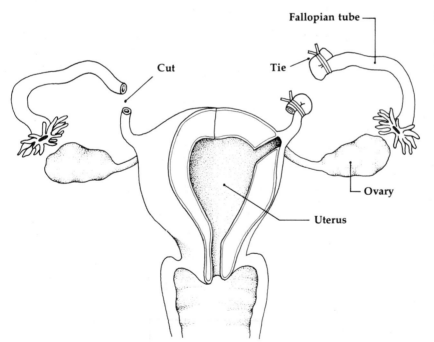

Figure 7.2

Internal female reproductive organs showing tubal ligation

Figure 7.2.) In women who have not recently been pregnant the incision is made much lower, often hidden along the upper edge of the pubic hair. In a vaginal tubal ligation the incision is made in the upper vagina just behind the cervix. This method is not suitable immediately following pregnancy because vaginal tissues are too congested and the tubes are high up in the abdomen, out of reach. Advantages of vaginal tubal ligation are less discomfort after the procedure than with the abdominal method and no visible scar. From the physician's point of view the procedure is technically difficult, and there is some risk of infection of the abdominal cavity with vaginal bacteria.

Laparoscopy Laparoscopy requires only one, more commonly two, puncture wounds and has been labeled in the press as "Band-Aid" or "bellybutton" surgery. A *laparoscope,* a "slender tube shaped like a telescope and equipped with a bright heatless light," is passed into the abdominal cavity through a tiny puncture that frequently is hidden within the folds of the navel. When the tubes can be clearly seen through the laparoscope, a coagulating instrument is inserted through the same puncture wound or through a second puncture in the lower abdomen. Each tube is gently lifted with the operating scope and seared in two or three places. Sometimes a portion of the tube is also removed. Laparoscopy is often performed under general anesthetic but also can be done with less risky local anesthetic. Before the laparoscope is introduced into the abdomen, the abdominal cavity is inflated with carbon dioxide gas to separate the internal pelvic organs and expose the uterus and tubes. After the procedure the gas is allowed to escape. Any that remains is harmlessly absorbed. Hospitalization for tubal ligation by laparoscopy is minimal. Some hospitals and clinics do the procedure on an outpatient basis, and the woman is released the same day. In others an overnight stay is the rule. Even so, the procedure should not be considered a minor one. Occasionally there are serious complications, such as internal bleeding or perforation of the bowel, that require further surgery (Lanson, 1975).

Hysteroscopic Sterilization One other procedure is worthy of mention. In hysteroscopic sterilization a narrow, telescopelike instrument is passed through the cervix and into the uterine cavity, where the tiny openings of the two Fallopian tubes are located and sealed with a tiny cauterizing instrument that is passed through the telescope. The physician can directly view the tubal openings through this instrument. This procedure has many advantages: it takes less than five minutes, requires no incision or elaborate equipment, and can easily be done in a doctor's office.

The newest method of hysteroscopic sterilization involves blocking the Fallopian tubes by injecting two drops of liquid silicone in each tube.

Blockage occurs about five minutes later when the silicone solidifies. This procedure requires no surgery, hospitalization, or general anesthesia. Another advantage of the procedure is the possibility that it may be reversible if the woman later wants to become pregnant. However, reversibility has not been proven in humans (*San Diego Union,* September 30, 1979).

Effects on Sexuality   Women can resume sexual activity as soon as they wish after abdominal tubal ligation or laparoscopy. About four to six weeks of abstinence from vaginal intercourse is needed to assure proper healing of an upper vaginal incision. Tubal ligation provides immediate sterility because ova can no longer pass through the tubes and reach the uterus. Other than that, reproductive and sexual functioning should be unaffected. Hormones continue to circulate via the bloodstream after tubal ligation. The menstrual cycle is unaffected. Ovulation still occurs, but the ovum disintegrates in the upper end of the Fallopian tube through which it can no longer pass.

Failure Rate   The failure rate for tubal ligation is between one-tenth and two per hundred operations, usually because the woman has an undetected pre-existing pregnancy or because a surgeon mistakenly identifies a round ligament as a Fallopian tube (Wortman and Piotrow, 1973, p. C-17).

Male Sterilization

Vasectomy, cutting of the *vas deferens* (sperm-carrying duct), is a minor surgical procedure that permanently eliminates fertility in the male. The technique is simple enough to be performed in a physician's office or outpatient clinic.

In the late nineteenth century vasectomy was occasionally used to prevent *epididymitis* (swelling of the epididymis, a tube within the testicle) after prostate surgery. Not until early in the twentieth century was the value of the procedure for sterilization and fertility control recognized. Adverse publicity about the pill in 1969 and 1970 led to increased emphasis on male responsibility for fertility control, and the number of vasectomies performed in the United States leaped from a quarter of a million in 1969 to about three-quarters of a million in 1970 and 1971, leveling off to about half a million by late 1973. Vasectomy is now a major technique in voluntary family planning.

Procedure   Vasectomy can be done with a local anesthetic. Once the anesthesia has been administered, the entire operation usually takes no   228

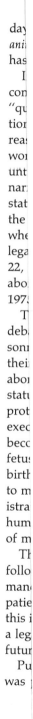

day
anii
has
I
con
"qu
tior
rea:
woi
unt
nar
stat
the
whe
lega
22,
abo
197:
T
deb
son
thei
abo
stat
prot
exec
becc
fetu:
birth
to m
istra
hum
of m
Tl
follo
man
patie
this i
a leg
futur
Pu
was

*A mobile vasectomy
unit in India*
Agency for International
Development

more than ten to twenty minutes. A small incision is made in the scrotal
sac, and a vas drawn out, sometimes producing a sensation of abdominal
pulling. Once the vas is cut, the surgeon may tie, coagulate, and/or clip
the ends; the favored technique varies from physician to physician. The
procedure is repeated on the opposite side, the incisions closed, and the
operation is complete. (See Figure 7.3)

Effects on Sexuality   How soon can intercourse resume? Some doctors
advise their patients to wait at least until they are out of the office or clinic.
Others are somewhat more conservative and recommend waiting five to
ten days in the belief that this allows the vas stump to heal before pressure
is placed on it by ejaculation. They believe this healing makes less likely
the formation of *sperm granulomas,* an inflammatory response to the leakage of sperm into surrounding tissues. Usually there are no symptoms,
but sometimes a granuloma can be felt as a hard lump, actually a mass of
sperm, or can become infected.

Vasectomy does not result in immediate sterility. Sperm still remain in
the vas deferens between the site of the surgery and the outside world.
Until all these sperm have been ejaculated, the man is capable of causing a
pregnancy. For most men this will be somewhere between ten and twenty

229

An
tom
fou
phy
any
the
Ho
sid
thr
con

Vas
bee
effe
duc
mor
nee

A
tub
atte

Ab
Abo
poir
(Ch
folk
fron
writ
life
abo
A
the
medi
"ani
tion
tury

decision and has continued somewhat more gradually in a positive direction since then. At the same time, organized opposition to abortion has grown, pushing for legislation banning the use of federal money for abortions. In 1977 the Supreme Court ruled that states are not required to fund abortions for women who cannot afford them; this decision was reversed in February 1980. Lobbying is under way for a Constitutional amendment prohibiting abortions altogether (Adler, 1979).

There have also been an increasing number of antiabortion demonstrations, including violence against abortion clinics. This violence has included fire bombing, throwing flammable liquids on clinic staff, destruction of operating equipment, and firing bullets into clinics. One researcher, from an analysis of cross-cultural data and voting records in the United States Senate, found a high correlation between opposition to abortion and acceptance of various forms of human violence (Prescott, 1978). From the results of this study one may predict that violent antiabortion demonstrations will continue.

In spite of the controversy, abortion is being used increasingly to terminate unwanted pregnancies. In 1977 and 1978 nearly three of every ten pregnancies ended in abortion; there were 1.32 million legal abortions in the United States in 1977 and a projected 1.37 million in 1978 (*San Diego Union,* January 20, 1980).

Even when abortion is legal, it affects not only the woman who has the abortion but also her family and the father of the aborted fetus. Abortion leaves some women with a sense of relief and freedom; others may experience extreme guilt and depression. Probably most have to deal with some negative reactions from themselves or other persons (Adler, 1979).

A woman in her early twenties reports on her abortion experience: I was so surprised that the nurses and the doctors were so nice to me — just like I was a real patient and not there for something awful like an abortion. . . . I don't feel so bad about it now, but my mother never will let me forget. Like now I have been having headaches and she says it's because of "that thing" that I did — she won't ever use the word *abortion.* My brother didn't say much except that I was just "too flip" about it all. I think he wanted me to get hysterical and really feel bad as a kind of punishment.

From the authors' files

Also, there is some evidence that women who have had abortions tend to have more miscarriages and other problems in subsequent pregnancies, but most women do not have such problems. (*Sexuality Today,* August 28, 1978).

Different techniques are used for abortions at different stages of pregnancy, as appropriate for the size of the embryo or fetus.

234

Menstrual Extraction

This procedure can be done within the first few weeks after a late menstrual period when there is suspicion of pregnancy, and can provide reasonable assurance of a nonpregnant condition several weeks before the standard pregnancy tests now available can be used reliably. In *menstrual extraction,* a thin, hollow, flexible plastic tube is inserted through the cervix into the uterus, suction is applied, and the endometrium (uterine lining) is removed. Advantages of the procedure are that determination of pregnancy is unnecessary, complications are minimal, and the procedure can be done in a few minutes without hospitalization and without general anesthesia, or any anesthesia at all in most cases. The equipment is simple and inexpensive, and the technique can be performed by a trained paraprofessional as well as by a physician. Some clinics prefer to wait until a period is about two weeks late to perform the procedure, because only about half the women who have menstrual extraction before the seventh day after a delayed menstrual period turn out to be pregnant, whereas between the seventh and fourteenth days, about 85 percent are pregnant (Van der Vlugt and Piotrow, 1974).

Effects   A woman who undergoes this procedure may have intermittent menstrual-like flow during the following week, varying from spotting to regular flow. There may be cramps comparable to menstrual cramps, although this is not usually a problem. Some clinics recommend that the patient avoid intercourse for one week following the procedure and that her partner use a condom if there is intercourse the following week, because of the increased risk of infection. Conception is possible, and contraceptive measures should be used. If a menstrual period does not occur within four to five weeks after menstrual extraction, a woman should consult a physician to ascertain that no products of the pregnancy remain in the uterus and that no ectopic pregnancy exists. Absence of bleeding following the procedure may indicate that the woman was not pregnant. The relatively small amount of endometrial lining in the nonpregnant uterus is usually completely removed during the extraction (Van der Vlugt and Piotrow, 1973).

Avoidance of Menstruation   Some women have used menstrual extraction at the time of their menstrual periods, not because a pregnancy was suspected, but to eliminate menstrual bleeding and cramps and shorten the periods from several days to several minutes. When performed infrequently, this procedure is probably harmless if done by a trained person under sterile conditions. However, repeated menstrual extractions may damage the uterus. The uterine lining is pulled off with considerable

235

force, and more of the lining may be removed than would be shed during the regular menstrual flow. There is always some slight risk of infection. A woman should never try to perform the procedure herself (Cherniak and Feingold, 1973, p. 12).

Suction Abortion

Suction abortion, sucking the fetus out of the uterus through a narrow tube, is the most widely used method of abortion performed up to the twelfth week of pregnancy. This method is sometimes called *vacuum curettage* or *vacuum aspiration.* The procedure is rapid and simple, blood loss is slight, and the risk of complications is low. Local anesthetic is usually sufficient to prevent severe pain, and the risks of general anesthesia are unnecessary. The procedure is similar to that of menstrual extraction except that the suction is stronger and the suction tube larger. Because of the larger tube, it is necessary that the cervix be dilated before the tube can be inserted. Sometimes this is done by inserting a laminaria "stick" into the cervix a day or so before the abortion. The *laminaria,* a form of seaweed, expands as it absorbs moisture and causes the cervix to dilate. In another procedure, local anesthetic is injected near the cervix at the time of the abortion, and the cervix is then dilated by the insertion of increasingly larger rods.

Once the cervical opening is wide enough, the plastic suction tube, which is about one-third of an inch in diameter, is inserted into the uterus until it touches the fetus. Suction is applied for twenty to forty seconds. This breaks up the fetus and sucks it out into a vacuum bottle. The physician then scrapes the inner walls of the uterus with a spoonlike instrument called a curette to be certain that none of the fetus or placenta remains. (See Figure 7.4.)

Effects   Some women, especially those who have never previously given birth, may experience menstrual-like cramps during the procedure. Most women also experience a short period of cramping after the abortion. These cramps are usually not severe and last only a few hours. The abortion is followed by menstrual-like bleeding that lasts from one day to a week. Douching should be avoided because the cervix remains slightly dilated for a few days, and water or air forced into the uterine cavity could cause complications. After an early, uncomplicated abortion, intercourse can be resumed as soon as the woman feels ready. Ovulation will usually occur within ten to thirty-five days, so contraception should be used. Women who have Rh-negative blood should receive Rh-immune globulin (Rhogam) at the time of the abortion (Cherniak and Feingold, 1973, p. 45).

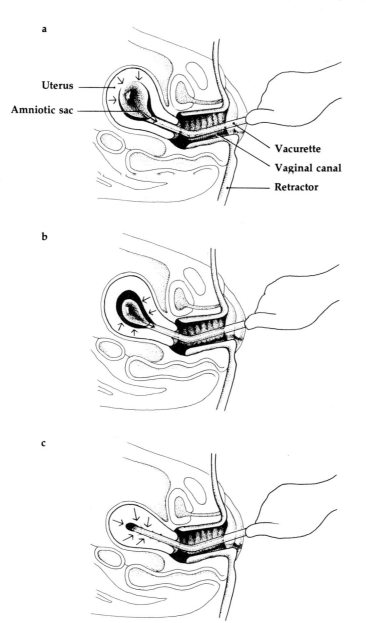

Figure 7.4

Side view of internal female reproductive organs showing suction abortion (vacuum aspiration)

a

Uterus

Amniotic sac

Vacurette

Vaginal canal

Retractor

b

c

Risk of Infection About fifteen women per thousand who have abortions develop pelvic infection following a suction abortion. Symptoms are usually fever, lower abdominal pain, and sometimes nausea and vomiting.   237

Antibiotic treatment is usually rapidly effective. In rare instances, small bits of the fetus or placenta remain in the uterus after the abortion and cause continuous bleeding and cramping. In these cases the suction procedure is repeated. Very rare complications of suction abortion are perforation of the uterus, which may require surgical repair, or heavy bleeding, which may require a blood transfusion. In a two-year period, between 1970 and 1972, the mortality rate in New York City was 1.5 per 100,000 suction abortions. Childbirth causes the death of a mother in about 23 per 100,000 pregnancies (Cherniak and Feingold, 1973, p. 46).

Many physicians feel that after about twelve weeks of pregnancy the fetus is too large and the uterus too soft for suction abortion to be performed safely. Many other physicians, however, use this method even in the twentieth week of pregnancy, combining suction with the use of crushing forceps and cervical dilatation by graduated dilators (*Medical World News*, January 10, 1977). After sixteen weeks the uterus and amniotic sac are large enough to permit abortion by a method that will stimulate the uterus to contract and expel the fetus.

Saline Abortion

In a *saline abortion* the usual procedure is to kill the fetus within the uterus by injecting a salt (saline) solution through the abdominal and uterine walls. The death of the fetus stops production of pregnancy-supporting hormones, and about six to forty-eight hours after the injection, contractions of the uterus usually begin. The cervical canal then gradually dilates, the amniotic sac eventually breaks open and releases the salty fluid through the vagina, and the contractions become harder and harder until the fetus is pushed out through the cervix and vagina.

Effects   A woman will have menstrual-like bleeding and cramps for several days following a saline abortion. Intercourse should be avoided until this bleeding has stopped. If symptoms such as severe menstrual cramps, lower abdominal pain, fever, heavy bleeding, nausea, or vomiting develop, they should be reported immediately to a physician. Because of possible complications from the use of the concentrated salt solution, saline abortion is not suitable for women who have severe high blood pressure or severe heart or kidney disease (Cherniak and Feingold, 1973, p. 46).

Complications   A saline abortion is both physically and psychologically more difficult for a woman than vacuum aspiration. Whenever possible, abortion should be performed before the twelfth week of pregnancy. Mortality rates for saline abortion are about the same as those for normal   238 childbirth. Possible complications include infection, incomplete abortion, heavy bleeding, and blood clots. Most of these are discovered and treated while the woman is still in the hospital (Cherniak and Feingold, 1973, p. 47).

Prostaglandins

Prostaglandins are naturally occurring chemical substances that contribute to contractions of smooth muscles such as those of the intestines and uterus. Prostaglandins also can cause degeneration of the *corpus luteum* (progesterone-secreting body) and therefore act as an *abortifacient* (abortion-causing agent). Prostaglandins are now frequently used instead of saline to induce abortion beyond the twelfth week of pregnancy and may ultimately replace saline for this purpose. They are now available in a vaginal suppository. These suppositories are limited to hospital use and are considered safer than saline for second-trimester abortion (*Medical World News*, December 26, 1979).

Hysterotomy

A less-used procedure that could be called a small Caesarean section, *hysterotomy* is a major surgical procedure in which incisions are made through the abdominal and uterine walls, and the fetus and placenta are removed. This procedure requires a hospital stay of about one week.

A hysterotomy usually is performed only when the fetus is more than twenty-four weeks old and is too large to be safely removed by other methods. A hysterotomy is difficult for both the woman having the abortion and the hospital personnel involved, because the fetus that is removed is alive and may move or cry before it dies.

Conclusion

Whether to use contraceptives and which ones to use are significant decisions, with implications for the individual, for personal relationships, and for society. On the individual level, the planned use of contraceptives indicates acceptance of oneself as a sexual being and a willingness to take responsibility for one's life and the life of potential human beings. In the context of a relationship, the careful planning of contraceptive use, the sterilization of one or both partners, and the use of abortion are the result of important mutual decisions that can have profound effects on the relationship in the present and in the future.

239

At the level of society, the sum of individual childbirth decisions is the birthrate, which is one of the primary determinants of the direction of society itself. The successful limitation of birthrates has international implications for decreasing poverty, famine, and distress among the world's people. Few individual and interpersonal decisions are as socially significant as those concerning contraception, sterilization, and abortion.

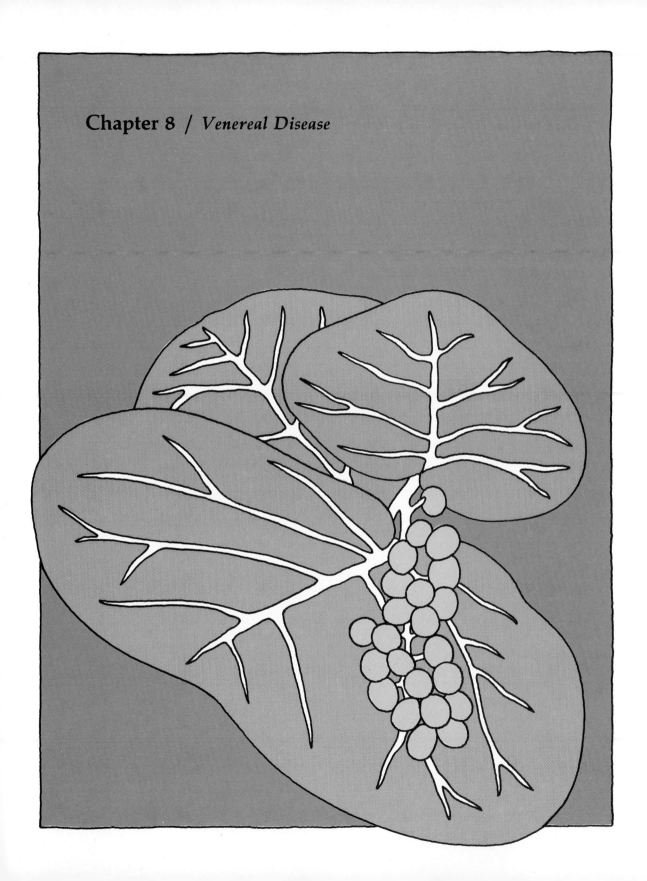

Chapter 8 / *Venereal Disease*

Venereal disease (VD) is often called a social disease because it is contracted and passed along by means of the social activity of sexual contact. There are several types of venereal disease, of which the most commonly known are gonorrhea and syphilis. The incidence of these and other types of venereal disease has outpaced the growth of population in the industrial nations of the twentieth century. Venereal disease has proved particularly difficult to bring under control, despite continually improved medical techniques and antibiotics that can prevent and cure it. Resistance to treatment is probably related to the peculiar combination of social and moral factors associated with venereal disease.

Venereal Disease as a Social Problem

At one level, venereal disease is simply a disease — amenable, like any other disease, to epidemiological measurement, cure, or prevention. However, attempts to measure the true incidence of venereal disease in a given population tend to be frustrated, because the number of cases reported is probably much lower than the actual incidence of the disease.

Even though disease symptoms may be checked free of charge at most public health facilities, some people do not seek medical care because they do not recognize the symptoms or because they are afraid of doctors. Most people who avoid treatment, however, do so because of the social stigma attached to VD or because of the requirement that they report all their sexual contacts.

Reporting Contacts

When an individual reports VD symptoms to a public health clinic, she or he is required to report the names and addresses of all persons with whom he or she has had sexual contact, in order to stop the spread of the disease. This may be so embarrassing that people either will not report the disease at all, or if they do, they will go to a private doctor who will not report contacts. Many homosexuals, for example, have regular VD checkups with private doctors who themselves are gay.

A male in his late twenties states: Every month I go to my doctor and have a checkup. I must have had VD a hundred times in my life. He is gay too, so he understands. I don't know what I would do if he was straight. . . . I call all the people up that I have had sex with if I know their names. Often I don't.

From the authors' files

242

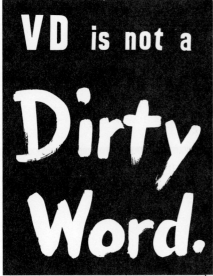

Get tested and treated confidentially and FREE

VENEREAL DISEASE CLINIC

VD will be less of a problem when people forget their embarrassment and seek immediate treatment for themselves and their sexual contacts.

Center for Disease Control, Atlanta, Georgia

On the other hand, some people may be less reluctant to go to a public health service than to a private doctor, or they may see both as stigmatizing.

A man in his mid-thirties recalls: When Rose told me she had VD, I was just horrified. I went to the public health service, and I sat there and felt perfectly humiliated. But I did not want to go to my regular doctor. That was worse because he knew me.

From the authors' files

243

Venereal Disease and Social Stigma

Unfortunately, venereal disease is not only a medical condition, it is also a social disease. The sexual interaction that preceded the infection is often itself stigmatized — premarital, promiscuous, extramarital, homosexual, or commercial — and the person is ashamed or afraid to admit such behavior to medical authorities or to family members.

In addition, the venereal disease itself is a stigma; a spouse infected by a wife or husband, for example, may feel as afraid or ashamed as a person who has had promiscuous contacts. Although people may be aware of their ethical responsibilities to warn contacts and public health authorities about infection, they may be unwilling to do so because of possible stigmatization.

In a society in which sexuality is glorified in the private media and yet hidden from the public eye, it is not surprising that people are reluctant to get treatment for a sex-related disease, despite the individually and socially damaging results of not reporting it. When the kinds of sexuality and sex partners that must be revealed are stigmatizing or even illegal, concealment becomes even more likely. Venereal disease is unlikely to become less of a problem, despite advances in medical technology, until the moral and legal approaches to sexual interaction are totally separated from the medical approach.

Types of Venereal Disease

There are many types of venereal disease, of varying degrees of seriousness. The degree of seriousness, however, varies from great to extreme. No venereal disease should be left untreated, because all are potentially dangerous to the diseased man or woman and, if untreated, to unborn children.

Gonorrhea

Gonorrhea is one of the oldest known diseases. Symptoms of gonorrhea are described in detail in the Old Testament in the Book of Leviticus, written about 1500 B.C., and descriptions of what may be gonorrhea are found in ancient Egyptian and Chinese writings. Today, more than three thousand years later, gonorrhea is one of the most often reported communicable diseases in the United States. A total of 874,161 cases were reported in the fiscal year ending June 30, 1974. Many more cases were not detected, and many others that were detected and treated were not

244

reported. The Public Health Service estimates there were actually around 2,700,000 new cases of gonorrhea in the United States in fiscal year 1974 (*Today's VD Control Problem*, 1975), about one new infection every twelve seconds (*VD Fact Sheet*, 1974). For the year 1978 the number of reported civilian cases of gonorrhea in the United States had increased to 1,013,056 (United States Public Health Service, January 2, 1979). It is estimated that 70 to 85 percent of cases are never reported, so the actual figure for 1978 may be around 4 million (*Science Digest*, July, 1979, p. 80). Some 230,000 women in the United States have gonococcal pelvic inflammatory disease (*PID*) each year and 10,400 consequently require surgical sterilization. Another estimated 40,000 to 50,000 become sterile because of tubal scarring and other damage from pelvic inflammatory disease resulting from gonorrhea (*Sexuality Today*, April 21, 1980).

The disease was named *gonorrhea* (Greek: *gonos*, seed; *rhoia*, a flow) because the disease-caused discharge in the male was originally thought to be loss of semen. Gonorrhea is also called "clap" and, by the French, *"la chaude pisse"* (hot piss) (*VD Handbook*).

Transmission   The causative agents of gonorrhea are bacteria, *Neisseria gonorrhoeae.* Commonly called gonococci, these were identified in 1879 by the German bacteriologist Neisser. They are sensitive and require conditions of warmth, moisture, and lack of oxygen in order to survive. These conditions are found in the mucous membranes: the moist linings of the mouth and throat, vagina, cervix, urethra, and anal canal — the parts of the body frequently brought into contact during sexual activity. Gonorrhea is transmitted through sexual relations, both heterosexual and homosexual, although it is not always caught during a single sexual contact with an infected partner. A man has a 20 to 50 percent chance of catching gonorrhea from a single sexual contact and a woman a greater than 50 percent chance. Repeated intercourse with an infected partner greatly increases the possibility of becoming infected. Gonorrhea can also be transmitted during the birth process to the eyes of a newborn as it passes through the birth canal.

Female Symptoms   Men and women are affected differently by this disease. About 80 percent of infected females have no apparent symptoms, even though in their abdomens the gonococcal infection is progressing unnoticed. Women with symptoms may notice a mild burning or smarting in the genital area, with or without a slight discharge. The vagina and cervix may be mildly inflamed. The endometrium, or inner lining of the uterus, is not usually conducive to multiplication of the bacteria except during menstruation, when the bacteria can multiply rapidly in the dead

245

cells and discharged blood of the uterine lining. During menstruation the infection will frequently move up the sides of the uterus and into the Fallopian tubes, where it will attack the inner walls. Pus forms and leaks out into the pelvic cavity and onto the ovaries. Pelvic inflammatory disease *(PID)* results. Frequently the tubes are left blocked by scar tissue. Symptoms may be severe pain and fever or only a feeling of heaviness and a dull aching of the groin or back. Menstruation may become irregular and painful, with PID symptoms peaking a few days after each period. Ovaries can be affected and production of ovarian hormones disrupted. Early treatment may prevent permanent tube blockage but cannot repair damage already done.

Most treated women experience no further symptoms, but some, even though the infection is no longer present, experience chronic residual pain due to scarring, adhesions, and other damage. Sometimes this is so severe that removal of the uterus and tubes becomes necessary for relief (*VD Handbook*, pp. 17–18). An untreated infection usually subsides after a few weeks, but it is followed by a chronic infection that may last for years and cause extensive damage to the reproductive organs. Unfortunately, in most cases symptoms in the female are so slight and mild that they arouse little or no concern and the internal damage goes unnoticed. Many women first become aware of their own infection when a partner develops symptoms.

Other possible, but infrequent, complications of gonorrhea in both men and women include pimplelike lesions on the extremities, arthritic inflammation of the joints and membranes around the tendons, spinal cord, and brain, and inflammation of the heart lining and valves. Gonococcal infection of the throat can be experienced as a sore throat and tonsillitis. Anal infection rarely has noticeable symptoms, although sometimes there may be mild irritation or mucous discharge, or, more rarely, burning pain in the anus and blood or pus in the feces.

Male Symptoms About 85 percent of infected males notice gonorrhea symptoms within seven days after exposure, most within two to four days. The urethral canal becomes inflamed, causing a sharp, burning pain during urination. There is a discharge from the penis because of the presence of white blood cells destroying the gonococci. This is thick at first, later thinner and watery.

A male in his early thirties recalls: The only time I ever got anything was when I was in Vietnam. It didn't seem like much — just a burning when I urinated — but at least I knew enough to go right away and get some penicillin for it. . . . I wasn't surprised. It was my own fault because I knew I should have used rubbers in a situation like that, but I just hate those things.

From the authors' files

246

If there is no treatment, these symptoms usually subside after two or three weeks. However, the disease is still present and contagious, and may affect the prostate gland and testicles, which can become inflamed and tender and sometimes abscessed. If the testicles become infected and remain untreated, sperm passage becomes blocked and sterility results (*VD Handbook*).

A new gonococcal strain has recently been identified that produces urethral infections with no apparent symptoms in white males, but rarely infects nonwhites (*Medical World News*, March 7, 1977). Control of gonorrhea is very difficult because asymptomatic carriers are difficult to identify without routine screening of all high-risk persons.

Diagnosis and Treatment Gonorrhea is diagnosed through the culturing of material taken from the cervix of a woman or from the urethra of a man, or sometimes from the anal canal or throat.

The preferred drug for treatment of gonorrhea is either penicillin or ampicillin. When both are contraindicated, spectinomycin or tetracycline are usually used. It may take as long as five days for the infection to clear completely, and sexual activity should be avoided for a minimum of five days after treatment so that partners are not infected or reinfected. In the male, permanent or residual damage is rare; total recovery is the rule. However, strains of a so-called super gonorrhea are being reported that are resistant to all antibiotics currently used in the treatment of VD (*San Diego Union*, January 17, 1980).

Cure rate after initial treatment for gonorrhea is about 90 percent. This means up to 10 percent of people treated will require further antibiotic treatment. If the disease is not completely cured, symptoms may disappear, but the disease can cause internal damage and still be passed on to sexual partners. Therefore, it is essential that a follow-up culture be done. One source (*VD Handbook*, p. 26) recommends that three separate negative cultures be obtained before treatment is considered complete, one within a week of receiving treatment and the second and third the following week. Use of a condom provides some, but not total, protection against gonorrhea.

Syphilis

The disease rate of gonorrhea has been increasing constantly for nearly twenty years; the number of cases reported in fiscal year 1974 was the greatest number reported since the Public Health Service began keeping records fifty-five years ago (*Today's VD Control Problem*, p. 11). The number of cases of syphilis, however, has remained about the same — around

247

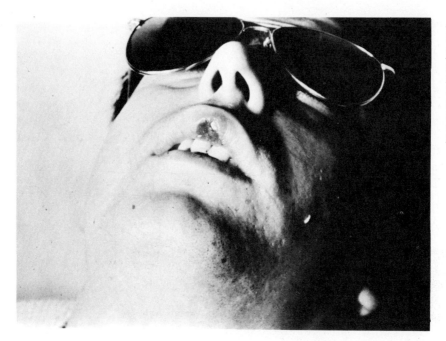

twenty-five thousand annually in recent years. The Public Health Service estimates the number of actual new cases, both reported and unreported, to be about eighty thousand each year.

Treponema pallidum is the delicate, corkscrewlike spirochete that causes syphilis. It requires warmth and moisture to survive and can be washed from the skin and destroyed with soap and water. However, *Treponema pallidum* can enter the body through intact skin, reach the blood stream a few hours after entry, and begin spreading throughout the body. Syphilis, if untreated, then develops in several stages.

Primary Syphilis In the first stage a *chancre* (lesion) appears at the site where the organism invaded the body between ten days and three months after sexual contact with the infected person. The chancre starts as a red bump that soon becomes an open sore, and may be covered with a gray or yellow crusty scab. It does not bleed easily and is painless. It may be surrounded by a thin pink border, the edges may be raised and hard, and the whole area may feel hard. If untreated it will heal in one to five weeks after it appears. In men the chancre usually appears on the glans or coronal area of the penis and may also appear around the opening, on the shaft, or on the scrotum. In women the chancre usually appears on the cervix or inner vaginal walls and often goes undetected. It may also appear on the lips of the vagina, the clitoris, or the urinary opening. In both

248

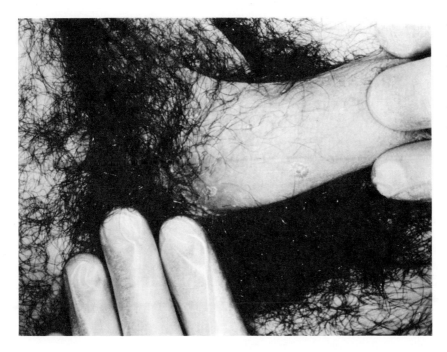

A syphilitic chancre on the shaft of the penis.
Photo by Nicholas J. Fiumara, M.D., M.P.H., Director, Division of Communicable Diseases, Department of Public Health, the Commonwealth of Massachusetts

A chancre on the lips of the vagina, a symptom of primary syphilis.
Photo by Nicholas J. Fiumara, M.D., M.P.H., Director, Division of Communicable Diseases, Department of Public Health, the Commonwealth of Massachusetts

249

men and women chancres resulting from oral-genital contact may appear on the lips, tongue, or tonsils, and occasionally on other parts of the body, usually where a bite or scratch was acquired during lovemaking. If infection resulted from anal contact, the chancre may appear around or in the anus. In most cases only one chancre will appear; occasionally there are more.

Secondary Syphilis When primary syphilis is not treated, the disease continues into the secondary stage. After the chancre heals, the infected person has no outward symptoms for a while but can still infect others. Between two weeks and six months after the chancre appears, a generalized skin rash develops. It may last a few days or a few weeks and may or may not be accompanied by headaches, loss of appetite, nausea, constipation, aching bones, muscles, or joints, and a slight persistent fever. Symptoms are usually distressing enough that medical treatment is sought, although the disease may not be recognized. Syphilis has been called the great masquerader because its symptoms are similar to those of so many other diseases.

Treatment with penicillin during either the primary or secondary stages is rapidly effective, and the infected person recovers without permanent effects. Without treatment secondary syphilis symptoms disappear within two to six weeks, occasionally longer, and the disease enters a more dangerous stage.

Latent Syphilis During the latent stage the disease is hidden. About 25 percent of untreated individuals re-experience the primary chancre and secondary symptoms sometime during the first two years of latent syphilis. These disappear in a few weeks, and the disease once again becomes hidden. After about a year the disease is no longer contagious, except in cases of women who become pregnant. Women with latent syphilis can pass the disease to their unborn children. Treatment in early pregnancy can prevent congenital syphilis in the child. Most untreated women miscarry, have stillborn infants, or give birth to children with the congenital disease.

Late (Tertiary) Syphilis About two-thirds of those who remain untreated have no further problems with the disease. The other third develop the further complications of late syphilis, which include ulceration of an internal organ (three to seven years after infection), fatal heart and major blood vessel damage (ten to forty years), or spinal cord and brain involvement leading to paralysis, insanity, and eventually death (ten to twenty years).

Diagnosis and Treatment   Diagnosis of syphilis is accomplished through microscopic examination of fluid from a chancre or through a blood test. Routine blood tests are performed on all people who enter a hospital, apply for a marriage license, give blood, or enter the military, and on all pregnant women. Penicillin is the preferred treatment for syphilis, with tetracycline or erythromycin used for those who are penicillin-sensitive (*VD Handbook*).

Nongonococcal Urethritis

Nongonococcal urethritis (NGU), also called *nonspecific urethritis (NSU),* is any inflammation of the male urethra not caused by the gonococcus organism. NGU is probably not one disease, but a set of symptoms that can be caused by one of a number of organisms. Most NSUs have in common that they do not respond to penicillin but can be cured by tetracycline. The condition may also sometimes be caused not by an organism but by chemical irritation from soaps, deodorant sprays, or vaginal contraceptives. Symptoms are a thin, usually clear, discharge from the penis. The discharge may be continuous but in many cases is noticed only in the morning before urinating. Some men experience a thick, white, creamy discharge. Mild to moderate pain is usually experienced when urinating. Usually sex partners have no sign of infection, although in some cases a partner will be found to be asymptomatically carrying a causative organism.

NGU has become our most common sexually transmitted disease. It is estimated that $2\frac{1}{2}$ million Americans will be afflicted by it during 1980. Although the symptoms of NGU are mild or may go unnoticed, its effects may be serious. Men may develop inflammation of the seminal ducts and testes, narrowing of the urethra, and prostate inflammation. In infected women the disease may cause blockage of the Fallopian tubes and pelvic inflammation. For infants born to infected mothers, the risk of eye infection is 40 to 50 percent, and the risk of a pneumonia-like illness is about 5 to 10 percent (Galton, 1980).

Vaginitis

Vaginal infection *(vaginitis)* is attributable to *Trichomonas vaginalis, Hemophilus vaginalis,* or *Candida albicans* in more than 95 percent of cases (Burmeister and Gardner). Chemical irritation can also cause vaginal inflammation.

251

Trichomonas Vaginalis   A profuse, frothy white or yellow discharge with an unpleasant odor and accompanied by itching, inflammation, and a vaginal pH of 5 or higher is strong evidence of trichomoniasis. This disease is usually transmitted through sexual contact; however, *Trichomonas* can survive for several hours at room temperature on moist objects, such as toilet seats, washcloths, and towels, and can infect a woman whose genitals come into close contact with them. The organisms can be carried under the foreskin of an uncircumcised male and can infect the male prostate. Most infected males are carriers with no symptoms and pass the organisms into a woman's vagina in their semen. Treatment is with metronidazole, a drug produced under the brand name Flagyl; both partners must receive treatment. To prevent re-exchanging the organism back and forth, a condom should be used or intercourse avoided during treatment.

Candida Albicans   The microscopic yeastlike fungus *Candida albicans* (monilia; yeast) is present on the skin and in the mouth, vagina, and large intestine of many healthy people. Only when conditions are right for the organisms to flourish in large numbers does a disease state result. Many women carry *Candida* in their vaginas without active vaginitis. Some of the ways the organisms can reach the vagina are from a woman's own anus, from the foreskin of an uncircumcised male, or from a partner's throat during oral-genital contact. Profuse discharge and disagreeable odor are *not* features of this disease. The most significant symptom is intense vaginal and vulval itching. The vagina is usually red and dry with the pH of vaginal secretions between 3.8 and 5. Discharge, which is not heavy, is thick, white, and curdlike, somewhat like cottage cheese. Most often, treatment is with vaginal tablets or creams; sometimes oral tablets are also taken. The condition can be quite persistent and difficult to control.

Conditions like pregnancy, diabetes, and the taking of birth control pills with more than 0.05 milligrams of estrogen cause an increase in the amount of sugar in vaginal cells and thereby create an environment in which the yeast organisms can thrive and multiply. Any woman who is not pregnant and has repeated yeast infections should be tested for diabetes. Fatigue, malnutrition, stress, emotional upset, and any other conditions that lower a woman's natural resistance to disease can also make her more susceptible to *Candida* vaginitis (*VD Handbook*; Burmeister and Gardner). Some women treat themselves with yogurt whenever they experience vaginal discharge or itching. This can be unwise because yogurt is not the best treatment for every type of vaginal problem.

A forty-two-year-old woman reports: I was feeling a good deal of itching in my vaginal area, and a friend told me about yogurt so I bought some and spread it on. It seemed to work and the itch went away. But next time I got an itch there

From the authors' files

the yogurt didn't work and when I went to the doctor he said I should forget about the yogurt and get to him right away when I have these symptoms.

Taking antibiotics will destroy certain beneficial vaginal bacteria that normally keep yeast organisms from flourishing. Yogurt contains some of these same bacteria, and some women use a small amount of unsweetened yogurt in their vagina several times a day when they are taking antibiotics as a preventive measure to keep yeast from flourishing.

Hemophilus Vaginalis The most common sign of *Hemophilus vaginalis* is a gray discharge with a pH of 5 to 5.5 and a characteristic disagreeable odor. The discharge may be scant or heavy, but is usually less profuse than that of trichomoniasis. Hemophilus is a venereal disease, and reinfection can be anticipated if sexual partners are not treated. Vaginal suppositories are usually prescribed for the vaginitis, and ampicillin is taken orally by both partners (Burmeister and Gardner).

Genital Warts

Genital warts are caused by a virus similar to the one that causes common skin warts on other parts of the body. It is currently believed that venereal warts are usually transmitted by sexual contact, although they have been found on individuals whose only sexual partner had no sign of the condition. Genital warts appear one to three months after intercourse with an infected partner. In men they most commonly appear on the glans, foreskin, opening, or shaft of the penis, or the scrotum, in that order of frequency. They may also appear around the anus after anal intercourse. Women usually have the warts on the lower part of the vaginal opening, but the lips, inner vagina, and cervix can also be affected. Small warts are usually treated with a chemical that causes the warts to dry up and fall off; larger warts are removed surgically *(VD Handbook).*

Herpes Genitalis

There are two types of *Herpes simplex* virus. Type 1 usually causes cold sores, fever blisters on the face, and eye infections. Type 1 causes only about 10 percent of genital herpes infections. *Herpes simplex Type 2* is usually acquired through sexual contact and is the predominant cause of genital herpes infections. In women, genital *Herpes* will most frequently appear on the vaginal lips. Other sites may be the clitoris, outer portion of the vagina, the anus, and the cervix. The glans and shaft of the penis are the most common sites in men. Sometimes blisters will appear around the anus of men who experience anal intercourse. The sores may be ex- 253 tremely painful for four or five days, and the healing process generally takes ten to twenty days.

When the *Herpes* virus invades the body, it causes symptoms for only a short time and then becomes dormant and continues living in the body cells, usually without producing symptoms, for the rest of the person's life. In some people infections do recur, usually when resistance is low due to other illness, fever, emotional upset, stress, fatigue, and so on.

Women who are taking oral contraceptives have significantly fewer recurrences than women not on the pill. Patients not taking the pill had an average of one recurrence every fifty-one days as compared to a recurrence every eighty-two days for pill users. Severity and duration of symptoms were the same in both pill users and nonusers. Women using birth control pills were three times more likely to stay free of recurrence than those not on the pill (*Medical World News,* April 4, 1977).

Women with Type 2 *Herpes simplex* are eight times more likely to get cervical cancer than are women who do not have the infection (Blough and Giuntoli, 1979). A routine Pap test (a smear taken from tissues at the tip of the cervix) every six months can permit early enough detection of cancerous or precancerous conditions of the cervix, if they should occur, to make these conditions curable. An infant can acquire *Herpes* during birth passage through an infected cervix or vagina. It may be that some babies are infected while still in the uterus and that *Herpes* infection is the cause of some stillbirths and miscarriages. Some infected newborns recover completely, and others develop fatal brain infection.

No antibiotic yet available kills the *Herpes* virus. Most treatment is focused on relieving pain, speeding healing, and preventing additional infection by other organisms *(VD Handbook).* A new drug called 2-deoxy-D-glucose has been found effective against *Herpes* in 95 percent of the cases tested (Blough and Giuntoli, 1979). However, it is still experimental and has not been licensed by the Food and Drug Administration for use by practicing physicians.

Because *Herpes genitalis* continues to live in the body cells and may cause recurrent infections, it can be a very discouraging illness for both the infected person and the physician.

A nurse-practitioner at a university health clinic reports: Doctor Smith says he just won't take any more VD patients with herpes because it is getting him down too much. He has some now that keep getting the symptoms over and over again — sometimes every time they have intercourse it makes it start up again — and there is just *nothing* we can do about it. There's no cure. We can give them medication for the symptoms but we can't stop it from coming back.   From the authors' files

254

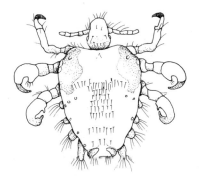

Figure 8.1
Pubic louse

Pubic Lice (Crabs)

A pubic louse is yellowish gray and about the size of a pinhead. (See Figure 8.1.) It attaches its claws to a pubic hair and inserts its mouth into the skin, where it remains, feeding from tiny blood vessels. When filled with blood it may appear as a rust-colored speck. A female louse will lay about three eggs a day during her thirty-day lifetime. She cements each firmly to a pubic hair, near the skin, where it will remain for seven to nine days until it hatches.

   Pubic lice are transmitted by close physical contact and sometimes through clothing, a sleeping bag, or a bed belonging to an infected person. The most common symptom is an intolerable itching, probably caused by an allergic reaction to the bites. Some people develop a rash that appears as small, sky-blue spots. Others experience no symptoms. Scratching usually does not relieve the itching but often carries the lice under the fingernails to other hairy parts of the body. One or two treatments with an appropriate nonprescription cream, lotion, powder, or shampoo will bring rapid relief from the itching and will kill the lice and eggs *(VD Handbook)*.

Conclusion

The seriousness of venereal disease varies from the itching annoyance of crabs to the deadly, often hidden scourges of syphilis. Shame, however, may occur with only the suspicion of any of these diseases. To the extent that sex and sex-related diseases are still considered shameful or dirty in our society, changes in social attitudes will have to accompany progress in medical technology if venereal disease is ever to be prevented and cured.

Part III / *Sexuality and the Life Cycle: Typical Patterns*

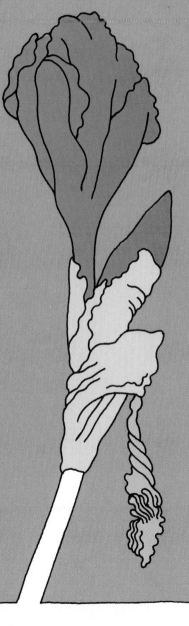

The typical life cycle in the United States has a certain pattern. People are expected to engage in certain sexual behavior at certain ages, and refrain from the same behavior at other periods of the life cycle. Some of these expectations are tied to biology: for example, girls are not expected to menstruate at age six, nor women to give birth at age seventy. Other expectations, however, are more directly social. A woman may be capable of giving birth between the ages of twelve and fifty, but in our society she typically limits her childbearing to her twenties and thirties, with some overlap into her teens and early forties.

The Life Cycle

In addition to different social expectations in regard to sexuality and reproduction, societies have different definitions of the life cycle itself, which, again, are only partly tied to biological factors. Aries (1962), for example, notes that in preindustrial societies childhood was not recognized as a distinct part of the life cycle; children were portrayed in pictures and statues as miniature adults, and were sometimes married and living away from their biological families as early as four or five years old.

Few societies aside from industrialized ones have an "adolescent" stage between childhood and adulthood. In the typical hunting-and-gathering or agrarian society, children undergo "rites of passage," either formal or informal, that signal their entry into adulthood. Children may undergo these rites as early as thirteen, or younger   257 (as in the case of the Jewish bar mitzvah and bat mitzvah), or well into biological maturity. For example, rural Irish small-farm owners are not entitled to many of the perquisites of adulthood until they inherit the family farm, which may not occur until the "child" of the family is in his forties.

In our society, the life cycle is very roughly divided into five phases: childhood, adolescence, young adulthood, middle age, and old age. These phases tend to shade into one another rather than being marked by definite rites of passage, and there may also be extreme social and biological variations within each category. For example, a person of sixty and a person of ninety might be considered "elderly"; they are considered "the same" socially but they could be quite different physiologically and psychologically. A child of six months, however, is different socially, as well as physiologically and psychologically, from a child of six; yet both are categorized as "children."

Childhood in our society ends approximately with the onset of puberty. The childhood category is often divided into phases beginning with infancy and going through toddler and other stages. As indicated in Chapter 2, childhood is considered an active phase in the development of sexuality by psychologists and others influenced by the Freudian theory of childhood sexuality. However, as Gagnon (1974) notes, at this point in the life cycle the child's sexuality is part of a series of other types of learning, such as the learning of basic motor and language skills, and basic social categories, including family affiliation and gender identity.

Adolescence is a time of physiological, sexual, and reproductive-system changes, as outlined in Chapter 10, and also of psychological and social stress, at least in industrial societies. During adolescence, the child is gradually metamorphosed into an adult member of society, moving through the educational system into a job and a marriage, the twin symbols of Western adult status.

In our society, young adulthood tends to begin with financial independence from parents or with marriage. Therefore, young adulthood does not begin at a definite age, but can vary from the late teens into the early thirties or even later.

At least until recent times, middle age in industrial society has been a time of "settling down" and "settling in" to marriage, occupation, child rearing, and financial responsibility. It is the longest-lasting phase in the life cycle (unless the aged phase lasts a good deal longer than usual), continuing generally from the late twenties to the sixties.

Old age in our society, like middle age, is defined primarily in relation to occupation. Women are often required to retire from their jobs at sixty-two, and men at sixty-five. Like the other phases, old age is marked by physiological changes that enable the aged to be identified visually.

Sexuality and the Life Cycle

As indicated in subsequent chapters, each of these five phases of the life cycle is defined sexually by a series of assumptions about "appropriate" and "inappropriate" sexual, romantic, and marital behavior, feelings, and attitudes. Some of these appropriate and inappropriate behaviors and attitudes are clearly definable, such as the appropriateness of getting married sometime between the teens and the thirties, or the inappropriateness of marrying one's grandparent. Other behaviors and attitudes are more ambiguous.

In our society heterosexual genital sexual intercourse between married partners is considered to be the sexual norm. However, there are certain other activities that have a marginal acceptance within the norms, and that are somewhat widespread; for example, premarital sexual intercourse, extramarital sexual interaction, oral-genital contact, and masturbation.

Although extramarital sexual interaction is very common, it is included in Part 4, since it does not seem to have gained much widespread public acceptance. On the other hand, premarital sexual intercourse seems to be on the margin of social acceptability, at least among the adolescents and young adults who practice it, so we include it in Part 3.

As an alternative form of sexual interaction, oral-genital contact is common enough, and accepted enough in the public's attitudes, to be included as an institutionalized part of the sexual life cycle. Similarly, masturbation is considered "normal" by most people today, particularly in adolescence. Contemporary acceptance of these forms of noncoital sex is in contrast with nineteenth-century attitudes, which condemned oral sex and masturbation as perverted and likely to have dire medical and social consequences (Bullough, 1975). Earlier prohibitions against oral sex, of course, are still entrenched in the legal codes of many states. Interestingly, masturbation is not illegal in any state.

In the following three chapters, the typical sexual patterns associated with the five stages of the life cycle are analyzed. The data on sexuality in old age are included in the chapter on adulthood, mainly because such data are rather sparse. This sparsity itself suggests the interdependence of behavior, social definitions, and scientific analysis: sexuality among the elderly is somewhat stigmatized in our society, so the lack of data on it may be attributable either to a lack of such sexual behavior, a lack of willingness to admit to it, or a lack of scientific attention to it. Such an interdependence is an inevitable feature of any discussion of sexuality and the life cycle.

Chapter 9 / *Sexuality in Infancy and Childhood*

When a baby is born it is declared to be either a boy or a girl. In most instances the label of gender greatly influences the baby's life chances starting with birth and continuing until death, because society prescribes different treatment for the sexes. Differences in treatment of males and females in our culture are based in part on physical differences between the sexes. Other differences in treatment are based on traits whose link with biology is more open to question; for example, the assumptions that men are more logical and more aggressive and that women are more emotional and more nurturing.

Gender Identity

It is important to examine assumptions about maleness and femaleness in light of recent scientific findings concerning the developing of gender identity and gender role. *Gender identity* is a persistent conviction that one is either a male or a female. *Gender role* is everything a person says or does to indicate that he or she is either male or female. Gender role is the public expression of gender identity; gender identity is the private expression of gender-role (Mazur and Money, 1980, p. 4). The individual's concept of maleness and femaleness, and hence her or his gender identity, will depend largely on the cultural definition of appropriate masculine and feminine behavior.

The awareness that one is a female or a male, usually called *core gender identity,* occurs between the ages of eighteen months and three years. This early identity is modified and expanded through social interaction with other people in childhood, adolescence, and adulthood. Gender identity of a mature person may be elaborated in terms such as "I am a very feminine female" or "I am a somewhat masculine female."

This section will focus on the means by which an individual develops both gender identity and the behavior appropriate to it. Although the discussion centers on the development of a gender identity culturally appropriate to the ascribed sex, one should be aware that this does not always occur. A male who is physiologically male in every respect may be convinced that he is really a female trapped in a male body; a biological female may have a male gender identity. Instances of this type of culturally inappropriate gender identity are discussed in more detail in Chapter 13.

Biological Differences Between Males and Females

The development of gender identity begins with the sex chromosomes. The X or Y sex chromosome of the male parent, when added to the X   262 chromosome always supplied by the female parent, determines the genetic sex of the offspring. When a Y chromosome is added and development goes according to plan, male differentiation of the fetus occurs. When an X chromosome is added and development goes according to plan, female differentiation occurs.

Prior to the sixth week of gestation, the fetus has undifferentiated and primitive gonads that are capable of developing into either typically female reproductive organs or typically male reproductive organs. As internal structures, all fetuses have both Mullerian ducts, from which ovaries, Fallopian tubes, upper vagina, and uterus can develop; and Wolffian ducts, from which testes, vas deferens, seminal vesicles, prostate, and ejaculatory ducts can develop. (See Figure 9.1.) The external genitals of all fetuses appear identical in the very early gestation period, and may develop either a male or a female appearance.

Beginning around the sixth week of gestation the Y chromosome, if present, programs the undifferentiated gonads toward development of testes by means of an H-Y antigen. The male testes then secrete androgen and Mullerian inhibiting substance *(MIS)* at about the sixth week of gestation. Androgen assures that the Wolffian ducts develop into male internal reproductive organs; MIS ensures that the Mullerian ducts do not develop.

In the absence of a Y chromosome, no H-Y antigen is secreted, testes do not secrete androgen and MIS, and the Mullerian ducts develop into the internal female reproductive organs. As far as is known, the fetal ovaries do not secrete hormones. The mechanism in females that causes Mullerian development and suppresses Wolffian development is not known (Mazur and Money, 1980, pp. 5–6).

Whereas the male and female internal genital structures develop from two separate primitive structures, the external genitals develop from identical beginnings. (See Figure 9.2.) If the fetus is female and produces no androgen, the genital tubercle (nodule) becomes the clitoris and the skin around it forms the hood of the clitoris and the labia minora. The labioscrotal swellings remain separate and form the labia majora.

If the fetus is male and produces androgen, masculinization of the external genitals begins about the eighth week of life. The genital tubercle enlarges to become a penis and the skin surrounding it wraps around the penis to form the foreskin. The labioscrotal swellings fuse and form the scrotum.

The presence or absence of fetal androgen programs not only the differentiation of the internal and external genitalia, but also the differentiation of sex-related pathways in the brain. It is not known exactly how androgen causes brain differentiation (Mazur and Money, 1980, p. 7). Apparently, androgen affects the organization of the hypothalamus, which among other things is responsible for controlling the pituitary

Fetus Before Sixth Week of Pregnancy (Sex Organs Identical)

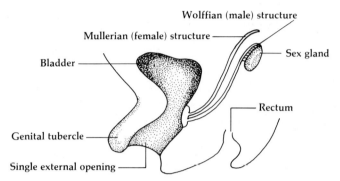

Wolffian (male) structure

Mullerian (female) structure

Sex gland

Bladder

Rectum

Genital tubercle

Single external opening

Figure 9.1

Three stages in the differentiation of internal genital organs

Fetus After Sixth Week of Pregnancy

Female

Male

Fallopian tube

Uterus

Mullerian structures

Sex gland ovary

Genital tubercle

Male remnants

Female remnants

Sex glands

Wolffian structure or vas

Prostate

Genital tubercle

Female remnants

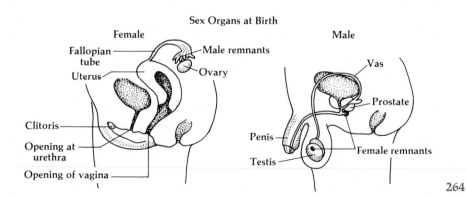

Sex Organs at Birth

Female

Male

Fallopian tube

Uterus

Clitoris

Opening at urethra

Opening of vagina

Male remnants

Ovary

Vas

Prostate

Penis

Testis

Female remnants

Fetus Before Sixth Week of Pregnancy (Sex Organs Identical)

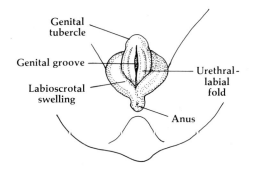

Genital
tubercle

Genital groove

Labioscrotal
swelling

Urethral-
labial
fold

Anus

Figure 9.2

*Three stages in the
differentiation of the
external genital
organs*

Fetus After Sixth Week of Pregnancy

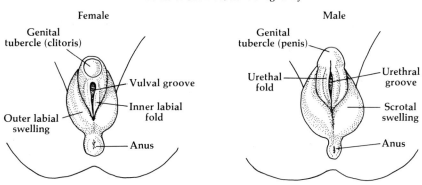

Female

Genital
tubercle (clitoris)

Vulval groove

Inner labial
fold

Outer labial
swelling

Anus

Male

Genital
tubercle (penis)

Urethal
fold

Urethral
groove

Scrotal
swelling

Anus

Sex Organs at Birth

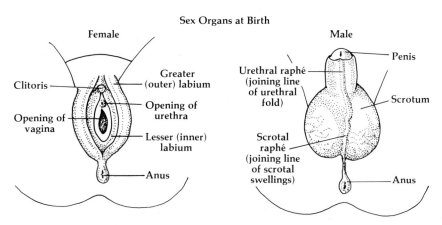

Female

Clitoris

Opening of
vagina

Greater
(outer) labium

Opening of
urethra

Lesser (inner)
labium

Anus

Male

Urethral raphé
(joining line
of urethral
fold)

Scrotal
raphé
(joining line
of scrotal
swellings)

Penis

Scrotum

Anus

gland. The pituitary gland in turn causes a cyclic hormonal pattern in females but not in males, as it stimulates the ovaries in the female and the testes in the male.

In addition to the obviously different sexual organs, males and females develop many other physical differences. For example, in most countries males are the weaker sex in terms of life expectancy. Although 120 males are conceived for every 100 females, only 105 of the males live to be born. During the first year of life the death rate for males exceeds that for females by about 25 percent. The average life expectancy of white females in the United States today is seventy-three years while that for males is approximately six years less (Dengrove, 1973).

Although weaker in terms of life expectancy, in every known human society the average male is taller, heavier, and stronger than the female. He has a higher metabolic rate, requires more food, and produces more physical energy than the female does. His heart pumps more forcibly and his blood contains more red corpuscles, giving him a greater oxygen supply for physical exertion. In contrast to the male's physical strength is his developmental retardation. His growth velocity lags nearly two years behind the female's, and physiological maturity is achieved about two and one-half years later than the female's (Hutt, 1972; Dengrove, 1973).

These differences between males and females are only arithmetic averages for the two sexes; they are not true of every male compared to every female. Some females are taller and stronger than some males; some males mature faster than some females. Furthermore, the average female in the United States is taller and heavier than the average male in India.

Behavioral Differences Between Males and Females

Differences between males and females in life expectancy and growth are usually accepted as innate and biological. Behavioral differences are not so clearly tied to male and female physiology. In childhood, for example, girls have a greater preference for indoor and more sedentary activities. In contrast, boys tend to be more active, aggressive, and unruly than girls (Dengrove, 1973). It is possible that the greater incidence of aggressive behavior in boys is the result of social learning rather than of innate biological differences between the sexes. There is some evidence that in our culture dependent behavior is less rewarded for males and physically aggressive behavior is less rewarded for females (Kagan, 1977). One study of seventh-grade boys and girls revealed that girls more often than boys reported that their parents were affectionate. The boys more often reported that parents were rejecting, hostile, and ignoring. More research is needed to clarify the relationships between the way children are raised and their development of gender identify (Mischel, 1966).

Very young children often freely express loving feelings toward each other. Older boys may not do this if they are taught that it is not proper behavior for males.

Suzanne Szasz

Physiological Factors in Gender Identity

Nevertheless, some evidence indicates that behavioral differences between males and females have some physiological basis, at least for animals. Researchers have found that female laboratory animals given androgen during a critical developmental period will exhibit patterns of activity that are most often found in the male of the species. For example, androgen-treated female monkeys initiated play, engaged in rough-and-tumble play, and threatened more frequently than untreated females. (The threat response of rhesus monkeys involves stiffening of posture, staring at the other monkey, flattening the hair on top of the head, retracting the lips, and baring the teeth.) When placed with a normal receptive female, the androgen-treated females attempted the mounting and pelvic-thrusting motions typical of the male during copulation (Young, Goy, and Phoenix, 1964).

Studies of humans yield results similar to those in studies of lower mammals. Human females exposed to abnormally high levels of fetal androgens show a low interest in some aspects of maternal behavior. In one study of androgenized females, a majority stated that having children usually did not enter their thoughts, dreams, or fantasies. Only a very few stated a desire to be affectionate to small infants. In contrast, females with one missing sex chromosome (XO instead of normal female XX chromosomal pattern) or genetic males who were insensitive to androgens in the

267

fetal state exhibited a maternal response considered typically female. All of them stated that having children frequently entered their thoughts, dreams, and fantasies, and a majority stated they strongly desired to cuddle and hold a small infant (Ehrhardt, 1973).

A similar conclusion as to the importance of biological factors affecting gender identity and behavior was reached through a study of patients who had normal-appearing genitals at birth, but who felt they were of the opposite sex and often behaved in ways more associated with the opposite sex, even though they were raised in a manner appropriate to their apparent gender. At puberty it was discovered that in spite of normal-appearing genitals, they were genetically of the opposite sex and had internal organs and hormones typical of the opposite sex. Apparently their gender identity and behavior had been influenced by their genetic sex (Stoller, 1968, pp. 17–28). A consideration of evidence of this nature leads one author to conclude:

From the moment of birth onwards, differences in structure, in metabolism, in physiological and psychological functions characterize the development of the two sexes. Many of these noncognitive differences are shared not only with other societies which manifest very different culture patterns but with other primates as well. The similarity in many attentive, exploratory, and social behaviors between monkeys, chimpanzees and children is remarkable, and this fact alone makes a purely environmental interpretation of sex differences difficult to countenance.

Hutt, 1972, p. 112

Social Factors in Gender Identity

An equally impressive body of evidence exists for the argument that gender is determined by social rather than biological factors. One group of researchers analyzed the development of gender identity by studying children with external genitals that appear to be of one gender while their internal and chromosomal sex is of the other. In one instance they studied two children, both of whom were genetically and endocrinologically female with the normal internal sex structures of females, but with external genitals that appeared masculine. At birth one of these children was correctly designated as a female and the other incorrectly labeled a male. By the time they were five years old, the one who was believed to be a girl felt no doubt that she was a girl, and the one believed to be a boy was equally certain that he was a boy. Their mannerisms and behavior were correct for their assigned sex even though the boy had the biological make-up of a female. From a number of studies of this type the researchers have concluded that all people have the potential for either male

268

*When we give little
girls lots of affection
and pretty dresses, we
are teaching them what
we think is proper for
females in our culture.*
Henri Cartier-Bresson/
Magnum Photos, Inc.

or female behavior and identity at the moment of birth. It is not biological sex but life experiences that determine gender identity and behavior (Money, 1965b; Hampson and Hampson, 1961).

Anthropological studies also lend weight to this argument. The expectation in our culture is that males are more sexually active, more dominant, more aggressive, less nurturant, and less emotionally expressive than females. The existence of these differences in the United States has been fairly well documented (Gadpaille, 1973). But in some cultures many of the differences between men and women that we so readily accept as natural do not exist. And in others these stereotyped differences are actually reversed. Among the Tchambuli, for example, women are more highly sexed, more aggressive, and more businesslike than men. In this tribe the women control the important business of fishing while the men spend their days gossiping, bickering, primping, and haggling in the

269

When we emphasize physical strength and courage for little boys, we are training them to fit our ideas of proper masculinity.
Leonard Freed/Magnum Photos, Inc.

marketplace for bargains (Mead, 1935, pp. 170–182). There is no reason to suppose that the Tchambuli differ from us in any biological way. Yet, given the same biological make-up, they have quite different ideas of what constitutes appropriate masculine and feminine behavior. Apparently their development of gender identity and appropriate sex-role behavior is based more on social factors than on biological ones.

Nature Versus Nurture

There is considerable evidence that the presence or absence of androgen in the blood stream of the fetus during critical stages of development affects the organization of the fetal brain in ways that are still being discovered. These discoveries lend weight to the argument that some of the differences between feminine and masculine behavior may be due to innate differences in brain structure. For example, neurologists have had evidence for some time that in right-handed adults damage to the right hemisphere of the brain disrupts nonverbal, spatial abilities and that damage to the left hemisphere disrupts language. Very recently they have

270

discovered that a woman's verbal and spatial abilities are more likely to be duplicated in both sides of the brain, while a male's are not. Because women's brain hemispheres may be less specialized for spatial and linguistic functions, it may be easier for them to combine the two in a single activity, such as reading or understanding a person's behavior from her or his facial expression. Men's brains may make it easier for them to keep separate cognitively different activities performed simultaneously, such as operating machinery while talking (Goleman, 1978).

Two neuropsychologists have summarized the findings of the growing body of literature regarding brain-based competencies of the sexes. They found that men are likely to excel in depth perception, have faster reaction times, tend to be more interested in objects than in people, are more skilled at gross motor movements, and engage more in rough-and-tumble play. In contrast, women have better hearing; are more sensitive to touch; excel in verbal skills, manual dexterity, and fine coordination; and are more socially responsive and empathic (McGuinness and Pribram, summarized in Goleman, 1978, p. 59).

Although it is apparent that prenatal hormones cause different brain organization in males and females, it would not be correct to assume that persons are born "masculine" or "feminine." Hormones alone are not capable of going quite that far, particularly in humans. The prenatal hormones may alter the threshold for some behavior traits defined as masculine or feminine, but they do not preordain behavior; instead they may establish a predisposition for behavior traits that are shared by both sexes but have different thresholds in males and females (Higham, 1980).

In humans it is not always easy to distinguish an innate predisposition from a trait that has developed as a result of having been expected and taught and rewarded. Studies of animals clearly show sex-linked behavior traits. Evidence for sex-linked traits in humans is found in studies of persons with clinical syndromes with a known history of inappropriate prenatal androgenization. After considering evidence from animal studies and studies of persons with certain clinical syndromes, one researcher compiled the following list of behavior traits that are apparently sex linked (Money, summarized in Higham, 1980, p. 24):

1. A high level of energy expenditure is more characteristic of males than of females.

2. Competitive rivalry and assertiveness is more prevalent in males than in females.

3. A tendency toward roaming and exploring is more characteristic of males than of females.

271

4. Defense of the group against intruders is more characteristic of males than of females.

5. Guarding and defending the young is more prevalent in females than in males.

6. Nesting and homemaking behaviors are more prevalent in females than in males.

7. Parental care of the young is more prevalent in females than in males.

8. Sexual mounting and thrusting is more characteristic of male play activities, while spreading and containing are more prevalent in females.

9. Erotic arousal is more dependent on visual stimuli in males and more dependent on tactual stimuli in females.

Gender, Society, and Individuals

For many people biological sex is consistent with assigned sex at birth and with the way one learns to fill a certain sex role. They seldom have reason to be self-conscious about whether they are masculine or feminine or whether their behavior is the result of social or biological factors. But the recent interest in the women's liberation movement and the gay liberation movement has raised some questions about the particular attitudes and behaviors assumed to be natural for men and women.

Biological factors set limits on what can be learned by social training; also they make some activities easier to learn than others. But what is "natural" is still largely a matter of what people in a society at a given point in time feel is natural. These ideas influence the subtle and not-so-subtle ways in which we raise our children to be proper males or females. When we give boys guns and trucks and give girls dolls and dishes, we are teaching them what we feel is their appropriate role in the world as we see it. When we punish a boy who plays with a doll or a girl who makes a flying football tackle, we are teaching them our idea of appropriate femininity and masculinity. Usually these lessons are well learned. If they are consistent with an individual's unique biological make-up, they are learned fairly readily. If they are not consistent with innate capacities, the cost of learning them may be much greater.

In females alone there is probably as much variation in innate biological capacity for behavior as there is in all people, males and females combined. The same holds true for males. We all know it is foolish for a father to push his 120-pound daughter to become a star halfback. It is probably equally foolish for him to push his 120-pound son toward the same goal. But both of them might enjoy driving a truck; both might like to bake bread. It appears that the interests of these assorted human beings

A man may enjoy feeding a baby, and a girl may enjoy playing baseball. Probably the welfare of all persons is served best when they are free to pursue their interests without too much concern for what is considered proper masculine or proper feminine behavior.
Read D. Brugger/Picture Cube

could be served better if we asked of them that they develop their unique capacities without an excessive concern for whether they are being masculine or feminine. The interests of our society could also be served better if all persons were free to exercise all their talents, even if this meant stepping outside their stereotyped masculine or feminine role.

Sensual-Sexual Development of Children

Erotic development in infants and children takes place at different rates and in different ways in each individual. Some of these developmental variations are influenced by heredity and nutrition; others are influenced by the types of stimulation and repression present in the child's environment.

Infancy

A warm physical relationship between mother and infant is important in the sensory and affectional awakening of the infant, arousing sensitivity in the body and stimulating the growth of sexual consciousness. When mother-infant contact is positive, most infants manifest genital play

273

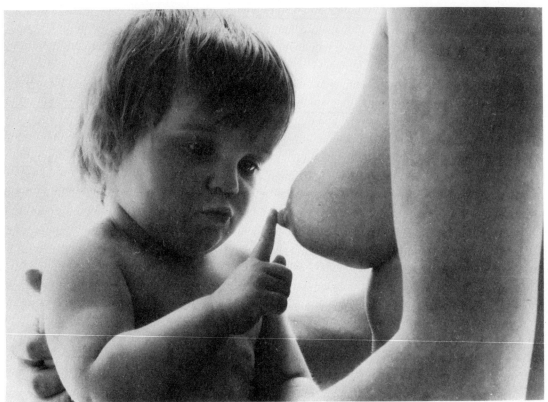

A warm physical relationship between mother and child is important to the physical and emotional development of the child.

Will McBride-Stern/Black Star

within the first year. When mother-infant encounters are rare or problematical, total development is slowed, genital play is much rarer, and activities such as rocking or head banging tend to replace it (Higham, 1980). Adults who were deprived of warm physical contact in infancy are more likely to exhibit retarded sexual development, violent-aggressive behavior, and social-emotional problems (Prescott, 1979).

The mouth is the principal source of sensual pleasure for infants, but they respond also to genital and general body contact, and may engage in genital stimulation when their development is normal and the activity is not forbidden. By two years of age the child has usually learned to channel his or her impulses for sensual gratification into the modes of expression permitted by society. In the United States, where direct genital manipulation is discouraged, the sensual-erotic activities of two-year-olds usually include such things as kissing and hugging family members, friends, and toys, as well as rhythmic motor activities such as riding a toy horse or swinging (Gesell and Ilg, 1946, pp. 270–366; Martinson, 1973, pp. 5–6).

274

Ages Three and Four

By the age of three or four, children become aware of the genital differences in males and females and may develop childhood romances. These romances are characterized by much the same behavior one observes in adults who are in love: hugging, kissing, sitting close, giving gifts, seeking out each other, and grieving at being separated (Bell, 1902).

My little nephew of three and a little neighbor girl of the same age had a most affectionate love for each other, and were not at all shy about it. They would kiss each other when they met, and seemed to think it all right. The little boy used to tell me that they would marry when grown. This continued about two and a half years; then the girl's parents moved away, much to the grief of both children. The little boy would often climb up and take the girl's photograph from the mantle and kiss it.

Higham, 1980, p. 18

Besides displaying affectionate and sexual behavior, children aged three to four are curious about sex differences and reproduction. They are interested in knowing where babies come from and how babies can get out of their mother's stomach. They may be fascinated by other people's bathrooms and bathroom activities, particularly by different postures for urination. Boys of this age may propose marriage to their mothers, and girls to their fathers (Martinson, 1973, pp. 25–26).

Ages Five Through Seven

At age five through seven, interest in bathrooms decreases, and there is increased interest in more subtle differences between the sexes, such as beards in men and breasts in women. Interest in having a baby may be expressed, and there is considerable role rehearsal in "playing house." Most five-year-olds know that they are expected to select as an eventual mate someone of the opposite sex from their own age group who is not in their family, and a majority of them are already committed to the idea that they will marry someday (Broderick, 1966).

Mild sex play, exhibition of one's own genitals, and inspection of genitals of other children are common between the age of five and seven, often under the guise of playing "doctor." A young man reports a childhood experience:

When I was six years old, I consciously experienced my first erection with a neighborhood girl of the same age. My curiosity increased when I saw a small glimpse of her genital area when we played "doctor" and my desire to know more about the female sex increased tremendously. One day after school, the girl came over to my house. We proceeded up to my bedroom where I told her, "You

Martinson, 1973, p. 31

275

can see me if I can see you." After she agreed, we both pulled down our pants. She asked me what my penis was. I told her that it was my "weiner," and that she didn't have one — only boys had weiners. I then proceeded to touch my weiner to her "doop" [rear]. This contact lasted for only a short time, yet I noticed for the first time that my penis was stiff.

Children are naturally curious about sex differences and reproduction.
Frederick D. Bodin/Stock, Boston.

276

Ages Eight and Nine

By the age of eight or nine interest in sex exploration and sex play are less common than at age six, but sex interest is high and curiosity about reproduction continues. Girls are interested in learning about menstruation, and both sexes seek more information concerning details of fertilization, pregnancy, and birth (Martinson, 1973, pp. 75–76).

At eight and nine, boys and girls begin to play separately while maintaining a high interest in members of the opposite sex (Broderick, 1971).

A young college man reports: I was living out in the country when I was about eight. I kept noticing that there were certain times when I would have an erection — when I sat next to Rhonda in school or when I was looking at Rhonda's legs across the aisle. Another time it happened was when Joanie, a junior high girl, would gallop her stallion, Midnite, down the road in front of our farm.

From the authors' files

Interest in the opposite sex is evidenced by peeping, sex jokes, provocative giggling, and the whispering and writing of sex-related words. In addition, boys and girls begin to rate themselves and others in terms of physical attractiveness. Self-consciousness about their bodies may progress to the point of not wanting to be seen nude by a parent of the opposite sex or siblings. When mixed play does occur, kissing games or teasing about boy friends and girl friends is a frequent outcome (Gesell and Ilg, 1946, pp. 321–370; Martinson, 1973, pp. 75–76).

Ages Ten Through Twelve

Ten- to twelve-year-olds demonstrate interest in sex through preoccupation with body changes and telling sex jokes. (See Selection 9.1.) Apparently ages eleven and twelve are the high point for interest in sex jokes among children in the United States (Ilg and Ames, 1956, p. 207).

Same Jokes, Different Kids/Jim Wood

Selection 9.1

A serious-minded University of California researcher has been spending a lot of her time recently listening to children tell dirty jokes.

The idea, according to Rosemary Zumwalt Elrick who delivered a paper yesterday to the California Folklore Society, was to learn how jokes reflect children's attitudes toward adult sexuality.

The jokes she gathered from white middle class girls aged 7 to 10, were the same ones the researcher herself had heard in her own girlhood.

San Francisco Sunday Examiner and Chronicle, April 13, 1975, A-11.

277

A graduate student in anthropology at Berkeley, Elrick found the much-talked-of sexual liberation among adults has yet to make itself felt in children's jokes.

In her paper, she analyzed seven children's dirty jokes and their variations. Collected over the past four years, the jokes involve children being kept in ignorance of adult sexuality.

The pattern of the jokes involved children contriving to see their parents naked for the first time — for instance, in the shower or bath.

The children in the jokes would then ask the names of the adult sex organs. The response in the jokes was that the parents would avoid a direct, truthful answer and instead give fanciful names to the sexual parts.

(Asked the name for breasts, the mother might reply "Those are my headlights.")

"The fanciful names given to the sexual organs are associated either with power, food or animals," Elrick said. They include car, garage, headlights, banana, fruitbowl, plug and socket.

Using these safe words, the punchline might be something like "Mommy, why don't you turn on your headlights so daddy can put his car in your garage."

In the jokes, the children pretend sexual ignorance but in fact they coyly draw upon their basic knowledge of sex.

What do such jokes reveal about children's attitudes toward adult sexuality?

The jokes reveal that children at times see their role as potentially damaging to adult sexuality, according to Elrick.

The jokes recognize the taboo of adult sexuality — the way in which parents may pretend to their children that there is no such thing as sex — by having the child promise not to look at the adult's sex organ while the adult and child are bathing.

The children, naturally, look anyway, then ask the questions that set up the humor.

Because of the conspicuous body changes associated with approaching puberty of some children in this age range, most of them are interested in and even awed by their own and others' bodies. A young man remembers early adolescence:

A friend and I or even a group of us would sit around and compare penises. During most of these comparisons, we would experience erections, which we thought was funny. We watched to see if our hairs had started to grow. For several weeks we watched closely (once in a while checking with a magnifying glass). Finally the big day came for me. I was so proud and excited that I showed many of my friends and even my sister who was just a year younger than I was.

Martinson, 1973, p. 77

278

A young woman recalls:

One morning in the fifth grade I noticed humps appearing on my chest. I was amazed, scared, and pleased all at the same time. To show how pleased I was, I called all of my girl friends' attention to this phenomenon and let them "feel" my breasts.

Martinson, 1973, p. 81

Ten- and eleven-year-olds appear to be prejudiced against members of the opposite sex, but this prejudice exists side by side with a definite romantic interest. At ages ten and eleven, about 60 percent of boys and 80 percent of girls have already decided they want to get married some day. In one urban community 86 percent of boys this age reported having a girl friend, and 96 percent of the girls reported having a boy friend, although in most cases the romance was secret and not reciprocated. Approximately half these children reported having been in love at least once (Broderick, 1971).

Sexual Activities in Infancy and Childhood

It is difficult to analyze childhood sexuality using adult definitions of sexual behavior. Many activities of children that might appear sexual to an adult may be the result of curiosity about bodies and bodily functions that is not sexually focused. For example, a child who is exploring his or her own genitals or the genitals of another child, may be motivated more by curiosity than by sexual urges. In contrast, an activity that does not appear sexual to an adult, such as climbing a rope or riding a horse, may be engaged in by a child precisely for the sexual excitement and orgasm that she or he has discovered it can produce (Martinson, 1976).

We consider activities in infants and children as sexual ones when they lead to physical changes that are commonly accepted as indicators of sexual arousal, such as swelling sex organs. Obviously if a child is too young to talk we can only assume the child is sexually aroused by using such physical cues. Even for children with considerable verbal skills, sexual excitement usually must be inferred from nonverbal cues, since young children do not often have the experience to describe particular physical sensations as specifically sexual ones. Children may know simply that some activity is pleasurable; only when they remember it in later years will they be able to define it as having been a source of sexual pleasure.

279

Masturbation

The sexual activities of children and the sources of sexual stimulation they discover are almost as varied as those of the most sensual and imaginative adult. The most common sexual activity is masturbation. We will use the term *masturbation* to mean deliberate self-stimulation leading to sexual arousal and often to orgasm. Sometimes young children will idly fondle their genitals, but this is not masturbation as we have defined it. We refer to a deliberate activity done for pleasure. It is usually accompanied by intense concentration, heavy breathing, rhythmic body movements, muscle tension, and a decreased awareness of the immediate environment. In some instances a definite orgasm occurs; sometimes only a state of relaxation and satisfaction comparable to the postorgasmic state is achieved (Elias and Gebhard, 1969; Kinsey et al., 1948, pp. 157–161).

There are two types of autoerotic activities during early childhood. During the early months of development the masturbatory activities are random, without a specific object, and not accompanied by fantasy. Sometime between sixteen and eighteen months a second type of autoerotic activity develops that is accompanied by some form of fantasy. At this stage the child is able to reach the genitals more easily and the masturbation is closer to adult masturbatory activities. Squeezing, pinching, and rapid rhythmic movements of the hand are usually accompanied by flushing, rapid breathing, and perspiration. Boys tend to start genital play several months earlier than girls. Boys' sexual activities appear to be more focused, more intentional, and more frequent even though the discovery of the anatomical differences seems to come at the same time, about fourteen to fifteen months (Modaressi, 1980).

Sexual Potential in Children   Contrary to what many people think, at least some young children and infants are quite capable of masturbation with definite sexual response, orgasm, and in some cases even multiple orgasms. Kinsey and his associates reported four cases of females under one year of age coming to orgasm and a total of twenty-three cases of females three years of age or younger reaching orgasm (Kinsey et al., 1953, p. 105). It is accepted that most females — children and adults — are capable of multiple orgasms when they are properly stimulated. Some adult females have masturbated to orgasm as often as ten, twenty, or even a hundred times within a single hour (Kinsey et al., 1953, p. 163). Very few adult males have the capacity for multiple orgasm, but some infants and young boys exhibit a surprising capacity for several orgasms in a short time span. Among a sample of preadolescent boys on whom masturbatory data are available, more than half reached a second climax within a short time, and nearly one-third were able to have five or more orgasms in quite rapid succession. The youngest male in this study was aged five   280 months and had three orgasms within an unspecified time period. The record-holder for this particular study was an eleven-month-old boy who had fourteen orgasms within thirty-eight minutes (Kinsey et al., 1948, pp. 177–181).

The potential for sexual response in children can also be seen by analyzing societies that are sexually permissive. In their study of thirty-two societies that were permissive with regard to prepubescent sexuality, Ford and Beach found that most boys and girls progressed from absent-minded fondling of their genitals in the early years to systematic masturbation by age six to eight (Ford and Beach, 1951, p. 195). In the societies where children are allowed to observe adult sexual activities, even prepubescent youngsters will attempt oral-genital contacts and coitus. Boys and girls in some cultures, such as the Trobrianders of Melanesia or the Chewa of Africa, often engage in full sexual relations before puberty, sometimes as early as six or seven years of age (Ford and Beach, 1951, pp. 197–198; Broderick, 1966).

Nature and Incidence of Childhood Masturbation   Completely accurate data on the incidence of masturbation among children before puberty are difficult to obtain. In a study of 432 prepubescent white boys and girls 56 percent of the males and 30 percent of the females reported masturbation before puberty (Elias and Gebhard, 1969). For females, masturbation is the most frequent source of preadolescent orgasm. Boys more often experience their first orgasms by other means such as intense emotional situations or physical stimulation in play. These include such things as sliding down a banister or a rope, wrestling, reciting in front of a class, or seeing a frightening movie (Reevy, 1973).

Masturbation Techniques   The techniques for masturbation are much the same as those used by adults, and usually involve manual stimulation of the genitals. However, female children are less likely than adult females to insert fingers or other objects in the vagina; they concentrate almost exclusively on stimulation of the clitoris. Besides manual stimulation, the technique most used by children is rhythmic movement of the buttocks while lying face down with the genitals pressed against some object, such as a blanket or toy (Reevy, 1973).

Most of the young girls who masturbate discover the technique accidentally through their own exploration (Kinsey et al., 1953, p. 137).

A female university graduate student recalls her first orgasm at age twelve: One night after I had gone to bed I was sort of feeling around down there because I could not go to sleep and was bored just lying there. I noticed it felt good when I stuck my finger in and slid it out slowly — particularly sliding

From the authors' files

281

it out. For some reason I tried sliding it in and out faster and faster, and the faster I did it the better it felt. All of a sudden it seemed like the muscles in my stomach and legs were twitching and a funny feeling came over me — sort of like stepping in a warm shower — and I felt very relaxed. I thought it must have been an orgasm and I was amazed and terribly proud of myself. I had no idea they came so easy like that.

In contrast, nearly all boys have heard about masturbation before they try it themselves, and a large proportion have seen friends masturbating (Kinsey et al., 1948, p. 501).

A young college man recalls: I learned to masturbate without knowing about it from my friend Art. . . . One day Art said that Jerry taught him how to do something that really felt good, and he thought I ought to try it. . . . He said all you had to do was to put your fingers on your dick and move them up and down forty times and then jump into the pool. That seemed odd to me but I tried. I put my thumb and forefinger on each side of the penis and carefully counted 40 strokes and then jumped into the pool. Nothing happened. Well, Art thought maybe I needed to do it eighty times. . . . Later at home I tried it eighty times and a hundred times, especially when I was taking a bath. I began to notice that it felt good, but not as good as Art implied and he seemed to genuinely feel that it was really good. I was also now having an erection when I did it. One day I decided I wasn't going to stop until something happened. I firmly grasped the penis, and began to furiously move my clenched hand up and down. On the thirty-sixth stroke it happened — a real good feeling came over me and some whitish stuff came out of the end of the penis. I thought that was strange. I kept trying it and every time the whitish stuff came out, I felt good.

From the authors' files

Homosexual Activities

As children reach grade-school age they tend to play mostly with children of their own sex, so it is not surprising that many of their sexual activities are with playmates of the same sex. When Kinsey and his associates interviewed a sample of white boys and girls aged four to fourteen, they found that 52 percent of males and 35 percent of females reported homosexual prepubertal sexual activity (Elias and Gebhard, 1969). In fact, during late childhood and early adolescence, sex play with members of the same sex is probably more common than sex play with members of the opposite sex (Comfort, 1963, p. 42). If genital exhibition can be considered sex play, then roughly 99 percent of females and virtually all males report homosexual activity during childhood (Reevy, 1967).

Kinsey found that after genital exhibition, handling the genitals of the other person was the next most frequent type of childhood homosexual activity. Three percent of females and 16 percent of males reported oral-

282

genital contacts with childhood companions of the same sex. Vaginal insertions were reported by 18 percent of girls in homosexual encounters before puberty; 17 percent of boys reported having anal intercourse (Kinsey et al., 1953, p. 140; Martinson, 1973, p. 95). For example, a man reports a sexual experience at age twelve with another boy:

I remember him asking if I would itch his "cock." I guess it was more curiosity at his big organ than anything that led me to comply and I did. . . . Anyway, I was stimulating him and he all of a sudden insisted that I stop. I didn't know why at the time, but I did what he said. He then suggested that he return the favor. Well, he began to manually stimulate me, and the sensation was so great at orgasm I honestly remember that I made him stop for a second. Then I asked him to start again and the sensation came back and I made him stop again. I was too young to ejaculate anything, but it sure felt good.

Martinson, 1973, p. 95

Most parental admonitions against sexual experimentation are directed at heterosexual activities, and parents usually chaperone play among children of mixed sexes more closely than that of children of the same sex. Because sexual contact with the same sex is not as likely to be the subject of sexual warnings and concern, many children are unaware at the time that this is as forbidden as contact with the opposite sex. In most cases childhood homosexual activities are confined to a relatively brief period and are rather quickly forgotten in the excitement of the heterosexual activities that usually accompany the adolescent years. Sometimes the more intense homosexual experiences are a source of guilt in later years.

A young female graduate student reports: I had a really close girl friend who was about three years older than me — she was about fourteen at that time. . . . We started just by spending the night together on weekends and having slumber parties like all girls do. But she started showing a physical interest in me — hugging and stroking me a lot. I did not know it was a disapproved thing to do because my family is very physical and demonstrative — like my mother would hug and kiss us a lot. Since she was older than me, I really thought she was great to be so interested in me, and we got to doing a really lot of heavy petting and things. It even got to the point of her putting her finger in my vagina and stroking my genitals. It was at that point that I thought maybe it was not the right thing to do, but I still enjoyed it and I felt really close to her. Right after that we moved to another part of town and I did not see her again. I really missed her when we moved and I could not really understand all my feelings about her and missing her and being lonely and wanting someone to touch me. My feelings were really baffling to me. Later I learned that homo stuff was not the right thing to do and I really felt guilty about it. I was baffled about my feelings about her until I started dating boys and had the same feelings and then I did not feel funny or guilty anymore.

From the authors' files

Heterosexual Activities

There is also some heterosexual sex play among young children. Kinsey and his associates found that 34 percent of males and 37 percent of females reported sex play involving members of the opposite sex, usually with companions of approximately the same age (Elias and Gebhard, 1969). Genital exhibition is the most frequent activity, but manual manipulation, oral-genital contacts, and attempted intercourse also occur.

A woman in her early twenties remembers: My brother and I used to take baths together until we were about nine or ten years old. In the tub we used to play with each other and touch each other quite freely. We were curious and we explored each others' bodies. Once he asked if he could stick his weewee in my weewee and I said, "No, no, because I will get pregnant!" You see my Mom had told me about things like that but she had never told him even though he was just about eighteen months younger than me. But after that I didn't want to take baths with him.

From the authors' files

Sexual activities among preadolescents may take the form of teasing and rough play.
Joel Gordon

Sexual or romantic activities among preadolescents also may take the form of teasing and rough play as an excuse for physical or verbal contact between the sexes. For boys there is a gradual increase in heterosexual childhood sex play until adolescence, but girls tend to drop out of such play as they near puberty. This could be because girls become more aware of the social implications of sex play, or it could be because girls are supervised more carefully in their contacts with boys as they approach adolescence (Broderick, 1968).

Sex Education for Children

Most persons think of sex education in relation to adolescents; few realize that most learning about sexuality takes place in infancy and childhood. Children aged four to six ask more sex-related questions than do children of any other age, even including the adolescent years (Strain, 1948, pp. 106–108). Thus the period of infancy and childhood is quite important in the development of sexual attitudes. In this early period the parents' attitude toward sexuality has a strong influence on the developing child. Even when the parents do not answer specific sex-related questions and do not discuss sexuality directly, children pick up feelings that are conveyed by many nonverbal means as the actions of their parents reveal their attitudes toward bodies, bodily functions, and bodily pleasures.

Parental Sanctions   A mother or father diapering an infant provides the child's first lesson in sex education when the child touches his or her own bare genitals. A parent whose anxious facial expression and quick movements to cover the exposed area with a dry diaper indicates her or his own horror of childish genital exploration, cannot keep from conveying this to the impressionable child. These attitudes can be perceived and absorbed by the child even before she or he has the language to express them, so that a small child may understand there is something awful, fearful, and untouchable about her or his genitals before parental warnings of "not nice," "nasty," or "don't touch" have a real meaning.

As the child grows older, verbal and physical sanctions reinforce early learning about sexuality. These can make a particularly lasting impression when they are carried out without adequate explanation of specifically what is forbidden and why. A young man recalls:

Later my mother asked what we were doing in the basement. I finally told her that we were showing butts. She told me never to do anything like that again. I felt almost certain that I had done something which would prove to be irreparably damaging to my future life.

Martinson, 1973, pp. 56–57

285

A young man reports:

When an erection would occur our mother would scold us and this tended to
frighten us. I remember one time I was visiting my grandmother. I had just taken
a bath and she wanted to see if I was clean or not. As she cleaned my navel I had
an erection. She said, "Oh, Gary!" and gave it a little slap. It just frightened the
sexual dickens out of me.

Martinson, 1973, p. 57

Attitudes Toward Childhood Sexuality   Many adults in our society are quite
concerned when they discover young children involved in sexual activities. They may fear that indulging in sexual activity will upset the child's
physical, emotional, or social development. Their concern for his social
development has some justification, because a child who is too open with
his sexual interests and activities may quickly be ostracized in some
neighborhoods — at least by the adults. But there is no evidence that early
sexual activities per se harm a child's physical or emotional development.
The problems arise when adults get upset, punish the child, or in some
other way reveal their horror at this very normal activity (Kinsey et al.,
1948, p. 115).

Attitudes in Other Cultures   The strict prohibition of childhood sexuality
found in most segments of our society is by no means universal. Neither
are the negative adult attitudes toward children's sex activities. In societies where there is a very permissive attitude toward sexual expression in
childhood, free and open sex play is quite common. In a few societies
adults may even participate actively in the sexual stimulation of infants
and young children. For instance, among the Kazak of central Asia, adults
playing with young children excite them by rubbing their genitals.
Mothers in Alorese society (an Oceanic island tribe) may fondle the
genitals of their babies while nursing them (Ford and Beach, 1951).

Even without adult stimulation, children in permissive societies quickly
learn a variety of sexual activities. Among the Pukapukans of Polynesia,
boys and girls masturbate freely and openly in public. Typical amuse-
ment for Trobriand girls and boys includes manual and oral-genital stimulation and attempts at sexual intercourse (Ford and Beach, 1951).

In societies where they are allowed to do so, children increase their
sexual activities at the approach of puberty and during adolescence. In
fact, in some cultures it is felt that early sexual experimentation by children and adolescents is important to their development. Among the
Chewa of Africa, for example, parents think that children can never have
offspring unless they begin to exercise themselves sexually very early in
life. The Lepcha of India believe that girls cannot mature physically unless
they practice sexual intercourse. Early sex play in this tribe involves

286

various forms of mutual masturbation and attempts at intercourse. Older men occasionally have sexual relations with girls as young as eight years of age, with no social repercussions. By the time they are eleven or twelve years old, most girls of this tribe regularly have intercourse (Ford and Beach, 1951).

The Ila people of Africa have an interesting attitude toward children's sexual behavior. They regard childhood as a time to prepare for mature sexuality and adulthood. Each girl is given a house where she takes her boyfriend, and there they play as man and wife. As a result of this practicing for adulthood, there are no virgins over ten years of age among these people (Ford and Beach, 1951).

Transmission of Attitudes   Most parents in the United States have basically the same problem in the early sex education of their children, regardless of whether their own personal sexual attitudes are very permissive, very strict, or somewhere in between. They must help a child learn to regulate his or her sexual impulses sufficiently so that he or she can survive comfortably in a society that expects certain forms of regulation. A good part of sexual therapy involves re-education for people whose parents emphasized regulation of sexual impulses more than gratification of them. (See also Chapter 5)

Even the most supportive parental attitudes and the most ideal developmental situation in childhood may not prepare a child to meet every situation. Norms concerning proper sexual behavior are specific to a particular culture, subculture, social class, and era. In most segments of lower-class slum society, for example, there is more open sexual behavior in children, teenagers, and adults than there is in the middle classes. Behavior appropriate in the slum setting may cause concern or even shock in a middle-class setting.

Even persons who remain insulated within a given culture may find that attitudes about sexuality change from one generation to the next. Individuals who absorbed the sexual attitudes of their parents may find these attitudes inadequate for equipping themselves or their children to live in a rapidly changing world where every generation experiences considerable change in sexual behavior and attitudes. Equally acute is the problem of a person who must sometimes live, visit, or do business in another culture where typical sexual attitudes and behavior are quite different from those she or he thought were innate or God-given.

The sexual attitudes acquired in childhood are amazingly durable. They are absorbed before a child has the experience to question them. They develop in interaction with adults who in a child's trusting eyes are all-powerful and all-knowing. And they continue to operate throughout life on an emotional level that is often quite resistant to intellectual arguments for adjustment. A rigid sexual value system supported by strong labels such as "sinful," "perverted," or "dirty" may not be the best to equip a growing child for the world in which he or she will eventually live, love, and reproduce. The world we live in is changing rapidly, and is composed of a variety of cultures and subcultures that, because of modern means of rapid transportation, are often not insulated from each other. Probably a fairly flexible and pragmatic system of sexual values and attitudes will better prepare a child for what she or he must face in the future. Life may be less complicated and more rewarding for those who feel that although there is nothing inherently evil about human sexuality in all its various expressions, conformity to prevailing norms (or at least discretion and the appearance of conformity) is one way to avoid the fairly strong sanctions associated with most sexual taboos.

Chapter 10 / *Sexuality in Adolescence*

The period of life we call adolescence is a complex of physiological, psychological, and social-role changes. Although the biological and reproductive maturation accompanying adolescence is universal in human societies, the definition of adolescence and the sexual interpretations given to childhood and adolescence vary from culture to culture. In our culture *adolescence* covers approximately the period from thirteen to about twenty years of age, although this varies according to social class and other factors.

Age, Sexuality, and Society

All societies have some working definition of a child and an adult, but only Western industrialized societies have developed the intermediate stage we call adolescence as a separate part of the life cycle. In Western societies in the past and in many agrarian societies today, young males and females, at ages ranging from seven to the teens, go through rites of passage that signal their transition from child to adult status. In societies such as India and preindustrial Europe, children in their preteen years may marry. Whereas our society frowns on sexual interaction or intercourse between adolescents and adults, this form of sexuality is the norm in some other cultures.

Because of these differences in customs and norms, it is difficult to differentiate the biological urges for sexual pleasure and fulfillment that occur at adolescence from the social permission given to such pleasure and fulfillment. Unlike children, adolescents in our society are usually perceived as sexual beings, but only as potential rather than actual sexual partners. Although both young boys and girls are theoretically expected to remain sexually inexperienced, immense latitude and opportunity are given to them to experiment sexually, in places ranging from the back seat of the car to the great outdoors. However, adolescent sexual experimentation, if it occurs, is expected to occur away from the knowledge and observations of adults and without the production of offspring, although adolescents are generally not given contraceptive advice.

Puberty

Adolescence is the socially defined period between childhood and adulthood in our society; *puberty* is the period of increased hormonal activity resulting in the physical changes necessary to the development of the

290

With the beginnings of puberty, children are often interested in the changes in their own and others' bodies.

Adolescence, 1932, etching by Gerald Brockhurst. Courtesy of the Syracuse University Art Collection.

ability to reproduce. The age at which puberty is said to begin depends partly upon the criteria used to determine onset. In females development of breasts and growth of pubic hair usually begin around age ten or eleven. Menstruation typically begins from eleven to thirteen years of age. In males pubic hair begins to grow and the testicles begin to enlarge around twelve to sixteen years of age. Enlargement of the penis and the

291

ability to ejaculate usually occur between ages eleven and fifteen. Whereas almost all females have had instruction regarding their first menstruation before it occurs, only about one-third of males have had any instruction prior to their first seminal ejaculation. About half of females report that they told their girl friends of their first menstruation, but only 12 percent of males told anyone of their first ejaculation and most tried to hide it (Levin, 1976).

Reproductive Capacity

One of the socially and biologically important consequences of puberty is that females begin to ovulate and males begin to produce sperm. There are not adequate data on precisely when people develop the capacity to reproduce. The first ejaculate for a male may contain viable sperm, but this is not a certainty for all males. First menstruation may signal the beginning of ovulation, but this also is not a certainty. Even though adolescent males may produce viable sperm and adolescent females may ovulate, their fecundity is considerably lower than it will be in early adulthood.

Bodily Change

In addition to development of the sexual organs, other body changes are associated with puberty. Some of these are of concern to adolescents because they may be used as criteria for physical attractiveness or sex appeal. In the female the breasts develop and the hips begin to widen, and in the male the shoulders become broader. Males also develop coarse body hair, coarse facial hair, and deeper voices. Both sexes experience a growth spurt. The growth spurt for females is typically between age ten and fourteen and for males between eleven and seventeen (Group for the Advancement of Psychiatry, 1968).

Masturbation

Related to increased hormonal activity in puberty there is an increased awareness of and interest in sexual activities. One fairly common sexual activity during adolescence is masturbation. Although it is difficult to obtain completely accurate data on a practice as private as masturbation, studies indicate that probably nearly all males and almost two-thirds of females in the United States have masturbated to orgasm by the time they complete adolescence (Kinsey et al., 1948, p. 506; Kinsey et al., 1953, p.

142; Sorensen, 1973, p. 131; Hunt, 1974, pp. 75–78). (For a discussion of the methodology utilized by these researchers, see the appendix.)

For the majority of males, masturbation slightly precedes or begins with puberty, after which the incidence rises markedly. During the early teens masturbation is most common among boys of lower social levels who do not plan to go to college. In later adolescence the active incidence of masturbation is highest among males of higher social levels who plan to attend college. Throughout adolescence masturbation is the primary sexual outlet, although by the late teens the frequency of masturbation drops. Among males not destined for college, masturbation tends to be replaced by coitus; among males who plan to attend college, it is replaced to some degree by petting (Kinsey et al., 1948, p. 507; Reevy, 1973).

By the age of thirteen, approximately two-thirds of males and one-third of females have masturbated to orgasm (Hunt, 1974, p. 77). (For a discussion of Hunt's research methods see the appendix.) In the early teens the incidence of masturbation for females is very much the same for all social and educational levels. In the late teens, girls from lower social and educational backgrounds masturbate less and become more interested in sexual intercourse. Girls who plan to go to college consider masturbation a more acceptable outlet than coitus. For females, as for males, masturbation is the primary sexual outlet during adolescence (Kinsey et al., 1953, pp. 142–143; Reevy, 1973).

Techniques of Masturbation

The techniques of masturbation used by adolescents are generally the same as those used by adults. Hand stimulation of the genitals is the method most frequently used by both sexes. Rubbing the genitals against objects, such as pillows or bedclothes, is occasionally used by either sex. Objects are sometimes inserted into the vagina by adolescent females, but this method is more likely to be used by adult females. Girls also occasionally use rhythmic thigh pressure or vibrators, techniques almost never employed by boys (Reevy, 1973).

Learning About Masturbation

Most males do not discover masturbation for themselves, but instead have heard about it before they attempt it. A fairly high proportion have observed companions masturbating (Kinsey et al., 1948, p. 501). It is not uncommon for young boys to engage in masturbation with a group of male friends — an activity sometimes called a "circle jerk." This may take the form of a game or contest to see who can ejaculate first or who can squirt semen the farthest.

In contrast to males, very few females observe or talk about masturbation with friends, and the majority of them discover it without any previous knowledge that any other person has been involved in a similar activity (Clifford, 1978). Some females first discover masturbation through reading books, usually moral and sex-education literature, or from hearing religious lectures designed to discourage it. Sometimes a heterosexual petting experience causes a girl to realize the pleasure that can be gained from manual stimulation, so that afterward she stimulates herself (Kinsey et al., 1948, p. 501; Kinsey et al., 1953, pp. 137–140).

Fantasies During Masturbation

Nearly all males and about half of females experience sexual fantasies while they masturbate. Males are more likely than females to have fantasies of unfulfilled or repressed desires, but for both males and females, fantasies usually involve thoughts of intercourse with a loved person. Reading erotic literature, viewing erotic pictures, or smoking marijuana may be combined occasionally with masturbation (Kinsey et al., 1948; pp. 509–511; Kinsey et al., 1953, p. 163; Hunt, 1974, pp. 91–94).

Masturbation Among College Students

A study of college students in Pennsylvania found that 97 percent of males and 78 percent of females masturbated at some time. In a study of college students in the New York metropolitan area, 89 percent of males and 61 percent of females reported they were currently masturbating (Arafat and Cotton, 1974). Most of these students began masturbating between the age of nine and sixteen, although about 17 percent began before age nine. (See Table 10.1.) The females in the sample were much

Relationship Between Sex and Age at First Masturbation   Table 10.1

Age at First Masturbation	Males	62.12%	Females	37.88%	Total	%
5–8 years	30	14.63	25	20.00	55	16.67
9–12 years	85	41.46	40	32.00	125	37.88
13–16 years	80	39.02	40	32.00	120	36.36
17–21 years	10	4.88	20	16.00	30	9.09
Number	205		125		330	

Source: "Masturbation Practices of Males and Females" by Ibtihaj S. Arafat and Wayne L. Cotton reprinted by permission from the *Journal of Sex Research*, 1974, 10, p. 165.

Intensity of Orgasm During Masturbation Versus Intensity of Orgasm During Intercourse   Table 10.2

Intensity of Orgasm	Males	62.12%	Females	37.88%	Total	%
Masturbation equal to intercourse	81	39.51	26	20.83	107	32.42
Masturbation less than intercourse	105	51.22	57	45.84	162	49.10
Masturbation greater than intercourse	19	9.27	42	33.33	61	18.48
Number	205		125		330	

Source: "Masturbation Practices of Males and Females" by Ibtihaj S. Arafat and Wayne L. Cotton reprinted by permission from the *Journal of Sex Research,* 1974, 10, p. 165.

more likely than males to report that masturbation produced more intense orgasms than did intercourse. Over all, 49 percent of the respondents reported less intense orgasms with masturbation than with intercourse. (See Table 10.2.) The frequency of reported masturbation for males and females is remarkably similar in the sample of college students, with most reporting that they masturbated from a few times a week to a few times a month. (See Table 10.3.) The most common feeling after

Frequency of Masturbation   Table 10.3

Frequency	Males	62.12%	Females	37.88%	Total	%
Several times a day	21	10.00	14	11.11	35	10.61
Once a day	14	6.67	7	5.55	21	6.36
Several times a week	68	33.33	42	33.34	110	33.33
Once a week	34	16.67	14	11.11	48	14.55
Several times a month	68	33.33	48	38.89	116	34.15
Number	205		125		330	

Source: "Masturbation Practices of Males and Females" by Ibtihaj S. Arafat and Wayne L. Cotton reprinted by permission from the *Journal of Sex Research,* 1974, 10, p. 165.

Feelings after Masturbation   Table 10.4

Feelings after Masturbation	Males	62.12%	Females	37.88%	Total	%
Guilt	30	12.71	15	9.74	45	11.54
Physical satisfaction	161	68.22	88	57.14	249	63.85
Depression	26	11.02	38	24.68	64	16.41
Perversion	11	4.66	2	1.30	13	3.33
Fear of becoming insane	8	3.39	11	7.14	19	4.87
Number	236		154		390*	

* Some respondents cited more than one response.

Source: "Masturbation Practices of Males and Females" by Ibtihaj S. Arafat and Wayne L. Cotton reprinted by permission from the *Journal of Sex Research,* 1974, 10, p. 165.

masturbation was physical satisfaction (for 64 percent of the sample), although 36 percent reported negative feelings such as guilt or depression. (See Table 10.4.)

Effects of Masturbation

Many people erroneously believe that masturbation is physically harmful. Some think it causes pimples, poor posture, weak eyes, mental dullness, or even insanity. (See Selection 10.1.) Masturbation causes none of these. The physical effects of masturbation are not fundamentally different from the physical effects of any other sexual activity.

Ladies' Guide in Health and Disease / J. H. Kellogg, M.D.   Selection 10.1

Effects of Solitary Vice in Girls

The victim of this evil habit is certain to suffer sooner or later the penalty which nature invariably inflicts upon those who transgress her laws. Every law of nature is enforced by an inexorable penalty. This is emphatically true respecting the laws which relate to the sexual organs.

Wide observation has convinced us that a great many of the backaches, sideaches, and other aches and pains of which girls complain, are attributable to

Originally published in the 1890s. Reprinted from Ms Magazine, November 1973, p. 108.

this injurious habit. Much of the nervousness, hysteria, neuralgia, and general worthlessness of girls originates in this cause alone.

The period of puberty is one at which thousands of girls break down in health. The constitution, already weakened by a debilitating, debasing vice, is not prepared for the strain, and the poor victim drops into a premature grave.

Signs of Self-Abuse in Girls

Mothers should always be on the alert to detect the first evidences of this vice in their daughters, since later nothing but almighty power seems competent to loosen its grasp. The only positive evidence is detection of the child in the act. A suspected child should be watched under all circumstances with increasing vigilance.

[But] aside from positive evidence, there are other signs which may lead to the discovery of positive evidence.

A marked change in disposition. When a girl who has been truthful, happy, obliging, gentle, and confiding, becomes peevish, irritable, morose, and disobedient, she is under the influence of some foul blight.

Loss of memory and loss of the love for study. The nervous forces are weakened, giving place to mental weakness and inactivity.

Unnatural boldness in a little girl. If she has previously been reserved, this is just ground for the suspicion of secret vice.

A forward or loose manner in company with little boys. Girls addicted to this habit are guilty of the most wanton conduct.

Languor and lassitude. In a girl who has possessed a marked degree of activity and energy, this should give rise to earnest solicitude on the part of the mother for the physical and moral condition of her child.

An unnatural appetite. Sometimes children will show an excessive fondness for mustard, pepper, vinegar, and spices. Little girls who are very fond of cloves are likely to be depraved in other respects.

The presence of leukorrhoea. Self-abuse occasions a frequently recurring congestion of the parts, together with the mechanical irritation accompanying the habit.

Ulceration about the roots of the nails. This especially affects one or both of the first two fingers of the hand, the irritation of the fingers being occasioned by the acrid vaginal discharge.

Biting the fingernails. The irritation of the fingers, which gives rise to the habit of biting nails, grows out of the irritable condition of the nails mentioned above.

The expression of the eyes. The dull, lusterless eye, surrounded by a dark ring, tells the tale of sin.

Palpitations of the heart, hysteria, nervousness, St. Vitus's dance, epilepsy, and incontinence of urine, giving rise to wetting the bed.

How to Cure Vicious Habits

The habit of self-pollution is one which when thoroughly established, is by no means easily broken. The victim of this most terrible vice is held in the most abject slavery, the iron fetters of habit daily closing the prisoner more and more tightly in their grasp. The effect is to weaken the moral sense perhaps more rapidly than any other vice, until there is little left in the child's character to which an appeal can be made.

The mother should first carefully set before the child the exceeding sinfulness of the habit, its loathsomeness and vileness, and the horrible consequences which follow in its wake. But in most cases, the evil is not so easily mastered. The little girl should be kept under constant observation every moment of her waking hours. Care should be taken that the child does not feign sleep for the purpose of gaining an opportunity to avoid observation.

It is much more difficult to cure this soul-destroying vice in girls than in boys. They are seldom as ready to confess their guilt as are boys, and then are less easily influenced by a portrayal of its terrible consequences. Sleepless vigilance must be coupled with the most persevering patience.

In obstinate cases, severe means must be adopted. We were once obliged, after every other measure had failed, to perform a surgical operation [clitoridectomy] before we were able to break the habit in the case of a girl of eight or ten years who had become addicted to the vice to a most extraordinary degree.

In the absence of guilt or other emotional conflicts, the effects of masturbation to orgasm can be beneficial. But because masturbation is so widely condemned, at least half of all adolescents who masturbate experience guilt or anxiety (Sorensen, 1973, p. 141; Hunt, 1974, pp. 72–75). (For a discussion of Sorensen's and Hunt's research methods see the appendix.)

For example, one woman, in recalling her first masturbatory experience, reports: "I was so disgusted with myself and frightened at the feelings it engendered that I threw up for a week."

From the authors' files

Adolescents are not alone in their negative feelings regarding masturbation; most adults also are more or less guilt-ridden if they masturbate, and are extremely secretive about it. Few people admit it to their closest friends or even their lovers, despite the fact that masturbation is certainly common: nearly all single males and a majority of single females masturbate, as well as substantial percentages of married people. Masturbation in private is not physically harmful and is devoid of social and interpersonal difficulties. Modern sex educators are now beginning to speak approvingly of masturbation and to recommend it for people without adequate sexual outlets (Hunt, 1974, pp. 75–87).

298

Attitudes of Adults (by Age, Gender, and Education) Toward Masturbation by 12- or 13-year-old Boys and Girls, in Percentages[1]

Table 10.5

Source: "The Distribution of Selected Sexual Attitudes and Behaviors Among the Adult Population of the United States" by W. Cody Wilson, reprinted by permission from the Journal of Sex Research, 1975, 11, p. 170.

Males (N = 911)		Age			Education		
Attitude	Total %	21–39	30–59	60+	Coll.	H.S.	Elem.
Punish (a)	5	1	7	6	2	4	14
Forbid but not punish (b)	12	6	13	15	6	15	14
Discourage but not forbid (c)	28	26	30	25	33	29	18
Discuss but not discourage (d)	34	50	31	25	42	32	24
Ignore (e)	8	8	8	7	12	7	3
Don't know (f)	11	8	9	18	4	11	22
No answer (g)	2	1	2	4	1	2	5
Summary:							
Forbid (a + b)	17	7	20	21	8	19	28
Discourage (c)	28	26	30	25	33	29	18
Not discourage (d + e)	42	58	39	32	54	39	27

Females (N = 1,370)		Age			Education		
Attitude	Total %	21–39	30–59	60+	Coll.	H.S.	Elem.
Punish (a)	4	4	2	8	1	3	13
Forbid but not punish (b)	10	7	10	16	5	11	17
Discourage but not forbid (c)	21	15	24	15	22	22	11
Discuss but not discourage (d)	36	51	35	24	48	35	19
Ignore (e)	8	7	9	6	10	7	8
Don't know (f)	16	13	14	25	9	17	26
No answer (g)	5	3	6	6	5	5	6
Summary:							
Forbid (a + b)	14	11	12	24	6	14	30
Discourage (c)	21	15	24	15	22	22	11
Not discourage (d + e)	44	58	44	30	58	42	27

[1] The complete wording of the item is: "Most children play with themselves sexually while they are growing up. If a young person does this and has a sexual climax, this is called masturbation. Suppose a 12- or 13-year-old boy or girl does something like this. Which one of these statements comes closest to your opinion of what a parent should do?"

Parental Attitudes

Many adults are now fairly tolerant of masturbation among young adolescents. A national survey made in 1970 (Wilson, 1975) revealed that only about 16 percent of adults felt a parent should forbid or punish masturbation in a twelve- or thirteen-year-old; 43 percent said they thought it should not even be discouraged. (See Table 10.5.)

One university-educated mother says of her thirteen-year-old daughter: I think Karen has masturbated — at least I certainly hope she has. I wouldn't want her to grow up ignorant about sex like I did. . . . Some of my friends who are really into women's lib say I should teach her about it, but I don't feel I can do that. But I have told her about sex and the parts of her body, and have talked about masturbation and intercourse in a very accepting way so she knows I don't disapprove.

From the authors' files

Petting

Another important adolescent sexual activity is petting. *Petting* includes all forms of erotic physical contact between two persons except coitus (penetration of the vagina by the penis). Petting typically proceeds in a fairly standard sequence as the partners become better acquainted. It usually begins with lip kissing and progresses to deep kissing, sometimes called "French kissing" or "soul kissing." This involves tongue contact and stimulation of the lips and interior of the mouth with the tongue. Typically, petting then advances to manual and oral stimulation of the female's breasts. It then may proceed to manual stimulation of the female genitals, and sometimes to manual stimulation of the male genitals. Next in the progression may be rubbing together the naked genitals, but without vaginal penetration. Petting may then advance to oral stimulation of female or male genitals. Not all petting follows this progression, and not all petting proceeds this far. For some couples petting may consist only of kissing. Other couples may experiment with every possible sexual activity, including orgasm, except coitus (Kinsey et al., 1948, pp. 540–541).

Incidence of Petting

Adolescents today start petting at an earlier age than those in previous generations, and the incidence of petting is greater. Almost all of today's youth experience some petting by the time they reach age twenty. Not many experience it before puberty, but there is a steady increase until late adolescence, which is the period of the highest incidence of petting. A

300

An important sexual activity of adolescents is petting, usually beginning with kissing.
Paul Fusco/Magnum Photos, Inc.

study of college students made in 1975 found that 80 percent of college men and 73 percent of college women had engaged in heavy petting, petting that involved genital stimulation (Leslie, 1978, p. 108).

Petting is more common among persons planning to go to college. Those who are not college bound are more likely to engage in coitus in their heterosexual relationships. College-bound youths consider petting more morally acceptable than coitus, even though the female who engages in extensive petting is sometimes slurringly referred to as a "technical virgin" or "demi-vierge." This means she still can claim to be a virgin because she has not experienced actual penetration of her vagina by a penis, but that she is sexually experienced because she has tried many other forms of sexual contact, often to orgasm. People of less education consider most of the petting activities as perversions, particularly if they are used as a substitute for coitus (Kinsey et al., 1948, p. 542; Kinsey et al., 1953, pp. 259–267; Reevy, 1973).

A male Ph.D. in his late thirties recalls: There was a guy in graduate school with us that was so lower class he even thought French kissing was perverted. We all

From the authors' files

laughed about it when he wasn't around. He really freaked out if someone mentioned getting a blow job.

Recent studies, however, indicate an increasing acceptance of various erotic techniques in the lower social and educational levels. There is also a decrease in the importance of petting for people of higher social levels as they increasingly move on to full sexual intercourse in their premarital relationships (Hunt, 1974, pp. 137–138).

Effects of Petting

Petting among adolescents is widely practiced and also widely condemned. It is not surprising to find young people expressing some guilt and anxiety over this activity. Often they are concerned about the physical effects of petting. When petting does not result in orgasm but produces a high degree of sexual arousal, it may leave the participants with some degree of general nervous tension as well as specific congestion or even pain in the genital area. As some have described it, "It is as frustrating as hell." Not all persons experience unpleasant aftereffects; many who do, relieve them by masturbation after they leave their petting partner (Kinsey et al., 1948, p. 542; Kinsey et al., 1953, p. 263).

When petting is part of an affectionate relationship and results in orgasm for both partners, its effects can be beneficial for sexual maturation. Sometimes the physical and emotional satisfactions are greater for adolescents who engage only in petting than for the adolescents for whom intercourse is fairly routine. The variety of activities possible with one's mouth, hands, and body produce a prolonged and intense sexual stimulation that may be missed in the hasty intercourse of inexperienced adolescents. Although physical satisfaction is very much involved in petting to orgasm, it is often not the only goal of the experience. Extended physical and verbal expressions of affection often result in a very satisfying experience. Petting can be an important form of communication and sharing between a boy and a girl (Sorensen, 1973, pp. 183–185).

Petting in adolescence is related to later sexual adjustment in marital or nonmarital intercourse. Petting educates both partners to the wide variety of pleasurable and erotic contacts besides intercourse that are possible between two people. Petting may help young people gradually to lose their inhibitions concerning different kinds of physical contact, and may help them to learn what is most stimulating to themselves and to others. Petting often is the source of the first orgasm attained by a female in a heterosexual relationship. Learning to have an orgasm from petting apparently makes it easier for females later to experience orgasm in intercourse (Kinsey et al., 1953, pp. 263–264).

302

Homosexual Activities

A fairly small proportion of people report having homosexual experiences during adolescence. However, this depends partly on how one defines a homosexual experience. It may be erotic arousal by a person of the same sex regardless of whether there is physical contact. It may include sexual contact with a person of the same sex regardless of whether there is erotic arousal. Or it may consist of arousal to orgasm by physical contacts with individuals of the same sex. Here we will use the term *homosexual experience* to refer to physical contacts between people of the same sex who are seeking sexual stimulation or satisfaction with each other.

Incidence of Adolescent Homosexual Activities

Of adolescents who report homosexual experience, the majority of males have their first experience when they are eleven to twelve years of age, the majority of females when they are six to ten. As boys approach late adolescence, they have more frequent homosexual experiences. By the end of adolescence about 20 percent of males have had a homosexual contact to orgasm. The likelihood of homosexual contacts for females does not increase with age, so that by the end of adolescence less than 10 percent have had a homosexual experience (Reevy, 1973; Sorensen, 1973, pp. 291–292).

Sometimes adolescent boys seek homosexual contacts with older men in exchange for money. In these contacts, typically the boy allows the man to engage in oral stimulation of his penis ("suck him off") but does not reciprocate in any way. For most of these boys this represents an easy way to pick up a little extra money. They deny that they enjoy the contacts, although they usually achieve orgasm (Reiss, 1963).

Adolescent Tolerance of Homosexuality

In spite of the visibility of gay liberation, most adolescents today do not expect to engage in homosexual activities. Roughly three-fourths say they have never had a homosexual contact and are sure they would never want to do so. But almost half are quite tolerant of such activities for other people provided they are willing participants. They explain their tolerance in several ways. One is as a concern for the total person rather than his or her sexual behavior. Another is a philosophy of "being yourself" rather than playing socially preassigned sex roles. Also, they contend that love is irrational and accidental so that no one can predict when or with whom it will occur (Sorensen, 1973, pp. 286–293).

303

Effects of Homosexual Activities

Typically, homosexual experiences in adolescence are transitory and do not lead to a preference for homosexuality in adulthood. Often they occur between very young persons who have learned only the adult distinction between "naughty" and "nice," but not the adult distinction between "perverted" and "normal." At such an early age children may be aware of the disapproval generally applied to heterosexual activities but unaware of the stigma surrounding homosexual activities. If they learn about the latter when they are older, they may experience considerable anxiety over these activities of their youth. A young man recalls:

My second homosexual experience was one with my older cousin. . . . The contact involved lying down on the couch and unzipping each other's pants and fondling, caressing, and masturbating each other's genitals. . . . These homosexual contacts at the time did not seem abnormal at that age, but as I look back upon it I can hardly believe I ever did such a thing. Today I would never consider doing such things.

Martinson, 1973, p. 99

The principal danger of homosexual experiences at any age is that others may give these experiences and those who participate in them the social label "queer" or "perverted." Adolescents detected in homosexual activities may be stigmatized by their families, friends, teachers, and potential employers. This could happen in spite of their heterosexual preferences and in spite of the fact that homosexual activity has been experienced by a sizable proportion of the self-identified normal heterosexual people in the United States.

Sex Dreams

Sexual dreams are not unusual in adolescence, particularly for males, but they constitute only a very small part of total sexual outlet. When sexual dreams include orgasm, they are accompanied in the male by ejaculation, and consequently are commonly called "wet dreams." Sexual dreams for the female may also include orgasm, although no physical evidence remains to confirm this.

By age twenty approximately three-fourths of males but less than 10 percent of females have had dreams to orgasm. The male peak in frequency of nocturnal dreams is reached in the late teens or early twenties, but the female peak is not reached until somewhere between ages forty and fifty-five. These sexual dreams, particularly for males, may include unconventional types of behavior unacceptable to the individual when awake. An individual's inhibitions are less likely to operate in sleep.

304

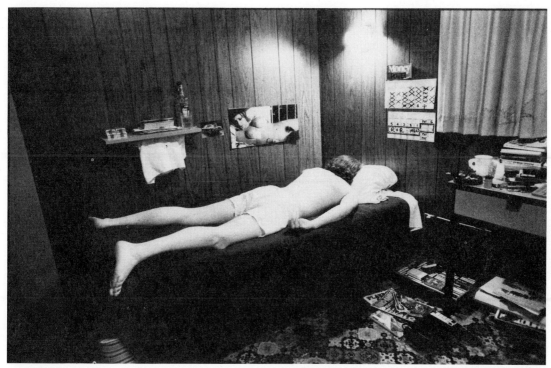

Sex dreams and sex fantasies are a common activity in adolescence.
Marcus Halevi

Nocturnal dreams usually proceed to orgasm quite rapidly, even in an individual who is slow to respond when awake. Occasionally an individual's earliest experience of orgasm may occur during a dream, although this is not typical (Kinsey et al., 1948, pp. 517–530; Kinsey et al., 1953, pp. 191–226).

Sexual Intercourse

Traditionally our society has proclaimed firmly that sexual intercourse before marriage is wrong. Under no conditions has premarital sex been officially approved or considered right and good. This is in contrast to the norms of other societies throughout history. Other societies have dealt with sex before marriage in various ways, but very few have completely banned it as we have (Hunt, 1974, pp. 109–111). Recently, however, various writers have expressed the opinion that a sexual revolution, both in attitudes and in behavior relating to premarital sexuality, has been occurring in the United States since 1900. (Cannon, 1971). This revolution has been attributed to many factors. Among them are the growth of individualism, the decline of traditional controls, the increased emphasis on science and existential philosophy, the anonymity of urban life, and the development of more effective contraceptives (Ehrmann, 1964).

Attitudes Toward Premarital Intercourse

Some writers argue that there has been a liberalization in sexual attitudes but that actual behavior has remained much the same. They contend that petting has increased but that the rate of premarital intercourse has not changed significantly. Instead, the real revolution has been in attitudes; now premarital sex is more accepted and less guilt-producing (Reiss, 1967).

In spite of the arguments, the sexual revolution has been slow in appearing. In both 1937 and 1959 a national sample of men and women were asked if "it is all right for either or both parties to a marriage to have had previous sexual intercourse." At both times more than half the respondents indicated they felt is was all right for neither the woman nor the man. As late as the mid-1950s more than half the college students believed sexual abstinence to be the proper premarital standard (Hunt, 1974, pp. 109–119).

Some signs of changes in attitudes began to appear by the beginning of the sixties. Studies showed some acceptance of premarital sex if the couple was engaged, in love, or even just felt strong affection. The percentage of college women approving of premarital coitus in a love relationship in 1958 was 17 percent; in 1968 it was 38 percent. In 1973 a national survey showed that 90 percent of women of college age approved of premarital sex for women "in love, but not engaged" (Hunt, 1974, pp. 109–119).

In spite of the sampling limitations of the surveys involved, the percentages represent strong evidence for a dramatic change in attitudes toward premarital sex. The new standard has been termed "permissiveness with affection," implying a liberation of sexuality within the context of love relationships (Reiss, 1968). This positive support for sexual liberation is not felt by all segments of the population. The new liberal attitude is much more common among the young. Of women aged fifty-five and over, only 23 percent approve of premarital intercourse for a woman in a love relationship, compared to 90 percent of young women (Hunt, 1974, p. 118).

Behavior Change

The increasing acceptance of premarital intercourse has not immediately resulted in behavior changes. Various studies of premarital coitus among college women indicate no significant change between 1929 and 1965. During that period, studies found that between 11 and 20 percent of   306 college women had experienced premarital intercourse (Cannon, 1971). In the late 1960s significant changes in sexual behavior began to appear. Several studies of college women in 1969 and 1970 found that the incidence of premarital coitus was between 37 and 56 percent (Cannon, 1971). Data published in the mid-1970s indicate that between 70 and 85 percent of college women have experienced coitus (Hopkins, 1977).

Increased rates of premarital intercourse are found among males also, though not to such a striking degree because they had a higher initial rate. The greatest change is for males who are college bound. In 1974, by age seventeen, half the males who would eventually go to college had had premarital sexual experience; this is more than double the figure for 1938. By age seventeen, nearly three-fourths of the males who did not plan to go to college had had intercourse, compared to a little over two-thirds of a comparable sample in 1938. Of married males aged eighteen to twenty-four, 95 percent had had coitus before marriage (Hunt, 1974, pp. 132–134).

The Double Standard

It is clear that the double standard of sexuality for young males and females has undergone some revision in recent years, with the incidence of female sexual experimentation coming closer to that of males (Peplau, Rubin, and Hill, 1977; King, Balswick, and Robinson, 1977). Nearly thirty years ago, most males — particularly lower-class ones — had their first sexual experience with prostitutes, or the local "peg board." Many girls who petted or had sexual intercourse did so to bargain for the favors of a boy they wanted to date, favors that disappeared soon after the girl became known as an "easy lay." For both males and females, early sexual experiences were linked with exploitation, competitiveness, and sometimes impersonality.

Today both males and females are more likely to experiment with petting and sexual intercourse voluntarily, sometimes recreationally, but often with mutual affection and respect. Males are less likely to experience their first intercourse with a prostitute or an impersonal sex partner, and females are less likely to experience petting or their first intercourse as part of the competitive struggle for desirable males. Young men are also less likely to perceive sexually active young women as "easy lays" and to demand that their wives be at least technical virgins (Hunt, 1974). For both males and females the percentage of those having premarital intercourse increases with increased emotional commitment (Lewis and Burr, 1975). (See Table 10.6)

In spite of revision of the double standard in recent years, there are still some important differences between males and females in their motivations for premarital sexual experimentation. In their peer group males

Percent Currently Having Premarital Intercourse, by Level of Commitment   Table 10.6

Level of Commitment	Males %	Females %	Number
On first date	21	2	1592
Infrequent dating	27	3	1532
Going steady	42	23	1235
Engaged	56	36	545
Number	560	1032	

Source: Robert A. Lewis and Wesley R. Burr, "Premarital Coitus and Commitment Among College Students," *Archives of Sexual Behavior* (New York: Plenum, 1975), p. 76.

have considerable support — perhaps even pressure — for their sexual activities, regardless of their emotional commitment to their partner (American Educator, Winter, 1979, p. 5). Females are much less likely to have peer support for premarital sex; their sexual activities depend to a great degree on their emotional involvement with their sexual partner (Miller and Simon, 1974). Put another way, it is "being in love" that makes sex acceptable for the female.

Conflicting Values

Despite the relative sexual liberation of young people today, they live in a society that is not wholly in favor of their liberation. Parental, religious, and social pressures for chastity before marriage have eased but not disappeared. (See Selection 10.2.) Attitude surveys indicate a fairly high current level of social acceptance of premarital sexuality. But national averages do not tell the story of the value conflict in which most adolescents are caught. Parents of adolescents are generally much less permissive in their attitudes than are the adolescent's peer group. One recent study found that although 30 percent of the mothers had premarital sexual experience, only 3 percent would be accepting of premarital sex for their daughters. Although 51 percent of the fathers had premarital coitus, only 18 percent would accept sexual permissiveness for their sons (Wake, 1969). Although most parents are not tolerant of sexual experimentation by their adolescent children, they maintain a double standard in their attitudes. Most parents are more likely to condone the sexual activities of a son than of a daughter (*American Educator*, Winter, 1979, p. 5).

Contemporary adolescents are caught between the very restrictive attitudes of their parents and the very permissive attitudes of their peers. In most instances the sexual standards of the peer group are more influential than parental or religious standards in determining sexual behavior of adolescents. There is a tendency for the adolescent to perceive parental permissiveness as a low point on a continuum, with peers' permissiveness as a high point. Her or his own attitudes fall between these two points but are much closer to the peers' (Reiss, 1967, pp. 129–139).

In addition to the conflict between parental and peer attitudes, the contemporary adolescent is caught between the fantasy of ecstatic liberation often portrayed by the mass media and the reality of his or her own tentative fumbling attempts to reach this ecstasy. Finally, realistic sex education is often still inadequate. Thus, it is not surprising that some males and many females find their first sexual experience less than ecstatic.

A young college woman reports: At the age of eighteen I lost my virginity after being brought up in a strict Catholic family and hearing from the age of one how I couldn't lose my virginity till I was married. I was so curious as to what virginity was all about that I'm surprised I didn't lose it earlier. It was a pleasant experience — not earthshaking as I had imagined, but much more painful than I expected.

From the authors' files

The lack of sensual pleasure in first intercourse is apparently due to a combination of many factors, such as nervousness, guilt, lack of skill, fear of failure, and fear of discovery. In one study over one-third of males and nearly two-thirds of females reported a feeling of regret after their first experience. This regret was often attributed to fear of pregnancy or moral conflicts. Also, they expressed disappointment because first intercourse did not meet their expectations for an ecstatic experience (Hunt, 1974, pp. 150–155).

Ann Landers

Selection 10.2

Dear Ann Landers: Where are all those advocates of premarital sex when it comes time to pick up the pieces after a "momentary mistake"? And what do the advocates do to help prevent such "mistakes"?

Do they tell the kids that though a relationship may be "meaningful" to one partner it may be purely self-satisfaction, an ego trip, or mere condescension on the part of the other?

Do they tell the kids that a "meaningful relationship" may be so meaningful that one partner may have an overwhelming desire to cement that relationship with a child?

Do they tell the kids they should NEVER count on the other person to take precautions — and that to be perfectly safe, both parties should count on themselves?

Ann Landers, *San Diego Tribune* (Chicago: Field Newspaper Syndicate), November 20, 1974.

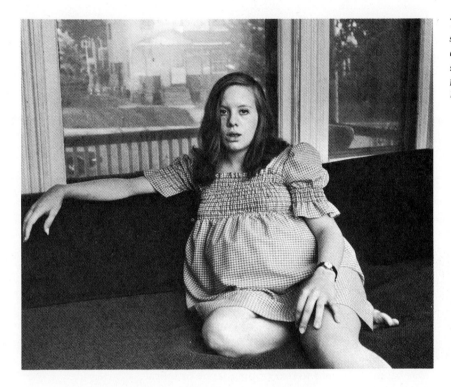

Do they tell the kids that a girl's most intense desires are very likely to accompany her most fertile times? ("Just this once?")

Do they tell the kids that a person's "love" might be severely dampened by resentment and turn to full-fledged hate should that person feel trapped?

Do they tell the kids that alternative solutions to an unwanted pregnancy are vastly more difficult to handle than coping with the challenges of virginity?

Do they tell the kids that the legality of abortion is insignificant compared to the emotional trauma?

Do they tell the kids that giving up a child for adoption is no simple matter for anyone who has had a "meaningful relationship"?

Do they tell the girls that keeping an out-of-wedlock baby goes far beyond the enjoyment of having a cute little bundle of joy to cuddle and take for a stroll in the perambulator?

Where are those advocates of premarital sex when it's time to mend lives suffering from their advice? — A Shoulder to Cry On

Thank you for a good letter. I'm glad you offered your shoulder to "cry on." Mine is already the wettest in the U.S.A. (Are you listening, students?)

Communication About Sex

The gap between parental expectations and the sexual attitudes and behavior of most adolescents is related to a lack of communication about sex. The great majority of adolescents say they do not talk freely with their parents about sex. They often feel their parents lie to themselves and are unwilling to acknowledge their children's sex problems or sexual behavior. Consequently, most adolescents have less respect for their parents' opinions about sex than about other matters.

A sixteen-year-old girl reports: Boy, my parents are really all screwed up about sex — particularly my mom. She keeps telling me how awful it is just because it just ruins your reputation and gets you pregnant. She acts like she never would do it except that she is married and she feels she has to. I know that's a lie. She keeps telling me not to neck or anything because we might get "carried away." If she really thought it was awful then she wouldn't be worried about me having those feelings and wanting to do it when I'm not married. She must think I'm really dumb.

From the authors' files

As adolescents grow older, disagreement with parental opinions on matters of sex increases. Most adolescents agree that many young people are leaving home these days because they are seeking sexual freedom (Sorensen, 1973, p. 240). It is not surprising to find that adolescents who are more involved in sexual activities have much less commitment to traditional adult authority, family, and religion (Vener, Stewart, and Hager, 1972; Miller and Simon, 1974).

Sex Education

The communication gap between parents and adolescents on sexual matters extends to sex education. The overwhelming majority of young people report that their parents never talked to them about sexual matters before or during their high school years. A male graduate student from a wealthy home says:

Neither of my parents ever really spoke to me about it. Mostly, I was warned about the potential of pregnancy; that was virtually all. Oh, there was a little hint of gentlemanly bragging by my father, to suggest he enjoyed sex, but it was all terribly vague.

Hunt, 1974, p. 124

This is as true for college-educated and white-collar families as it is for blue-collar or noncollege ones. Most young people get their sexual information either from their friends or from books and magazines (Hunt, 1974, pp. 120–130). (See Table 10.7)

311

Primary Sources of Sex Information[1]   **Table 10.7**

Source[2]	Males (Percent "Yes")	Females (Percent "Yes")
Mother	24	62
Father	30	12
Male Friends	81	10
Female Friends	15	70
Brothers	13	6
Sisters	4	15
Other Relatives	6	7
Clergymen	7	5
Teachers	14	22
Doctors	6	8
Independent Reading	67	67

[1] Students were given a card with the above list of options, and were asked: At the beginning of high school, which, if any, of the people listed on this card had given you a good deal of information about sex?

[2] Percentages total more than 100 percent because respondents could answer affirmatively to more than one category.

Source: "Sources of Sex Information and Premarital Sexual Behavior" by Graham Spanier reprinted by permission from the *Journal of Sex Research,* 1977, 13, p. 78.

Many schools now provide some form of sex education for young people.

Ellis Herwig/Stock, Boston

"The Board of Education requires me to give you some basic information on sex, reproduction and other disgusting filth."

Apparently, many parents avoid discussing sex with their children in an effort to prevent them from knowing about and, therefore, indulging in premarital sexual activities. Common parental attitudes are: "I try to keep them from knowing too much," or "I think sex education corrupts the minds of fifteen- to sixteen-year-olds" (Libby and Nass, 1971, p. 228). Ironically, the lack of parental sex education is related to adolescent promiscuity. When parents are the major source of sex education on the widest variety of sexual topics, their children are less apt to be promiscuous and they engage less often in premarital sexual intercourse. Rather than encouraging early sexual experimentation, parents who give their children extensive sex education may prevent premature experience (Libby, Gray, and White, 1978; Spanier, 1977). A sixteen-year-old girl comments:

My folks have never openly discussed the matter with me. I think I would have had my virginity longer if they would have — otherwise I felt I had to learn from experience.

Hass, 1979, p. 283

313

A New Sexual Ethic

In spite of these conflicts with parents and anxieties induced by faulty sexual education, over half of adults agree that young people today have healthier attitudes toward sex than do their parents (Wilson, 1975). And there is evidence that members of the current younger generation are in many instances developing more satisfying sexual relationships than have previous generations of Americans. They extend foreplay and intercourse for longer periods of time and employ a greater variety of techniques in both activities. For example, nearly all males aged eighteen to twenty-four today report mutual fondling of genitals in foreplay, and roughly 70 percent report oral-genital contact in premarital sex. Of a comparable group of males in 1938 only 33 percent had experienced fellatio and 14 percent had tried cunnilingus premaritally (Hunt, 1974, pp. 166-167). In contrast to the impression that premarital intercourse is usually rushed because of the male's lack of experience or control, young single persons today under age twenty-five spend about fifteen minutes in foreplay and another fifteen minutes in intercourse (Hunt, 1974, p. 160). This is in contrast to the finding reported in 1948, that a sizable majority of males reached orgasm within two minutes after the insertion of the penis into the vagina (Kinsey et al., 1948, p. 579).

There have also been increases since the late 1930s in the percentage of unmarried people who use positions in coitus other than the conventional posture with the male above and facing the female. Unmarried people now are at least twice as likely to use such variations as intercourse with the female above, or on-the-side, sitting, standing, or rear-entry vaginal intercourse (Hunt, 1974, p. 156).

Considering the extended duration of foreplay and intercourse, as well as the more imaginative techniques utilized in premarital sex, it is not surprising that young single females are more often orgasmic than their counterparts of a generation ago. In 1972 three-fourths of young women reported having orgasms in premarital intercourse, whereas less than one-half did so twenty years before (Hunt, 1974, pp. 147–148).

For adolescents in the United States today there is convincing evidence of a much greater incidence of premarital sexual activity of all kinds, and also evidence that these activities are enjoyed more freely than was possible in previous generations. Yet there does not seem to be any evidence of a persuasive mood of hedonism. On the contrary, the sex ethic of the great majority of adolescents today is essentially liberal romantic. Recreational sex is chosen only by a small minority (Peplau, Rubin, and Hill, 1977). Most younger persons now take pride in the ability to have good sexual experiences, but they have a conviction that these experiences are best when they are part of a committed and perhaps monogamous love relationship (Hunt, 1974, pp. 151–155).

314

CHAPTER 11 / *Sexuality in Adulthood*

Not all people in the United States marry, but most do at least once. Furthermore, most sexual intercourse takes place within marriage. Typically one of the concerns of early adulthood is choosing a marriage partner and developing a sexual relationship with this partner. Some young adults are involved in other types of relationships, such as living together, group marriage, homosexuality, or mate-swapping. These less typical sexual patterns will be examined in later chapters. Although this chapter focuses principally on sexual relationships within marriage, much of what is discussed here applies to enduring sexual relationships that fall outside legally constituted, heterosexual marriage.

Marital Sex as Pleasure

Western civilization has restricted the sexual pleasure of married couples more severely than almost any other culture. With the beginning of Christianity marital sex was viewed as evil, preferable to sex outside of marriage but inferior to chastity. This negative view of marital sex generally dominated Western society until modern times. In the late eighteenth and the nineteenth centuries its restricting effect on marital sexual pleasure was particularly strong. This was intensified by the prevalent middle-class view that the nice woman did not have lustful sexual desires or feelings. Some wives at the very highest or very lowest social levels probably did enjoy sex, but the typical middle-class or working-class wife of that era found it no better than a tolerable duty. A substantial minority found it revolting, shameful, or degrading (Hunt, 1974, pp. 175–178).

Contemporary Attitudes

By the early part of the twentieth century the legitimation of human sexual pleasure in the Western world had begun. Sexual intercourse began to be viewed as a healthful activity that made a positive contribution to the marital relationship. In the 1930s and 1940s sexual liberation began to have an effect on married sex, and Kinsey found that the differences between the marital sexual practices of the younger and older generations in his samples were consistently in the direction of greater pleasure, freedom, and mutual participation (Kinsey et al., 1948, pp. 563–582; Kinsey et al., 1953, pp. 346–408; Hunt, 1974, pp. 179–185). Data from the early 1970s indicate that this trend has continued (Hunt, 1974, pp. 179–185).

Most discussions of sexual liberation focus on its implications for the unmarried, unfaithful, or unconventional. But its greatest impact has been

Couples today have greater pleasure, freedom, and variety in their sexual life.
Owen Franken/Stock, Boston

on the large majority of persons involved in relatively stable and monogamous marriages. The principal effect of sexual liberation has been an increase in the freedom of husbands and an even greater increase in the freedom of wives to experiment with and enjoy a variety of sexual practices in their married life (Hunt, 1974, pp. 179–185).

Sexual Intercourse Within Marriage

In general, contemporary marriages involve higher frequencies of sexual intercourse than did those of a generation ago. Both husbands and wives report such increases, and the frequency is higher in every age group than it was for comparable groups in the 1930s and 1940s (Hunt, 1974, pp. 186–195). For example, as shown in Table 11.1, the median frequency of intercourse in the youngest age group has increased from 2.45 times per week in the 1940s to 3.25 times per week in 1972; in the oldest age group it increased from 0.50 times per week in the 1940s to 1.00 time per week in 1972.

317

Frequency of Marital Coitus per Week (Male and Female Estimates Combined), 1938–1946/9 and 1972   Table 11.1

1938–1946/9 (Kinsey)		1972 (Hunt)	
Age	Median Frequency	Age	Median Frequency
16–25	2.45	18–24	3.25
26–35	1.95	25–34	2.55
36–45	1.40	35–44	2.00
46–55	.85	45–54	1.00
56–60	.50	55 and over	1.00

Source: Reprinted with permission of Playboy Press. From *Sexual Behavior in the 1970's*, p. 191, by Morton Hunt. Copyright © 1974 by Morton Hunt.

Face-to-face interviews with a probability sample of 2,486 adults in the forty-eight contiguous states conducted in early 1970 (Wilson, 1975) confirm the findings of higher frequencies of intercourse. (See Table 11.2). The highest frequencies of intercourse are for younger rather than older persons and for better-educated as opposed to less-educated people. Also, females report lower frequencies of intercourse than do males, presumably because this sample includes unmarried (divorced, widowed, and never married) as well as married adults. As will be discussed in Chapter 12, unmarried women, particularly in older age ranges, have less opportunity and social support for sexual encounters than do unmarried men.

There is strong empirical and theoretical evidence that the significant increase in marital coital frequency is due in part to changes in the definition of female sexuality. Traditionally women's sexuality was not acceptable, but the current women's movement has challenged this idea. The liberalization of attitudes and behaviors among young women is quite likely a reflection of their receptivity to the women's movement and its redefinition of appropriate female sexuality (Mahoney, 1978).

Not only has frequency of marital intercourse increased in the United States since the beginning of the twentieth century, but also the regularity of orgasm for married women. A study in 1929 found that 46 percent of married women had "a very inferior or wholly lacking orgasm capacity" (Hunt, 1974, p. 210). By early 1970 a dramatic change is indicated. In a sample of married white females only 7 percent reported that orgasm occurred in intercourse "almost none or none of the time" (Hunt, 1974, p. 212).

Frequency of intercourse or orgasm is not the only indicator of sexual pleasure. But subjective evaluations of marital sexual pleasure confirm the conclusions suggested by the more objective measures. In a national sample in the early 1970s, 99 percent of males and 88 percent of females

Frequency of Marital Intercourse, by Gender, Age, and Education, in Percentages[1] Table 11.2

Males (N = 911)		Age			Education		
Frequency of Intercourse	Total %	21–29	30–59	60+	Coll.	H.S.	Elem.
Not at all	8	8	3	25	8	6	17
Some, but less than 1 per month	16	10	12	34	14	14	21
1 or 2 times per month	17	8	20	18	17	16	16
1 or 2 times per week	35	34	45	6	35	39	25
More than 2 times per week	16	35	14	3	20	18	8
No answer	8	5	6	14	6	7	13
Females (N = 1370)		Age			Education		
Frequency of Intercourse	Total %	21–29	30–59	60+	Coll.	H.S.	Elem.
Not at all	20	12	13	50	21	14	38
Some, but less than 1 per month	11	4	11	15	9	10	16
1 or 2 times per month	12	10	15	6	13	13	8
1 or 2 times per week	30	34	37	5	29	34	17
More than 2 times per week	13	30	12	1	16	14	6
No answer	14	10	12	23	12	15	15

[1] The exact wording of the item is: "In the past six months how often, on the average, did you engage in sexual intercourse?"

Source: "The Distribution of Selected Sexual Attitudes and Behaviors Among the Adult Population of the United States" by W. Cody Wilson, reprinted by permission from the *Journal of Sex Research,* 1975, 11, p. 170.

in the youngest cohort termed their marital coitus either mostly pleasurable or very pleasurable. These positive reactions extended even to the oldest age group (fifty-five and older), with 94 percent of males and 83 percent of females giving mostly pleasurable or very pleasurable ratings to their married sexual relations (Hunt, 1974, pp. 215–216).

Sexual Practices

Not only are married couples in the United States today having intercourse more often and with greater enjoyment than their counterparts a generation ago, but they are also using sexual practices indicative of more open attitudes toward sexual experimentation within the marital relationship.

Foreplay   In the 1930s and 1940s, among married couples with no college education, mouth-breast contact and manual stimulation of the genitals were seldom used in sexual foreplay. Cunnilingus (oral contact with female genitals) and fellatio (oral contact with male genitals) were totally avoided in marriage by the majority of this lower-education group. College students in the 1930s and 1940s were more likely than older people to have used these techniques (Kinsey et al., 1948, pp. 572–578; Kinsey et al., 1953, p. 361; Hunt, 1974, pp. 195–196).

From data gathered in 1972 we conclude that every form of foreplay is now used at least occasionally in a larger percentage of marriages than was true in the previous generation. The stronger the former taboos against an activity, the greater the magnitude of the change. The most dramatic changes are those that have occurred in oral-genital acts, but because of the old taboos, initiation into these activities is not always easy.

A male in his late twenties reports: I had never gotten into oral sex until I met Betty. She would go down on me and finally I got to really like that. After a few months of us being together she told me that she never could have a vaginal orgasm and she wanted me to go down on her so she could have one. I just could not do it because I always thought it was dirty and smelly down there. We tried all sorts of things to make it seem better, like taking a bath together and her using perfumed douches and her shaving off her pubic hair. Finally I tried it and when I first put my face down there I thought it had a musky smell, but then I got busy with what I was doing and it had no odor or flavor and it was fine. Now I have gotten used to it and if I really like a woman, I go for it. Not that I get my kicks that way, but if I really like her then I like to do it for her.

From the authors' files

Both fellatio and cunnilingus are now used within marriage by a majority of high-school-educated persons and by a great majority of those with some college education. (See Table 11.3.) The growing freedom to use previously forbidden erotic techniques extends to a much lesser degree to anal intercourse and manual or oral stimulation of the anus (Hunt, 1974, pp. 197–200). Sometimes use of these more forbidden techniques is interpreted as evidence of greater intimacy and commitment than that involved in intercourse alone. One college-educated woman in her early

320

Selected Techniques of Foreplay Used Premaritally by Young White Males
With More Than Grade-School Education, in Percentages

Table 11.3

	Kinsey (Adolescent to 25)	Present Survey (18 to 24)
Male manual play with female genitals	91	90
Female manual play with male genitals	75	89
Fellatio	33	72
Cunnilingus	14	69

Source: Reprinted with permission of Playboy Press. From *Sexual Behavior in the 1970's*, p. 166, by Morton Hunt. Copyright © 1974 by Morton Hunt.

thirties describes her experience with anal intercourse in relationship to her strong feelings for the man involved:

I even tried anal sex with him. I had been afraid to but I did it because he wanted to and it is not bad. Except I cannot have a climax that way and he does not either. But he says he likes it because it is tighter there. I would not do it with just anyone, though. I do it with him because I really like him.

From the authors' files

There has also been a small increase in the past decade in the typical duration of marital foreplay among the college educated, and a substantial increase at the noncollege level. Kinsey and his associates found that foreplay of less-educated husbands was typically very brief, in many instances limited to the most perfunctory sort of body contact, such as a single kiss or genital pat. Only the college-educated husband was likely to extend precoital petting for five to fifteen minutes or more (Kinsey et al., 1948, pp. 572–573). Today prolonged foreplay is as much a part of marital sex as it is for those still in the unmarried courtship stage. The median duration of foreplay for both single and married people under age twenty-five is fifteen minutes (Hunt, 1974, p. 201).

Coitus In coitus, as well as in foreplay, contemporary American married couples apparently have considerably more freedom and pleasure than did their counterparts a generation ago. Today's married couples practice more variety in positions in intercourse. For example, three-quarters of married couples have coitus with the female on top of the male at least occasionally, compared with about one-third a generation ago. Vaginal intercourse with the penis inserted from behind is now used by 40 percent of married couples, compared to 10 percent in the 1930s and 1940s. Anal

321

intercourse is now used occasionally by some married people, particularly in the younger age groups (Hunt, 1974, pp. 202-204).

Not only do contemporary couples prolong foreplay more than previous generations did, but they also prolong coitus itself. Kinsey and associates found that in the 1930s and 1940s probably three-quarters of all males reached orgasm within two minutes after beginning coitus, and many reached climax in less than a minute or even within ten or twenty seconds after vaginal penetration (Kinsey et al., 1948, p. 580). Data from the early 1970s show that the median duration of coitus for married couples is about ten minutes. It is the younger couples who prolong coital sex the longest, in contrast to the stereotype of the young man who supposedly lacks orgasmic control because of his urgent drive and inexperience (Hunt, 1974, pp. 204–206).

Masturbation Many people assume that married persons have no need to masturbate because they have a spouse who can provide them with coitus as a sexual outlet. Data indicate, however, that about three-fourths of married men and two-thirds of married women under the age of thirty-five masturbate (Williams, 1980, p. 106).

For many married men masturbation functions as a supplement to their usual marital sex life. These men may masturbate as a matter of routine before brushing their teeth in the mornings. Others may do so to relieve physical tension during periods of stress. One husband in his late thirties reports:

I masturbated a lot when I prepared for my examinations — by God, I did it all day long. If I didn't eat or smoke, I masturbated — and then I could go on studying.

Hessellund, 1976, p. 137

Many wives who masturbate report they do so as a supplement to their marital sexual relationship. One wife in her thirties reports:

It is periodical, but normally every third day, even if we are together. . . . Well, I tell him about it and say it is sad that it has to be like that. But it is as if he doesn't realize that I want to be with him more often.

Hessellund, 1976, p. 137

Most married persons who masturbate keep it a secret from their spouse. When a spouse does know of the masturbation, some are upset about it, some accept it, and some will help the partner. One husband in his late thirties reports that he masturbates

"four to five times a month when my wife has her periods. Our relationship is so good that she also helps me sometimes"

Hessellund, 1976, p. 138

Married persons who masturbate do not have more positive attitudes toward masturbation than those who do not masturbate. Many of these persons feel their masturbatory activities are an unnatural substitute that is morally wrong, and describe the activity as impersonal and cold, causing a sense of guilt (Hessellund, 1976).

Sexual Pleasure and Marital Satisfaction

Evidence points to greater freedom and pleasure in marital sexual relations in the United States today than in previous generations. There is more variety in both foreplay and coitus, and both are engaged in more frequently and for longer periods. Now more women are able to achieve orgasm more often in their marital relations, and the reported level of pleasure in marital sex is quite high for nearly all married persons (Hunt, 1974, pp. 230–232). At the same time, standards for sexual performance are going up. The new freedom to talk and write about sex has made more people aware of the possibilities for sexual pleasure that they may be missing. Now that more women are free of the old idea that nice women don't enjoy it, they are likely to be trapped by the notion that women should have multiple orgasms at every sexual encounter. Men are equally trapped by this expectation, for they feel they must try harder to give their partner and themselves more ecstasy. The current American emphasis on greater sexual achievement has led some social scientists to conclude that sex has become work, with performance standards and objective criteria for success, and published manuals for achieving the elusive sexual peak experience (Lewis and Brissett, 1967).

There remains the question of whether the pleasure of marital sex contributes to the overall success of the marital relationship. Although in this case it is difficult to separate cause and effect, data indicate there is a high positive correlation between subjective ratings of closeness in the marital relationship and pleasure in marital sex. (See Table 11.4.) For example, of the couples who rated their marriage as "very close" about 97 percent rated their sexual relationship as "mostly pleasurable" or "very pleasurable." In marriages that persons rated as "not too close or very distant," the marital sex life was described as neutral or unpleasurable by roughly half the respondents. This appears to support the conclusion that sexual pleasure to some degree depends upon and is productive of emotional closeness and love in human relationships. Couples who have a free and pleasurable sexual relationship are much more likely to feel emotionally close than those who do not. And a close, loving relationship is much more likely than a distant one to involve free and pleasurable sexual expression (Hunt, 1974, pp. 230–232).

323

A close loving relationship usually involves a pleasurable sexual expression.
Joel Gordon

The merging of the sexual and emotional aspects of a relationship is beautifully described in the following excerpts from an interview with Diane Pike, widow of the late Bishop James A. Pike:

I think it was the third time we were intimate together sexually that I discovered the transcendent — or divine — aspect of the sexual relationship. We had talked for about two hours about the subject and Jim was the first person I had ever met, and certainly the first man I had ever met, who understood what I was talking about in this transcendent realm. It was incredible to me that someone could really understand what I meant and could feel very much the same. Well, when we made love with one another that night I had a transcendent experience in orgasm. It was a fantastic thing. . . . I discovered that I could give such physical pleasure to Jim that it would somehow just lift me into this loss of self. It was like to give him pleasure physically gave me pleasure at all dimensions of my being, and therefore I would be lifted into a thing where I could have orgasm without his even touching me. It was as if sexual orgasm became an expression of the joy of my whole being.

Otto and Otto, 1972, pp. 291–294

324

Percentage of Sexual Pleasure by Marital Closeness   Table 11.4

Married Males	Marital Relationship		
	Very Close	Fairly Close	Not Too Close or Very Distant
Marital sex life in past year was:			
Very pleasurable	79	45	12
Mostly pleasurable	20	50	47
Neither pleasurable nor nonpleasurable	1	2	17
Mostly or very nonpleasurable	—	3	24
Married Females	**Marital Relationship**		
	Very Close	Fairly Close	Not Too Close or Very Distant
Marital sex life in past year was:			
Very pleasurable	70	30	10
Mostly pleasurable	26	58	28
Neither pleasurable nor nonpleasurable	1	8	45
Mostly or very nonpleasurable	3	4	17

Source: Reprinted with permission of Playboy Press. From *Sexual Behavior in the 1970's*, p. 231, by Morton Hunt. Copyright © 1974 by Morton Hunt.

Factors Affecting Sexual Pleasure

Even though a couple may feel very close and have relatively few inhibitions concerning sexual expression within their relationship, yet they may, at any point in their relationship, find that their sex life is not as satisfying or exciting as they would like it to be. Some sexual problems require professional help for their solution. (See Chapter 5.) Others, to be discussed here, are more transitory in nature and may be resolved by a couple who are truly concerned about each other's feelings and who understand the biological, psychological, and social factors influencing sexual response.

Cultural Conditioning

One set of problems stems from the different cultural conditioning of American males and females. The female is usually taught that her most important role in life is to be a wife and mother. Her energies are channeled into preparing herself for this role and attracting a man who will marry her. She is taught that sex should be confined to the marriage relationship or at least to a love relationship that is expected to lead to marriage. Sexual feelings not associated with a love relationship must be suppressed or denied. Although the women's liberation movement has changed, and is still changing, the typical pattern of female socialization to some degree, the old pattern is still predominant in our culture. Because of early training, most females enter courtship and marriage with "person-centered sex," or sex with affection, as their preference (Reiss, 1973). Their friends reinforce this pattern because they typically give the highest status to the girls who are the most attractive as potential wives. Females are rewarded most by their peers when they can get the most evidence of love from their dates in exchange for the least amount of sexual contact (Gagnon and Simon, 1973).

Typical male cultural conditioning in our society is quite different from that of females. Most males are taught that their most important role is achievement within the masculine world (Gross, 1978). The goal of being a good husband and father is rarely emphasized as their primary one. One proof of achievement in the man's world, besides occupational success, is number of sexual conquests. The male's peer group is most likely to give him high status if he can get the most sexual access from his dates in exchange for the least evidence of love (Gagnon and Simon, 1973). Accordingly most males seek "body-centered sex," or sex just for fun (Reiss, 1973).

Attitudes Toward Love and Sex

The different attitudes that males and females in our society have toward love and sex are an expected part of courtship in most instances. It is expected that the male will try to get all the sexual favors he can without being trapped into a commitment to a more permanent relationship. And it is expected that the females will try to get as much evidence of commitment as possible without giving very much sexual access. Although these differences in male and female sexual orientation are expected in early stages of courtship, a more compatible set of attitudes is important in an enduring marital relationship. Unfortunately, once these roles are well learned, they are not easy to dismiss after the wedding is over.

Many wives, particularly in the lower social classes, do not want to risk 326 losing their sexual inhibitions because they worry about what their husbands would think of them if they did so. One twenty-eight-year-old married woman expresses her concerns about oral sex:

I always feel like it's not quite right, no matter what Pete says. I guess it's not the way I was brought up, and it's hard to get over that. He keeps telling me it's OK if it's between us, that anything we do is OK. But I'm not sure about that. How do I know in the end he won't think I'm cheap?

Rubin, 1976, p. 144

Although their husbands may reassure them, many working-class wives remain fearful of expressing their sexuality or experimenting with new techniques. Partly these women have difficulty forgetting the prohibitions instilled in their upbringing, and partly they are aware of the ambivalence many husbands have about their wives' sexuality. When asked about fellatio, one young working-class husband said:

No, Alice isn't that kind of girl. Jesus, you shouldn't ask questions like that. She wasn't brought up to go for all that fancy stuff. You know, all those different ways and that oral stuff. But that's OK with me. There's plenty of women out there to do that kind of stuff with. You can meet them in any bar any time you want to. You don't have to marry that kind.

Rubin, 1976, p. 144

Generally, middle-class husbands are less ambivalent about their wives' sexuality and tend to think less often in stereotypical good girl–bad girl terms. Their wives live in an atmosphere that more readily accepts or encourages them to be sexually uninhibited within the marital relationship (Rubin, 1976, p. 144).

There is some evidence that the more dramatic differences between male and female sexual attitudes are diminishing. Both the women's movement and the zero population growth movement are concerned with de-emphasizing the wife-and-mother role and emphasizing occupational achievement for women. A move in this more equalitarian direction is under way and will probably continue. More similar life goals for men and women will affect attitudes toward premarital, marital, and extramarital sex. As women develop greater freedom in their premarital sexual relationships, they will expect sexual satisfaction in their marital relationship as well as an equal right to seek extramarital sex. As men are freed from the demands of their role as the tough, aggressive, sole breadwinner, they may allow themselves the luxury of emotions such as tenderness and love. The eventual result may be men and women with similar attitudes combining the best of the more traditional male and female attitudes, perhaps an acceptance of sex as a physically satisfying activity for men and women, with a preference for sex within an affec-

Women are now freer to take an active role in seeking sexual satisfaction in their relationships.
Abigail Heyman/Magnum Photos, Inc.

tionate and stable relationship (Reiss, 1973). There is some evidence that this view of human sexuality is increasing among American youth today (Reiss, 1973; Hunt, 1974).

Differences in Sex Drive

Differences in sex drive may cause some degree of discontent with the sexual aspects of a relationship.

A graduate student in her early thirties reports: I have a fairly strong sex drive and most men don't. Like I want to have sex every day. Now I am going with a man who is forty-two and his sex drive is really less than mine. So I finally had to learn to masturbate, and now that I learned how I can have a better climax that way. Except it is just physically better but it is not psychologically satisfying. He does not like it that I do that, though. But I need it and he cannot do it every day. He drinks a bit and I think that makes it worse.

From the authors' files

Sex drive is partially determined by biological factors such as androgen levels, thyroid function, and general health. If one's sex drive is felt by oneself or one's partner to be too low or too high, a medical checkup can determine whether some physical problem is involved that can be medically treated. A lengthy discussion of these medical problems is outside the scope of this text.

328

Differences in sex drive between men and women often result from cultural and social factors. Orgasms, particularly in females, involve a number of responses that may be developed or inhibited according to the culture in which one is raised. Only a few generations ago in the United States it was believed that a normal and well-brought up woman had little or no sexual feeling. Although this belief is not so strong now, women are not encouraged to have as strong a sex drive as men. At the same time men are expected to have an imperious need for frequent sexual outlets. If they do not give evidence of being always ready and eager, they run the risk of being considered unmasculine.

A man's apparently ever-present sexual readiness may be not simply an expression of urgent sexual need, but the result of a socialization process that constricts the development of the emotional side of his personality in all but sexual expression. Conversely, a woman's insistent plea for a nonsexual demonstration of love is the result of socialization that encourages the development of the emotional side of her personality in all but sexual expression (Rubin, 1976, pp. 147–148). One married couple in their late twenties expresses it this way:

The wife: I don't understand him. He's ready to go any time. It's always been a big problem with us right from the beginning. . . . I feel like that's all he wants sometimes. I have to know I'm needed and wanted for more than just jumping into bed.

Rubin, 1976, p. 146

The husband: She complains that all I want from her is sex, and I try to make her understand that it's an expression of love. I'll want to make up with her by making love, but she's as cold as the inside of the refrig. . . .

The wife: He keeps saying he wants to make love, but it just doesn't feel like love to me. Sometimes I feel bad that I feel that way, but I just can't help it. . . . I want him to talk to me and tell me what he's thinking about.

The husband: Talk! Talk! What's there to talk about? I want to make love to her and she says she wants to talk. How's talking going to convince her I'm loving her?

Not all persons in our society are exposed in equal degree to the type of sex-drive conditioning described above, but most absorb some part of it. It is not surprising that many young couples find they are somewhat sexually incompatible because the woman has less sex drive than the man. Usually the problem is a temporary one. Most women begin to discard many of their former inhibitions and learn to respond to sexual stimulation within the context of a loving, trusting relationship (Clark and Wallin, 1965; Gebhard, 1968).

Speed of Sexual Response

Another potential cause of sexual incompatibility is the relatively long period of physical stimulation necessary for most women in our culture before they are aroused to the point of orgasm. Typically the American male responds sexually to a wide variety of sexual stimuli, such as the sight of an attractive woman, pornographic materials, or watching his wife prepare for bed. Most young women in this country have been conditioned against acknowledging, even to themselves, that visual or auditory sexual stimuli are arousing (Schmidt and Sigusch, 1970). Whereas a husband may be sexually aroused by the sight of his wife changing clothes, he may not realize that she is not similarly aroused but instead requires considerable foreplay before her ardor can match his.

It appears that women are as capable as men of responding to all types of erotic stimuli, but the cultural acceptance of women's erotic response has been lacking in the United States. There is some evidence that this is changing and that women are now developing more erotic imagery. There is also evidence that males are becoming aware that their clothing and hair styles can evoke erotic imagery in females (Reiss, 1973). Most women gradually overcome their cultural conditioning, and through the years their general sexual response improves so that it more nearly matches (or even exceeds) that of their mates. This is probably the result of several factors. One is a redefinition by the woman of her role in relation to her sexuality. In other words, if she is married, then some degree of sexual feeling and sexual expression is acceptable in even the more repressive segments of our society. Another factor that usually increases sexual responsiveness of women is practice. Orgasm involves a number of responses that may be developed or inhibited by the cultural milieu. Because sexual experimentation during childhood and adolescence is usually strongly discouraged for females in the United States, a good deal of their sexual learning typically takes place after marriage. Studies show that the percentage of coitus resulting in orgasms for women rises steadily with the length of their marriage (Clark and Wallin, 1965; Gebhard, 1968).

One young college-educated woman described her experience this way: Before Bill and I were married we had done a lot of pretty heavy petting, and I had orgasms then sometimes. But I insisted we wait until we got married before we really had sex. And maybe if we had had sex before we got married, I would not have wanted to get married after all because sex really was not good for a long time. Maybe we were just trying too hard. But he always finished so fast and I pretended that I was all satisfied too because I was afraid it would make him feel bad to think that he had failed. But after a while I began to wonder what was wrong with me that I could have orgasms when we petted before we were married, but I could not have any with intercourse. It really made me depressed

From the authors' files

and I could not talk with anyone about it. Finally one night he decided to try to do it twice in a row, and the second time he was a lot slower to finish and I could tell he was going to be a lot slower so I just relaxed and had a real one for the first time. After that I knew I was all right as a woman, but it still was not easy for him to slow down and me to speed up. It took us a long time to figure out how to work our way around that one.

Marriage Versus Courtship

Several factors operate to increase sexual pleasure over time in an enduring relationship, but there are also some aspects of marriage that tend to decrease sexual enthusiasm. One is that a marital partner becomes associated with some of the less pleasant aspects of living. During courtship most couples keep their relationship separate from the duller or more unpleasant parts of life, such as earning a living or cleaning the house. Courting involves relatively more pleasant or recreational activities — movies, picnics, parties — than does marriage. A sexual relationship during courtship is associated with the other exciting and pleasurable facets of courtship. In contrast to courtship, marriage involves two persons sharing all of life, not just its more exciting and fun-filled dimensions. It is not surprising that the person who asks you to pay the overdue bills or wash the laundry or carry out the garbage is sometimes not as sexually stimulating as the person who asked only that you be an attractive date or

Marriage involves dealing with more of the practical aspects of life than does courtship.
Dave Sagarin/Editorial Photocolor Archives, Inc.

an interesting companion. The movie star Marlene Dietrich describes the shift from courtship to marriage this way:

> Your heart leaps when he notices you. . . At all times you and your heart wear your Sunday dress — and he falls in love with you. The world and life are wonderful. But every day is not Sunday and you soon take off your Sunday dress. You and your heart. And somewhere back in your fairy-tale-hungry mind you are disappointed. And you think it must be somebody's fault. . . . He does not necessarily have to be the reason. He just happens to be around when the constant Sundays become weekdays, with a few Sundays here and there and far apart, when you find out about life as you see it now in your weekday clothes.

Dietrich, 1961, p. 250

Simple boredom also takes its toll of sexual excitement in a marriage. In sex, as in any aspect of living, unrelieved sameness year after year, though it has its reassuring aspects, can lead to boredom and loss of the thrill of anticipation. Some couples try to overcome this by experimenting with new coital positions, new techniques for sexual arousal, erotic materials, or a new setting for lovemaking. Other couples try secret love affairs or consensual adultery as a means of preserving the security of a marriage while experiencing the excitement of a new sexual partner. These latter alternatives will be discussed in more detail in Chapter 12.

Role Relationships and Social Class

Social class and conjugal role relationships are related to each other and to marital sexual satisfaction. Conjugal role relationships can be described in terms of a continuum from segregated relationships to joint relationships.

Segregated conjugal role relationships refer to those "in which the predominant pattern of marital life involves activities of husband and wife that are separate and different but fitted together to form a functioning unit or that are carried out separately by husband and wife with a minimum of day-to-day articulation of the activity of each to the other" (Rainwater, 1965, p. 30). In contrast, *joint conjugal role relationships* are those "in which the predominant pattern of marital life involves activities carried out by husband and wife together (shared) or the same activity carried out by either partner at different times (interchangeable)" (Rainwater, 1965, p. 30). Role relationships in any given marriage may approach either the segregated or the joint end of the continuum, or may fall somewhere in between the two extremes.

The organization of conjugal role relationships is closely related to social class; in general, the higher social classes have more joint relationships and lower classes the more segregated ones. One study found joint relationships in 88 percent of upper-middle-class couples compared to segregated relationships in 72 percent of lower-class couples (Rainwater, 1965, pp. 32–33).

Both social class and conjugal role relationships are related to sexual satisfaction for both men and women and for both whites and blacks. Couples in higher social classes are more likely to report satisfying sexual relations than are couples in lower social classes. (See Table 11.5.) Couples with highly segregated role relationships are more likely to report less satisfactory sexual relationships than are those with less role segregation. (See Table 11.6.) These relationships are equally true for both sexes and both whites and blacks, but husbands on the average consistently report more enjoyment in sexual relations than do the wives, and blacks more than whites. The difference in sexual pleasure in males and females is especially true in marriages characterized by highly segregated conjugal role relationships. Rainwater (1965, pp. 68–70) found that the husband enjoyed sex more than his wife in 80 percent of white and 75 percent of black couples in which there was high role segregation (See Table 11.7.)

A partial explanation for these findings of the relationship of social class, conjugal role relationships, and sexual satisfaction may lie in the different attitudes expressed toward the function of marital sexual relations. (See Table 11.8.) In marriages in which there is high role segregation, both husband and wife tend to view the primary function of marital sex as physical pleasure and relief of tension. Characteristically many of these role-segregated couples view sex as the wife's duty, whether she enjoys it or not. One wife explains her feelings about sex:

I knew it was part of my married life and I wanted to do all any wife should do but I just couldn't help dreading nights when he would want to make love. . . . I could live happily the rest of my life without any sex except that I want more children. . . . I try to do my whole duty in the matter and I always expect to do that — I think that's only fair to your husband. . . . I think that's the way it is, probably, the husband is always in the mood, the wife isn't, and I think it's just the way people are, men always eager, women not near as much so.

Rainwater, 1965, pp. 89–90

A man with a role-segregated relationship expressed quite clearly his interest in obtaining physical satisfaction without any indication of an understanding of other functions of marital sexual relations:

Before I was married, I knew what sexual relations were. I knew how it felt and what was done, but that's about all. I guess I thought it was done just for fun. . . . To me it is just as important as any other part of marriage. I can't say what they do for me other than just to satisfy my desires, I guess, the same as they do for any man.

Rainwater, 1965, p. 98

333

Attitudes Toward Marital Sexual Relations, by Social Class   Table 11.5

Attitude	Social Class		
	Middle	Upper-Lower	Lower-Lower
Husbands			
Highly positive	78%	75%	44%
Mildly positive	22%	25%	56%
Number	56	56	59
Wives			
Highly positive	50%	53%	20%
Mildly positive	36%	16%	26%
Slightly negative	11%	27%	34%
Totally negative	3%	3%	20%
Number	58	68	69

Source: Lee Rainwater, "Sex in the Culture of Poverty," in Broderick and Bernard (eds.), *Individual, Sex, and Society,* copyright © The Johns Hopkins University Press, 1969, p. 131.

Attitudes Toward Marital Sexual Relations Among Lower-Class Couples, by   Table 11.6
Degree of Role Segregation and Race

Attitude	Degree of Role Segregation			
	Intermediate* Whites	Blacks	High Whites	Blacks
Husbands				
Highly positive	72%	90%	55%	56%
Mildly positive	28%	10%	45%	44%
Number	21	21	20	25
Highly positive	64%	64%	18%	8%
Mildly positive	4%	14%	14%	40%
Slightly negative	32%	18%	36%	32%
Totally negative	—	4%	32%	20%
Number	25	22	22	25

* Includes the few jointly organized couples.

Source: Lee Rainwater, "Sex in the Culture of Poverty," in Broderick and Bernard (eds.), *Individual, Sex, and Society,* copyright © The Johns Hopkins University Press, 1969, p. 133.   334

Table 11.7

Segregation and Comparative Enjoyment of Sexual Relations by Husband and Wife Lower-Class

		Husband Enjoys More	Equal Enjoyment or Wife Enjoys More
Whites	Number		
Intermediate segregation	21	38%	62%
Highly segregated	20	80%	20%
Negroes			
Intermediate segregation	21	33%	67%
Highly segregated	24	75%	25%

Source: Reprinted by permission from Lee Rainwater, *Family Design* (Chicago: Aldine Publishing Company, p. 69); copyright © 1965 by Social Research, Inc.

Attitudes Toward the Function of Marital Sexual Relations, by Social Class

Table 11.8

Function	Middle Class	Lower Class	
		Intermediate Role Segregation	High Role Segregation
Husbands			
Emotional closeness and exchange	75%	52%	16%
Psychophysiological pleasure and relief only	25%	48%	84%
Number	56	40	21
Wives			
Emotional closeness and exchange	89%	73%	32%
Psychophysiological pleasure and relief only	11%	27%	68%
Number	46	33	22

Source: Lee Rainwater, "Sex in the Culture of Poverty," in Broderick and Bernard (eds.), *Individual, Sex, and Society,* copyright © The Johns Hopkins University Press, 1969, p. 135.

In marriages with less role segregation, both husband and wife are more likely to view sex as a means for expressing and increasing emotional closeness. (See Table 11.8.) Consequently these couples express more affection, use more consideration to increase their partner's pleasure, and experience more pleasure themselves. One husband expresses his feelings about marital sex:

My wife and I both enjoy each other; we are compatible. The main satisfactions are physical, of course, and also emotional relaxation, and a sense of unity. That goes for both of us. . . . Sex is very important; it is the way the family grows bigger and closer in feeling between husband and wife.

Rainwater, 1965, p. 73

His wife's feelings about their sexual relationship are also quite positive:

My husband was very understanding. It was wonderful after the first couple of months and still is. . . . I know that I am pleasing my husband, I can tell, and he makes me feel that I am the best thing in the world. It makes him feel good, feel that he is a man and that he has made me feel good. I have an orgasm almost all the time.

Rainwater, 1965, pp. 73–74

Sex and Marital Tensions

An unsatisfactory sexual relationship can produce tensions in an otherwise happy marriage, and marital tensions can be reflected in an otherwise satisfactory sexual relationship. Usually sexual and marital satisfaction are closely related, although in some cases a couple may maintain a good sexual relationship when every other aspect of their life together is filled with tension. Some other couples may have a loving and harmonious marriage in spite of some glaring sexual incompatibilities.

The Clarks are an example of a sexually adjusted but otherwise unhappy couple (Komarovsky, 1962, pp. 95–98). Mrs. Clark is an untidy and unstable woman, unable to cope with her children or housework, and worried about her husband's periodic depressions. Their untidy apartment upsets her husband, who comes and goes without concern for her wishes. Yet their sexual relations are both frequent and satisfying:

His own preference was to be with her during one, two or three orgasms previous to his own and then to work them both up to a good climax. She said, "But we ain't always got time for that or if we are too tired. Saturday night's a good time after he gets his mind off things and relaxes. . . . Sometimes he wants it when I don't and I usually let him have it. But he really don't like that so much, and he wants us to come together. He understands real good what I need to get me going. Sometimes I don't want to start and he'll fool around until I do."

Komarovsky, 1962, p. 96

336

But the Clarks are an exception; most studies have found a positive correlation between sexual adjustment and general satisfaction with marriage (Komarovsky, 1962, pp. 94–95). A study of letters written to the national office of the American Association of Marriage Counselors found that sexual-affectional problems were cited as the cause of marital difficulties by over half the couples seeking help for their failing marriages (DeBurger, 1975). Husbands and wives differed somewhat in their description of sexual problems perceived to be central to marital disruption. The predominant complaints of a wife were that her husband was having an affair, wanted sex too often, or was sexually crude; that sex relations were disgusting; and that she did not have an orgasm. Sexual complaints of a husband were more often that sex relations with his wife were generally poor, that sex was infrequent, and that his wife was cold and unresponsive, and that he was worried about his low sex drive.

Sexuality in the Two-Career Family

Often the decision not to have children is combined with the wife's wish to have a career outside the home. Regardless of whether there are children in the home, two careers in a family will have an impact on the sexual relationship of a couple (Hall and Hall, 1979). In a family with a working mother and young children, time and energy for lovemaking are usually severely curtailed because one or both adults have a multitude of family and household responsibilities waiting when they arrive home. Most of these household chores are usually assumed by the woman, even when she has a professional career (Bryson and Bryson, 1975).

It is especially important for such couples to set their priorities carefully and plan time for intimacy. One woman reports the following in answer to a question concerning her biggest sexual difficulty:

Physically, there's only 24 hours in a day, and between ages 30 and 40, one can cope with only job, children and other responsibilities. The question is priority. The desire to get ahead in this world occurs in your 40s and believe me, now you need every ounce of energy to try to get there.

Pietropinto and Simenauer, 1979, p. 89

Many careers require geographic mobility for job advancement or even for job retention, as when one's company relocates. Marital and sexual difficulties can occur when the best career opportunities exist in a different location for each partner (Holmstrom, 1972, pp. 29–58; Bird, 1979). Some couples survive living in different locations and visiting each other periodically. But this arrangement assumes either some sexual deprivation or some freedom from the expectation of sexual monogamy (Kirschner and Walum, 1978). Even when both husband and wife have jobs in the same geographic area, their differing work schedules may interfere with their sex lives. One husband reports:

Presently biggest difficulty is due to time difference in our jobs and not being able to be alone for spontaneous sex. Cope by doing without a lot of times and just putting up with it.

Pietropinto and Simenauer, 1979, p. 97

Although it is becoming more acceptable for women in the United States to have careers, it is usually assumed that the man's career is the more important one. Among couples with the husband and wife in the same profession, it is not unusual for the husband to be more successful or productive in his career than is his wife. The typical reason for this difference in career success is that the wife was willing to make her career secondary to the needs of her family and of her husband's career (Heckman, Bryson, and Bryson, 1977).

If a wife is more successful in her job than her husband — however the couple choose to define success — he may feel emasculated in her eyes and in those of friends, family, and colleagues. If he is more successful than she is, she may feel resentment for the real or imagined advantages men have in the pursuit of careers. The tensions brought about by competitiveness in a two-career family can be highly destructive of a sexual relationship, as well as most other aspects of a marriage (Holmstrom, 1972, pp. 103–12).

Sexual Compatibility

There is no way to make generalizations about sexual relationships in early marriage. Sexual relationships are a part of all aspects of the relationship between two unique individuals influenced by their physiological and psychological make-up and their current social situation. A couple may develop during courtship a sexual relationship that is physically and emotionally satisfying. Yet this same couple may find their sexual relationship deteriorate sadly in their marriage because of problems stemming from a multitude of factors, some of which have been discussed in this chapter. In contrast, another couple may have little or no satisfactory sexual contact during courtship, but may develop a beautiful sexual relationship after some years of marriage. And even the most compatible relationship is not immune to outside disruptive influences such as illness, unemployment, an abnormal child, financial setbacks, and crises in the extended family. Because of the multitude of factors that can affect human relationships and sexual functioning, it should not be surprising that even happily married people may at some time experience some dissatisfaction with their sex lives. They may find that their partner has too much or too little sex drive, too many or too few inhibitions, sexual preferences that seem strange or annoyingly prosaic. Or they may discover that their mate no longer provides sufficient erotic stimulus for their continuing sexual arousal.

Over one million persons in this country have participated in marriage-enrichment programs in an effort to improve their marital relationship (Koch and Koch, 1976). These marriage-enrichment programs are usually weekend programs that teach husbands and wives how to be more accepting, more responsive to each other's needs, and more intimate. The programs are not intended to provide marriage counseling or sex therapy. Usually only couples who perceive their relationship as good are asked to attend. However, many couples learn to make their good relationship better. One authority believes the key to the process is to have couples find out that all married pairs experience conflict and dissatisfaction but that these can be used constructively to improve rather than destroy the relationship. Many couples attending these workshops

Within a caring relationship sexual incompatibilities can often be resolved.
Joel Gordon

find afterward they have an improved communication, a new level of intimacy, and an improved sexual relationship (Koch and Koch, 1976).

Within an otherwise good relationship apparent sexual incompatibilities often can be resolved if both partners are open to giving and receiving sexual pleasure in a variety of ways. For example, a man who cannot get an erection on some occasion need not leave his partner unfulfilled if he realizes that using his finger, tongue, or a vibrator can produce orgasm in most women. Or a woman can use oral or manual stimulation to bring her husband to orgasm if she does not feel like having intercourse. The increasing acceptance of oral-genital and manual-genital contact in foreplay opens the way to their acceptance and enjoyment as alternatives to coitus.

An unsympathetic and unloving person may find excuses to leave his or her partner sexually unfulfilled. Sometimes, effecting sexual adjustment requires professional help. But in a loving relationship between two persons with healthy attitudes toward their own sexuality, there is no reason for sexual frustration. With open communication, apparent sexual incompatibilities can often be resolved.

Sexuality and Aging

With advancing age, changes occur in the sexual organs along with the rest of the body. Decreased hormone production in later years affects the appearance of the sex organs and the manner in which sexual response occurs.

But physical changes alone cannot account for the sexual feelings and activities of the individual in the later years. In humans, sexuality is not the simple product of hormone levels. Many other factors enter into the equation. These include social attitudes toward the sexuality of older people, personal feelings about sexual attractiveness, availability of sexual partners, and fears of rejection or sexual failure. These factors, in combination with many others, make it difficult to describe the sexual behavior of the typical individual in the later years. There is as much variety in the sexual activities and responses of older people as in any other age range.

In the paragraphs that follow we will describe the typical physical changes that occur with advancing age in the male and female, and the way in which these changes may affect the sexual functioning of the older person. We will also discuss some of the sexual problems that aging may create. Throughout this discussion it is important to remember that although these patterns are typical of many people in the United States, they are not universal.

340

Sexual Changes in the Female

In the human female the most dramatic reproductive change associated with aging begins with menopause, when the monthly menstrual periods stop. The average age at onset of menopause is now around fifty, although menopause may occur any time between the mid-thirties and early sixties (AMA, 1972, p. 81).

Menopause Menopause is the result of diminished estrogen production and is accompanied by the gradual end of a woman's reproductive capacity and the atrophy of the reproductive organs. In the years after menopause the fat in the breasts decreases and the soft glandular tissue is replaced by fibrous cords. The tissues of the vulva become thinner and lose their engorgement response. The vagina shrinks in size and loses some of its elasticity. There is a decrease in the vaginal secretions important for lubrication during intercourse. The lining of the vagina tends to lose its normal acidity and thus becomes more susceptible to infection (Rubin, 1965, pp. 129–130). Sexual intercourse in the older woman may lead to a urinary tract infection through passage of bacteria into the entrance of the urethra. Women should urinate soon after sexual relations to flush out any organisms in the lower urinary tract (Charatan, 1978).

Some of the most distressing physical changes may be slowed through hormone therapy. The natural vaginal secretions, for example, may be replaced by application of creams or suppositories containing estrogen. This hormone is quite effective in overcoming vaginal dryness, restoring elasticity of the vaginal lining, and re-establishing normal acidity (Rubin, 1965, pp. 131–135).

About 40 percent of women experience additional symptoms during menopause that are probably brought about by the temporary imbalance of the endocrine system as the ovaries decrease their estrogen production. These symptoms include irritability, insomnia, "hot flashes," headaches, and depression. They can usually be relieved by supplemental hormones prescribed by a physician. Some physicians recommend oral hormones, others give hormone injections, and a few use hormone pellets implanted under the skin. Estrogenic hormones are often prescribed, but some prescriptions contain estrogen combined with a progestin (synthetic progesterone) and others contain estrogen combined with testosterone. There is some evidence that use of estrogen increases the likelihood of uterine cancer, although some researchers question these findings (Horowitz and Feinstein, 1978). Some physicians will not prescribe supplemental estrogen for menopausal women because of the possibility of increased risk of uterine cancer. The supplemental hormones also tend to prevent the changes in the vagina that may make sexual intercourse uncomfortable or even painful (Rubin, 1965, pp. 130–135).

The symptoms that we typically associate with the physical changes occurring at menopause are not found among women in all cultures. In one agricultural sect in India, for example, women do not experience any unpleasant secondary symptoms of menopause such as hot flashes, irritability, dizziness, and insomnia. These Indian women eagerly look forward to menopause because it brings an improvement in their status. Once these women can no longer bear children they may remove their veils, mingle freely with the men, and be treated with respect *(Sexuality Today,* August 7, 1978).

Reaction to Sexual Stimulation   After menopause the measurable physical reaction to sexual stimulation changes. Among women past age sixty the degree and duration of physical response to sexual stimulation are usually diminished. Breast engorgement and nipple erection are less pronounced. There is a decrease in vaginal secretions and in engorgement of the clitoris and labia. Contractions of the pelvic platform during orgasm are less vigorous and less frequent, declining from a typical frequency of five or six contractions at age thirty to two or three at age seventy. Sometimes these contractions are painful rather than pleasurable (Kaplan and Sager, 1971).

Even though most of the measurable physical indicators of sexual response diminish after menopause, subjective feelings of pleasure and satisfaction in intercourse remain the same or even increase for many women. This increased satisfaction may be the result of freedom from concern about possible pregnancy. Although menopause signals the end of a woman's reproductive capacity, it does not mean the end of a woman's sexual life. Research has shown that the capacity for sexual intercourse with orgasm does not necessarily diminish with age, particularly among women who enjoyed an active sex life during their procreative years. In fact the female orgasmic *refractory period* (the period of time after orgasm when sexual arousal cannot occur) remains very short throughout life (usually less than a minute) so that women retain their capacity for multiple orgasms. An eighty-year-old woman apparently has the same physiological potential for orgasm that she had at age twenty. This does not necessarily mean that her sexual interest or sexual activity is the same, however (Kaplan and Sager, 1971).

Sexual Changes in the Male

Men also experience sexual changes with increasing age. Androgen output declines steadily but slowly in most men until about age sixty, and thereafter remains relatively constant. In the healthy male, sperm production does not abruptly cease. Although fertility is gradually decreased, viable sperm can be found in very elderly men (Rubin, 1965, p. 117).   342

Hormone levels   The decline of hormone levels in men is slower and milder than in women, often becoming evident ten to fifteen years later than in women. In contrast to women, most men have a gradual reproductive decline usually without producing clinical symptoms and without a physiological readjustment comparable to menopause in the female. Some men, however, show symptoms so similar to those experienced by the menopausal woman that they have been regarded by many physicians as cases of "male menopause." This is a controversial subject in medicine; some physicians deny that it is possible to make such a diagnosis (Voigt and Schmidt, 1977).

Slowly decreasing hormone levels are associated with physical changes in the aging male. As the typical man ages, the amount of each ejaculate decreases and the ejaculatory jets are less forceful. With advancing years the testicles become smaller and less firm. Usually erections become less frequent and less rigid. By age fifty the typical male may require from eight to twenty-four hours after orgasm before erection may again be achieved (Kaplan and Sager, 1971, pp. 117–118).

Sexual Arousal   One change that comes with age may be a boon to many men and their sexual partners. As they become older most men require a longer period of stimulation to reach orgasm (Masters and Johnson, 1966, pp. 251–252). This enables the male to prolong intercourse and extend the period of pleasure for himself and his partner. This may enable his partner to enjoy multiple orgasms in coitus that she could not achieve with a man unable to sustain intercourse because of his own orgasmic urgency. Because sexual arousal occurs more slowly, the older man is more likely to engage in more leisurely foreplay, with greater pleasure for himself and his partner (Charatan, 1978).

Sexual Activities of Older People

Virtually all physical activities of older people are somewhat slowed or occur less frequently because of the body's decreased strength or vigor. A man in his eighties ordinarily cannot run a mile as easily as a much younger man; an elderly woman typically cannot cope with a demanding career plus several small children with the ease of a woman in her twenties. This decreased physical capacity of the aging is reflected in their sexual activities as well as in other spheres of life. But the relationship between sexual activity and advancing years is affected by many social, psychological, and interpersonal factors, which vary from person to person. Some may cease all sexual interaction after a certain age; others may continue at the levels of their younger years until death. In one study, 13 to 15 percent of people over age sixty-five reported increased frequency of sexual intercourse (Pfeiffer, 1975, p. 46).

343

Some older persons have a loving spouse and increased leisure time to enjoy their relationship. Joel Gordon.

Sexual Activities in Aging Women   The sexual activity of an aging woman is dependent on her past sexual enjoyment and the availability of a sexually capable partner. Women who enjoy sexual relations and who have an appropriate partner may continue to have an active sex life even in their eighties and nineties. On the other hand, women who previously found little or no pleasure in intercourse may use menopause and advancing age as an excuse to avoid sexual relations (Pfeiffer and Davis, 1972).

Even the woman who enjoys her sexuality may have lower levels of sexual activity in her later years because of ill health or lack of an interested and able partner. A study of a national probability sample of 2,486 adults in the United States in the early 1970s found that 50 percent of women over age sixty reported no intercourse at all in the previous six months (Wilson, 1975). (See Table 11.2.) However, studies that take into account frequency of masturbation and nocturnal dreams to orgasm find that the total sexual outlet for women does not decline appreciably with age. When women no longer have coitus or have coitus less frequently, they often compensate by masturbatory or dream activity (Van Keep and Gregory, 1977).

344

An overwhelming majority of older women report they stopped having sexual intercourse because their husbands had either died, became ill, lost interest, or lost their ability to have an erection. Even when the husband was still living, a large majority of the women blamed their husbands for the cessation of their marital sexual activities. Interestingly, their husbands blamed themselves also (Pfeiffer, 1969).

Sexual Activities in Aging Men   In all age groups, males report a higher level of sexual interest and sexual activity than do women. Although most men in good health continue to maintain some degree of sexual interest throughout their adult life, the proportion engaging in sexual intercourse does gradually decrease with advancing age. Data show that seven out of ten healthy married couples over age sixty are sexually active, some into their late eighties (Charatan, 1978, p. 155). Another study found that one-fifth of males in the United States are still sexually active in their eighties (Pfeiffer, 1969). Kinsey and his colleagues found that involuntary morning erections, which averaged twice per week for men in their early thirties, decreased to an average of about once a week for men in their early sixties (Kinsey et al., 1948, p. 230).

Men with positive attitudes toward sex and a history of positive sexual experiences are more likely to continue sexual activities in their later years. Others may experience a cessation of sexual activities because of worry over declining health, boredom with monogamy, and fear of failure or inadequacy (Pfeiffer and Davis, 1972).

Apparently it is easier for an older man than for an older woman to find a willing sexual partner or spouse. In a typical year 35,000 men but only 16,000 women over age sixty-five wed (Lobsenz, 1974). This can probably be explained by a variety of factors, some of which we discussed above. One is the higher death rate for males, which results in a greater number of women than men in the older age groups. Also, a generally greater social acceptance of male sexuality and sexual aggressiveness permits men to pursue a mate when they feel so inclined. One study found that almost 90 percent of women stopped having intercourse when their husbands became ill or disinterested, or died; in contrast, marital status had little or no effect on the sexual activity of men (Pfeiffer, 1968). Finally, social acceptance of older men seeking younger partners gives older men a variety of sexual opportunities not open to older women.

Even with the numbers on their side, however, not all men find sex partners readily available. One older man reports:

When you get to my age, your chances of finding a sex partner are pretty slim. So I just beat my meat whenever I get horny, which ain't too often these days.

Lopez, 1979, p. 66

Sexual Problems of Aging

It is difficult to discuss sexuality in the middle and later years without also considering the effects that common health problems often have.

Health   Any type of ill health that saps one's physical strength decreases the capacity for sexual activity. Also there are some surgical procedures fairly common in later years that directly affect sexual functioning for a time. For example, hysterectomy (removal of the uterus and sometimes the ovaries and Fallopian tubes in the female) or prostatectomy (removal of the prostate gland in the male) are not unusual in the older population.

Hysterectomy   Many people erroneously believe that a hysterectomy for a woman or a prostatectomy for a man means the end of sex life because sex organs are removed in these operations. This is not true. Removal of the ovaries, which may or may not be part of a hysterectomy, deprives the woman of an important source of estrogen and progesterone, causing symptoms of hormone deficiency similar to those in menopause. But these problems can be controlled by local or internal doses of supplemental hormones, as described earlier in this chapter in connection with physical changes associated with menopause. Removal of the uterus does not directly affect a woman's hormone balance and for most women has no appreciable effect on capacity for intercourse or orgasm. A few women, however, are disappointed after hysterectomy to find that part of the sensation of deep penetration is absent, since the penis can no longer stimulate the cervix and the abdominal muscles that are involved when the uterus is displaced during coital thrusting.

Prostatectomy   The prostate gland secretes the bulk of the fluids that, along with the sperm that develop in the testes and the fluid produced by the seminal vesicles, form the male ejaculate. Total prostatectomy usually results in the loss of ability to have erections because of nerve damage resulting from the surgery. But lesser surgical procedures need not interfere with erectile ability. However, many men will have *retrograde ejaculation* in which the seminal fluid is ejaculated into the bladder rather than out through the urethra. Retrograde ejaculation does not interfere with a man's sexual performance or sexual pleasure, but it does mean that he is not capable of causing pregnancy (Pearlman, 1978).

Sexual abstinence   Recovery from illness or surgery usually means some period of sexual abstinence for the ill person. This means the spouse is left without marital sexual release. Long periods of sexual abstinence for older persons often cause some deterioration of the sexual organs and some loss of sexual functioning (Rubin, 1965, p. 221). It is important for continued sexual functioning that sexual activity, even in a limited form, be resumed   346 as soon as possible. It is also important to physical and mental health for a person to feel comfortable using masturbation as a sexual release when poor health or other circumstances make other outlets unavailable or infrequent.

There is a common myth that too much sexual activity will sap a man's vital juices and leave him depleted and unable to perform in his later years. In fact the contrary is true. High levels of sexual activity in the earlier and middle years of life are associated with relatively high levels in later years and with physiological evidence of maintained sexuality (Martin, 1977).

Cardiac Problems   Often postcoronary individuals (those who have had a heart attack) are afraid to resume their sexual activity for fear the physical exertion will put too much strain on the heart. Sometimes physicians advise their cardiac patients to refrain from sexual activity. More likely a physician will not bring up the subject with older patients on the assumption that sex is no longer important for them. If the physician does not mention sexual matters, the patient will probably act according to fear and inadequate knowledge and reduce sexual activity, sometimes to the point of abstinence. Reduced sexual activity can lead to frustration and marital conflicts, factors likely to impede recovery or to increase cardiac stress (Wagner, 1975).

Most current research, however, indicates that the cardiovascular cost of sexual activity within marriages of long duration is relatively low, comparable to that of many other ordinary daily activities. The oxygen use in sexual intercourse is roughly equivalent to that in walking briskly. The heart rate ranges from 90 to 150 beats per minute, which is about the level during light or moderate exercise.

For male cardiac patients, position during intercourse is important because isometric contraction of muscle groups increases blood pressure in the heart. Because sexual intercourse with the male on top results in sustained arm and shoulder isometric muscle contraction, there may be additional stress on the heart of the male in this position. Side-by-side and female-on-top positions are more desirable for the male cardiac patient. For female cardiac patients the coital position is less important because the female superior position does not usually result in isometric arm or shoulder muscle contraction (Wagner, 1975).

Patients with heart disease may have a fear of having another heart attack or of dying during sexual intercourse. Reliable statistics are difficult to obtain, but a conservative estimate is that only 1 percent of coronary deaths occur during sexual intercourse. These deaths occur very rarely in marital relations, but are much more likely in extramarital relations. Apparently the anxiety that accompanies extramarital sex will increase cardiac stress (Charatan, 1978).

The average cardiac patient may feel his or her sexuality severely threatened. The return of sexual arousal may be a welcome sign of rehabilitation and of the potential for a normal life. It is not uncommon for the cardiac patient to masturbate while in the hospital. During masturbation the heart rate does not go above 130, so the cardiac stress during masturbation is less than that during intercourse. Physicians are being advised to suggest masturbation as a way of returning to sexual activity when the cardiac patient has recovered sufficiently that a heart rate of 130 beats per minute for a brief time is not contraindicated (Wagner, 1975).

Social Attitudes   There is a fairly widespread idea that old age is a sexless time in one's life or that if it is not, it should be. The prevalence of this notion may create concern among older persons who find that their normal sexual urges are taboo in the eyes of their younger friends, their children, and perhaps even their family physician. A further consequence of this rather general attitude is that older people themselves often accept this negative view of their own sexuality. Many elderly people who find they have strong sex desires are overwhelmed with guilt and feel they must be morally decadent or physically abnormal (Rubin, 1965, pp. 3–13). In contrast, some people accept and enjoy their sexuality in their later years as much as in their youth.

A widower in his seventies speaks with confidence of the future: I could marry again without the least fear of not making the new wife a satisfactory sex partner. I have not had any of the fears that most men my age have of losing their sex drive. This I know is due to the knowledge that I have on the subject. If I can pass this on to other aging men it will help.

From the authors' files

Men and women who live in nursing homes or retirement homes are probably those most affected by the attitude that older persons should be sexless. The environment in most of these homes is almost totally desexualized, with residential wings and sometimes even recreation rooms and dining halls strictly sex-segregated. Privacy is almost impossible to find (Kassel, 1976). Even married couples are typically separated and not allowed privacy even for conversation — and certainly not for sexual contact. One home actually had a rule forbidding any unmarried man and woman to watch television together late in the evening (Lobsenz, 1974). In another nursing home, resident's privileges are taken away if she or he is found in the room of a person of the opposite sex (Dressel and Avant, 1978).

Administrators in these homes find it less troublesome to ignore the sexual needs of the older people who live there than to cope with them. In this way the administrators avoid criticism from family members who

348

might be horrified at the so-called moral laxity of any home that would permit or provide for opportunities for sexual contact among the elderly.

One geriatric institution that previously had segregated the sexes tried a new arrangement with both men and women living on the same floor. The results of this arrangement were quite positive, indicated by a more cheerful atmosphere, better grooming by the males, and more cautious use of profane language by the males (Dressel and Avant, 1978).

The older person who has a sympathetic, healthy, and sexually accepting spouse may find social attitudes concerning sexuality and aging of little importance. At least they are of little importance as long as the couple never discuss their sexual activities with other members of their family. The unmarried, divorced, or widowed individual is not so lucky. Social attitudes toward their seeking a sexual partner outside of marriage are very strongly negative. Often marriage between older persons is treated as a joke, and it is usually labeled by others as a companionship-only arrangement.

Older people (over age sixty-five) and younger people have similar views on sexuality for people over sixty-five. Although 41 percent think of people over sixty-five as very physically active, only 5 percent think of them as very sexually active (Silny, 1980, p. 140).

The problems caused by social attitudes are more acute for older women than for older men. Because of the double standard that still prevails in our culture, society is more censorious of the sexual needs of the aging woman. Remarriage is the only alternative that does not meet with social scorn or ostracism. The problem of older women is aggravated by the relatively small number of men still alive in the older age range. Nonmarried older women outnumber nonmarried older men by three to one (Dressel and Avant, 1978, p. 16). Older men are six times more likely to get married than are single older women. This is partly due to the sex ratio among older persons and the fact that men often seek younger partners (Treas, 1975). The typical widowed or divorced woman has a much smaller chance of finding a mate than does a man of the same age (Rubin, 1965, pp. 165–167). A wealthy sixty-eight-year-old widow describes her desperation:

Now just listen: four months after my husband's death I went down into the street just like someone who is going to commit suicide. I had made up my mind to give myself to the very first man who would have me. Nobody wanted me. So I went home again. . . . [Marriage] is all I ever do think of. . . . I would rather have a decrepit invalid of a man than no man at all! — DeBeauvoir, 1972, p. 39

Because older women outnumber older men, some authorities have suggested legalization of marriage between one man and several women

349

(Dressel and Avant, 1978). However, strong sentiment against alternative sexual arrangements makes legal polygamy unlikely in the near future, despite its obvious economic, social, and sexual advantages for the persons involved.

One alternative life style for senior citizens that is gaining popularity is that of living together without being married. Many elderly couples who might like to marry choose instead to live together so they will not lose their Social Security benefits. However, many who do this are fearful of the reaction of their children if they find out. For example, one woman reports:

Every time my son comes to visit, I have to ask Sam to move out for a few days, which he spends with his cousin Sadie. But if my son should find out I was shacking up, he'd have maybe a hemorrhage. Now my daughter, she would understand. But my son expects me to be virgin.

Lopez, 1979, pp. 105–106

Daughters of elderly people are more tolerant than sons with respect to the cohabitation arrangements of their widowed parents. One study found that 80 percent of daughters would accept such liaisons for their parents, compared to only 45 percent of sons (Lopez, 1979, p. 106).

Male or female, married or unmarried, older people who have unfulfilled sexual needs usually have no understanding person with whom to discuss their concerns. Their only sexual outlet may be masturbation, which is widely condemned and often guilt-producing. All too often older persons are left to face in solitude their sexual frustration, their guilt, their fears, and their loneliness. This is doubly tragic because it is often so unnecessary.

The later years of life potentially can be very rewarding sexually. An older couple, freed of the responsibilities of raising children and pursuing careers, have for the first time in their married life the leisure to enjoy prolonged lovemaking. The rich and rewarding sex life of an older couple is described in the following correspondence:

Jim and Ellen report that old age is wonderful. They admit that Jim is a little slower to erect, "but who is in a hurry?" . . . They have sex four or five times each week. These parties last from twenty-five minutes to forty-five minutes. They each start out with the object in their mind to see how much sexual pleasure they can cause the other. If Ellen has a new trick she wants to try one day, the next day Jim will have something that he wants to try. Neither has ever refused to try what the other suggests.

William N. Bruce, March 9, 1975, personal correspondence

When two people can enjoy the loving exchange of pleasure, it is not important that both are slow to achieve sufficient arousal to permit intercourse. It is not even important that one or both partners may not feel like intercourse or orgasm. An unaroused partner who feels free to use fingers, tongue, or whatever else his or her partner enjoys can still give much sensual pleasure and plentiful orgasms to his or her mate, and in so doing derive considerable joy from the giving. Orgasm is important and beautiful at any age — but so are loving and giving and being loved in return.

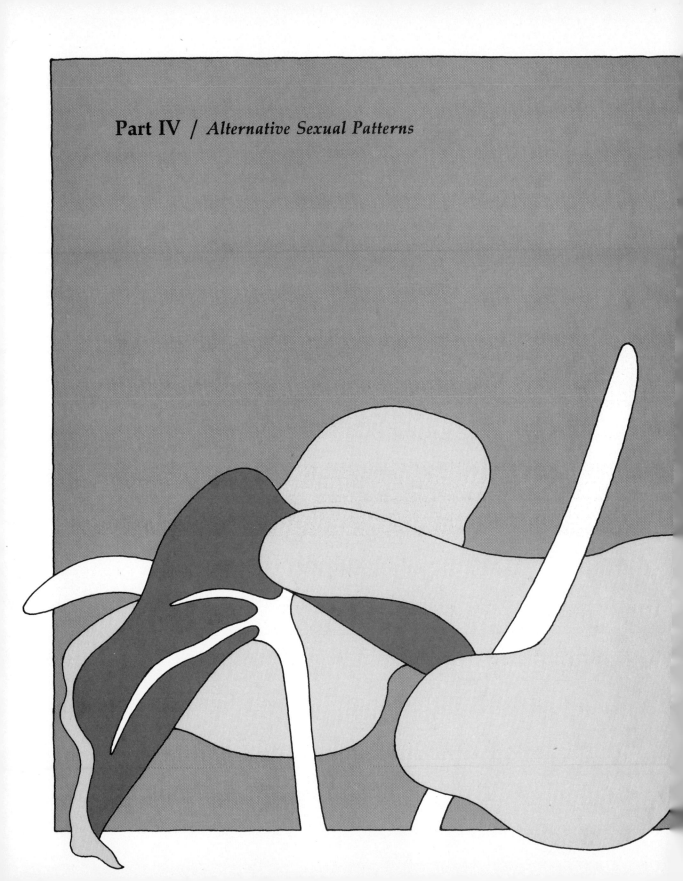

Part IV / *Alternative Sexual Patterns*

Not all individuals follow the typical sexual patterns outlined in Part A. To a degree, almost any deviation from these patterns can stigmatize an individual, who is then likely to be penalized in ways ranging from simple gossip and ridicule to imprisonment, or even castration or execution. For example, the few women who never marry may be derogatorily labeled spinsters, old maids, or abnormal. At the other end of the spectrum, the small minority of men who engage in bizarre sex crimes are labeled sick, twisted, criminal, perverted, or abnormal.

Normality and Abnormality

The term *abnormal* conjures up the entire range of deviations from typical patterns, from "old maids" to "perverted" sex criminals. Conversely, the term *normality* implies — perhaps erroneously — that the majority of individuals conform to the typical sexual patterns of the life cycle. But it is necessary to clarify the several bases upon which people are seen as normal or abnormal. Wardell Pomeroy (1966) has described the various definitions that the term *normal* can have when applied to sexual behavior.

1. *The statistical definition.* Behavior that is common is considered normal and that which is uncommon is abnormal. By this standard, premarital intercourse, adultery, and masturbation would be considered normal. Virginity in adults and anal intercourse are examples of behavior that would be considered statistically abnormal.

2. *The phylogenetic definition.* Since humans are a species of mammal, another definition

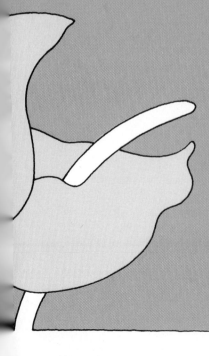

353

of normal sexual behavior is based on whether or not the behavior is found among mammals. By this definition it is very difficult to find a human sexual behavior that would be defined phylogenetically as abnormal.

3. *The moral definition.* By this definition anything that is considered morally wrong is defined as abnormal. Since our religious heritage has left us with a very restrictive sexual moral code, almost every sexual act except marital intercourse is considered morally wrong.

4. *The legal definition.* By the legal definition any sexual act that violates a law is labeled a perversion. In most cases the legal code closely parallels the moral code in our society. By the legal definition oral-genital contact, adultery, incest, and anal intercourse are some of the sexual acts considered abnormal in most states.

5. *The psychological definition.* By the psychological definition any sexual behavior is abnormal when it results in a lowered sense of self-esteem. By this definition even marital intercourse may be considered abnormal for some individuals or under some circumstances. A variation of the psychological definition of normality has been suggested by Stoller (1970) who defines *perversion* as any sexual activity accompanied by hostility. Normal sexual interaction, therefore, is nonhostile sexual interaction.

6. *The social definition.* By the social definition, sexual behavior that harms society or another person is abnormal. Any sexual acts between consenting adults are normal, but an act involving coercion or directed against a child by an adult is harmful and hence abnormal. Although this social definition of sexual normality sounds very straightforward on the surface, it leaves room for considerable debate regarding what, if any, sexual behavior is harmful to other people.

The term *social* is somewhat misleading in this definition based on interpersonal harm, since all concepts of sexual normalcy are set within the social and cultural context. Even within a particular culture one is often faced with overlapping subcultures with conflicting and changing standards for which sexual acts are healthy or unhealthy, mature or immature, idealized or perverted (Ruitenbeek, 1967; Ellis, 1962). Furthermore, there is some overlap between all these standards of normality. For example, a sexual act like anal intercourse, which is condemned by most church codes, is also condemned by the legal codes of many states, and is statistically relatively uncommon.

Social Norms

The ideal norms regulating sexual behavior in our society are based on all six concepts of normality, but most particularly on the moral or religious norms of the Judeo-Christian heritage. In Part 4 we analyze contemporary data on some of the major violations of the sexual mores. Each of these variations may be contrasted with an ideal moral norm that restricts sexual contact:

NORM	VIOLATION
SEXUAL PARTNER	
Non-kin	Incest
One	Extramarital intercourse, bigamy, polygamy, promiscuity
Other sex	Homosexuality, bisexuality, transsexualism
Emotionally related	Commercial sex, prostitution, casual sex
Adult	Pedophilia, statutory rape
Human, living	Necrophilia, bestiality
Voluntary	Forcible rape, sadomasochism, voyeurism
Sexual Aim	
Procreation/gratification	Celibacy
Moderate gratification	Nymphomania, satyriasis
Intercourse (marginal: fellatio, cunnilingus, masturbation, premarital sex)	Unusual orificial sexuality, sexual devices, fetishism, transvestism
Private gratification	Public sex, pornography, nudity

All the sexual activities in the right-hand column are stigmatized to some degree. All are practiced by some people, although the number varies for different activities: for example, a majority of men and women report extramarital sexual interaction, while very few people admit to incestuous interaction.

The type of stigma attached to the given violation is also variable, covering a range of legal and social penalties: imprisonment, fines, confinement to a mental hospital, enforced therapy, divorce, loss of job, loss of family and friends, gossip, ridicule, and so on. Adaptations to stigma also vary. Individuals who violate the norms may deal with the problem of stigma by keeping their behavior secret, or they may engage in it openly, with different results for their lifestyles and identities.

In the chapters that follow, the alternative sexual patterns listed are discussed in several contexts, including both the medical and the subcultural perspectives. The medical approach focuses on the etiology, epidemiology, and therapy of sexual variations; we include contemporary data on these, and criticisms of the medical approach. In addition, we present the individual, identity, and subcultural aspects of the variations that have a considerable sociological as well as psychological or physiological significance. Throughout, the extent and implications of alternative sexual patterns are considered as they affect the people who adopt them and the society in which they live.

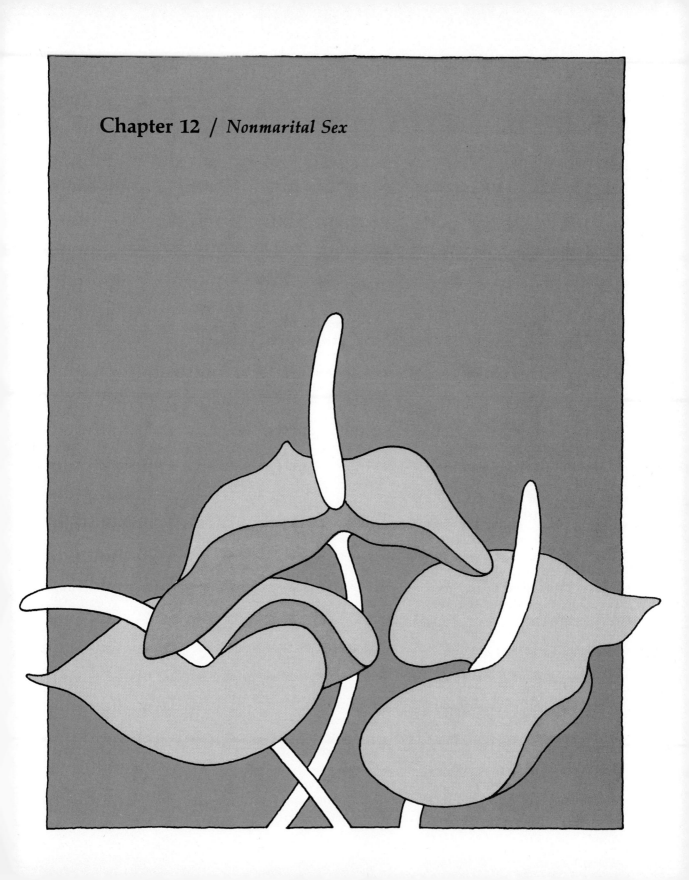

Chapter 12 / *Nonmarital Sex*

As of September 1978 there were an estimated fifty-two million unmarried adults in the United States (*Newsweek,* September 4, 1978, p. 76). Over thirty million of these have never been married; between thirteen and fourteen million are widowed, and a little over eight million are divorced. These persons constitute a large number of adult Americans who have no socially accepted sexual outlet.

Although counselors, clinicians, clergy, and lay people emphasize that sexual intercourse with orgasm is important for the physical and emotional health of married people, there is often silence on the topic of sexuality for the unmarried. The usual escape from the contradictions in our attitudes toward unmarried sexuality is to ignore and minimize the issue as much as possible. When forced to take a stand, most tend to condemn it publicly and condone it privately. In meeting their sexual needs, unmarried persons have little alternative than to ignore conventional morality, which demands that sexual relations take place only within marriage (Gebhard, 1970).

Other people are married but for various reasons choose to seek sexual experiences outside their marital relationship. In this respect, these people also are involved in sexual experiences that many adults consider socially unacceptable. Most of these married people have secret extramarital affairs, but some have extramarital experiences with the approval and agreement of their spouses.

The Divorced and the Widowed

Sexual needs are similar for the divorced and the widowed, who have been conditioned by years of marriage to expect and desire both the physical release and emotional closeness of a continuing sexual relationship. Although their needs may be similar, there are important differences between the widowed and the divorced with respect to their social situations.

Sexual Adjustment

During the last months or years of a marriage that ends in divorce, sexual relations usually deteriorate or are terminated. The recently divorced person has therefore often gone through a period of relative sexual deprivation (Waller, 1967, pp. 56–81). Also, most people are left after a divorce with a sense of having failed in an interpersonal relationship. Divorced people may compensate for both their recent sexual deprivation and their bruised ego by seeking sexual encounters.

Recently widowed people are in a somewhat different situation. They typically have not experienced a deterioration of their marital relationship 358

just prior to their spouse's death, and consequently do not have the sense of having failed in their most important sexual relationship. Also, the widowed are less likely than the divorced to have experienced sexual deprivation prior to the death of their spouse, except in cases where the mate had a long terminal illness.

Another factor that may affect the sexual adjustment of the widowed and the divorced differently is the quality of the emotional tie to the absent mate. Widowed people seldom feel hostile toward their deceased mate and may retain strong emotional ties with her or his memory. Over time, the survivor may exaggerate in memory the good qualities of the deceased and selectively forget all the shortcomings. This memory can be a deterrent to the establishment of new sexual relationships because no living person can possibly equal the exalted image of the deceased (Geb-hard, 1970).

Most divorced people have some positive feelings toward their ex-mate, but they are seldom troubled by unrealistically positive memories. Typically the pain surrounding a divorce gives both parties sufficient reason to feel some hostility toward each other, which usually balances or outweighs the positive feelings. In most instances the divorced can more readily develop new sexual relationships than the widowed because they are less haunted by love for their absent spouse. However, a strong degree of hostility toward one's divorced spouse may carry over into all new relationships. This transferred hostility may lead a divorced person to avoid contact with the opposite sex for a time, or it may lead him or her to seek only degrading or uninvolved sexual contacts (Waller, 1967, pp. 56–81).

The friends and family of the widowed often exert a subtle (or not so subtle) pressure on them to remain faithful to the deceased, because many feel that a new love would be disloyal and even sexually immoral. The widowed person more often than the divorced one will have a supportive group of in-laws and married friends who encourage maintenance of previous patterns of behavior. Although possibly not intending to do so, well-meaning friends and relatives by their moral support lessen the chances that a widow or widower will soon seek new relationships (Gebhard, 1970).

Divorced people are much more likely than widowed people to have had extramarital relationships. Undoubtedly this extramarital experience facilitates developing (or continuing) sexual relationships after divorce (Gebhard, 1970).

Resumption of Sexual Activity

Data from the early 1970s indicate that celibacy in divorced men and women today is a rarity. The median rate of frequency of coitus for divorced men is a little higher than that of married men of the same age, and the median frequency of coitus of sexually active divorced women is approximately the same as the rate for married women in the same age range (Hunt, 1974, pp. 240–246).

There is some evidence that most divorced persons find their postmarital coitus more sensuous, free, and varied than their marital coitus. For example, 90 percent of divorced men and over 80 percent of divorced women report some oral-genital experience — a proportion higher than that for married people. As for experimenting with coital positions, divorced people are much more likely to have tried such variations as rear-entry vaginal intercourse or anal intercourse. Approximately 90 percent of divorced persons rate their postmarital sex as mostly pleasurable or very pleasurable. Further evidence of sexual pleasure is indicated in the fact that over 80 percent of divorced women report reaching orgasm in most or all of their postmarital coitus, a figure higher than that for married women (Hunt, 1974, pp. 246–249). Because divorced women typically have more education than married women, and because more educated women are more likely to be orgasmic than less educated women, the higher frequency of orgasm among divorced women may be related to their education rather than to their divorce.

Although the preceding discussion indicates that divorced individuals typically have an active, varied, and physically satisfying sex life, this is not meant to imply that their development of postmarital relationships is free of problems. Divorce is traumatic in nearly all respects, including postmarital sexual adjustment. Moving from a relatively monogamous married state to the sexually liberated world of the divorced is often anxiety-producing and sometimes even shocking. Not only are recently divorced men and women often unsure of themselves, but they also are unfamiliar with the unwritten rules of a sexual marketplace that is often quite different from the one they knew before they were married (Hunt, 1974, pp. 249–253; Welch and Granvold, 1977). One young woman reports:

The men I met, being older, had a wider repertoire of sexual lifestyle. I was a virtual baby — they expected things that I thought were whorish. My sex life was a big adjustment.

Greenberg, 1979, p. 320

A middle-aged man reports:

The first date was a disaster. She was a young single girl. I couldn't tell whether she wanted to rape me or what. It was completely different. I didn't know how to handle it. I was completely at loose ends; women were more aggressive than I was used to. I was totally lost.

Greenberg, 1979, p. 320

Because of the trauma of marital failure, divorced men and women are often afraid of emotional involvement. They may be torn between a desire for intimacy and commitment and a fear of involvement in another disastrous relationship. Eventually many divorced people reconstruct their lives and are able to enter into intimate relationships that may endure, deepen, and be formalized in a new marriage. But until they develop an emotional commitment to another person, many find that postmarital sex involves physical pleasure but lacks emotional fulfillment. For many, a sexual relationship with a loved partner is more rewarding than that with a sexually more exciting but unloved partner (Hunt, 1974, pp. 248–253).

Many persons go through a series of stages in their sexual adjustment after divorce. For a time many are celibate because they are not ready emotionally for sexual relations or do not know of willing sex partners. A majority of divorced men are not celibate for longer than three months and a majority of women for no longer than a year (Hunt and Hunt, 1977, p. 132). Once they begin to have sexual relations, many newly divorced persons go through a stage of experimentation with casual sex with a variety of partners. This stage helps reassure them that they are desirable and can function sexually. But sooner or later the period of exploration leads to the discovery that sex is better when it is linked with affection (Hunt and Hunt, 1977). A thirty-year-old writer describes his transition:

For about a half year I screwed anything that wasn't dead. I cruised the bars, I went to parties, I picked up girls at short-order counters. I really felt freed from having to have it mean anything except a good fuck. Then I began to find it sort of boring, a waste of time and effort. One night I asked myself why the hell I was

Hunt and Hunt, 1977, p. 154

screwing a girl I wouldn't even want to spend the time to have a cup of coffee with, and I cut out. After that I began to get choosier and started to look for girls I would be interested in.

Single Parents   Widowed or divorced persons who have young children still living with them often feel that the children's presence seriously constrains their development of new sexual relationships. Most single parents report feeling that they must conduct their sexual relationships away from home. Those who do have sexual encounters in their home feel that fear of intrusion by their children restrains their pleasure. Many single parents feel that if their children knew of their sexual activities it would be emotionally traumatic for the children (Greenberg, 1979). One young mother of three comments:

I think children look at their mothers differently. They never think of their own mothers as "doing it." I think exposing children to your sexual activities is a heavy thing to lay on a kid. One of my friends did this and her girls started at very young ages, thirteen and fourteen, to bring boys in for sex.

Greenberg, 1979, p. 317

Divorced and Widowed Females   There is a scarcity of current data on the sexual life of the widowed. One study of divorced and widowed women interviewed between 1939 and 1956 found that widowed women were slower than divorced women of the same age to resume an active sex life after losing their spouse. More widowed than divorced women in all age ranges remained celibate. When widowed women did resume coitus, their frequency of intercourse was lower than that of divorced women of the same age. Widows, however, were equally as likely as divorcees to reach orgasm in their postmarital sexual intercourse (Gebhard, 1970).

Divorced and Widowed Males   Comparable data for divorced and widowed men are not available, but we would assume that the percentage who have postmarital coitus, the frequency of postmarital coitus, and the speed with which postmarital coitus is begun after the end of marriage are all higher than the comparable figures for widowed women. This assumption is based on three facts. First, sexual aggressiveness in our society is more acceptable in men than in women; hence a widower is less likely to be criticized for pursuing new partners than a widow. Second, the higher male death rate means there are more women than men in the middle and later years. A widow may have more difficulty than a widower in finding a new partner because of the scarcity of men in her age range. There are almost five widows for every widower (Clayton and Bornstein, 1976, p. 31).

   Third, it is socially acceptable for a man to date a younger woman, but a woman who dates a younger man is often regarded as lewd. This means the widow of middle age or older is less likely than the widower to find an acceptable mate, because the few men in her age range may seek younger women. Often the choices of the single woman in the middle or later years are limited to men who are much older than she is. A widow may feel reluctant to become involved with an older man who is likely to become senile and ill and to die before she does. Once widowed, a woman may hesitate to risk being widowed again.

A sixty-eight-year-old widow describes her feelings concerning remarriage: I nursed Jim myself all the time he was sick and right up till the time he died. But that was okay because he was my husband and we had been together all those years. But I don't want another old man to take care of! . . . I do feel sorry for old Tom because I know he's lonely and doesn't have anyone to chase around with, but none of us [widows] wants to date him. It *is* lonely sometimes at night, but I can always call Ann or Steph to come watch TV with me. I had just rather be lonely than be bothered with some old man to look after.

From the authors' files

The Never Married

The number of people in the United States over age eighteen who have never married jumped from an estimated 12,900,000 in 1960 to 16,200,000 in 1970. The age group under twenty-five accounted for more than its share of the growth of singles whereas the percentage of people over thirty who have never been married has declined in the past fifteen years (Jacoby, 1974).

In the United States in the past, the person who never married was typically characterized as a lonely, emotionally shriveled loser, particularly if the individual was female, hence the derogatory terms "spinster" or "old maid." Now the single man or woman is likely to be stereotyped as carefree and happily promiscuous. Probably neither stereotype is accurate. But a single who hopes to find another individual with whom to develop a sexual or emotional relationship may have to contend with one or both of these images.

Availability of Partners

The opportunities for meeting other singles vary greatly, depending to a large degree on an individual's sex, age, occupation, and domicile, as well as personal attractiveness. Probably the most disadvantaged in this respect is the older female with a low income living in a small town or rural area. Almost all the factors that limit the availability of sexual partners for widowed and divorced women also are applicable in the case of the

Some unmarried persons lead very lonely lives, while others find sociability in places where singles gather.

Left: Charles Harbutt/ Magnum Photos, Inc.; right: © Eric A. Roth 1979/Picture Cube

woman who has never married. And the never married woman, because she has remained unmarried, also may have to contend with an image of being either totally frigid or wildly promiscuous. If she is young and attractive, her chances are better. Also if she lives in a large city she may find singles clubs, singles apartment complexes, computer dating services, or singles bars, where she may encounter others in the same situation. She will be more likely to find casual sexual partners than a marriage partner and the likelihood of finding either decreases with age. A thirty-five-year-old woman, for example, has a 34 percent chance of ever marrying, and a fifty-year-old woman has only a 6 percent chance (Roy and Roy, 1968, p. 139). (See Table 12.1.)

Percentage of Never Married Women Who Will Marry   Table 12.1

Age	Percentage Who Will Ever Marry	Percentage Who Will Marry Within a Year
25	78.5	18.9
30	55.3	9.6
35	34.3	4.9
40	20.2	2.7
45	11.3	1.5
50	6.1	0.8
55	3.2	0.4

Source: W. D. Sprague, "Patterns of Adultery" (Washington, D.C.: U.S. Bureau of the Census).

A male who has at least an upper-middle-class income and who lives in a large urban area is the most likely to find many opportunities for either casual or committed sexual relationships. This is especially true for those living in apartment houses that cater to singles (Proulx, 1973).

Attitudes

Attitudes of singles toward their never married state vary widely. Some, both male and female, are desperately looking for any kind of committed or casual sexual relationship to enrich their lonely and sexless lives. Others vehemently deny that they could ever give up the joys of their single life for the burdens and boredom of marriage. One thirty-six-year-old male described his feelings:

I'm into playin' and lovin' and not givin' a damn for the rest of my life. Comin' home to the same pair of tits and the same corned-beef hash every night — hell that just ain't what I was born for.

Proulx, 1973, p. 25

Probably many singles are enthusiastic about their life at one time, but after a few years some want to find a more permanent relationship. A twenty-nine-year-old woman summarizes her attitude this way:

If you'd asked me about being single four years ago, I would have said it was the greatest thing in the world. I still think it's great for a lot of people, especially in contrast to immature marriages. But quite frankly, I want to get married now. I want children. . . . I can be alone, often I want to be alone, but I don't want to stay alone for the rest of my life. I'm not desperate to get married, but marriage is the big, tantalizing, unanswered question in my life.

Jacoby, 1974, p. 43

Cohabitation

There is a growing trend for unmarried couples to live together. The Census Bureau found 654,000 unmarried couples in 1970 and 1,320,000, or double that amount, in 1976. One study estimated that 2 million persons were cohabiting in 1977, and the trend is expected to continue (Newcomb, 1979). Although cohabiting persons are drawn from all groups of unmarried people, they are more likely to be under age thirty and less committed to traditional religion. One study of students at fourteen state universities found that one-fourth of the sample had cohabitated at some time (Newcomb, 1979).

Most males who cohabit cite sexual gratification as their reason. Most females cohabit because they hope the relationship will lead to marriage. However, most cohabitants do not get married to each other, although almost all of them indicate they would like to get married sometime. (Newcomb, 1979).

365

The most significant positive consequences for cohabitants are companionship, sexual gratification, and economic benefit. The most significant negative consequences are the problems of resolving property rights when the relationship ends and the risk of disappointment for female cohabitants who expect marriage and sexual exclusivity to result from cohabitation. Apparently the cohabiting experience does not alter sex roles in marriage nor increase the quality of the mate selection process (Newcomb, 1979).

Extramarital Sexual Interaction

Extramarital sexual interaction involves a married person engaging in sexual relations with someone other than his or her spouse. Extramarital sex is often secret because a spouse would disapprove, be hurt, or be angry if he or she knew. It is important to expand our connotation of extramarital sex to include situations in which it is not secret and in which the spouse may even approve. Clanton (1973) distinguishes among three types of extramarital sex, which constitute different types of behavior with different implications for the people involved. *Clandestine extramarital sex* refers to an extramarital sexual relationship the participant keeps secret from the spouse on the assumption that the spouse would disapprove if she or he knew about it. *Consensual extramarital sex* refers to extramarital relationships that the spouse both knows about and accepts — perhaps approves enthusiastically. *Ambiguous extramarital sex* refers to situations in which the spouse knows but chooses not to confront the participant or issue an ultimatum that might precipitate a divorce rather than end the extramarital affair. Most of the extramarital sex in our society is ambiguous or clandestine.

Incidence of Extramarital Sex

A number of social conditions in the United States lead one to expect a rising incidence of extramarital relationships. One is the increased life expectancy, resulting in marriages with an average duration of forty to fifty years if not ended earlier by divorce (Sprey, 1972). A second social condition contributing to extramarital sex is our mobile urban environment with a sizable proportion of working women, which maximizes opportunities for discreet sexual encounters. Effective birth control and the increasing acceptance of nonprocreative sexuality also add to the feasibility of extramarital relationships (Sprey, 1972).

366

In the past few years the mass media have added fuel to the argument that monogamous marriage is outmoded. A proliferation of popular books, magazine articles, and guests on TV talk shows suggest that exclusiveness in our sexual relationships is archaic, even within marriage. All the talk of sexual freedom for married couples, plus the social conditions that facilitate extramarital relationships, convince most people that extramarital sexuality is becoming more common. Data do not confirm this assumption, however. Morton Hunt's study in the early 1970s found the overall incidence of reported extramarital sex for married men over twenty-five basically unchanged from that found by Kinsey a generation before. In both periods about one-half of married men had ever had extramarital intercourse. Only among men under twenty-five was there a small increase (Hunt, 1974).

Among married women over twenty-five, Hunt found no overall increase in incidence compared to a generation ago, when about one-fourth of married women reported they had had extramarital sex. Among wives under twenty-five there was a very large increase (from 8 percent to 24 percent), which makes the incidence for these young women as high as that of the women over twenty-five (Hunt, 1974). It is estimated that eventually about half of this group of young wives will probably have extramarital sex during the course of their life, indicating a convergence with the current male rate of extramarital sex (Atwater, 1979, p. 35).

From a survey of readers of *Redbook* magazine, Robert Bell concluded that the incidence of extramarital sex for married women is now almost 40 percent (Bell, 1975). Because his sample includes a greater proportion of younger, better-educated, and more financially secure women than are found in the population as a whole, his estimate is probably high. (For a discussion of Bell's methodology, see the appendix.)

Life Situations and Extramarital Sex

In addition to the social conditions that foster extramarital relationships, there are numerous personal reasons for engaging in these relationships in spite of the risks often involved. Among the things people may hope to find in an extramarital relationship are excitement and romance, variety in sexual partners or techniques, a more satisfactory sexual outlet than the marital partner, peer status, and reaffirmation of youth or attractiveness.

Sue is 32, has three children and recently completed the training to become a computer analyst. She has been married 14 years to an insurance executive. . . . "I simply had this feeling," she says, "that there had to be more to life than what I know. I didn't know what it was or how to find it, but I just knew I had to look. And it wasn't a question of work or a career either because I had that." Feeling

Los Angeles Times, August 21, 1975, p. 29

strongly attracted to her physician (who is married) and feeling that the attraction was mutual, she decided to tell him frankly how she felt. The result has been an affair which is extremely desultory: they have been together only twice in a year. She finds it "thrilling" (he is more aggressive than her husband) but frustrating (he is difficult to reach by phone). "There have been times when wanting to talk to him has been an obsession and I couldn't get through," she says.

Although many married people have what some would consider good reasons for pursuing an extramarital relationship, only a relatively small proportion do so. In one study of a midwestern suburban sample of middle-aged, middle-class couples, 78 percent of the men and 41 percent of the women agreed with the statement that most happily married persons would like to experience sexual intercourse with another person (Johnson, 1970). These respondents all denied ever having had an extramarital sexual relationship.

A variety of factors may explain this apparent disparity between interest and action in extramarital sex. For those who are interested in finding extramarital sex, opportunity is undoubtedly one factor in determining who does or does not engage in extramarital encounters (Johnson, 1970). Occupations that necessitate considerable travel and have coworkers of the opposite sex offer more opportunities for sexual adventuring than do those with no travel and coworkers mostly of the same sex. Although opportunity is a necessary condition for extramarital sex, it is not a sufficient one. For example, when married couples have to live apart for periods of time because of their work situation, they are not more likely to have affairs than when they shared a single home. Apparently a person's attitude toward affairs is the important variable that permits or does not permit utilization of an opportunity for extramarital sex (Gerstel, 1979).

Opportunity is also an important factor even when people are happily married and not necessarily interested in or seeking sexual involvement outside their marriage. A man and a woman who spend considerable time together professionally or socially may find their social or professional relationship deepening into a more intimate relationship. A woman and man in this situation are faced with several alternatives: discontinuing or restructuring their original relationship in order to avoid further contact and involvement; continuing the relationship, knowing the developing emotional involvement alone is a threat to their respective marriages even without sexual intimacy; or developing an emotionally and sexually intimate relationship. Any of these alternatives may have long-term implications for the work life, social life, and marital life of the participants. As women are increasingly released from their domestic role and enter the work force, this form of unintended extramarital sex may occur more often.

368

Another factor in a person's trying extramarital sex is knowing a person who has already done so. One woman reports:

My girlfriend in Texas — she's a gal who's had great influence on me. She's the most unleashed person I know of. Four years ago when I first met her — we were all out there together, without our husbands and children — she proceeded to pick up a guy about ten years younger than herself and trot right off to bed with him and brag about it the next morning. I had never met anybody like this, who was so open about it. . . . it was just unreal. I never met anybody like that. So she was influential in my coming around. I knew it could be done.

Atwater, 1979, p. 45

One study found that half the women involved in extramarital sex had known such a person. Most of these influential persons were peers of the women, but a few were parents or other relatives (Atwater, 1979, p. 45).

Common sense tells us that dissatisfaction with the sexual or emotional aspects of marriage is an important motive for seeking extramarital sex. Although there are exceptions, data offer some support for this assumption. Several studies find that marital dissatisfaction is one factor that may lead to extramarital sex (Glass and Wright, 1977; Walster, Traupmann, and Walster, 1978; Atwater, 1979). A poor sexual relationship at home is the primary reason husbands give for saying they would consider looking for outside substitutes. However, a poor sex life ranked third among wives as a reason for infidelity. Emotional incompatibilities such as constant fighting and lack of understanding ranked first and second among wives (Pietropinto and Simenauer, 1979, p. 282).

People who are dissatisfied with their marriage must deal with their own values in resolving their problem; those with strong moral prohibitions against extramarital sex tend to seek fantasy involvement rather than actual sexual involvement. Dissatisfied people who do not have strong moral prohibitions may find their missing satisfactions through actual emotional or sexual involvement outside the marriage (Neubeck and Schletzer, 1962).

The Extramarital Sex Experience

It is difficult to characterize the extramarital sex experience. Some researchers conclude that extramarital sex is less pleasurable than marital sex (Hunt, 1974, p. 278); others conclude that it is as good as or better than marital sex (Atwater, 1979). The range of individual reactions varies greatly. One woman reports her first extramarital sexual experience as very positive:

It was right out of the romantic novels of the 19th century! Oh, it was just fantastic!

Atwater, 1979, p. 55

Overall Pleasure of Marital and Extramarital Sexual Relations for Married Respondents with Extramarital Experience, in Percentages   Table 12.2

	Males		Females	
	Marital	Extramarital	Marital	Extramarital
Very pleasurable	67	47	55	37
Mostly pleasurable	30	43	35	37
Neither pleasurable nor nonpleasurable	2	6	7	14
Mostly nonpleasurable	1	1	2	8
Very nonpleasurable	1	2	1	5

Source: Reprinted with permission of Playboy Press. From *Sexual Behavior in the 1970's,* p. 278, by Morton Hunt. Copyright © 1974 by Morton Hunt.

Some persons find excitement and romance in extramarital sex, while others find that guilt and fear of discovery weigh heavily against their pleasure.
Burt Glinn/Magnum Photos, Inc.

In contrast, another woman reports her guilt and trauma:

It was pretty traumatic the first time, because I couldn't believe that it really happened. . . . Afterward I felt kind of strange. I really felt something was wrong with me.

Atwater, 1979, p. 55

Undoubtedly, for some people an extramarital relationship provides a satisfying physical and emotional experience. For others it is a miserable and unsuccessful attempt temporarily to transcend their usual existence. Probably for most participants, the problems of guilt and fear of discovery are weighed against the delights of recaptured youth and desirability and the rediscovery of excitement and passion. Apparently the sexual revolution has not made the widespread changes in extramarital sexuality that it has in premarital and marital sexuality. A 1977 study of a nationwide cross section of American adults found that 87 percent felt extramarital sex was always or almost always wrong. Only 3 percent felt it was not wrong at all (Glenn and Weaver, 1979).

Consensual Extramarital Sex

Consensual extramarital sex refers to extramarital relationships of which the spouse knows and approves. It includes several different forms of behavior, each associated with different motivations, gratifications, and problems.

Open-ended Marriage

One form of consensual extramarital sex has been called "open-ended marriage" (Clanton, 1973). In an *open-ended marriage* both spouses are free to develop close relationships outside the marriage with persons of either sex. For some couples it is understood and accepted that these relationships may include extensive sexual and emotional involvement. Other couples may have an agreement that their outside relationships will include only transitory sexual encounters with no deep emotional involvement. A study of seventeen sexually open marriages found that only one male and one female usually had sex without emotional involvement even though their philosophies favored sex with affection. The other participants reported deep affection or love for their sexual partner outside the marriage (Knapp, 1976).

In some open-ended marriages there is an understanding that each partner can have sexual and nonsexual relationships outside the marriage as long as she or he is discreet and does not tell the spouse any details of

371

the outside relationships. In other open-ended marriages there is open discussion of outside relationships, and the sexual partners outside the marriage may be included in many activities with the married couple. If the couple has dependent children, the latter alternative may pose some problems when the children (and their friends) realize their family relationships are unusual.

An interesting example of an open-ended marriage was reported in *Newsweek* magazine in a brief article on Christina Paolozzi Bellin, a model who became an instant celebrity when a topless picture of her was printed in *Harper's Bazaar* in 1962:

... Afterwards she modeled for a few more years, flopped as a Hollywood starlet, married a young doctor in 1964 and has since settled into a free-spirited domestic life in which she and her husband openly engage in extramarital affairs. "So far," she says, "all I ever wanted I got: a successful husband, two wonderful children and a fantastic lover." Christina and her husband, Dr. Howard Bellin, live in a Park Avenue apartment with their two young sons. Bellin, a plastic surgeon, pilots his own jet plane and helicopter and often flies the family on vacation trips. His wife's present lover, a young Israeli, goes on some of the trips and has dinner with the Bellins at their home three nights a week. Christina says she has been "faithful" to her lover for five years, but her husband does not necessarily limit himself to one affair at a time. He, too, introduces some of his paramours to his spouse and children. Sometimes, as Christina admits to TV's Barbara Walters on a forthcoming "Not For Women Only" program, the Bellin children find the adult relationships a bit confusing.

Some of the reported benefits of a sexually open marriage are better fulfillment of personal needs, the excitement of new experiences, increased communication and enjoyment of sex with spouse, a lessening of jealousy and possessiveness, a feeling of freedom combined with security, and the ability to be fully oneself and to end the need for role playing. Reported difficulties are jealousy, time-sharing problems, guilt, resentment, fear of hurting others, and lack of private meeting places. Most persons involved in sexually open marriages feel that the advantages of the arrangement significantly outweigh the disadvantages (Knapp, 1976). However, most researchers who have studied the phenomenon agree that very few married couples can successfully manage the stresses of open marriage (Hunt, 1977; Clanton, 1979).

Mate Swapping

Another form of consensual adultery has been termed *mate swapping* or *swinging,* in which married couples exchange spouses with other married couples for sexual relations with the full consent of all involved. Mate swapping can be distinguished from open-ended marriage because it is a sexual exchange in which husband and wife are participating simultaneously and in the same place, although perhaps in different rooms. Thus it is an activity in which spouses engage together, and the quest for new sexual partners is a joint undertaking rather than an independent one as in an open-ended marriage. Mate swapping may be of several types depending on the degree of intimacy and emotional commitment wife and husband have with their extramarital sexual partners.

In spite of the difficulties of researching mate swapping, information from widely scattered studies can be pieced together to give us some understanding of the kinds of individuals engaging in this activity, the forms their activities may take, and the possible effects of this behavior. In contrast, there is a scarcity of scientific data on open-ended marriages.

Age The age range of people who engage in mate swapping is quite wide, with the youngest reported as eighteen and the oldest as seventy (Bartell, 1970). Any one gathering, however, is unlikely to include a wide age range. Apparently, parties are quite segregated by age, probably as a result of the emphasis on physical attractiveness prevalent among swingers. Although informants often say that age is unimportant, they tend to reject couples more than ten years older than they are (Rosen, 1971; Bartell, 1970; Varni, 1972).

Another reason that swingers in the middle age range stay within their own age group is that they are afraid of venereal disease, which they think is prevalent among very young swingers (O'Neill and O'Neill, 1970).

Social Class and Ethnicity Although the age range is wide, the social-class range of the swinging groups studied so far is fairly narrow: predominantly middle class and upper middle class (Bartell, 1970; Smith and Smith, 1970; O'Neill and O'Neill, 1970). The educational level is above that of the general population, with one study reporting that 25 percent of males had some college education (Bartell, 1970), and another reporting over 80 percent with some college education (Smith and Smith, 1970). The racial composition of the swinging groups studied is largely Caucasian (Bartel, 1970; Smith and Smith, 1970). Estimates of the number of married people who have tried mate swapping run as high as 25 percent of couples in the United States today. Recent data, however, indicate that probably only 2 percent of couples have tried swinging (Hunt, 1974, p. 271; Spanier and Cole, 1975).

Generally speaking, the swingers studied to date are not wild-eyed, long-haired bohemians who spout radical political and social ideologies. On the whole they are fairly conventional couples with bureaucratic jobs, suburban homes, and well-manicured lawns. Their only major deviation from the usual life style of middle America is this one aspect of their sex

373

life — namely, swinging (Rosen, 1971). And with respect to their swinging, they perceive themselves as members of an avant-garde group that has transcended the strictures of the conventional puritanical morality by which the rest of society is still bound.

Although not vastly different from nonswinging couples of similar socioeconomic backgrounds, swingers have more liberal attitudes on a variety of sexual topics, such as abortion, sex education for children, contraceptives for adolescents, premarital sex, and nudity. Three-fourths of swingers in one study also described their political views as liberal. But swingers do not translate this liberalism into political activism; more than half were not affiliated with any political party — a fact not surprising in view of their relative detachment from parents, community, church, and other traditional social institutions (Gilmartin, 1978).

Initiation into Swinging   In most instances, when married couples decide to try mate swapping, the idea is initiated by the husband and the wife agrees to try it only after considerable discussion (Rosen, 1971; Smith and Smith, 1970; Henshel, 1973). One wife expresses her reactions this way:

Swinging was something Don and I had read about and occasionally joked about, and I must admit the idea was somewhat intriguing at that point. But when Don suggested that we ask Jim and Myrna if they would be interested, I was horrified. It was a fun thing to joke about, but when I had to think of it in terms of actually switching off and having sex with friends, it suddenly seemed unthinkable. I insisted it would be impossible for me to respond in bed with someone I did not really love. But Don kept bringing up the subject. . . . Finally I agreed that we might just go over to Jim and Myrna's house to see some porno movies he had just gotten, but if I did not feel like switching partners, we did not have to. That made me feel a little better, but I was still nervous.

From the authors' files

Usually the couple approach their first experience with some misgivings but if it is a fairly positive encounter they may leave it with a heady sense of new freedom. They then pursue one new experience after another in a fairly indiscriminate manner until they have satisfied their curiosity. After this they may become more selective, and probably swing less often (Palson and Palson, 1972). Apparently many couples tend to drop out of swinging either partially or completely after a period of several years. Others may continue actively swinging for twenty years or more (O'Neill and O'Neill, 1970).

Swinging Contacts   The ways that couples interested in mate swapping contact other couples vary greatly. Occasionally couples who are close friends simply drift into a sexual exchange as an extension of the closeness of their friendship. Or a couple interested in mate swapping may proselytize among their friends and convince nonswingers to join them.

More often, however, swingers contact people they have not previously met. These contacts can be made in a variety of ways. Sometimes contact is made through personal referral by a couple that knows both couples, has swung with both, and feels they would be compatible. Contacts may also be made through advertisements in swinging magazines or the underground press, or at swinging parties or bars (Bartell, 1970; Bell, 1971; Varni, 1972).

Regardless of how contact is made, swingers always emphasize that no one has to have sexual relations with any particular person if she or he does not wish to do so (Smith and Smith, 1970; O'Neill and O'Neill, 1970). When sexual contacts are made at a large party, anyone is free to accept or reject advances, although it is understood that rejection should be tactful (Symonds, 1968; Varni, 1972). When contacts are made by answering an advertisement placed by another couple, quite often the initial contact is purely social and involves no sexual exchange. If everyone concerned is willing after the initial meeting, a date is made to get together at another time for sexual exchange (Bartell, 1970).

Swinging Parties   Mate-swapping parties may assume several forms. A party may be of the "closed," or "soft swing," type, which at first glance resembles any other cocktail party, with well-dressed couples sipping drinks and casually chatting with each other. The difference is that couples occasionally drift off to the bedrooms, returning later, fully dressed, to resume their socializing.

At the other extreme is the "open," or "hard swing," party, commonly called an *orgy*. At these parties the attitude is that anything goes. After the party gets under way, nudity is the rule, and one may see piles of writhing human bodies in the middle of the floor, enjoying touching and being touched by whatever and whoever comes within their reach. Any given party may fall somewhere between the soft and hard or may include both open and closed swinging in different rooms of the house (Bartell, 1970; Bell, 1971; Palson and Palson, 1972).

Some degree of homosexual activity is present at most large parties. The homosexual contacts are almost invariably between females; male homosexuality is usually frowned upon (Bartell, 1970; O'Neill and O'Neill, 1970; Palson and Palson, 1972; Varni, 1972). Ordinarily the men encourage the women in their sexual activities and experience erotic stimulation from observing them (Symond, 1968). Many women report they derive as much sexual pleasure from the other women as from the men, once they overcome their initial hesitation.

Swingers vary greatly in the types of physical and interpersonal experiences they seek in their sexual activities. To distinguish among them, it is useful to divide mate swappers into five categories: hard-core, egotistical, recreational, interpersonal, and communal (Varni, 1972).

At an orgy one may see piles of persons on the floor, touching and being touched by whomever comes within their reach.
Stern/Black Star

Hard-Core Swingers Hard-core swingers want no emotional involvement with their partners, and, with very little selectivity, swing with as many couples as possible. They seek variety for its own sake, with little or no concern for other aspects of swinging. They may participate in large impersonal parties, or they may continually seek other couples for sexual exchanges of brief duration.

Egotistical Swingers Egotistical swingers want sexual-sensual experiences, with little or no emotional involvement with their partners. They are usually fairly selective and are primarily seeking to gratify their own emotional need to feel desired. Swinging is a separate part of their lives, and they have very few social relationships with their swinging partners.

Recreational Swingers Recreational swingers are primarily concerned with the social aspects of swinging activities. They are members of fairly stable groups that engage in nonswinging activities with one another. Swinging is viewed as a hedonistic activity in which emotional involvement with the partner is neither needed nor desired. They have both swinging and nonswinging friends.

376

Interpersonal and Communal Swingers   Interpersonal swingers seek close emotional relationships with their partners. They desire friendships with couples with whom they can share themselves emotionally in an open and honest manner. They are usually quite selective in the partners they swing with, and almost invariably avoid large swinging parties. However, many of their friends may be swingers. Communal swingers are very similar to interpersonal swingers except that they advocate some form of group marriage, an idea rejected by almost all other swingers.

Motives for Swinging   The preceding classification indicates some of the motives for mate swapping. One motive may be simply to obtain sexual variety without threatening an otherwise rather conventional marriage and life style. Another motive may be ego enhancement through having one's sexual attractiveness continually reaffirmed. A third motive may be to expand one's social life by means of a new form of recreation.

You can meet and be with physically the most attractive, good, intelligent people with your wife's consent and be as sexually stimulated as you want to be and still have a great home life — dinner cooked when I get home from work, a beautiful mother for our children, and have my wife as a great bed partner and still have all the variety any man could want when it comes to sex.

Margolis and Rubenstein, 1971, p. 54

Some swingers want to obtain something similar to an extended family that would include other compatible couples in addition to the nuclear family. Group marriage may or may not be part of this extension of family. Even when the couples all maintain separate homes and separate financial arrangements, the emotional closeness fostered by the sharing of interests, social activities, and sexual intimacies creates an emotional, if not legal, extension of the nuclear family (Comfort, 1972).

Because not all people are seeking the same things from their consensual extramarital sex, it follows that the effect of these experiences on their marriages, personalities, and total life style must vary, depending to some degree on what they seek in the experiences.

The Experience of Mate Swapping   For the hard-core or egotistical swingers who seek an emotionally uninvolved physical experience with a succession of partners, swinging can provide the variety and impersonality they seek. But the continual search for new partners can be time-consuming, except perhaps for the relatively indiscriminate hard-core swinger who resides in a large metropolitan area. Egotistical swingers, because they are more selective, have more difficulty finding new partners. This alone can lead a couple to drop out of swinging when they have exhausted the supply of compatible swingers in their area or have tired of the continual search (Bartell, 1971, p. 239).

Another thing that bothered me a lot was the constant need to go after new couples as if this was a way to make sure that real friendships would never grow out of these relationships — just the exchange of sexual partners. I didn't feel like wandering around to meet new people for the sake of sex alone. I think I'm a fairly gregarious guy, but this thought of compulsion or obsession to meet new people turned me off.

Margolis and Rubenstein, 1971, p. 68

For egotistical swingers who are reasonably young and attractive, swinging may provide the ego satisfaction they seek when they discover that many sexual partners find them desirable. However, the reverse may occur when a person's fantasies of his or her sexual prowess or attractiveness exceed reality. The male is particularly vulnerable to this kind of ego-shattering experience. According to one study of swingers, less than 25 percent of men become sexually aroused regularly at large parties, although most report they get turned on more frequently at small parties (Bartell, 1970). Often the wife of a swinging couple becomes more enthusiastic about mate swapping than her husband after she overcomes her initial timidity and anxiety (Palson and Palson, 1972; Smith and Smith, 1970). A woman may enjoy being sought after by a number of men and women whether or not she consistently experiences orgasm (Bell, 1971). On the other hand, her husband may find that he does not live up to his fantasies of being a great lover romping gleefully, penis erect, through a roomful of nude women, satisfying each of them in turn. Instead, his inability to respond sexually to every woman can become quite apparent and can be a real threat to his image of himself. A woman, however, is capable of having many orgasms in one evening, and her failure to become sexually aroused is not as visible and is not as likely to be defined as ego-shattering (Symonds, 1968; Palson and Palson, 1972). Another reason men may experience some distress at swinging parties is that they typically must take the initiative more often than women in suggesting sexual relations, and hence they experience rejection more often.

The interpersonal and communal swingers, who want close personal relationships with couples they swing with, have a somewhat different experience. They are seeking not a continuing succession of new faces for variety or ego enhancement but couples with whom they can be compatible for a long time in many different activities. Such couples may not be easy to find. It is probably more difficult to match two couples who are socially, emotionally, and sexually compatible than it is to find two compatible individuals. When swingers who want an interpersonal relationship use parties, advertisements, or swinging bars to contact other swingers, they are likely to become disillusioned after a time by the superficiality and impersonality of their relationships.

378

There are several problems related to swinging, in relation both to society and to the marital partner. For anyone involved in mate swapping the possibility of discovery is a constant hazard, with attendant risk of job loss, social ostracism, and family condemnation. The possibility of contracting a venereal disease is an additional social concern.

Jealousy A problem for most people involved in consensual adultery is the management of jealousy. One way to minimize jealousy is to keep all extramarital relationships completely nonemotional, which means that a couple cannot have a sexual exchange with another couple more than a few times and does not mix socially with them. Or a couple with an open-ended marriage may agree to limit their outside relationships to brief and unemotional, purely sexual, encounters. This approach serves to minimize jealousy because no intense emotional involvement is ever given a chance to threaten the marriage relationship. Jealousy, however, often does not follow rules and may appear despite an open marriage.

A woman in her mid-thirties reports: I don't usually get jealous — maybe some — a kind of creepy feeling at first. But then it subsides because I know he always comes back to me even though he has been with someone else. Sometimes I wish he would find somebody else so he wouldn't get so upset with me. Not so he would go off and live with her or something, but so he would find something special to relieve some of the tension at home so he would not mind my seeing my friend. He says he is not jealous, but right after I see my friend, then my husband always finds something to get really mad about — but he always says it is not because he is jealous. I guess I never really felt insecure about him leaving me so maybe that's why I am not much jealous. He is more afraid that I might leave him and it makes him more jealous.

From the authors' files

Individuation Whereas increasing intimacy between couples brings an increase in emotional satisfactions, it also brings an increase in problems, particularly those relating to jealousy. For couples who form lasting friendships with other couples, those who do not experience jealousy have often gone through a process that has been termed *individuation* (Palson and Palson, 1972), which implies that each person is seen and appreciated as an individual with a unique combination of desirable and undesirable qualities. This means that a spouse is not seen simply as a good provider or a good cook who can readily be replaced by another equally good provider or skilled cook. For a secure and compatible married couple, intimate friendships pose no threat to the marriage because each person knows his or her spouse perceives her or him as a unique and therefore irreplaceable individual with the qualities she or he desires in a permanent relationship (Ramey, 1976).

379

Effects of Consensual Extramarital Sex

The total impact of consensual extramarital sex on the people involved is difficult to assess because most studies are of couples presently involved in these activities and include few or no couples who have dropped out. This means that most respondents are still reasonably satisfied with their experiences, or else they too would have dropped out. Thus, most people who engage in consensual extramarital sex report that it has had a favorable effect on their marriage and their sexuality (Rosen, 1970; Palson and Palson, 1972; Ziskin and Ziskin, 1973; Knapp, 1976).

Most couples report an increased sexual interest in their mate, an increase in honesty and openness in their marriage, and a new area of shared interest with the spouse (Bartell, 1970; Varni, 1972). Many women in particular say they learned to shed some of their sexual inhibitions and develop a more positive feeling toward their own bodies (O'Neill and O'Neill, 1970). Both men and women report that sex with other partners has taught them new sexual techniques. Some couples report an increase in understanding and appreciation, not only of each other but of other people as well (Bartell, 1970; O'Neill and O'Neill, 1970; Palson and Palson, 1972; Ziskin and Ziskin, 1973; Constantine and Constantine, 1973).

Most couples who drop out of swinging report jealousy, guilt, and a threat to the marriage as their primary problems. Some couples drop out because their children were beginning to question their activities. This was especially a problem for couples with teenage children (Denfeld, 1974).

Some of the couples who choose to discontinue consensual extramarital sex do so because of having had several negative experiences and because of fear of being found out by their family, friends, or employers. Some simply experience a waning interest in the activity as they would in any other. And some find it too difficult to manage the jealousy that arises. Perhaps others drop out because they find that it is too mechanical and impersonal. They feel they are used as a sex object rather than appreciated as a total human being. They find there is a loss of identity and lack of emotional involvement that is for them the antithesis of sexual pleasure (Bartell, 1970).

It all seemed so mechanical. There was no emotion, really. The woman took off her clothes, and pulled back the covers and sort of jumped in and waited for me to do the same. When I did get into bed, I waited for her to make the first move, and that didn't take long. She told me what a nice body I had and was there anything in particular I wanted her to do to get me started. . . . When it was all over she asked me if I wanted to stay in bed with her a little longer. I told her that if it were just the same to her we should get dressed and go back into the living room.

Margolis and Rubenstein, 1971, p. 62

380

In contrast, some who continue to enjoy their expanded sexual relationships report that these have provided a unique experience and a greater intensity of communication between human beings (O'Neill and O'Neill, 1970).

The long-term effects of consensual extramarital sex on a couple, their marriage, and their children will not be known for many years; however, at this point some tentative conclusions are possible. To the degree that consensual adultery can provide sexual variety without disrupting marital relationships, it is a conservative institution that serves to preserve rather than destroy families (Denfield and Gordon, 1970; Palson and Palson, 1972). When mate swapping provides a new source of recreation that couples can share, it can have welcome consequences. When a sexual exchange provides a couple with a new network of close relationships extending beyond their immediate family, it gives them an important source of warmth and emotional support that is largely lacking in a highly urbanized society such as ours (Comfort, 1972). On the other hand, when consensual extramarital sex exacerbates feelings of personal inadequacy, threatens the stability of a satisfying marital relationship, or increases the sense of alienation from fellow human beings, the pain of the consequences may outweigh the potential for personal growth.

Although swinging will probably always have some enthusiastic participants, there is some evidence that it is now declining in popularity in the United States. Although figures on swinging have always been imprecise, an estimate for 1972 was 1 million to 1.5 million participants. Current estimates are considerably lower, and swinger bars and clubs have been decreasing in number (Fang, 1976).

Multilateral Sexual Relations

When intimacy and involvement with particular people outside the marriage continue over time, there is frequently some move to restructure the original marriage or marriages. The restructuring may take the form of divorce and remarriage with the other partners, or it may involve bringing all intimate people together in a multilateral sexual relationship, or what is commonly called group marriage. A *multilateral* or *group marriage* is defined as "a voluntary family group of three or more persons, each of whom is committed to and maintains a relationship with more than one other person in a manner regarded by the participants as being 'married' " (Constantine, Constantine, and Edelman, 1972, p. 268). A multilateral marriage can result from increasing involvement with outsiders either by members of an open-ended marriage or by participants in intimate friendships. It differs from bigamy and polygamy in that it does not   381

involve the deception of partners as bigamy may, and it is not legally binding in the United States.

Group marriages vary considerably in form. The increasing involvement of a couple with one other woman or man can lead to a three-person marriage. When two or more couples become increasingly involved with each other emotionally and sexually, they may enter into a multilateral relationship. The inclusion of children and other adults can yield a very complex family arrangement.

Group marriages may be the basis of communal living arrangements in which there is a wide range of human relationships.
Cary S. Wolinsky/Stock, Boston

Motivations for Entering Multilateral Marriages

The reasons for entering multilateral relationships are at least in part the same as those for entering any other marital relationship. One man involved in a three-person marriage described his reasons:

To state the matter in purely emotional terms, I simply found myself loving two women, of similar temperament, demeanor, and character (but with interesting differences), who, as I appraised it, had a liking and a need for one another. . . . I

From *Face to Face to Face* by Gordon Clanton and Chris

382

also found myself intellectually curious about the effects such a combination experience-experiment might have on each of us personally. What transformations might be forthcoming and what kind of a group might we be for ourselves and for others? To me, it also seemed socially daring, sexually interesting, and a personal challenge.... A group marriage, as I conceived it, held ever so much more promise for personal development, companionship, sexual variety, and differentiation in style and identity and family function than the ordinary model of the conventional, or even the unconventional, marital dyad.

Downing. Copyright © 1975 by Gordon Clanton and Chris Downing. Reprinted by permission of the publisher, E. P. Dutton.

Many people seek in group marriage an expansion of the benefits of two-person marriage plus the unique advantages for personal growth found when marital interaction includes a larger number of people (Constantine and Constantine, 1971).

Perceived benefits come from the additional persons in the household with whom one may relate intellectually, socially, emotionally, and sexually. Pooled economic resources and work efforts can provide more freedom to pursue creative interests. Additional sibling and parent figures in the household can provide the children in a group marriage with many more opportunities for affectional relationships (Constantine and Constantine, 1973; Ellis, 1970). Multilateral marriage provides a wider range of relationships than is possible in most monogamous marriages. People can have multifaceted sex, love, child rearing, and other human relationships that they might never otherwise experience; they may see themselves as developing in a more fulfilling manner than if they had limited themselves to monogamy (Ellis, 1970). A man living in a two-man, one-woman threesome summarizes the advantages of their arrangement as he sees it:

The chief advantage is since we have had a baby, with three persons to take care of it — I can't conceive of how traditional parents take care of children. It's beneficial for us financially — we had a combined income of $35,000 and we were able to afford things we couldn't afford otherwise. I think it gives us all more freedom in that if I want to go and do something there are no feelings of leaving someone at home alone.... If I come home and I have something to talk about I've got a fall back if someone's in a bad mood. If I want to be alone John and Alice can talk to one another. If we have fights the third person can act as a referee — more than a referee, a translator.

From the authors' files

Difficulties in Multilateral Relations

Multilateral marriage involves many difficulties as well as advantages. Problems can come from differences regarding life styles, child-raising practices, money management, need for privacy, division of work, and

383

stigmatization by other people, to mention a few. Relations with the larger society can also be a problem as a group marriage has to deal with reactions of neighbors, friends, relatives, employers, and even lending institutions. Jealousy is a fairly common problem, but much less so among people who are older and in groups that are comparatively well established (Constantine and Constantine, 1973).

Even very well-adjusted individuals in our society encounter difficulties in finding and living harmoniously with one other adult. These difficulties are compounded in multilateral marriages when several adults must find each other compatible and attractive in a long-term relationship. The common problems of adjusting schedules to accommodate everyone's needs are compounded as the household increases in size. Scheduling of everyday activities such as eating, cleaning, sleeping, and listening to music means that some individuals must sacrifice their preferences for the good of the group (Ellis, 1970).

Sexual Relations in Group Marriages

Scheduling of sexual relationships often presents a problem in group marriages. The question of who sleeps with whom on a given night must be resolved in some way. Even though the participants may make a sincere effort to form emotionally equitable ties with all other members of the group, inevitably some relationships are closer than others, and some people are more attractive than others as sex objects or love objects. Spontaneous pairing off each night gives the most freedom of expression and also presents the most problems, since several of the group may choose the same partner and others' choices may not be reciprocated. To avoid the problems associated with spontaneous pairing, some group marriages set up a system of sexual rotation. This reduces friction by limiting the sexual options within the group to a more manageable number; it also limits freedom of choice, which is often seen as a disadvantage of sexual rotation (Ellis, 1970; Salsberg, 1973; Clanton and Downing, 1975, pp. 222–224).

The loving atmosphere provided by the multilateral family composed of a variety of adults and children with whom one can relate may offer more emotional and sensory input than one can expect in the typical monogamous nuclear family. But for some persons this results in sensory overload. The emotionally charged atmosphere associated with continuous intimate interaction among many persons is similar to being in a continuous encounter group. Unless there are provisions for family members to have some occasional privacy and solitude, sensory overload can become a problem (Salsberg, 1975).

Duration of Multilateral Marriages

Multilateral marriages typically do not last long. Most groups remain together for several months to a few years, and then break up for one reason or another (Ellis, 1970; Constantine et al., 1972; See, 1975). Probably those that have a high degree of financial security and are highly structured with regard to work routines and leadership for specific tasks are likely to endure the longest (Mowery, 1979). In spite of the problems and the relatively short life of most group marriages, most persons who have tried them report that they would try again, though under somewhat different conditions. Many feel that the right relationship with the right people could induce them to enter another, similar relationship (Constantine and Constantine, 1973, p. 207).

I realize now how very socialized I am for pairs, couples, and one-to-one relationships. I can visualize realistically the many disadvantages and limitations of a couple isolated in a house and having no function by today's standards and demands except to interact with each other. . . . I do, however, see group marriages becoming more common and workable but perhaps with certain factors different from what was true of our situation.

Clanton and Downing, 1975, p. 183

The problems of multilateral relationships tax the capacities of most persons to deal with them; yet the majority who have tried it report it as a positive growth experience that left them with a greater capacity to love, increased self-awareness, and enhanced self-esteem (Salsberg, 1973).

Conclusion

In spite of the sexual revolution in attitudes in the United States, sex outside marriage is not widely accepted. The most liberal attitudes are those toward premarital sex. A recent national survey of adults found that 41 percent felt sex for unmarried persons was always or almost always wrong. The same survey found that 87 percent felt extramarital sex was always or almost always wrong (Glenn and Weaver, 1979).

The youngest and best educated segments of the population have been the most liberal in their sexual attitudes and the most experimental in their sexual behavior. This group is the most willing to experiment with premarital sex and to live together without being married. However, research on college students indicates a high level of commitment to egalitarian marriage. Most are not willing to participate in alternatives such as extramarital sex (Strong, 1978).

Some elements within our society are disenchanted with traditional marriage and family institutions. Their motives range from lofty idealism to irresponsible adventurism. Their questioning of traditional family structure with its rigid sex roles and hierarchical power structure apparently has not led to a total rejection of marriage. Instead there appears to be a move toward companionship or egalitarian marriage as an ideal, rather than toward alternative life styles (Mace, 1979). The old double standard of sexuality for men and women is disappearing. It is no longer assumed that the male's nature is sexual and promiscuous while the female's is pure and chaste. Women's sexual needs are accepted as being as important as men's, not only within marriage but also in premarital and extramarital sex. This is perhaps our most profound sexual revolution (O'Neill, 1977).

Chapter 13 / *Homosexuality, Bisexuality, and Transsexualism*

In the United States the ideal norms for sexual behavior specify partners of the opposite sex. Homosexual and bisexual behavior clearly violate this norm because they involve sexual relationships between people of the same sex. *Homosexual behavior* means engaging in sexual relationships primarily with others of the same sex. *Bisexual behavior* means engaging in sexual relationships with individuals of both sexes.

Transsexualism also represents a deviation from the heterosexual norm, since transsexuals have sexual relations with partners of the same biological sex. Transsexuals can be distinguished from homosexuals and bisexuals by their unique gender identity: transsexuals consider themselves people who have bodies of the wrong sex. A transsexual with a male body feels he is really a female; a transsexual with a female body feels she is actually male. Transsexuals feel their body is wrong, but their sexual behavior is appropriate; homosexuals and bisexuals know their sexual behavior is socially stigmatized, but they do not question the appropriateness of their bodies.

In any analysis of homosexuality, bisexuality, and transsexualism it is important to distinguish behavior and identity; it is also important to differentiate gender identity from sexual identity. *Gender identity* is one's identity as a biological male or female (see Chapter 9). *Sexual identity*, on the other hand, is one's identity as a sexual type of person — as a homosexual, heterosexual, or bisexual. An individual can engage in homosexual behavior, yet have a heterosexual identity; and vice versa. Finally, identity may be asserted by oneself or labeled by others; an individual with a heterosexual identity and homosexual behavior may be labeled a homosexual or a lesbian by others.

Homosexuality

Homosexuality in both males and females can refer to sexual behavior, emotional states, or definitions of self. In this section we will describe the sexual behavior associated with the homosexual label and show its relation to important questions of definition of self, identity, and community or group membership.

Incidence

With reference to sexual behavior over a lifetime or a number of years, Kinsey and other sex researchers use a seven-point scale in which one extreme refers to males or females with a history of exclusive heterosexuality and the other extreme refers to those with a history of exclusive homosexuality. Near the exclusively homosexual end of the scale are people who are almost entirely homosexual in their activities or reactions, but who have had incidental sexual experience with or reactions to someone of the opposite sex. Further along the scale is predominant homosexual activity with more than incidental heterosexuality. Those in the middle of the scale have experienced homosexual and heterosexual contacts equally.

Next on the scale are people whose activities or reactions have been predominantly heterosexual but often homosexual. Last before exclusive heterosexuality is the category of predominantly heterosexual behavior or reactions with only isolated instances of homosexuality (Kinsey et al., 1948, pp. 639–641).

Much sexual behavior in males and females falls between the two extremes of exclusive homosexuality and exclusive heterosexuality. Kinsey's data from the 1940s and 1950s and Morton Hunt's data from the early 1970s indicate that roughly 25 percent of American males and 15 percent of American females have had at least one homosexual experience, and a considerable number of other persons have responded erotically to persons of the same sex but without actual physical sexual contact. However, only about 2 percent of females and 3 percent of males beyond age fifteen rate themselves as mainly or completely homosexual (Kinsey et al., 1948, pp. 610–666; Kinsey et al, 1953, pp. 446–501; Hunt, 1974, pp. 303–319). Furthermore, in a sample of men that was gathered from gay bars and organizations in the United States, Weinberg and Williams (1974, p. 112) found that about half the respondents did not classify themselves as exclusively homosexual. (See Table 13.1.) (For a discussion of Williams and Weinberg's samples and methodology, see the appendix.)

Until fairly recently most people in the United States assumed there were at most three categories of people — homosexuals, heterosexuals, and a few bisexuals who enjoyed both types of sexual contacts. The stereotype was that a heterosexual was sexually normal and all others

Sexual Preferences of Respondents from Gay Bars and Organizations, in Percentages	Table 13.1

Exclusively homosexual	50.6
Predominantly homosexual, only insignificantly heterosexual	29.8
Predominantly homosexual but significantly heterosexual	13.1
Equally homosexual and heterosexual	4.4
Predominantly heterosexual but significantly homosexual	2.1
N = 1,057	

Source: From *Male Homosexuals: Their Problems and Adaptations*, p. 112, by Martin S. Weinberg and Colin J. Williams. Copyright © 1974 by Oxford University Press, Inc. Reprinted by permission.

were sexually perverted, objects of pity and scorn in need of medical attention or perhaps institutionalization. With the publication of some of the findings of the Institute for Sex Research at Indiana University, it is now apparent that the dichotomy of normal or queer is inadequate for describing what actually exists in this country. Even though questions have been raised about some aspects of the methodology of Kinsey and his associates (Hobbs and Lambert, 1948; Terman, 1948; Wallin, 1949; Cochran et al., 1953; Hunt, 1974, pp. 303–319), the fact that such a large percentage of the Kinsey sample did not fall into either the exclusive heterosexuality or exclusive homosexuality category must challenge previous concepts. More recent data tend to confirm the Kinsey findings (Hunt, 1974, pp. 303–319).

Although there are many similarities between male and female homosexuality, some differences have been found with respect to their homosexual activities. Erotic responses to people of the same sex have been reported in about twice as many males as females, and sexual contacts with the same sex that proceeded to orgasm have been reported in about a third as many females as males. Kinsey reports that a large proportion (71 percent) of the females he interviewed who have had homosexual contact have restricted their homosexual activities to one or two partners. Only half the males with homosexual experience have so restricted their contacts, and many of the males have been highly promiscuous, sometimes with literally hundreds of partners (Kinsey, 1953, pp. 487–501).

Culture and Homosexuality

Morton Hunt's survey in the 1970s found that roughly half his sample of adults agreed with the statement "There is some homosexuality in all of us," and half felt that homosexuality should be legal. A recent Gallup poll found that 56 percent of Americans think homosexuals should have equal rights in terms of job opportunity, although a significant proportion would deny a homosexual the right to be an elementary school teacher, a member of the clergy, or a doctor (Morin, 1978, pp. 34–35). This partial tolerance of homosexuality now found in the United States is not universal, nor has it been at any time in recorded history. Attitudes toward homosexuality have included a tolerant view implying some moral inferiority but not unqualified moral degradation, a view of homosexuality as equal to heterosexuality, and a view of it as superior. One civilization that viewed homosexuality as superior, of course, was classical Greece, in which emotional and sexual relationships between men and between men and boys were regarded as more meaningful and enduring than those between men and women.

390

Tolerant Cultures   In some cultures homosexual behavior is both common and acceptable. Certain Melanesian communities, for example, are very permissive about homosexual acts. Young boys commonly engage in mutual masturbation and sodomy with their friends and brothers. After marriage only a small proportion of men entirely give up their homosexual activities. Homosexual behavior is expected from most men as long as they still fulfill their wives sexually. There is no secrecy about homosexuality, and boys discuss it in front of parents and friends without shame (Karlen, 1971).

Other cultures not only tolerate or accept homosexuality but also accord homosexuals a special status. Among the Koniag of Alaska, the Lango of East Africa, and the Tanala of Madagascar it is not uncommon for certain men to dress like women, perform women's tasks, and even become the "wife" of a man. These men enjoy considerable social prestige and many become powerful shamans believed to possess supernatural powers. These tribes believe that sexual contact with a shaman will confer religious and magical benefits (Churchill, 1967).

The United States and Western Europe, however, are not the only cultures that condemn homosexuality. In Nicaragua homosexual behavior was penalized by stoning; all the pre-Columbian Mayan nations had laws against homosexual contact (Churchill, 1967).

Law, Health, and Religion   As Pomeroy (1966) points out, normality may be defined with reference to social harm, self-fulfillment, the law, religion, and a number of other authorities. Conceptions of the abnormality of homosexuality have arisen in the contexts of law, religion, and health.

Being homosexual is not against the law; but certain acts commonly performed by homosexuals are illegal in all but thirteen states. In most states oral-genital and anal sexual acts are illegal even if performed in private by heterosexual married couples. In practice, few heterosexuals are arrested for such private sexual behavior; the majority of homosexuals are arrested for statutory violations in public places such as rest rooms, beaches, and parks. In the seven states where private homosexual behavior between consenting adults has been decriminalized, the dire predictions of some conservative groups have not been fulfilled. Decriminalization has had no effect on the involvement of homosexuals with minors, the use of force by homosexuals, or the amount of private homosexual behavior (Geis et al., 1976).

In the context of the moral heritage of Western society, both homosexual acts and a homosexual identity are stigmatized as immoral and perverted. That heritage lies within the Judeo-Christian tradition, in which any sexual act that cannot lead to procreation is condemned. Not only are

391

homosexual acts illegal, but the very identity of homosexuality also is stigmatized within the moral and religious framework as evil.

In the eighteenth century, medical concepts about sexual deviation reinforced traditional religious concepts that were under attack. These ideas were amplified in the nineteenth century until all forms of nonprocreative sexuality were viewed as illness (Bullough, 1974). Gradually it was realized that childbearing was not the only healthy goal of sexuality. Persons who desired contraception were eventually accepted as not pathological. The medical community long ago rejected the naive assumptions that labeled homosexuality as an illness. Until recently, however, homosexuality was on the American Psychiatric Association's list of diagnostic mental illness categories along with schizophrenia and paranoia. Judd Marmor, president of the APA in the early 1970s, was instrumental in having the term *homosexual* removed from the diagnostic categories used by professionals (although it remained within the categories of symptomatology). The removal was accomplished with great conflict within the psychiatric discipline, and a movement was immediately begun to have it reinstated.

An increasing body of evidence supports the view that homosexuality is not an illness. Studies comparing homosexual and heterosexual populations on a variety of measures of emotional health find no greater neuroticism among gays than among straights (Riess, Safer, and Yotive, 1974; Adelman, 1977; Ferguson and Finkler, 1978; Bell and Weinberg, 1978).

The Medical Definition of Homosexuality

Today, although many persons still believe that homosexuality is evil in biblical terms, many more believe that it is a sickness beyond the rational control of the persons involved. This definition of homosexuality as a sickness is one part of a general social movement to redefine evil as sickness and discover its causes, incidence, and cure through the application of the medical model (see also Chapter 16). The medical view is that homosexual behavior or a homosexual identity is a sickness whose cure, incidence *(epidemiology)*, and cause *(etiology)* should be discovered through research, just as doctors seek to find the causes, incidence, and cure of diseases such as cancer.

Epidemiology of Homosexuality   Prior to Kinsey's work the relatively large amount of homoerotic experiences of the so-called normal population in the United States was not really known. Most scientific writings on the subject of homosexuality were by psychologists or psychiatrists whose reports were based on their clinical experience. Because their clinical practice was necessarily composed of persons with emotional problems of   392 one sort or another, they concluded that homosexuals were neurotic persons who needed to be helped with, or cured of, their emotional problems. Their writings focused mainly on the causes of homosexuality. Because these writers were often steeped in Freudian tradition, these causes were sought in the pathological childhood and family situation of the patient.

Etiology of Homosexuality   The therapists are not alone in their search for the causes of the so-called illness or sexual perversion of homosexuality. Other writers have attributed homosexual behavior to various other sources. One popular theory locates the causes of homosexuality in family dynamics (Bieber, 1962). Some suggest it is the result of a glandular malfunction and hormonal imbalance. Others have suggested a genetic predisposition in the form of a chromosome disorder. Recent research, however, does not support the idea that homosexual behavior results from hormonal or genetic predisposition (Brodie et al., 1974). One recent study indicated subtle differences in hormone levels between heterosexual and homosexual males, but there was extensive overlap between the groups (Newmark et al., 1979). The majority of research concludes there are no consistent differences in hormonal levels between heterosexuals and homosexuals (Meyer-Bahlburg, 1977; Ross, Rogers, and McCulloch, 1978; Meyer-Bahlburg, 1979).

The medical view of homosexuality is implicitly based on the assumption that man has an inborn instinct or tendency to be heterosexual. Scientific studies of other cultures or of animals do not lend any support to an instinctual theory of human sexuality. Human sexual behavior varies widely and is dependent on learning and conditioning. For this reason the causes of homosexuality are best sought not in a search for some malfunction that has led to the so-called perversion, but in a more general theory that explains how sexual preferences are acquired (Acosta, 1975). It is just as meaningful to inquire into the causes of heterosexuality as into the causes of homosexuality. Perhaps it is most meaningful to explain sexual behavior in behavioral terms — in other words, what in a given situation developed a given sexual act — rather than in terms of predispositions and traits (see Tripp, 1975).

At this point it is possible to discuss the ways in which homosexual behavior is related to definition of self and identity, but to do so we must engage in separate discussions of male homosexuality, lesbianism, and bisexuality. This separation is necessary because there are some known (and probably even more unknown) differences in the developmental aspects of male homosexual, lesbian, and bisexual identities and communities. In addition, there are wide differences in the literature about male and female homosexuality and bisexuality. Homosexuality remains   393 shrouded in some mystery, like all sexuality in our society, but much more is known about male than female homosexuality, and more is known about homosexuality than about bisexuality.

Male Homosexuality

Some males who have experienced homosexual contacts or fantasies label themselves homosexual, some bisexual, and some heterosexual. The males whose definition of self is heterosexual despite homosexual contacts may be married men who engage in casual homosexual contacts (Humphreys, 1970), lower-class males who allow other males to perform fellatio on them for pay (Reiss, 1964), institutionalized males who have no heterosexual outlet, and males who do not choose to adopt a homosexual or bisexual identity even in the face of a predominant homosexual sexual and/or romantic interest (Warren, 1974; Cass, 1979).

Coming Out   *Coming out* is the process through which gay persons recognize their sexual preferences and integrate this knowledge into their lives. The coming out process is marked by a series of milestones. The first of these experiences is awareness of same-sex attractions. This awareness is often part of an enjoyment of fantasies involving same-sex persons. The second stage is engaging in sex with others of one's own sex. For women, these first sexual experiences are often in the context of a loving relationship, but are usually relatively casual or impersonal encounters for men (Monteflores and Schultz, 1978). During this second stage persons are often very secretive about their homosexual activities. They may have a homosexual identity or they may still retain their heterosexual identity.

The third stage involves acknowledging to other persons that one is a homosexual. These other people quite often are also homosexual. Later the individual may "come out" to straight friends and to family members.

The fourth stage is the development of a gay identity. A gay identity involves rejecting the negative social stereotypes associated with being homosexual. Usually this process is facilitated by the individual's becoming part of a gay community and becoming acquainted with a number of homosexuals who can be perceived as acceptable people similar to himself, rather than the sick perverts envisioned by most persons.

The last stage involves acknowledging to the public that one is gay. This is often accomplished through active involvement in gay rights organizations (Lee, 1977).

There are differences in the coming out process for men and for women. Gay men tend to engage in same-sex activities about two years after they become aware of their attraction to males. Women tend to wait about six years before they act out their homosexual attractions (Monteflores and Schultz, 1978).

394

Homosexuality is expressed through sexual and affectionate relationships with persons of one's own sex.
Steve Stone/Picture Cube

Once men engage in homosexual behaviors they often avoid a homosexual identity by denying that they feel any emotional attachment to their sex partners. They rationalize that it was just for money or just for sex kicks or just because they were too drunk to know what they were doing. In contrast, women avoid a homosexual identity at first by emphasizing the very personal and special nature of their love relationship with their sex partner. By this means a woman may identify herself as a person who loves this one special woman, and thus avoid identifying herself as a

395

lesbian. Thus, whereas men avoid identifying themselves as homosexual by denying their feelings, women avoid a homosexual identity by emphasizing their feelings (Monteflores and Schultz, 1978).

The coming-out process is easier for women than for men. Because our society has traditionally valued the male role over the female role, violation of roles through homosexual behavior represents more of a loss for a male. In addition, the women's movement facilitates coming out for lesbians. The sense of solidarity provided for women has no counterpart among men. Not all aspects of the women's movement support lesbianism, but the criticism of women being forced into stereotyped sex roles provides implicit support for some aspects of lesbianism (Monteflores and Schultz, 1978).

When a man first comes out he may be more likely than at any other time to affect the effeminate mannerisms most people commonly associate with the male homosexual stereotype (Gagnon and Simon, 1968). Some self-avowed homosexuals never adopt these mannerisms; some do for only a time and then drop them when their homosexual identity is more secure. Some maintain extravagant mannerisms throughout their homosexual career — at least in situations where they do not have to hide their homosexual identity. In addition to adopting mannerisms that caricature those of the opposite sex, many homosexuals enjoy dressing in clothing different from that usually expected of their sex. A gay male might enjoy occasionally "going camp," or wearing something like a lacy shirt and tight black velvet pants (Gagnon and Simon, 1968; Warren, 1975).

A common belief is that a male homosexual may be easily recognized because he is effeminate; in addition it is assumed that effeminate males always take the receptor role in sex acts. Both stereotypes are wrong. Although some male homosexuals are effeminate, many others are indistinguishable from so-called normal males, and some are hypermasculine. There is some evidence that homosexual males who are masculine in their dress and mannerisms are not tolerated as well in the straight community as those homosexual males who fit the effeminate stereotype (Storms, 1978). Interestingly, it is rarely the effeminate male who is the most sought by gay men as a sex partner (Laner and Kamel, 1978). An analysis of personal ads in a gay newspaper indicated that 45 percent specifically mentioned a straight or masculine appearance as the quality desired in a partner (Lee, 1976). (See Table 13.2.) Appropriate age range and a desire for a lasting relationship were the only two qualities that ranked higher than masculine appearance. Like heterosexuals, the appearance and social role of homosexuals may vary independently of sexual preferences.

Activities and Roles The sexual options open to homosexual males include fellatio (oral-genital contact), anal intercourse, oral-anal contact, 396

Desired Characteristics of Partners Specified in 248 Advocate *Advertisements*   Table 13.2

Rank Order	Quality Desired in Partner	Percentage Seeking Desired Quality
1	Age within a specified range	73
2	Partner must want a faithful, lasting relationship	53
3	Straight or masculine appearance	45
4	Specific kind of physique (height, weight, build, musculature, etc.)	42
5	Sincerity, honesty, seriousness	40
6	Interest in specified social activities, hobbies, sports, arts, etc.	33
7	Warm and/or affectionate	31
8	Specified race	23
9	Preferred sex role (e.g., butch, top man)	22
10	Handsome, good looking	20
11	Qualities of character (sensitivity, stability, etc.) that are not listed above	19
12	Not a drug user	18
12	Not into sadomasochism (S & M)	18
13	Intelligent and/or educated	16
13	Not fat	16
14	Size of penis or type of penis (e.g., "uncut")	15
15	Discretion	14
16	Smooth or hairy	12
16	Socioeconomic status	12
17	Not frequently at the bars	10

hand stimulation, friction of the penis against the thigh or other part of the partner's body *(interfemoral intercourse),* use of vibrators and dildos for anal stimulation, and insertion of fingers into the anus. These sexual contacts may be one-sided or reciprocal; they may be restricted to just one form or a combination of several forms.

Williams and Weinberg (1974), in a survey of homosexual males in the United States, found that over 50 percent of the respondents had experienced each of the following types of sexual activity at least three times: mutual masturbation, insertee fellatio, insertor fellatio, insertee anal intercourse, and insertor anal intercourse. (See Table 13.3). Tripp (1975) points out that for many males interfemoral intercourse is the preferred form of sexual contact. The terms *insertor* and *insertee* are more accurate for describing male-male sexual contacts than the active-passive contrast used in describing male-female and female-female sexual contacts. The   397

Sexual Practices   Table 13.3

Which of the Following Homosexual Practices Have You Engaged in at Least Three Times?*

Mutual masturbation and/or received fellatio and/or performed anal intercourse	13.0%
Has in addition performed fellatio	20.9
Has in addition received anal intercourse	11.5
Has experienced all of the above	54.6
N = 1,057	

* The original response categories were coded into the form presented here.

Source: From *Male Homosexuals: Their Problems and Adaptations,* p. 111, by Martin S. Weinberg and Colin J. Williams. Copyright © 1974 by Oxford University Press, Inc. Reprinted by permission.

insertor is the male who inserts the penis into the mouth or anus. The *insertee* is the male who receives it. The effeminate-appearing male homosexual may prefer the insertee role in fellatio, which cannot be appropriately described as passive. The homosexual whose self-image is heterosexual will often refuse to take any but the insertor role in fellatio or anal intercourse, and may additionally refuse to kiss or hold his partner tenderly. The most popular set of sexual preferences is for all roles combined, both insertor and insertee, oral and anal. It is difficult simply to categorize most gay males as insertors or insertees (Harry, 1976).

In using the term *social role*, we refer to the demeanor, attitude, and occupation of male homosexuals. Most male homosexuals in our culture are traditionally masculine in appearance, demeanor, and occupational role, but some are generally (or occasionally) effeminate, and a few others are supported by other men or act as male prostitutes — occupational roles traditionally assigned to women.

Jeffrey and Joe: Jeffrey is a well-known Republican political figure, while Joe is his self-described "wife" — a golden-colored, much younger black man who stays hidden from the public view in their mutual home. While Jeffrey is a typically masculine if highly conservative-appearing man, Joe is slight, and quite effeminate, with flamboyant clothes, flips of the wrist, and use of the word "she" to describe himself. Joe has lived with Jeffrey for two years without working, and seems content to stay home, cook gourmet food, and keep an immaculate house.   From the authors' files

Raymond and Jim: Raymond and Jim are both medical doctors, and both are conservatively masculine in appearance. Raymond is still in the internship   From the authors' files

398

stage of practice, and they have been separated for a while, but will soon be living together again. They divide the cooking and household chores about equally. Both are very self-conscious about any attribution of effeminacy or masculine-feminine role playing to them, and they strive to maintain absolute equality in all things.

Secret and Overt Homosexuality   Jeffrey and Joe and Raymond and Jim belong to the secret end of the secret-overt continuum that describes the gay world. Within this continuum — ranging from public media announcement of homosexuality at the overt extreme to total secrecy in contacts with straights at the other — there is some discrete division in the

Some persons seek greater social acceptance of gays through political activism.
Charles Gatewood/Magnum Photos, Inc.

399

types of gay communities. The secret gay world is embodied in cliques and communities that are generally middle class (with some blue-collar membership), relatively middle-aged (late twenties, thirties, and forties), nonactive and relatively conservative politically. They keep their homosexuality secret from most straight friends, coworkers, and family (Warren, 1974).

The overt gay world, on the other hand, is represented by either the underworld described by John Rechy (1963) or by the politically activist gay community (Humphreys, 1972). Like the black movement, which ranges from the NAACP to the Black Panthers, political activism among male and female homosexuals ranges from the conservative Mattachine Society to the radical Gay Activists Alliance. Members of all groups, however, are committed to the declaration of their homosexuality to at least a limited — and sometimes a wide — audience of straight friends, acquaintances, coworkers, and family. Just as many middle-aged secret gays are indistinguishable from straight businessmen, professors, lawyers, and construction workers, many gay activists look like any other bearded, long-haired, jean-clad counterculture activist.

The other overt sector of the gay world is composed of those homosexuals whose homosexuality or effeminacy is either very obvious or is their stock in trade: male prostitutes (Rechy, 1963), female impersonators (Newton, 1972), gay-bar bartenders, or flamboyant hairdressers. Though not a single community, the gay underworld encompasses many communities of those who share common interests and common problems.

The Gay Bar Between the underworld and the middle-class secret community is the male gay-bar community, whose members go to gay bars and often to gay steam baths, motels, and other places where gays congregate publicly. Many male and female homosexuals go to gay bars occasionally, but many bars have a hard-core clique of patrons whose entire social and sexual life — and sometimes their entire life — is tied up with bar functions, schedules, and activities (Warren, 1974).

As researchers in the field have consistently found, homosexuality has no definite characteristics, location, or boundaries. Homosexual behavior can occur in any social class, ethnic group, or situation. Self-defined homosexuals are found in every community, and gay communities are found wherever a large enough number of gays reside. Homosexuality is as various as heterosexuality in its sexual, cultural, and social aspects.

Lesbianism

Lesbianism, like male homosexuality and bisexuality, can be conceptualized as a form of sexual behavior, an emotional preference, or a definition

Techniques Preferred by Lesbians to Reach Orgasm   Table 13.4

Response	Number of Responses
Oral sex	147
Manual stimulation	117
Vaginal stimulation	88
Masturbation	50
Tribadism	50
Anal stimulation	36
Other	17
Total *	505

* Total number of respondents was 286, but some respondents indicated they had more than one technique they preferred to use to reach orgasm. Consequently, the total number of responses is greater than 286.

Source: Pat Califia, "Lesbian Sexuality," *Journal of Homosexuality*, 4 (1979), p. 260. Copyright © 1979 by the Haworth Press, Inc. All rights reserved. Used by permission.

of self. As a type of sexual behavior lesbianism can include hand stimulation of the genitals, cunnilingus (oral-genital contact), rubbing the genitals against the thigh or other parts of the partner's body, use of vibrators on the internal or external genitals, anal stimulation, and insertion of dildos or other articles into the vagina. These activities in any one sexual encounter may be mutual or one-way.

Although there is a wide range of potential types of sexual activities possible for women in their same-sex contacts, a recent study of lesbian sexuality found that most women preferred manual or oral clitoral stimulation in their sexual encounters (Califia, 1979). (See Table 13.4.)

Definition of Self   A person who engages in lesbian sexual activities may or may not have an emotional as well as sexual involvement with another woman. Women with intense emotional involvements with other women, without sexual acting out, may be labeled lesbian by themselves or others. In addition, observed lesbian sexual activity or emotional preference may be accompanied by definition of oneself as a lesbian, a heterosexual, or a bisexual (Ponse, 1978). In studies by Warren and Ponse (1976) and by Blumstein and Schwartz (1974), subjects who have had sexual experiences with other women provide examples of all three types of self-definition. Illustrative cases are given below to show the very complex interplay between sexual experience, emotional direction, and definition of self.

Kim, lesbian definition of self: Although I have had sexual experiences with males, I am a lesbian — I prefer the term "gay." Emotionally I have had a crush on or fallen in love with — whichever you prefer — dozens of women and only one man. I have had lasting romantic-emotional relationships only with

From the authors' files

401

women (two of them: one relatively immature and one relatively mature). I prefer sex with women, although sex with men does not turn me off. I have experienced orgasm only in a relatively mature relationship with a woman. If for some reason (which I cannot conceive) I had to have relationships with men, or marry one, I would still be gay. If my present relationship with a woman ended, I would not totally reject men as such (some of my best friends have been straight men in the past, and many of them now are gay men), but I would probably seek sex only with women because I am used to that, and I would not want to mess with birth-control devices or pills. I would seek a committed sexual-emotional relationship only with another woman, so far as I can judge at this time.

Dana, heterosexual definition of self: Dana and her boy friend, who usually posed as a married couple, were members of several swinging groups for couples. After a few experiences in the groups, Dana observed that female-female sexual interaction took place, as well as male-female. After talking with her boy friend, whom she consulted with in all things, she decided that she would try this new experience at a party, which she did. She soon became quite keen on female-female sexual interaction, so much so that some of the men at the swingers' parties got rather annoyed with her. She and her boy friend then went to lesbian bars, where Dana picked up women with whom she had sex at home, with her boy friend in the next room. Throughout these experiences she continued to assert that she was completely heterosexual, her rationale being that she remained emotionally faithful to her boy friend. *From the authors' files*

Dulcie, definition of self without labels: At the age of twenty-seven, after many satisfactory sexual encounters with males, Dulcie had a sexual experience with a lesbian who took her to a gay bar, and later herself initiated a short sexual liaison with a seventeen-year-old girl. After these encounters she declared that she liked both men and women sexually, but did not approve of labels such as "gay," bisexual," or "straight." She liked women and men around the age of seventeen or eighteen, and desired short-term relationships with no deepening emotional commitment; however, she required her male partners to have undergone vasectomies, which limited the male field quite a bit. *From the authors' files*

As little is known about the psychological and social characteristics of lesbians as about their sexual behavior, possibly because many lesbians are married, have children, and are highly secretive about any lesbian affairs they do have. However, some research has been done on types of lesbian communities and on identities, role playing, and femininity in the lesbian community (Gagnon and Simon, 1973; Ponse, 1976; Warren and Ponse, 1975; Warren, 1973).

Lesbian Initiation of Sexual Activity

Table 13.5

Response	Number	%
Respondent initiated sex equally as often as her partner	208	73
Respondent initiated sex more often than her partner	36	13
Respondent's partner initiated sex more often than respondent	27	9
No data	15	5
Total	286	100

Source: Pat Califia, "Lesbian Sexuality," *Journal of Homosexuality,* 4 (1979), p. 260. Copyright © 1979 by the Haworth Press, Inc. All rights reserved. Used by permission.

Roles and Activities   According to available data, there are several dimensions to role playing among lesbians, both sexual and social. Most lesbians play mutual lovemaking roles in their sexual activity. A large majority report they initiate sex·as often as their partner does (Califia, 1979). (See Table 13.5.) More rarely they may assume passive-active roles based on their own male-female or "butch-femme" stereotype of lovemaking. A *butch* is a masculine female; a *femme* plays the wife role. A *one-way butch* is a butch who makes love to her female partner but does not allow or encourage reciprocal lovemaking.

Some of the data on one-way butch and femme encounters comes from Ward and Kassebaum's study of imprisoned women (1965). Some prisoners take the masculine or active role in lovemaking either always or generally, which may or may not be symbolized by their social role. In a similar vein, outside of prison some lesbian sexual relationships may be almost entirely one-way. One "active" lesbian put it this way:

Joan: I prefer to make love to Kristin rather than the other way around. I get so much more pleasure out of making love to her, and she gets so much more out of being made love to. And I take so long.

From the authors' files

In other instances sexual practices may be spelled out in masculine-feminine terms:

Viva: Little boys (referring to her female sexual partners) should be tanned and little girls (referring to herself) should be white and soft.

From the authors' files

In lesbian relationships several kinds of mutual and masculine-feminine role combinations may occur: neither partner appears more masculine in dress or demeanor, and sexual activity is generally mutual; one partner appears more masculine socially but is sexually more passive; one

403

partner appears more masculine and takes the more aggressive role sexually; both partners appear fairly masculine and either both or one is sexually active. Occasionally both women desire to be sexually passive.

Dallas and Simone have lived together for seven years. Dallas takes the more dominant social role, with short cropped hair and tailored shirts; she makes the drinks at parties and lights Simone's cigarettes. Simone is long-haired and wears dramatic makeup and floating-chiffon type clothes; she does the cooking and defers demurely to Dallas. However, she complains: "We have had sex only once for the past six months. Both of us want to be seduced and be made love to."

From the authors' files

Sometimes an individual's sexual and social roles are fairly fixed, no matter what the situation, but often they vary according to the particular sexual or emotional partnership in which the individual is currently involved. Most lesbians are not involved in sexual and social role playing and are indistinguishable from the general population of women (Ponse, 1976a; Tuller, 1978).

Most lesbians are not distinguishable from the general population of women in mannerisms or appearance.
Joel Gordon

Social Roles   Social role, as opposed to sexual role, is a complex of appearance and style, demeanor, and occupation, which may vary together or independently. In the following cases the social roles and the sexual roles vary much as do those of a traditonal marriage — in the eyes of the participants as well as the observer.

Joan and Kristin: Joan and Kristin are both attractive brunettes, tall and slim, but Joan is decidedly more masculine in appearance, if only by contrast to Kristin. Joan's hair is very short, while Kristin's is long and full. Joan wears tailored shirts and levis while Kristin wears bare-midriff pants outfits; Joan wears little make-up while Kristin wears a considerable amount. Joan works as a hospital technician, and prefers that Kristin stay at home and look after the house, which she does reluctantly. Joan lights Kristin's cigarettes and buys her flowers, and expects Kristin to do the cooking, housekeeping, sewing, and marketing. Many of their friends have the same type of social-role arrangement to a greater or lesser degree, and collectively refer to the role incumbents as "the girls" and "the boys."   *From the authors' files*

Lauren and Kim: Lauren and Kim are both very feminine-appearing women, with soft hair, make-up, and high-style clothes. Both work as secondary-school teachers, and both contribute to the housework and cooking. Kim tends to do more housework and cooking, while Lauren does more of the handywork and gardening, but they both try very consciously to arrange this work rather exactly between them so they both develop skills in everything. Their sexual exchange is always mutual.   *From the authors' files*

As indicated, the type of sexual and social roles can vary with the type of lesbian setting. Although many — perhaps most — lesbians are not part of any lesbian community or group, there appear to be several types of lesbian communities: the lesbian-bar community, the overt-lesbian feminist activist community (political and/or religious), a lesbian affiliation with the gay male community, and lesbian and "familial" organization in women's prisons (which will not be discussed here).

Lesbian Organizations and Communities   Overt-lesbian feminist groups may differ from all-lesbian organizations in various ways: they may be affiliated with the male gay rights or gay church movement, feminist gay-straight alliances, or bisexual organizations. All these activist movements, however, are feminist and are on the overt end of the overt-secret gay continuum.

In addition, all these groups are committed to sexual and social feminism, which denigrates both the playing of traditional male-female social roles (by members of either sex) and one-way butch arrangements. Sexually, lesbian feminists are encouraged to explore every aspect of their

Some lesbians are active in organizations seeking legal and social acceptance of their life style.
Ellen Shumsky/Jeroboam

own female sexuality and to satisfy their partner's sexual needs freely and frankly — even if this includes a movement away from exclusive lesbianism into bisexuality (Warren and Ponse, forthcoming). Socially, lesbian feminists are encouraged to forsake both traditionally masculine and traditionally feminine types of appearance and demeanor: the butch-masculine and the traditional-feminine. The typical lesbian feminist tends to scorn traditional feminine, seductive dress, make-up, and body language, but is also likely to scorn the uniform of the butch lesbian-bar community: cropped hair, men's pants or even ties, and the aping of male body language and chivalrous, chauvinist behavior. Some members of the feminist movement assert the advantage of sexual independence from men that can come from celibacy, masturbation, or homosexual activities. Those who choose homosexual activities rather than relating sexually to men, whom they consider their oppressors, are referred to as "politica-lesbians" (Lessard, 1970).

The Lesbian Bar The lesbian-bar community is quite different from the lesbian feminist community; although the clientele of a given lesbian bar

406

may include everyone from lesbian feminists to straight males to married women, the core group of any bar has the characteristics of a community or a series of interlocking cliques. Members of this bar community may be lower- or lower-middle class, somewhat hostile to gay and feminist activism, and "masculine-masculine" or "masculine-feminine" in appearance and demeanor.

Many of the core members of the bar clique spend a considerable amount of their leisure time in bar and bar-related activities, just as do the male "career" gays. Bar-related activities may include beach picnics and softball matches with other bar clientele. Heavy drinking is the norm, much as in the male homosexual community that is its counterpart.

Among some of the cliques and membership groups of the upper-class male gay community are a few women, a small percentage of the clique membership of such communities. Generally the women in the male gay community, who consist of both heterosexuals and lesbians, are quite different in social role from either the feminist activists or the lesbian-bar groups. In general, the females in the male gay community are not feminist, but rather adopt a fairly traditional female social role in all areas but their sexual preference (Warren, 1976).

Bertha and Pauline: Bertha and Pauline have one lesbian couple as friends, but all the rest of their many friends and acquaintances are gay males, many of long standing. They go out to the theater, dinner parties, and restaurants with these men — but rarely gay-male bars and never lesbian bars. They are both in their early forties, dressed in extremely conservative fashion with hair done in the beauty parlor, nylons and high heels, and knit suits with very expensive gold jewelry. Pauline in particular detests what she calls "dykes" — butch or masculine lesbians.

From the authors' files

The Lesbian Life Style   In one study of young, well-educated lesbians, 85 percent of respondents reported committed relationship with a female lover at the time of the study; slightly more than half lived with their lover. The typical lesbian in this study reported involvement with an average of one to four lovers in her lifetime; almost none engaged in one-night stands. Their current relationship was reported by an overwhelming majority as stable, happy, and satisfying, and 93 percent characterized their relationship as a permanent commitment (Albro and Tully, 1979).

Although many of these women occasionally went to gay bars or belonged to gay organizations, their social activities most frequently consisted of dining with friends or entertaining at home. Most of them reported they met other lesbians through mutual friends or through women's-group meetings (Albro and Tully, 1979).

Most of these women consider society's acceptance of them as lesbians as important to them, but they feel isolated from straight society as a result of their sexual orientation. Slightly over half reported they usually attempt to present themselves as heterosexual at work and in public.

Most have not told their parents of their gayness because they were afraid of rejection or other negative repercussions, and they very rarely tell employers, work acquaintances, teachers, or neighbors (Albro and Tully, 1979).

Gay Males and Lesbians

By itself, the common fact of their gayness does not lead to close relationships and a community of interests between lesbians and gay males. It is surprising to many straight persons that relationships between many lesbians and gay males are marked by antagonism.

Some women, however, are a part of the same social world as gay men, and maintain close relationships with them. Gay males enjoy having females as part of their social circle because they feel the women add a touch of glamour and variety to an otherwise all-male party. Female friends sometimes accompany the men to family or business functions where the male needs to appear to be straight by taking along a female date. Also some men feel the presence of women at their parties helps make wild behavior more unlikely (Warren, 1976).

The gay women who prefer to socialize mostly with gay men do so because they find the men more accomplished at sociability and less inclined toward bitchiness than lesbian groups. These lesbians found other compatible women at mixed male-female gay parties more than they did at social gatherings consisting only of lesbians. Like the men, the women also used males as straight fronts in straight settings (Warren, 1976).

Some of the women who socialize regularly with gay men are heterosexual. Gay men often refer to these women as "fag hags," feeling they are too undesirable to get attention from straight men and therefore seek it from gay ones (Warren, 1976).

Gay Parents and Role Models

At least one-fifth of all lesbians and one-tenth of all gay men have children (Bell and Weinberg, 1978). In most cases the homosexual parent takes an active role in raising his or her children, and the vast majority of gays perform quite adequately as parents. Problems with child rearing occur for gay parents, but no more often than for heterosexual parents (Riddle, 1978; Miller, 1979). The sexual preference of parents appears to have no negative effect on children. The children of gays are no more   408 likely than other children to have emotional problems, adopt opposite-sex-typed behaviors, or become gay themselves (Riddle, 1978). A gay man reports on his influence on his daughter:

The school board was debating whether homosexuality should be discussed in family-life classes. My sixteen-year-old daughter, who is on the Student Council, asked me my position. Then she went before the board and told them, "Why not teach about homosexuals? For ten years I've known my dad is one, and it hasn't hurt me or our relationship." I think she blew their minds.

Miller, 1979, p. 250

Not only do gay parents provide role models for their children, but many children experience meaningful relationships with gay adults. By the time they reach adulthood most persons have encountered at least one gay teacher, doctor, or religious leader. Rather than posing a menace to young persons, gays may facilitate important developmental learning. One study found that college students who were exposed to openly self-identified gays as class lecturers showed increases in self-esteem. Gay role models demonstrate a variety of alternative adaptations to traditional sex-role behavior. Children exposed to gays become exposed to the concept of cultural and individual diversity as positive rather than threatening. Presumably an increased comfort with diversity results in a greater freedom from social pressures to conform to rigid sex-role expectations (Riddle, 1978).

Bisexuality

Like homosexuality or lesbianism, bisexuality can refer to behavior or to identity. Like gayness, too, bisexuality may evolve into a life style or a personal style. Researchers such as Humphreys (1970) prefer the term *ambisexual* to describe persons who have sex with both males and females, because *bisexual* has connotations of anatomical hermaphroditism (see Chapter 3). However, *bisexual* remains the more widely used term.

Bisexual Behavior and Identity

Bisexuality is the experiencing of sexual interaction with both males and females during a particular period. Like homosexuality or heterosexuality, bisexuality can occur at any point in the life cycle. To refer to an individual who has had experiences with both males and females over the entire life span as bisexual may be misleading. This same category can encompass those who have had such contacts continuously over the life span and those who have alternated between homosexual and heterosexual

409

activities for long periods of time, as well as those who have had simultaneous or group sex with both males and females.

In contrast to a straight or gay identity, a bisexual identity is a relatively new phenomenon. Interestingly, both scientific observers and participants in the gay world often deny credence to the viability of a truly bisexual identity (Warren, 1974; Tripp, 1975). Blumstein and Schwartz point out

the distinction between *behavior* which scientists label as bisexual and respondents who label themselves as *bisexual persons.* This distinction highlights a very difficult definitional problem: we have encountered many women whose behavior immediately invokes in us the label bisexual, but who adamantly claim to be either homosexual or heterosexual; also women who claim to be bisexual, but whose behavior seems not to support such a self-definition.

Blumstein and Schwartz, 1974

For example:

I am bisexual. I have never actually had sex with a man, only with another woman, but I believe that all creatures are basically bisexual, including myself.

From the authors' files

Stylistic Bisexuality

Today, people claiming a bisexual identity are becoming increasingly common. Some are former heterosexuals and some, former homosexuals. It is possible that some of them are influenced by the role models of stylistic bisexuality prevalent in today's mass media.

A phenomenon of the 1970s, *stylistic bisexuality* is distinguished by its public aspect: the identification of themselves as bisexual by media figures. Stylistic bisexuality may involve the same type of sexual interaction as any other bisexual orientation. The difference is that it has become a part of public consciousness through the television, film, and printed media, and thus can become a force for social change. Publicly declared bisexuals include folk singer Joan Baez, comedienne Lily Tomlin, actress Maria Schneider, feminist writer Kate Millett (who later redefined herself as lesbian) and author Dorothy Thompson. A subcategory of media bisexuality is rock music bisexuality, which introduces a further distinction between stylistic and life-style bisexuality.

Several rock stars, such as David Bowie, have declared their bisexuality in song lyrics and public statements. According to Kopkind (1973) David Bowie (a married man with a young child) and Lou Reed "came out in word and deed, in lyric and performance. . . . Many of [Bowie's] songs express gay love and its special pain. . . . He and his lead guitarist exchange erotic glances, gestures and grasps." Others, such as Alice Cooper,   410

Joan Baez is one of a number of media figures who publicly proclaim their bisexuality.
Bob Fitch/Black Star

insist that their flamboyant make-up and sequined costumes are simply a stylistic device and do not denote bisexual behavior.

From Heterosexual to Bisexual

Whether it be stylistic or behavioral, young people interested in the rock scene are imitating bisexuality, from male groupies who engage in sex with male rock stars, to Hollywood discotheques where fourteen-year-old boys wear drag and dance with both girls and other boys. As *Newsweek* points out: "Not surprisingly, students who passed through puberty watching rock star Mick Jagger sing love songs to his drummer are pushing hardest at the perimeters of sexuality" (May 27, 1974, p. 90).

The open bisexuality of many media idols prompts the pursuit of bisexual activities by persons who are eager to appear sophisticated and cosmopolitan. Previously predominantly heterosexual, these people increasingly made acceptable the appearance of bisexuality in some of the most chic nightclubs and restaurants in Europe and the United States (Carroll, 1974; Humphreys, 1974).

411

Men and women differ in the ease with which they incorporate bisexual behavior into a previously strictly heterosexual life style. Women tend to find initial experiences much less traumatic than men, and are less likely to allow a single experience or a few experiences to lead them to an exclusively homosexual identification. Women often feel that such activities are a natural extension of affectionate behavior. Men, on the other hand, may fear that any same-sex experiences have serious implications for their masculinity. It is much more comfortable for most women to integrate bisexual activities and a bisexual identity with their self-concept (Blumstein and Schwartz, 1977).

From Homosexual to Bisexual

In addition to people moving away from exclusive heterosexuality, the new bisexuality attracts people moving away from exclusive homosexuality. Some bars and clubs that were once exclusively gay have become more bisexually oriented (*Newsweek,* May 27, 1974). Many gay males linked to both the gay liberation movement and the youth counterculture are turning toward bisexuality, while their older counterparts remain exclusively homosexual (Humphreys, 1971). Similarly, some women in gay activist organizations are shifting from exclusive lesbianism to bisexuality. These women believe that bisexuality is more liberated than exclusive heterosexuality or homosexuality, because human beings are naturally bisexual (Ponse, 1976a, 1976b).

However, many gay groups are not very receptive to the heterosexual activities of a gay person. Sometimes gays who engage in bisexual behavior are told that their heterosexual attractions are only an affectation or a cop-out as a denial of their true sexuality, and result from their inability to accept their homosexuality (Blumstein and Schwartz, 1977).

Feminism and Bisexuality

The feminist movement has contributed to the growth and acceptance of bisexuality. Common concerns of the women in the gay liberation movement and in the women's liberation movement were recognized early. To some degree, both are rebelling against roles predetermined by sex, and both feel oppressed by the chauvinistic heterosexual male. Both are working to develop a sense of self-worth and to escape the condition of second-class citizenship. The relationship between the two groups, however, is not always positive. Some women become involved in bisexual activities, not as a movement away from men, but as a movement toward women. As consciousness of sisterhood is raised to a love of all women who have endured the same problems in life, love may sometimes be given physical expression (Harrison, 1975).

412

The women's movement was critical in that it allowed me to express my feelings for women. I knew other women were trying things, so it didn't seem weird and far out. . . . I wish I could say the movement has helped me to be less silly and less needy with men. It hasn't — but it's released my feelings for women. . . . in bed with women, I have warm loving feelings. . . . I have lust for men and love for women. I made random love to men who don't care, who don't matter. I couldn't pick up a woman for sex. All my strong loyalties are with women. When I need comfort and understanding, I go to a woman; there isn't a single man I can call in the middle of the night.

Harrison, 1975, pp. 55–56

The Counterculture and Bisexuality

The so-called counterculture is not specifically a bisexual life style movement, but it does involve an institutionalized sexual permissiveness that facilitates the development of bisexuality. Those who are most committed to a counterculture way of life are the commune dwellers. Most communes are predominantly heterosexual, although a few are truly bisexual in lifestyle. Even in the predominantly heterosexual communes, if nonmonogamous relationships are permitted or expected, there is usually the freedom to develop sexual relationships with persons of either sex.

Swinging and Bisexual Behavior

At the opposite end of the cultural continuum from the counterculture, bisexuality is practiced by many swinging couples, although this is not generally institutionalized in the life styles or identities of the participants. Swinging couples rarely permit male-male sexual interaction, but they usually condone and often promote female-female sexual interaction. Like the activity of swinging itself, the swingers' bisexuality is engaged in secretly and furtively. Although a woman may experience sex with another woman in a mate-swapping situation, both women usually continue to see themselves as heterosexual rather than as bisexual. (See Chapter 12.)

The most important aspect of bisexuality today, however, is its increasing institutionalization as an alternative life style and identity. As a life style it is becoming increasingly visible, and its participants increasingly vocal and ideological. Bisexuals can be almost religious in their ideology, stressing the universality of human love and the naturalness of the sexual expression of love for everyone (Carroll, 1974; *Newsweek*, May 27, 1974). In the phenomenon of media bisexuality, this ideology is imprinted on the public consciousness. At this level, publicists of bisexuality are sometimes bitterly opposed by both the advocates of traditional morality and the older members of the gay subculture (Humphreys, 1971; Warren, 1974; Carroll, 1974; Blumstein and Schwartz, 1976).

413

Transsexualism

Transsexuals consider themselves to be of the sex opposite to their biological sex. A biological male who is a transsexual feels that he is really a woman who happens to be trapped in a man's body. Similarly, a female transsexual feels she is really a man encased in the body of a woman. Transsexuals are relatively rare in this society and the causes of transsexualism are not known. Many researchers feel that gender identity is the result of the way a person is raised. Others have found some evidence that transsexualism is associated with abnormal hypothalamic or pituitary function (Seyler et al., 1978). Researchers in West Germany found that an H-Y antigen, which is normally found in male tissues and sperm was absent in a group of male-to-female transsexuals. This H-Y antigen was found to be present in a group of female-to-male transsexuals (*Sexuality Today*, March 24, 1980).

Even though transsexualism is not a common phenomenon in any known culture, records of it can be found in the distant past and in widely separated cultures. Greek mythology designated the goddess Venus Castina as the one who responded with sympathy and understanding to the yearnings of feminine souls locked in male bodies. Among the Mohave Indians, boys who were destined to become shamans (priest-doctors) would pull their penises back between their legs and assume the name and mannerisms of a woman. They would marry a man, act as his wife, and imitate menstruation, pregnancy, and childbirth. In paleo-Asiatic, ancient Mediterranean, Indian, Oceanic, and African tribes, men who assumed the ways and dress of women enjoyed high esteem as shamans, priests, or sorcerers. All were revered and considered to have supernatural powers.

Although the sexual preferences of the transsexual are oriented to his or her biological sex, most transsexuals do not identify with the homosexual community and may even be hostile to it. Whereas a homosexual is attracted to people of the same sex, transsexuals consider themselves heterosexual because they feel they do not belong to their biologically assigned sex and are therefore actually attracted to people of the opposite sex. In addition, most transsexuals fervently desire to change the physical evidence of their sex, whereas homosexuals are quite content to keep the sex to which they were born. Transsexuals also resent being labeled transvestites (see Chapter 14) because transsexual cross-dressing is not fetishist; the transsexual feels she or he is dressing in a manner appropriate to his or her true sex.

Transsexualism and Childhood

Most transsexuals report that their gender identity has been opposite to their biological identity or confused since early childhood. Male-to- 414 female transsexuals report more early certainty about opposite gender identity, and female-to-male transsexuals report more confusion:

A biological female reports: I'm in limbo. I've always felt like I was asexual, very much a loner. I didn't play with the girls, I always had cowboy hats and guns, I never played with dolls.

From the authors' files

A second female says: I was brought up as a feminine female; I was not a tomboy but I tried to be.

From the authors' files

It is difficult to know whether or not transsexuals actually experienced gender confusion, for several reasons. First, people often strive for consistency in their biographies and like to see their past as leading inevitably to their present desires and identities. Second, psychiatrists and surgeons make it a prerequisite for the transsexual operation that the motivation for gender change originated in early childhood. The payoff for a consistent biography is the desired operation.

There is some evidence from young children, especially males, that sometimes youngsters do grow up identifying with and behaving like members of the opposite gender — from as young as one year old. There are documented cases in which young boys imitate girls by wearing female clothing, playing with dolls, and learning to cook and sew (Block and Tessler, 1973). Similar cases among young girls have rarely been documented, since masculine behavior in females can be dismissed as "tomboyish."

In many documented cases of both male and female transsexualism, the individual has fought his or her tendencies toward cross-gender identification to the extent of getting married and having children according to her or his biological gender role. In her book *Conundrum,* Jan Morris (once the travel writer James Morris) tells of her marriage to an understanding woman, her own surgical conversion to female in early middle age, and the development of a new relationship with her children as a "female" father. In a similar vein, a pseudonymous "Jane Fry" (see the appendix) described how, as a man, she had watched her wife's pregnancy and developed all the symptoms herself:

The more pregnant my wife got, the more sick I got. Morning sickness and the whole bit. I knew what was happening to me psychologically — I was starting to relate to myself like I was having the baby. . . .

Bogdan, 1974, p. 100

I thought that I should be having the baby. I looked on Joan as the masculine part of the twosome. She had a better job than I had; she made more money; she was more domineering. . . . You might think that having a child would make me feel more like a man and make me feel good, but it actually built up self-loathing in me. Looking back on it now, I see that over the years of my childhood [and]

415

adolescence — that whole bit — I built up kind of a mask around myself, a mask of masculinity.

From Male to Female

Male-to-female transsexuals may or may not have undergone a sex-change operation. "Pre-op" transsexuals are those who have not been able to raise the money, the motivation, or psychiatric and medical support for the costly and complex sex-change operation. Pre-op male-to-female transsexuals sometimes form small communities in major cities and compete with one another in such matters as breast size, lack of hair on body and face, attractiveness to heterosexual males, and limpness of penis. In fact, a term of insult from one pre-op male-to-female transsexual to another is to say that "she is soft as a chair" meaning the penis still attains erections and serves as a source of sexual gratification. To the true transsexual, the penis is a source of shame and anxiety to be eliminated, not a source of pleasure.

Dr. Richard Raskind before hormone treatment and sex-change surgery.
Wide World Photos

416

Most pre-op male-to-female transsexuals use female hormones to suppress their penile sexual urges and to promote female skin tone and secondary sexual characteristics. They may also have silicone implants in their breasts. On the other hand, the biological females who wish to become males generally have their breasts surgically removed.

Some pre-op male-to-female transsexuals lead relatively conventional female lives with understanding boy friends; others act as "female" prostitutes, performing oral acts with their male customers; they may also sometimes appear before the men nude, with their genitals strapped backward between their legs. However, many seek to avoid the gender

Dr. Renee Richards, who was formerly Dr. Richard Raskind, now shown after a sex-change operation.
United Press International

417

revelation that would come about with genital or anal intercourse, and transsexual prostitutes sometimes get into fights with customers who find out that they are biological males.

A "post-op" transsexual (one who has had the sex-change operation) has undergone the surgical removal of testicles and penis and the construction of a vagina. The genitals of a male who becomes a female are said to be indistinguishable from those of a biological female, except by a gynecologist. The surgeon constructs labia, clitoris, and vaginal walls from the tissues and skin of the penis. The nerve endings of the penis are retained and laid in the vagina, so that the new "woman" can experience orgasm.

The transsexual male-to-female can experience intercourse with a man, but to do so she must constantly stretch the vagina after the operation to prevent its closing up, and because she usually has no natural vaginal lubrication she must use a lubricant during intercourse. She must also continue to take regular doses of female hormones to ensure continued breast development and impede the growth of hair on face and chest.

The post-op transsexual may, like Jan Morris, be open about her condition but have a fairly conventional life style. Others may continue to seek constant male attention as a prostitute, showgirl, or stripper. Still others (far from the eye of the prying researcher, so less known about) vanish completely into the mainstream of women and are known to nobody as a transsexual. Although a proportion of transsexuals settle down into stable relationships with a man, including marriage, many go through a honeymoon period of promiscuity right after the operation, and still others remain promiscuous for a much longer time.

From Female to Male

The female transsexual has many of the same problems and goals as the male transsexual. She feels trapped in the wrong body and describes herself as unable to adjust to the expected female behavior pattern. Although tomboyism in girls is more tolerated than effeminacy in boys, in this society a female transsexual suffers a dilemma in adolescence as frustrating as that for a male transsexual. Typically she is disgusted by the obvious manifestations of her body — breasts and menstruation — and is unable to relate romantically to males. If she seeks the company of lesbians, she still feels isolated because they do not share her goal of transforming her body into that of a man (Ehrhardt, 1973).

My previous contacts were primarily gay. I developed a tremendous hostility to gays — I lived with a butch woman and we clashed, because I'm male and she's butch.

From the authors' files

418

When the female transsexual seeks medical treatment her goal is androgen therapy to obtain some male characteristics, such as beard growth and a lower voice. She may also want to have her breasts, ovaries, and uterus removed to eliminate estrogen hormone production, menstruation, and the typical female breasts.

I wanted to have the sex change that I'd read about, so I went up to Stanford. I knew there was something inside of me saying I want to be a man — I've had a hysterectomy. I'm going to be starting on hormone therapy. By July I'm going to completely take on a new identity. From the authors' files

Most female transsexuals do not now seek surgical construction of a penis. Such an operation is very lengthy and complex, and it does not produce a penis capable of erection. When a surgeon does construct a penis he usually uses skin from the abdomen. The procedure requires several operations before the tube of skin hangs down in the position of a penis. The urinary tube inside the penis may be made from a segment of the small intestine so that the urinary opening is at the tip of the penis; in other cases it may be at the base of the penis. The clitoris is preserved and embedded in the base of the artificial penis so it can continue to serve as a source of sexual stimulation and orgasm in intercourse. The new penis cannot become erect and needs to rest in some form of support to insure penetration of the partner's vagina (Money, 1968, pp. 85–88).

Sex-Change Operations: The Contemporary Situation

With the increasing publicity given to transsexualism, there is likelihood of an increase in those seeking the transsexual operation who previously would have let the desire to change gender remain a secret, unarticulated wish. The present increase in the rates of those undergoing the operation, however, should not be read as an increase in the number of people who feel that they are trapped in the body of the wrong gender (we cannot know historically how many have felt this way), but rather as an increase in the number of people willing, able, and motivated enough to translate that desire into reality. As in any other area of life, role models, transsexual or otherwise, are useful devices to enable wishes to become fulfillment.

At the beginning of 1979 it was estimated that between 3,000 and 6,000 adult Americans have been hormonally and surgically sex-reassigned. Until fairly recently most transsexuals had to go to Europe for this type of surgery. Now there are approximately forty centers in the Western Hemisphere offering sex-reassignment surgery (Berger et al., 1979).

Several hospitals in the United States are equipped and willing to do transsexual surgery, but only after careful study of each case. Most re- 419 quire that an applicant first undergo hormone therapy and live as a member of the opposite sex for periods ranging from several months to several years to assess whether the desire for the more permanent changes brought about by surgery is sufficient to warrant it. Even with these precautions, not all transsexuals are able to make a satisfactory postsurgical adjustment (Stoller, 1968, pp. 246–251; Restak, 1979).

The concept of sex-change operations raises some interesting legal problems. For instance, the surgeon may be prosecuted under "bodily mayhem" laws that prohibit deliberate mutilation of the body to avoid the armed services. Also some physically changed people may find it impossible to get their legal sexual status changed on their birth certificates, although others are able to accomplish this. In spite of the medical, legal, and personal problems involved, the more humane professionals agree that sex change is the only course of treatment for many transsexuals. Conventional psychotherapy has not been successful in changing their sexual identity to fit their body (Block and Tessler, 1973).

Conclusion

Transsexualism, like homosexuality and bisexuality, may best be understood as a complex matter involving the identity, behavior, and life style of individuals who are stigmatized by the larger society. On the behavioral level, homosexuality relates to sexual acts with members of one's own sex, and bisexuality to sexual acts with members of both sexes. In this context a transsexual is equivalent to a homosexual.

In terms of self-identification, a transsexual is someone who believes she or he is of the opposite gender to his or her biological gender. In the same terms, a gay person is someone who identifies herself or himself with both homosexual behavior and a gay identity, and a bisexual is sexually responsive to both sexes.

Bisexuals, transsexuals, and gays in our society are stigmatized by those who identify themselves as heterosexual. Like any other stigmatized or minority group, these groups have developed their own ways of adapting to their stigma, ranging from secrecy to activism. This choice of adaptation in turn profoundly influences the life style of all who are involved in transsexualism, bisexuality, or the gay world.

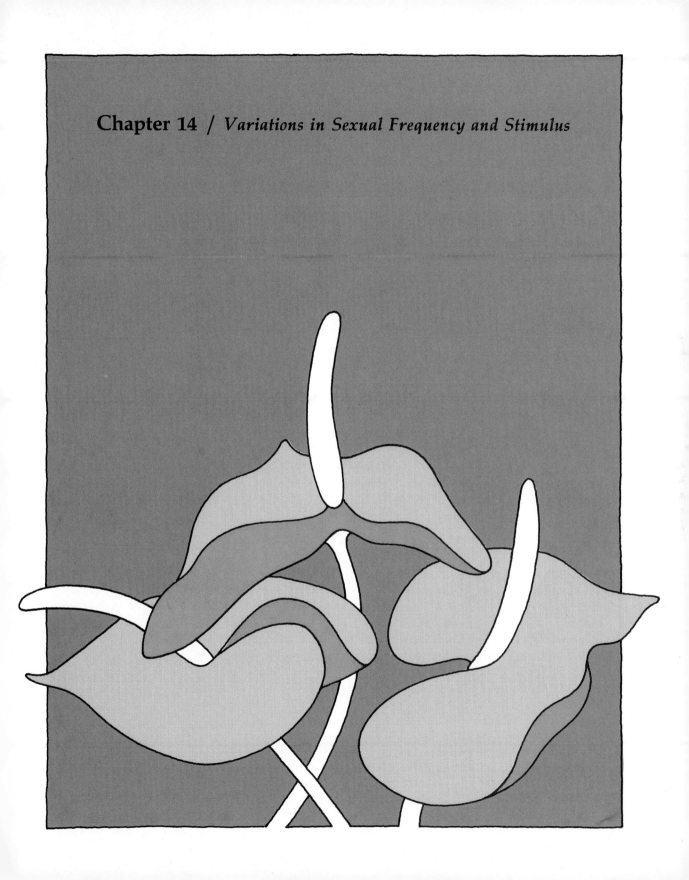

In the United States the ideal norms of sexual behavior prescribe that the sexual stimulus should be a sexual partner to whom one has an emotional commitment, and that people should engage in sexual relations with moderate frequency — not too often and not too seldom. Many deviations from these norms may go unnoticed, since they are practiced in private by consenting adult couples or by a single individual. Deviations from the norm prescribing moderate frequency include celibacy and promiscuity; deviations from the norms prescribing the correct stimulus include fetishism and the use of objects for sexual stimulation. When such deviations from the norms are noticed by others, they are likely to result in criticism or ostracism rather than legal sanctions. Also, because the proscription against immoderate sexual release is vague in its definition of "too often"or "too seldom," only the more extreme deviations from the prescribed norm become apparent.

Celibacy

Because human beings have a physiological capacity for sexual behavior, they are sexual beings. As such, *celibacy*, a decision to refrain from sexual activity, is a sexual option that is available only in societies that provide one or more ways of being celibate. Those eligible for the social label "celibate" include only adults capable of choosing celibacy as a sexual option.

Degrees and Styles of Celibacy

In our society there are many degrees of celibacy, and several institutionalized social forms. *Complete celibacy* means refraining from any volitional sexual release, including masturbation, although it cannot by definition include involuntary sexual responses, such as orgasm during erotic dreams.

Interpersonal or *partial celibacy* allows masturbation as a sexual activity, but not any form of sexual activity that involves other people. Those who engage in sexual interaction with others short of intercourse, including oral, anal, and manual stimulation, are not considered celibate. The social styles of celibacy in our society are experiential, religious, feminist, and health-related.

Experiential Celibacy   *Experiential celibacy* is practicing celibacy simply as another sexual option, before or after experiencing other varieties of sexuality. Put another way, people can try celibacy much as they experiment with group sex, homosexual behavior, or premarital intercourse.

422

A middle-aged man says: My sex life could be described as a shifting sea of   From the authors' files
desires and fantasies of varying turbulence and power. They have pressed
towards either heterosexual, autoerotic, homosexual, or even on rare occasions
towards sadomasochistic expression, though in the latter case an unconscious
alert has never allowed the possibility to become action. I explored these ways
and means to pleasure as far as I cared to and needed to discover their limitations. But gradually my concerns with potency and pleasure became a quest for
an ever deeper experience, in fact, for some Ultimate Experience of power,
pleasure, and union in love from which I would never again retire back into my
shell of separateness. It was as I came to see that this was the goal of my drive to
pleasure that I came into contact with the notion of celibacy as a value.

Experiential celibacy of this type does not involve a community of the
celibate or a special ideology of celibacy as do many of the other types.

Religious Celibacy   Religious celibacy, like some other types of celibacy,
is related to an ideology, or belief system. Celibacy is enjoined upon those
who choose the Roman Catholic priesthood or the Roman Catholic, and
some Protestant, orders of nuns and monks. In the Christian tradition
celibacy is required of religious functionaries because they are supposed
to love all humanity rather than particular individuals, and because their
attention and time must be spent in religious duties that embrace all
people (or at least their parish) rather than just spouse and children.

*Celibacy is expected in
some religious orders.*
*René Burri/Magnum Photos,
Inc.*

423

A nun says: As a member of a religious order, I find that celibacy or virginity is   From the authors' files
a positive quality indicative of a consecrated way of life. It is a grace enabling
me more easily to devote my entire being to God with an undivided heart,
viewing life from a sacred perspective, as a means of growing in love and
perceiving truth. What might seem to some an unnatural way of life has
become second nature to me over the years, a life that spiritualizes the natural
by means of intention. The rationale for my being celibate is to be like Jesus
Christ, who was not tied to the cares of this world by marriage, so that he could
be free to follow the will of his Father.

There is some debate in Roman Catholic circles as to whether celibacy
should be complete or partial, at least for men. Nuns are expected to be
completely celibate and to refrain from masturbation as well as sexual
interaction with others. Monks and priests, on the other hand, may be
partially or completely celibate. Although most Roman Catholic priests
interpret the law of celibacy as prohibiting masturbation, some believe
that the male sexual urge can become so pressing that it may be legitimately relieved by masturbation, though not by sexual interaction with
another person. If the extension of love to the whole world were the only
reason that the clergy were enjoined to be celibate, it would be logical to
allow them to masturbate, since masturbation is not part of an interpersonal relationship. But the expansion of love is not the only reason.

Unlike the Jewish heritage, the Christian heritage has until recently
glorified celibacy above the marital state. Both Judaism and Christianity
encouraged marital sexuality directed toward reproduction, since they
were both agrarian religions. But the early Christians, led by Saint Paul,
glorified chastity above the married state, something the early Jews had
never done (Tripp, 1975). Today Roman Catholic priests are still expected
to be celibate, although they may become priests after they are widowed.
This is not true in Protestant denominations, and it was not true of the
Roman Catholic priesthood until about the sixth century. The enjoining
of celibacy on the priesthood is based on a negative evaluation of sexuality as well as a duty to love all equally.

Feminist Celibacy   Feminist chastity is also ideological, but is based on
social or political rather than religious factors. Most feminists do not
practice celibacy as a conscious ideological choice; a few, however, deliberately refrain from sexual interaction with any other person. The logic
behind complete feminist celibacy is that sexual interaction with another,
in a sexist society, drains energies that would otherwise be channeled into
the struggle for female equality. The logic behind partial celibacy (refraining from sexual interaction with men, but engaging in masturbation)   424

is that men are not able to engage in egalitarian sexual and love relationships with women in a sexist society, and that therefore heterosexual sexual relationships should not be attempted by feminist women.

Some feminists extend the ban on sexual interaction with men to a further ban on love relationships. These very militant feminists believe that the romantic mystique of love, perhaps even more than sexual domination, is at the root of male oppression of women. Therefore, women should not form love relationships with men (Firestone, 1971) or women (Ponse, 1976a).

Celibacy for Health   Complete, partial, or limited celibacy can be practiced for medical reasons. Some heart attack victims, for example, are cautioned against becoming sexually excited in order not to overstrain their hearts.

Intermediate between medical celibacy and religious celibacy is the celibacy of health-medicine belief systems, such as yoga. Among many varieties of yoga are some that stress celibacy as a means to maximize the energy levels in the body and achieve a higher level of consciousness.

A young man asks: Why celibacy? I can only speak to you out of the body of information which has moved me to find out for myself. It falls squarely into the category of what is usually labeled the mystical and occult, or metaphysical sciences. The schools of thought I am most familiar with are the assorted schools of yoga coming out of India. . . . Self-realization or the manifestation of all one's human potential is the principal goal of celibacy. In more down-to-earth terms, that human potential can be mined. The practical application of different practices can purify, strengthen, and prepare the body, the emotions, and the mind — most especially the nervous system and the brain — to accommodate an increasingly subtler, simpler, greater degree of energetic order, and a vaster awareness, a keener intelligence.

From the authors' files

Celibacy as Choice

The distinction between celibacy and other forms of sexual abstinence is a fine one. What of a married couple who do not have sex? A man who has difficulties maintaining an erection and therefore does not attempt intercourse with anyone? A woman who is never asked to go to bed with anyone and does not herself ask? None of these would be considered celibates by our definition of conscious choice; a celibate is one who makes an ideological choice, not one who simply refrains from sexual interaction.

425

Promiscuity, Nymphomania, and Satyriasis

Dictionaries define *sexual promiscuity* as engaging in sexual intercourse indiscriminately. By this definition there are very few promiscuous persons; it is quite rare that a person is truly indiscriminate in the choice of sex objects. Most individuals will reject some willing sexual partners, either because they are of the wrong sex, too old, too young, or physically and personally repulsive. The term *promiscuous* today commonly refers to having many sex partners. What constitutes many partners is a highly subjective matter. Some people would label as promiscuous anyone who had more than one sex partner in a lifetime; others feel that promiscuity refers only to having sexual relationships with several partners in a given time period. Regardless of the criteria used for defining promiscuity, all the common-sense definitions carry a value judgment as to what constitutes too many sex partners (Ellis, 1969).

Closely related to our notions of promiscuity are the medical diagnostic categories of *nymphomania* (insatiable sexual appetite in females) and *satyriasis* (insatiable sexual appetite in males). In defining what constitutes too much sex drive or a desire for too frequent sexual intercourse, we again encounter value judgments. There are no objective medical or scientific criteria for determining what constitutes a normal sex drive or a normal frequency of sexual intercourse (Pumpian-Mindlin, 1967).

Sex Drive and Frequency of Intercourse

Sex drive in humans is highly variable and is influenced by physiological, cultural, and psychological factors (Kirkendall, 1973). Physiological factors influencing one's sex drive include the action of androgenic hormones (see Chapter 3) and one's general health. The cultural definition of appropriate sex drive often affects subjective feelings of desire as well as behavior with respect to these desires. In Victorian times, for example, when so-called nice women were not expected to enjoy sex or feel sexual desires, many of them were not only nonorgasmic but were actually repulsed by their sexual relationships.

In the United States today frequency of intercourse is highly variable, influenced by such factors as age, education, personal preference, and availability of an acceptable and willing partner. A study of a probability sample of adults in the United States in early 1970 found that approximately 16 percent reported no sexual intercourse at all in the preceding six months, while approximately 15 percent reported frequencies of more than twice a week (Wilson, 1975). Younger and more educated people reported higher frequencies than older or less-educated ones. (See Chapter 11, Table 11.2.)

American sexual behavior is not typical of all human beings; higher or lower frequencies are common in other societies. The Aranda of Australia have intercourse three to five times each night, and the Chagga of Tanganyika do not consider it unusual to have intercourse ten times a night (Chesser, 1971, p. 184). But in the United States someone who desires intercourse ten times in a typical evening is quite likely to be labeled abnormal — a nymphomaniac or a satyr.

The Psychological Perspective on Promiscuity

Psychological criteria for determining promiscuity focus on the nature of the relationship between the sexual partners rather than on the intensity or insatiability of the sex drive or on the number of sexual partners. Many experts define *sexually promiscuous behavior* as that in which many sexual partners are sought for reasons of power, self-aggrandizement, or escape from self without concern for a personal relationship and sometimes without concern for sexual release (Willis, 1967; Auerbach, 1968; Ellis, 1969). By this definition promiscuous behavior stands in contrast both to the commonly accepted ideal of intimacy and commitment as important components of a sexual relationship and to the less common ideal of sexuality as recreation (Golden, 1968; Ellis, 1969).

Typically in the United States promiscuity for a man is accepted or even exalted. Many of the heroes of fiction enjoy one sexual conquest after another — but not the heroines. For a woman the label of promiscuous or "nympho" usually has definite pejorative connotations, in spite of the fact that men may joke about how they would like to meet one someday.

Not only are women more likely than men to be called promiscuous if they have more than one sex partner (Cloyd, 1976), but their physiological capacity for multiple orgasms in a short time period makes them quite vulnerable to the label of insatiable nympho. Casual use of these labels by people who do not fully understand the nature of human sexuality can be psychologically and socially damaging to those so labeled. Similarly, use of the term *fetishism* to describe another's sexual behavior may be problematical, since fetishism, like promiscuity, is dependent upon interpretation.

Fetishism

Originally the word *fetish* meant an idol or an object with some magical significance. *Sexual fetishism* refers to a kind of erotic idolatry in which a person obtains sexual excitement or satisfaction from the sight of or   427 contact with a particular part of the human body or an inanimate object. When the fetish acts as a stimulus to masturbation or intercourse, it is called a *partial fetish;* when the fetish object brings on orgasm either with or without object contact but without additional stimulation, it is called a *complete fetish* (Chesser, 1971, p. 41).

Fetish Objects

Fetishes are usually articles of female clothing — underwear, gloves, shoes, and handkerchiefs — because fetishism occurs almost exclusively in men (Caprio, 1973, p. 435). But a fetish also may be any part of the body, such as breasts, ankles, or hair, or any kind of object that sexually arouses the individual. The list of possible fetishistic objects is inexhaustible, although some are more common than others. Shoes, gloves, rubber, fur, silk, and breasts are particularly popular in our culture (Thorpe, Katz, and Lewis, 1961, pp. 324–325).

Fetishism may involve active pursuit of the object, such as hair-snipping or stealing women's clothing; some fetishists may even derive erotic satisfaction from the act of stealing the desired object. Sometimes the fetishist becomes so obsessed with his favorite objects that he becomes a

Some commonly used fetish objects may be sold in sex supermarkets.
Jan Lukas/Editorial Photocolor Archives, Inc.

collector, keeping careful books about the date and origin of the acquisitions. Some fetishists may fondle, manipulate, smell, or kiss the objects to produce arousal and orgasm; others may look at the object to stimulate a fantasy sequence while masturbating; still others may use the object as a masturbatory device (Caprio, 1973).

The Fetish Continuum

Most individuals experience fetishism to some extent. One woman may be turned on by the big, blond, teddy-bear type, while another prefers slim brunettes. One man may find freckles particularly erotic, and another may be overwhelmed by a china-doll complexion. There is nothing unusual in finding certain things more erotic than others. The loving person can accept his or her partner's erotic preferences to enhance their sexual relationship. Consider this example:

The husband was fascinated by elbow-length gloves. Unless his wife wore white kid gloves during intercourse he was practically impotent. As soon as she drew them on, however, he was powerfully stimulated. They kept a number of pairs of gloves in a special drawer. It was ceremoniously unlocked before going to bed as though beginning a sacred rite. This preliminary was a kind of symbolic love-play.

Chesser, 1971, pp. 42–43

It is difficult to differentiate objectively between a preference and a fetish. Most of us have been told that only certain types of sexual activities are normal, and any variation is labeled as unnatural. It is as though we cannot respond to our own inclinations but must let society decide what is natural for each of us in our sexual activities. In many cases, the loneliness of the fetishist might have been avoided if she or he could have found someone who would have uncritically accepted and loved him or her (Chesser, 1971, pp. 48–55). However, it is often difficult to match a fetishist desire with a willing partner as the following excerpt shows:

When sexuality reawakened in the adolescent, KS was attracted not to women but to the leather or fur wraps they happened to wear. The attraction spread from coats and capes to gloves and shoes, women's riding boots particularly. . . . Real female skin seemed revolting. Breasts and female genitalia were repulsive and roused intense feelings of guilt. A woman's bare foot was lifeless; that same foot in a shoe. . . . Then . . . could KS feel true sexual desire and exert full potency. Nevertheless, KS did fall in love and marry. . . . She could not understand . . . his "holy ceremony of love" which required her to put on furs or bearskin gloves before the love act, or his total impotence without resort to his fetishes. KS found that his wife could not come into his fantasy world. . . . Without them, he was impotent. With them, he knew his wife's revulsion.

Ruitenbeek, 1974, p. 103

Today, people who seek partners for fetishist or other unusual sexual acts can facilitate their search by advertising in gay and straight underground newspapers. Advertisements for almost every imaginable sexual fetish or preference are printed in such newspapers; for example:

TOY BALLOONS — BiWM [bisexual white male] professional with unique fetish — kids' balloons turn me on! If you have some or complementary turn on, would like to hear.

WM wants young, moderately aggressive black for S&M [sadomasochism], w/s [water sports — urolagnia], scat [scatology — sexuality involving feces], boot licking. No addicts, hustlers.

MALE FEET — sought for adoration by attractive WM, 35. Can travel.

CHUBBY CHASER — WM, 5'10", 150, wl/blt, very gdlkg, who travels for a living, looking for WM's 21–39, tall, with lrg gut. I am FF [fist fucker] top, S&M dom, & like wkg over really huge guys. Your location no problem.

BOXING FANS — WM univ grad, turned-on by prizefights, leather boxing gear, etc., wishes to hear from avid ringsiders, any age. Object: Friendship. Also research amateur boxing hist. Seek info and pics of stag smoker battle royals, clandestine newsboy B.A. fight shows, etc.

Transvestism

The term *transvestism* literally means cross-dressing or putting on the garments of the opposite sex. This term, therefore, refers to a concrete piece of behavior and appears relatively unambiguous. But because the meaning of this behavior is different for different persons, its function for human sexuality cannot be clearly understood without further distinctions. People may cross-dress for many different reasons, some of which have little or no sexual connotation.

Fetishist Cross-Dressing
Fetishist cross-dressing refers to putting on clothes of the opposite sex for the purpose of producing genital excitement, generally leading to masturbation or intercourse and orgasm. There is some consensus that the term *transvestism* should be used only for this phenomenon (Stoller, 1971). We will follow this usage, which treats transvestism as one form of fetishism.

There are two different types of transvestites. Some are excited by a single garment or a few garments, and this preference remains relatively   430 constant throughout life. For example, a man may find it particularly exciting to don a pair of women's lace panties, and may wear them often under his usual masculine outer garments. Other transvestites may start with only a few garments and gradually include more and more garments until on occasion they dress completely in the clothes of the opposite sex. They may be successful in passing as a member of the opposite sex and enjoy the thought that they are fooling the world and may at any moment reveal their secret (Stoller, 1971).

Apparently women do not indulge in fetishist cross-dressing, or if they do so, the cases have not been reported in studies of sexual behavior. Although some women do dress in men's clothes, they do not become sexually excited by this act, so by our definition they do not belong in the category of transvestites (Stoller, 1971).

Fetishist cross-dressing is enjoyed primarily by men whose preferences and fantasies are largely heterosexual. They prefer women as sex objects; most are married and have children (Prince and Bentler, 1972). Their penises are the source of their erotic pleasure. They do not act stereotypically effeminate when in men's clothes, and they work in typically masculine occupations (Stoller, 1971). Their hormone levels are not significantly different from those of males who are not involved in cross-dressing (Buhrich et al, 1979). The following case is typical of a man who indulges in fetishist cross-dressing.

This patient, in his 30's, married, the father of three children, and a precision machine operator, remembers his first cross-dressing as a tremendously exciting sexual experience in which, as a punishment, an aunt forced him to cross-dress at age 7. . . . From puberty on, sexual excitement was invariably and intensely induced by putting on women's shoes, and as the years passed, this gradually progressed so that with each episode of cross-dressing he now dresses completely as a woman and, with proper makeup to hide his beard, passes in society as a woman for a few hours at a time. He has never had a homosexual relationship and has no sexual interest in male bodies; he is interested in female bodies, but though looking excites him, lying next to a woman is more complicated: he can then only maintain full potency either by putting on women's garments or fantasizing that he has them on.

Stoller, 1971, p. 231

Drag

Homosexuals may also cross-dress ("go in drag") on occasion. This is not sexually arousing to them and may have little or no sexual motivation. Among gay males, there are three possible meanings for wearing female attire: (1) transvestism; (2) professional female impersonation — female impersonators are the star entertainers in some nightclubs (Newton, 1972)

431

and (3) casual "camping," that is, having fun as a "drag queen." Among gay males the drag queen represents a humorous caricature of femininity and effeminacy (Warren, 1974).

Individual gay males may be quite hostile to those who wear female attire for a different reason than is acceptable to them. For example, some gays dislike all drag, and others like it only in the casual sense (Warren, 1974). Similarly, female impersonators may disdain transvestites:

432

Female impersonators do not refer to themselves as transvestites. Sometimes in interviews one would reluctantly say, "Well, I guess I'm some sort of transvestite," but then he would quickly add, "but I only do it for a living," or "this is my job." To female impersonators, the real transvestites are the lone wolf isolates whose individual and private experiments with female attire are described as "freakish." To them, the transvestite is one who dresses as a woman for some "perverted" sexual purpose.

Newton, 1972, p. 51

Whereas transvestites may make a genuine attempt to look like women and wear ordinary clothes, drag queens and female impersonators generally wear flamboyant, outrageous, and out-of-the-ordinary evening costumes, with elaborate hair styles and glittering make-up (Newton, 1972).

Like male homosexuals, female homosexuals sometimes enjoy getting into drag to attend a gay costume party or drag ball. There are very few professional male impersonators (Newton, 1972, p. 500). A minority of female homosexuals dress always or in their leisure hours as men; unlike male drag queens, their male attire mimics the blue-collar, jean-clad male rather than the elegant male. Lesbians who consistently dress as men often have very feminine sexual partners with whom they play out traditional male-female social, and sometimes sexual, roles (see Chapter 13).

Sexual Devices

Sexual devices are devices used to reach orgasm or enhance sexual pleasure. As such, they are generally designed for application to the male or female genital or anal areas. It is not always easy to distinguish a sexual device from certain types of fetishes, and indeed the same object may be both. Whereas the purpose of a sexual device is to enhance sexual pleasure or produce orgasm, a fetish is an object, sometimes the sole object, of sexual arousal. A woman who uses an electric vibrator to reach orgasm may eventually become aroused by the sound, sight, and feel of the device itself.

There are four main types of sexual devices: artificial genitals, vibrators, penis erectors and extenders, and masturbatory devices.

Artificial Genitals

Artificial genitals include artificial vaginas and *dildos* (artificial penises). Contrary to stereotypes, most dildos are not used by lesbians but rather by male homosexuals (and perhaps heterosexual couples). The dildo may be inserted in the vagina or anus; some come equipped with devices for

433

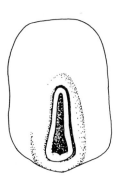

Figure 14.1
An artificial vagina

ejecting "semen" in the form of warm milk or other liquids. Artificial vaginas (see Figure 14.1) are generally attached only to fake female genitals, but may occasionally be part of an entire female doll or blow-up form, generally used by males for masturbatory purposes. Artificial penises may also be incorporated in a life-size male doll, sometimes including a penetrable anus.

Vibrators

Vibrators (see Figure 14.2) come in electrical or battery-operated form and in a variety of shapes and colors. Some are shaped like penises, while others have a variety of attachments for different massage depths. Most vibrators are sold through ordinary retail outlets as instruments for face massage or soothing body tensions. They can also be found in sex supermarkets and adult book stores that stock artificial genitalia.

Vibrators are used by females and males for solitary masturbation, and in heterosexual and homosexual encounters with a sexual partner. Females may use vibrators inside the vagina or on the clitoris or mons veneris; sometimes two vibrators are used to stimulate the vagina and clitoris at the same time. Males use vibrators on the genitals or in the anus. Vibrators have also been used successfully to help previously nonorgasmic women attain orgasm (see Chapter 5).

Penile Aids

Penis extenders are designed for heterosexual or homosexual males who wish to give their sexual partner the sensation of penetration by a larger penis. These extenders consist of a piece of rubber or plastic shaped like a penis but only an inch or two in length. Extenders are worn at the tip of the male's penis and are attached to a condom or a series of straps that keep them in place throughout sexual interaction (see Figure 14.3.) Some

434

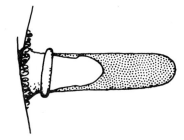

Figure 14.3
A penis extender

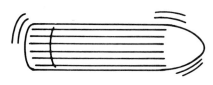

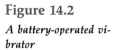

Figure 14.2
A battery-operated vibrator

penis extenders have small projections on them that presumably create additional stimulation.

Penis erectors are designed for use by men who cannot always achieve an erection when they wish to. They vary in design, but most consist of a firm rubber or plastic splint, curved to fit underneath a flaccid penis and support it. These splints are kept in place by small straps that fit over the penis and larger straps that go around the male's torso. Penis erectors are also used by female-to-male transsexuals who have undergone a sex-change operation.

There are also rings that fit over the head of the penis just behind the glans, equipped with fringelike projections for added stimulation. Rings or extenders with these projections are often referred to as "French ticklers." They can be attached to a penis-shaped vibrator as well as to a penis.

Cock rings may also be used by male homosexuals and heterosexuals in sexual interaction with a partner. A *cock ring* fits around the base of the penis after erection and maintains the erection as long as the ring is in place.

A twenty-seven-year-old homosexual explains: A cock ring . . . pushes the penis and testicles forward, making them more protuberant. Some gay guys will wear them for that reason alone: it allows them to show a big basket. A cock ring is also worn during sex to maintain erection after one or more ejaculations. . . . In fitting a cock ring, care must be taken to get one that is neither too loose nor too tight. If it is too loose, it might fall off the flaccid penis or fail to prolong erection after coming. If it is too tight, it might bruise the base of the penis. This happened to me, with the first cock ring I bought: I had a small ring of bruises on the upper part of my penis, extending down the sides. So I went and bought the next larger size of metal ring. Some cock rings are adjustable: they are made

From the authors' files

of leather with snaps at various intervals, or occasionally of chain. These latter two seem quite popular with butch or S and M crowds. The more usual type is a plain metal ring.

Masturbatory Aids

Sex supermarkets in the United States and other nations stock a variety of devices as masturbatory aids in addition to artificial genitals and vibrators. Among devices designed primarily for use by women is an artificial penis attached to a motor that moves the vibrator in a thrusting manner simulating intercourse. Similar in concept are automatic masturbation machines designed for use by males. These machines have a sleeve that fits over the penis and provides a massaging action through alternating air suction and compression.

Ben-Wa balls have been used by Japanese women as a masturbatory aid for centuries. One of the two Ben-Wa balls is solid and is inserted

Many kinds of sexual devices are sold in sex supermarkets found in large cities throughout the world.
Edo Koenig/Black Star

deep in the vagina, touching the cervix. The second ball, which is filled with mercury, is placed in the vagina in contact with the first ball. The slightest body movement causes the mercury-filled ball to jostle the solid ball, which in turn stimulates the cervix, uterus, and vagina. With the Ben-Wa balls a woman could enjoy a leisurely afternoon rocking in a hammock. The American version of this ancient device usually has a cord attaching the balls to an electrically operated vibrator (which is not meant to be inserted).

Ordinary household items may also be drafted into use as masturbatory devices. "J," the author of *The Sensuous Woman,* recommends female masturbation by holding the genitals against a washing machine (while it is operating, of course).

The boundless ingenuity of woman and man in supplementing natural equipment with mechanical has resulted in an endless variety of other subtypes of specific devices and machines. As yet, however, most of them are variations on artificial genitals, vibrators, penis extenders and masturbatory equipment.

Antisexual Devices

In contrast to the sexual devices manufactured and sold today were the antisexual devices manufactured and sold in the eighteenth and nineteenth centuries. Some antisexual devices had contraception as their major purpose, such as the male chastity belts sold in Germany after the publication of Malthus's famous warning in 1830 about overpopulation (Malthus, 1958).

Other antisexual devices have as their sole or major purpose the prevention of sexual activity or access. Female chastity belts have been used for centuries to preserve female virginity by preventing access to the vagina. For males, physicians have devised antimasturbatory girdles and devices designed to prevent involuntary seminal emissions (Bullough, 1975, p. 300).

Unusual Orificial Sexuality

Any animate or inanimate object and any part of the body can have erotic significance for an individual. For some people orifices of the body other than those commonly associated with sexual sensitivity may have such erotic significance that their stimulation can produce arousal and orgasm. While most of these sexual variations are rare in the general population, they occur often enough to have been given medical diagnostic labels.

Because people with these preferences are not often encountered they have not been extensively studied, and little is known about them except that they receive sexual stimulation from their practices.

Sexual Urethralism

In *sexual urethralism* the individual enjoys stimulation of the urethra by some object. Because urethral stimulation is a private act it usually causes no social difficulties. Medical problems may arise, however, because the objects used may slip through the urethra into the bladder. Because the urethra of the male is longer than the female urethra, this accident is less common among males. However, almost every type of small object has been surgically removed from both male and female bladders at one time or another — including a small snake (Allen, 1969, p. 107).

Closely related to sexual urethralism is an erotic interest in urine. This is called *urophilia, undinism,* or *urolagnia* by sex researchers; participants may use the term "water sports." This preference may take the form of enjoying watching persons or animals urinate; for others it may take the form of wishing to urinate upon another person, to have someone urinate on them, or to drink urine (Allen, 1969, p. 111). Occasionally people who receive sexual stimulation from acts involving urine will advertise in the underground press for a sexual partner who is also interested in this activity.

WET PANTS, WET BEDS, DIAPERS — Are you turned on by wetting your pants or bed, wearing diapers & rubber pants? Let's make contact! Esp Florida wetters! W/m, 40, 6', 32" waist.

One of the best known early sex researchers, Havelock Ellis, practiced urolagnia. Brecher describes its origin and development:

More than forty years earlier, when Ellis was a boy of twelve, walking by the side of his mother along a gravel path in an unfrequented part of the London Zoological Gardens, his mother had "stood still, and soon I heard a very audible stream falling to the ground. When she moved on I instinctively glanced at the pool on the path, and my mother, having evidently watched my movements, remarked shyly, 'I did not mean you to see that.'"

The experience was repeated a little later. . . . Thereafter, Ellis reported in *My Life,* he enjoyed a "light strain of what I may call urolagnia."

Brecher, 1969, p. 55

One of Ellis's female companions, Francoise Delisle, writes of experiencing his urolagnia:

Francoise went into the bedroom to use the chamber pot. Havelock unexpectedly "followed me to minister himself to my needs . . . and did this in so unexpected a fashion as to reduce me to utter bashfulness, but delicious bashfulness, wistful and alluring if puzzled, as I stood in front of him, and he, on his knees, let me caress the glorious head fully accessible to my hand. . . .

Brecher, 1969, p. 57

"Of the full meaning of his delicate attention I was then ignorant. Nor did he say anything that could enlighten me. Least of all did I know the name given to it in his sexological books . . . urolagnia."

Sexual Analism

Sexual analism refers to obtaining sexual pleasure from stimulation of the anus. The anus and the sexual organs have the same nerve supply, and some persons derive considerable pleasure from this very sensitive area (Allen, 1973, p. 804). Some males experience both pleasure and orgasm from anal penetration by another male or from the insertion of a dildo in their anus by a male or female. Many heterosexual couples enjoy anal intercourse on occasion. Females sometimes may reach orgasm during anal intercourse. Males commonly reach orgasm while penetrating the anus in either a heterosexual or homosexual relationship. Additionally, many people enjoy anal stimulation as a part of foreplay or as an added stimulation during other sexual activities (see Chapter 4). Because of fairly widespread enjoyment of anal stimulation, companies that sell sexual devices carry very slender anal vibrators and slender dildos designed to be strapped on in a position for anal stimulation during intercourse. The makers of X-rated movies cater to the interest in anal eroticism by producing movies with scenes of sexual play involving such things as anal intercourse, masturbation during an enema, or intercourse combined with the act of defecation.

Klismaphilia Some individuals obtain erotic pleasure from enemas, a condition referred to as *klismaphilia.* Often these persons discovered this pleasure in childhood when they were forcibly given an enema to relieve constipation. As adults they may continue the practice, either secretly and privately or with the aid of their sex partner (Denko, 1976).

Coprophilia, Coprophagia, and Mysophilia *Coprophilia* refers to an erotic interest in feces; many authorities consider it a special case of sexual analism. Closely related to coprophilia is *coprophagia,* which is a craving for eating dirt, leaves, rocks or other substances usually deemed dirty, inedible, and without nourishment. This craving is presumed to have erotic overtones related to sexual oralism or analism, although some authorities

439

suggest it is brought on by vitamin or mineral deficiencies rather than by sexual interest (Allen, 1969, pp. 108–110). *Mysophilia* refers to a sexual interest in nonfecal dirt and is presumed to be a variety of sexual analism (McCary, 1973, p. 393).

Coprolalia

Coprolalia means obtaining sexual pleasure from using so-called filthy language (Allen, 1969, p. 111). It is not unusual for people in the throes of sexual passion to utter words or phrases that might be considered filthy language, but this does not constitute coprolalia. Coprolalia refers to instances where an individual cannot obtain sexual pleasure without using certain words or hearing his or her partner use them. Many authorities consider writing poison-pen letters, scribbling sexual graffiti on walls, and making obscene phone calls as additional instances of coprolalia if the individuals performing these acts receive sexual pleasure from them (Allen, 1969, pp. 111–115).

In both heterosexual and homosexual contexts, some individuals receive sexual gratification from talking on the telephone — generally in sexual terms — while masturbating.

I met this girl at a gay bar and she was really wild sexually. We made it a few times, and then she kept calling me up. When she called me up she kept saying sexy things, so I got all hot and sexy. I began to get the idea, and one time when she called I began to masturbate, breathing heavily. When she heard me, she got excited and said she was beginning to do the same thing. I had an orgasm as she continued to talk, and I guess she did too. She wanted to do this again, but I felt too embarrassed and self-conscious. I told another lesbian about this episode, and she said the same thing had happened to her with a woman.

From the authors' files

People also may seek partners for such activities by placing advertisements in the underground press:

GAY OBSCENE PHONE CALLER! — I love to say what you want to hear while you (and I) get off! Together! I love to call only those guys sincerely desiring mutual satisfaction. No fakes, please! Send your first name, favorite topic and $2 cash. Don't forget to include your phone number!

Although some telephone coprolalia is by mutual consent, other individuals seek sexual gratification through making obscene telephone calls to unsuspecting strangers.

Conclusion

Variations in sexual stimulus and sexual frequency in our society meet with a variety of social and legal reactions. So-called excessive sexual frequency, if it meets criteria of consent, privacy, and heterosexuality, is not against the law, but it may bring about stigmatization, especially for women. Celibacy or infrequency of sexual interaction may also be stigmatizing for both women and men; although celibacy and abstinence are not illegal, they can have law-related implications. For example, refusal to have sex with a spouse can be grounds for divorce. In addition, in some places spouses with a degree of sexual activity that is perceived as unhealthily low (or high) may be denied the right to adopt children.

Variations in sexual stimulus are more likely to come under legal controls. Public transvestism is forbidden under many local misdemeanor statutes that make it illegal to dress in clothing of the opposite sex. In some jurisdictions female impersonation on the stage may be forbidden or the impersonators may be required to wear articles of male as well as female clothing.

I went to a drag show in Los Angeles in the late 1960s. It was truly weird: the men wore wigs, make-up, and long sequined gowns with suits, shirts, and ties underneath! When I asked why, I was told that local ordinances required the wearing of full male dress under female attire.

From the authors' files

The use of nonliving or nonhuman objects as sexual fetishes or stimuli is not regulated by law, as indicated in Chapter 16. However, indirect control of sex apparatus may be exerted by legislative control of sex shops, pornography stores, or mail-order advertising. Because the use of sexual devices and fetishes or unusual orifices is often private, the individuals concerned are less likely to be publicly stigmatized for their preferences than are transvestites or the promiscuous. Telephone coprolalia may bring about social stigmatization or legal action if the receiver of the call is nonconsenting.

In our society, variations in sexual frequency and sexual response also vary in the degree of legal and social stigmatization attached to them. A promiscuous "satyr" male may be mildly condemned, thoroughly condemned, or praised and admired, depending upon the audience. At the other end of the continuum, eating feces or drinking urine is considered disgusting and perverted by many individuals, although the acts do no direct harm to society and involve no unwilling victims. The sexual prohibitions in our society cover both acts considered harmful to society and their victims, and acts that are seen simply as immoral or disgusting.

441

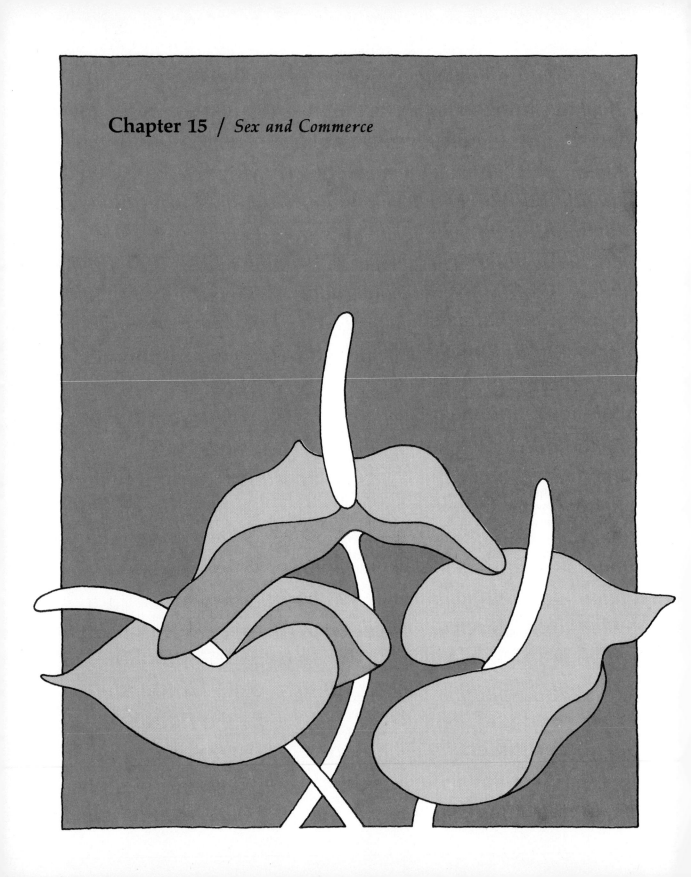

Chapter 15 / *Sex and Commerce*

Throughout history, sex in Western society has been closely linked with money and commercialism. Contemporary examples of the link between sex and commerce include prostitution, pornography, and the eroticization of the mass media. Like other forms of commerce in industrial society, sexual commerce has various modes of organization, distribution, and consumption, and it has links with government agencies, such as the police and the Internal Revenue Service. Sexual commerce also has many other characteristics of commercial activity in an industrial society.

As Ruitenbeek (1974, p. 32) comments, during the Industrial Revolution the Victorians·equated the sexual loss of semen with loss of power and money. Even today, sexual orgasm may be described as "spending" and premarital chastity as "saving oneself for marriage," using the commercial terms of the Victorian era.

Extravagant young men "sowed their wild oats" with the help of the army of girls driven on the street by starvation wages — or, thriftier, they soothed themselves by masturbating. And they reaped, it was claimed, a harvest of insanity, debility, and disease. Their more cautious contemporaries did their utmost to conserve money and seed alike.

Ruitenbeek, 1974, p. 32

Today, sexual imagery in our society is losing some of its monetary and thrifty-capitalist connotations. However, prostitution, pornography, and other kinds of commercialized sex are used by individuals and organizations to make money. In this text we are concerned with both the commercial aspects of sex and the sexuality and life styles of people whose bodies are bartered and sold — the prostitutes.

Prostitution

By dictionary definition, a *prostitute* is a person who engages in sexual relations for money. To this rather narrow definition one should add that such relations are promiscuous, fairly indiscriminate, largely without affection, often anonymous, and not made legitimate by marriage. Even with these qualifications there are still ambiguous cases: mistresses, girl friends, and wives may often accept money or gifts in exchange for sexual favors (Gebhard, 1969).

Prostitutes usually are women who offer their sexual services to men. However, there are also male prostitutes who service men with homosexual preferences. Less common are services for women provided by either female prostitutes or male gigolos. Because female prostitutes for male clients are the most numerous of the categories, there are more data available on them than on any other type of prostitute. However, even

443

these data are limited because it is difficult to obtain a representative sample of prostitutes. Most of the information concerns prostitutes who are in prison or in psychotherapy; however, these two categories are not representative of all prostitutes.

Types of Female Prostitutes

The female prostitutes who cater to male clients may be roughly divided into four categories based on the means by which they conduct their business. These categories also bear some relation to the prostitute's expected income.

Streetwalkers   One category is the "streetwalker," or "bar girl." Among prostitutes these are probably lowest on the social scale in terms of income and prestige. The streetwalker plies her trade by approaching men who walk along the streets of particular areas of a city, while the bar girl approaches men who come into the particular bar she frequents. In both cases the prostitute must approach the man in a manner that indicates to him that she is willing to exchange sexual service for money. But she does not dare be too direct in her approach in case the man is a police officer in

This store in Alaska forbids prostitutes to go inside to keep warm while waiting for the next customer.
Marcus Halevi

444

plain clothes who would arrest her for soliciting. One bar girl describes her way of soliciting a customer:

I catch his eye and hold it for a few seconds. Then I slowly drop my gaze to his zipper. I hold my eyes there for a few seconds and then I slowly raise my gaze again until I meet his eyes again. He usually gets the message.

Atkinson and Boles, 1977

Once she and her customer have agreed that she will give him a sexual service in exchange for money, they go to her place, a nearby hotel, or perhaps his apartment or hotel room (Woolston, 1969).

Prostitutes in Brothels   Other female prostitutes may work in a brothel, or whorehouse. These women share a portion of their fees with the owner of the house, and in exchange they receive a place to conduct their business as well as some measure of protection from arrest or brutal clients. Houses vary in their setup, but usually they have a large living room where the client makes his choice among women who are available at that time. The chosen woman takes him to her room. The activities she performs, the time she gives him, and the price she charges are agreed upon either in the living room or as soon as they get to her room (Woolston, 1969).

Prostitutes in Massage Parlors   A third category is women who work in massage parlors. Ostensibly the customer goes to a massage parlor for a

Most massage parlors offer sexual services to customers who request them.
Magnum Photos, Inc.

445

massage. However, in most instances these massages are conducted in small private rooms where it is quite possible and quite likely that sexual services can be sold to the customer. To protect herself legally, the masseuse does not directly offer sexual services, but it is generally understood that they are available in most massage parlors when the customer requests them (Rasmussen and Kuhn, 1976). Intercourse is somewhat less likely in a massage parlor because by law they may not have beds, but fellatio and hand stimulation are quite common. The fee charged the customer depends on the services offered in addition to the massage for which the customer presumably came to the establishment. The advantage of a massage parlor for both the woman and her customer is that it is not illegal in most places, whereas houses of prostitution are illegal in all states except Nevada (Winick and Kinsie, 1971).

Call Girls   The call girl is usually at the top of the economic hierarchy of female prostitutes. She does not solicit customers on the streets or work in a brothel or massage parlor, but gets clients either through personal referral or as part of an organized escort service. Contact is made when a client calls her or the escort service and tells what kind of arrangement he would like. It is not unusual for a call girl to ask a prospective customer for his name, driver's-license number, and place of business. With this information she can check to see if he is a real customer or a member of the vice squad. Also, she feels she has more protection against the possibility that he may be brutal or psychopathic. The type of client is always a concern to any prostitute because she has little or no legal recourse if she is beaten up by one of her clients.

The call girl may go to her client's place or she may perform her sexual services at her apartment. Sometimes she and perhaps several other call girls are asked to entertain a group of men and serve as their dates for a private party. Large corporations sometimes use call girls in this way to entertain prospective clients or other business associates. Ordinarily the call girl spends more time with her clients than other types of prostitutes, and may provide them with services other than direct sexual ones — such as serving as an attractive date for an evening on the town or for a weekend excursion (Winick and Kinsie, 1971; Greenwald, 1970, pp. 48–52).

Female Prostitutes and Social Class

Prostitutes may also be roughly classified by their socioeconomic class origins or life style: street walkers are generally lower class; prostitutes in brothels may be lower class or upper middle class, depending upon the type and location of the brothel; call girls and women who work in massage parlors are generally middle class in background and orientation.   446

Lower-Class Prostitutes   Jackman et al. (1963) subdivide lower-class prostitutes into two subtypes: criminal world and alienated. The criminal-world prostitute has ties to the criminal subculture, and may make an adequate income and express enjoyment of the criminal life, which she perceives as exciting. She typically rejects middle-class values and disdains her middle-class clients.

The alienated prostitute is alienated from both middle-class society and from the criminal subculture. She often lives alone and is an alcoholic or supports a drug habit (Jackman, 1963). Both alienated and lower-class criminal prostitutes are likely to be in and out of jail on a routine basis.

Middle-Class Prostitutes   An interesting contrast in life style can be found among many of the prostitutes who work in massage parlors outside the central city or in legal houses of prostitution. These women have regular working hours and a good income. As long as they conduct their business carefully, they are not likely to be arrested. Therefore, they are not so involved in the criminal subculture and may have a fairly typical middle-class life style (Rasmussen and Kuhn, 1976).

Jackman et al. (1963) refer to middle-class prostitutes as dual-world prostitutes, because they belong neither to the middle-class world nor to the prostitute subculture but have ties to both. Many strongly reject the world of prostitutes but cannot find complete acceptance among the straight middle class. Dual-world prostitutes are family oriented; many are currently married or divorced and have children in their care.

Lesbian Prostitutes   Besides catering to men, females may work as prostitutes to serve women with homosexual preferences. However, this is not very common, and there have been fewer studies of this particular aspect of prostitution. From the little that has been written on the subject, apparently lesbian brothels are similar to heterosexual ones in their setup, except for the decor. The furnishings tend to resemble those of an expensive boudoir with pictures showing scenes of lesbian lovemaking. Female prostitutes for women may also seek customers in bars, although they confine themselves to gay-female bars (Benjamin and Masters, 1964).

The Career of the Female Prostitute

In addition to types and social class of prostitutes, sociologists are interested in the moral careers of prostitutes. The term *moral career* is used by Howard Becker (1963) and Erving Goffman (1961) to describe the sequence of stages through which stigmatized individuals typically pass.

Like the data on types of prostitution, the data on moral careers of prostitutes give a highly variable picture (Laner, 1974); part of this variability may be due to the fact that little empirical study has been made on   447 prostitutes, and the work that has been done varies by type of prostitute, region, and historical time. However, data indicate that the typical moral career of the prostitute includes most of the following elements: entry, presence of and relationship with pimp, income, training, relationships with clients, and termination of prostitution.

Entry A variety of psychological aberrations have been cited to explain entry into prostitution; at the same time, a variety of economic motivations have been cited by the prostitutes themselves. As Laner notes, these explanations are not mutually exclusive; prostitutes might seek as the rewards of prostitution both "feelings of personal worth as desirable women and financial proof of that worth" (1974, p. 414). Other possible motivations for prostitution include the chance to earn a substantial income in nonroutine work, the chance to live a glamorous life and mingle with clients of a higher socioeconomic level, and the excitement of an illegal profession. For some women it is the only way to earn enough money to finance a drug or alcohol habit. Sometimes a woman with a very high sex drive will seek prostitution as a logical way to earn money at the same time she satisfies her sexual needs (Gebhard, 1969; Woolston, 1969).

Women may enter prostitution almost by accident, by deliberately seeking contacts, or by any combination of both; as Young (1970) points out, in the Western world very few women are forced into prostitution. Jackman et al. (1963) found that among fifteen call girls interviewed, all but one had entered prostitution by making contact with another call girl. At the other end of the continuum, Young (1970) reports that many drift into prostitution through occupations such as restaurant or hotel work.

Pimps *Pimps* are males — and more rarely, females — who live in whole or in part off the earnings of prostitutes (Benjamin and Masters, 1964). Criminal-subculture prostitutes are most likely to share a pimp with other prostitutes (Benjamin and Masters, 1964); on the other hand, dual-world prostitutes are more likely to have husbands who may or may not act as pimps (Jackman et al., 1963). Call girls are least likely to have pimps, but may have them for protection from clients and the police.

And before I even could open my mouth, they'd made a deal for monthly payoffs of $1,100 to the police for protection. When I complained about the high monthly figure, Abe told me I'd better cooperate, since I needed the protection, or else I would get deported.... Meanwhile, another "deal" was made. This had to do with my previous arrest. After discussions back and forth with Abe and the arresting police officer, Nick fixed a price of $3,500 to get me off the hook completely. Originally the arresting officer had suggested wryly that the "golden goose" ought to pay $10,000 to get her case dismissed, but as that figure was

Hollander, 1972, pp. 303–304

A prostitute who has a pimp often depends on him for emotional reasons as well as for protection and help.
Joel Gordon

rather outrageous, they settled for $3,500. Again, there was really nothing I could do about it other than get up the money.

When a prostitute has a pimp, he typically lives on her earnings and acts as her protector, lover, and emotional anchor. Sometimes the pimp also acts as a procurer, obtaining customers for the prostitute or finding a position for her in a good brothel. A pimp may also provide an underworld connection for getting drugs and for protecting her from arrest or conviction (Benjamin and Masters, 1964; Woolston, 1969). In the criminal-world subculture the pimp's fancy clothes and car function as symbols of the prostitute's prestige and earning power (Young, 1970).

Sometimes a prostitute stays with a pimp because she is afraid he will brutalize her if she leaves him. Prostitutes have been beaten, branded, starved, kidnapped, and tortured by their pimps for trying to leave his protection. Michelle, a twenty-seven-year-old ex-hooker who suffered a ruptured spleen at the hands of her pimp, stated: "You stick with him out of fear. You have no place to go and no one to turn to. You're a criminal yourself. And they tell you they'll kidnap you for a month and hold you and beat you up until you agree to work for them" (*Sexuality Today,* February 6, 1978). Pimps have a large financial stake in the prostitutes they control. For example, it is estimated that there were 750 to 1,000 pimps working in New York City in 1978, and their collective earnings were $135,000,000 a year (*Sexuality Today,* February 6, 1978).

Income and Expenses   The amount of money a prostitute can earn depends upon a variety of factors: her attractiveness, her sexual skills, the variety of sexual services she will perform, her initiative, the amount of time she puts in, where she works, and the socioeconomic level of her customers. The lowest-priced prostitutes in the United States are the older and less attractive women working in slum areas, who may get only a few dollars from a customer. Other, more desirable streetwalkers often get as much as twenty to forty dollars per customer. At the top of the economic scale are the call girls, who receive from fifty to over a hundred dollars for each session, and occasionally even more (Greenwald, 1970, pp. 57–58).

Although prostitutes usually pay few or no taxes on their income, they have relatively high business-related expenses, such as an attractive wardrobe and frequent visits to a beauty parlor. If the prostitute takes customers to her apartment, then she may also have to give generous tips to the apartment manager, doorman, and elevator operator.

Training   In an interview study of thirty-three call girls, Bryan (1965) found that they underwent a period of training and apprenticeship after entry into prostitution. This apprenticeship took place under the direction of another call girl or — more rarely — a pimp. During the training period the new call girl either bought lists of clients' names from other prostitutes or was referred to clients by other call girls, who then took 40 to 50 percent of the call girl's fee.

Although the prostitutes being trained received little in the way of instruction about sex techniques, they did receive instructions in hygiene. Sometimes the call girls training them transmitted a value code: exploit the clients, be fair to the other call girls, and defer to the pimp. However, the teaching of these values tended to be haphazard, and trainees did not necessarily follow them. Bryan (1963) found little occupational stability or subcultural unity among his call-girl sample.

Prostitutes who work in a brothel are often trained by the madam, who instructs them both in the rules of the house and in means by which they can make more money from their customers. For example, one madam reports:

They find that I am teaching them how to make money, to dress tastefully, to converse and be poised with men, to be knowledgeable about good hygiene, to

Heyl, 1979, p. 105

have good working habits, such as punctuality, which will help them whether they stay in the rackets or not, and to have self-respect.

Customers The female prostitute's customers are often unmarried youths, or men who are geographically separated from their wives or girl friends. However, a large number of a prostitute's clients are married men who are living with their wives (*Medical World News,* July 12, 1976, p. 31). For men who have no other sexual outlet readily available at the time, the motivation for visiting a prostitute may be simply to relieve sexual tension. For young men the visit may also involve other factors, such as the desire to gain sexual experience or to prove their manhood (Winick and Kinsie, 1969).

The man who has a wife or girl friend available for his sexual satisfaction could have a variety of motives for seeking the services of a prostitute. Probably one important attraction of a prostitute is that she will do many things that other women refuse to do because they think of them as perverted or repugnant. Oral sex is paramount among the types of contact that men often seek from prostitutes (*Sexuality Today,* October 29, 1979), although the complete list would include virtually every sexual practice physically possible for humans. Other motivations include a desire for variety or a desire for sex without emotional entanglement (Simpson and Schill, 1977). Also, a visit to a prostitute may be a social occasion with a group of male friends. Another important motivation is that a man need not fear that his initiative with a prostitute will be rejected. Many men also claim that intercourse with a prostitute is cheaper than intercourse obtained in any other way (Kinsey et al., 1948, p. 351).

There is a variety of evidence about the prostitute's relationship with and perspective on clients. The prostitutes studied by Young (1970) expressed dislike and disdain for their clients, especially the "kinky" ones. According to Jackman et al. (1963), many criminal-subculture prostitutes disliked middle-class values, the alienated prostitutes were apathetic, and the dual-world prostitutes had a rather ambivalent attitude both to the middle class and to clients.

In contrast, Bryan (1966) found that the call girls he studied distrusted their fellow call girls, and many formed friendships with their clients. He found that the women had higher esteem for their clients than for other call girls. In general, prostitutes' attitudes toward their clients correspond to the social class of the client; that is, prostitutes who service lower-class men are less likely to like them than those who service upper-class men.

Sexuality Like other women, prostitutes may be heterosexual, lesbian, or bisexual; some are highly sexed and others are uninterested in sex. Gebhard (1969) found that prostitutes as a group report more sexual

451

response with their husbands or boy friends than the average woman does. On the other hand, sexual responsiveness with customers is much more problematical; few women go into prostitution in order to satisfy an indiscriminate or enormous sexual appetite.

Undoubtedly there is a considerable element of fantasy for both client and prostitute in most sexual transactions (Laner, 1974). Many of the sexual requests made to prostitutes are fantasy trips into sadomasochism or necrophilia. (See Chapter 16.) As Young (1970) indicates, prostitutes learn to pretend sexual pleasure with undesired clients; at the same time, clients may not perform sexual acts by which prostitutes can obtain orgasm.

The Termination of Prostitution Although very little is known about prostitutes who give up the life, it is doubtful that many of them go into more respectable professions or fulfill the common dream of using their savings to start a legitimate business venture. The married woman who used prostitution for a time to supplement the family income most likely resumes her former role when she leaves prostitution. For the unmarried woman, marriage is probably the most common way out, since most of them receive marriage proposals from their more regular customers (Benjamin and Masters, 1964; Young, 1970).

As Bryan (1965) points out, prostitution is not a stable occupation, and recruitment and termination of prostitutes are a continuous process. However, it is clear that aging provides one, perhaps unwanted, termination of prostitution; some aging prostitutes may become madams in a brothel or trainers of new girls.

In our discussion of the moral career of the prostitute, we have concentrated on the female rather than the male prostitute. However, there are several types of male prostitutes: gigolos, who are patronized by women, and male homosexual prostitutes, who perform sexual services for men.

Male Heterosexual Prostitutes (Gigolos)

Gigolos are male prostitutes who perform sexual services for women. They are not very common and have not been extensively studied. Gigolos usually do not seek clients in the same open manner as do other prostitutes. Instead they frequent bars, resorts, or vacation spots that are popular with wealthy middle-aged women. Their approach is usually more subtle than that of other prostitutes, and they pretend to be personally or romantically attracted to the woman. Typically gigolos are young and handsome, whereas their customers are older and concerned about retaining their physical attractiveness. In addition to direct sexual gratification, gigolos usually provide their customers with flattery and attention and serve as escorts for various social occasions. In return they receive money and gifts. Male prostitutes may also work in massage parlors that cater to women, be part of an organized escort service, or work in an occupation that allows them considerable contact with lonely women.

A part-time college student in his mid-twenties reports: I guess you would say that I am a male prostitute. Except that I am not really — I am a bartender. The way it got started was that three girls came into the bar one night when I was working. I knew two of them as regulars but one of them was new to me. She kept looking at me and looking at me all the time, and so I stopped to talk to her whenever I passed by the spot where she was sitting. . . .

From the authors' files

When I closed up the bar and cleaned up that night, I found that she had left a note for me in the ladies room asking me to meet her after we closed. She wanted to go to my place . . . When I straightened up my place next morning I found a matchbook cover on the table by my bed with a lipstick print on the outside and a five-dollar bill folded up inside. I knew she had left it and I felt real funny about it. . . . She says she wants to pay me because that makes her conscience feel clear because it's not like being unfaithful to her husband or loving anyone else, but it's just for sex and nothing more. She told one of her friends about it, and now she comes to me too. . . . But I am going to give it up. I feel funny about it all. And I think it is affecting my personal sex life too.

Male Homosexual Prostitutes

Males who work as prostitutes to serve the sexual needs of other males are quite common in the United States and the rest of the Western world. Most of these male prostitutes do not consider themselves homosexuals. Instead, they believe themselves to be motivated by a desire for money rather than sexual pleasure (Reiss, 1964). Most of the "hustlers," as they are often called, abandon prostitution as they reach their mid-twenties and thereafter lead typical heterosexual lives. They have marriages and children, and apparently most do not move into the gay life when they stop hustling (Benjamin and Masters, 1964).

"Heterosexual" Hustlers   Hustlers are sometimes lower-class teenage boys who are members of street gangs in large cities. They are introduced to hustling by older boys as an easy way to make money. In contrast to most female prostitutes, they usually have very strict unwritten rules concerning what is allowable and what is not. Generally they allow no demonstration of affection whatever and insist that sexual activities with the customer be confined to fellatio. Even though hustlers usually have an orgasm in their contact with their customer, they do not admit to themselves that they enjoy it, but firmly maintain that they do it only for the easy money it involves (Reiss, 1964).

453

Gay Hustlers   Gay male hustlers are those who identify as homosexual but who seek to earn a living, or perhaps some additional cash, as a male prostitute. Such male prostitutes are likely to be willing to engage in a variety of sexual acts with their clients, including fellating them, in contrast to lower-class "heterosexual" hustlers. Gay male hustlers may meet their clients in gay bars, baths, or other meeting places, or visit the homes of clients allegedly to model in the nude, give massages, or other services.

How about a fantastic full body massage by
                DEAN JOHNSON?
21, trim, tanned, and well-built. . . . B. of A. and Master Charge accepted. New offer: Have 6, get 1 free. A sensuous rub!

   The male hustler's usual method of making contact with a customer is through advertisements, or through loitering on street corners, in all-night movie houses, parks, public toilets, and gay bars. Their mode of operation is similar to that of the female prostitute with two exceptions — their fees are usually lower, and they more often adjust their fees in favor of younger, and more attractive customers (Benjamin and Masters, 1964).

Male Homosexual Organizations

Male homosexual prostitution is not the only route to paid gay sex; other routes include various profit-making organizations oriented to homosexual sex. Among these are modeling or masseur agencies and steam baths.

Modeling or Masseur Agencies   By the modeling-agency or masseur-agency route, customers wishing homosexual sex simply call a telephone number given in the advertising section of one of the many gay publications and ask for the services of a masseur or male model. The man will then come to the client's home and perform sexual services for a fee, which is split between the masseur or model and the organization:

W/m, 33, wishes to do modeling in your home or mine. From 8 a.m. to 2 p.m. $3. per hour, with or without clothes. Write Harold, Box 324.

LOW RATES!
massage by tall, slender, endowed young man. L.A. area. John, Box 257.

Masseur, Hot, hung stud. Films, enemas, toys, Accu-Jac, locker room. Box 386.

Steam Baths   Although there are heterosexual prostitution rings that send masseuses to private homes, there is no heterosexual equivalent of the male steam baths. Males who want inexpensive sex with other men can pay a fee as low as one or two dollars and gain access to dozens or   454 hundreds of potential sex partners in one of the many steam baths or Turkish baths that have proliferated in urban areas of the United States (Weinberg and Williams, 1975). The baths vary from the simple to extremely luxurious. Some feature dancing, restaurants and bars, and even entertainment. Many have color TVs, swimming pools, saunas, whirlpool baths, and gyms.

The environment of the steam bath is arranged by sexual preferences and activities. Many steam baths have an "orgy room" designed to entertain multiple participants in sexual encounters. All have private rooms in

Males who want sex with other males can often find it for the price of admission to a steam bath.
© *Eric A. Roth 1979/Picture Cube*

455

which potential sex partners may sit or lie while other potential partners walk down the corridors looking into rooms. Some baths include rooms for specialized preferences such as "leather" or sadomasochistic rooms equipped with chains, whips, and restraints (see Chapter 16).

Prostitution and Society

Prostitution and commercial sex organizations such as the steam baths are highly stigmatized in our society. In other cultures, responses to prostitution vary from tolerance to religious or ritual sacralization (Young, 1970). Although there are a few societies without prostitution, they are rare; prostitution flourishes in all industrial nations despite various attempts to stamp it out.

Tolerance   In the Hellenic world, prostitution was part of a triad often condemned today: slavery, pederasty, and prostitution (Young, 1970). Unruffled tolerance of prostitution prevailed, along with tolerance and some idealization of *pederasty* (sexual relations between a man and a boy). (See Chapter 16.) The paid *hetaerae* (prostitutes) of ancient Greece were, in many periods of Greek history, culturally valued as the intellectual as well as sexual companions of great men.

Religious Rituals   In some cultures in recorded history relations between a prostitute and customer were treated as a religious act and took place within the temple. In Mesopotamia around the middle of the fifth century B.C., for example, every woman had to give herself once to a stranger in the temple before she married. This obligatory prostitution was regarded as a purely religious act, a sacrifice to the goddess Ishtar, to whom every woman must belong for a night. The goddess selected a lover for her and thus provided a mystical juncture with divinity (Lewinsohn, 1958, pp. 30–31).

In some parts of the Near East, the temples had a special house for priestesses who performed sexual services for male worshipers. This is the temple prostitution that often scandalized early Christians. But those who took part in this sexual transaction did not regard it as lustful or sensual; to the participants it was a sacred and uplifting act of communion with the gods (Taylor, 1970, pp. 228–229).

Temple prostitution was introduced into Greece from the East, but apparently only Corinth adopted it to any extent. There temple prostitution was combined with the cult of Aphrodite. It is said that at the time of Augustus, over ten thousand hetaerae were employed in the temple of Aphrodite in Corinth, where their fame for charm and piety was unexcelled (Lewinshon, 1958, p. 57).

456

Stigmatization As Young (1970, p. 65) points out, in contemporary Western society "prostitution is specialized, mercenary, and reprobated." Prostitution has not always been stigmatized, as the examples of toleration and sacralization indicated. Nor has prostitution always been specialized; women's sexual services have been used in many cultures to repay debts or express goodwill:

The custom whereby a man lends his wife or daughter to a guest is a form of prostitution; in return for her kindness the family or the clan expect to receive his good will, or even sometimes the good will of the gods, expressed in fertility of crop and of people. But the wife or daughter does not thereby become a prostitute.

Young, 1970, p. 65

In the United States today, prostitution is illegal in all states but Nevada (though the law is not enforced in some states) and is condemned in the context of middle-class norms. Where prostitution is against the law, the prostitute without adequate protection from the police may make a continuous circuit from the streets to the county jail, with numerous pay-

Where prostitution is against the law, the prostitute who works on the street may be arrested many times during her career.
Wide World Photos

ments of fines in between. At the same time, the female prostitute's customer is generally not liable to arrest, although he may be stigmatized by family and employers if found out. Both participants in a homosexual-prostitution encounter are liable to legal and social stigmatization.

Adaptation to Stigma   Prostitutes adapt to stigma in a number of ways. Jackman et al. (1963) note that many prostitutes are ambivalent toward middle-class norms that proscribe prostitution. They rationalize stigma in several ways.

One common rationalization of prostitution by prostitutes is the reiteration that straight housewives are really prostitutes because they sell their sexual services to their husbands for financial support. Therefore, prostitutes are not only better than housewives, they are more honest, because they deliver value for money (Young, 1970).

It is also common for prostitutes (and some social scientists) to argue that prostitution serves the sexual needs of some people in our society in a manner that is probably less socially destructive than most other alternatives (Davis, 1937; Benjamin and Masters, 1964). One prostitute explains her function in this way:

Okay, lately I have "sinned" by selling my body to men, by trading the bodies of my girls to more men. But it hasn't been strictly commerce. I *have* tried to give some happiness to those men, even though they paid for it. I have been honest with them and filled a lost hour of loneliness by giving them a warm smile, a cold drink, soft music in the background, and then a warm and young body to hold, to press, to kiss, to make love to. . . . The man was satisfied, and for the time he was in my house, at least, he was no longer lonely and miserable.

Hollander, 1972, p. 309

A third way of adapting to the social stigma is to focus on values other than middle-class sexual ones. Many prostitutes stress the money and material goods they are able to obtain for themselves and their pimps. Others focus on their unselfishness in providing support for dependent children, parents, or spouses (Jackman et al., 1963).

Often the prostitute is portrayed as having extremely low feelings of self-worth as a result of stigmatization or of prostitution itself. However, Bryan (1966) found that the self-esteem of call girls was higher than their regard for their colleagues, but equal to their regard for clients and for straight men and women. Furthermore, in spite of the occupational hazards of prostitution, nearly two-thirds of the prostitutes questioned in one study reported no regrets whatever about their choice of an occupation (Gebhard, 1969).

No matter what the legal or social status of the prostitutes — individual or organization, male or female — the name of the prostitution game in

458

our society is money. Some of the money earned in prostitution goes to the prostitutes, but a good share goes to the male parasitic participants — pimps, bellboys or bartenders who refer clients, corporations, landowners and landlords, and corrupt police or organized crime. Similarly, the connection between money and pornography in contemporary western society is very close.

Pornography

Pornography is extremely difficult to define. The federal and state criminal justice systems in the United States have consistently failed to provide a watertight definition of pornography that will insure convictions of the producers or distributors of pornographic material. Rather than attempt to enter the debate on the definition of pornography, we will rely on our reader's common-sense understanding of *pornography* as the written, visual, or spoken presentation of sexual interaction or genitals.

Purpose of Pornography

What we would today define as pornography has had different social meanings throughout history. Some of the artifacts from historic and prehistoric cultures that depict sexual interaction, such as the bas-reliefs that adorn some Indian temples, have a religious basis, celebrating life and fertility. Others, such as statues depicting sexual intercourse from African cultures, have a magical basis, directed toward insuring male or female fertility. In our culture, most generally, the purpose of pornography is a blend of entrepreneurial economics and sexuality; the making of money by the production and distribution of depictions of sexuality that will sexually arouse the consumers.

Money Making In Western history the major purpose of the production of pornography has been to sexually incite and thus cause money to be spent. For centuries, prostitutes have incited reluctant customers by showing them pornography, and have inspired other customers to more expensive sexual heights by depictions of more expensive sexual acts. But not all pornography has an economic base. Noneconomic examples include graffiti in rest rooms and pornography created by prisoners.

Masturbation Pornography created by prisoners, such as the books written by Jean Genet when he was in prison, has as its major purpose the fantasy accompaniment to masturbation. Much economically purveyed   459 pornography is also used in this manner, ranging from magazines people buy and then read while alone, to pornographic movies people watch in a darkened theater.

Graffiti in rest rooms, particularly in the public rest rooms catering to males, may also have an element of fantasy as an accompaniment to masturbation. However, sexual graffiti in rest rooms can also have the purpose of communication, as in the case of a male homosexual who lists his telephone number and genital endowments for the attraction of other male homosexual clients.

Nevertheless, most pornography costs money, and this has been the case since the earliest pornography disseminated by the mass media. The mass media, are in fact, a vital factor in the development of a body of pornography. Without printing presses and audiovisual equipment, pornography is limited to statues and artwork, and is generally confined either to public places or to the few who can afford it for their private delectation.

Development of Pornography

The first pornography, of course, was probably in the form of erotic art and statues and stories passed from person to person by word of mouth. The invention of the printing press then made possible written pornography. Only since the age of mass literacy in industrial nations, during the last two hundred years, has written pornography become available to anyone. Steven Marcus, in *The Other Victorians,* has described the quantity and quality of visual and written pornography collected by prominent, wealthy, and literate Victorian men — a quantity and quality that would amaze those who still think of *Victorian* as synonymous with *asexual.* Before the Victorian era there were novels such as *Fanny Hill,* which is today available to a mass readership rather than a limited and underground one.

A new development in pornography since the industrial era has been motion-picture pornography. The first motion-picture pornography developed with the first motion pictures, and consisted of a series of photographic cards that, when flipped very fast, gave the illusion of motion. Next came the invention of silent films, which included some pornographic silents.

Today pornographic products include all the historical varieties: statuary, pictures, written words, flipped cards, and sound movies. Recently there has been increased private ownership of pornographic movies for home viewing. Pornography has not yet invaded television in the United States, but pornographic movies are shown on television late at night in Japan.

Laws Regulating Pornography

There are now five federal laws prohibiting distribution of obscene materials in the United States. *Obscene material* is extremely problematical to define legally, and its definition is generally much narrower than our definition of pornography. One federal law prohibits the mailing of such material, another prohibits importation of obscene materials, another prohibits broadcast of obscenity, and two prohibit the interstate transportation of obscene materials. In addition, forty-eight of the states have statutes that generally prohibit the distribution of obscene materials (Commission on Obscenity and Pornography, 1970). The problem of enforcing these laws is that no one seems able to determine in the courtroom which pornographic materials are really obscene and which are not, because labeling pornographic materials as obscene involves subjective value judgments. For example, Supreme Court decisions have established that material cannot be prohibited on grounds of obscenity unless it meets three criteria: (1) the dominant theme of the material must appeal to a "prurient" interest in sex; (2) the material must be "patently offensive" to "contemporary community standards"; and (3) the material must lack "redeeming social value." The key decision in 1966, concerning the sale of *Fanny Hill,* established that before a work could be considered obscene, it had to meet all three criteria.

But there are no simple rules for determining what are community standards, what has redeeming social value, and what appeals to prurient interests. As case after case has been won by defendants in the lower courts, and as trials become more expensive and time-consuming, attempts to enforce the assorted federal, state, and local pornography laws have become fewer (Bowers, 1971). As a result there has been a boom in publicly available pornography, such as magazines, newspapers, films, and books. Special stores cater to the selling of "adult books," films, and other media for home consumption, while special movie theaters show an endless run of pornographic movies. The trend toward public availability of pornography is most advanced in large metropolitan areas, and may be successfully curtailed in some small local communities by determined and persistent judges and local leaders (Kirkpatrick, 1974; Zurcher and Kirkpatrick, 1976). In February of 1980, four hundred FBI agents in ten cities wound up a massive investigation of the pornography industry with the arrest of what one FBI official called "every major producer and distributor of pornography in the country" (*Newsweek,* February 25, 1980, p. 37). The special agent in charge claimed that the investigation and indictments will have a debilitating impact on the $4-billion-a-year pornography industry.

In some communities the debate over what is and is not obscene may at times seem a bit ridiculous:

461

A twenty-five-year-old male college student reports: When I lived in Portland, there was a theater there that featured nude male dancers. The city fathers said that was okay as long as no display of a turgid penis was made. So this whole debate started trying to define when a penis stops being flaccid and becomes turgid. At what point can the difference be legally defined and evaluated by visual inspection were the questions. It was really funny. Here was a group of grown men sitting around trying to decide when a guy does or does not have a hard on.

Exposure to Pornography

As pornography has become more widely disseminated in the United States, social scientists as well as citizens have become interested in its effects. Prior to 1969 there was very little factual knowledge about the consequences of exposure to explicit sexual materials. This lack of information left people to speculate and project their own fears to fill the void. People who had the least experience with sexual materials were the most likely to attribute fearful consequences to their use (Abelson et al., 1970).

Exposure to explicit sexual materials is widespread in the United States. A recent study with a representative national sample of adults found that 84 percent of men and 69 percent of women had been exposed to written or pictorial versions of explicit depictions of sexual activities (Abelson et al., 1971). Exposure to sexual materials is not confined to adults. On the basis of several studies, one may conservatively estimate that 85 percent of boys and 70 percent of girls have seen visual depiction or read textual descriptions of sexual intercourse by the time they reach age eighteen (Wilson, 1971).

Sexual Stimulation   There is overwhelming evidence that pornography is sexually stimulating for substantial proportions of both males and females. It is commonly believed that women are less aroused by sexually explicit materials than are men, but research does not clearly confirm this assumption (Hatfield, Sprecher, and Traupmann, 1978). When viewing erotic stimuli, women report physiological sensations associated with sexual arousal as often as do men, although the women are less likely than men to report subjective feelings of arousal (Schmidt and Sigusch, 1970). Young people are more likely than older ones to report that sexually explicit materials are arousing. People who are college educated, religiously inactive, and sexually experienced are more likely to report arousal by erotic materials than are persons who are less educated, religiously active, and sexually inexperienced (Commission on Obscenity and Pornography, 1970).

462

Many children and adolescents have seen sexually explicit materials.
© *Joel Gordon 1979*

The potential for sexual stimulation inherent in pornography can be socially utilized in a number of ways. We have already noted that prostitutes may use pornography to encourage reluctant or low-spending customers. Similarly, people involved in continuing sexual relationships may use pornography to revive a mutually flagging sexual interest, or simply as added spice to an established sexual relationship.

A middle-aged woman reports: When we first walked in the theatre I was really stunned because it was in the middle of the movie and we came in at the part with a man and a woman really going at it, and the camera was zoomed right in on the action. I felt funny about it and I wanted to leave and still I wanted to stay too. But we stayed and watched both features. Although I really didn't like the movies, I still had to admit that they turned me on — which was kind of a surprise to me since I'm not real liberal about sex and things. . . . Now Bill and I go to see X-rated films whenever we hear of a good one in town because frankly we like the added zing it gives us. Like when we get out of one of those movies, we can hardly wait to get home — just like when we were first married.

From the authors' files

463

Sometimes an individual may use pornography in an attempt to stimulate a sexual partner, or someone with little sexual interest may use it to turn on in preparation for a sexual encounter. Finally, as already indicated, pornography may be used as an aid to masturbation, particularly for prisoners, adolescents, and others without an immediate sexual outlet.

Public Opinions   Given that it performs these sexual functions, is pornography socially harmful? The debate on this question is endless, and the answers seem to take three forms: (1) pornography is neither harmful nor harmless but neutral; (2) pornography is socially beneficial because it channels what might be socially harmful sexual impulses into harmless channels; and (3) pornography is socially harmful because it stimulates people to sexual acts they might not otherwise perform, such as rape, group sex, or sadomasochism. Public opinion on this issue is diverse, to say the least. About two-thirds of adults in the United States think that explicit sexual materials excite people sexually and provide information about sex. Approximately half are of the opinion that sexual materials improve sex relations of some married couples. Approximately half think that they lead to rape or to a breakdown in morals (Abelson et al., 1970).

In 1970 the United States Commission on Obscenity and Pornography reported that explicit sexual materials have been used by people for many years with no apparent harmful effects either to themselves or to others. They also found that convicted sex offenders generally had had significantly less experience with explicit sexual materials in adolescence than the average person (Commission on Obscenity and Pornography, 1970, pp. 36–37). Several recent studies have analyzed the effects of exposure to explicit sexual materials. Based on the findings of these studies, it appears that for most people exposure to sexual materials produces no change in attitude regarding what is acceptable sexual behavior and no change in the type of sexual behavior in which they engaged (Wilson, 1971).

Evidence from other countries also indicates few socially harmful effects of freely available sexual materials. In Denmark, for example, after the legalization of pornography, there was a decrease in sex crimes and a decline in sexual assaults on children (Sexuality Today, October 8, 1979). Official commissions in countries such as Denmark, Sweden, Israel, and the United Kingdom (as well as the United States) have recommended elimination of prohibitions upon distribution of sexual materials to consenting adults; these commissions all concluded that the exposure of consenting adults to explicit sexual materials causes no demonstrable damaging individual or social effects (Commission on Obscenity and Pornography, 1970, p. 49).

464

The musical revue Oh! Calcutta!, *featuring total nudity and simulated sex, opened in New York in 1969 and is still doing a steady business today despite some problems. Radio and television stations will not air its commercials, and police in three cities arrested the production on obscenity charges while the show was on tour.*
Courtesy of the 1980 production of Oh! Calcutta! at the Edison Theater, New York City

The atmosphere of shops handling sexually explicit materials and the attitudes toward these shops in countries where pornography is legally and socially accepted are often quite different from that now found in the United States.

A woman in her forties says: I had visited a pornographic bookstore once in the United States and never wanted to go back; it was too quiet, sinister appearing, and hole-in-corner. The pornographic shops in Amsterdam were a revelation: open to the street, with every conceivable sexual interest displayed proudly in the window. Customers jostling, talking, and going in and out, just like any other store, with smiling clerks and a fairly rapid and unembarrassed-appearing trade in all kinds of books and devices.

From the authors' files

The Pornography Debate   In spite of recent findings, a sizable minority of people in our society are opposed to the existence of explicit sexual

465

materials, even if these are shown to have no harmful effects and are only utilized by adults in their own homes (Abelson et al., 1970). One vocal minority argues that commercial pornography dehumanizes people by representing them as obscene animals. Others contend that society has a legitimate concern in maintaining moral standards and that censorship should be used to promote the quality of life that the laws of a democracy should defend and enhance (Kristol, 1971).

The opposite point of view is that censorship violates the First Amendment of the Constitution, which guarantees free speech, and that pornographic material should be unrestrictedly available to adults. Only a minority of people in our population hold to this viewpoint. The majority of people take a stance between the two extremes. Similarly, there is a debate over the social value or harmfulness of the eroticization of the mass media.

The Eroticization of the Mass Media

Pornography has existed for centuries, as has the religious or mystical depiction of sexual activities. Today, however, there are two major differences: the legitimate media of communication have become mass media, and the mass media themselves have become eroticized. This eroticization of the media has occurred in two contexts: advertising and programming. As Cuber and Harroff note: "It is a commonplace that sexual themes pervade American society. Popular literature and music express a frank preoccupation with sex, often in its rawest aspects. Madison Avenue incessantly exploits vulnerability to sexual stimuli" (1968, p. 171).

Advertising In advertising, sexual innuendo has become more and more direct as an aid to the selling of products, and objects associated with sexuality and the genitals are more prevalently advertised in the legitimate media. In recent years, advertisements for such products as sanitary napkins and underwear have been permitted on television, whereas formerly they were banned.

At the same time there has been a proliferation of suggestive advertisements on television, in magazines, and on billboards. For decades, scantily clad females posing in sleek automobiles have been used as a means of stimulating male fantasy associations and thus motivating men to buy cars. (See Selection 15-1.) Today, however, this mild eroticism has been replaced by a much more clear-cut version. A female voice advertises a French airline on the radio: "Have you tried it the French way?" Another female voice, on a television advertisement for shaving cream, purrs seductively: "Take it off — take it all off."

Mistress Versus Wife/Vance Packard

A classic example of the way motivation analysts found merchandising possibilities in our deeper sexual yearnings was a study Dr. Dichter made for Chrysler Corporation in the early days of M.R. [market research] His study is now known as "Mistress versus Wife."

Dr. Dichter was called upon to explain a fact puzzling marketers of the auto. While most men bought sedans and rarely bought convertibles they evidently were more attracted to convertibles. Dealers had found that they could draw more males into their showrooms by putting convertibles in the window. After exploring the situation Dr. Dichter concluded that men saw the convertible as a possible symbolic mistress. It set them daydreaming of youth, romance, adventure just as they may dream of a mistress. The man knows he is not going to gratify his wish for a mistress, but it is pleasant to daydream. This daydreaming drew the man into the auto salesroom. Once there, he finally chose a four-door sedan just as he once married a plain girl who, he knew, would make a fine wife and mother. "Symbolically, he marries the sedan," a spokesman for Dr. Dichter explained. The sedan is useful, practical, down to earth, and safe. Dr. Dichter felt that the company would be putting its best foot backward if it put its main emphasis on sedans simply because that was the car most men ended up buying. Instead, he urged the company to put the hope of mistress-adventure a little closer to males by giving most prominent display to the convertibles. The spokesman went on to explain Dr. Dichter's line of thinking. "If we get a union between the wife and mistress — all we sought in a wife plus the romance, youth, and adventure we want in a mistress — we would have . . . lo and behold, the hardtop!" The hardtop was soon to become the most successful new auto style introduced in the American market for several years, and Dr. Dichter's organization takes full credit for inspiring it by its "Mistress versus Wife" study.

Programming The media have been eroticized in program content as well as advertising in recent years, though media programming is not pornographic as the term was defined above. However, there has been an increasing eroticization of the content of movies, television, and magazines destined for mass public rather than clandestine pornographic consumption.

Magazines In recent years, magazines such as *Penthouse, Playboy,* and *Playgirl* have proliferated, and have also changed their policy from showing females with only their breasts nude, to showing pubic hair, to showing the female genitals, in full color. At the same time, these magazines have also adopted the policy of using male nudes with genitals exposed, and pictures of males and females (and occasionally couples of the same sex, triads, and groups) in sexual embraces once reserved for underground pornography.

Movies   Eroticization of the movies has gone beyond the proliferation of hard-core pornography. Films such as *Last Tango in Paris* and *Emmanuelle*, showing frontal nudity and sexual interaction, are screened in neighborhood movie theaters rather than local porno palaces. Not all contemporary movies with clearly erotic content are X-rated and thus restricted to adults; some are given R ratings.

Television   To many, the last bastion of media respectability is television, but it also is becoming eroticized. The content of soap operas has been increasingly sexual over the last few decades. Furthermore, situation comedies destined for the entire family now allow many formerly forbidden topics. For example, in "Rhoda" an unmarried heroine admits to taking birth control pills, and in "Karen" a woman has an affair with a married man without suffering painful consequences. Even gays and prostitutes are portrayed as full human beings on programs such as "Hot L Baltimore" attracting many letters of protest or approbation.

Puritanism   Paradoxically, the eroticization of the mass media in the United States coexists with an asexual puritanism grafted onto what Cuber and Harroff call the "Monolithic code" of the Judeo-Christian tradition (1968, p. 19). This code of "correct conduct and right thinking" stresses "chastity, fidelity, parenthood and various forms of attendant responsibility and restraint, all channeled through heterosexuality" (1968, pp. 19–20).

This uneasy coexistence of puritanism and flagrant eroticism gives rise to a rather cyclical and unpredictable succession of new legal restrictions on eroticism followed by the easing of such restrictions (Glaser, 1971). To some extent, the new eroticism and the older puritanism have their own publics who attempt to push the balance of legislative influence to one side or the other. The results of such competing interests are not only cycles of permissiveness and repression, but also the ironic coexistence, in one nation, of *Deep Throat* and the pasting of fig leaves over genitals in art textbooks.

When I was in the curriculum-planning division of the San Diego city schools, a ruling went out that genitals could not be displayed in high school textbooks, so we had to go through and ink all of them out. This was a response to pressure from parents in the John Birch Society.   .

From the authors' files

468

Conclusion

It is clear that there are many interest groups related to the commercial aspects of sexuality. Some groups are indirectly connected by the wish to preserve society from commercial sexuality: politicians and individuals or voter organizations who fight prostitution, pornography, or the eroticization of the mass media. Still other interests are the consumers or potential consumers of commercialized sex, who may either favor or be ambivalent toward legislative control. Finally, there are those who profit from the commercialization of sex: those who profit on a large scale, such as the mass media, corporations, landlords, and perhaps organized crime; and those who profit in a small way, such as call girls, hustlers, and pornographic-movie stars.

The government itself has a considerable interest in the commercial aspects of sexuality, both as the supposed representative of the people and as an interest group with powers of legislative and financial control. At the present time the government collects taxes from makers and distributors of pornography and undertakes some regulations through zoning and other ordinances. The mass media are under more stringent and complete government control. The government, however, exercises very little control over prostitution as a business enterprise, except for massage parlors, which pay taxes and are somewhat controlled by zoning laws. Individual prostitutes and their pimps may pay no taxes and receive no protection from government. The legal, economic, and social issues involved in business enterprises that flourish in the midst of stigma and illegality are extremely complex.

In a large-scale entrepreneurial, industrial society, it is likely that sex will always be the subject of marketing and manipulation, like all types of goods or services. All the forms of sexual commerce, indeed, are likely to flourish in an economy that encourages both sexuality and material gain.

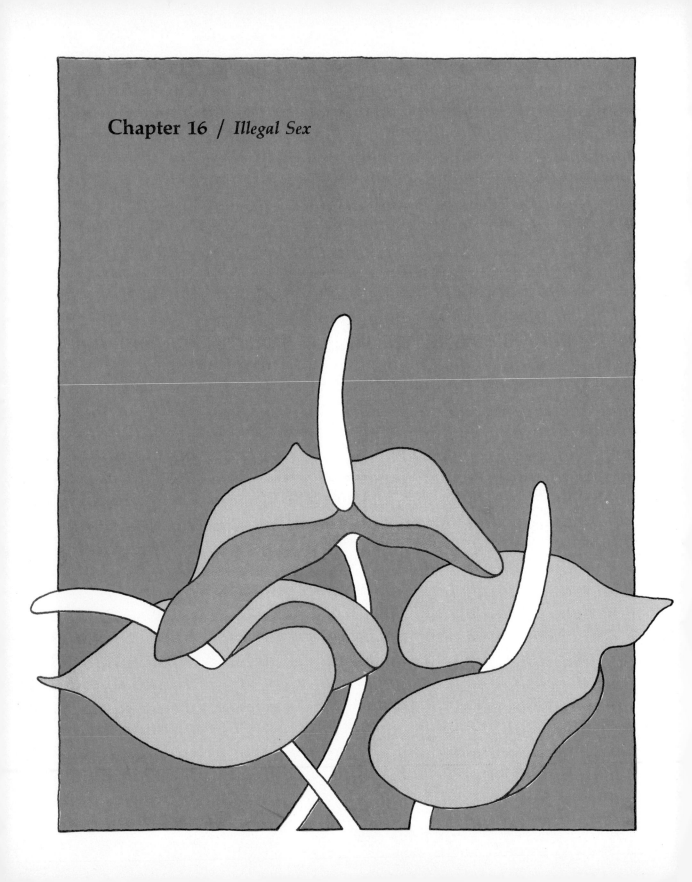

Chapter 16 / *Illegal Sex*

In our culture sexuality is connected with the concept of consent, both in law and in custom. Many aspects of sexual behavior covered in previous chapters are against the law but do not violate the norms of consent. Most married partners who engage in oral sex, prostitutes who service customers, and gays who have sex with one another are acting illegally but consentingly. However, certain acts do violate the concept of consent in our society: sex acts with those legally unable to consent, sex acts accompanied by force or violence, observation of the nakedness of others without their knowledge, and public nudity or display of genitals.

Certain types of sexuality involve the use of force or violence; forcible rape and undesired sadomasochistic acts come within this definition. At the same time, there are other types of sexual interaction in which the concept of consent is more complicated, both socially and legally, such as in mutually consenting sadomasochistic acts and in mutually consenting sexual interaction with minors, whom the law regards as legally unable to consent.

Legal Nonconsent

There are three types of sexual behavior that are considered illegal because one partner is involved without consent, even though no force is used:

1. In sexual relations with animals or dead human beings, consent is assumed to be impossible because the sex object cannot either consent or protest. The notion of consent is not applied to vegetable or mineral products that are frequently used as masturbatory or fetishist devices. Even though candles or fur gloves cannot give consent to use for sexual purposes, there are no laws against such use.

2. All sexual relations with minors are legally considered as sex without consent because presumably minors have not reached an age at which they have sufficient knowledge of the consequences of their acts to give or withhold consent meaningfully.

3. Sexual acts involving looking at another's genitals or displaying one's own genitals to another person are legally punishable when these acts are performed without the consent of the other people involved, in public or in private settings. There are no penalties attached to these acts when they are done within a consenting relationship that does not violate any other laws or norms.

Sex with Animals

The use of animals as sex objects is commonly called *bestiality, bestiosexuality,* or *zoophilia*. Many different types of animals and of sexual contact may be involved. Bestiality is generally stigmatized in our society; nevertheless, animal contacts may form the first source of sexuality for people brought up in rural areas. As many as 17 percent of male adolescents who live on farms have sexual contact to orgasm with animals, and probably as many more have sexual relations that are not carried through to climax (Kinsey et al., 1948, p. 459). Usually these contacts become less frequent with age and as the adolescent encounters more available human sexual partners. It is not surprising that sexual contact with animals is less common for males raised in urban areas, where there is less access to animals. The incidence for city males is only one-half to one-fifth that found among rural males (Kinsey et al., 1948, pp. 459–463).

Males also have sexual contacts with dogs and cats. They are most likely to masturbate the animal or to have coitus with it; some have the animals lick or suck their genitals (Kinsey et al., 1953, p. 509).

Females in the United States are less likely than males to engage in erotic activities with animals; the reported incidence for women is about 4 percent, with very few of these incidents involving contact to orgasm (Kinsey et al., 1953, p. 509). Females are most likely to have contacts with dogs and cats. This usually involves general body contact, but may include the animal's licking her genitals, masturbation of the animal, or intercourse (Kinsey et al., 1953, p. 509).

Some ancient codes and laws, such as the Hittite laws, prescribed penalties for males having sexual contacts with animals, but most ignored the possibility of females doing so. In contrast, the Talmudic code specifically prohibits bestiality for both sexes, and prohibits a female from being alone with an animal (Kinsey et al., 1953, p. 507). In the United States virtually all the states have laws prohibiting sexual relations between humans and animals of other species. In all states except New Hampshire, bestiality is a felony or its equivalent, and in some states the maximum sentence is life imprisonment (Kinsey et al., 1953, pp. 505–509).

It is not unusual for the person engaging in sexual activities with his or her pet to have some feelings of affection for the animal. Quite often, though, the contact is made simply through curiosity, desire for novelty, or desire for sexual release when other sex objects are unavailable. Occasionally the bestiality involves sadistic elements that may result in injury or even death to the animal. In cases involving cruelty to animals, some legal sanctions seem justified. In cases where there is no discomfort to the animal, the penalties for bestiality appear unduly harsh and based more on religious concepts of sin than on a realistic evaluation of damage to persons or animals or society as a whole.

472

Sex with a Corpse

The use of a dead body as a sex object is usually called *necrophilia.* Some men enjoy contact with simulated corpses. A few large cities have prostitutes who cater to this preference; they use wax or powder to give their skin a lifeless appearance, dress in a shroud, and lie in a coffin for the benefit of the client (Allen, 1969, p. 256).

A client took me back to his place, and as soon as I got in the door there was a dirty great coffin standing open. He put me in a white nightie with a rosary in one hand and a Bible in the other and a wreath of roses on my head. Then I had to lie down in the coffin ... he started nailing the lid down and all the time he was shouting out: "You're dead now, God damn you to hell." He told me his wife had died.

Young, 1964, p. 65

Sex with Children

An adult who has sexual relations with a child has committed one of the most serious sex offenses in our society and is regarded as extremely degenerate. In many states the penalty for the offending adult is life imprisonment; in a few it is death (Thorpe, Katz, and Lewis, 1961, p. 332). In spite of the strong penalties, adult-child sex is not uncommon. It is estimated that one out of every four girls is sexually abused in childhood, primarily by close family members or family friends (*Sexuality Today,* October 1, 1979).

Age Definitions   The definitions of *child, adult,* and *adolescent* in our society tend to be ambiguous; however, the relevant statutes of each state specify the ages at which a given sexual act is defined as child molestation, statutory rape, or a consenting sexual act. The social response to sexual acts with minors varies according to the sex, age, and difference in age between the participants. Sexual interaction between a female who has not reached puberty and an adult male is highly stigmatized, as is sexual interaction between a pubescent or prepubescent male and any other male. In general, the younger the child and the older the adult involved, the greater the stigma arising from the sexual interaction. Sexual contact with a prepubescent child is generally defined as *child molestation;* when a pubescent or older adolescent is involved, the act is legally redefined as *statutory rape.*

   Particularly in lower-class subcultures, sexual interaction with a pubescent female is regarded as appropriate, although contact with a prepubescent female is almost universally condemned. The law defines sexual contact with a biologically mature female under the adult age of sixteen or eighteen as statutory rape rather than child molestation, but many mem-

473

bers of society regard this legal category as rather ridiculous, particularly when the sexual participants are close in age, as in the case of an eighteen-year-old boy and his fifteen-year-old girl friend.

Attitudes Toward Adult-Child Sex   The typical American's horror at adult-child sexual relations remains even when no force is involved and when the child is either the aggressor or a willing participant. This horror is apparently based on the assumption that all children are sexually pure and innocent and that the adult is corrupting this innocence. The assumption of childhood purity persists despite massive evidence that infants and children are capable of sexual arousal and in some cases even orgasm (see Chapter 9).

The attitude that sexual interaction between adults and children is a criminal act by the adult is not found in all cultures; in fact it is difficult to find another culture in which childhood sexuality has as many taboos as in our society (Ullerstam, 1966, pp. 68–69). Among the Balinese, for example, manipulation of their genitals is used to comfort babies, and there is general delight among adults in stimulating a baby to see him or her respond (Martinson, 1973, p. 15). The ancient Greeks considered it an older man's duty to have sexual relations with boys as a prerequisite for their education to good citizenship.

All sexual relations between an adult and a child are viewed as criminal in the United States, regardless of the degree of force used by the adult.
David White/Black Star

474

All sexual relations between adults and children are viewed as criminal in the United States, even though there are varying degrees of coercion by the adult and the child's reaction may range from strong resistance to enthusiastic cooperation or seduction. When force is used on the child the act is called *rape*. When no physical force is used, the common term is *child molesting*. This term is judgmental and reflects the common assumption in our culture that the child is an unwilling victim even when she or he is cooperative or aggressive. The medical diagnostic term *pedophilia* is commonly used to refer to the "aberration in which the adult individual gains sexual satisfaction from engaging in sexual activities with immature children" (Thorpe, Katz, and Lewis, 1961, p. 321). Sexual activity between an adult male and a boy is commonly known as *pederasty*. *Statutory rape* is the term typically used to describe an adult's sexual relations with an adolescent who is a willing participant but has not reached the legal age of consent. In most states the legal age is eighteen.

Adult-Child Homosexual Contacts   One study of men convicted of sexual activities with boys under the age of twelve found that most of these men were fairly young (average age, thirty-one) and that only 16 percent were married at the time. Most of these men also indicated interest in sexual contacts with adolescent boys (age thirteen to eighteen) and very young girls; some were interested in reaching orgasm with any warm-blooded animal and would use whatever was convenient (Gebhard et al., 1965, pp. 272–297).

The boys who were sexually approached averaged about age ten. In almost half the cases the boys looked upon the offenders as friends; almost one-third were strangers. The boys resisted the sexual overtures in one-fourth to one-third of the cases; however, only 7 percent of the boys reported the matter to the authorities (Gebhard, et al., 1965, pp. 272–297).

The most common form of sexual contact (45 percent of cases) was masturbation — usually performed on, rather than by, the boy. Fellatio occurred in 38 percent of cases, anal intercourse in only 4 percent (Gebhard et al., 1965, pp. 272–297). Even fondling, without fellatio, anal intercourse, or masturbation, can lead to a charge of pederasty or child molesting.

One Saturday afternoon there was two of them, two little boys, I said all right they could come out with me because they'd helped me push my boat down into the water from the shed. A very hot day it was. They went over the side for a swim. They'd no costumes on. . . . And I did, you know, I must admit I did go so far as to forget myself, I laid hands on them. Nothing serious, please don't think that, I didn't attack them or anything of that kind. Only playing about, touching them, that was as far as it went. They didn't object, they didn't complain. . . .

Parker, 1972, p. 70

475

That was why it was such a surprise to me the next week-end. . . . These two plain-clothes policemen . . . asked me exactly what it was had happened . . . and I told them. . . . The police took me to court straight away for it, and I was given six months.

According to a study of self-identified pederasts willing to be interviewed (Rossman, 1973), many pederasts never come to the attention of the law because they tend to have impersonal sex with young male prostitutes when away from home and affectionate nonsexual relationships with boys at home. Most of those who have sexual contacts with boys who are not prostitutes are careful to secure the boy's affection first and become sexually active only as the affection grows and the boy wishes. Most of them claim, "You never really have to seduce a boy. Give him time and he will seduce you" (Rossman, 1973, p. 34)

One study of males convicted of sexual assault against children found that, regardless of the sex of their child victim, the offenders were heterosexual in their adult orientation. The study suggests that homosexuality and homosexual pedophilia may be mutually exclusive and that the adult heterosexual male constitutes a greater risk to the underage child than does the adult homosexual male (Groth and Birnbaum, 1978).

The motivations of the boys who participate in sexual activities with adults are much like adult motives for sexual interaction. Some become involved because of the love they feel for the man or because they are hungry for demonstrations of affection from any adult; others are simply seeking the money or other material gifts that they are often given. Some of these boys enjoy the thrill of doing something forbidden, the adventure of trying something new. Many of them enjoy the sexual contact itself and the sexual satisfaction they get from being masturbated or from having fellatio performed on them (Rossman, 1973).

One study followed for a period of ten to thirty years a small sample of boys who had experience with an older homosexual. It concluded that such involvement on the part of adolescent boys did not have lasting negative effects such as inducing homosexuality or neuroticism in adulthood (Tindall, 1978).

Adult-Child Heterosexual Contacts When an adult male sexually approaches a prepubescent girl the act is commonly called *child molesting.* One common stereotype of the child molester is an old man who is approaching or has reached senility. Statistics do not support this stereotype. In a study of child molesters convicted for heterosexual offenses against girls under age twelve, the offenders averaged thirty-five years of age, with only one-sixth of them over age fifty. Roughly one-third were married at the time of the offense. Although about one-fourth of the men were drunk at the time of the offense, most of the acts were obviously planned in advance (Gebhard et al., 1965, pp. 148–151).

Contrary to general opinion, most of the child molesters were not strangers lurking around a dark corner; over half the offenders were friends or acquaintances of the child. Oral-genital contact occurred in about 16 percent of the cases; intercourse was attempted in only 6 percent of cases, and intromission (insertion of the penis into the vagina) was effected in 2 percent. In a great majority of cases the sexual contact was limited to petting and fondling (Gebhard et al., 1965, pp. 69–73).

Always the same age group, six to eleven; no younger and no older, outside those limits it didn't appeal to me at all. Playing about with them with my hands under their skirts, tickling their bottoms [buttocks], getting them to let me take their knickers [panties] down. . . . I'd sit them on my knee and play with them, and at the same time I was able to masturbate myself without using my hands. Five, ten minutes at the outside, then I got my ejaculation and that was it.

Parker, 1972, pp. 27–28

Most of the heterosexual child molesters were men unable or unwilling to defer gratification until a more suitable sexual partner could be found. Although a few were admittedly amoral, most were moralistic, conservative, and extremely guilt-ridden as a result of their sexual activities with children. However, even the guilt-ridden tended to repeat their acts.

It is difficult to determine the degree to which the young girls encouraged or resisted the sexual advances. Most of the offenders, when interviewed, reported passive cooperation or encouragement on the part of the children; according to the official court records most of the children resisted the sexual advances. (See Table 16.1.) In interpreting these data it is important to keep in mind that a lack of resistance by the child does not necessarily indicate the same degree of complicity in the act that it might in the case of an adult. In any relationship between a child and an adult there is an understanding that the adult is stronger and in a position of authority relative to the child. Compliance by children may occur simply because they have been taught to do as they are told without any backtalk, whether they like it or not (Gebhard et al., 1965, pp. 54–55).

Reactions of Female Children to Adult Sexual Advances   Table 16.1

	Resisted	Passive	Encouraging	Number
According to record	75.4%	8.2%	16.4%	61
According to offender	14.6%	36.9%	48.4%	157

Source: Paul H. Gebhard et al., *Sex Offenders* (New York: Harper & Row, 1965), p. 72. Reprinted by permission of the Institute of Sex Research.

Kinsey and his associates asked a sample of twelve hundred women about prepubescent sexual activities. Twenty-eight percent reported a sexual experience with an adult before age thirteen, but in only 6 percent of the cases could the subject recall that the event was reported to the police. In less than 2 percent of the cases did the women report they were coerced in this childhood encounter, and less than 8 percent collaborated in the sexual activity. The remaining 90 percent were accidentally involved by someone exposing himself to them or unexpectedly fondling or patting their genitals (Gagnon, 1965).

A very large majority of the women reported they had reacted negatively to the experience. Most were simply frightened as they would be if they had seen a spider; a few had extreme negative reactions such as hysteria or vomiting; some reacted positively with sexual arousal up to and including orgasm. Of the 333 women reporting sexual contacts with adults in their childhood, only 3 had severely damaged adult lives that they attributed to their early sexual experience (Gagnon, 1965).

From the data gathered by Kinsey and his associates it is estimated that between 20 and 25 percent of girls reared in a middle-class environment experience sexual interaction with an adult while they are still children. Most of these experiences involve no more than exhibition or genital touching.

A woman in her late twenties recalls: It was about the time I was in the third grade that I sort of got raped. My brother and I used to chase lizards near the beach every afternoon, and this one afternoon a man helped us look for lizards. At least at that time I thought of him as a man, but I guess he was only seventeen years old or so. Anyway, he kept pointing out farther-away places for us to look for lizards. Finally, we got close to a cave on the beach and he said there were some good rocks in there. When we got in he pulled out a knife and said he would kill us if we cried or called out or anything. He stripped off my brother's clothes and tied him up. Then he stripped off my clothes and laid them aside very carefully. He kissed me and put his finger in my vagina and in my anus. He didn't ever take his penis out or take off his clothes or really try to have sex with me. Most of all he was interested in my ruffled cotton panties and held them up to his face and caressed them. We were both scared, but we never told anyone about it because he said he would kill us if we did.

From the authors' files

Girls in a lower-class environment are exposed to a higher risk, including offenses of a more intimate sexual nature, such as intercourse and oral-genital contact. Most of these incidents are not reported to the police. Given the structure of our legal system, this may be a wise decision. The initial interrogation by authorities and the adversary proceedings of the courtroom may be more traumatic for the child than was the sexual contact, and may indelibly imprint on his or her mind an event that might otherwise be quickly forgotten (Gagnon, 1965).

Child Sexuality Organizations   The actual incidence of child-adult sexual contact is unknown. Most people in our society, including most of the adult participants in such interactions, feel that child-adult sex is shameful and guilt-provoking. However, there are a few small organizations dedicated to the promotion of childhood sexuality, and specifically child-adult sexual interaction. For example, the Rene Gunyon Society of Los Angeles works to bring about decriminalization of child-adult sexuality; their slogan is "Sex by age eight, or else it's too late!" Similarly, the Better Life organization wishes to legalize and promote child-adult contacts.

Better Life is an educational service organization serving the interests of pedophiles and children's sexual rights worldwide. For the record, a pedophile is an adult who enters into emotional/physical relationships with children under the age of 15 or 16.

Wright, 1975, np

Incest

Incest is sexual relations between individuals who are too closely related to contract a legal marriage. Although some type of incest taboo is found in virtually every known society, the definition of which relatives are included within the taboo varies from society to society. In some societies the definition of taboo relatives extends far beyond blood kin and may include so many persons that a given individual may find it extremely difficult to find any potential marriage partner (Ford and Beach, 1951, p. 112). Even within the United States the definition of incest varies from state to state, as do the penalties for it. In some states the definition includes cousins, uncles, aunts, and step-parents. Penalties for violating laws prohibiting incest range from a five-hundred-dollar fine and/or a six-month jail term to fifty years' imprisonment (Cavallin, 1973). In addition, marriage to someone close — such as a godparent or an in-law — may be socially unacceptable though not illegal.

Convicted Incest Offenders

Studies of incest in the United States are based mostly on interviews with people institutionalized after arrest and conviction for incest. This methodology imposes severe limits on the findings since they cannot be generalized to the noninstitutionalized population. Undoubtedly many

479

instances of incest are unreported, and even those that are discovered among the higher social classes are more likely to be handled quietly within the family without intervention by legal authorities. Social scientists know very little about the participants in incest who have not come to the attention of the law (Sagarin and MacNamara, 1970, pp. 167–168). And yet it has been estimated that there are 25 million incest victims in the United States (*Sexuality Today*, July 3, 1978).

Because of the overrepresentation of the lower social classes among those arrested and convicted for incestuous activities, it is not a surprise that studies of convicted incest offenders report that they come from a dependent or marginal socioeconomic group (Weinberg, 1955, p. 52; Gebhard et al., 1965, pp. 207–271). The most exhaustive study of reported incest offenders concluded that incest is symptomatic of a serious family disorganization (Weinberg, 1955, pp. 49–110). In some of the cases, family members were so interdependent that the children found it difficult to establish or sustain extrafamilial relationships. In other cases the family was so loosely organized that the children never learned the importance of sexual restraints. The incestuous fathers and brothers were mostly unskilled workers with little education (five to six years average) and below-normal intelligence. Many of the incestuous fathers were widowed, separated, or sexually rejected by their wives (Weinberg, 1955, pp. 49–110).

Types of Incest

Of the cases of incest that reach the courts, 40 percent are father-daughter, 40 percent are stepfather-daughter, 18 percent are sibling, and the remaining 2 percent are mother-son, mother-daughter, and father-son (*Ob-Gyn News*, May 1, 1977). The father usually initiates the sexual relationship with the daughter, although in many cases the daughter is a willing participant. Father-daughter incest is usually detected when the daughter tires of the relationship or gets angry at the father and reports it (Weinberg, 1955, pp. 121–156).

Sibling incest between brother and sister who are in their early teens or younger is the most frequent type, but is rarely reported. It is seldom discovered and, when discovered, is usually not treated as a serious matter. Sibling incest among older participants is sometimes reported, usually by the female. Brother-sister incest occurs most often in families in which the children are given considerable sexual freedom, in which one of the participants cannot find acceptable sexual partners outside the family because of personal inadequacies and social isolation, or in which the brothers and sisters share the same bedroom. Incestuous sisters are more likely to be willing participants or even sexual aggressors than are incestuous daughters (Weinberg, 1955, p. 148).

480

Incidence of Incest

Morton Hunt's recent national survey gives some idea of the incidence and types of incestuous activities in the United States. (For a discussion of Hunt's methodology see the appendix.) About 15 percent of respondents indicated some sexual contact with relatives, including petting as well as coitus. (See Table 16.2.) Most of this contact was with siblings or cousins; rarely was it between parent and child. (See Table 16.3.) Much of this

Percentage Who Ever Had Any Sexual Contact With Relatives*   Table 16.2

	Under 35	35 and over
Males	18.9	13.4
Females	12.6	11.3

* Corrected to allow for experience by half of nonrespondents.

Source: Reprinted with permission of Playboy Press. From *Sexual Behavior in the 1970's*, p. 342, by Morton Hunt. Copyright © 1974 by Morton Hunt.

Percentage Who Ever Had Any Sexual Contact with Relatives: Total National Sample, by Sex and Relationship of Partner   Table 16.3

Had Incestuous Contact with:	Relationship	Males	Females
Nuclear	Father	0	0.5
family	Mother	0	0
	Son	0	*
	Daughter	*	0
	Brother	*	3.6
	Sister	3.8	0.7
Other	Uncle	*	0.6
close	Aunt	*	0
relatives	Nephew	0	0
	Niece	*	0
	Grandfather	0	*
	Grandmother	0	0
Marginally	Male cousin	*	3.2
consanguineous	Female cousin	9.2	*
and	Brother-in-law	0	*
nonconsanguineous	Sister-in-law	*	0
relatives	Stepfather	0	*
	Stepmother	0	0

* Less than 0.5 percent.

Source: Reprinted with permission of Playboy Press. From *Sexual Behavior in the 1970's*, p. 344, by Morton Hunt. Copyright © 1974 by Morton Hunt.

Percentage Who Ever Had Heterosexual Coitus with Relatives by Sex and by Relationship of Partner, Total National Sample **Table 16.4**

Had coitus with:	Males	Females
Sister	1.5	
Aunt	*	
Niece	*	
Sister-in-law	*	
Female cousin	3.9	
Brother		0.8
Uncle		*
Stepfather		*
Male cousin		0.5

* Less than 0.5 percent.

Source: Reprinted with permission of Playboy Press. From *Sexual Behavior in the 1970's*, p. 346, by Morton Hunt. Copyright © 1974 by Morton Hunt.

incestuous contact was in the nature of childhood sex play, as evidenced by the fact that one-third of the males and nearly half the females had these experiences before age twelve. Over a quarter of the males and over half the females went no further than light petting in these activities (Hunt, 1974, pp. 336–345).

Omitting incestuous contacts involving petting, and considering only coital activity, Hunt found about 7 percent of his sample reported coitus with relatives. This occurred mostly between siblings or between cousins. (See Table 16.4.) A woman in her forties recalls:

Looking in my brother's room I found him asleep also, but the covers of his bed had fallen to one side, and I could see my brother lying down, wearing nothing but an undershirt which was worked up above his waist leaving the rest of his body exposed. I stood for about 20 minutes just looking at his fairly well-developed penis and testicles. . . . My brother actually possessed more than my husband. . . . I removed my night clothes, went into bed with him and snuggled up close, molding my body with his. I must have dozed off for when I awoke it was four o'clock. My brother had changed his position and was now facing me. He was awake and also sexually excited. Without any warning I forced one leg under him and the other over him, sliding his penis into me. Although I had to help him all the way to his release he completed the act beautifully, and we had sexual intercourse two more times that day.

Greenwald and Greenwald, 1973, p. 236

In contradiction to the findings of studies based on institutionalized incest offenders, Hunt found incestuous acts are more common among

482

better-educated and white-collar people than among the blue-collar population or those who had not attended college (Hunt, 1974, pp. 345–350).

Incest in Other Cultures

Although some kind of incest taboos are found in almost every culture, the definitions of incest are often quite different from our own. In the Trobriand Islands, for example, a girl who has intercourse with her mother's brother is committing incest, but if she has intercourse with her father she is not (Ramey, 1979). Many societies permit violation of their incest taboos by particular persons or on particular occasions. For example, among certain Polynesian tribes where incest is subject to severe sanctions, sexual intercourse with otherwise forbidden relatives forms part of a ceremony in religious festivals (Ullerstam, 1966, p. 44). Among Egyptians, sibling marriage was common among the royalty in the first century A.D., and later spread to some segments of the rest of the population (Cavallin, 1973, p. 19). Even where sanctions are severe and incest is not permitted for any persons under any circumstances, incest occurs. For example, although incest was prohibited among the Greeks and Romans, Caligula had sexual relations with his three sisters and Nero with his mother (Cavallin, 1973, p. 19).

The Incest Taboo

The incest taboo is very strong; the mere mention of incest in our society today evokes expressions of disgust and horror among most persons. Members of the scientific community advance many arguments for the necessity for an incest taboo: incest prohibitions are instinctive, incest taboos are necessary to maintain family structures, or incestuous breeding causes biological degeneration (Meiselman, 1978). Examination of these arguments for incest taboos reveals a lack of solid foundation for them.

Apparently there is no instinctive wish for incest and no instinctive prohibition against it. There is abundant evidence that a child has sexual desires and when presented with the opportunity for sexual contact within the family, may participate quite willingly. Children have no natural revulsion to incest, but are taught this as they grow older (Bagley, 1968, p. 514).

Genetic Inbreeding A prevalent argument is that incest will cause a deterioration of genetic quality by increasing sickliness, degeneracy, idiocy, and sterility. Experiments of inbreeding among animals and studies of children born of incestuous relationships largely contradict this claim. Inbreeding intensifies the inheritance of traits, both good and bad, but the

483

risk of defective offspring from recessive hereditary diseases is negligible if the disease has not previously manifested itself in the family (Ullerstam, 1966, pp. 48–49; Bagley, 1968, p. 21).

Intrafamily Rivalry The most forceful argument against incest is that it will create situations of intense rivalry that will disrupt the family structure and destroy its effectiveness in carrying out its basic functions. This argument is based on the assumption that sexual jealousy and conflict are a necessary result of multiple sexual involvements within the family group. Our society's accepted attitudes toward sexual possessiveness and sexual jealousy lead most persons to conclude that both father and son or both mother and daughter could not have a sexual relationship with the same family member without creating serious interpersonal problems. This assumption has been challenged by some who study relationships and the management of sexual jealousy within group marriages. The Constantines conclude that the difficulties concomitant with multiple sexual relations are not inevitable; where multiple relations are permitted, the energy consumed in resolving interpersonal issues is less than the energy that otherwise would have been spent in suppression or avoidance of sexual attraction (Constantine and Constantine, 1973, pp. 218–227).

One study found that when incest also involves abuse, the incest experience is often negatively perceived by the participants. But when incest is entered into with mutual consent, it is likely to be perceived as a positive experience. Data from the study indicate that whenever incest led to isolation of the incestuous family members, they felt some guilt and negativity. In contrast, whenever the participants felt they had the support of their family, their experience was generally quite positive (Ramey, 1979).

Exhibitionism

An *exhibitionist* is a person who exposes his or her sexual organs to the opposite sex in situations defined as socially inappropriate and when the exposure is, at least in part, for the purpose of his or her own sexual arousal and gratification. This definition rules out instances in which the exposure is seen as appropriate, such as in petting, coitus, or at nudist camps.

This definition differs from the more general meaning given it by common usage. Quite often people will use the word *exhibitionist* to refer to anyone who enjoys showing off his or her body and being admired for its attractiveness. By this definition, many people who go to nude beaches, 484 public beaches, or even cocktail lounges could be called exhibitionists because their manner of dress (or degree of undress) is designed to call attention to the sexual attractiveness of their bodies. This exhibition of the body is distinguished from illegal exhibitionism because of its motivation and its appropriateness; it is motivated by a desire to attract the attention of potential sex partners, and it is done in a manner that society considers reasonably appropriate for the situation. This is in contrast to the exhibitionist, whose genital exposure is highly inappropriate — as on a public street or in a subway — and whose motive is the arousal and, in some cases, orgasm that results from the exposure. Masturbation often accompanies or follows the exposure when the act of exposing does not itself produce orgasm.

Incidence

Among people arrested for sexual offenses, 35 percent of all arrests are for exhibitionism (Ellis and Brancale, 1956; Allen, 1969, p. 185). Virtually all people arrested for exhibitionism are males, although a few cases of female exhibitionism are reported in the psychiatric literature. Convicted exhibitionists are fairly young, with an average age of thirty for the first offense. Less than one-third are married, and many are judged to have difficulties in relating to members of the opposite sex (Gebhard et al., 1965, pp. 394–399). Most are rated as emotionally immature, with 63 percent evaluated as having a severe emotional disturbance (Ellis and Brancale, 1956, pp. 49 and 59).

Nearly all exhibitionists expose themselves to strangers — sometimes very young or adolescent girls, sometimes women. The great majority (86 percent) of instances of exhibitionism are obviously premeditated, with only a few the result of impulse or drunkenness (Gebhard et al., 1965, p. 395).

Response of Victims

Often the victims of exhibitionists are shocked or frightened by the experience. A young girl may be horrified if she has never seen an adult erect penis or if she has been taught that genitals are disgusting objects to be kept hidden. A woman may share some of these reactions and in addition may fear she is in danger of being raped or in some way harmed by the man who is exposing himself to her.

I was walking home just minding my own business, just concerned about getting home . . . and I come up to this corner and I had to stop because there was this car that was going really slow and he was way over on the right hand side. I mean,

This excerpt from "Meaning and Process in Erotic

485

apparently it looked like he was going to make a right hand turn. And I had to stop for him. . . . And, uhm, I just stood there and I waited for him to pass [so] I could be on my way. . . . I naturally just looked in his window and he was masturbating and he looked up at me and he looked, really, he was drooling . . . and really nasty looking . . . and I really felt threatened . . . I didn't like it happening.

Offensiveness: An Expose of Exposees" by Sharon K. Davis and Philip W. Davis is reprinted from *Urban Life and Culture*, Vol. 5, no. 3 (October 1976), pp. 377–396, by permission of the publisher, Sage Publications, Inc.

He ended up turning left, he was way over on the right hand side and he ended up turning left. And I kept walking and it started bothering me. And I was thinking, you know, I didn't see that, you know, I'm just going to go home and close the door and it'll all be gone, it won't be there any more. And then . . . he came around the second time. I plainly saw him and I got really paranoid. . . . I was turning to go down a long block and he came by very slow again. He turned left and I could see his hand movements. . . . (he) sort of had his face pressed up towards the window just glaring at me. And his eyes were really wet looking. It made me paranoid because I didn't know if he knew me and if he knew that I lived by myself.

I don't know where his head was at so I don't know if he was desperate enough to drive down an alley and grab some little kid and pull him in the car. . . . Maybe he was sick, maybe this was the only way he could get his jollies. . . . Maybe he never bothered anybody. . . . I think there's always going to be a certain amount of people that are lewd, crude, and outrageous. There's nothing you can do with them. I was offended. I felt that I shouldn't have to be exposed to it.

Fears of rape or harm are largely unfounded, since the exhibitionist rarely is violent or aggressive, and he is often at some distance from his victim. But although he does not want to harm her physically, he usually hopes to see some reaction of shock or fright and is disappointed if he makes only a slight impression:

Middle aged women, smartly dressed, no one else. Someone who reminds me of my mother, a doctor said once, he pointed that out to me, and I think that might be right, that I'm still trying to insult her. No, it's not a prelude to a sexual assault, there's never anything like that in my mind. Just to shock. If a woman looks disgusted and turns away, then I'm satisfied. A woman smiled at me once and came towards me instead; I ran away from her as hard as I could. . . . I can't tell you why I do it; when it's happening I'm not conscious of anything except this feeling of being contemptuous towards women and wanting to give one a shock.

Parker, 1972, pp. 218–219

If the female reacts strongly, he may construe this as a compliment to his virility, believing that his large penis caused her reaction (Chesser, 1971, pp. 225–235).

Exhibitionists are generally quiet, submissive people who do not want to hurt anyone. And there is nothing inherently harmful in seeing another individual's genitals if one chooses to do so. But in exhibitionism the element of choice is taken away from the victim, and she or he is unwillingly used by the exhibitionist for his or her sexual stimulation and gratification. We would all like protection from being sexually used without our consent. Yet imprisonment is a harsh penalty for a person who has assaulted neither person nor property.

Nudity

The rationale for generally prohibiting public nudity in our society is the same as that for prohibiting exhibitionism: the display of one's genitals to another individual without his or her consent. However, in the past, places have been set aside for social nudism, a practice by which adults and sometimes children mutually consent to congregate without clothes.

Although organized social nudism is not a new phenomenon, it has always been limited in the United States to private, secluded settings. Today the trend is toward less organization of nudity and more doffing of clothes in relatively public settings. This new public nudity can result in legal and social stigmatization of the participants and has stimulated public debate. (See Selection 16.1.)

Nudist Camps

Nudist camps are generally governed by very strict rules of conduct. Singles are either forbidden or discouraged from joining, and new members and visitors are carefully screened. Contrary to what one might imagine, sexual arousal at nudist camps is reportedly rare, partly due to the atmosphere in most camps, which is self-consciously asexual and perhaps prudish by most nonnudist standards. Sexual suggestiveness is quite restricted, and accentuation of the body is frowned upon, as is making inviting remarks or sitting with the legs spread. Telling dirty jokes is discouraged, and body contact is usually taboo. In most nudist camps in the United States, alcoholic beverages are forbidden, although this is not generally true in other countries (Weinberg, 1971).

As a group, nudists are fairly heterogeneous. Their attitudes with respect to sex, politics, and religion vary from very conservative to very liberal. Contrary to what is generally imagined, there is also a wide assortment of body builds and degrees of physical attractiveness. Psychologically, nudists exhibit comparatively sound mental health with above-average levels of self-esteem and security. From an analysis of the nature and extent of their sexual practices, nudists appear to be very

487

sexually active, with higher than average reported participation in premarital and extramarital sex, masturbation, oral-genital contact, and
group sexual behavior. It appears that an interest in social nudism is
related to an interest in sensuality (DeMartino, 1969).

About 25 percent of the respondents in one study report being more
interested in sexual relations with their spouse as a result of their experience with social nudism, and about 33 percent report that their sexual
happiness in life has increased to some extent. There is also some increase
in desire for extramarital sex relations reported by some nudists, although
the majority report no involvement or no change (Hartman and Fithian,
1971).

In most cases men learn of nudism from magazines or from friends, and
they then convince their wives to try it. Most couples go to nudist gatherings the first time largely out of curiosity, although the man's curiosity is
usually more specifically sexual. Many of the men say they thought it
would be interesting to see lots of nude girls (Weinberg, 1971).

Most people are surprised, upon first visiting a nudist camp, to find that
they readily adjust to nudity and experience little or no self-consciousness
without their clothes in this situation. This is partly facilitated by unwritten rules that make it improper to stare at anyone's body (Weinberg,
1971).

The effects of practicing social nudism for a couple are not easy to
gauge because most studies of nudists do not include the dropouts who
felt it was a negative experience. It is not surprising, therefore, that most
nudists report that nudism is a positive experience. Among the reasons
reported for participation in social nudism are relaxation and sociability:
many nudists speak of a sense of closeness and family with their fellow
nudists that they rarely find with their other friends. Probably the sharing
in a nonconforming and disapproved activity is a factor in fostering their
togetherness (Weinberg, 1971; Hartman and Fithian, 1971).

Practicing social nudism is not accepted in most social circles. The
majority of nudists keep their nudity secret because they fear the social
consequences if it were known. About 25 percent of the respondents in
one study report they were afraid of occupational reprisals if their employers knew of their activities. Because of the stigmatization of nudists
by many others in society, it is not surprising that most nudists, like
others who violate sexual taboos, lead something of a double life and feel
isolated from much of the rest of society (Weinberg, 1971).

Nudity on the Beach

Nudity is permitted in the United States at some public beaches that are
relatively inaccessible and out of view. Because these beaches are open to
the public, rather than private like nudist camps, they cannot maintain the

488

same type of rules for proper conduct. Body contact or displays of affection are not forbidden at these beaches, but are not often encountered. Drinking alcoholic beverages or smoking marijuana, while illegal at most beaches, may sometimes be seen on nude beaches, but intoxication is very rare.

Public Nudity: Does It Threaten Public Morals?

Selection 16.1

Yes / Jaquie Davison

When there were only two people in the Garden of Eden, they felt the need to cover themselves and made fig-leaf aprons.

San Diego Evening Tribune,
December 6, 1974, p. 3

God did not feel that fig leaves were sufficient, so he made them clothes of animal skins.

With public nudity, the people of our society would be narrow-mindedly consumed with thoughts of sex. Without public nudity, our minds can reach out to spiritual, intellectual and cultural ideas.

When I opposed legalization of Black's Beach last year, a young man said to me:

"You're wrong, Mrs. Davison. Those people have the right to go nude at Black's Beach if they like." He spoke to me of personal rights and free agency.

A week later he said:

"Mrs. Davison, you're right. I went to Black's Beach to see for myself. When a boy and a girl at the beach rub suntan oil on each other, there is always a scrap of material to stop your hands in certain areas. At Black's Beach there is nothing to stop your hands and the things I saw happening there should be reserved only for the bedroom."

Throughout history, cheap money-makers have capitalized on the fact that men are instinctively, sexually aroused by sight of the nude female body. A gyrating, nude dancer attracts men to the cocktail lounges, where their prurient natures are stimulated. Therefore they sit longer and drink more.

Nudity is the prime mover of sex magazines. One "7-11" store manager told me that sex magazines are a $500-a-month business for him, so he doesn't want to hide them under the counter.

It is interesting to note that most nude scenes in movies pertain to premarital, extramarital and promiscuous behavior.

Public nudity stimulates our sexual desires which must be restrained   Last year a man was picked up in San Diego and charged with child molesting. He had in his possession full-color magazines of nude young girls from age 3 or 4 to early teens.

I went to the police department to see the books. They were like other nude magazines except the models were children. The man would show the pictures to little girls, then molest them.

The natural instinct to cover oneself goes back to the time of Adam and Eve, but that natural instinct is being broken down by the public school system in San Diego County.

My daughter fretted all summer in 1973 about going to junior high. She dreaded going because there is no privacy in the shower room.

My older son said he had never had privacy in the showers either and that you do get used to it although, when he first had to shower in front of others, he hated it and was sick a whole week so he wouldn't have to go to school.

Don't our children have the right to privacy of their bodies?

Because of good law enforcement in our area here, we are not exposed to blatant displays of public nudity, but we have another problem that does not fall under the jurisdiction of the law. That is, near-nudity.

It is appalling to see so many junior and high school girls wearing shorts and halter tops. The sad thing about it all is that they think it is attractive. They just don't know what it does to the minds of men looking on.

Men are stimulated sexually by the near-nude female body. Many good men will not admit this to their wives or the women they love, but they talk about it to each other.

In San Diego, rape is one of the fastest-growing violent crimes, and it seems to be more prevalent along the beach areas where young women wear nearly nothing.

We must put our sexual desires into some framework of restraint and it is much easier to do if we are not constantly being exposed to sexual stimuli.   490

Women have always inspired the higher and finer morals and ideals, yet it seems that someone has left the door to immorality open. Now it is up to us to close that door and return this country to "one nation under God."

It might well be remembered that the first rule for a Communist revolution is: "Corrupt the young. Get them interested in sex. Make them superficial. Destroy their ruggedness."

No / David Irving

America is currently undergoing a vast social change regarding public acceptance of nudity.

For the past century, public (and even private) nudity has been a big no-no. In the last few years there has been an increasing amount of nudity in movies, in magazines and on the beaches.

The result has not been, and will not be, an immediate bacchanalian orgy, for nudity itself is not really erotic.

It is only by forbidding nudity, by treating certain portions of the body as both mysterious and "dirty," by creating a curiosity where none should exist that we make the nude body (or the thought of it) so sexually stimulating.

Reverse the process, make nudity commonplace and acceptable, and the erotic stimulation disappears. (The truth of that came out sharply to me the day I was on Black's Beach talking with several nude friends — and caught myself eyeing the girls who walked by in bikinis. There's no question about it, a little bit of clothing is a lot sexier than no clothing at all.)

The bathing suit has had a very short history as it was not invented until the late 1800s. For thousands of years before that, whenever people wanted to go swimming, they did so in the nude.

We should revert to the age-old custom and discard the bathing suit, a rather ridiculous piece of clothing. In the water it hampers your swimming; out of the water it quickly becomes cold, clammy and a magnet for sand; while sunbathing it's only a useless covering which keeps you from getting an even tan.

Swimming and sunbathing nude bring a sense of freedom and relaxation. By shedding clothing and inhibitions, we shed, at least temporarily, the worries and frustrations of a too hectic life.

For the past few years a growing multitude of people of all ages, including many families, has thronged to Black's Beach, most of them to enjoy it in the nude. This summer the crowds ran in excess of 10,000 on a typical weekend day.

Yet Black's Beach is no den of iniquity.

The police officers and lifeguards who patrol the beaches report that there are fewer problems on Black's Beach than on the other beaches in the city. The crowds are mellower, there is less trouble with drugs and alcohol, there are fewer fights or disturbances.

491

Despite the claims of critics, who seem to know all about the beach without ever going there themselves, there's no sexual activity taking place on Black's Beach. Clearly there's no threat to public morals here.

Rather than being a threat, an increase in and greater acceptance of public nudity would have a beneficial effect on public morals and mental health.

Numerous psychological studies have revealed that sex offenders — rapists, child molesters, etc. — generally have had sexually repressive childhoods and experiences. A relaxed public attitude and casualness with respect to nudity (and sex in general) would go a long way toward reducing the incidence of such perversions and the resulting violent crime against innocent individuals.

In addition, most otherwise well-adjusted people today have an excessive fear concerning the attractiveness of their own body. General public nudity, as at Black's Beach, eliminates these ridiculous insecurities as people learn that almost everyone, he or she included, is about average in looks. Without clothing, the concentration on physical attractiveness is actually reduced. You find yourself focusing on the individual and his or her personality once the lure, mystery and eroticism of the clothing and what it's hiding are gone.

A relaxed public attitude with respect to nudity would be healthful Much has been made about the supposedly harmful effects public nudity would have on children, yet they are the ones who would be least bothered by it.

Children are not born with a sense of shame about the human body nor inhibitions about exposing it. They acquire these traits only through a repression of their natural feelings by a society that is confused and afraid of its own sexuality.

Confronted with public nudity, children easily respond with a natural instinct of seeing nothing unusual in it. They don't associate nudity with sexuality nor place a heavy sexual tension on exposure of the body — and they are better off not learning to make such associations.

Voyeurism

Voyeurism, or *peeping-Tomism,* means obtaining sexual gratification from looking at the bodies, sex organs, or sex acts of other persons. In contrast to other people who may enjoy looking at naked bodies, voyeurs obtain all their sexual satisfaction from the act of peeping and the masturbation that usually accompanies it.

The term *peeping Tom* comes from the legend of Lady Godiva. When her husband proposed to raise his tenants' taxes in eleventh-century Mercia (part of what is now England), Lady Godiva rode through the town naked in protest, covered only by her long hair. Out of respect, all the towns-   492

people shut themselves in their houses and did not look at her, except for one man, Tom of Coventry. As punishment for his peeping, Tom was struck blind by a miracle.

The Law

Voyeurism may in some instances be labeled a criminal act and in other instances be accepted as normal behavior. Pleasure in looking at the bodies of others, particularly those of the opposite sex, is socially accepted. Beauty contests, striptease shows, and a great deal of commercial pornography cater to the desire for sexual arousal from looking. Legal penalties are imposed not for watching others but for the surreptitious watching of people in the privacy of their own homes, cars, or hotel rooms. The voyeur can be distinguished from the average man- or woman-watcher in our society, not only by a willingness to violate another's privacy, but also by a willingness to run risks while doing so. In pursuit of a good view a peeping Tom may have to scale fences, cling to narrow window ledges, patiently wait for hours, or run from irate neighbors and police officers. In fact it is the very element of danger and risk that is sexually exciting to the peeping Tom. One might suppose that a nudist camp would be absolute heaven for a peeper, but this is not so because the element of risk and forbiddenness is missing in an environment where observation of nude bodies is acceptable. The peeper wants to see what he has no right to see, and so must remain outside and surreptitiously peep in (Sagarin, 1973).

Characteristics of Voyeurs

Convicted voyeurs are almost invariably males. Peeping Toms almost never watch women they know well; it is extremely rare to find them peeping at a girl friend, relative, or spouse. Apparently this is not a precaution against being recognized, but instead is a preference for the novelty and forbidden quality of seeing a stranger (Gebhard et al., 1965, p. 360).

Convicted peepers tend to be young, twenty-six years old on the average. Slightly less than half have ever been married. Habitual peepers typically have a relatively stunted heterosexual development; for instance, few have petted, and most attempt their first coitus at a later age than most other males (Gebhard et al., 1965, pp. 368–379; Smith, 1976).

Peepers are not always harmless individuals; some commit rape or burglary. Rape is more common among habitual than occasional peepers. Most voyeurs are always on the outside looking in, hoping to observe without detection. But those who enter dwellings in order to peep or who deliberately try to attract the woman's attention are more likely to try rape than the others (Gebhard et al., 1965, pp. 375–378).

Not only are persons usually frightened when they discover they are the object of a peeper's attention, but they rightfully resent the invasion of their privacy. But in protecting our privacy, our legal processes often do more harm to the peeper than is warranted by the harm he has done to society or his victims.

A typical example is that of a clergyman, age forty-six, who was caught spying on a nudist colony through binoculars. . . . He was a married man with two teenage children and even if the incident had been kept a close family secret the shame he felt was unbearable. . . . In despair he attempted suicide. It might have been kinder to let him succeed. He left the Church and found employment in an East End hostel, but although he made heroic efforts to live down the scandal his family relationships were irretrievably ruined.

Chesser, 1971, p. 226

494

Sex in Public

In our society, norms prescribe that sexual interaction should take place in private, away from the view of audiences that do not give consent to the observation of sexual interaction. A certain amount of sexual contact occurs in public places: people kiss and neck in darkened movie theaters or drive-ins, or make love in deserted parks, beaches, or buildings. It is difficult to specify exactly when a romantic encounter in public becomes a sexual one, since the laws and norms of our society do not proscribe holding hands or kissing on the mouth in public. Although the topic of public sex is a potentially interesting one for sociological analysis, little has been done in the area; a notable exception is Laud Humphreys's *Tearoom Trade: Impersonal Sex in Public Places.*

In *Tearoom Trade,* Humphreys describes the sexual interaction between males in public rest rooms, or "tearooms," and examines the social characteristics of the participants. (See Chapter 3.) His methods have been the subject of much ethical controversy (see the appendix), but his findings have undeniable interest.

There are a variety of roles played in tearoom encounters, from the insertee and insertor in fellatio to the police who may enter and break up the action. Humphreys took notes on typical tearoom encounters.

Y was very tough looking . . . (is he a hustler, a tough, or a straight?) He went into second stall, unzipped pants and began to masturbate with his back to me. I went to door (which was stuck open with the humidity) and peered out. X moved swiftly, and Y turned around to facilitate X's masturbating him . . . (Now we can identify some players, but which is the insertee and which is the insertor?)

X sucked Y, after unfastening his pants and pulling them down so that his stomach, pubic hair, and testicles were exposed, for about five minutes (This is the payoff, X is the insertee — Y the insertor).

Humphreys, 1975, p. 53

By noting participants' license plates and obtaining their home addresses by tracing their cars, Humphreys went to their homes a year later and interviewed them as part of another social science project. He found that the majority of participants were married and living with their wives (54 percent). He subdivided his total sample into types: bisexuals, gays, closet homosexuals, and "trade" — men who defined themselves as heterosexuals because they played only the insertor role, not the insertee.

Humphreys argues that the tearooms do not really qualify as public places when they are being used for sexual purposes, because the participants employ a system of observation and signaling that breaks up the action upon the approach of a minor, a nonparticipating adult, or a police officer in uniform. However, his conclusions are not shared by most legislative bodies: sexual or exhibitionist interaction is punishable in all

495

states under either felony or misdemeanor statutes such as those prohibiting lewd conduct or solicitation.

Sex with Violence

Sex with violence ranges from sex with extreme force, to sex with wanted violence, to boisterous sexual interaction with consent. However, the two major types of sexuality that involve violence are forcible rape and sadomasochism.

Sadomasochism

Sexual sadism is obtaining sexual pleasure from pain inflicted upon another person; *sexual masochism* is obtaining sexual pleasure from having pain inflicted upon oneself. The two terms are often linked to form the one word, *sadomasochism,* because it is generally believed that persons who are sexually stimulated by one activity will also be stimulated by the other (Moore, 1969).

The work *sadism* is derived from the name of the French author, the Marquis de Sade, who wrote extensively of his cruel erotic fantasies and exploits. One of his favorite pastimes was to whip women hung from the ceiling while his servant manually stimulated his genitals. The term *masochism* was derived from the name of an Austrian novelist, Leopold von Sacher-Masoch, whose greatest sexual pleasure came from being mistreated by the women in his life (Ullerstam, 1966, p. 85). (See Selection 16.2.)

Sadomasochism is sometimes referred to by the term *algolagnia,* which means that the sexual urge has become linked to the experience of pain or to the rite, punishment, or act of violence that causes pain (Ullerstam, 1966, p. 81). *Algolagnia* is a more accurate term because both *sadism* and *masochism* are fairly common words in our language that are loosely used to refer to many acts having little or no sexual arousal associated with them.

A Sadomasochistic Contract

The following is the agreement that Leopold Baron von Sacher-Masoch drew up and made Madam Wanda von Dunajew sign. It specifies the conditions of his "slavery" to her.

Selection 16.2

Aurelia Sacher-Masoch, *Confessions* de ma vie avec deux portraits (Paris: 1907)
496

"My slave,

"the conditions upon which I accept you as my slave and agree to tolerate you near me are as follows:

"Unconditional surrender of self.

"You have no will besides my own.

"You are a blind fool in my hands, executing all my commands without the least demur. Should you forget that you are a slave and fail to give me absolute obedience in all things I shall be entitled to punish and chastise you entirely at my discretion without any right of complaint on your part.

"Any pleasure and happiness I may grant you must be acknowledged by you as such; I am under no debt or obligation to you. You must be neither son, nor brother nor friend, nothing but a slave lying in the dust. Your body as well as your soul belongs to me, and no matter how much suffering this will cause you, you must subordinate your feelings and emotions to my will.

"I am entitled to practise the worst cruelties upon you and you must bear them without complaint. You must work for me like a slave and if I revel in plenty and nevertheless starve you and trample you underfoot, you must, without a murmur, kiss the foot that is trampling on you.

"I may dismiss you at any time, but you must never leave me without my consent, and should you attempt to escape you authorise me to torture you to death by every imaginable means.

"Apart from me you have nothing. I am your all, your life, your future, your happiness, your misfortune, your joy and your sorrow.

"You must carry out my commands for good or ill, and if I bid you to commit a crime you must become a criminal in order to carry out my will. Your honour belongs to me, like your blood, your spirit, your strength; to you I am mistress of your life and death. Should you at any time feel that you can bear my domination no longer, that my chains are too heavy for you, then you must kill yourself; I shall never liberate you."

Types of Sadomasochism   All sadomasochistic sex involves violence, but the meanings of that violence vary for different participants. Basically there are three identifiable meanings to sadomasochism: violent and forcible sadomasochism involving a real lack of consent, violent and perhaps forcible sadomasochism involving at least initial consent, and a type of sadomasochism that involves mock rather than real or painful violence or force. Any one of these types of sadomasochism may involve heterosexual, homosexual, or perhaps group participants.

Incidence   Although it may be inconceivable to some people that inflicting pain on someone else or being painfully treated by another individual can be pleasurable, it is not an uncommon phenomenon. Kinsey and his associates (1953, pp. 676–678) found that 3 percent of females and 10   497 percent of males reported a definite or frequent erotic response to sado-masochistic stories; over 25 percent of both males and females reported definite or frequent erotic response to being bitten in foreplay. More recent data, presented in Tables 16.5 and 16.6 show some interesting trends. Males are more likely to inflict pain; females are more likely to be the recipients of pain in erotic encounters. Both the inflicting and receiving of pain are much more common in the younger age groups and among the unmarried portion of the sample. Bondage and discipline (being tied and being whipped), described in the literature as classic sadomasochistic activities, are relatively rare in this sample. Most deliberate infliction of pain is by biting; some respondents also report activities such as hitting, scratching, and pinching. A few people report activities that result in pain but are not deliberately done for that purpose, such as unduly hard kissing or anal intercourse (Hunt, 1974, pp. 332–336).

Many of the milder forms of sadistic or masochistic pleasure are quite accepted in our culture, particularly since cruelty need not necessarily be physical. Humiliating sarcasm can hurt more than a physical blow and can be kept up much longer. It is not unusual for some couples to report they have their best lovemaking after a big fight. A similar pattern is found in the animal kingdom. Some monkeys, for example, engage in battle before

Percentage Who Ever Obtained Sexual Pleasure from Inflicting or Receiving Pain, by Age and Sex, Total National Sample **Table 16.5**

	Males		Females	
	Under 35	35 and over	Under 35	35 and over
Inflicting pain	6.2	2.9	2.5	1.5
Receiving pain	3.7	1.0	5.4	3.5

Source: Reprinted by permission of Playboy Press. From *Sexual Behavior in the 1970's*, p. 334, by Morton Hunt. Copyright © 1974 by Morton Hunt.

Percentage Who Ever Obtained Sexual Pleasure from Inflicting or Receiving Pain, by Marital Status, Total National Sample **Table 16.6**

	Males		Females	
	Single	Married	Single	Married
Inflicting pain	10.3	2.5	5.2	*
Receiving pain	6.3	*	10.0	2.1

* Less than 1 percent.

Source: Reprinted by permission of Playboy Press. From *Sexual Behavior in the 1970's*, p. 335, by Morton Hunt. Copyright © 1974 by Morton Hunt.

beginning copulation; at the conclusion of mating the female monkeys may be severely wounded (Chesser, 1971, p. 73).

Sadomasochistic Games Somewhat less prevalent in our society is the deliberate use of sadomasochistic games by couples as a part of their lovemaking rituals. These games are done by mutual consent and are not carried to the point of injury. They may involve such things as enacting a rape scene in which one partner pretends to force the other to submit while she or he vehemently protests this indignity. The use of sadomasochistic games of this type is based on a tacit understanding that the partner playing the sadistic role will not inflict punishment beyond the point at which the other partner's protests and fears become real rather than feigned (Comfort, 1972, pp. 153–160). The following advertisement illustrates the fantasy element in sadomasochism (and also its commercialization):

If you've ever done S&M in a fully equipped game rm., then you know how great the scene can be. But if you're new to the scene, you probably have not & you are missing out. An all-mirrored training center complete with leather wear, toys & heavy equip., & a model who is S&M to show you around present a great opportunity that you should not pass up!

Sadomasochistic activities may involve the use of devices designed for physical restraint or the infliction of pain.
Sepp Seitz/Magnum Photos, Inc.

499

Sadomasochism and Prostitution   Often people (particulary heterosexual males) who enjoy sadomasochistic activities do not have a sexual partner who is similarly inclined, and must seek prostitutes who are willing to cater to their tastes. Houses of prostitution that specialize in a clientele with sadomasochistic preferences may be furnished with torture chambers where the prostitute will not only inflict or receive pain (within limits) as the client prefers, but also feign sexual pleasure while doing so. Similarly, homosexual gathering places such as steam baths may have "S and M" rooms for clients so inclined. People without a partner may use pornography with sadomasochistic themes while masturbating.

Sadomasochistic behavior with a consenting adult partner, a prostitute, or in fantasy during masturbation poses no social problem. The most extreme expression of sadomasochistic preferences, however, may involve the use of force to the point of serious injury or even murder for the satisfaction of erotic needs. In a lust murder, intercourse never takes place; the murderer reaches orgasm as a result of the acts of violence, killing, and mutilation.

Many people may be somewhat sexually aroused by fantasies or behavior involving sadomasochistic activities; but it is relatively rare for a person to be totally dependent on these activities for sexual arousal and release. It is also rare to feel that one must utilize force to satisfy these needs.

Rape

The legal definition of *rape* varies somewhat from state to state in the United States, but most legal definitions include the idea that rape involves sexual intercourse without the consent of the other person, whether the intercourse occurs by force, trickery, or because the other person is not competent to give consent (too young, mentally defective, or unconscious). This definition includes both *forcible rape* — intercourse without consent when the victim has reached the legal age of consent, age eighteen in most states — and *statutory rape,* which is intercourse with a person under the age of consent, both with and without consent. Almost without exception, rape is an act committed by a man — occasionally against another man, but usually against a woman — rather than by a woman.

Incidence   The scientific study of rape and rapists, like the study of other illegal sexual variations, is limited because most of the data are derived from cases that come to the attention of the law. Statistics concerning reported rape cases are especially biased because rape is an underreported crime, probably by as much as 80 percent (Amir, 1971, pp. 27–29). In 1973   500

there were fifty-one thousand reported rapes in the United States, but it is estimated that the true figure is about 276,000 (*Sexuality Today*, October, 1, 1979). In order to make these statistics more meaningful, crime and census statistics for the city of Los Angeles were used to estimate that the chances of a Los Angeles woman meeting a rapist at some time during a thirty-year period is conservatively estimated as about one in ten. (Offir, 1975).

Victims   The victims of reported rape may be of any age, from small infants to very elderly women, but the majority are between fifteen and twenty-five years of age. Most come from lower social classes and most are unmarried. Like their victims, the majority of convicted forcible rapists are between fifteen and twenty-five years of age and from lower social classes. Unlike their victims (about one-fourth of whom are married), more than 40 percent of the rapists are married. About half of rapists have previous arrest records for rape and other offenses (Macdonald, 1971, pp. 49–110). A large majority are judged to be of at least average intelligence, but severely emotionally deprived during their childhoods (Ellis and Brancale, 1965, pp. 26–74). Most of them feel rejected, hurt, and humiliated in their relationships with women. As a result they have strong feelings of hostility. Rape is more an expression of anger and power than of sexual passion (Groth and Birnbaum, 1979). The erotic responses of rapists and nonrapists to audio presentations of sexual scenes have been compared. Rapists show minimal response to nonviolent, mutually enjoyable intercourse scenes, but develop erections when presented with sexual rape scenes. Nonrapists responded erotically to mutual lovemaking but not to rape scenes (Abel et al., 1977).

Degree of Force   Forcible rape is the type that usually comes to mind when one thinks of rape; it is highly feared by most women and regarded as reprehensible by most people. But not all cases labeled as forcible involve the use of physical force sufficient to produce injury. It is debated how much force must be used to label clearly an act of sexual intercourse as forced upon a victim. Many people in our society feel that a virtuous woman should appear to resist intercourse with a man to whom she is not married, even though she may actually desire a sexual relationship with him. Similarly, many men feel they are expected to use both persuasion and coercion in trying to seduce a woman as proof of their virility and masculinity, and as a means of allowing the woman to have pleasure of intercourse while maintaining her appearance of virtue. Because of these notions of appropriate behavior for men and women in their initial sexual encounters, it is not surprising that some misunderstanding can arise as to the precise degree of force and degree of resistance necessary in a given case to label it as rape. For example, the resistance given by a tiny and mild-mannered woman may be felt by her to be a real fight for her life and purity, but her assailant may interpret it as no more than a coy, ritual protestation of virtue.

Date Rape   Sometimes a male may forcibly undress a woman he is dating and make her submit to sexual intercourse, yet not consider his acts as rape. Many of these sexually aggressive males feel that force in securing sexual intercourse is justified if the female suggests by her words, actions, manner of dress, or reputation that she may be sexually accessible, even though she rejects his advances (Kanin, 1967). Approximately 50 percent of a sample of women enrolled at a midwestern university reported being victims of sexual aggression during the academic year (Kanin and Parcell, 1977). It has been estimated that 35 percent of all rapes are of this type, but most of these are not reported to the police (Storaska, 1975).

Rape and the Law   The law reflects the cultural ambiguity concerning the degree of force by the man and the degree of resistance by the woman involved in a case of rape. Compounding this ambiguity is the erroneous opinion of many experts in the field of legal medicine that "rape cannot be perpetrated by one man alone on an adult woman of good health and vigor" (Ploscowe, 1951, p. 210). The older rape laws were greatly influenced by this skepticism and demanded a very high degree of resistance by the woman to a sexual assault before such assault could be termed forcible rape. For example, in the 1938 case of *State of Wisconsin* v. *Hoffman,* the Court took the position that "the voluntary submission by the woman while she has the power to resist, no matter how reluctantly yielded, removes from the act an essential element of the crime of rape" (Ploscowe, 1951, p. 211). In most states, however, the law demands much less resistance on the part of the woman: she must show some physical resistance, but her opposition need only demonstrate that she did not agree to the act of intercourse. For example, in the 1945 case of *Keeton* v. *State of Texas,* a man and woman had been drinking and necking together in a tourist cabin when he demanded intercourse and she refused. A struggle of some kind took place, but after a time the woman ceased resisting and passively submitted. He was found guilty of forcible rape and sentenced to twenty-five years' imprisonment (Ploscowe, 1951, pp. 212–214).

Underreporting   Because of ambiguities in the legal and social definition of forcible rape, the data on rapists and their victims describe people involved in acts in which varying degrees of force were used. Data on rape are further limited by underreporting. Sometimes a woman does not report being raped because she is afraid of the publicity and the stigma associated with being a rape victim, or because she fears that the court will conclude that she did not sufficiently resist the sexual advances, and therefore was not legally raped. Some women do not want to be subjected to the rigorous and sometimes brutal cross-examination by the mostly male personnel in the police or district attorney's office. Because these fears are so common, rape crisis centers have been opened recently in some cities so that rape victims will have a place to go for a sympathetic hearing of their experience and advice on how to proceed with further legal action.

Stages in Rape   In more than half the cases of reported forcible rape, the rapist is a stranger to his victim. In these cases the rape usually follows a discernible pattern of stages (Selkin, 1975). The first stage is locating the victim. Some rapists choose victims vulnerable to attack, such as mentally retarded girls, elderly or handicapped women, or women who are intoxicated. Other rapists, in looking for a defenseless victim, may search out isolated or easily entered locations, such as the run-down section of town where residences are in poor repair and many women live alone.

After locating a likely victim, the next stage is testing her reactions to see if she can be easily intimidated. Rapists may test a woman by making suggestive remarks or by caressing her to determine if she will react fearfully or submissively. Once he knows he has intimidated her, he is assured that she is likely to submit to his demands.

503

In the third, or threat, stage of rape the rapist tells the victim what he wants from her and what he will do to her if she resists; he says he will not harm her if she submits. It is important that he frighten her into submission so that he secures from her controlled behavior that permits him to carry out the sexual act. The fourth stage in rape is the sexual transaction itself. Vaginal intercourse occurs in about half the rape cases, oral and anal intercourse in most of the others (Selkin, 1975, p. 76).

There was a sort of shed, a big shed where you keep garden tools and things. I caught hold of her arm, I said, "Come on, come in here." She started yelling. I said, "Keep quiet, I won't hurt you, I'm not going to hurt you if you keep quiet." She said "What do you want, do you want money, I've got some money in the house . . . I'll give it to you if you want it." I said . . . "I don't want money, you can keep your money. Just keep quiet and then I won't hurt you." There was a lot of room in that shed, a big place it was; all garden tools and a big lawn-mower and a lot of old sacks. I said "Get down on those, you'll be all right, I just want a bit quick and then I'll leave you alone." . . . She didn't make any noise, then I had intercourse with her.

Parker, 1972, p. 264

Avoiding Rape   Authorities on the topic of rape do not agree on the best method a woman should use to deter a would-be rapist. Some authorities recommend loud and violent resistance (Sanders, 1980); others recommend avoidance of struggle (Storaska, 1975). Recent research indicates that the tactic that is effective in deterring a rapist in one situation may not be effective with another man in another place. Rapists who are dominant, aggressive, and highly assaultive usually agree that physical and verbal resistance by the woman only served to excite them more and encourage them to more violence. A few of these men have indicated that passivity, crying, and signs of personal distress would distract them from rape. On the other hand, rapists who had been tentative in their approach reported that signs of weakness and distress served to increase their sexual excitement. In the latter instances women may be more successful in avoiding rape by active rejection and verbal or physical attack (Brodsky, 1976).

If approached by a would-be rapist, women are advised to keep calm, avoid struggling or screaming, and *most important*, treat the rapist as a worthwhile human being. By these tactics she can avoid becoming the target of his hostility against women. The woman should gain his confidence, talk to him, go along with what he wants until she can safely get out of the situation. If it is impossible to avoid sex with him, she should pretend to cooperate, gently fondle his penis and testicles, and then suddenly squeeze one of his testicles (*not* the penis) *very* hard. The pain will send him into instant shock, giving the woman some time to escape (Storaska, 1975).

504

Female Rapists There are some rare instances in which a woman is charged with rape because she has assisted a man in raping another female. In one case a man and his wife were both charged in the rape of their thirteen-year-old niece. The girl reported that her aunt took her by force to her uncle's bedroom, took off her pajamas, and held her down while her uncle raped her (Macdonald, 1971, p. 74). In some states an adult female who entices a boy under age eighteen to have sexual relations can be prosecuted for statutory rape. Forcible rape of a man by a woman is quite rare and often considered physically impossible because some degree of erection in the male is necessary for penile-vaginal intercourse. It is possible, however, for a woman to rape a man, as illustrated in the following passage describing sexual assaults by women of Vakuta (in northwestern Melanesia) on men from other villages:

First they pull off and tear up his pubic leaf, the protection of his modesty and, to a native, the symbol of his manly dignity. Then, by masturbatory practices and exhibitionism, they try to produce an erection in their victim and, when their

Macdonald, 1971, p. 75

505

maneuvers have brought about the desired result, one of them squats over him and inserts his penis into her vagina. After the first ejaculation he may be treated in the same manner by another woman. ... Sometimes these furies rub their genitals against his nose and mouth, and use his fingers and toes, in fact, any projecting part of his body, for lascivious purposes.

Male Victims   Even though a man runs very little risk of being raped by a woman, a man may be raped by another man who desires anal intercourse. Such rapes are not uncommon in men's prisons, where a new prisoner may be raped repeatedly by older prisoners unless he is particularly strong or quickly locates another prisoner who will help him defend himself. Prison rape is as much a part of the power struggle in the institution as it is a sexual release.

Social Consequences of Rape   It is undeniable that rape is an unpleasant experience for most women. Some suffer physical injuries sufficiently severe to require medical attention or hospitalization; a few women are brutally murdered by the rapist. Although the pregnancy rate for rape victims is lower than one would expect, some women do become pregnant as a result of rape. Regardless of the decision these women make with regard to their pregnancy — to bear the child or have an abortion — they risk rejection by their friends and family, as well as personal emotional conflicts.

Even among women who are not physically injured and do not become pregnant, most suffer some emotional trauma, such as feelings of terror or degradation. Most women report that during the incident they were more afraid of dying than anything else. After rape many women report having nightmares and difficulty sleeping as well as loss of appetite (*Medical World News*, March 8, 1976, p. 58) and a decrease in sexual interest and sexual pleasure (*Sexuality Today*, April 2, 1970). In addition to the misery of the rape itself, most women who report it are subjected to the additional humiliation of the legal proceedings and sometimes even rejection by friends and family who regard her as somehow unclean.

Although a man is unlikely to be raped, he may be falsely accused of rape and subsequently imprisoned, castrated, or executed as punishment. Sometimes a woman who willingly enters into a sexual relationship will later accuse the man of rape because she feels guilty or was caught by her father or husband, or because her lover has found someone else and she is angry. In other instances a woman may accuse a man of rape or attempted rape when she has in fact never had any kind of sexual relationship with him. The accused is usually someone fairly close to her, such as a stepfather, teacher, employer, or landlord; her motivation may be the desire for attention or a wish to punish the accused (Macdonald, 1971, pp.

506

207–231). Because proof of rape is difficult to establish, it is sometimes difficult for a man to prove his innocence, as it is sometimes difficult for a woman to prove his guilt in rape cases. The laws in most states, however, protect the innocent man more effectively than the raped woman.

Conclusion

Although apparently simple, the concept of consent to sexual interaction is rather difficult to apply, both legally and socially. Particular areas of difficulty are statutory rape and sadomasochism. Whereas it is clear that forcible rape is within the area of nonconsent, statutory rape frequently involves a willing, sexually active, adolescent female with a male sometimes only slightly older. Similarly, many cases of sadomasochistic contact, such as the much publicized Manson murders and mutilations, are entirely without the consent of the participants. On the other hand, some sadomasochistic adventures proceed as games or staged events — or even as genuinely painful episodes — with the consent of all concerned.

The legal and social definition to this point in time has focused mainly on the issue of ability to consent: legally, a child, an adolescent, an animal, a dead body, someone bound and strapped to the wall (however she or he got there), and an unwilling observer of public sex are all socially powerless or unable to consent. In some cases this inability to consent is a legal fiction; in others it is a true description of the situation. The direction of law and social policy in the future will determine how, if at all, our social institutions will redefine consent to separate genuine issues of consent from those that are legal fictions.

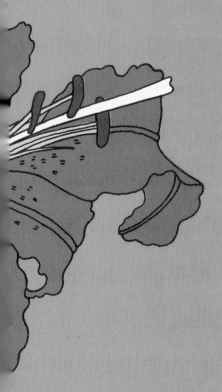

Change is inherent in the nature of reality: all things in nature are in a state of perpetual flux and motion. Sexuality is no exception. Despite an appearance of equilibrium, all societies and individuals are at all times undergoing a continual process of change.

However, societies and individuals differ in the way they *define* change and in the extent to which they *sanction* change. For example, in many traditional societies change is perceived as threatening and negative, and social groups and individuals are encouraged to cling to the status quo. Today, change is accepted to a degree unparalleled in previous history. Concepts such as "growth" and "movement" are not only seen as tolerable; they are glorified by some groups as good and right, in and of themselves.

Society today is changing not only in one direction but in many directions, branching toward a future of even faster change and even greater diversity. Change today emphasizes alternatives: alternative futures, alternative possibilities, alternative life styles, alternative ethical choices. Ours is a society in which the idea of alternatives and the necessity for choice among them are becoming institutionalized, replacing earlier certainties and restrictions upon choice.

The questions of love and emotions, and ethics and values in relation to sexuality illustrate both continuities and changes in the relation between society and the individual. The definiton of love and the relation of love and other emotions to sexuality have preoccupied people for centuries; as Van den Haag (1962) notes, "the Romans sometimes wondered if love would not blunt and tame their sexual pleasures, whereas the troubadours fretted lest sex abate the fervor of love's longing." At the same time, concepts of the relationship of love to sexuality today are changing as people explore a variety of emotional, sexual, and emotional/sexual relationships outside of marriage (Ramey, 1976).

Sexual values and ethical dilemmas have also been debated throughout history, in part because of the heritage of religious and moral prescriptions and proscriptions relating to sexuality. On the other hand, today's sexual values are influenced by technological imagery of sexuality not available to preindustrial generations, while ethical dilemmas have been compounded by the disaffiliation of some people from the traditional patriarchal family.

Love and sexual ethics illustrate not only the dialectical nature of social change and social equilibrium but also the interrelationship of individual and social change. Changes that occur in the society as a whole — such as an increase in the number of people who do not practice exclusive monogamy — affect individual consciousness and can play a part in modifying individual behavior. At the same time, individual consciousness and behavioral change reflect back and modify the direction of general social change.

Change, alternatives, and the interdependence of the individual and society are all interrelated with sexuality in the present, and probably the future. The following chapters summarize some — but by no means all — aspects of those changes and alternatives that influence the direction of individual sexuality today.

Love is a word with a multitude of meanings. People speak of love with reference to pets, warm climates, ice cream, and orange marmalade. But the kind of love that concerns us here is love between human beings.

Types of Love

The meaning of sexual love is differentiated in our society from other meanings of love. In distinguishing sexual or erotic love from other types of love between human beings, it is common to distinguish familial love and love of humanity *(agape)* from sexual love *(eros)*.

Agape, a predominantly religious or political kind of love, refers to the love a person has for all other people simply because they are human. Theoretically, agape is both selfless and nonsexual and can inspire self-sacrifice for the benefit of humanity. A second type of theoretically asexual love is the love that occurs between family members and friends, which, while not generally expected to be selfless, is strongly expected to be free of libido. Finally, *eros* is a sexual attraction between two people who, in our society at least, are not closely related by blood and are not members of the same sex.

One kind of love is that which family members have for each other.
Michael Serino/Picture Cube

As Freud pointed out over a century ago, these types of love may differ more in degree than in substance. According to Freud, the life force, or eros, is present in all interpersonal relationships and attractions. An element of sexual ecstasy can exist in the fervent self-sacrifice of agape, and a mother can experience sexual satisfaction from nursing her child. In reverse, an element of selflessness can enter into even the most erotic of relationships.

Love and Infatuation

In our society it is common to differentiate types and degrees of erotic love in terms of the perceived degree of involvement and social characteristics of the people concerned. For example, the erotic love experiences of a child of twelve will almost always be trivialized as "infatuation," whatever the perceived degree of involvement, because real "falling in love" is not appropriate for twelve-year-olds in our society. Similarly, an experience of falling in love by certain adults may be declared invalid by

Love between two very young persons is often labeled as infatuation by most adults.
Jean-Claude Lejeune/Stock, Boston

513

others under certain social circumstances. For example, if a young woman falls in love with a very rich and very old man, a prostitute with her client, or a homosexual with another homosexual, the ensuing relationship will usually be labeled as something other than love by most persons. The social characteristics of the persons involved may negate the perceived degree of involvement and cause the behavior to be labeled infatuation, rationalization, opportunism, and so on.

The legitimacy of the expression "falling in love" is conferred in our society only when certain conditions are met: when the parties are adult, of opposite sexes, and considered "suitable" for one another in such matters as race, ethnicity, age, height, weight, personal attractiveness, education, and socioeconomic class. If these conditions are met, even the condition of "falling in love at first sight" may be accepted by others as true love and not infatuation. From the lover's perspective, "love" describes the present relationship, and "infatuation" those that are past (Kephart, 1967, p. 178).

These social meanings of falling in love in our culture may or may not be shared by those who think of themselves as in love. Psychologists, sociologists, and other behavioral scientists, however, have attempted to give more empirical foundation to theories of love. In some instances love has been the subject of typological classification; in others, of explanatory theories. To provide a background for the various categories and theories of love that have been developed in recent times, we must go back to the origins of romantic love as it developed in the Middle Ages.

Romantic Love

Romantic love has been celebrated in Western literature and society since the Middle Ages, when courtly love was established as the conventional system of relationships between men and women.

Courtly love In the mythology of courtly love, a young man who adored the lovely woman of high social class was supposed to adore her from afar, chastely, and to put himself at her disposal as a knight sworn to her protection and allegiance. The knight might die for his lady, but he would never have sexual relations with her. Courtly love in the Middle Ages had many of the attributes of romantic love today, except that today marriage rather than platonic adoration is the aim of romance. Capellanus, writing in the twelfth century, defined love as:

a certain inborn suffering derived from the sight of and excessive meditation upon the beauty of the opposite sex, which causes each one to wish above all things the embraces of the other and by common desire to carry out all of love's precepts in the other's embrace.

Capellanus, 1959, p. 28

514

Romantic love usually includes elements of suffering, excessiveness, a focus on physical beauty, and a desire for complete physical and mental union.
Andy Mercado/Jeroboam

The elements of love mentioned by Capellanus are still part of romantic love today: suffering, excessiveness, a focus on physical beauty, and a desire for complete physical and mental union. Like some contemporary writers, Capellanus in the twelfth century noted that romantic love depends upon difficulties: seeing one another rarely and with difficulty, secrecy, and observing others trying to win one's partner. Romance, then and today, requires unrequitedness, lack of fulfillment, and separation; it may die when these obstacles are no longer a part of the sexual situation.

Other Types of Romantic Love   In his research into types of sexual or romantic love, John Alan Lee (1974) found six primary varieties of love, with most actual romantic experiences having the characteristics of several types. Lee's types are Eros, Ludus, Storge, Pragma, Mania, and Agape.

1. *Eros.* Erotic love is the staple of romantic fiction and fantasy. The erotic lover often falls in love at first sight and very quickly gets sexually involved. She or he is very concerned with the physical beauty of the loved one, and desires to know completely the loved one's body and mind. Erotic lovers are miserable while apart, and although they prefer an exclusive relationship, they do not suffer from extreme jealousy or despair.

2. *Ludus.* Ludus, on the other hand, is playful love — love as a game. The ludic lover keeps a distance between him or herself and the partner, in order to keep love at the game level and prevent a deeper involvement. People who like ludic love often have several partners at once, and prefer recreational sex to emotionally intense experiences.

515

3. *Storge.* Like erotic lovers and unlike the ludics, storgic lovers take love seriously. However, love as *storge* does not depend on passion, love at first sight, or ideal beauty. Storgic lovers often become lovers after the development of a deep and lasting friendship, which quietly develops a sexual component. Marrying the person next door is an example of storgic love.

4. *Pragma.* Pragmatic lovers are similar to storgic in that their approach to love is balanced rather than passionate or fervid; as Lee puts it, their love is "love with a shopping list" (1974; p. 49). A pragmatic lover might go to a computer dating service, because what he or she is most concerned with is "shopping" for a list of compatible qualities or traits. An example is the young businesswoman who sets out to find a husband who can fit into her life style.

5. *Mania.* Mania is a sort of unbalanced eros. The manic lover is consumed as a person by the loved one; given over to extremes of all kinds of emotion: jealousy, ecstasy, misery, rapture, possessiveness. The manic lover often destroys the tie he or she has with the loved one by excessive jealousy and possessiveness. Like erotic love, manic love is the stuff of fiction: "its components — furious jealousy, helpless obsessing, and tragic endings — are the stuff of human conflicts" (Lee, 1974, p. 48).

Theodore Reik also writes of what he calls "erotomania," or the "psychotic form of love" — "raving love." (1963, p. 41). He claims that erotomania is mostly love from afar: "erotomania has in most cases a platonic character." Further, erotomania often takes the form of an unrequited love for another, coupled with the delusion that one *is* loved (1963, pp. 41–44).

6. *Agape.* A sixth type of love according to Lee is *agape,* not exactly in the Christian sense of love for all fellow human beings, but in the sense of loving one person selflessly, without making demands for love in return. As Lee points out, "I found no saints in my sample. I have yet to interview an unqualified example of agape" (1974, p. 50).

Love and Psychological Need

Despite its rarity, selfless love is something of an ideal in Western society; psychologists and others often contrast it with love based on psychological need. Maslow (1962), for example, distinguished between "D-love" and "B-love." D-love is deficiency love; it arises from a deficiency in the lover, who seeks to fulfill previously unfulfilled needs by contact with the love object. Most of these psychological needs arise from early parent-child relationships. B-love occurs between two self-actualized persons who are not dependent on each other; it is based on an appreciation of the qualities of the other person.

Similarly, C. S. Lewis (1960) distinguishes "gift-love," which has no strings attached, from "need-love," which is based on need, like deficiency-love. Maslow and Lewis point out that deficiency-love or need-love makes many demands upon the loved one, and is linked to the zero-sum view of love.

The *zero-sum* view of love is that there is a limited quantity of love, which, if spent on one person, will leave nothing for another. In our culture, the zero-sum view is appropriate, and even mandatory, when describing marital love. For example, it is quite common that if a wife tells her husband she has fallen in love with someone else, he will feel deprived and lost. In countries that sanction polygamous marriages, on the other hand, the concept of zero-sum is absent from marital love. In our society, a mother who declares she does not love her second child because all her love has been squandered on the first is likely to be severely sanctioned. The zero-sum view of love is not appropriate to parent-child or friendly love in our culture, but only to romantic or marital love.

Possessive Love

Because we expect the zero-sum view of love to apply to romantic love, we also expect jealousy to be associated with love. The heritage of romantic love, in fact, links love with a variety of emotions such as guilt, anger, and jealousy. In the twelfth century, Capellanus cited jealousy as a way of increasing love: "Love increases . . . if one of the lovers feels real jealousy which is called, in fact, the nurse of love" (1959, p. 153). Today, in opposition, the O'Neills comment: "Jealousy is never a good or a constructive feeling. It may show you care but what you are caring for is too much for yourself and not enough for your mate" (1972, p. 246). Although surprisingly little has been written about the emotion of jealousy, it is clear that it is a powerful emotion commonly experienced in Western culture throughout the centuries (Clanton and Smith, 1977).

There are several types of jealousy that may occur in romantic relationships, although all can intrude on a variety of friendship and family interactions. *Possessive jealousy* involves defining the partner as a possession or projection of the self, and feeling jealous when the partner expresses independence.

Fear jealousy is related to possessiveness and insecurity. To the extent that one's own sense of worth depends upon another person's devotion, one will be subject to fear of losing that devotion.

Exclusion jealousy is the experience of being left out of a critical or lovely experience of someone loved. Even couples with sexually open marriages who do not experience fear jealousy or possessive jealousy may experience exclusion jealousy; for example, if a woman has her first orgasm with a lover rather than her husband.

517

Possessiveness, jealousy, and a feeling of incompleteness when apart may be based more on feelings of insecurity than on love.
Bruce Davidson/Magnum Photos, Inc.

I have never had an orgasm with my husband Al. When we go to a swinging party, I have several orgasms generally with the men or the women there. Al and I have tried every kind of sex together for me, but it doesn't work. He never says anything about it, but I know it makes him feel just terrible — really rejected by me emotionally.

From the authors' files

When a relationship is based more on romantic love than on mature love, it is likely to be subject to jealousy. Many contemporary writers view jealousy as an emotion based on selfishness and insecurity rather than on mature love.

Mature Love

Romantic love is based on a sense of need or lack of completeness so that an individual desperately seeks the one perfect person who will give the love that will fill that need. In contrast, mature love proceeds, not from need, but from a sense of wholeness and from self-acceptance. Mature

518

love honestly respects the total individuality of each person, including fears and faults as well as joys and strengths. Because mature love is based on acceptance of a total person rather than unrealistic idealization, it can increase with continuing intimacy.

A romantic lover wants to possess the loved one completely. In mature love there is no idea of possession. Each person allows the other complete freedom to grow and develop her or his potential to the fullest, even when this means they have less time to spend together. Mature lovers know that time together can be more enjoyable when each person has more interests and joy of life to bring to the relationship.

Because mature love is based on acceptance of a total person rather than romantic idealization, it can increase with continuing intimacy.
Joel Gordon

519

When romantic lovers are apart they may suffer real pain or "withdrawal" symptoms because without the other person each is incomplete (Peele and Brodsky, 1974). In contrast, mature lovers feel complete whether alone, together, or in the company of others.

Romantic lovers expect to feel love and passion only for each other. But mature love is a part of the love one feels for all persons. It is not expected to be exclusive. There may be a commitment that the sexual relationship will be reserved for the two partners, but loving feelings will be shared with all others.

Within a relationship based on mature love, sexual expression can reach its greatest potential. In these relationships, sex is a means of physically expressing the high degree of caring, acceptance, and intimacy of both the physical and the emotional aspects of the relationship. In this setting it can reach its most complete and joyous expression.

Many relationships between couples who love each other involve elements of both romantic and mature love. Often the earlier stages of a relationship involve many aspects of romantic love. Later stages will involve more elements of mature love if the relationship continues beyond the early period of idealization (Parron and Trole, 1978).

There is some debate about whether romantic love should be or is the basis of a happy marriage. Most persons in this country agree that some form of love (either romantic or mature) is an important element of any long-term sexual relationship — married or unmarried. Most people also agree that love alone is not enough, and that similarity in life goals and basic values is also important if a relationship is to continue for very long. Relationships based only on romantic love are likely to be of a relatively short duration (*Newsweek,* February 25, 1980, p. 89). Persons who hope to have an enduring relationship are more likely to find it when the basis is mature love involving many areas of mutual interests and values.

Psychological Aspects of Love

Love and Rewards

A common psychological explanation of love is that one develops love for another person when he or she has been a source of (or associated with) many different kinds of rewarding emotions and experiences (Miller and Siegel, 1972). This explains the love that one feels for friends and relatives as well as spouses and lovers. For example, a young child may develop a love for his parents and siblings because usually they are the source of the things he enjoys — food, fun, affection, and so on. Typically, in love relationships with friends or relatives, sexual arousal or sexual satisfaction is not one of the rewards one expects and seeks. The importance of sex as a rewarding aspect of romantic love relationships distinguishes love for friends from the love one feels for a lover.

In some instances it appears that the reward theory does not hold true and that romantic love increases in a negative or threatening emotional situation. For example, a person may feel stronger love when he or she has been rebuffed or made jealous. This occurs because an individual is more prone to strong emotional response when his or her flow of adrenalin increases. Fear, anger, and many other negative feelings may cause a surge of adrenalin. The emotional response to the increased adrenalin may be interpreted as strong feelings of love. Many positive feelings, such as sexual arousal, also may cause a surge of adrenalin (Walster and Berscheid, 1971).

The Search for the Ideal

An important psychological theory of love in our society is the search for the ideal. In childhood or adolescence most people develop an image of their ideal lover or mate. So-called love at first sight occurs when a person encounters another person who appears to meet his or her image of the ideal mate. If this initial feeling of attraction is reciprocated to some degree, the two people will seek opportunities to be together and interact.

In the early stages of romance both people try to appear at their best and try to live up to the other's ideal. Both seek to continue their relationship and be together at every possible opportunity because each anticipates that the other can fill all of his or her needs for affection, sexual pleasure, emotional security, demonstration of personal worth, or whatever else is important in his or her own hierarchy of requirements (Miller and Siegel, 1972).

When a romance proceeds smoothly, very intense feelings of love will be an important aspect of the relationship. But problems can arise, because two people rarely fit perfectly each other's image of the ideal love. At first each attributes to the other all the qualities of her or his ideal, and each tries to live up to this ideal. But over time, discrepancies between the ideal and the real become too obvious to overlook, and the effort of trying to live up to someone else's ideal becomes tiring. When disillusionment sets in, quite often the relationship is ended, and each partner seeks someone else who appears to fit his or her ideal better (Miller and Siegel, 1972).

For some people, this falling in and out of love in search of their ideal may continue throughout life. Others will end their search at some point and settle for one person who, though not perfect, offers them more rewards than others.

521

Projection

Projection is a related psychological concept used to account for the making and breaking of love relationships. In *projection,* the person attributes qualities present or desired in the self onto the other person. For example, a wife trained to suppress her own cravings for power and influence may project onto her husband idealized powerfulness and strength that he may or may not have. When he does not live up to her ideal for herself, the relationship becomes strained because he seems weak; when he does live up to it, the relationship is also strained because she resents and envies him. Or the qualities projected onto the partner may be one's own negative qualities: the husband accuses the wife of sloppiness when he really fears sloppiness in himself, or the wife nags the husband about economic security when she fears insecurity.

Complementary Neuroses

Love has also been seen as the product of complementary neuroses (Reik, 1963, pp. 31–33). For example, a couple meets at a party and there is immediate mutual attraction. They date and fall quickly in love. Each person has sensed in the other some complement to his or her own neurotic needs: the manipulators respond to the easily manipulable, the masochists to the sadists, those who want to be needed to those who need, and so on. If a lasting relationship develops based on these mutual needs, the relationship remains stable if the needs remain unchanged. But should the needs of one of the partners change, say through individual psychotherapy, the relationship will be strained and may eventually break.

Most of the psychological explanations of love focus on the parents — generally the mother — as the source of future romantic and sexual patterns. Freud's Oedipal theory, for example, assumes that love is the product of frustrated sexual longing for the parent of the opposite sex, who is then reproduced as the loved object in adulthood. More recently, the old adage about marrying "a gal just like the gal who married dear old Dad" has been extended to women too: women, like men, seek the characteristics of their mothers rather than their fathers, in their sexual partners.

Love and the Life Cycle

Different classifications and explanations of love are used for different stages in the life cycle, from infatuation in adolescence through companionship in old age. Certain types of love are regarded as particularly appropriate or inappropriate at stages in the life cycle. In a study of over a

Perceptions of Infatuation and Love, by Sex, in Percentages   Table 17.1

	Females	Males
Age at first infatuation	13.0	13.6
Age at first falling in love	17.1	17.7
Number of times infatuated	5.6	4.5
Number of times fallen in love	1.3	1.2
N = 1,000		

Source: William M Kephart, "Some Correlates of Romantic Love," *Journal of Marriage and the Family*, 29, August 1967, pp. 470–481. Copyright © 1967 by National Council on Family Relations. Reprinted by permission.

thousand young men and women, Kephart (1967) found that people reported infatuations more frequently and at earlier ages than they reported falling in love. (See Table 17.1.) He suggests that the distinction between love and infatuation may be arbitrary, and that people report past loves as infatuations.

Types of love other than the erotic may also be defined as appropriate to different stages in the life cycle. Stanton Wheeler (1972), for example, suggests that people learn different types of love at different ages. Between one and six years of age, the child learns how to receive love and be affectionate in return. Between six and twelve she or he learns about the love and give-and-take of friendship in the peer group, while between twelve and twenty-one, says Wheeler, the individual begins to learn empathy, and thereby develops the ability to love altruistically.

Love and the Adolescent

The presence of an interpersonally directed sex drive is relatively novel to the adolescent and serves as a strong reward in romantic interaction. Although not all adolescent romances involve sexual contact to the point of orgasm, they usually include some degree of pleasurable sexual arousal that serves as a motive to continue the romance. If the physical relationship includes sexual contact to orgasm, the additional physical pleasure and release may increase both the rewards of interaction and the feeling of love.

Acceptance and Attraction   Sexual interaction provides more than physical pleasure for adolescents. Because premarital sexual activities meet with some degree of disapproval in our society, willingness to engage in them is usually interpreted as a proof of the very special quality of the other person. Sexual surrender, particularly by a young woman, is one of the clearest ways to show acceptance of another person. The knowledge of   523 mutual acceptance is highly rewarding (Miller and Siegel, 1972). For most adolescents the love relationship adds immensely to the sexual pleasure of the relationship, and the sexual pleasure adds to the feelings of love. Not only does a romantic relationship hold the promise of direct sexual rewards through sexual arousal and release, it also affirms to the couple, as well as to the world, that they are attractive to members of the opposite sex. In a society such as ours, where sexual attractiveness is so highly valued, this is a powerful reward.

The Expression of Affection   Romantic love relationships also provide an opportunity for expressing affection physically. In most instances adolescents are considered too old to be cuddled freely by their parents and relatives the way they were as small children. This is even more true for males than for females in our culture. So adolescents' natural needs for affection must usually be met in their peer relationships. Because of the fairly widespread taboos against demonstrations of affection between persons of the same sex — particularly males — almost the only socially acceptable way to give and receive physical affection is within a heterosexual love relationship.

Sexual pleasure, proof of sexual attractiveness, and an opportunity to express and receive affection are some of the rewarding aspects of romantic interaction. Because of the depth and variety of the needs most adolescents bring to their love relationships, these relationships are experienced very intensely. Often being with one's beloved seems more important than anything else because the interaction is more rewarding than any other experience.

A thirteen-year-old female describes love in this fashion: Love is the feeling you get when you know you're with the right person. Love is unknown until it reaches you, but when it finally gets there you know what it is. Knowing that you want him and he wants you. Being able to express your feelings toward one another without having to verbalize them.

From the authors' files

Romantic love relationships are an important aspect of adolescent development in our society. Typically, most sexual learning takes place within romantic relationships. And young people use "being in love" to legitimate their sexual activities, whether these activities involve only light petting or proceed to coitus. Not only does love increase the pleasure of sexual contacts, but often it decreases the guilt surrounding them.

In adolescence most people learn, within their love relationships, the joy of giving as well as receiving sexual pleasure. For an adolescent it is a heady experience to discover that she or he can cause a strong sexual response in another individual, particularly when this response is part of the partner's love for him or her as a unique individual, rather than just physical reaction to sexual stimulation. In childhood, sexual contacts, if they occur, are largely self-seeking. Pleasure in sexual giving usually is learned first in adolescent love relationships. Even though the relationship may not endure for very long, pleasure in giving may carry into other romantic love relationships and hopefully will flourish in more enduring ones in later years.

Intimacy Adolescent romance provides experience in relating intimately outside the family, not only in a physical, sexual sense, but also as a total person. In romantic love relationships, young people learn the pleasures and problems of maintaining close relationships (Lieberman and Jackson, 1973). An individual may find the security of having a steady boy friend or girl friend more or less important than the freedom to date anyone. Through the experience of a series of romances with different persons having different attributes, adolescents refine their conception of the kind of individual they would find most compatible for a long-term love relationship. For example, one person may discover that big blue eyes are not as important in the long run as a sense of humor, and another may find that neither blue eyes nor a sense of humor is as appealing as a good tennis backhand.

The experience gained in romantic love relationships can help an adolescent move from the self-centered and relatively nonsexual interpersonal-love relationships of childhood to the intimate sexual-love relationships of adulthood that typically are the bases for marriage and parenthood.

Adult Love

In our society much is expected of adolescent love, but the freight of expectations borne by adult love is greater still. Adult love is supposed to survive until death, whereas adolescent love, or infatuation, is allowed to die after a short interval. Furthermore, adult love is supposed to leave room for the partners to develop and mature without disrupting that love, and to survive the emotional and physical storms of childbearing and child raising. Many people even expect the sexually titillated, excited love of courtship and adolescence to carry through from the wedding ceremony to the Social Security check.

The Love Ideal There is some debate as to how extensively the love ideal permeates our society and how extensively adults are influenced by it in their expectations and experience of marriage. On the one hand, William Kephart says, "It is certain that, as compared to other societies, America has a special place in its heart for romantic love" (1973, p. 92), whereas Linton claims, "In any ordinary population the percentage of individuals with a capacity for romantic love of the Hollywood type was about as large as that of persons able to throw genuine epileptic fits" (1936, p. 175).

Given that most marriages in this country are between people of the same economic, religious, racial, and educational background, it is clear that many factors other than romantic love are operating in mate selection, particularly clan, racial, and ethnic identifications (Goode, 1959). The selection of mates from within close social groups, as in the United States, is called *endogamy;* the opposite practice is called *exogamy.*

For a few couples in love, their emotions may be strong enough to lead them to brave social differences and adverse conditions. Most people in the United States, however, view romantic love as only one criterion for choosing another person for a long-term sexual and emotional relationship. Marriages based only on romantic love may be more unstable than those that include other areas of compatibility; therefore, many of the functions of marriage — such as economic and child-raising functions at the social level, and emotional security at the personal level — might be undermined in a romantic marriage. On the other hand, marriages based only on rational considerations but omitting romantic love may not provide the degree of emotional satisfaction expected from marriage.

Love and Intimacy   The relationship between love and the development of intimacy over time is the subject of some disagreement among experts. Some assert that romantic love and the development of intimacy are strongly related.

The main human task and dilemma is forming an ability to fuse the passionate, the tender, the intimate, and only when this is possible and achieved can love be said to exist. Characteristic of such love is a posture of concern for the beloved that is as great as concern for the self. And if this kind of relatedness to the sexual partner is achieved, a wide variety of other subtle psychological needs are satisfied, such as the need for self-esteem or self-effectuation, and the establishment of patterns of interpersonal security.

Bartz and Rasor, 1972, p. 54

Love increases the pleasure of sex. It does this by singling out the love object as the focus of an individual's erotic desire and of his need for closeness and intimacy with another person. This focus upon a single individual raises the level of sexual tension.

Lowen, 1972, p. 18

Others suggest that romantic or sexual love and intimacy tend to be mutually exclusive.

526

Sex can thrive without an intense personal relationship, and may erode if it exists.

Van den Haag, 1962

It is worth emphasizing that the benefits of smooth togetherness are bought at the price of dwindling erotic tensions. . . . Conversely, a genuine closeness is notable by its absence in the most intense forms of erotic interest. . . . Thus, it is in new relationships and in marriages torn by fights and clashes — that is, where . . . the details of compatibility have *not* been worked out — that the highest erotic excitements flourish. Throughout a multitude of examples it becomes apparent that the comforts of a personal closeness, and the stuff of sexual attractions are at cross purposes.

Tripp, 1975, pp. 59–60

The relationship between romantic love and the development of long-term intimacy is undoubtedly different for different individuals or couples, but it is also clear that intimacy brings about a diminution of excitement and the feeling of elation characteristic of being in love. In addition, the definition of what is pleasurable about sexual encounters in the context of intimacy of romantic love can be variable.

I have affairs with men other than my husband every now and then. . . . It is not so satisfying as our sexual relationship in terms of orgasm, but on the other hand the process that leads up to the orgasm is so much more exciting.

From the authors' files

Love, Sex, and Commitment

Sexual release is pleasurable even in the absence of any relationship. If it were not, masturbation would not be such a widespread practice. Most people, however, find sex more enjoyable when another person is involved in the experience. Most also find that sex with another is best if they have a love relationship with the other person. If, in addition to mature love, the relationship is characterized by a mutual total commitment to the relationship, then sexuality can reach its most complete expression.

Persons who do not have an ideal relationship within which to express their sexuality must resolve the question of how much commitment and love they expect in a relationship before they are willing to become sexually involved. Some individuals are quite comfortable having sex with someone they know only slightly. For most persons casual sex is relatively easy to find and may be a pleasurable release in the absence of, or in addition to, more committed sexual relationships. People who are not

Sexuality can reach its most complete expression in a relationship based on mature love and a mutual life-long commitment to the relationship.
Cynthia Benjamin/Black Star

comfortable with relatively casual sex may have times when they have to go without a sexual relationship until they establish a committed love relationship.

The maximum commitment involves a life-long marriage with complete sexual fidelity. Individuals who have or who are considering making this kind of commitment have some questions to resolve. Some persons feel that a total commitment of this nature may limit their personal growth because it limits their sexual and interpersonal options. They may choose to make no commitments at all, or they may make only limited commitments. Limited commitments may have any form. A commitment to love and life-long marriage but not to sexual fidelity is one option. Another option is a commitment to caring and fidelity on a short-term basis for as long as the relationship seems good to both persons. There may perhaps be only a commitment to pleasure for the duration of a summer vacation. Whatever the decision, there is generally some choice to be made between the security of commitment and the freedom of noncommitment.

528

Sexuality and Society

Sexuality is valued differently by different persons in contemporary society. An individual — or a society — may place a high or low value on sexuality itself; give high value to either male or female sexuality, or to both; and rate sexual interaction and satisfaction below or above such other values as money, prestige, intellectual fulfillment, or parenthood. At the same time, an individual or society espouses a set of sexual ethics that may or may not correspond with the value placed on sex. For example, an individual who values sex very little may have a definite and well developed code of sexual morality, whereas an individual who places a high value on sex may have only a rudimentary moral code.

To discuss sexual values and ethics, it is necessary to take into account that people see human sexual interaction from many different perspectives. To paraphrase a witty saying, "One man's pervert is another man's husband." Sexual values and ethics may be viewed from the perspective of the relationship between society and sexuality *(functionalism)* or the relationship between sexuality and the individual in interaction with others *(humanism)*. The distinction is more academic than real; society and the individual in interaction are separable only for purposes of analysis. We will discuss first the functionalist viewpoint and its application to society, and then the humanistic viewpoint and its application to the individual.

Functionalism

The functionalist perspective is concerned with the survival of society and its institutions; behavior is evaluated with reference to its *function* in the perpetuation of the existing system. For example, a rising divorce rate may be seen as dysfunctional for a social system because of the costs entailed in court and child-custody procedures. Similarly, frequent sexual intercourse may be seen as functional for the maintenance of a marriage.

In deciding what aspects of sexual experience are valuable, one may ask several questions: Is sexual experience a valuable kind of human experience? If so, what kinds of sexual experience are most valuable? How does sexual interaction compare in value to other types of experience? And, finally, what forms of sexual interaction are ethically acceptable?

There are not only different values put on sexual interaction, but there are different ethics, or standards, of what moral codes are functional for oneself and others. Ethics, though usually defined in terms of the moral censure of the behavior of others, can also involve the development of a moral code for one's own personal conduct and relationships. Contrary to some popular thinking, as options become more open and sexual choice less simple, the problem of personal sexual ethics becomes more pressing. 529

Social Values and Sexuality

As indicated in earlier chapters, sexuality is interpreted socially in ways that are in general consistent with the prevailing value systems. In the Victorian era, for example, people were preoccupied with making and saving money; as Ruitenbeek (1974) indicates, the Victorians used many monetary metaphors to describe sexual matters, such as "spending" to describe male and female orgasms, and "saving oneself for marriage."

Sex and Repression   The Victorians believed that semen and sexual energy, like money, should be saved. During the Victorian era the prevailing response to sexuality among most persons was one of repression. Sexuality was legitimate only in marriage, for the purposes of procreation, and in moderation. The actual sexual interaction that took place between couples was not a legitimate topic of discussion. Between the Victorian era and the 1970s, sexuality became obsessed by technique.

The Technicalization of Sex   In the post-Victorian era, between the two world wars, technology developed rapidly and entered the realm of sexuality. The decades between the wars and the 1950s and 1960s saw the proliferation of marriage manuals that attempted to teach respectable married couples how to achieve sexual satisfaction. As Brecher comments, "The focus of most of these marriage manuals was . . . to give instructions on 'the specific bodily techniques — the kisses, the caresses, the thrusts — by means of which readers could [attain] . . . orgasm' " (1971, p. 102).

This new approach to sexuality, based on rules, instructions, and manuals, was appropriate to the technological society that was growing out of the industrial era — it was sex by technique. Many of these manuals were so thoroughly rational and technical in their approach to sex that they tended to remove it from the context of emotions, subjectivity, and interpersonal relations (Stokes, 1971, pp. 92–98). Many sexual partners, trapped by the rhetoric of science into a definition of sexuality as rule-guided and difficult, would probably agree with Dennis Brissett, who writes:

[Sex is] a human function to enjoy, not an awesome task to be mastered. Sex in this society has been so scrutinized, so analyzed, and so worried about that it has taken on an almost non-human quality. It has lost much of its subjective and human basis.

Brissett, 1971, p. 80

As Brissett and Lewis note, technological themes were continually stressed in marriage manuals, from the correct setting for the task of sex, to the correct techniques, and finally to the correct product — the orgasm. They point out that the manuals use many of the concepts appropriate in   **530** the sphere of work, such as striving, straining, pacing, technique, learning, skill, practice, study, methodology, control, and equipment. They cite one manual that advised the new bridegroom to compare his new wife's genitals with an anatomical sketch: "It should be studied, on the bridal night . . . the husband should compare the diagram with his wife's genital region" (Lewis and Brissett, 1969, p. 78).

The Organization of Sexuality Society in the 1970s is not only technicalized, it is also bureaucratized and organized. Sociologists since the nineteenth century have commented on the increasing bureaucratization, organization, and rationalization of social systems, and the lessening of mystical, nonrational, and intuitive forms of social organization. Sexuality is no exception to this general trend: since the turn of the century, sex has become increasingly the subject of organization.

Sex-related organizations are not a new phenomenon, but they are blossoming and springing up, with a quantity and membership that are unprecedented. The term *sexual organizations* refers to organizations dedicated to the pursuit of goals linked with sexuality or gender identity. Most of these organizations have their main offices in the larger cities of the United States, but they are by no means limited to such cities. The types of organization include sexual matching services and sexual freedom organizations.

Sexual matching services may match people for dating, for sexual swinging, or for other sexual variations. Matching services may be heterosexual, homosexual, or bisexual, and may be administered by a small, personally run office or a large-scale, computerized operation.

Sexual freedom organizations may also vary in size and may be homosexual, bisexual, or heterosexual. The best-known organization of this type is probably the Sexual Freedom League, which, as its literature states, is dedicated to freeing sexuality from traditional Western restrictions. (See Selection 17.1.) The aims of other sexual freedom organizations are more specialized. One sexual freedom society in Los Angeles seeks the destigmatization of adult male sexual contacts with young boys. Many sexual freedom organizations are dedicated to the destigmatization of sexual acts considered deviant or illegal, and consequently overlap with organizations seeking political rights related to sex and gender, such as the gay liberation and feminist organizations.

Freedom and Destigmatization There is a curious paradox in the juxtaposition of the terms *organization* and *freedom*. Organization, especially of the bureaucratic kind, can be seen as inimical to the development or expression of personal freedom. In turn, freedom implies lack of organizational or other restraints on personal choice and behavior.

531

Today, however, people join together to seek sexual freedom mainly on the basis of some kind of stigmatized behavior or status, such as swinging, gayness, or femaleness. For example, a solitary gay or feminist will be unable to achieve personal freedom in a society that blocks and restrains gays and women; collectively, gay and feminist organizations hope to challenge the limits set by society upon their freedom.

A Statement of Position / The Sexual Freedom League

Selection 17.1

Sexual Expression

We believe that sexual expression, in whatever form agreed upon between consenting persons of either sex, should be considered an inalienable human right. We believe this because we feel that sex without guilt and restriction is good, pleasurable, relaxing, and promotes a spirit of human closeness, compassion, and goodwill, and because sex is intrinsically a part of every human being. We believe that sexual activity, heretofore little explored in the West, has a wealth of potential for making life more livable and enjoyable. . . .

Sexual Freedom League, San Diego, 1975

Wife and Husband Swapping, Group Sex, Sex in Public

Because sex is good, these forms, if mutually agreed upon between indulging parties, are also good. They are bad if unwilling persons are coerced into them. It is not the concern, right, nor should it be in the power of any who find no satisfaction in these forms to impose their will on those who do. All laws which make such forms illegal should be abolished.

Nudity

As all people were born naked with all the beauty of adornment that nature saw fit, they should have the prerogative of continuing so through life according to their own wishes. That the sight of the natural human body offends some people is really no reason to grant them the monopoly of dictating their wishes on everybody else, some of whom may have, for their own good reasons, not the least desire or need to be so restricted. Thus we feel that the question of nudity is essentially the right to come and go without having one's own desires restricted by others who are unwilling to adopt the same desires. We also believe that the body is naturally invigorated by sunshine, fresh air, and water. That nakedness excites others in an unwanted and prurient way and abets sex crimes is a myth resulting in the perpetuation of the dirty aura and guilt-ridden climate of sex, which in turn is the very thing that brings into being sex criminals and molesters and in the end seems to constitute every good reason for believing in the myth. Yet, the acceptance of nudity and human sexuality in general would quickly break the vicious cycle which produces sexual criminals and gives us our obstinate reason for supporting the myth. Persons with genuine respect for human sexuality are not offended by the sight of another's naked body, nor are they, when erotically stimulated, inclined to impose themselves sexually onto another. However, as far as sexual excitement itself is concerned, we believe that such is good, normal, and may be construed as a compliment if no coercion or force is involved. In conclusion, we feel that all laws which prohibit nudity in public (unless for special exceptional reasons) should be abolished....

Youth

We feel that the fuss against children being exposed to sex or indulging in it is just so much nonsense based upon much misinformation. The sex organs of children are not injured by sex indulgence, any more than the sex organs of adults are so injured. Nor are the minds of children hurt by sex indulgence — neither by trauma or by permanent fixation on sex. Trauma results only from shocking or painful experience in injurious conflict against personal conscience or feelings. Fixation results from the socially-imposed value of denying or repressing something which one is nevertheless interested in or unable to rid from the unconscious mind. If there is any single statement which aptly expresses our views concerning sexual activity among children, it is this: *we believe that a sex organ in the hand of a child is more desirable than a toy machine gun.* Further, we believe also that murder committed in playful effigy is far worse and less moral than sex indulged in with pleasure in reality. That "sex is corrupting" we believe is sheer nonsense. It can only be corrupting when an equation is perpetuated between sex and dirt, sex and crime, or sex and guilt. Otherwise it is uplifting. All laws, in any state, which militate against sex activity by children should be re-evaluated.

Obscenity and Pornography

Sex depicted in writing, photography, or spoken of in "four-letter words," as well as publicly witnessed in the form of naked or copulating persons, is neither necessarily obscene nor, in any derogatory sense, pornographic. Writing which focuses on sex does not need anything of "redeeming social import" in order to justify such a focus on sex. Sex itself, where no one is forced against his will, is redeeming in and of itself. Sex is universally one of the main biological and social principles of humanity. Redemption from sex guilt is the only redemption currently needed and can only be attained when the climate which nourishes guilt is eliminated. Postal regulations which make it illegal to send certain sexual matters through the mails should be rescinded, as they militate against an essential aspect of freedom. Censorship of materials with

533

sexual content should also be eliminated, and all laws that imply that sex is derogatorily obscene and pornographic, and as such illegal, should be abolished.

Sexuality and the Individual

In addition to the functionalist perspective, sexual ethics includes the contemporary Western humanistic belief that human beings each have a unique worth; ethically, this means that they should not be treated as objects, or as means to an end. Most of those concerned with the development of their own sexual ethics would give at least lip service to this idea, although they might violate it behaviorally.

Humanism

A humanistic view of the self most often takes the form of the quest for self-fulfillment, authenticity, or self-actualization. Whatever the content of self-fulfillment, many people believe that an individual should maximize his or her intellectual and emotional capacities, talents, and enjoyment of life. An authentic, fulfilled individual will not make of herself or himself an object to please someone else, like the woman who fakes orgasm to please her husband or the man who fakes tenderness to please his wife.

Although treating oneself and others as worthwhile individuals is a key humanistic ethic, it is violated extensively today, and has been in the recent past, in the areas of sexual and family relationships. In the contemporary Western world, men have pursued women purely as sexual objects (and sometimes vice versa), and women have pursued men as a means to a source of income. Men have used women as childbearing machines, and women have used men as a protection from independence. Today the use of people by others for their own ends is recognized as a major problem of interpersonal and sexual relationships.

Contemporary concern for women's and men's self-actualization in traditional or alternative sex roles is a relatively new phenomenon as compared with continuing social concern about the maintenance of family and social systems. Until the present century, concern with sexuality — or any other facet of human experience — was always in terms of functions and dysfunctions in society.

Today, however, there is a movement away from the functionalist stress on the relation between sexuality and society toward a focus on the 534 individual, as a person and in interaction with others. Furthermore, sexuality is taking on an increasing value as the expression of interest in others and as a component of self-expression and self-actualization.

The Personalization of Sexuality

During the 1960s and 1970s sexuality became reinterpreted not as a technical or bureaucratic matter, but as a means of expression and communication between people. Personalized sex is sex related to the total personality of the participants, and an expression of their relationship to one another. As Alex Comfort comments, "Sex is the one place where we today can learn to treat people as people" (1972, p. 9). Similarly, Rosemary Reuther in "The Personalization of Sexuality" states:

Sexuality as love remains a deeply creative development of communication between two persons. If we can open ourselves to the beloved on the deepest level and make our body-selves the sacrament of personal communication, the result will be the transfiguration of our total creative powers that must restore to our society those deepest powers of personality hitherto alienated as the "spiritual realm."

Reuther, 1974, pp. 42–49

The personalization of sexuality in this manner is not simply a variation of the motto of the permissive 1960s "sex with affection." Although Comfort and other humanists stress the joys of sex with love, even temporary relationships are seen as having a legitimate expression in sexual interaction.

The evidence collected by William Simon and his associates concerning premarital sexuality among young people provides evidence for increasing personalization. As indicated in earlier chapters, sexuality for young males is becoming more humanized than in earlier decades. In the 1940s, the young man's first sexual encounter was likely to be with a prostitute or a promiscuous girl. In the 1970s it is more likely to be with a female with whom the young man has a friendly relationship.

For the young female in the 1940s, the first sexual encounter was likely to be the result of a romance-sex bargain: the male provided romance, and pressured the female into increasing degrees of sexual intimacy. Today the female's first sexual encounter is more likely to be mutually agreed upon and less the result of the romance-sex bargain.

I very quickly saw the fun that could come from being with boys. It was new and exciting to be liked by them. I forgot my old thinking about kissing and found pleasure in the games we would play. It was also very nice to be held in the arms

Ribal, 1973, p. 24

535

of the boys while they kissed. . . . When I was sixteen I met the boy who gave me my first sexual intercourse. . . . When I first danced with him at a party, I knew he would be my first love in bed.

The personalization of sexuality removes the focus of sexuality from the genitals. Comfort argues for a return to what Freud called the polymorphous perverse sexuality of childhood, in which any part of the body can give sensual pleasure:

Our idea of sex wouldn't be recognizable to some other cultures, though our range of choice is the widest ever. For a start it's over-genital . . . "sex" for our culture means putting the penis in the vagina. Man's whole skin is a genital organ.

Comfort, 1972, p. 10

Similarly, Leonard asserts that we need a "new sexuality" that involves the sexualization of "every aspect of sensing and thinking" (1974, pp. 26–27).

Sexuality and Individual Values

Sexuality, however, is only one part of life. Even a Don Juan would be reluctant to claim that sexual interaction is the sole purpose and value of life. The contemporary young adult, therefore, is faced with the problem of the placement of sexual fulfillment and variety among life's other values, such as emotional intimacy, individual autonomy, a vocation or career, security, freedom, reputation, intellectual pursuits, child rearing — the list is endless. And, as we have seen in earlier chapters, the choice of sexuality's place in the hierarchy is partly conditioned by the physiological facts of puberty, partly by maturity and aging, and partly by the environmental conditions of socioeconomic class, ethnicity, religion, and subculture. Different choices may be made at different points in the life cycle, and with different people and in different situations. However, within this framework is a set of options. To make a well-thought-out, personal choice, the young adult must be aware of the impinging cues that may affect an individual's evaluation of the importance and scope of his or her own sexuality.

Some of these cues point in the direction of the sexualization of the whole of life; others, in the direction of desexualization. Advertising represents an example of sexualization, and the structure of everyday life an example of desexualization.

There is an implicit value bias in advertising that lures us from the first moment the television is turned on. Sexuality in advertising is entwined with other values: wealth, youth, physical attractiveness, leisure, and sometimes even violence and speed. Viewers and readers learn that sexuality is optimally possible only to those who possess the stereotyped attributes; conversely, people who do possess the attributes learn that sexuality must be a primary value for them. Young, beautiful people may feel sexually inadequate if they do not value sexuality very highly, whereas older, unattractive people fear that they are oversexed if they take "too much interest" in sex.

On the other hand, people are taught by a variety of social arrangements in everyday life that sex is incompatible with nonsexual areas of life such as work and parenting, so if it is to be indulged in, time and space must be set aside for it. Children are not permitted to observe parents' sexual interaction as they are in some cultures; therefore, parents must find time for sex when the children are asleep or out of the house. Sex is not supposed to disturb the work life or the household routine.

From these two examples it is clear that the growing child receives contradictory cues as to the appropriate value to be placed on sexuality; the resulting accommodation may reflect, underemphasize, or overemphasize the person's individual physiological-psychological sex drive. As a result, placement of sexuality in the individual's hierarchy of values can often be difficult and may remain unsatisfactory throughout much of life.

The contradictory emphasis on sexuality in our society can be analyzed differently from the functional and humanistic perspectives. Functional logic asserts that unchecked sexual activity is dysfunctional and destructive for the social system, and that the checks to sexuality built into the family support the social system. To the extent that the stable family in our society is still important, and despite the fact that sexual activity between spouses takes place within the family, it remains a restraining force on sexuality.

The message of the mass media, however, as well as much of the educational system and some political and religious ideology in our society, is that sexual satisfaction is an aspect of self-fulfillment. We can clearly see, now, that functionalism for society can be a quite different thing from functionalism for individual self-actualization. The dictates of self-fulfillment through sexual expression can lead to the disruption of families in which the spouses' sexual relationships are not satisfactory, and thence to social disorganization.

Monogamy and Sexual Variety

Sexual and other values and needs are not always compatible and may be opposed to one another. Marriage has been described as a tragedy because it attempts to balance the incompatible human needs for freedom and security. Freedom versus security is one pair of alternative potential 537 values that relates primarily to sexual behavior; another is self-fulfillment versus commitment, which goes beyond the question of sexual behavior to the problem of the nature and purpose of human relationships.

Freedom and Security   In *Open Marriage* (O'Neill and O'Neill, 1972), the authors suggest a marriage based on the freedom of each of the partners to pursue her or his own self-fulfillment. But they leave unresolved the question of the extension of this freedom into sexuality. A marriage (or a committed living-together arrangement) that is open and free in the sexual sense may create problems for one or both partners in the area of security and belonging. But if the freedom for sexual adventures is structured by rules (no emotional commitment to the casual partner, always sleep at home), then the situation is no longer free — and the adventuring partners may trample on other peoples' feelings, using them as means to ends. A requirement of complete sexual fidelity, however, can lead to sexual boredom and a lack of sexual fulfillment, to unrealistic fantasies about the marvels of other sex partners, or to secret affairs that undermine the foundation of the marital relationship.

Commitment and Self-Actualization   Although most people pay lip service to the ideal of self-fulfillment for each individual, there is much debate as to how commitment to another fits with self-realization. Without a close, intimate, and committed relationship — or more than one, in the case of a communal marriage — the partners may be free to pursue goals, but goals often become empty of meaning when their triumph is unshared. This may be self-actualization, but it can also lead to alienation and loneliness. On the other hand, commitment to the needs and goals of the partner can stultify the development and realization of one's own goals and needs as an independent human being.

Whether heterosexual or homosexual, married or unmarried, a salient question for many couples — but not all — is the choice between monogamy and sexual variety. For some, there is a second choice between secret and open sexual variety.

Permanence and Exclusiveness   Recent ethical commentaries on marriage, such as Whitehurst and Libby's reader *Renovating Marriage* (1973) and the work of the Francouers (1974), stress the value of permanence in marriage but not the value of exclusiveness. Using the humanistic perspective, social thinkers such as the Francouers and the contributors to *Renovating Marriage* argue that exclusiveness in marriage is antithetical to the goal of self-fulfillment in the sexual, and possibly in the emotional, sphere of life. Others argue that sexual exclusiveness is a vital part of the mutual emotional commitment of marriage.

538

Mature lovers know that time together can be more enjoyable when each person has developed interests to bring to the relationship.
Jim Scherer

On the other hand, not all social ethicians or sociologists are in agreement on the value of permanence in marriage — or on the value of exclusiveness. The Roys point out that marriage should be more easily terminated than it is today: "A reform of the total system of marriage *must* provide for a much less destructive method for terminating one. The first change required in our present ideal is to recognize that a good divorce can be better than a poor marriage" (Roy and Roy, 1973, p. 71).

There is a functionalist argument explicit or implicit in some of the writings on sexual ethics and values in a technological society. McLuhan and Leonard (1974) for example, argue that a more flexible sexuality is vital to the adaptability of humankind in postindustrial society. Others

539

assert that sexual exclusiveness in marriage leads to conflict and divorce, and thus to the disruption of a stable family structure; on the other hand, extramarital sex may improve or stabilize marriage.

If a husband cares for his wife and children but harmlessly and enjoyably enter- Ellis, 1971, p. 74
tains his secretary on the office sofa every once in a while, and if this secretary helps preserve her own basically good but sexually unsatisfying marriage by this kind of momentarily unremunerated "overtime" . . . their mates may actually be benefited.

Conclusion

Sexuality in our society has been unchained from the earlier demands of a patriarchal, agrarian society; people have the option of new freedom and new cultural forms. The unchaining of sexuality has freed people from the unchallenged tyranny of ancient demands and has led to the questioning, if not the acceptance, of every expression of human sexuality. Monogamy, childbearing, the double standard, stereotyped sex roles, exclusive heterosexuality, marriage — all these are no longer automatically judged as good. Casual sex, bisexuality, homosexuality, masturbation, illegitimate childbirth — all these are no longer automatically judged as bad.

A question has been raised. But within that question is a continuing moral choice: if casual sex is not always dehumanizing, then it is not always self-fulfilling either. If marriage is sometimes an authentic partnership, it can also be an escape from selfhood. Individuals must answer these questions for themselves, either randomly and without pattern or guided by a set of values worked out in personal experience and growth.

The human task is not simple. It involves understanding one's own personal values and resolving any contradictions among them. It means developing a personal ethical system consistent with these values. It means choosing options that are consistent with one's values and ethics. It also means recognizing the consequences of the choices on the larger social group, on one's friends and family, and on one's sense of self-worth. And then one must be willing to live with the consequences.

The old chains on human sexuality came from the unquestioned authority of economic, religious, and familial institutions. Now sexuality has been unchained from these. But there are new chains, sometimes forged slowly and painfully, that come from the human experience.

Chapter 18 / *Current Trends and Alternative Futures*

Current trends in sexuality tend to be elusive, because some of them are fads, but others are deeper and more lasting, with consequences for the future. At the same time, any of today's trends can by changed at any moment by unpredictable major events, such as war or natural disaster.

World War II, for example, changed much of the social structure of the nation, including the family and related sexual behavior. During the war, with men on the battlefields and factories at full operation manufacturing war goods, women experienced only as housewives and mothers moved into jobs formerly reserved for men. As a result, there was a backlash in the 1950s, with a re-emphasis on women's place in the home with the children. However, the war had left a residue of changed sex roles that has had consequences for all the decades since.

Further consequences of the war were an increased divorce rate and a greatly but temporarily increased birthrate. When the war ended, there was an increase in divorces as men came home to wives who had become different people. Although the divorce rate fell in the postwar years, it never returned to pre-World War II levels. The second demographic consequence of World War II and optimistic economic conditions was the postwar baby boom, which peaked in 1957 and has had a profound impact on the age structure of the United States ever since (see Table 18.1).

Birthrate Trends Table 18.1

Year	Birthrate per 1,000 Population
1940	19.4
1950	24.1
1955	25.0
1960	23.7
1965	19.4
1967	17.8
1968	17.5
1969	17.8
1970	18.4
1971	17.3
1972	15.6
1973	15.2
1974	14.8
1975	15.0

Source: U.S. Bureau of the Census, *Statistical Abstract of the United States, 1974*, 95th ed., (Washington, DC: U.S. Govt. Printing Office, 1974), p. 66; U.S. Department of Health, Education, and Welfare, *Monthly Vital Statistics Report*, vol. 24, no. 9 (November 21, 1975).

Unusual, unforeseen events of magnitude always threaten to upset current trends and to change radically the drift of society. At the same time, a careful examination of the patterns underlying the sexual interaction covered in previous chapters yields some insight into trends that might develop in the future.

Demographic Changes

One of the first and most important factors on which to base empirical future projections is the age structure of the population. Since the so-called baby boom of the post-World War II period (see Table 18.1) the population of the United States has grown steadily younger. But today, as the birthrate becomes smaller and smaller, the trend has reversed toward a population with a continually growing proportion of older people. Meanwhile, the vast number of people born in the early 1950s are approaching middle age, and in the next fifty years will enter old age. By the year 2030 there should be 32 persons over the age of sixty-five for every 100 adults aged eighteen to sixty-four in the United States, unless we have either another baby boom or a surge of immigration (Morrison, 1979).

What implications does this changing age structure have for the future of sexuality? In the first place, much (if not all) of the sexual experimentation characteristic of recent years is associated with the youthful segment of the population. In the second place, history records that the younger generation of any given age structure tends to be more experimental than the older generations.

The age structure of the population, then, is not expanding in a unilinear direction toward a stable or increasing proportion of youth; it is beginning a new cycle of an expansion of the middle-aged and aged proportions of the population. One probable consequence of the aging of the population is a reversal of the trend toward sexual and marital experimentation, and a return to more conservative and traditional forms.

Birthrates

Changing age structures are dependent upon changing birth and death rates. Together with a changing age structure has come a decrease in the reproductive role of women, both a decrease in the birthrate (see Table 18.1) and a shortening of the time span that women devote to child rearing. In 1900, for example, the average female life span was forty-eight, with ages twenty-two to forty devoted to the bearing and rearing of infants. Today the average female life span is seventy-four, with childbearing limited in general to the period between twenty and twenty-six (Ramey, 1976, p. 6.)

Family size also has decreased. The number of live births for the average American fertile female dropped from eight at the end of the eighteenth century to three in 1970 (Winch, 1970). The average size of a household was 5.4 in 1790, 4.2 in 1900, and 3.1 in 1971 (Eshleman, 1974, p. 6).

There is some contemporary argument as to whether the birthrate will continue to decline or whether it will take a cyclical upturn. The most reasonable forecast, made by the Census Bureau, projects an average of 2.1 births per woman during her childbearing years. By this projection the population will increase slightly during the 1980s, with 2.2 million live births each year. Thereafter the annual increase will moderate to between 1.5 to 2.0 million during the 1990s (Morrison, 1979).

Two-Worker Families

Closely related to the trend toward smaller families is the increase in the number of women who are working. In 1950 only 24 percent of wives were working, compared to 46 percent in 1977. By 1979 almost 60 percent of families that included both a husband and a wife had at least two wage earners. According to the Department of Labor's Bureau of Labor Statistics, "The rising number of multi-earner families has been one of the most important socioeconomic developments of the 1970s." Also, an increasing number of wives are expecting to have careers rather than temporary jobs to supplement the family income or relieve the monotony of housework. They are starting work earlier in life and continuing to work after children arrive and on into their older years. They are increasing their representation in higher paying professional occupations. For example, women now account for one of every eight physicians, compared to one of every eighteen in 1962 (Morrison, 1979).

The trend toward smaller families and economic equality between women and men should have profound influences on intimate relationships in the future. One short-term effect of the trend toward women working is an increased family income, which allows for more luxuries and more leisure time.

Leisure

The twentieth century in the United States has seen an expansion in the amount of leisure available to the growing middle class, if not to the upper or lower classes (Wilensky, 1973). In the near future at least, the trend toward leisure is expected to continue (Harvey, 1975).

One use of leisure is the experiencing of, and perhaps experimentation with, sexual interaction. With increasing acceptance of leisure as valuable, the work ethic may come to be applied less often to sex. Perhaps in the future we will cease to make orgasm the only goal of sexual interaction. Instead, orgasm may be a delightful interruption in an otherwise continuous process of generating pleasurable sensations. Orgasm may not be the goal of every erotic encounter, but rather a possible outcome that often arises naturally as the lovemaking proceeds (Slater, 1977).

Dual Careers and Commuter Marriages

The phenomenon of two career-bound persons in one family has been called the dual-career family, and it brings with it special problems and adaptations (Hall and Hall, 1979). Many of the careers to which greater numbers of women are now aspiring involve intermittent traveling or moving (Bird, 1975). When both a woman and a man have prestigious careers that demand moving to another location, it is unlikely that the required moves will coordinate very easily. Many families, therefore, are instituting such adaptations as the commuter, or long-distance marriage.

In the *commuter,* or *long-distance, marriage,* spouses live at some distance from each other. They may arrange to travel back and forth on a regular monthly or weekly basis, or just a few times a year, or in some cases they

The fact that more wives now have careers of their own is causing changes in marriage relationships and the traditional roles of husband and wife.
Joel Gordon

545

simply do not see each other for whatever period is required. In such families either the wife or husband assumes responsibility for the children; at the present stage of social development, the responsible one is most often the wife.

One middle-aged husband in a two-career family reports: My wife did not want to give up her job in San Francisco and I could not stay here, so I went to Minneapolis while she stayed in San Francisco — we were actually only separated for four months. . . . She kept the two children here. . . . I flew back about four times during that period.

From the authors' files

The sexual adaptations made by such a couple range from abstinence to secret extramarital sexuality or an agreement that each may have sexual interaction with others (with whatever strings or rules might be attached by the partners). The husband just quoted comments:

There was never any discussion of what we would do sexually because there was never any question. . . . We would go and deal with whatever happened when we got back together. . . . I did not get involved with anyone during the period we were separated because it would be too emotionally involved and complex. . . . I don't know about my wife, you would have to ask her.

From the authors' files

Whatever sexual adaptation is made is likely to affect the experience of sexuality and the institution of marriage itself, at least among those classes in which women are moving into responsible careers.

Changing Sex Roles

As women have increasingly assumed careers in positions where their income and prestige are equivalent to those of most men, the relationships between the sexes have changed. Liberation for women is also resulting in liberation for men.

There has been a movement in today's society toward depolarization of sex-role relationships and role symbols. Today there are more role relationships that differ from those of the traditional patriarchal family than there were several decades ago. Women no longer automatically desire and bear children and do the housework; men no longer automatically make decisions for their wives, compete in the rat race, and take out the garbage. Some women hold high-paying professional jobs, prefer to be unmarried, and change the oil in their cars; some men take care of babies, are tender and soft in their relationships, and do the ironing.

Cultural symbols of role are also depolarizing; males and females are not so completely divergent in appearance, voice, and body language as they once were. Hair lengths may be short or long for either sex; women

546

Today there is a movement away from the polarization of sex roles and toward more sharing of responsibilities and duties in the marriage relationship.
Elizabeth Crew/ICON

can wear pants, and men, caftans and necklaces. The trend to unisex in fashions has created a greater variety and range of fashions for both males and females. As McLuhan and Leonard (1974) see it, the styles of male and female personality, like their clothes, need to become more alike for a future in which an "emotional range and greater psychic mobility" are required.

Economic Changes

At present only the upper-middle and middle classes are influenced to any great degree by changes in sex roles and high-powered careers for women, but the ramifications of such changes tend to spread over time to lower social classes and to disadvantaged ethnic minorities. Such spread of social movements from the upper to the lower classes tends to be a feature of the dissemination of social behavior in general; at the same time, there are processes at work in society that appear to draw the lower classes and the disadvantaged into the cultural world of the middle classes.

Affluence The growing affluence of our society, of which increasing leisure is one product, was both an absolute and a relative phenomenon for   547 several decades before the economic problems of the 1970s. Absolutely, median average income has risen faster than the rising cost of living; relatively, a progressively smaller percentage of the population has incomes below the poverty line. Talcott Parsons (Johnson, 1975) called the betterment of previously disadvantaged sectors of the population *inclusion,* a process by which more and more people are included in the American dream of abundant material goods, prosperity, and equality.

Embourgeoisement Inclusion is linked to the theory of *embourgeoisement,* which proposes the inclusion of previously lower-class or nonwhite people into the white middle class. In general, the theory of embourgeoisement has not been borne out by empirical evidence. As Goldthorpe et al. point out, "Very little *direct* evidence . . . (supports) the specific proposition that manual workers and their families were in the process of being assimilated on a relatively large scale into middle class ways of life and middle class society" (1967, p. 66).

On the other hand, the culture of the lower classes and of ethnic minorities is undoubtedly influenced somewhat by the mass media and by contact with middle-class society through education and other social institutions. To the extent that lower-class sexual behavior and attitudes differ from those of the upper classes, and black or other minority behavior and attitudes from those of whites, we can expect lower-class sexual interaction to continue to become increasingly like the white middle-class standard (see Chapter 1).

A comparison of the Kinsey data with the Hunt data shows that there has been some embourgeoisement of the sex habits of the lower classes. During the past generation, the sexual attitudes and behavior of Americans in general have shifted considerably in the direction of greater latitude. This shift, particularly among younger adults, has tended to narrow the gap between white-collar and blue-collar people, and between people with college educations and those without. There is, today, something close to a consensus or dominant sexual ethic among the young, regardless of their social class (Hunt, 1974, pp. 28–36).

Technological Changes

Contemporary society is characterized by continued technological innovation, in sexuality and reproduction as well as in other areas. Francoeur comments:

Within a decade or two our technology has plunged us into the midst of *manmade* sex: artificial insemination, frozen sperm and egg banks for humans, embryo

Francoeur, 1974, p. 5

548

transplants, surrogate mothers, genetic selection and modifications, predetermination of fetal sex, conception control, legalized abortion and transexual [sic] operations are already in use. And tomorrow holds the probabilities of artificial wombs, asexual forms of human reproduction, and genetic engineering.

Research on Reproduction

Among the most significant technological innovations related to sexuality and the future are new species, cloning, test tube babies, multiparents, and genetic engineering.

New Species   New species midway between plants and animals have been created in the cellular stage. A frog with a new chromosome code differing from either the male or female code has been bred. Mice embryos have been frozen and thawed, and have continued normal development. Ovaries and vaginas have been transplanted successfully in both human and animal females (Francoeur, 1974).

Cloning   *Cloning* refers to the propagation of a life form by duplicating it from a single cell of its own being. Because every human and animal cell contains an entire genetic code, cloning is considered a feasible scientific operation within the near future. The possibility of cloning means that humans would have the potential of reproducing themselves indefinitely, or of reproducing famous or brilliant people to benefit society. The possibility of mutations and the technical difficulties of manipulating living micro-organisms in a laboratory make perfect cloning difficult to achieve. (See Selection 18.1.)

A Human Clone? Prospects vs. Risks Weighed

Selection 18.1

A human clone would, at best, be a carbon copy, Dr. H. Eldon Sutton points out. But, he says, because of mutations and/or the inability to duplicate the nurturing environment, the chances are slim.

   The chances for mutation depend on what kind of cell is used to fertilize the egg. A sperm cell has a good chance of producing a direct replica, without mutation; but, because it carries only 23 chromosomes (half of the normal total per cell), the offspring would be created from only half of that parent and would not be a direct genotype. Also the chance for a lethal gene, normally recessive, to become activated in this case, is very high, according to Dr. William Bennett of Cambridge, Mass.

   A cell from another part of the body — the skin or internal organ — would provide a full number of chromosomes for duplication but poses a high risk of

Science Digest, June 1978, p. 3. Reprinted by permission from *Science Digest*. Copyright © 1978 The Hearst Corporation. All Rights Reserved.

549

mutation, says Dr. Bennett. Every skin cell has undergone many multiplications; and the more cell divisions, the higher the chance for mutation.

Choosing the donor cell is, however, only one of several risky stages of the cloning process which have not yet been perfected in documented experiments, although many scientists acknowledge the possibility of success.

First you need an ovum, or egg. The injection of a "fertility" drug such as Pergonal can induce eggs to ripen *in vivo*, in the uterus, where experimenters say they have the best chance for survival. Usually about 32 hours following the injection, the almost ripened eggs can be removed from the surface of the ovary, using a delicate instrument called a laparoscope, and then placed in a special culture.

Most scientists agree that the next step presents the biggest challenge. The nuclei of both the egg cell and the donor's sperm or body cell must be separated from their surrounding cytoplasm. Then the donor's nucleus must be implanted into the empty cytoplasm of the egg cell, and the resulting embryo must, finally, be activated to reproduce.

This process has been performed successfully on mice and tadpoles using micromanipulation — physically manipulating the cells — but the chances for success with human eggs are "extremely low," most scientists believe, because these eggs are so much smaller and more delicate. Dr. Landrum Shettles of Randolph, Vt., reports performing three successful nuclear exchanges, but he has not yet published his results.

Dr. Bennett points out that the other method, cell fusion, is "plausible": the ovum nucleus can be "knocked out" by irradiation, and then certain substances such as viruses are known to work on cells to make them fuse. With fusion, however, some of the cell material from the ovum — mitochondria, for example — can get mixed up in the fusion process, and its minor genetic effect would ruin the carbon copy.

Assuming that the nucleus has been implanted without causing great damage to the ovum, the embryo must grow to the blastocyst stage . . . in a culture and then be implanted into the wall of the uterus. Dr. Douglas Bevis of England states he has accomplished this task, but will not publish his results.

Many scientists agree that a cloned person is possible. Some have been convinced enough to speak openly about the potential dangers of cloning and eugenics, and others have taken political or legal steps to control genetic engineering. They want to know who will be in control and what those people will want to produce.

Multiparents Another reproductive innovation has been accomplished in animals: the blending of two fertilized embryos to form one, which then grows into a hybrid with multiparents. As Toffler puts it: 550

A typical multi-mouse, born of two pairs of parents, has white fur and whiskers on one side of its face, dark fur and whiskers on the other, with alternating bands of white and dark hair covering the rest of the body. Some 700 mice bred in this fashion have already produced more than 35,000 offspring themselves. If multi-mouse is here, can "multi-man" be far behind?

Toffler, 1979, p. 241

Test Tube Babies In 1978 the first confirmed test tube baby was born in England and christened Louise Brown. Louise had been conceived on November 10, 1977, in a medical laboratory by Doctors Edwards and Steptoe, who used an ovum from Lesley Brown and a sperm from John Brown. The fertilized egg was allowed to continue dividing in the test tube for two and a half days and was then inserted into Lesley Brown's uterus. This time, unlike some previous attempts with would-be mothers, the pregnancy continued. Nine days before her due date the mother-to-be developed toxemia, and Dr. Steptoe decided to deliver the baby by Caesarean section — a healthy five-pound, twelve-ounce girl.

Although the birth of Louise is a major medical breakthrough, it poses some important problems. Thousands of infertile women have been given hope, but only a tiny proportion of these hopes can be satisfied under even the best of circumstances. Very few medical teams possess the skills of Doctors Steptoe and Edwards in this controversial field. Even these two men tried their procedure more than eighty times before they produced a test tube conception that resulted in a successful birth (Gwynne, 1978).

In addition, there is no guarantee as to the health of babies conceived in test tubes. Although Louise is free of gross physical and mental defects, she cannot be considered free of all developmental anomalies that may occur as she becomes older. There is a fear that the success with Louise occurred only by chance and that future test tube babies may be genetically or physically less than perfect at birth.

A difficult legal question involves the status of the fertilized egg before implantation in the mother's uterus. Is this fertilized egg to be considered a human being whose life must be saved at any cost? Or can defective eggs or unused eggs simply be thrown down the drain as unnecessary or undesirable laboratory products?

Surrogate Pregnancy The possibility of babies being conceived in a test tube leads to the question of a fertilized egg being implanted in the uterus of a woman other than the biological mother who produced the egg. Thus women who could not carry a pregnancy to term or who did not want to bother with pregnancy might pay another woman to nurture a fetus in her womb for nine months. Legal and interpersonal questions might arise when the baby was born if both women claimed to be its mother.

Other combinations of sperm, egg, and uterus can be imagined. For example, a woman who cannot ovulate might ask for an egg from a fertile woman (possibly her sister) to be fertilized in a test tube with her husband's sperm and then implanted in her own uterus. Again questions arise, such as the legitimacy of a child whose biological mother is not married to the biological father.

Artificial Wombs   Embryo mice have been sustained in the test tube almost halfway through their normal gestation period. Artificial wombs have been developed that will successfully nurture a lamb fetus that would otherwise die (Gwynne, 1978, p. 11). Eventually these two techniques might be combined to produce an artificial womb that could successfully carry a human pregnancy from conception to birth — motherless gestation. When an artificial womb is perfected, the production of human beings can be almost completely separated from sexuality and parenting. Women may donate their eggs to a laboratory egg bank, and men donate semen to a sperm bank. The laboratory personnel would then take over, fertilizing eggs in test tubes and producing children in laboratory wombs. After birth these children could be placed for adoption or raised in institutions.

Genetic Engineering   Test-tube fertilization also provides the option for some form of genetic engineering. For example, if a father has a hereditary disease, he may ask that another man contribute sperm to be used to fertilize his wife's egg. The couple might feel that a child produced in this manner, making it half theirs, would be preferable to an adopted child who did not carry the genes of either parent.

With the emergence of such techniques as recombinant DNA technology, which allows scientists to replace individual genes, even more sophisticated genetic engineering might be developed. One would hope that genetic engineering might eliminate such problems as mental retardation, physical abnormalities, and inherited diseases. Also one might imagine that eventually a couple could select before conception all the characteristics they want in their child; for example, a baby girl who will have her father's brown eyes and artistic ability plus her mother's intelligence and fair complexion. This would raise some problems if the technology slipped a bit and the couple discovered years later that their engineered child inherited the mother's lack of artistic ability and the father's lack of intelligence. Could they sue the genetic engineers? Or perhaps send back the faulty product for replacement, as one does with TV sets or lawn mowers?

If genetic engineering takes place in a laboratory, apart from parental concerns, to produce fetuses that are nurtured in artificial wombs, then   552 the laboratory scientists may have the option of selecting the characteristics they wish to see reproduced. They could decide what qualities will be screened out and what qualities will be bred in. They would be faced with the awesome task of deciding what constitutes a desirable human being for the world in the future (Cornish, 1980).

Brain Research

A major sexual theme in science fiction is that in the future interpersonal sexuality will be replaced by stimulation of the pleasure zones in the brain. Brain stimulation to pleasure has in fact been accomplished in animals, but it is not yet known whether all the erotic and psychological associations of human sexuality can be reproduced or improved by brain pleasure-center stimulation.

Some recent research suggests that there may be links between brain function and human sexuality. Scientists are exploring a group of brain substances known as endorphins. These substances are now being isolated, analyzed, synthesized, and scrutinized in an effort to understand their effects. They apparently modulate a variety of feelings such as loneliness and sexual arousal. For example, animal studies have shown that separation of mother and infant seems to disrupt the release of endorphins and causes literal suffering. Researchers are suggesting that the endorphins may affect the intimate relationships of adults as well as mother-infant bonding (*Brain Mind Bulletin*, December 18, 1978). This leads one to speculate whether sometime in the future one may take a pill to increase or decrease sexual desire, improve feelings about relationships, or alleviate loneliness.

Research on Contraception

In the past two decades science has made considerable progress in developing effective means of contraception. Yet the perfect contraceptive has not been found. So far all have some drawback such as side effects, cost, or inconvenience of use. Research continues worldwide in the race to develop a means of preventing conception that is inexpensive, easy to use, inoffensive, safe, and easily reversible.

Cervical Cap Cervical caps for prevention of conception are not a new idea, but caps devised previously could easily be dislodged. Now a dentist and a gynecologist have collaborated and developed a technique for custom fitting cervical caps so they will not dislodge. It is a relatively simple procedure. The gynecologist takes an impression of the cervix, and a dental laboratory takes this impression and makes a cap that will pre-   553 cisely fit the woman's cervix. The cap fits snugly over the cervix, riding on a film of mucus. It is equipped with a one-way valve so that menstrual flow may come out of the uterus, but semen may not enter.

This cap has not been extensively tested and is not widely available. One of the women testing the cap has worn her for two years. Among the one hundred women testing the cap, there have been two pregnancies. One pregnancy apparently occurred when one woman removed the cap to look at it shortly after she had sexual intercourse. The other pregnancy occurred when the valve had a hole in it *(Sexuality Today,* April 7, 1980).

Contraceptive Sponge   A collagen sponge containing zinc is being tested as a contraceptive. The sponge is inserted, either by fingers or by an applicator, inside the vagina and covering the cervix. It is retained in the vagina for the twenty-four to twenty-seven days that the woman does not have a menstrual flow. It may be removed, washed, and reinserted at any time. It cannot be felt by the woman or her partner when it is in place. The sponge is not dislodged during intercourse or by the contractions of orgasm. Apparently its resiliency keeps it in place. It absorbs the semen before it can reach the cervix, and the collagen and zinc possess spermicidal properties. An added advantage is that the zinc inhibits the replication of Type 2 *Herpes simplex* virus.

If this contraceptive sponge proves effective, it has a tremendous potential, particularly in underdeveloped areas, because it can be purchased and used without the woman seeing a doctor, getting a prescription, or having a special fitting *(Medical World News,* October 17, 1977, p. 29).

Gossypol   Chinese scientists claim they have developed a male contraceptive pill that is highly effective, has no serious side effects, and does not interfere with sexual activity. The pill, called *gossypol,* is derived from the seeds and other parts of the cotton plant. In order to suppress sperm production, men must take it daily for three months and then continue taking a maintenance dosage. A man can regain his fertility within a year after he stops taking the pill *(Sexuality Today,* January 22, 1979).

Vaginal Rings   The research team of the International Committee for Contraception Research is working on a vaginal ring containing estrogen and progestin that will inhibit ovulation in the same manner as do oral contraceptives. The hormones will be absorbed by the lining of the vagina and go directly into the blood stream, thus reducing the dosage needed and reducing side effects.

The rings, smaller than a diaphragm, are made of silicone rubber with a core of a thin, hormone-impregnated layer that permits time release of the steroids. The ring should be effective for about six months and can be left in place until it needs to be replaced *(Sexuality Today,* October 23, 1978).   554

Contraceptive Implants The International Committee for Contraceptive Research is also developing a pellet that releases estrogen and progestin gradually into the blood stream when it is implanted under the skin. This small dosage of hormones inhibits ovulation with a minimum of undesirable side effects (*Sexuality Today,* October 23, 1978).

Scientists at the Worcester Foundation for Experimental Biology are working on a contraceptive implant for men. It is made of a small plastic tube filled with three milligrams of the hormone prostaglandin. The slow release of prostaglandin from the end of the tube has caused sterility for six months when placed in the scrotums of test animals. More animal tests are planned before tests can begin on human beings (*Sexuality Today,* September 18, 1978).

LHRH Luteinizing hormone-releasing hormone (LHRH) is one of more than twenty peptides identified in the last decade that form the basis for the brain's control of many bodily functions. The brain uses LHRH to signal the pituitary gland, which in turn releases leutinizing hormone that triggers ovulation. Hundreds of synthetic versions of LHRH are being developed in academic and commercial laboratories around the world in an effort to create a new generation of contraceptives. It is quite possible that this research will produce a variety of new contraceptive agents, including a male pill, a so-called morning-after pill, and a pill to induce menstruation after a missed period. LHRH also is being tested for a new oral contraceptive that will suppress ovulation but will not produce the side effects characteristic of contraceptives containing estrogen and progestin.

A research team at the Salk Institute is testing LHRH to determine its effectiveness in preventing pregnancy in several ways. In one method, a small daily dosage is administered as an under-the-tongue capsule or as a vaginal insert, which prevents ovulation. A second method is a once-a-month larger dose administered six or seven days after ovulation. This dosage would induce menstruation several days early and would begin the degeneration of the corpus luteum, the part of the ovary that secretes progesterone and is necessary for maintaining a pregnancy.

In Uppsala, Sweden, LHRH is being tested by daily administration in the form of a nasal spray. A Canadian group is testing the same LHRH in a once-a-month dose to induce early menstruation. If tests continue to be positive, it is predicted that some form of this new contraceptive will be on the market in this country in less than five years (*San Diego Union,* December 12, 1979).

Testosterone Injections Researchers at the University of Houston have completed tests using injections of testosterone for male birth control. Men become sterile within two weeks after their first injection, and will   555 remain sterile if they receive similar shots every ten or twelve days. When the injections are discontinued, fertility soon returns. Although preliminary tests were successful, it will probably be several years before testosterone injections will be approved by the Federal Drug Administration and available to the general public (*Los Angeles Times*, January 28, 1980).

Sexual Scenarios for the Future

Technological research will undoubtedly continue and increase in the future. The outlook for economic and social change, however, is not so clear. Several viewpoints are presented here, taking into account the likely effects of economic and technological changes on life styles and sexual scenarios in the future.

Scarcity

It seems unlikely that the unprecedented prosperity experienced in the United States during the past few decades can continue without limit. Already our desire for an increasingly better material life is beginning to strain the limits of our finite resources. It is possible that future generations will have to work harder and yet adjust to having fewer material goods. A great many economists are predicting that the world will experience a major depression during the 1980s (Cornish, 1979).

In the recent past, periods of economic prosperity have been associated with an exploration of new sexual life styles. For example, a sexual revolution occurred in the United States during the economic upsurge of World War I and the Roaring Twenties. Again during the prosperity of the 1960s and early 1970s there was an explosion in experimentation with sexual life styles.

On the other hand, in times of economic hardship we have usually experienced a move back toward conservative, traditional values in marriage and sexual behavior. At the onset of the Great Depression, for example, women lowered their hemlines, dressed more conservatively, and became more respectful of a "meal ticket." The sexual code was no longer flouted, and family became more highly prized. There was less tolerance of deviant social behavior, and the younger generation became more respectful of their parents and traditional values. People stayed home and spent more time with their families (Stoken, 1980).

In trying to predict the future of sexuality in the United States, it is tempting to use the past as a model and predict that an economic decline will result in sexual conservatism. Some writers have suggested this as   556 one possible scenario for the 1980s. If we assume that personal relationships and life styles remain linked in the historic manner to the economic cycle, then we may conclude that American society will retrench and pull back toward traditional values when a downturn occurs (Francoeur, 1980). In this case we would describe the future as follows.

Sexually Conservative Scenario

The energy crunch and inflation will seriously cut into the spendable income of the majority of persons. As the average age of the population rises, this older majority's conservatism will be reinforced by the deepening economic slide. There will be less money for leisure activities, the younger generation will lose much of its mobility, and the home will gain strength as the focus of social activity (Francoeur, 1980).

Women will lower their hemlines, tighten their morals, and become more willing to assume traditional female roles. Sexual adventurousness and drug use will diminish. The younger generation will be less rebellious and less scornful of traditional marriage and family life (Stoken, 1980).

Marriage-preparation and marriage-enrichment workshops will proliferate, as will tighter marriage and divorce laws as an antidote to the high divorce rate of the 1960s and 1970s. Monogamous marriage and premarital virginity will gain popularity as women's liberation and gay liberation become very subdued or almost dead. The media and the educational systems will ignore anything other than lifelong, sexually exclusive, patriarchal marriage (Cornish, 1979; Francoeur, 1980).

Sexual Pluralism Scenario

If we assume that many of the social changes that have occurred since the turn of the century are irreversible, then we would expect quite a different future for sexuality in America. This view of the future acknowledges the impact of an economic downturn on many aspects of life, but considers irreversible the changes brought about by effective contraception, antibiotics for venereal disease, and the economic and psychological liberation of women. In this scenario the frequency of divorce, extramarital relationships, and single-parent families will continue to increase each year. As these realities become more visible, the formal values will shift to reflect the fact that few Americans achieve a lifelong, sexually exclusive marriage.

Institutions such as churches, courts, and schools will develop means for administering to the needs of persons in nontraditional relationships. The skyrocketing cost of land, housing, and heating will result in multifamily homes with communal sharing of costs, work, and responsibility.

One scenario for the future includes the possibility of more single-parent families.
Jean Claude Lejeune/Stock, Boston

Gay relationships, childless couples, unmarried couples, single-parent families, and multiadult households will become increasingly acceptable (Ramey, 1976; Cornish, 1979; Francoeur, 1980).

Although the duration of relationships may decrease, the intimacy of these relationships may increase. The old idea of lifelong marriage "for better or for worse" may be replaced by an emphasis on "for better only" in a relationship, however short its duration. The marriage vow might take the form of a renewable contract that would expire automatically if the marriage quality did not warrant its renewal. Parenting might not be the automatic privilege of marriage, but would require licensing of persons deemed suitable. "Professional parents" might raise children, with biological parents visiting and enjoying their children in the kind of relationship now enjoyed by grandparents and grandchildren (Stinnett and Birdsong, 1978).

If marriages become shorter and less binding and if parenting becomes less tied to marriage, the whole concept of family as we know it may begin to disappear. In this scenario many people would find themselves without a family to relate to. With family members very widely scattered and the family no longer serving its traditional functions, artificial or intentional families might be able to fill the void (Dudley, 1979). These artificial families might be formed on the basis of similar interests, such as church affiliation, occupation, or hobby. Other artificial families might be geographically based, such as a common neighborhood in an urban area or a common farm in a rural area (Cornish, 1979).

The disintegration of the family might also be accompanied by the elimination of interpersonal sex as well. If technology makes it possible to have bigger and better orgasms through drugs or brain stimulation, many persons may choose these means of sexual satisfaction in preference to the less certain methods using primarily genital stimulation (Cornish, 1979). Such a development could reduce sex therapy to a simple medical problem of how to change the dosage for one's chemically induced orgasms.

Creative Advancement Scenario

A more optimistic view of the future portrays the United States as meeting the challenges of economic scarcity with a creativity that can cope with change. In this scenario the throwaway society with its "me first" approach to consumption and relationships is replaced by an appreciation of cooperation and conservation. The need to share and conserve is evidenced in a variety of cooperative living arrangements with multiadult households. The pluralism of adult and family life styles that developed in the 1970s becomes fully recognized by law. Churches find rituals for covenanting and giving support to a variety of human relationships, including monogamous marriages, sexually open relationships, gay relationships, and celibate unions. Fidelity becomes defined in personalized terms of faithfulness to the commitment made to another person or persons. With more emphasis on sharing and less emphasis on private property in the economic sphere, sexual love becomes less of a limited commodity and more of a life force that can be shared (Francoeur, 1980).

Because of all the options available, individuals engage in serious consideration of the life styles open to them. The divorce rate drops for those

According to the creative advancement scenario, relationships will be characterized more by cooperation than by a "me first" approach, and fidelity will be defined more in terms of the commitment made to another person or persons.

Carol Palmer/Picture Cube

who choose marriage, and parenting is taken seriously by people who choose it. Individuals become aware of the value of their interpersonal relationships as a haven and as a buffer against an economic world that is increasingly uncertain (Francoeur, 1980).

Conclusion

No one knows what lies in the future. Unforeseen events such as a major war or catastrophe may make all predictions untenable. Unexpected technological developments may have far-reaching and quite unpredicted consequences. A long period of scarcity may have an unforeseen impact on generations accustomed to prosperity.

A few things seem certain, however. The years ahead probably will not be tranquil. We will face many challenges and will have to make many crucial choices. And the choices that are made will shape the world we live in for many years to come. But if challenge is inevitable, we may also expect excitement. In the sexual sphere, as in all other spheres of life, the decade of the 1980s promises to be full of excitement. Whatever our future is, it certainly will not be dull.

Appendix / *Methods and Methodological Problems of Sex Research*

The covert and sensitive nature of most sexual behavior in our society accentuates the methodological problems that accompany any social research and thereby increases the importance of both exploring these methodological problems and developing procedures designed to overcome them.

In their broadest sense, the terms *methodology* and *methodological procedures* refer to all methods used to obtain and analyze systematically information from subjects. These procedures can be evaluated from two perspectives: their effect upon the validity of different types of conclusions and their effect upon the respondents (ethical considerations).

To analyze the effects upon validity, it is helpful to classify methods by two different criteria. First, it is useful to distinguish between surveys or laboratory studies that analyze many cases and case studies that describe single cases. Second, it is useful to separate studies based upon respondents' reports of attitudes and past behavior from studies based upon direct observations of behavior by the investigators. These two dichotomies produce the four possibilities presented in Table A.1.

In Cell 1 are surveys based upon questionnaires or interviews, such as Hunt (1974) and the Kinsey reports (1948 and 1953). Such surveys represent the most common type of sex research. In Cell 2 are surveys or laboratory studies of direct observations of behavior. These are rare, but are well exemplified by the pioneering work of Masters and Johnson (1966). In Cell 3 are case studies based upon in-depth interviews, such as Bogdan's (1974) autobiography of "Jane Fry," a transsexual. Finally, in Cell 4 are studies employing direct observation and focusing upon individuals or sex-related communities, such as Warren's (1974) ethnography of the gay world.

By
Douglas Kirby

Table A.1

	Respondents' Reports of Attitudes and Past Behavior	Direct Observations of Behavior
Surveys/Laboratory studies	1	2
Case studies	3	4

563

Survey Research

An important difference between surveys and case studies is that *surveys* typically obtain a small amount of information about each of a large number of people or groups, whereas *case studies* typically obtain much more information about a smaller number of people or groups. The purpose of survey research in sexuality is to provide descriptive generalizations about the social attributes, sexual attitudes, and sexual behavior of specified populations. Surveys describe the attributes and behavior of a population and relate the attributes to the behavior, but ordinarily they do not provide an in-depth understanding of either the behavior or its meaning to the participants. Well-constructed surveys allow generalizations to large populations, such as American adolescents, American white adults, or American women.

Sampling

Most scholars conduct surveys in order to make statements about rather large populations of people, but they commonly have the resources to study only a few people. To overcome this limitation, many researchers employ sampling techniques and then generalize from the sample to the population. If the sample is selected properly, the scholars have the best of both worlds — reduced expenses and valid statements about the entire population. If the sample is selected improperly, the scholars may be able to keep sampling expenses quite low, but their generalizations will be invalid. Because of the overall importance of sampling, and also because some major studies in sexual behavior are based upon flawed samples, some of the basic principles of sampling are described below.

Representativeness   It is common in social research, and especially in sex research, for scholars to try to estimate the characteristics of some defined population. For example, they try to estimate the proportion of all American adults who have engaged in premarital intercourse or homosexual behavior. When samples are used to make generalizations to populations, it is essential that the composition of the sample closely resemble the composition of the population. If the composition of the sample does not approximate that of the population, then the sample may be biased and the inferences made about the population may be erroneous.

An example may illustrate the importance of this principle. Suppose a scholar wants to estimate the proportion of all American adults who engage in extramarital intercourse. If the proportion of men to women in the sample exceeds the proportion of men to women in the population, and if men tend to have more extramarital sexual activity than women, the generalizations to the entire population of men and women will be too   **564** high. Similarly, if a sample contains a disproportionately large (or small) number of people with liberal attitudes, with authoritarian parents, with greater education, with greater leisure time, and so on, and if these groups of people tend to have more (or less) extramarital experience, then generalizations will tend to be erroneous. Thus, it is imperative that all groups that have either more or less extramarital experience should be proportionally represented in the sample.

Probability Samples   Unfortunately there does not exist any sampling method that assures perfect proportional representation. However, whenever the toss of a coin, the throw of a die, a table of random numbers, or some other random process determines whether a particular person is added to the sample, then each person in the sample will have an equal chance or probability of being selected in the sample. In turn, whenever each person has a known probability of being in the sample, the sample is appropriately called a probability sample and the following occurs: (1) sample proportions will closely parallel those of the population whenever the sample size is sufficiently large; (2) deviations from proportionate representation will be random and will tend to cancel each other; and (3) the size of errors in inferences about the population can be determined by statistical calculations.

Nonresponse   After some sampling process has been used to identify desired subjects, a major sampling problem arises: namely, the problem of nonresponses. In some studies of sexual activity, only 20 percent of those people asked to participate actually do so. Such low response rates raise a crucial question: are those people who do not respond significantly different from those who do respond? They are obviously different in that they either are not capable of responding or are not motivated to respond. Whether this capability and motivation are linked to sexual behavior is not known. Do respondents participate because they view their own sexual activity as normal and common, whereas nonparticipants refuse to participate because they do not wish to reveal greater homosexuality, extramarital intercourse, sodomy, or other activities defined as either illegal or deviant by American society? Or is the reverse more generally true? Do people who have explored less common forms of sexual activity consider themselves avant-garde and therefore wish to participate? Do those with extensive sexual histories wish to brag or tell about their sexual activity while those with little sexual activity feel more embarrassed and consequently do not wish to participate?

Generalizations   Several conclusions can be reached about the representativeness of participants, and therefore about the validity of generaliza- 565 tions to the entire specified population. First, in the vast majority of studies on sexual behavior, the final sample actually observed does not constitute a good probability sample of the specified population. Second, the differences between participants and nonparticipants and the differences between sample proportions and population proportions are not well established. Third, for purposes of describing sexual behavior some of these differences are undoubtedly unimportant, and others may cancel each other out. Fourth, important differences undoubtedly remain and confound matters by varying from place to place and time to time. For example, decades ago when the topic of sex was usually taboo, differences between respondents and nonrespondents may have been greater than now, when sexual behavior can be more openly discussed.

Surveys of Respondents' Reports

All social scientists face the problems of obtaining accurate and complete information from human respondents, but once again the sensitive and covert nature of sexual behavior accentuates the difficulties. Because many studies on sexual behavior seek information about sexual behavior during specific life situations (for example, adolescent sexual behavior, premarital sexual behavior, and extramarital affairs), and also because the personal nature of sexual activity usually prevents outsiders from observing the sexual activity of any representative sample of Americans, most surveys of sexual behavior have required that respondents describe their past sexual behavior. Thus questionnaires and interviews rather than direct observation must be used.

Validity of Respondents' Reports   The reliance of much survey research upon respondents' reports of past behavior raises another crucial question already mentioned in Chapter 1: how do self-reported accounts of sexual behavior differ from actual sexual behavior?

Concealment   For a variety of reasons, respondents may wish to conceal experiences. Some respondents may have had sexual experiences that they subsequently perceive as exploitative or painful and may not wish even to think about those experiences, let alone describe them. Other respondents may feel considerable guilt about some experiences and may not wish to admit fully either to themselves or to social scientists that they engaged in such behavior. Still others may fear some external reprisal — either disapproval from the interviewer or possible exposure. After all, if the extramarital or homosexual activities of many people were revealed to the public, the marriages and/or careers of these people could greatly

566

suffer. Still others, especially older people, may simply forget about sexual experiences that occurred early in their lives.

For these reasons it is absolutely essential that the respondent be put at ease when answering questions, that some type of rapport be established, that questions be asked in an objective scientific manner without the biases of the investigators affecting the responses, that hints of unexplored sexual activity be fully explored, and that both privacy and anonymity be assured.

Enlargement Some respondents may introduce a different type of error; they may enlarge upon their past experiences. They may feel ashamed about their lack of sexual prowess and may compensate by greatly exaggerating past events or describing totally fictitious events. Others may do this unconsciously. For them, long-held fantasies may have become reality.

To avoid errors of this type, questionnaires or interviews can provide cross-checks on accuracy, and interviewers can ask detailed questions rapidly so that the respondent deliberately lying may be caught doing so. Of course, the best strategies are preventative; rapport should be established, and the need for totally honest answers should be emphasized, in the hope that the respondent will strive to answer honestly.

Errors due to concealment or enlargement may be systematic rather than random. That is, they may be related to social attributes of interest. For example, in the American culture men may be more likely to exaggerate, women more likely to conceal; young people may be more open and candid, and older people more restrained.

Evidence Many scholars have analyzed the effects of the interview upon responses. Ideally, reports of past behavior will reflect only that past behavior and not the features of the interview situation. However, the reverse appears to be true. Maslow and Mintz (1956) found that the physical surroundings of the interaction had an effect: respondents in visually more aesthetic rooms responded differently from respondents in less aesthetic rooms. Many researchers have focused upon the similarity of the social attributes of the interviewer and subject. For example, Hyman (1954) reported that the responses that white interviewers received from blacks seemed geared to what blacks perceived as socially acceptable answers. Similarly, Lenski and Leggett (1960) reported that lower-class blacks were especially likely to express agreement with agree-disagree items, even when agreement was inappropriate. Clark and Tifft (1966) found that errors in reporting occurred most frequently when unreported behavior violated personal or peer-group norms. More in the realm of sex research, Ehrlich and Riesman (1961) and Benhy et al. (1956)   567 reported that the similarity of age and sex influenced the frankness of sexual discussion. Least-inhibited discussions involved subjects and interviewers of the same sex; most inhibited discussions involved different sexes of similar age.

Survey Interviews Versus Questionnaires

Accounts of past sexual behavior are solicited through either interviews or questionnaires and thus are either oral or written. Each of these two methods of obtaining reports has its advantages. In a survey interview, much greater rapport can be established and many features of the interview can be varied to meet the needs of the respondent and the situation. For example, the order of questions can be varied; questions about sexual activities that might unnecessarily offend some respondents can be omitted; vocabularly can be adjusted to suit the respondent better; the meaning of particular words or the intent of questions can be clarified when necessary; and responses suggesting unexplored sexual activity can be more fully probed. In sum, the interview has the many advantages associated with greater flexibility and personal interaction.

On the other hand, the administration of written questionnaires is much cheaper, less time-consuming than interviewing, and is anonymous. Anonymity may reduce efforts to impress the interviewer, and may solve problems of confidentiality. Questionnaires can be made identical so that personal characteristics of interviewers and their interviewing strategies do not influence responses. They also provide a written record that can subsequently be re-examined, whereas oral responses cannot be directly re-examined unless they are taped. In sum, survey questionnaires have the advantages associated with standardization and impersonal or indirect interaction.

Nine Major Surveys of Sexual Behavior

The methods and problems of surveys presented above can now be applied to nine major studies, which are discussed in greater detail. These nine studies are frequently cited in this text; all asked many questions of hundreds or thousands of people; and all are national or international in scope.

The Kinsey Reports

Kinsey, Pomeroy, Martin, and Gebhard produced the two most widely quoted, most widely discussed, and for their time most definite studies of human sexual behavior, *Sexual Behavior in the Human Male* and *Sexual*   568

Behavior in the Human Female. Because the methods of the two volumes were very similar, both volumes are discussed simultaneously.

The Samples   For the first volume, Kinsey, Pomeroy, and Martin interviewed 5,300 white men. For the second volume, Kinsey, Pomeroy, Martin, and Gebhard interviewed 5,940 white women. Although these sample sizes are large by most standards, the failure to employ the principles of probability sampling discussed above has led to many criticisms of these samples (Cochran, Mosteller, and Tukey, 1954). In a scientifically haphazard (but not random) manner, Kinsey and his colleagues made contacts in different communities and asked them to participate. They then asked these initial respondents to convince their friends to participate. Many did so. Kinsey and colleagues also asked entire groups or organizations, such as college classes, fraternities and sororities, professional groups, and residents of rooming houses, penal institutions, and mental institutions, to participate. Thus, they developed community interest and used peer-group assurances or pressures to obtain 100 percent participation, so that 26 percent of the male sample and 15 percent of the female sample came from such 100 percent groups. It is clear that the samples selected by Kinsey and his colleagues are not random.

Their explanation for not utilizing randomization procedures is important. According to their experience, attempts to secure sex histories from lone individuals chosen by random sampling methods would have resulted in refusal rates sufficiently high to destroy the randomness of the samples. Instead they used friendship patterns and group pressures to reduce the errors resulting from nonresponses. Their sampling methods may also have increased the validity and completeness of the interview reports by increasing the initial rapport and confidence of the subjects.

The final sample included respondents from ages two to ninety, from all occupational and educational levels, from several religions, and from both urban and rural backgrounds. Moreover, it included at least fifty respondents from each of the forty-eight contiguous states.

Despite the heterogeneity of the samples, the failure to employ randomization procedures caused some groups to be either underrepresented or overrepresented in the samples. In one or both of the samples, college students, young people, better-educated people, Protestants, urban residents, residents of Indiana and the Northeast, and other groups were overrepresented. Conversely, manual workers, less-educated people, older people, Roman Catholics, Jews, rural residents, and people living west of the Mississippi were underrepresented. Consequently, when these samples were used to make inferences to the entire population of Americans, unknown errors were introduced.

To improve the quality of the male sample, Kinsey, Pomeroy, and Martin used statistical procedures to give extra weight to the members of groups that were underrepresented. For some types of sexual activity, this weighted or corrected sample suggested greater sexual activity. For other types of sexual activity, the original sample suggested greater activity.

The Interviews   Given their samples, Kinsey and his colleagues chose to interview respondents rather than administer written questionnaires. In contrast to their sampling procedures, their interview techniques have been highly praised (Cochran, Mosteller, and Tukey, 1954; Ernst and Roth, 1948). They appear to have been adept at using language appropriate to the respondent, at accepting descriptions of acts commonly considered deviant without condescension, and in general at establishing rapport and acceptance. They asked questions briskly to encourage honesty, but did not produce a feeling of being hurried. They developed a sense of which types of respondents found which types of questions most sensitive and then asked them at the optimal time. They learned when probes were likely to be successful in eliciting additional information and which probes were most successful. They also developed crosschecks for accuracy.

Reliability   In their analyses, Kinsey and his colleagues employed several methods of checking the reliability of their methods and data. First, they recognized that the individual personalities of the three major interviewers may have affected interviewing techniques and elicited different information. To test this possibility fully, all three could have interviewed the same respondents, or respondents could have been randomly assigned. Unfortunately neither of these procedures was used. However, the reports of hundreds of respondents of each of the interviewers were compared, and for the most part they were quite similar. Where significant differences occurred, they could be explained by the methods of assigning subjects to the interviewers. For example, older and more sexually active respondents were sometimes intentionally assigned to Kinsey.

Second, to measure the reliability of information, 319 respondents were interviewed twice with an elapsed time of at least eighteen months. The two reports from each respondent were then compared. Information about incidences of sexual activity (for example, did the respondent ever engage in a particular activity) and information about vital statistics (age of marriage, religion, and educational background and so on) were very reliable. On the other hand, information about the frequency of engaging in particular sexual activities was much less reliable.

Third, for 706 married couples, both members were interviewed and their reports compared. Once again, vital statistics and incidences of types of sexual activity were reliable, whereas frequencies of types of sexual activity were much less reliable.

570

Fourth, the stability of interviewing techniques was examined by comparing the reports obtained by Kinsey during the first four years of interviewing with reports obtained during the last four years. Once again the two groups were very similar, and discrepancies could be explained by differences in the sample over time.

Finally, the heterosexual activities of all sampled men were compared with the heterosexual activities of all sampled women. Because heterosexual activities involve both men and women, the reports by women of the frequency of these activities should resemble the reports by men. The male reports of marital sexual intercourse closely parallel those of women. However, on premarital intercourse the two groups differ; women report substantially less activity. Part of this discrepancy may have been caused by sexual intercourse between men represented by the sample and women outside the scope of the women's sample, such as prostitutes. However, the two major factors in producing this discrepancy were probably the nonrepresentativeness of the male and female samples and the greater refusal of women to report premarital sexual experiences.

In sum, Kinsey, Pomeroy, Martin, and Gebhard employed poor sampling methods, and consequently inferences to the entire populations of white men and white women should be made with caution. However, good interviewing techniques were used, and consequently many of the data, especially the vital statistics and incidences of activity, appear quite reliable, valid, and complete.

Morton Hunt

In the early 1970s the Playboy Foundation commissioned Research Guild, Inc., a market-survey and behavior-research organization, to survey American sexual behavior. The foundation then asked Morton Hunt to analyze the data. Hunt presented his findings in *Sexual Behavior in the 1970's.*

The Sample The Research Guild selected twenty-four urban areas that presumably represent the diversity of American cities, and within each city they randomly selected names from the phone book. These people were telephoned and asked to participate anonymously in small private panel discussions on sexual behavior. About 20 percent agreed to do so. Because selecting names from phone books caused young people to be underrepresented, an additional sample of several hundred young people was questioned separately and added to the original sample. After extensive discussions, the panel members were asked to complete written questionnaires then and there. Everyone did so.

The final sample contained 2,026 individuals, and according to Hunt, its composition closely matches the composition of all Americans over   571 eighteen according to sex, race, age, marital status, educational level, occupational status, and rural-urban background. The use of phone books to provide lists of names did cause a few groups to be underrepresented if not ignored: inmates of prisons or mental institutions, the very poor, the illiterate, isolated individuals in rural areas, and people in communes.

Despite the parallels between the sample composition and the population composition, and despite the use of random sampling methods to identify people who were asked to participate, the fact that only 20 percent of those asked to participate did in fact do so seriously calls into question the representativeness of the final participants. As discussed in the section on sampling, participants may be very different from nonparticipants. They may be more willing to discuss sex, more interested in sex, and in general more sexually experienced.

To determine whether respondents were more liberal in general than the overall population, respondents were asked questions about their attitudes and behavior in nonsexual areas such as drugs, boycotts, women's rights, and socialization patterns. Once again, according to Hunt, the sample closely represented the total adult population. However, Hunt does not present empirical evidence for any of these statements.

The Questionnaires Four versions of the questionnaire were prepared: for men, married and unmarried, and for women, married and unmarried. The questionnaires asked between one thousand and twelve hundred questions. Although blocks of questions were undoubtedly inappropriate for some respondents and were properly skipped, this was still an enormous number of questions to ask. Undoubtedly the respondents did not give thoughful answers to all the questions, and their errors may have been substantial.

When using written questionnaires instead of interviews, it is not possible to vary the vocabulary and the order of the items, to probe where a probe seems profitable, or to use many of the techniques that Kinsey and his associates used so well. The researchers did attempt to create rapport and honesty during the panel discussions prior to the completion of the questionnaires. These sessions are not described by Hunt, however, and it is not clear that group definitions of deviancy did not affect the responses of individuals. Thus, the reports of the respondents may have differed significantly from their actual behavior.

The Redbook Report

The largest survey reviewed here is that conducted by Levin and Levin and Redbook magazine. The October 1974 issue of *Redbook* included a questionnaire that was returned by readers and provided the basis for the subsequent articles.

572

The Sample   More than a hundred thousand women returned the questionnaire. Although a sample size this large is extraordinary, a smaller, more random sample might have been better. Two flaws affect the representativeness of the *Redbook* sample.

First, only those people who read *Redbook* were exposed to the questionnaire, and *Redbook* readers do not constitute a random sample of all American women. However, it may be unfair to assume that the population of interest must necessarily be all American women. This is a study by *Redbook*, for and about *Redbook* readers, and the audience may well find the population of *Redbook* readers to be a population of genuine interest. If so, the fact that *Redbook* readers do not constitute a random sample of American women is irrelevant to those readers, but the study is still limited for scholarly purposes.

Second, of those women who saw the questionnaire, those who were motivated to return it without being asked probably differed in many respects from those who chose to ignore it. Respondents, in comparison with nonrespondents, may have had more open, more comfortable, and more positive feelings about sex; or perhaps they simply had more time on their hands.

The representativeness of the sample can be partly estimated by comparing sample attributes with national statistics. In comparison with the population of all American women, this sample underrepresents women over fifty, women with a low education, women with low incomes, unmarried women, and nonwhite women. In terms of religion and political attitude, the composition of the sample more closely parallels that of all American women. This comparison is somewhat unfair if the population of interest is defined as *Redbook* readers rather than American women, for the *Redbook* population in comparison with all American women also has smaller proportions of women over fifty, women with a low education, women with low incomes, and so on. Thus, inferences to *Redbook* readers may be valid, although those inferences to the entire population are less valid.

The Questionnaire   The questionnaire contained only sixty items. These items focused primarily upon sexual attitudes and behavior, and had been pretested to the extent that they had been used in previous studies. The certainty of anonymity and the fact that respondents completed the questionnaire without external pressure probably improved the quality of the information obtained.

Pietropinto and Simenauer

The only major national study focusing upon married couples is *Husbands and Wives* by Pietropinto and Simenauer (1979). Although they are the authors, Crossley Surveys, Inc., completed the survey research.

The Sample   Crossley Surveys, Inc., selected forty-one cities or areas in nineteen states and the District of Columbia. Within each of these areas the research firm distributed questionnaires at ten or fewer sites such as shopping centers, hotel lobbies, airports, universities, and office buildings. All these were selected to yield a cross section of the population with respect to age, race, and socioeconomic status. At the sites the research firm randomly selected thousands of individuals and asked them to complete the questionnaire. Some people declined to complete the questionnaire, others completed the questionnaire at the testing site, and still others completed the questionnaires at home. Altogether, 3,880 people filled out the questionnaires, yielding a response rate of 57 percent.

Because procedures were employed to obtain a random sample and because the sample size and response rate are reasonably high, this sample is among the better ones of opinion reviewed here. Nevertheless, two questions should be raised about the validity of the sample. First, how did the people at these testing centers differ from a random sample of Americans? If they were at airports, were they richer or more likely to be away from home? If they were at shopping centers, were they less likely to be employed and more mobile? If they were at universities, were they better educated? Each of the testing centers had its own biases. Possibly they canceled each other, but maybe they did not. Pietropinto and Simenauer failed to present any statistics comparing the sample with census data on age, race, income, or other factors. Second, how did the 43 percent who did not respond differ from those who did respond? Did they have better marriages or worse? Did they have different reasons for getting married? Were they less comfortable with their marriage? Once again, the authors provide no evidence for the answers.

The Questionnaires   The questionnaires included two types of questions, fifty closed-ended questions answered by all respondents, and thirty-two open-ended questions that were rotated on the questionnaires and were answered by only some of the respondents. This combination of questions provided the authors with useful data and quotable material. Because many spouses answered the questionnaires separately, the answers of one spouse were compared with those of the other spouse. This enabled the authors to assess the amount of agreement about different aspects of the marriage.

The questionnaires were reasonably short, and the questions were clear. Thus, the resulting data are probably valid. However, many of the questions violate a basic principle of questionnaire design: namely, possible responses in closed-ended questions should be mutually exclusive and exhaustive. In this questionnaire many responses were not mutually exclusive and they reflected several different questions that were in

574

fact squeezed improperly into one question. For example, Question 22, dealing with the respondents' sex lives with their spouses, provides categories involving quality ("Very good," "Good"), variability ("Variable"), dullness ("Generally dull"), and quantity ("Never or rarely have sex"). It is theoretically possible that some respondents' sex lives are variable and generally dull and infrequent; such respondents would not be able to answer the question validly.

The text of the book suggests that the closed-ended questions produced less interesting data and that the open-ended questions provided richness of content. It is clear that a number of married couples responded in some depth to the essay questions, and their insights and experiences enhance the book.

The Hite Report

Shere Hite directed the most widely acclaimed study of female sexuality, *The Hite Report,* in 1976. The study has produced more insight than previous ones into women's perceptions of their sexual behavior.

The Sample   The statistics in *The Hite Report* are based on a sample of 1,844 women; this sample provided most of the quoted material. However, an additional sample of about 1,200 women also provided some of the quoted material. The basic sample of 1,844 women is a large one, and it includes women from different parts of the country, of different ages, of different marital statuses, and with different religious, educational, and professional backgrounds. Nevertheless, the sample is definitely not random, for several reasons. First, questionnaires were sent to approximately 100,000 women, and thus the response rate is very low. The women who did answer them represent only a small minority of those receiving the questionnaire and must have been unusually motivated to respond. What sexual patterns of these select women may have motivated them to respond? Second, many of the questionnaires were mailed to members of women's groups (e.g., chapters of the National Organization for Women), abortion rights groups, university women's centers, and women's newsletters. After notices appeared in *The Village Voice, Mademoiselle, Brides, Ms.,* and church newsletters, people requested and received questionnaires. Finally, *Oui* magazine included the entire questionnaire in one of its issues and thereby produced 253 replies. Although these groups and journals have wide followings, it is clear that they do not provide a representative sample of American women. The women in the sample are probably more liberated than most American women, and their heightened consciousness may affect both their sexual behavior and their perceptions of their behavior. Third, these sampling problems are further

575

aggravated by the fact that the questionnaire encouraged respondents to "skip around" the questionnaire and to answer only those questions that interested them. Such encouragement is unusual, if not unique, in survey research. It again raises the question: How do women that are motivated to answer a particular question differ from those who are not motivated? Are they less or more satisfied with their sexual behavior? Are they more open about their behavior and thus different in other ways? In sum, the severe sampling problems in *The Hite Report* make it dangerous to generalize from its sample to most or all American women. In fairness to the author, it should be emphasized that she does not emphasize statistics in her book, and her goal is not to make inferences to all American women. Instead, her goal was to gain greater insight into the sexuality of some American women.

The Questionnaires   The four questionnaires used in the study were exploratory and open-ended. That is, the questions did not ask the respondent to choose the best of several possible answers; instead, they asked the respondent to describe some behavior or feeling or to explain various activities. Some of the questions required a page or more to answer fully; others required only a few words or sentences. Although there were about sixty questions in the questionnaires, each of them had several probes that requested additional information and thereby lengthened the questionnaire. No one could thoroughly answer all the questions in less than several hours. Thus, it was necessary for the respondents to choose only the questions they wanted to answer.

Open-ended essay questions do not have the same reliability and validity problems that characterize closed-ended questions. The respondents' answers to open-ended questions can be invalid or misleading if they are confused or not fully honest. In this study, the use of fairly sophisticated words, such as *cunnilingus,* may have confused some of the respondents, particularly those who were younger or less educated. In many questions these terms were used without definitions and may have confused some individuals. However, this problem is not substantial, for two reasons. First, the people who completed the questionnaires were probably fairly familiar with this terminology. Second, whenever respondents did not understand questions, they could skip them. Similarly, numerous answers to the question "How did you like this questionnaire?" suggest that most respondents answered the questions thoughtfully and honestly. For some it was a welcome opportunity to explore their own sexuality.

In sum, this study has some of the characteristics of case studies. There is substantial information from many of the respondents, and this information is probably accurate, but it is difficult to generalize to other women.

576

Robert C. Sorensen

For his volume, *Adolescent Sexuality in Contemporary America,* Sorensen employed some of the best available survey procedures, and produced one of the best studies of both male and female teenagers.

The Two-Stage Process   In collecting information on adolescent sexuality Sorensen employed a two-stage process. The first stage was exploratory. Sorensen and others engaged in in-depth interviewing of two hundred adolescents. These interviews were unstructured, but covered a broad variety of topics. Many of them lasted as long as three hours. All of them were taped and subsequently reanalyzed. However, they did not directly form the basis for the tables in the book; rather, they provided information about the choice of vocabulary commonly used by adolescents and the sensitivity of certain topics. Equally important, they generated numerous insights into adolescents' sexuality and suggested many hypotheses.

In the second stage the knowledge gained about vocabulary, sensitivities, and so on was used to help test the many hypotheses. In this stage a written questionnaire was completed by a sample of 411 American adolescents and then analyzed by the researchers.

The Sample   The sampling procedures for the second stage were quite complex and are beyond the scope of this appendix. In essence the procedures involved two steps. First, 200 urban, suburban, and rural areas were chosen by randomization techniques. Second, from these areas, 2,042 households in which 839 adolescents lived were selected, again by randomization procedures. Because some of the 200 areas contained more people than others, the probabilities of different groups of people entering were different, but known. Consequently, the sample was corrected by statistically weighting its members. This corrected sample of 839 adolescents closely approximates a true probability sample, with all its advantages. Only two groups of adolescents are knowingly undersampled or omitted in the corrected sample: runaways whose whereabouts are unknown and people in institutional housing, such as reformatories, college dorms, and military housing.

To safeguard the respondents, Sorensen required that prior to administration of the questionnaire, written permission be obtained first from the parents and then from the respondents. Parents of 60 percent of the adolescents provided this written consent, and of the remaining adolescents, 77 percent participated. That is, 393 of the 839 adolescents asked to participate actually did so. Somewhat later, 18 nonrandomly chosen adolescents also joined the sample, yielding a final sample size of 411.

Once again, the crucial question needs to be asked. How do the respondents differ from those adolescents who were asked to participate   577 but did not do so? On many measurable variables the two groups were very similar: namely, sex, age, race, parental income, number of people in the household, locality size, and geographic distribution. On other important variables there may have been differences. For example, parents who refused to allow their adolescent children to participate probably raised their children in a more authoritarian, stricter, less open, and more sexually conservative atmosphere. Consequently, those adolescents that were asked to participate but did not do so may have been less sexually experienced and may have had more traditional attitudes.

On the other hand, it should be realized that the problem of nonresponse occurs in almost all studies of human behavior, that 77 percent of adolescents allowed to participate did so, that this is a very high response rate, and finally, that overall this is one of the best samples discussed in this appendix.

Sample Size   Sorensen's sample size deserves comment. In comparison with others, which contain thousands or tens of thousands of cases, Sorensen's sample of 411 seems very small. Even if it constituted a perfect random sample of all adolescents, sampling error alone would produce significant error in the statistical inferences. However, this error can be estimated statistically. With 95 percent confidence, it can be stated that Sorensen's estimates of true population characteristics will be correct to within six percentage points. That is, if identical sampling procedures were used to select one hundred samples from a population, in ninety-five of them the sample's percentages would be within six percentage points of the true population percentages. For example, when Sorensen states that 48 percent of the sample respondents claim to be virgin, it can be concluded at the 95 percent confidence level that the true percentage lies between 42 percent and 54 percent. This is a significant amount of error. Moreover, the error is even greater for those subsamples with smaller sizes, such as the subsamples of males and the subsamples of females.

The Questionnaires   As already indicated, material from the first-stage interviewing was used in the Sorensen study to produce the second-stage questionnaire. This initial questionnaire was also pretested and revised. Its clarity and easiness to answer are noteworthy. Like the Hunt questionnaire, its major unresolved problem was its length — thirty-eight pages. It is probable that few adolescents gave thoughtful consideration to the last few pages.

The presence of interviewers or administrators during the completion of the questionnaire overcame some of the deficiencies of the questionnaire method. The questionnaire administrators established rapport and motivation for completing the questionnaire and answered any questions.   578

Confidentiality and anonymity were nevertheless assured by immediately placing the completed questionnaire in an envelope and mailing it.

Aaron Hass

The second major study on teenage sexual behavior is the study by Hass titled *Teenage Sexuality.*

The Sample   Although Hass makes numerous inferences to American teenagers in general, his sample of 625 teenagers is definitely not representative. It does include a roughly proportionate number of minority teenagers, but it is extremely limited geographically. About 90 percent of the participants live in California and the remaining 10 percent live in New York, Michigan, Texas, and New Jersey. Thus, the sample excludes most of the Midwest, the Northwest, and the Southeast. Notably it appears to exclude rural America and the Bible Belt. Moreover, its focus, southern California, is particularly well known as a region that probably has sexual values and sexual activity that are different from those elsewhere in the United States.

The need to obtain parental permission produced a second sampling problem. Although the biasing effects of obtaining parental permission are not known for certain, conservative parents are probably less likely than liberal ones to provide permission.

Hass does not describe his procedures for selecting teenagers. Apparently he did not try to select teenagers randomly even in the limited geographic areas of his sample. Thus, poor sampling procedures rather than bizarre teenage behavior probably produced some of the counterintuitive statistical findings in the book. For example, the statistical data indicate that fifteen- and sixteen-year-old boys are almost twice as likely as seventeen- and eighteen-year-old boys to want to have sexual intercourse on the first or second date. Similarly, according to the data, a greater percentage of fifteen- and sixteen-year-old boys than seventeen- and eighteen-year-old boys have had intercourse with ten or more sexual partners. Because people can only increase the number of their sexual partners as they grow older, this result is undoubtedly due to poor sampling. Thus, in general, all the statistical data should be viewed with great caution.

The Questionnaires   Hass administered two questionnaires, one for females and one for males. They contained a useful mix of both closed- and open-ended questions. The closed-ended questions provided statistical data, whereas the open-ended questions provided insight into the teenagers' perceptions and behavior. The answers to the latter questions form   579 a substantial portion of the text of the book. Although Hass pretested the questionnaires, they nevertheless contained several flaws. First, some of the questions were undoubtedly not clear to all respondents. In a few cases the use of large words may have confused some teenagers. For example, the word *masturbate* is not understood by all teenagers. In other cases, the language is not clear even to adults. For example, one question deals with same-sex sexual experience. *Sexual experience* can refer to a great many different activities and may be interpreted differently by different teenagers. Second, the questions were not well organized by content, and this may have added to confusion.

On the other hand, Hass used several procedures to enhance the quality of the data. First, all teenagers were assured of anonymity. Because the questions were of a sensitive nature to teenagers, this assurance was essential. Second, proctors were present while the respondents completed the questionnaires; thus, they could answer any questions the teenagers might have about the meaning of the questions. This may have reduced the impact of the confusion inherent in the questionnaires.

Zelnick and Kantner

Melvin Zelnick and John Kantner are professors in the Department of Population Dynamics at Johns Hopkins University. During the 1970s they received large grants from the National Institute of Child Health and Human Development, the U.S. Department of Health, Education and Welfare, and the Ford Foundation to study the sexual behaviors of young women. In 1971 they commissioned the Institute of Survey Research at Temple University to conduct a national probability survey. In 1976 they had the Research Triangle Institute conduct a second national probability survey. Because these surveys received substantial funding and because they were conducted by academics for scholarly purposes, the resulting data are probably the best available. They are certainly the most widely quoted data of their type.

The Samples   Both samples were probability samples of females from the ages of fifteen through nineteen living in households in the continental United States. They included both married and unmarried women. Both samples were also stratified by race in order to assure sufficient numbers of minority respondents. The first sample contained 4,392 respondents; the second contained 2,193. Although Zelnick and Kantner have provided very little information about specific sampling procedures, they have indicated that they selected residences throughout the country and then gave questionnaires to the fifteen-to-nineteen-year-old women living there.

The Questionnaires Zelnick and Kantner carefully developed and pre-tested the questionnaires so that the resulting data would help answer a number of important questions on teenage sexual behavior. In general, the questionnaires focused upon female sexual, contraceptive, and pregnancy behavior. Although the two surveys contained some different questions, they also included many identical questions so that researchers could properly compare behavior in 1971 with the same kind of behavior in 1976.

Weinberg and Williams

In their volume *Male Homosexuals,* Weinberg and Williams both narrowed the focus on sexual behavior by studying only male homosexuals and broadened it by studying adults in three countries: the United States, the Netherlands, and Denmark. Both these changes in focus produced definite problems in their sampling designs and their subsequent analysis.

A second difference between this volume and the surveys described above is the use of two distinct methods, participant observations and survey research. The first part of the volume contains ethnographic material on the homosexual world in four cities: New York, San Francisco, Amsterdam, and Copenhagen. The second part contains the results of surveys of homosexuals and a comparison group of heterosexuals in these same areas.

The Ethnologies In the ethnologic descriptions of the homosexual communities in the four cities, Weinberg and Williams describe past and present formal homosexual organizations, the gay bars and private clubs, the relations between the police and the homosexual communities, and the general legal and social reactions of the heterosexual society. For these descriptions they employed a variety of methods: they visited many gay bars and clubs and observed firsthand the interaction within them; they both formally and informally interviewed customers of bars, leaders in the homosexual organizations, and the police; and they read and discussed the laws pertaining to homosexuals and previous accounts of past relations with the police. In sum, they used whatever methods appeared most useful in gaining understanding and insight.

The Samples Because the populations of interest consisted of homosexuals in three countries, several samples were selected. The nature of the homosexual population prevented random sampling; instead, a variety of nonrandom methods were used to obtain a cross section of homosexuals. In the United States, questionnaires were sent to some 2,700 men on the mailing list of New York's major homosexual organization, the Mattachine Society of New York. About a third of this sample lived in New York. Similarly, 200 questionnaires were sent to men on the mailing list of the Mattachine Society of San Francisco. An additional 258 questionnaires were given to members of another major San Francisco homophile organization, the Society for Individual Rights. These questionnaires were distributed to half the members who attended any of the organization's social functions during a ten-day period. Finally, 234 and 225 questionnaires were given to a random sample of people in gay bars in San Francisco and New York, respectively. Of the questionnaires distributed, 1,117 or 38.7 percent were returned.

In Europe the sampling procedures resembled those for the United States. Questionnaires were mailed to members of the major homosexual organizations of both Denmark and the Netherlands. In Amsterdam and Copenhagen additional questionnaires were given to members of homosexual clubs and to people at homosexual bars. In the Netherlands, 1,077 or 45.1 percent of the questionnaires were returned. In Denmark, 303 or 24.2 percent of the questionnaires were returned.

In addition to these twelve samples, the authors took a random sample of 300 cases from the phone books of Amsterdam and Copenhagen in order to compare the homosexual populations with the heterosexual populations. Similarly, they compared their homosexual samples in the United States with a random sample of 3,101 Americans collected by Melvin Kohn (1969).

Although the total number of men in the samples is large, several features of the sampling procedures mar the representativeness of the samples: some questionnaires were distributed and returned by mail, and others were delivered and collected in person; the authors collected most of the data, but Kohn collected the American heterosexual data; selecting cases was scientifically haphazard rather than random; and finally, questionnaires were given to varying proportions of people on mailing lists, in clubs, and in bars. For example, questionnaires were sent to all people on some lists, but given to only half the people in some bars.

Although in general it is impossible to determine which types of groups of homosexuals are either overrepresented or underrepresented, it appears likely that the samples contain proportionately more open and organizationally active homosexuals than the populations of all homosexuals. Moreover, homosexuals that returned the questionnaire may have better accepted and adjusted to their own homosexuality than those homosexuals who failed to return the questionnaire.

To overcome some of these problems, Weinberg and Williams controlled some of these sampling variables. For example, when comparing New York homosexuals with Amsterdam homosexuals, they compared each of the three New York samples with the respective Amsterdam samples. Moreover, on many important psychological variables such as self-acceptance and depression, all the samples produced similar results, suggesting that within this realm sampling problems may not have obscured important relationships or artificially created new ones.

The Questionnaire   Because questionnaires were distributed in three different nations with different languages, three different versions had to be prepared. The English version was created and tested first. It was then independently translated into the other languages by different translators, and the results compared and modified. Finally, an independent third party translated the questionnaire back into English for comparison with the original. Obtaining correct translations was especially important, because in the area of homosexuality subtle nuances of various words can become quite important.

The questionnaire was reasonably short and clearly worded. Unlike the previous studies reviewed, the Weinberg and Williams survey made extensive use of scales and indices that enabled them to measure an entire domain or group of attributes with a single measure. For example, six different questions on loneliness were combined to create a single index of loneliness.

Uses of Survey Data

These studies, as well as others, can be used to reach different types of conclusions about American sexual behavior. First, a single study may be examined in order to make a statement about the distribution of a single variable over the entire population. For example, Sorensen presents the proportions of all adolescents who are virgin and nonvirgin, and *Redbook* estimates the proportions of women who feel marital sex is very good, good, fair, poor, or very poor. These proportions are vulnerable to sampling error, and consequently their accuracy is suspect.

Second, within a single study, two variables may be related to each other; that is, one subsample may be compared with another subsample. For example, the sexuality of men can be compared with that of women. These types of statements are less affected by sampling error and are more valid because the absolute proportions of each subsample are not important; the differences in proportions are important. Differences are less affected by sampling error because each subsample is likely to be affected approximately equally.

Third, the distribution of a single variable in one study may be compared with the distribution of the same variable in a different study taken at a different time. These comparisons are especially invalid and suspect. If a difference is found, it may be caused by a difference in reality, or it   583 may be caused by differences in sampling techniques, the amount of rapport established, the method of eliciting information (written or oral), the form of the question, or the openness and honesty of the respondents. For example, it has been commonly noted that the incidence of reported premarital sexual intercourse has increased over the last few decades. However, it has not been ascertained whether actual premarital intercourse has increased or simply the reporting of such intercourse.

Laboratory Studies Using Direct Observations: Masters and Johnson

The advantages of observing behavior directly rather than relying upon reports of past behavior are both major and obvious. First, the many problems of respondents' reports, such as enlargement and concealment, are eliminated. Second, directly observed behavior can sometimes be recorded on tape or film and subsequently reanalyzed to check the accuracy of codifications of the behavior or to test new hypotheses.

Observations also produce major problems, however, especially in the area of sex research. As noted earlier, few people are willing to have their sexual activity directly observed by investigators. Second, even if permission is granted, the presence of the observer may dramatically affect the behavior being observed. For example, consider how you, the reader, would behave sexually if people were observing you. Third, the cost of observing the behavior of many people in a survey is likely to be substantially greater than the cost of interviewing them. Finally, if observations are used without accompanying interviews, much of the motivation behind the behavior and the meaning of the behavior may not be measured.

In the area of sex research, only Masters and Johnson (1966 and 1979) have directed major studies based upon direct observation in the laboratory. They have focused upon both the physiological changes that occur in men and women during effective sexual stimulation and the causes of these changes.

The Samples

Their first volume, *Human Sexual Response,* was based upon eleven prostitutes from St. Louis, Missouri, and volunteers primarily from the academic community affiliated with a St. Louis university hospital. Moreover, Masters and Johnson kept only those volunteers who had normal sexual organs, were sexually responsive, and could communicate

584

minute details of their sexual reaction. Consequently, the final sample of 382 women and 312 men is not a probability sample of American adults: most of the members were from one city; the members were above average in intelligence and education; they had a higher than average socioeconomic background; and they probably had somewhat unusual attitudes about sexuality. Nevertheless, the physiological responses that characterized most of these volunteers probably also apply to most other Americans. That is, there is no good reason to believe that the physiological responses of these volunteers differ substantially from those of other Americans.

For their third volume, *Homosexuality in Perspective*, Masters and Johnson studied 176 homosexuals and compared them with two control groups of heterosexuals with sample sizes of 114 and 567 respectively. The first control group was selected specifically as a control group for the study; the second control group contained some of the participants from the first study described above. Because of the difficulty in obtaining homosexual volunteers in the St. Louis area, they included volunteers from various parts of the country. Like the participants of the first study, the volunteers in this study had a higher-than-average education and had a history of easily obtaining orgasm. They were also disproportionately likely to be between twenty and forty years old and to have a committed relationship with another person. Thus, this sample is also not a random one. In *Homosexuality in Perspective*, Masters and Johnson do not attempt to estimate parameters of the entire American population; this would be inappropriate. However, they do compare the homosexual sample with the heterosexual sample, and they also observe the changes in the homosexual after treatment; these comparisons are appropriate, given the nature of the sample.

Measurement Procedures

For both volumes, the research team used many of the same procedures. Prior to observing the volunteers in the laboratory, they carefully interviewed the participants, obtained psychosexual histories, and administered medical exams. In the laboratory they observed episodes of masturbation, mutual masturbation, fellatio, cunnilingus, intercourse, and anal intercourse. They used direct observation and film to collect data on overt body reactions, such as voluntary and involuntary muscle tension, presence of sex flush of skin on the trunk of the body, perspiration reaction, and respiratory rate. The research team also used direct observations and film in an imaginative way to record changes in the primary and secondary sex organs of men and women. Because all female sex organs are not visible during intercourse, the team used an artificial coition machine created for their research project. It was equipped with a clear plastic penis containing cold light illumination and photographic equipment capable of recording changes in the vagina and the lower portion of the uterus during sexual response. Finally, the team used standard medical equipment to record covert body reactions, such as blood pressure and cardiac rates. To aid in their interpretations of these physiological changes, the research team intensively interviewed the participants after their sexual experiences in the laboratory.

Masters and Johnson's laboratory analyses of sexual responses of men and women, both homosexual and heterosexual, are important because (1) they are the first studies to analyze what actually happens during sexual stimulation, rather than what respondents think or say happens; and (2) they demonstrate similar physiological responses for both homosexual and heterosexual sexual activity.

Case Studies Using Reports of Respondents

Case studies are in-depth investigations into a single unit, such as one person, a particular group or community, or a specific nation. Whereas surveys collect a small amount of information about each of many cases, case studies contain a great deal of information about single cases. This major difference provides the major advantages and disadvantages of case studies. On the one hand, case studies can provide a more complete exploration of a particular case. They can provide greater insight into the important cases of interaction, the sequences of interaction, and the meaning assigned to the interaction. On the other hand, case studies do not provide generalizations to a larger population. Obviously it is not possible to make inferences from a sample with one member, especially when randomization procedures are not used, and when cases are sometimes chosen for analysis because of their dramatic and unusual qualities, not because of their typical and commonly found qualities.

As indicated earlier, the reports of respondents may be elicited either through questionnaires or interviews. When conducting case studies, researchers rarely use questionnaires; far more often they use in-depth interviewing. Moreover, these interviews are not limited by previously prepared questionnaires with their precoded, closed-ended questions. Rather, most questions are open-ended, and the unsolicited comments of the respondents are more fully explored. This flexibility can provide greater insight into phenomena rarely explored by surveys: namely, the important causes of previous behavior and the meaning that this behavior has for the respondent. In other words, in-depth interviews can provide a real sense of understanding as well as generate new hypotheses.

586

However, conclusions reached through in-depth interviewing are susceptible to interviewer biases (Isaac and Michael, 1971) for at least two reasons. First, the investigator must subjectively interpret behavior, judge its importance, and place it within a particular theoretical framework. However, Cicourel (1964) points out that the term *bias* is misleading, because in-depth interviews share the interactive features of everyday life. Second, many of the procedures for conducting case studies have not been well codified or taught, and many statistical procedures developed to measure the quality of data or the nature of relationships between variables cannot be applied.

In the realm of sex research, case studies have provided data on the major influences upon sexual behavior, the varying respondent-generated definitions of those events, and the sequential unfolding of sexual behavior. For example, Tony Parker's (1964) book of case studies of sex offenders gives several vivid accounts of the family background of these men as well as of their offenses, such as rape and exhibitionism. Similarly, Bogdan's (1974) autobiography of "Jane Fry" depicts the life history of a transsexual from early childhood through heterosexual marriage and hormone treatment. Finally, in this book there are quoted materials from case studies that the authors obtained by conducting in-depth interviews.

Case Studies Using Direct Observation

A crucial characteristic of case studies employing observation is the direct involvement of researchers in the interaction, behavior, or community under observation. Although direct observation is an essential and perhaps most important ingredient in this involvement, rarely is direct observation used alone. Rather, interaction with the subjects and observations of events are commonly combined with informal and perhaps formal interviewing, some systematic counting, and some analysis of documents or artifacts (McCall and Simmons, 1969). This blend of methods is commonly called *participant observation* or *field research.*

Because the methods of participant observation do not rely on randomization, their results are not generalizable (external validity). However, the results of in-depth interviews or participant observation provide more and closer data on the texture of social life (internal validity).

The ethnographies or descriptions produced by participant observation rely much more heavily upon the abilities of the researchers than upon methodological recipes. Therefore, the data gathered by field researchers tend to be only as reliable, valid, and interesting as the researchers' training and personal abilities allow.

Homosexual Communities

In sex research, participant observation has been especially useful in the study of gay communities. Recent observational studies of gay communities are cited in this book (Newton, 1972; Warren, 1974; Humphreys, 1972, 1975). A few studies, such as Humphreys's, actually observed sexual activity. More commonly, sexual activity occurred in private, and the studies focused upon the public dimensions of these sexual relationships.

Worthy of special methodological attention is Humphreys's *Tearoom Trade* (1975), an ethnology of homosexual encounters in men's public rest rooms. Humphreys's methodology had two phases: observation of sexual interaction, and follow-up interviewing of the participants.

Playing the role of a "watchqueen" alert to the approach of police or minors to the rest room, Humphreys made detailed observations of the sexual activities, typically fellatio, of males in the rest rooms. In addition, he interviewed twelve rest-room participants to whom he revealed himself as a researcher.

After observing males in tearoom encounters, Humphreys recorded their car license-plate numbers and traced their names and addresses. A year later, wearing a disguise, Humphreys interviewed the participants in their homes as if they were part of a routine survey; his subjects were unaware that he had observed them in tearoom encounters. He observed their social situation and asked them questions about their marital status, religion, attitudes toward homosexuality, and sexual relationships with their wives. Humphreys's methodology stimulated critical attention from sociologists and other persons concerned with the ethics of his methods.

Swinging

Participant observation has also been widely used in the study of swinging (Bartell, 1970; Palson and Palson, 1972). Using this method, researchers with their spouses have contacted swinging couples by claiming to be interested in a sexual exchange. In some cases the research team actually participates in sexual activity; in other cases they simply discuss the possibility with the swinging couple. Because the swinging couples commonly remained unaware that they were being studied, many of them either provided fairly honest answers to the researchers or engaged in sexual activity typical of a first encounter. Unfortunately, because swingers are generally selective and often prefer other swinging couples similar to themselves, only those subjects similar to the researchers can be studied. Also the researcher cannot ask too many questions of the other swingers without arousing their suspicions.

Effects of Methods upon Respondents: Ethical Considerations

The previous sections of this appendix discussed the ways in which various methods affect the validity of conclusions. This section focuses on the ways in which various methods may affect the respondents. Just as the sensitive nature of sexual activity increases the problems of reaching valid conclusions, it also increases the problems of protecting the respondents. During the last decade, both professional organizations, such as the American Sociological Association, and government agencies, such as the National Institute of Mental Health, have expressed concern over the protection of subjects. This protection involves two principles: protection from harm, and informed consent.

Protection from Harm

Either the participation of human subjects in research must cause the subjects no harm, or the degree and probability of harm must be outweighed by the potential social benefits to the respondents or to society as a whole. Two principal concerns of the researcher who attempts to protect his subjects are *anonymity* (protection from external social stigma) and *emotional distress* (protection from internal psychological harm).

Anonymity In sex research perhaps the greatest concern must be the assurance of anonymity. If private information about homosexual or extramarital relationships is somehow leaked to the public, marriages and careers can be destroyed. Surveys based on questionnaires returned by mail provide the greatest protection because the answers of a particular respondent cannot be identified unless questionnaires are specially marked or the sample size is very small. Personal interviews introduce greater problems of confidentiality.

Kinsey and his colleagues were perhaps the most careful in this regard. All information was immediately written in a code that was developed by a cryptographer, memorized by only a few people, and never written down. The coded data were then keypunched, and the resulting IBM cards were kept carefully locked. The researchers had pre-established procedures for destroying information if the courts should demand it.

Case studies create the greatest problems of confidentiality. Although care may be taken to hide the identity of the person, organization, or community being studied, that identity may nevertheless be recognized through other characteristics presented in the analysis. Moreover, if investigators are subpoenaed in court, they can deny their knowledge of the subject only with difficulty.

589

Emotional Distress   All methods using either formal or informal interviews have a common problem: questioning that produces emotional responses. It is the explicitly stated purpose of the interviewer to obtain complete information from the respondent, and to this end the interviewer uses whatever reasonable methods are deemed necessary, including sophisticated techniques. This goal of obtaining complete information may directly contradict the desire of some respondents to avoid thinking about or talking about certain sensitive topics. The stable, mature, sophisticated respondent may well resist pressures to reveal information, but the unstable, immature, unsophisticated respondent may not be able to resist the subtle and carefully designed techniques of the well-informed and capable interviewer. Such respondents may, in effect, be pressured to examine and describe past painful experiences. In turn, this remembering and re-examining may in some cases be painful and destructive. For other subjects, past innocuous experiences may be redefined as deviant. For example, childhood activities with friends may be subsequently labeled as homosexual and thereby produce concern about both one's homosexuality and one's guilt. For still other subjects, a multitude of questions about sex may emphasize their lack of sexual experience and lead to doubts about their sexuality.

In most methods, except surveys based on written responses to questionnaires, the trained investigator tries to establish many features of a close friendship, such as rapport, trust, personal interest, and openness. However, the research situation lacks a crucial element of a friendship; namely, a genuine long-term concern for the well-being of the respondent. Thus, there is an element of dishonesty and perhaps exploitation involved. The good investigator is accommodating, friendly, and seemingly concerned until the desired information is obtained, and then, typically, the relationship, the friendship, and the concern abruptly end. This can be damaging to unstable, naive subjects who reveal their well-hidden thoughts and feelings and subtly, or not so subtly, ask for friendship or professional help that is not forthcoming.

Adolescent Naiveté   Questions and interviews can have a different type of effect upon naive, uninformed respondents such as young adolescents. When respondents are in a period of attitude formation or flux or in a period of sexual experimentation, questions about various sexual activities may in fact suggest such activities to the respondents, or the asking of questions in a matter-of-fact manner may be interpreted as authoritative sanctioning of activities deemed immoral or deviant by the respondent's community.

Sorensen paid special attention to these matters in his study of adolescent sexuality. First, he obtained written consent from the parents and the   590 respondents. Second, he removed from the final questionnaire all questions on sodomy and oral-genital sex.

Informed Consent

A second major issue in the protection of human subjects is *informed consent,* or ensuring that participants in a study are cognizant of the use to which their information will be put. Sometimes the principles of protection from harm and informed consent come into conflict. For example, to protect gay respondents from social stigmatization, it is best to keep data anonymous. On the other hand, the optimum condition for informed consent is represented by a signed consent form filed and stored by the researcher.

Misrepresentation   Some researchers misrepresent the purposes of the respondent's participation. For example, the Research Guild, which collected data for the study by Morton Hunt (1974), asked potential subjects to participate in panel discussions when in fact the guild actually wanted them to complete questionnaires.

Covert Research   *Covert research* involves the concealing of the research purpose from respondents. In sex research the most ethically controversial case study is Humphreys's *Tearoom Trade* (1975). The ethical issues involved in this study include: (1) tracing tearoom participants' names and addresses; (2) concealing part of the purpose of the survey interviews at the respondents' homes; and (3) the definition of the tearoom as a public or private space, and the need for the researcher to explain his presence there as a researcher.

Conclusion

By this point it should be clear that there are three major criteria by which methods and the resulting data should be evaluated: the data should provide a real sense of understanding and explanation; the methods should allow inferences to larger populations of people; and methods should maintain the welfare of the respondents.

It should also be clear that no single method is best. Different methods produce different insights and different types of conclusions. Our understanding of the sexual world is maximized and our hypotheses are best validated when all methods are employed.

One final suggestion: An important methodological principle is that theories are best validated when different methods produce similar conclusions. When different methods produce conflicting conclusions, one or both of the methods may be in error. Your own personal experiences constitute one basis for making generalizations. Use the method of generalizing from your experiences even though it has obvious limitations. If you own life experiences produce conclusions similar to those reached by these authors, you should have greater faith in these conclusions. If they differ, you may want to question both the methods employed by these scholars and the representativeness of your own life experiences. Whereas the experiences of an individual may either cast light upon or raise questions about the findings of a given study, generalizing to the whole population from your own experiences involves considerably more methodological risks than the risks associated with the studies cited here.

And one final caution. All the studies evaluated herein include paragraphs in which the limitations of the results are clearly stated. Once made, these disclaimers are seldom repeated. Nevertheless, they should be kept in mind by the reader.

Glossary

Abortion Induced termination of a pregnancy or of the life of the fetus.

Adultery Sexual intercourse between a married person and someone other than her or his marriage partner.

Agape Greek word meaning love of humanity or love for *all* other people.

Algolagnia The linking of sexual urge to the experience of pain.

Amenorrhea Unusual absence of menstruation.

Amniotic fluid The watery fluid in which the developing embryo or fetus is suspended.

Ampulla An enlargement of the upper end of the vas deferens which serves as a pre-ejaculatory reservoir for the sperm.

Anal sex Sexual intercourse by insertion of the penis into the anus of another person.

Androgen A hormone influencing the development of male sex characteristics and the sex drive.

Androgynous Having both male and female characteristics.

Anima The masculine element of the collective unconscious as described by Jung.

Animus The feminine element of the collective unconscious as described by Jung.

Anorgasmia The inability of a woman to achieve orgasm.

Apomorphine A poisonous, white, crystalline substance derived from morphine which produces nausea and vomiting.

Arcadia A utopia which re-creates some past golden era in a setting of rustic simplicity.

Areola The dark circle of tissue surrounding the nipple of the breast.

Artificial genitals Any artificial reproduction of male or female sex organs, such as dildos (artificial penises) and artificial vaginas.

Autoerotic Producing sexual response in one's self.

Aversion therapy Association of unpleasant stimuli with behavior to be extinguished.

Bartholin's glands Small mucous-producing glands located in the groove between the hymen and the labia minora in the female.

Ben-Wa balls One solid and one mercury-filled ball inserted in the vagina for the purpose of erotic sensation.

Bestiality Sexual activity between a human and an animal other than a human.

Bigamy Marriage to two individuals at the same time.

Biofeedback A technique for giving an individual information regarding certain of her or his bodily processes not usually part of conscious awareness, thereby making it possible for the individual to develop conscious control over bodily processes not ordinarily under conscious control.

Bisexuality Sexual attraction to members of both sexes.

G-1

Bladder   The stretchable sac in which urine is stored prior to release from the body.

Blastocyst   A hollow ball of cells that after several days of floating in the uterine fluid begins implantation into the uterine lining.

Bulbourethral (Cowper's) glands   Tiny pea-shaped organs located below the prostate on either side of the urethra that secrete an alkaline fluid during sexual arousal.

Butch   A masculine or aggressive role played by a female. Generally associated with lesbians.

Candida albicans   A yeastlike fungus infection of the vagina in which the most significant symptom is intense vaginal and vulval itching.

Capillaries   Minute blood vessels between the termination of the arteries and the beginning of the veins.

Castration   Surgical removal of all or a portion of the male's external genitalia.

Celibacy   Abstention from sexual activity.

Cerebrovascular accident   Rupture of blood vessels of the brain.

Cervical cap   A contraceptive device that covers the cervical opening, permitting menstrual flow to come out but not permitting semen to enter the uterus.

Cervix   The neck of the uterus, which opens into the vagina at its lower end.

Chancre   A dull-red, hard, insensitive lesion of the skin; a first indication of syphilis.

Chloasma   Commonly called "pregnancy mask"; characterized by brown spots and dark blotchy areas on the face.

Cilia   Short, hairlike processes found within the Fallopian tubes which help conduct the egg to the uterus.

Circumcision   Surgical removal of the foreskin of the penis.

Climax (sexual)   A term for orgasm.

Clitoris   A small, very sensitive sexual organ located just above the urinary meatus in the female.

Clitoroidectomy   Surgical removal of the clitoris.

Cloning   Pertaining to genetically identical cells descended from a single ancestor; a means of producing genetically identical beings.

"Cock ring"   A metal or leather ring worn at the base of the scrotum that pushes the penis and testicles forward and maintains the erection.

Coitus reservatus   Withholding of male orgasm during penile-vaginal intercourse. Also called *coitus interruptus.*

Collective unconscious   Described by Jung as the part of the unconscious mind containing the remote past of all human experience.

Concubine   A woman who has a sexual relationship with a man and is often financially supported by him although they are not legally married.

Condom   A plastic or thin rubber sheath worn on the erect penis during intercourse to avoid the passage of semen into the female's body.

Consensual adultery   Adultery with the consent of marriage partner.

Contraception   Using any device or means to allow sexual intercourse but prevent or greatly reduce the likelihood of conception.

Coprolalia   Sexual pleasure derived from using "filthy" language.

Coprophagia   A craving for eating dirt or other substances usually considered dirty and inedible.

Coprophilia   Excessive erotic interest in feces.

Copulation   Sexual intercourse or coitus.

Corona   The ridge at the base of the glans of the penis.

Corpora cavernosa   Two cylindrical masses along either side of the penile shaft

Corpus luteum   The portion of the ovarian follicle that remains after ovulation and that produces progesterone.

Corpus spongiosum   A cylindrical mass running along the bottom of the shaft of the penis.

Corticosteroids   A steroid that controls such processes as the body's water and salt regulation and sugar metabolism.

Cremasteric muscle   The muscle within the scrotum that suspends the testes.

Cryptorchidism   A condition in which one or both of the male testes do not descend from the abdomen into the scrotum.

Culture   The ways of living developed by a group of persons.

Cunnilingus   Stimulation of the external genitals of the female by use of the mouth and tongue.

Dartos   A sac within the scrotum containing each of the two testes.

Demographic   Relating to the study of characteristics of human population, such as size, growth, or density.

Diaphragm   (1) The muscular membranous partition separating the abdominal cavity from the chest cavity. (2) A rubber caplike contraceptive device that fits over the cervix of a woman.

Diethylstilbestrol (DES)   A synthetic estrogen used as an estrogen substitute. Used as a "morning after" pill.

Dildo   (1) Any object used as a substitute for an erect penis. (2) An imitation penis.

Ducts   Tubular passages through which a fluid substance is carried.

Dysmenorrhea   Difficult or painful menstruation.

Dyspareunia   Painful sexual intercourse.

Dystopia   A negative utopia or vision of future disaster.

Ectopic pregnancy   A pregnancy in which the fertilized egg implants somewhere other than in the upper section of the uterus.

Edema   Swelling caused by excessive accumulation of blood and fluid in the tissues.

Ego   The rational part of the human psyche that experiences and reacts to the outside world.

Ejaculation   The expulsion of semen from the penis, usually accompanying orgasm in the male.

Ejaculatory ducts   Tubes formed by the fusion of each seminal vesicle with the ampulla of its respective vas deferens that carry sperm through the prostate and into the posterior urethra.

Electra complex   Described by Freud as a daughter desiring sexual relations with her father and hating her mother as a rival.

Embourgeoisement   The theory of inclusion of previously lower class or non-white persons into white middle-class culture.

Embryo   A baby in its early stages of development in the uterus, until the end of the second month, after which it is called a fetus.

Endogamy   Marriage within a social class, caste, or group in accordance with custom and law.

Endometriosis   Presence of uterine lining in other parts of the pelvis, causing cysts, adhesions, and pain.

Endometrium   The inner lining of the uterus developed monthly to nourish the embryo if conception occurs and shed as menstrual flow in the absence of conception.

Endorphins   A group of brain substances that modulate a variety of feelings.

Epididymis   A coiled tube that serves as an organ where sperm mature, extending from the seminiferous tubules to the vas deferens.

Episiotomy   Incision in the vaginal area to facilitate passage of the baby through the birth canal.

Erectile dysfunction   Inability to achieve an erection.

Erectile tissue   Tissue that ordinarily fills with blood during sexual excitement.

Erogenous zones   Areas of the body sensitive to sexual stimulation.

Eros   (1) A fundamental human drive described by Freud as the source of the instinct for survival. (2) Greek word meaning sexual love or erotic love.

Erotic   Pertaining to sexual feeling and desire.

Estrogen   A group of hormones that produce female sex characteristics and affect the functioning of the menstrual cycle.

Estrus   A regularly recurrent period of ovulation and sexual interest in female mammals other than humans. Also called "heat."

Ethinyl estradiol   A synthetic estrogen available in pill form.

Excrement   Waste material, particularly feces, discharged from the body.

Exhibitionism   The exposing of a person's sexual organs, usually to a member of the opposite sex, in socially defined inappropriate situations.

Exogamy   The custom of marrying outside one's own social class, caste, or group.

Fallopian tubes   A pair of tubes in the female providing passage from the ovaries to the uterus.

Feces   Waste discharged from the intestines.

Fecundity   The ability or capacity for producing offspring, especially in abundance.

Fellatio   Taking the penis into the mouth for the purpose of sexual stimulation.

Femme   A feminine role played by a lesbian.

Fetish   The object of an erotic fixation in an individual

Fetishism   Sexual excitement associated with an object or part of the body generally considered as inappropriate for sexual purposes.

Fetus   A baby developing in the uterus from the third month to birth.

Fimbria   The fingerlike projections at the outer ends of the Fallopian tubes lying close to the ovaries.

Follicle Stimulating Hormone (FSH)   A hormone secreted by the pituitary gland which stimulates ovarian follicles to mature and produce ova and estrogenic hormones in the female, and which stimulates spermatogenesis in the male.

Frenulum   The thin fold of skin on the lower surface of the glans of the penis where the glans connects to the foreskin.

Frigid A label often attached to women who are not sexually responsive.

Functionalism A theoretical system which assumes that every component of a social system makes some contribution to the system's equilibrium, and that any element of a system can be examined with respect to the function it has in maintaining the system.

Futurology The study of what will happen in the future.

Gigolo A man who sells his sexual services to a woman.

Glans The tip or head of the penis in the male and the tip or head of the clitoris in the female.

Gonad The testes in the male or the ovaries in the female.

Gonadal Pertaining to the gonads.

Gonorrhea A common form of venereal disease.

Gossypol A contraceptive pill developed by Chinese scientists suppresses sperm production in the male.

Graffiti Crude drawings and inscriptions on walls of public buildings.

Haemophilus vaginalis A venereal disease characterized by a gray discharge with unpleasant odor.

Hedonism Behavior motivated by the desire for pleasure.

Herpes genitalis The condition of painful bumps or blisters on the sexual organs.

Heterosexual Sexual activity and feelings directed at individuals of the opposite sex.

Heuristic Guidance to discovering and learning.

Homosexual Sexual activity and feelings directed at individuals of the same sex.

Human Chorionic Gonadotropin (HCG) A hormone secreted by the embryo in the third or fourth week of pregnancy.

Humanism The belief that human beings have a unique worth, not to be treated as objects.

Hymen The thin, stretchable membrane partially covering the vaginal opening.

Hypertension Abnormally high arterial blood pressure.

Hyperventilation Very rapid and deep breathing.

Hypothalamus The portion of the brain that acts as a control center for certain bodily functions.

Hysterotomy A type of abortion similar to a small caesarean section in which incision is made through the abdominal wall and the fetus removed.

Id The part of the human psyche that is the source of instinctive energy and repressed material as defined by Freud.

Imperforate hymen A hymen with no openings, tears, or perforations.

Incest Sexual relations between close relatives (not husband and wife) who are generally considered as inappropriate sexual partners because of their familial or tribal relationship.

Inguinal canal A passage in the male from the abdomen to the scrotum through which the testes ordinarily descend prior to birth.

Intercourse (sexual) Sexual relations between two persons, usually involving penetration of the female vagina by the male penis.

Interfemoral The area between the thighs.

Intrapsychic   Processes occurring within the mind of an individual.

Intrauterine device (IUD)   An inorganic object inserted into the uterus for the purpose of preventing conception.

Intromission   Time of insertion of the penis into the vagina.

Klismaphilia   Erotic pleasure obtained from enemas.

Labia majora   The larger folds of fatty tissue on either side of the vaginal opening.

Labia minora   The smaller folds of erectile tissue framing the sides of the vaginal opening.

Lamaze technique   Birth preparation method involving both father and mother as active participants.

Laparoscopy   Tubal ligation by use of a laparoscope that makes possible one or two very small abdominal incisions; often called "the Band-Aid operation."

Leukorrhea   A vaginal discharge containing mucous and pus cells.

Leydig cells   Cells located in the intertubular connective tissue of the testes which produce testosterone, estrogenic hormones, and other androgenic hormones.

Libido   Sexual energy which includes all the impulses that deal with love in its broadest sense.

Ludus   Love as a game, or playful love.

Luteinizing Hormone (LH)   A substance secreted by the pituitary gland causing ovulation in the female and affecting testosterone production in the male.

Luteinizing Hormone Releasing Hormone (LHRH)   A peptide that is found in the brain and that signals the pituitary gland to release luteinizing hormone, which triggers ovulation.

Macrophages   A defensive cell reaction activated by a foreign body in the uterus.

Mania   Word meaning an unbalanced kind of eros (love); given to extremes of emotion.

Masturbation   Stimulation of one's own body to produce sexual pleasure and (often) orgasm.

Matriarchy   A family structure in which the adult female is dominant.

Matrilocal   A family structure in which the family resides with the mother and her kin.

Menarche   The first menstrual flow.

Menstrual cycle   The rhythmic reproductive cycle in the female involving preparation of the uterus for pregnancy, release of a mature ovum, and discharge of the uterine lining if conception does not occur.

Menstruation   The (approximately) monthly discharge of the blood and tissue comprising the uterine lining in the mature, premenopausal, nonpregnant woman.

Mestranol   A synthetic estrogen available in pill form.

Mittelschmerz   Mild abdominal pain occurring in some women at the time of ovulation.

Monilia   Yeast infection in the vagina.

Monogamous   A sexual relationship between two persons which excludes any other sexual relationships.

Mons veneris The rounded mound of flesh at the lowest part of the abdomen, also known as mons pubis.

Multiparous Having had more than one childbearing experience.

Myometrium The thick muscled walls of the uterus.

Myotonia Muscle tension.

Necrophilia Sexual attraction to a corpse.

Neisseria gonorrhoeae (gonococci) Bacteria responsible for gonorrhea.

Neurosis An emotional disorder that dominates all or part of the personality.

Nocturnal emissions Dreams involving orgasm and ejaculation by a male; often called "wet dreams."

Noncoital Sexual activity not involving sexual union of male and female sex organs through penile-vaginal intercourse.

Norm A guide to conduct specifying what is appropriate or inappropriate.

Nulliparous The state of having had no children.

Nymphomania "Excessive" sexual desire in a woman.

Obscene Defined as offensive to accepted standards of decency or modesty.

Oedipus complex Described by Freud as a son desiring sexual relations with his mother and hating his father as a rival.

One-Way Butch A lesbian who does not receive lovemaking.

Oogonium The primordial sex cell, or premature ovum, from which a mature ovum develops.

Oral-genital contact Contact between the mouth and the genital organs.

Orgasm (climax) The peak of pleasure in sexual excitement.

Orgasmic platform Area formed by outer third of the vagina and the labia minora when they are engorged with blood during sexual excitement.

Os A mouth or opening. The cervical os is the small opening in the cervix providing passage between the uterus and the vagina.

Ovaries The pair of glands in the female which provide ova (eggs) and certain hormones.

Ovum The egg produced by the ovaries which is capable of developing into an embryo when fertilized by a sperm.

Patriarchy A family structure in which the adult male is dominant.

Pederasty Sex relations between a man and a boy.

Pedophilia An adult's desire for sex with a child.

Pelvis The basinlike cavity in the lower part of the trunk of the body of humans.

Penile erector A firm rubber or plastic splint formed to fit under or around a non-erect penis and support it.

Penile extender A piece of rubber or plastic shaped like a one- or two-inch penis worn at the tip of the penis and attached to it by straps.

Penis A cylindrical organ in the male, located above the scrotum and below the pubic bone; it serves as a reproductive organ by which semen can be deposited within the female vagina.

Perimetrium The outer wall of the uterus, consisting of elastic fibrous tissue.

Perineum The area between the anus and the vulva in the female, and between the anus and the scrotum in the male.

Peritoneum The membrane lining the abdominal cavity.

G-7

Pessary   Devices used for contraception or support worn in the vagina.

Phylogenetic   Development or evolution of a race.

Pimp   A person, usually male, who secures clients for a prostitute in exchange for a portion of her earnings.

Pituitary gland   A small oval endocrine gland attached to the base of the brain which secretes several hormones.

Placebo   A substance used to imitate medication but having no medicinal content.

Placenta   The organ formed in the uterus to nourish the fetus and remove its wastes.

Polygamous   Marriage involving more than one husband or wife at the same time.

Polymorphous   Consisting of many forms or parts.

Polymorphous perverse   When sexual energy is not focused on the genitals but can attach itself to any site of the body or use of any object found to be pleasurable.

Pornography   Written, graphic, or other forms of communication intended to arouse sexual desires, lust, lasciviousness.

Postpartum   The period of time following the birth of a baby, during which the mother's body gradually returns to its nonpregnant state.

Pragma   Pragmatic or practical love, that which fits into one's "scheme of things."

Premature ejaculation   Inability of the male to control or slow his escalating sexual tension and progress toward orgasm.

Prepubescent   A person who has not reached puberty.

Prepuce (foreskin)   The fold of skin that covers the glans of the penis in the uncircumcised male; the fold formed by the labia minora that covers the glans of the clitoris in the female.

Priapism   A rare condition in which penile erections become painful and prolonged.

Progesterone   Hormone produced by the corpus luteum which, together with estrogen, causes development of the uterine lining in preparation for pregnancy.

Progestins   Synthetic hormones that resemble and are often used as supplement to progesterone.

Prostaglandin   Hormone important in maintaining pregnancy.

Prostate   A chestnut-sized organ in the male, located below the bladder, which secretes the fluid that is part of semen.

Prostitute   A person who engages in sex relations for money.

Psychoanalysis   A method, based on Freudian theory, for relieving emotional problems.

Psychotherapy   A form of treatment, largely verbal, by which a therapist aids an individual in overcoming psychic blocks to healthy personal functioning.

Psychotic   A person who suffers severe mental disorder characterized by deterioration of normal intellectual and social functioning and withdrawal from reality.

Puberty   The period of physiological change from a young child not capable of reproduction to a young adult capable of sexual reproduction.

Pubescent A person who has reached puberty.

Pubic lice ("crabs") A yellowish-gray louse that attaches to the pubic hair and feeds from the skin; the most common symptom is severe itching.

Pubococcygeus muscle The master sphincter muscle of the pelvis, extending from the os pubis in front to the coccyx in the rear.

Raphe A seamlike union between the two halves of the scrotum visible on its surface as a median ridge.

Rapport A mutual trust relationship or an emotional affinity.

Rapprochement Conciliation or return to cordial relations between two groups.

Recanalization The growing back together of the vas after a vasectomy.

Rectum Lower part of the large intestine through which feces are eliminated.

Refractory period A period of time following orgasm during which sexual stimulation is resisted or is ineffective in producing sexual arousal.

Repression A process by which material is forced into the unconscious part of the human psyche.

Retarded ejaculation Inability of a male to reach orgasm even after development of a high level of sexual tension and protracted stimulation usually considered sufficient to produce orgasm.

Rhogam A substance injected into the body of an RH− mother who delivers an RH+ child.

Rudiment An incompletely developed organ or part.

Sacralization Treating some act or object as sacred or as having religious significance.

Sadomasochism The association of pain with sexual arousal.

Satyriasis "Excessive" sexual desire in a male.

Schizophrenic A diagnostic category generally referring to a person who exhibits reactions of withdrawal from reality and variable behavioral disturbances.

Scrotum The external sac in the male lying between the upper thighs and containing the testes.

Self-actualization Developing one's fullest human potential.

Seminal fluid (semen) The fluid discharged by the male from the urethra just prior to orgasm and which contains sperm.

Seminal vesicles A pair of glands in the abdomen of the male which provide a portion of the ejaculate that contributes to the nourishment and activation of sperm.

Seminiferous tubules Coiled canals in the male testes in which sperm are produced.

Sensate focus A therapeutic exercise devised by Masters and Johnson by which a couple learns to focus on the sensations involved in giving and receiving sensual pleasure through touching nongenital areas of the body.

Sex flush Reddish splotches on the body that sometimes occur during sexual excitement.

Sibling rivalry Competition between brothers and sisters of a family.

Smegma A cheesy substance formed in both males and females where the foreskin covers the glans.

Sociosexual Pertaining to the relationship between social conditioning and sexual functioning.

Sodomy Sexual relations involving inserting the penis in the anus of another person.

Sperm (spermatozoa) The male reproductive cell that can fertilize an ovum.

Spermatic cord The cord suspending a testicle in the scrotum and composed of the vas deferens, nerves, lymphatics, and blood vessels within its sheath.

Spermatids Immature sperm cells that form in the seminiferous tubules.

Spermatocytes Cells in the seminiferous tubules capable of dividing and forming immature sperm cells.

Spermatogenesis Formation of sperm in the testes of the male.

Spermatogonia The outer cell layer of the seminiferous tubules, which are undifferentiated germ cells capable of becoming spermatocytes.

Spermicidal Sperm killing; usually referring to a cream or jelly used in the vagina as a contraceptive (a "spermicide").

Statutory rape Sex relations with an adolescent who has not reached the legal "age of consent," usually eighteen years of age.

Sterilization (male and female) Removal or alteration of all or part of the internal sexual organs for the purpose of making reproduction impossible.

Stigmatized To label or brand as disgraceful or undesirable.

Stilbestrol (also diethylstilbestrol) A synthetic estrogen used as an estrogen substitute.

Stirpiculture Production of special strains by careful breeding.

Storge Serious love that is not dependent on passion; a developing love.

"Streaking" A short-lived fad in the early 1970s involving people running very fast through a crowded setting without any clothes on.

Sublimation The rechanneling of sexual energy from its original goal into a more socially accepted goal.

Superego The part of the human psyche that acts as the conscience or moral monitor.

"Swinging" The practice of exchanging sex partners between various consenting couples.

Syphilis A common form of venereal disease.

Technicization (of sex) The new approach to sexuality based on rules, instructions, manuals, and so forth, appropriate to technological society.

Testes Two oval glands located in the scrotum of the male that produce sperm and testosterone.

Testosterone The hormone secreted by the testes of the male that affects development of male sex characteristics and sex drive; one of the androgenic hormones.

Thanatos A fundamental human drive described by Freud as the destructive drive toward death.

Thromboembolic disorders Blood clots in the circulatory system.

Thrombophlebitis Inflammation of the veins combined with clot formation.

Transsexualism A strong feeling that one's biological sex is not one's "real" sex; a strong desire to be of the opposite sex.

Transvestism The act of dressing in the apparel of the opposite sex for the purpose of deriving sexual pleasure from this behavior.

Treponema pallidum A corkscrew-like spirochete that causes syphilis.

Trichomonas vaginalis A frothy white vaginal discharge with an unpleasant odor accompanied by itching and inflammation.

Trimester A period of three months.

Tubal ligation Surgical procedure by which the Fallopian tubes are severed, tied, or cauterized to prevent sperm from reaching an ovum, thereby preventing conception.

Tumescence Swelling, induced by congestion with blood and other bodily fluids.

Unilinear (change) Presumption of continuation of existing trends.

Urethra The tube through which urine travels from the bladder out of the body; in males it is also a passage for semen.

Urethralism Deriving sexual excitement from stimulation of the urethra or urinary meatus.

Urinary meatus The opening of the urethra through which urine is excreted.

Urophilia (also undinism, urolagnia) Deriving erotic pleasure from urine or urination.

Uterus The stretchable, pear-shaped organ in the female in which a baby develops.

Vagina The canal-shaped organ in the female extending from the vulva to the cervix that receives the penis during coitus and provides a passage for the infant during birth.

Vaginismus A condition in which strong vaginal muscle contractions prevent insertion of the penis into the vagina making coitus painful or impossible.

Vaginitis A vaginal infection caused by trichomonas vaginalis, haemophilas vaginalis, or candida albicans.

Vas deferens A muscular tube in the male extending from the epididymis to the prostate which serves as a passage for sperm.

Vasocongestion Engorgement of tissues with blood and other bodily fluids.

Venereal disease Any of the contagious diseases contracted through coitus or oral-genital sexual activities.

Venereal warts Warts appearing on the genitals.

Vestibule The area of the female vulva which is surrounded by the labia minora.

Voyeurism (also scotophilia, inspectionism, peeping-Tomism) Sexual gratification from looking at the bodies, sex organs, or sex acts of other persons.

Vulva The external female genitalia.

Bibliography

Abel, G. G.; Barlow, D. H.; Blanchard, E. G.; and Guild, D. "The Components of Rapists' Sexual Arousal." *Archives of General Psychiatry* 34 (1977):895–903.

Abelson, H.; Cohen, R.; Heaton, E.; and Slider, C. "Public Attitudes Toward and Experience with Erotic Materials." *Technical Reports of the Commission on Obscenity and Pornography,* Vol. 6. Washington, D.C.: U.S. Government Printing Office, 1970.

Acosta, Frank X. "Etiology and Treatment of Homosexuality: A Review." *Archives of Sexual Behavior* 4 (1975):9–21.

Adams, Joe K. "The Hidden Taboo on Love." In *Love Today,* edited by Herbert A. Otto, pp. 27–41. New York: Dell Books, 1972.

Adelman, Marcy. "A Comparison of Professionally Employed Lesbians and Heterosexual Women on the MMPI." *Archives of Sexual Behavior* 6 (1977):193–201.

Adler, Nancy E. "Abortion: A Social-Psychological Perspective." *Journal of Social Issues* 35 (1979):100–119.

Albro, Joyce C., and Tully, Carol. "A Study of Lesbian Lifestyles in the Homosexual Micro-Culture and the Heterosexual Macro-Culture." *Journal of Homosexuality* 4 (1979):331–344.

"All About the New Sex Therapy," *Newsweek* (November 27, 1972):65–72.

Allen, Clifford, *A Textbook of Psychosexual Disorders.* London: Oxford University Press, 1969.

Allen, Clifford. "Sexual Perversions." In *Encyclopedia of Sexual Behavior,* edited by Albert Ellis and Albert Abarbanal, pp. 802–811. New York: Jason Aronson, 1973.

Alpert, Hollis, "Whither the Erotic Film?" *Sexual Behavior* 2 (1972):45.

Amelar, Richard D. "Therapeutic Approaches to Impotence in the Male." *Journal of Sex Research* 7 (1971):163–167.

American Medical Association Committee on Human Sexuality. *Human Sexuality.* Chicago: American Medical Association, 1972.

American Social Health Association, *Today's VD Control Problem 1975.* New York: American Social Health Association Press, 1975.

Amir, Menachim. *Patterns of Forcible Rape.* Chicago: University of Chicago Press, 1971.

Arafat, Ibtihaj S., and Cotton, Wayne L. "Masturbation Practices of Males and Females." *Journal of Sex Research* 10 (1974): 293–307.

Ard, Ben N., Jr. "Premarital Sexual Experience: A Longitudinal Study," *Journal of Sex Research* 10 (1974):32–39.

Ard, Ben N., Jr. "Sex in Lasting Marriages: A Longitudinal Study." *Journal of Sex Research* 13 (1977):274–285.

Aries, Philippe. *Centuries of Childhood.* New York: Alfred A. Knopf, 1962.

Arnstein, Helene S. "The Crisis of Becoming a Father." In *Sexual Issues in Marriage,* edited by Leonard Gross. New York: Spectrum Publications, 1975.

Athanasiow, Robert, and Shaver, Phillip. "Correlates of Heterosexuals' Reactions to Pornography." *Journal of Sex Research* 7 (1971):298–299.

Atkinson, Maxine, and Boles, Jacqueline. "Prostitution As an Ecology of Confidence Games." In *Social Deviancy in Social Context,* edited by Clifton Bryant, pp. 219–231. New York: New Viewpoints, 1977.

Atwater, Lynn. "Getting Involved." *Alternative Lifestyles* 2 (1979):33–68.

Auerbach, Alfred. "The Battle of the Sexes." *Medical Aspects of Human Sexuality* 1 (1967):6–8.

Auerbach, Alfred. "Satyriasis and Nymphomania." *Medical Aspects of Human Sexuality* 2 (1968):39–41.

Avers, C. J. *Biology of Sex.* New York: John Wiley & Sons, 1974.

Bach, George M., and Deutsch, Ronald M. *Pairing.* New York: Peter H. Wyden Co., 1970.

Bagley, Christopher. "Incest Behavior and Incest Taboo." *Social Problems* 16 (1968):505–508.

Barbach, Lonnie G. "Group Treatment of Preorgasmic Women." *Journal of Sex and Marital Therapy* 1 (1974):139–145.

Barbach, Lonnie G. *For Yourself: The Fulfillment of Female Sexuality.* New York: New American Library, 1975.

Barclay, Alfred M. "Sexual Fantasies in Men and Women." *Medical Aspects of Human Sexuality,* 7 (1973):209–212.

Barclay, Kathryn, and Gallemore, Jonny L. "The Family of the Prostitute." *Corrective Psychiatry and Journal Social Therapy* 18 (1972):10–13.

Bardwick, Judith M. *Psychology of Women. A Study of Bio-Cultural Conflicts.* New York: Harper & Row, 1971.

Barlow, David H. "Increasing Heterosexual Responsiveness in the Treatment of Sexual Deviation: A Review of the Clinical and Experimental Evidence." *Behavior Therapy* 4 (1973):655–671.

Barlow, David H. "The Treatment of Sexual Deviation: Toward a Comprehensive Behavior Approach." In *Innovative Treatment Methods in Psychopathology,* edited by Karen L. Calhoun, Henry E. Adams, and Kevin M. Mitchell, pp. 121–147. New York: John Wiley & Sons, 1974.

Bartell, Gilbert D. "Group Sex Among the Mid-Americans." *Journal of Sex Research* 6 (1970):113–130.

Bartell, Gilbert D. *Group Sex.* New York: Peter H. Wyden Co., 1971.

Bartz, Wayne R., and Rasor, Richard A. "Why People Fall In and Out of Romantic Love." *Sexual Behavior* 2 (1971):33–36.

Beach, Frank A. *Sex and Behavior.* New York: John Wiley & Sons, 1965.

Beauvoir, Simone de. "Joie de Vivre." *Harpers Magazine,* (January, 1972):33–40.

Behrman, S. J. "Which 'pill' to choose?" *Hospital Practice* 14 (1969):34–39.

Beigel, Hugo G. "Romantic Love." *American Sociological Review* 16 (1951):326–334.

Beigel, Hugo G. "The Meaning of Coital Postures." *International Journal of Sexology* 4 (1953):136–143.

Beigel, Hugo G. "The Hypnotherapeutic Approach to Male Impotence." *Journal of Sex Research* 7 (1971):168–171.

Bell, Alan P., and Weinberg, Martin S. *Homosexualities.* New York: Simon & Schuster, 1978.

Bell, Daniel. *The Radical Right.* New York: Doubleday, 1964.

Bell, Robert R. "Swinging, The Sexual Exchange of Marriage Partners." *Sexual Behavior* 1 (1971):70–79.

Bell, Robert R., and Bell, Phyllis L. "Sexual Satisfaction Among Married Women." *Medical Aspects of Human Sexuality* 6 (1972):136–138.

Bell, Sanford. "Childhood Romances." *American Journal of Psychology* 8 (1902):325–354.

Belliveau, Fred, and Richter, Lin. *Understanding Human Sexual Inadequacy.* Boston: Little, Brown & Co., 1970.

Belsky, Raymond. "Vaginal Contraceptives—A Time for Reappraisal?" *Population Reports,* H (3), (January, 1975), H-37–H-56.

Bender, Lauretta, and Blau, Abram. "The Reaction of Children to Sexual Relations with Adults." *American Journal of Orthopsychiatry* 7 (1937):500–518.

Benjamin, Harry, and Masters, R. E. L. *Prostitution and Morality.* New York: Julian Press, 1964.

Benney, Mark; Reisman, David; and Star, Shirley. "Age and Sex in the Interview." *American Journal of Sociology* 62 (1956):143–152.

Berbey, Barry R. "Psychiatric Sequelae of Sexual Deprivation." *Medical Aspects of Human Sexuality* 5 (1971): 176–179.

Berezin, Martin A. "Sex and Old Age: A Review of the Literature." *Journal of Geriatric Psychiatry* 2 (1969):131–135.

Berger, Jack C.; Green, Richard; Laub, Donald R.; Reynolds, Charles L.; Walker, Paul A.: Wollman, Leo. *Standards of Care.* Galveston, Texas: Janus Information Facility, 1979.

Bernard, Jessie. "Infidelity: Some Moral and Social Issues." In *Science and Psychoanalysis,* Vol. 16, edited by Jules H. Masserman, *The Dynamics of Work and Marriage,* pp. 99–126. New York: Grune and Stratton, Inc., 1969.

Berne, Eric. *Games People Play.* New York: Grove Press, 1964.

Berne, Eric. *Sex in Human Loving.* New York: Simon & Schuster, 1970.

Bernstein, Barbara E. "Effect of Menstruation on Academic Performance Among College Women." *Archives of Sexual Behavior* 6 (1977):289–297.

Biblarz, Arturo, and Biblarz, Dolores. "The Sociology of Fantasy," (unpublished manuscript, 1976).

Bieber, Irving. *Homosexuality: A Psychoanalytic Study.* New York: Basic Books, 1962.

Bieber, Irving. "The Lesbian Patient." *Medical Aspects of Human Sexuality* 3 (1969):6–8.

Bieber, Irving. "The Psychoanalytic Treatment of Sexual Disorders." *Journal of Sex and Marital Therapy* 1 (1974):5–15.

Bindrim, Paul. "Nudity as a Quick Grab for Intimacy in Group Therapy." *Psychology Today* 3 (1969): 25–28.

Bird, Caroline. *Born Female: The High Cost of Keeping Women Down,* rev. ed. New York: Basic Books, 1971.

Bird, Caroline. *Two-Paycheck Marriage.* New York: Rawson, Wade Publishers, 1979.

Birk, Lee; Williams, Gordon H., Chasin, Marcia; and Rose, Leslie I. "Serum Testosterone Levels in Homosexual Men." *New England Journal of Medicine* 289 (1974):1236–1237.

"Birth Control Deaths." *Newsweek* (March 1, 1976):60.

Blau, Theodore H. "The Love Effect." In *Love Today,* edited by Herbert A. Otto, pp. 151–164. New York: Dell Books, 1972.

Block, Norman L., and Tessler, Arthur N. "Transsexualism and Surgical Procedures." *Medical Aspects of Human Sexuality* 7 (1973): 158–161.

Blood, Robert O., Jr., and Wolfe, Donald M. *Husbands and Wives.* New York: Free Press, 1960.

Blough, Herbert A., and Giuntoli, Robert L. "Successful Drug Treatment of Genital Herpes." *Journal of the American Medical Association* 235 (1979):421–425.

Blumstein, Philip W., and Schwartz, Pepper. "Lesbianism and Bisexuality." In *Sexual Deviance and Sexual Deviants,* edited by Erich Goode and Richard Froiden. New York: William Morrow, 1974.

Blumstein, Philip W., and Schwartz, Pepper. "Bisexuality in Males." *Urban Life* Special Issue: *Sexuality: Encounters, Identities and Relationships,* edited by Carol A. B. Warren. Beverly Hills, Calif.: Sage Publications, October, 1976.

Blumstein, Philip W., and Schwartz, Pepper. "Bisexuality: Some Social Psychological Issues." *Journal of Social Issues* 33 (1977): 30–45.

Bogdan, Robert. *Being Different: The Autobiography of Jane Fry.* New York: John Wiley & Sons, 1974.

Bohannon, Paul, ed. *Divorce and After.* New York: Doubleday, 1970.

Boston Women's Health Book Collective. *Our Bodies, Ourselves.* New York: Simon & Schuster, 1973.

Bowers, John. "The Porn is Green." *Playboy.* (July, 1971):78–82, 182–188.

Brecher, Edward M. *Sex Researchers.* Boston. Little, Brown & Co., 1969.

Brecher, Edward M. "He Taught a Generation How to Copulate." In *People as Partners,* edited by Jacqueline P. Wiseman. San Francisco: Canfield Press, 1971.

Brecher, Ruth, and Brecher, Edward, eds. *An Analysis of Human Sexual Response.* New York: Signet, 1966.

Breedlove, William. "Swap Clubs and the Law." *Magazine of Modern Sex* 1 (1964):124.

Breedlove, William, and Breedlove Jerrye. *Swap Clubs.* Los Angeles: Sherbourne Press, 1964.

Brenner, Paul, and Greenberg, Martin. "The Impact of Pregnancy on Marriage." *Medical Aspects of Human Sexuality* (June, 1977):14–22.

Brenton, Myron. "Sex Therapy for College Students." *Sexual Behavior* 2 (1972):52–55.

Brissett, Dennis. "Comment" in *Sexual Behavior* 1 (December 1, 1971):13–14.

Brissett, Dennis, and Lewis, Lionel S. "Guidelines for Marital Sex: An Analysis of Popular Marriage Manuals." *Family Coordinator* 70 (1970):41–48.

Broderick, Carlfred B. "Sexual Behavior Among Preadolescents." *Journal of Social Issues* 22 (1966):6–21.

Broderick, Carlfred B. "Dating and Mating Among Teenagers." *Medical Aspects of Human Sexuality* 2 (1968):16.

Broderick, Carlfred B. "Preadolescent Sexual Behavior." *Medical Aspects of Human Sexuality* 2 (1968):20.

Broderick, Carlfred B. "Heterosexual Interests of Suburban Youth." *Medical Aspects of Human Sexuality* 5 (1971):83–100.

Brodie, H. K. H.; Gartrell, N.; Doering, C.; and Rhue, T. "Plasma Testosterone Levels in Heterosexual and Homosexual Men." *American Journal of Psychiatry* 131 (1974):82–83.

Brodsky, Stanley L. "Prevention of Rape: Deterrence by the Potential Victim." In *Sexual Assault,* edited by Marcia J. Walder and Stanley L. Brodsky. Lexington, Massachusetts: D. C. Heath, 1976.

Brown, M.; Amoroso, D. M.; and Ware, E. E. "Behavioral Effects of Viewing Pornography." *Journal of Social Psychology* 98 (1976):235.

Bryan, James H. "Apprenticeships in Prostitution." *Social Problems* 12 (1965):278–297.

Bryan, James H. "Occupational Ideologies and Individual Attitudes of Call Girls." *Social Problems* 13 (1966):441–450.

Bryant, Clifton D. *Sexual Deviancy in Social Context.* New York: New Viewpoints, 1977.

Bryce-Laporte, Roy Simon. "Review Symposium." *Contemporary Sociology* 4 (1975):353–361.

Bryson, Rebecca B.; Bryson, Jeff B.; Licht, Mark L.; and Licht, Barbara A. "The Professional Pair: A Survey of Husband-Wife Psychologists." *American Psychologist,* in press.

Buckley, T. "The Transsexual Operation." *Esquire* (April, 1967):111–205.

Buhrich, N.; Theile, H.; Yaw, A.; and Crawford, A. "Plasma Testosterone, Serum FSH, and Serum LH Levels in Transvestism." *Archives of Sexual Behavior* 8 (1979):49–56.

Bullough, Vern L. "The American Brothel." *Medical Aspects of Human Sexuality* 7 (1973):198.

Bullough, Vern L. "Homosexuality and the Medical Model." *Journal of Homosexuality* 1 (1974):99–110.

Burchinel, Les. "The Premarital Dyad and Love Involvement." In *Handbook of Marriage and the Family,* edited by Harold Christensen, pp. 665–670. Chicago: Rand-McNally, 1964.

Burgess, Anthony. *A Clockwork Orange.* New York: W. W. Norton, 1963.

Burmeister, Ronald E., and Gardner, Herman L. "Vaginitis: Diagnosis and Treatment." *Postgraduate Medicine* (August, 1974):159–163.

Burnhill, M. S., and Birnberg, C. H. "Improving the Results Obtained with Current Intrauterine Contraceptive Devices." *Fertility & Sterility* 20 (1969):232–240.

Burnside, Irene M., ed. *Sexuality and Aging.* Los Angeles: University of Southern California Press, 1975.

Burufaldi, Linda L., and Culpepper, Emily E. "Androgyny and the Myth of Masculine/Feminine." In *The Future of Sexual Relations,* edited by Robert T. Francoeur and Anna K. Francoeur, pp. 140–145. Englewood Cliffs, New Jersey: Prentice-Hall, 1974.

Butler, Sandra. *The Conspiracy of Silence: The Trauma of Incest.* San Francisco: New Glide Publications, 1978.

Byrne, Donn. *The Attraction Paradigm.* New York: Academic Press, 1971.

Byrne, Donn. "A Pregnant Pause in the Sexual Revolution." *Psychology Today* (July, 1977):67–68.

Calderone, Mary S. "Foreword." In *Family Life and Sex Education*, edited by Esther D. Schulz and Sally R. Williams, pp. v–vii. New York: Harcourt, Brace and World, 1968.

Calhoun, Karen S.; Adams, H. E.; and Mitchell, K. M., eds. *Innovative Treatment Methods in Psychopathology*. New York: John Wiley & Sons, 1974.

Califia, Pat. "Lesbian Sexuality." *Journal of Homosexuality* 4 (1979):255–266.

California State Department of Health. *Gonorrhea Screening Manual*. Sacramento: Health and Welfare Agency, Department of Health VD Control Unit, 1973.

California State Department of Health. *VD Fact Sheet. Basic Statistics on the Venereal Diseases Problem in California, 1974*. Sacramento: Department of Health VD Control Unit, 1974.

Campbell, Angus. "The American Way of Mating: Marriage Si, Children Only Maybe." *Psychology Today* 8 (May, 1975):37–43.

Campbell, M. F., and Harrison, J. H., eds. *Urology 1*. Philadelphia: W. B. Saunders Co., 1970.

Cannon, Kenneth L., and Long, Richard. "Premarital Sexual Behavior in the Sixties." *Journal of Marriage and the Family* 33 (1971):36–39.

Capellanus, Andreas. *The Art of Courtly Love*. Translated with an Introduction by John Jay Parry. New York: Frederick Ungar, 1959. Originally published in 1184–1186.

Caprio, Frank S. "Miscellaneous Variations in Sexual Behavior." *Variations in Sexual Behavior*, pp. 325–328. New York: Jason Aronson, 1955.

Caprio, Frank S. "Fetishism." In *Encyclopedia of Sexual Behavior*, edited by Albert Ellis and Albert Abarbanel, pp. 435–438. New York: Jason Aronson, 1973.

Carden, Maren L. *New Feminist Movement*. New York: Russell Sage Foundation, 1974.

Carrier, J. M. "Family Attitudes and Mexican Male Homosexual Behavior." *Urban Life* Special Issue: *Sexuality: Encounters, Identities and Relationships*, edited by Carol A. B. Warren. Beverly Hills, Calif.: Sage Publications, October, 1976.

Carroll, John. "Bisexual Chic." *Oui* 3 (February, 1974):48, 115–117.

Carson, Josephine. *Silent Voices*. New York: Delacorte Press, 1969.

Cass, Vivienne C. "Homosexual Identity Formation." *Journal of Homosexuality* 4 (1979):219–235.

Cavallin, Hector. "Incestuous Fathers: A Clinical Report." *American Journal of Psychiatry* 122 (1966):1132–1138.

Cavallin, Hector. "Incest." *Sexual Behavior* 3 (1973):19.

Chafetz, Janet S. *Masculine/Feminine or Human?* Itasca, Illinois: F. E. Peacock, 1974.

Charatan, Fred B. "Sexual Function in Old Age." *Medical Aspects of Human Sexuality* (September, 1978):150–164.

Cherniak, Donna, and Feingold, Allan. *VD Handbook*. Montreal: Montreal Health Press, 1972.

Cherniak, Donna, and Feingold, Allan. *Birth Control Handbook*. Montreal: Montreal Health Press, 1973.

Chesser, Eustace. *Human Aspects of Sexual Deviation*. London: Jarrolds Publishers, Ltd., 1971.

Christensen, Harold T. "A Cross-Cultural Comparison of Attitudes Toward Marital Infidelity." *International Journal of Comparative Sociology* 8 (1962):124–134.

Christensen, Harold T., and Johnson, Leanor B. "Premarital Coitus and the Southern Black: A Comparative View." *Journal of Marriage and the Family* 40 (1978):721–731.

Churchill, Wainwright. *Homosexual Behavior Among Males.* Englewood Cliffs, New Jersey: Prentice-Hall, 1971.

Cicourel, Aaron V. *Method and Measurement in Sociology.* New York: Free Press, 1964.

Cipolla, Carlo M. *The Economic History of World Population,* 5th ed. Middlesex, England: Penguin, 1970.

Clanton, Gordon. "The Contemporary Experience of Adultery: Bob and Carol and Updike and Rimmer." In *Renovating Marriage,* edited by Roger W. Libby and Robert N. Whitehurst, pp. 95–115. Danville, Calif.: Consensus Publishers, 1973.

Clanton, Gordon. "A Conversation With Albert Ellis." *Alternative Lifestyles* 2 (1979):243–253.

Clanton, Gordon, and Downing, Chris. *Face to Face to Face.* New York: E. P. Dutton and Co., 1975.

Clanton, Gordon, and Smith, Lynn G., eds. *Jealousy.* Englewood Cliffs, New Jersey: Prentice-Hall, 1976.

Clanton, Gordon, and Smith, Lynn G. "The Self-Inflicted Pain of Jealousy." *Psychology Today* (March, 1977):44–80.

Clark, Alexander L., and Wallin, Paul. "Women's Sexual Responsiveness and the Duration and Quality of their Marriages." *American Journal of Sociology* 71 (1965):187–196.

Clark, Don. "Homosexual Encounter in All-Male Groups." In *Perspectives on Encounter Groups,* edited by Laurence N. Solomon and Betty Bergon, pp. 368–382. San Francisco: Jossey-Bass, 1972.

Clark, John P., and Tifft, Larry L. "Polygraph and Interview Validation of Self-reported Deviant Behavior." *American Sociological Review* 31 (1966):516–523.

Clayton, Paula J., and Bornstein, Philipp E. "Widows and Widowers." *Medical Aspects of Human Sexuality* (September, 1976):27–53.

Clifford, Ruth E. "Development of Masturbation in College Women." *Archives of Sexual Behavior* 7 (1978):559–573.

Clifford, Ruth E. "Subjective Sexual Experience in College Women." *Archives of Sexual Behavior* 7 (1978):183–197.

Clor, Harry M., and Hettlinger, Richard F. "Debate: Should There Be Censorship of Pornography?" *Sexual Behavior* 1 (1966):66–69.

Cloyd, Jerald. "The Marketplace Bar: Pairing Rituals of *Homo Ludens.*" *Urban Life* Special Issue: *Sexuality: Encounters, Identities and Relationships,* edited by Carol A. B. Warren. Beverly Hills, Calif.: Sage Publications, October, 1976.

Cochran, William G.; Mosteller, Frederick; and Tukey, John. *Statistical Problems of the Kinsey Report on Sexual Report in the Human Male.* Washington, D.C.: The American Statistical Association, 1954.

Cohen, Jean. "The Effects of Oral Contraceptives on Sexual Behavior." In *Progress in Sexology,* edited by Robert Gemme and Connie C. Wheeler, pp. 375–383. New York: Plenum Press, 1976.

Cole, Charles L., and Spanier, Graham B. "Comarital Mate-Sharing and Family

Stability." *Journal of Sex Research* 10 (1974):21–31.

Cole, Theodore M. "Sexuality and Physical Disabilities." *Archives of Sexual Behavior* 4 (1975):389–403.

Collins, Glenn. "The Good News About 1984." *Psychology Today* (January, 1979):34–48.

Collins, Randall. "A Conflict Theory of Sexual Stratification." *Social Problems* 19 (1971):38–41.

Colton, Helen. *Sex After the Sexual Revolution.* New York: Association Press, 1972.

Colton, Helen. "Weekend Marriages." *The Futurist* 7 (1973):60–61.

Comfort, Alex. *Sex in Society.* London: Duckworth, 1963.

Comfort, Alex. *The Joy of Sex: A Gourmet Guide to Lovemaking.* New York: Crown Publishers, 1972.

Comfort, Alex. "Sexuality in a Zero Growth Society." *Center Report* 8 (1972):38–40.

Comfort, Alex. "Institutionalized Adultery." *The Futurist* 7 (1973):56–58.

Comfort, Alex. *More Joy of Sex.* New York: Simon & Schuster, 1973.

Committee on Adolescence, Group for the Advancement of Psychiatry. *Normal Adolescence: Its Dynamics and Impact.* GAP 6, 1968.

Constantine, Larry L., and Constantine, Joan M. "Sexual Aspects of Multilateral Relations." *Journal of Sex Research* 7 (1971):204–225.

Constantine, Larry L., and Constantine, Joan M. *Group Marriage.* New York: Collier Books, 1973.

Constantine, Larry L.; Constantine, Joan M.; and Edelman, Sheldon K. "Counseling Implications of Comarital and Multilateral Relations." *Family Coordinator* 72 (1972):267–273.

Coombs, Robert H. "Sex Attitudes of Physicians and Marriage Counselors." *Family Coordinator* 20 (1971):269–277.

Cornish, Edward. "The Future of the Family: Intimacy in an Age of Loneliness." *Futurist* (February, 1979):45–58.

Cornish, Edward. "An Agenda for the 1980's." *Futurist* (February, 1980):5–13.

Crépault, Claude; Abraham, Georges; Porto, Robert; and Couture, Marcel. "Erotic Imagery in Women." In *Progress in Sexology,* edited by Robert Gemme and Connie C. Wheeler. New York: Plenum Press, 1976.

CSC Nusletter (sic) 1, No. 4, October 1975.

Cuber, John F. "Adultery: Reality Versus Stereotype." In *Extra-Marital Relations,* edited by Gerhard Neubeck. Englewood Cliffs, New Jersey: Prentice-Hall, 1969.

Cuber, John F. "The Mistress in American Society." *Medical Aspects of Human Sexuality* 3 (1969):81–82.

Cuber, John F. "The Sexless Marriage." *Medical Aspects of Human Sexuality* 3 (1969):19–20.

Cuber, John F. "Alternate Models from the Perspective of Sociology." In *The Family in Search of a Future,* edited by Herbert A. Otto, pp. 72–83. New York: Appleton-Century-Crofts, 1970.

Cuber, John F. "Sex in Five Types of Marriages." *Sexual Behavior* 2 (1972):74–77.

Cuber, John F., and Harroff, Peggy B. "Other Involvements." In *The Significant*

Americans, edited by John F. Cuber and Peggy B. Harroff. New York: Hawthorne Books, 1965.

Cvetkovich, George; Grote, Barbara; Bjorseth, Ann; and Sarkissian, Julia. "On the Psychology of Adolescents' Use of Contraceptives." *Journal of Sex Research* 11 (1975):256–270.

Dalton, Katharina. *The Menstrual Cycle.* New York: Pantheon Books, 1969.

Dalton, Katharina. *Once a Month.* London: Hunter House, 1979.

Danfield, D., and Gordon, M. "The Sociology of Mate Swapping: Or the Family That Swings Together Clings Together." *Journal of Sex Research* 6 (1970):85–100.

Dank, Barry M. "Coming Out in the Gay World." *Psychiatry* 34 (1971):180–185.

David, Jay, ed. *Growing Up Black.* New York: William Morrow, 1968.

Davis, Gary L., and Cross, Herbert J. "Sexual Stereotyping of Black Males in Interracial Sex." *Archives of Sexual Behavior* 8 (1979):269–273.

Davis, Kingsley. "The Sociology of Prostitution." *American Sociological Review* 2 (October, 1937):744–755.

Davis, Sharon K., and Davis, Phillip W. "Meaning and Process in Erotic Offensiveness: An Exposé of Exposees." In *Urban Life* Special Issue: *Sexuality: Encounters, Identities and Relationships,* edited by Carol A. B. Warren. Beverly Hills, Calif: Sage Publications, October, 1976.

Day, Beth. *Sex Life Between Blacks and Whites.* Cleveland: World Publication, 1972.

DeBurger, James E. "Sex in Troubled Marriages." In *Sexual Issues in Marriage,* edited by Leonard Gross, pp. 65–73. New York: Spectrum Publications, 1975.

"Delayed Menses. 35% Pregnant When Period 5 Days Late." *Family Planning Digest* 3 (1974):12.

DeMartino, Manfred F. *The New Female Sexuality.* New York: Julian Press, 1969.

Denfield, Duane. "Sex Tabloids." *Sexual Behavior* 3 (1973):18–19.

Denfield, Duane. "Dropouts from Swinging." *Family Coordinator* 23 (1974):45–50.

Denfield, Duane, and Gordon M. "The Sociology of Mate Swapping: Or the Family that Swings Together Clings Together." *Journal of Sex Research* 6 (1970):85–100.

Dengrove, Edward. "Behavior Therapy of Impotence." *Journal of Sex Research* 7 (1971):177–183.

Dengrove, Edward. "Sex Differences." In *Encyclopedia of Sexual Behavior,* edited by Albert Ellis and Albert Abarbanel, pp. 931–938. New York: Jason Aronson, 1973.

Denko, Joanne D. "Erotic Enemas." *Medical Aspects of Human Sexuality* (December, 1976):37–38.

Diamant, Louis. "Premarital Sexual Behavior, Attitudes, and Emotional Adjustment." *Journal of Social Psychology* 82 (1970):75–77.

Diamond, Milton. "A Critical Evaluation on the Ontogeny of Human Sexual Behavior." *Quarterly Review Biology* 40 (1965):147–175.

Dickey, Richard P., and Dorr, Clyde H. "Management of Minor Side Effects of Oral Contraceptives," Chapter 7 in *Progress in Contraception Control, 1968,* edited by Dean L. Mazer; pp. 87–94. Philadelphia: J. B. Lippincott Co., 1968.

Dickey, Richard P., and Dorr, Clyde H. "Oral Contraceptives: Selection of the Proper Pill." *Obstetrics and Gynecology* 33 (1969):273–287.

Dietrich, Marlene. *Marlene Dietrich's ABC.* New York: Doubleday, 1961.

Downey, Gregg W. "The Next Patient Right: Sex in the Nursing Home." *Modern Healthcare* (June, 1974):55–60.

Dressel, Paula L., and Avant, N. Ray. "Neogamy and Older Persons." *Alternative Lifestyles* 1 (1978):13–36.

Driscoll, James P. "Transsexuals." *Trans-action* 8 (1971):28–31.

Dudley, Ellen. "Rainbows and Realities: Current Trends in Marriage and Its Alternatives." *Futurist* (February, 1979):23–31.

Dumm, John J.; Piotrow, P. T.; and Dalsimer, Isabel A. "The Modern Condom — A Quality Product for Effective Contraception." *Population Report,* H (2), (1974), H-21–H-36.

Eastman, Nicholson J. *Expectant Motherhood.* Boston: Little, Brown & Co., 1957.

Edwards, John N. "Extramarital Involvement: Fact and Theory." *Journal of Sex Research* 9 (1973):210–225.

Eggers, Oscar R. "An Answer to Monotonous Marriage?" *The Futurist* 7 (1973):61–63.

Ehrhardt, Anke A. "Maternalism in Fetal Hormonal and Related Syndromes." In *Contemporary Sexual Behavior: Critical Issues in the 1970's,* edited by Joseph Zubin and John Money, pp. 99–116. Baltimore: Johns Hopkins University Press, 1973.

Ehrlich, June, and Riesman, David. "Age and Authority in the Interview." *Public Opinion Quarterly* 23 (1961):39–56.

Ehrmann, Winston. "Marital and Non-Marital Sexual Behavior." In *Handbook of Marriage and the Family,* edited by H. F. Christiansen, pp. 585–622. Chicago: Rand McNally, 1964.

Eichenlaub, James E. *The Marriage Art.* New York: Dell Books, 1961.

Elias, James, and Gebhard, Paul. "Sexuality and Sexual Learning in Childhood." *Phi Delta Kappan* 50 (1969):401–405.

Ellis, Albert. *Sex Without Guilt.* New York: Appleton-Century-Crofts, 1958.

Ellis, Albert, "What is 'Normal' Sex Behavior?" *Sexology* 28 (1962):364–369.

Ellis, Albert. *Sex and the Single Man.* New York: Lyle Stuart, 1963.

Ellis, Albert. "Wife Swapping." In *Suppressed,* pp. 88–89. Chicago: Rand-McNally, 1965.

Ellis, Albert. "Sexual Promiscuity in America." *Annals of the American Academy* 378 (1968):58–67.

Ellis, Albert, "Sexual Promiscuity in America." *Annals of the American Academy* 379 (1969):282–285.

Ellis, Albert. "Group Marriage: A Possible Alternative?" In *The Family in Search of a Future,* edited by Herbert A. Otto, pp. 71–83. New York: Appleton-Century-Crofts, 1970.

Ellis, Albert. Untitled. In *Sexual Latitude: For and Against,* by Ronald Atkinson *et al.,* pp. 67–83. New York: Hart Publishers, 1971.

Ellis, Albert, and Brancale, Ralph. *Psychology of Sex Offenders.* Springfield, Illinois: Charles C Thomas, 1956.

Ellis, Albert, and Sagarin, Edward. *Nymphomania.* New York: Gilbert Press, 1964.

Ellis, Havelock, *Psychology of Sex.* New York: Mentor, 1954.

Ellison, Carol. "Sexual Needs of the Disabled and Chronically Ill." Paper presented to Society for the Scientific Study of Sex, Las Vegas, 1977.

English, O. Spurgeon. "Positive Values of the Affair." In *The New Sexuality*, edited by Herbert O. Otto, pp. 173–192. Palo Alto: Science and Behavior Books, 1971.

Ernst, Morris L., and Roth, David. *American Sexual Behavior and the Kinsey Report.* New York: Educational Book Company, 1948.

Eshleman, J. Ross. *The Family: An Introduction.* Boston: Allyn & Bacon, 1974.

Estlake, Allan. *The Oneida Community.* New York: AMS Press, 1973. From the 1900 London edition.

Evans, Hilary. *Harlots, Whores and Hookers.* New York: Taplinger Publishing, 1979.

Fang, Betty. "Swinging in Retrospect." *Journal of Sex Research* 12 (1976):220–237.

Fensterheim, Herbert. "Behavior Therapy of the Sexual Variations." *Journal of Sex and Marital Therapy* 1 (1974):16–28.

Ferguson, K. D., and Finkler, Deana C. "An Involvement and Overtness Measure for Lesbians." *Archives of Sexual Behavior* 7 (1978):211–227.

Finch, Stuart M. "Sex Play Among Boys and Girls," *Medical Aspects of Human Sexuality* 3 (1969):58–61.

Fink, Paul Jay. "Response to Inquiry." *Medical Aspects of Human Sexuality* 5 (1971):82.

Fink, Paul Jay. "Causes and Effects of Nonorgasmic Coitus in Women." In *Sexual Behavior*, edited by Leonard Gross, pp. 241–247. New York: Spectrum Publications, 1974.

Firestone, Shulamith, *The Dialectic of Sex.* New York: William Morrow, 1970.

Fisher, C.; Gross, J.; and Zuch, J. "Cycle of Penile Erection Synchronous with Dreaming (REM) Sleep." *Archives of General Psychiatry* 12 (1965):29–45.

Fisher, Seymour, *Female Orgasm: Psychology, Physiology, Fantasy.* New York: Basic Books, 1973.

Flowers, C. E. "New Advances in the Use of Oral Contraceptives." Paper given in Jefferson Medical School, unpub. 1963. Reported in *Handbook on Oral Contraception*, edited by Eleanor Mears, p. 70. Boston: Little, Brown & Co., 1965.

Fogel, Robert W., and Engerman, Stanley L. *Time on the Cross: The Economics of American Negro Slavery.* Boston: Little, Brown & Co., 1974a.

Fogel, Robert W., and Engerman, Stanley L. *Time on the Cross: Evidence and Methods.* Boston, Little, Brown & Co., 1974b.

Fonzi, Gaelon, and Riggio, James. "Modern Couple Seeks Like-Minded Couples. Utmost Discretion." *Philadelphia* 60 (1969):76–89.

Ford, Clellan S., and Beach, Frank A. *Patterns of Sexual Behavior.* New York: Harper & Row, 1951.

Forer, Bertram R. "Use of Physical Contact." In *New Perspectives on Encounter Groups*, edited by Laurence N. Soloman and Betty Berzon, pp. 195–210. San Francisco: Jossey-Bass, 1972.

Fox, Cyril A. "Orgasm and Fertility." In *Progress in Sexology*, edited by Robert Gemme and Connie C. Wheeler, pp. 351–355. New York, Plenum Press, 1976.

Francoeur, Robert T. "The Sexual Revolution." *Futurist* (April, 1980):3–12.

Francoeur, Robert T., and Francoeur, Anna K. "Hot and Cool Sex: Fidelity in Marriage." In *Renovating Marriage: Toward New Sexual Lifestyles*, edited by Roger W. Libby, and Robert N. Whitehurst, pp. 19–37. Danville, Calif.: Consensus Publishers, 1973.

B-11

Francoeur, Robert T., and Francoeur, Anna K., eds. *The Future of Sexual Relations.* Englewood Cliffs, New Jersey: Prentice-Hall, 1974.

Francoeur, Robert T., and Francoeur, Anna K. "The Pleasure Bond: Reversing the Antisex Ethic." *Futurist* (August, 1976):176–180.

Freud, Sigmund, "Some Psychological Consequences of the Anatomical Distinction Between the Sexes." *International Journal of Psycho-Analysis* 8 (1927):133–142.

Freud, Sigmund. "The Transformation of Puberty," *The Basic Writings,* edited and translated by Dr. A. A. Brill. New York: The Modern Library, 1938.

Freund, K. "Some Problems in the Treatment of Homosexuality." In *Behavior Therapy and the Neuroses,* edited by H. J. Eysenck, pp. 312–326. New York: Macmillan Company, 1960.

Friday, Nancy. *My Secret Garden.* New York: Pocket Books, 1974.

Friday, Nancy. *Men in Love.* New York: Simon & Schuster, 1980.

Friedman, Leonard J. "Unconsummated Marriage." *Medical Aspects of Human Sexuality* 4 (1970):16–18.

Frishauf, Peter. "Today's Health News." *Today's Health* 52(5), (1974):6–7.

Fromm, Erich. *The Art of Loving.* New York: Harper & Row, 1956.

Fromme, Allan. *The Ability to Love.* New York: Farrar, Strauss & Giroux, 1963.

Fuchs, Karl; Abramovici, Haim; Hoch, Swi; Fimor-Fritsch, Ilan; and Kleinhaus, Morris. "Vaginismus — The Hypnotherapeutic Approach," *Journal of Sex Research* 11 (1975):39–45.

Gadpaille, Warren J. "Research into the Physiology of Maleness and Femaleness: Its Contributions to the Etiology and Psychodynamics of Homosexuality." *Archives of General Psychiatry* 26 (1972):193–197.

Gadpaille, Warren J. "Innate Masculine and Feminine Differences." *Medical Aspects of Human Sexuality* 7 (1973):40–46.

Gagnon, John H. "Female Child Victims of Sex Offenses." *Social Problems* 13 (1965):176–192.

Gagnon, John H. "Sexual Conduct and Crime." In *Handbook of Criminology,* edited by Daniel Glaser. Chicago: Rand McNally, 1974.

Gagnon, John H., and Simon, William. "Homosexuality: The Formulation of a Sociological Perspective." In *Approaches to Deviance: Theories, Concepts and Research Findings,* edited by Mark Lefton, pp. 349–361. New York: Appleton-Century-Crofts, 1968.

Gagnon, John H., and Simon, William. *Social Sources of Human Sexuality.* Chicago: Aldine Publishing Co., 1973.

Galton, Lawrence. "VD: Outbreak of a New Variety." *Parade* (February 24, 1980):16.

Garrett, Thomas B., and Wright, Richard. "Wives of Rapists and Incest Offenders." *Journal of Sex Research* 11 (1975):149–157.

Gebhard, Paul H. "Factors in Marital Orgasm." *Medical Aspects of Human Sexuality* 2 (1968):22–27.

Gebhard, Paul H. "Misconceptions About Female Prostitutes." *Medical Aspects of Human Sexuality* 3 (1969):24–26.

Gebhard, Paul H. "Postmarital Coitus Among Widows and Divorcees." In *Divorce and After,* edited by Paul Bohannon, pp. 81–96. New York: Doubleday, 1970.

Gebhard, Paul H.; Gagnon, John H.; Pomeroy, Wardell B.; and Christenson, Cornelia V. *Sex Offenders.* New York: Harper & Row, 1965.

Geis, Gilbert; Wright, Richard; Garret, Thomas; Wilson, Paul R. "Reported Consequences of Decriminalization of Consensual Adult Homosexuality in Seven American States." *Journal of Homosexuality* 1 (1976):419–428.

Gerstel, Naomi. "Marital Alternatives and the Regulation of Sex." *Alternative Lifestyles* 2 (1979):145–175.

Gesell, Arnold, and Ilg, Frances L. *The Child from Five to Ten.* New York: Harper & Row, 1946.

Gillespie, D. L. "Who Has the Power? The Marital Struggle." *Journal of Marriage and the Family* 33 (1971):445–458.

Gilmartin, Brian G. "That Swinging Couple Down the Block." *Psychology Today* 8 (February, 1975):55–58.

Gilmartin, Brian G. *The Gilmartin Report.* Secaucus, New Jersey: Citadel Press, 1978.

Gilmore, C. P. "Something Better than the Pill?" *New York Times Magazine* (July 20, 1969):6–7.

Ginsberg, George L.; Frosh, William A.; and Shapiro, Theodore. "The New Impotence." In *The Future of Sexual Relations,* edited by Robert T. Francoeur and Anna K. Francoeur, pp. 112–117. Englewood Cliffs, New Jersey: Prentice-Hall, 1974.

Ginsberg, Kenneth N. "The Meat-Rack: A Study of the Male Homosexual Prostitute." In *Social Deviancy in Social Context,* edited by Clifton Bryant, pp. 160–176. New York: New Viewpoints, 1977.

Glaser, Daniel. *Routinizing Evaluation.* Rockville, Md.: National Institute of Mental Health, 1971.

Glass, Shirley P., and Wright, Thomas L. "The Relationship of Extramarital Sex, Length of Marriage, and Sex Differences on Marital Satisfaction and Romanticism: Athanasiou's Data Reanalyzed." *Journal of Marriage and the Family* 39 (1977):691–703.

Glenn, Norval D., and Weaver, Charles N. "Attitudes Toward Premarital, Extramarital, and Homosexual Relations in the United States in the 1970's." *Journal of Sex Research* 15 (1979):108–118.

Glick, Paul C. "A Demographer Looks at American Families." *Journal of Marriage and Family* 37 (February, 1975):15–26.

Goffman, Erving. *Asylums.* New York: Doubleday/Anchor Books, 1961.

Goldberg, Martin, "What Sex Means in a Happy Marriage." *Medical Aspects of Human Sexuality* 3 (1969):111–113.

Golden, Joshua. "What Is Sexual Promiscuity?" *Medical Aspects of Human Sexuality* 2 (1968):47–53.

Goldman, Marion. "Prostitution and Virtue in Nevada." *Society* 10 (1972):32–35.

Goldstein, Bernard. *Human Sexuality.* New York: McGraw-Hill, 1976.

Goldthorpe, John. "The Affluent Worker and the Thesis of Embourgeoisement: Some Preliminary Findings." *Sociology* 1 (1967):11–31.

Goldzieher, J. W., and Rudel, H. W. "How the Oral Contraceptives Came to Be

Developed." *Journal of American Medical Association* 230 (1974):421–425.

Goleman, Daniel. "Special Abilities of the Sexes: Do They Begin in the Brain." *Psychology Today* (November, 1978):48–59.

Goleman, Daniel, and Bush, Sherida. "The Liberation of Sexual Fantasy." *Psychology Today* (October, 1977):48–53.

Goodall, K. "Die Live." *Psychology Today* (December, 1972):10–13.

Goode, William J. *After Divorce.* Glencoe, Illinois: Free Press, 1956.

Goode, William J. "The Theoretical Importance of Love." *American Sociological Review* 24 (1959):38–41.

Gordon, Sol; Scales, Peter; and Everly, Kathleen. *The Sexual Adolescent,* 2nd ed. North Scituate, Massachusetts: Duxbury, 1979.

Graber, Benjamin, and Kline-Graber, Georgia. "Clitoral Foreskin Adhesions and Female Sexual Function." *Journal of Sex Research* 15 (1979):205–212.

Grant, Igor. "Anxiety About Orgasm." *Medical Aspects of Human Sexuality* 6 (1972):14–15.

Greenberg, Judith B. "Single-Parenting and Intimacy." *Alternative Lifestyles* 2 (1979):308–330.

Greenhill, J. P. "Use of Oral and Intrauterine Contraceptives: An International Panel Reports." *International Surgery* 49 (1968):312–318.

Greenson, Ralph R. "On Sexual Apathy in the Male." *Medical Aspects of Human Sexuality* 3 (1969):25–27.

Greenwald, Harold. *The Callgirl.* New York: Ballantine Books, 1958.

Greenwald, Harold. *The Elegant Prostitute.* New York: Walker, 1970.

Greenwald, Harold, and Greenwald, Ruth. *The Sex-Life Letters.* New York: Bantam Books, 1973.

Gross, Alan E. "The Male Role and Heterosexual Behavior." *Journal of Social Issues* 34 (1978):87–107.

Groth, A. Nicholas, and Birnbaum, H. Jean. "Adult Sexual Orientation and Attraction to Underage Persons." *Archives of Sexual Behavior* 7 (1978):175–186.

Groth, A. Nicholas, and Birnbaum, H. Jean. *Men Who Rape.* New York: Plenum Press, 1979.

Gusfield, Joseph R. *Symbolic Crusade: Status Politics and the American Temperance Movement.* Urbana: University of Illinois Press, 1966.

Guttmacher, Alan F. "How to Succeed at Family Planning." *Parents Magazine* 44 (1969):54–55, 82, 84.

Gwynne, Peter. "Was the Birth of Louise Brown Only a Happy Accident?" *Science Digest* (October, 1978):7–13.

Hall, Calvin S., and Lindzey, Gardner. *Theories of Personality,* 2nd ed. New York: John Wiley & Sons, 1970.

Hall, Francine S., and Hall, Douglas T. *Two-Career Couple.* Reading, Massachusetts: Addison-Wesley, 1979.

Hampson, John L., and Hampson, Joan G. "The Ontogenesis of Sexual Behavior in Man." In *Sex and Internal Secretions,* edited by William C. Young, pp. 1401–1432. Baltimore: Williams and Wilkins, 1961.

Harlow, Harry F. "The Nature of Love." *American Psychologist* 13 (1958):673–685.

Harrison, Barbara G. "Sexual Chic, Sexual Freedom and Sexual Confusion." In *Women in a Changing World,* edited by Uta West, pp. 48–63. New York: McGraw-Hill, 1975.

Harry, Joseph. "On the Validity of Typologies of Gay Males." *Journal of Homosexuality* 2 (1976–1977):143–149.

Hartman, William E., and Fithian, Marilyn A. *Treatment of Sexual Dysfunction.* New York: Jason Aronson, 1974.

Harvey, Edward B. *Industrial Society: Structures, Roles and Relations.* Homewood, Illinois: Dorsey Press, 1975.

Hass, Aaron. *Teenage Sexuality.* New York: Macmillan Company, 1979.

Hassett, James. "Sex and Smell." *Psychology Today* (March, 1978):40–45.

Hatcher, R. A.; Stewart, G. K.; Kline, R. W.; and Moorhead, F. L. *Contraceptive Technology.* Atlanta: Emory University School of Medicine, 1974.

Hatfield, Elaine; Sprecher, Sue; and Traupmann, Jane. "Men's and Women's Reactions to Sexually Explicit Films: A Serendipitous Finding." *Archives of Sexual Behavior* 7 (1978):583–591.

Hawley, Andy. "A Man's View." In *The New Women,* edited by Joanne Cooke, Charlotte Bunch-Weeks, and Robin Morgan, pp. 145–150. Greenwich, Connecticut: Fawcett, 1972.

Heckman, Norma A.; Bryson, Rebecca; and Bryson, Jeff B. "Problems of Professional Couples: A Content Analysis." *Journal of Marriage and the Family* 39 (1977):323–331.

Heilbrun, Carolyn G. "Recognizing the Androgynous Human." In *The Future of Sexual Relations,* edited by Robert T. Francoeur and Anna K. Francoeur. Englewood Cliffs, New Jersey: Prentice-Hall, 1974.

Heinlein, Robert. *Stranger in a Strange Land.* New York: Berkeley Publishing Corp., 1961.

Hellerstein, Herman K., and Friedman, Ernest H. "Sexual Activity and the Post Coronary Patient." *Medical Aspects of Human Sexuality* 3 (1969):70–74.

Henderson, Bruce, and Gagnon, John. *Human Sexuality: An Age of Ambiguity.* Boston: Little, Brown & Co., 1975.

Henderson, D. James. "Incest: A Synthesis of Data." *Canadian Psychiatric Association Journal* 17 (1972):299–311.

Henshel, Anne-Marie. "Swinging: A Study of Decision Making in Marriage." *American Journal of Sociology* 78 (November, 1973):885–891.

Herman, S. H.; Barlow, D. H.; and Agras, W. S. "An Experimental Analysis of Exposure to 'Explicit' Heterosexual Stimuli as an Effective Variable in Changing Arousal Patterns of Homosexuals." *Behavior Research and Therapy* 12 (1974):335–345.

Heron, William T. *Clinical Applications of Suggestion and Hypnosis.* Springfield, Illinois: Charles C Thomas, 1957.

Herskovits, Melville J. *The Myth of the Negro Past.* New York: Harper & Row, 1941.

Herskovits, Melville J. *The New World Negro.* Bloomington: Indiana University Press, 1966.

Hessellund, Hans. "Masturbation and Sexual Fantasies in Married Couples." *Archives of Sexual Behavior* 5 (1976):133–147.

Heuscher, Julius. "Vocational Celibacy and Authenticity." *Comprehensive Psychiatry* 13 (1972):445–457.

Heyl, Barbara S. *The Madam as Entrepreneur.* New Brunswick, New Jersey: Transaction Books, 1979.

Higham, Eileen. "Sexuality in the Infant and Neonate." In *Handbook of Human*

Sexuality, edited by Benjamin B. Wolman and John Money, pp. 15–28. Englewood Cliffs, New Jersey: Prentice-Hall, 1980.

Himes, Norman E. *Medical History of Contraception.* New York: Schocken Books, 1970.

Hirschfeld, Magnus. "Fetishism-General." In *Sexual Anomalies,* pp. 445–499. New York: Emerson Books, 1956.

Hite, Shere. *The Hite Report.* New York: Macmillan Company, 1976.

Hobart, Charles W. "The Incidence of Romanticism During Courtship." *Social Forces* 36 (1958):362–367.

Hobbs, A. H., and Lambert, R. D. "An Evaluation of Sexual Behavior in the Human Male." *American Journal of Psychiatry* 104 (1948):758–764.

Hochschild, Arlie. "Communal Living in Old Age." In *Future of the Family,* edited by Louise K. Howe, pp. 299–310. New York: Simon & Schuster, 1972.

Hoenig, J.; Kenna, J.; and Youd, Ann. "Social and Economic Aspects of Transsexualism." *British Journal of Psychiatry* 117 (1970):163.

Hoffman, Martin. *The Gay World: Male Homosexuality and the Social Creation of Evil.* New York: Basic Books, 1968.

Hoffman, Martin. "Homosexual." *Psychology Today* 3 (1969):43–45.

Hoffman, Martin. "The Male Prostitute." *Sexual Behavior* 2 (1972):17–19.

Hollander, Xaviera. *The Happy Hooker.* New York: Dell Books, 1972.

Holmstrom, Lynda L. *The Two-Career Family.* Cambridge, Massachusetts: Schenkman, 1972.

Hooker, Evelyn. "The Adjustment of the Male Overt Homosexual." *Journal of Projective Techniques and Personality Adjustment* 21 (1957):18–23.

Hooker, Evelyn. "Parental Relations and Male Homosexuality in Patient and Non-Patient Samples." *Journal of Consulting and Clinical Psychiatry* 33 (1969):140–143.

Hopkins, J. Roy. "Sexual Behavior in Adolescence." *Journal of Social Issues* 33 (1977):67–85.

Horn, Patrice. "Problems of a Not So Gay Old Age." *Psychology Today* (October, 1974):35.

Horn, Patrice. "RX: Sex for Senior Citizens." *Psychology Today* (June, 1974).

Horn, Patrice. "Behavior Mod in the Bedroom." *Psychology Today* (November, 1975):94–95.

Horowitz, Ralph I., and Feinstein, Alvan R. "Estrogen Pills and Uterine Cancer." *New England Journal of Medicine* (November 16, 1978):33–39.

Howard, J. L.; Liptzin, M. B.; and Reifler, C. B. "Is Pornography a Problem?" *Journal of Social Issues* 29 (1973):133–145.

Huber, S. C.; Piotrow, P. T.; Orlans, F. B.; and Kommer, G. "IUD's Reassessed — A Decade of Experience." *Population Reports,* Ser. B, #2, January, 1975.

Humphreys, Laud. "New Lifestyles in Homosexual Manliness." *Trans-action* 8 (1971):24–27.

Humphreys, Laud. *Out of the Closets: The Sociology of Homosexual Liberation.* Englewood Cliffs, New Jersey: Prentice-Hall, 1972.

Humphreys, Laud. *Tearoom Trade: Impersonal Sex in Public Places,* 2nd ed. Chicago: Aldine Publishing Co., 1975.

Hunt, Morton M. *The World of the Formerly Married.* New York: McGraw-Hill, 1966.

Hunt, Morton M. *Sexual Behavior in the 1970's.* Chicago: Playboy Press, 1974.

Hunt, Morton. "Why Open Marriage Failed." *Family Circle* (January, 1977):34–36.

Hunt, Morton, and Hunt, Bernice. *The Divorce Experience.* New York: McGraw-Hill, 1977.

Hutt, Corinne. "Neuroendocrinological, Behavioural, and Intellectual Aspects of Sexual Differentiation in Human Development." In *Gender Differences: Ontogeny and Significance,* edited by Christopher Ounsted and David C. Taylor, pp. 73–122. Edinborough and London: Churchill Livingstone, 1972.

Huxley, Aldous. *Brave New World.* New York: Bantam Books, 1972. Originally published in 1932.

Hyman, Herbert. *Interviewing in Social Research.* Chicago: University of Chicago Press, 1954.

Ilg, Frances, and Ames, Louise B. *Child Behavior.* New York: Dell Books, 1955.

Inman, W. H. W., and Vessey, M. P. "Investigation of Deaths from Pulmonary, Coronary, and Cerebral Thrombosis and Embolism in Women of Child-bearing Age." *British Medical Journal* 2 (1968):193–199.

Irwin, Theodore. "The Twenty Year Itch." *Sexual Behavior* 3 (1973):35.

Israel, S. Leon, and Rubin, Isadora. *Sexual Relations During Pregnancy and the Post-Delivery Period.* New York: Study Guide No. 6. Sex Information and Education Council of the United States, 1967.

Issac, Stephen, and Michael, William B. *Handbook in Research and Evaluation.* San Diego: Robert Knapp, 1971.

Jackman, Norman R.; O'Toole, Richard; and Geis, Gilbert. "The Self-image of the Prostitute." *Sociological Quarterly* 4 (1963):150–160.

Jacobson, Linbania. "Illness and Human Sexuality." *Nursing Outlook* 12 (1974):18–21.

Jacoby, Susan. "49 Million Singles Can't All Be Right." *New York Times Magazine* (February 17, 1974):37–43.

James, William H. "Marital Coital Rates, Spouses' Ages, Family Size, and Social Class." *Journal of Sex Research* 10 (August, 1974):205–218.

Janov, Arthur. *The Primal Scream.* New York: G. P. Putnam's Sons, 1970.

John Birch Society. *John Birch Society Bulletin.* Belmont, Massachusetts: John Birch Society, March, 1969.

Johnson, Benton. *Functionalism in Modern Sociology: Understanding Talcott Parsons.* Morristown, N.J.: General Learning Press, 1975.

Johnson, Jill. *Lesbian Nation: The Feminist Solution.* New York: Simon & Schuster, 1973.

Johnson, Ralph E. "Some Correlates of Extramarital Coitus." *Journal of Marriage and the Family* 32 (1970):449.

Johnson, Ralph E. "Attitudes Towards Extramarital Relationships." *Medical Aspects of Human Sexuality* 6 (1972):168.

Jones, G. S. "Menstrual Cycles—What's Normal?" *Consultant* (April, 1968):45–47.

Jung, C. G. *Essays on Analytical Psychology,* 2nd ed. Translated by R. F. C. Hall. Princeton, New Jersey: Princeton University Press, 1972.

Jung, C. G. *The Structure and Dynamics of the Psyche,* 2nd ed. Translated by R. F. C. Hall. Princeton, New Jersey: Princeton University Press, 1972.

Kagan, Jerome. "Check One: Male—Female." *Psychology Today* 3 (1969):39–41.

Kahn, Herman, and Wiener, A. J., eds. *The Year 2000.* New York: Macmillan Company, 1967.

Kando, Thomas M. "Role Strain: A Comparison of Males, Females, and Transsexuals." *Journal of Marriage and the Family* 34 (1972):459.

Kando, Thomas. *Sex Change: The Achievement of Gender Identity Among Feminized Transsexuals.* Springfield, Illinois: Charles C Thomas, 1973.

Kanin, Eugene J. "Reference Groups and Sex Conduct Norm Violations." *Sociological Quarterly* 8 (1967):495–504.

Kanin, Eugene J., and Parcell, Stanley R. "Sexual Aggression: A Second Look at the Offended Female." *Archives of Sexual Behavior* 6 (1977):67–76.

Kant, Harold S. "Exposure to Pornography and Sexual Behavior in Deviant and Normal Groups." *Corrective Psychiatry and Journal of Social Therapy* 17 (1971):5–9.

Kant, Harold S., and Goldstein, Michael J. "Pornography." *Psychology Today* 4 (1970):58–64.

Kaplan, Helen S. *The New Sex Therapy.* New York: Brunner/Mazel, 1974.

Kaplan, Helen S., and Sager, Clifford J. "Sexual Patterns at Different Ages." *Medical Aspects of Human Sexuality* 5 (1971):10–23.

Karlen, Arno. *Sexuality and Homosexuality.* New York: W. W. Norton, 1971.

Kassel, Victor, "Polygyny After Sixty." *Geriatrics* 21 (1969):137–143.

Kassel, Victor. "Sex in Nursing Homes." *Medical Aspects of Human Sexuality* (March, 1976):126–131.

Katchadourian, Herant A., and Lunde, Donald T. *Fundamentals of Human Sexuality.* New York: Holt, Rinehart and Winston, 1975.

Katzman, Marshall. "Obscenity and Pornography." *Medical Aspects of Human Sexuality* 3 (1969):77–83.

Katzman, Marshall. "Early Sexual Trauma." *Sexual Behavior* (1972):13–17.

Kaufman, Joseph J. "Organic and Psychological Factors in the Genesis of Impotence and Premature Ejaculation." In *Sexual Problems,* edited by Charles W. Wahl, pp. 133–148. New York: Free Press, 1967.

Kaufman, Sherwin A. *The Ageless Woman—Menopause, Hormones and the Quest for Youth.* Englewood Cliffs, New Jersey: Prentice-Hall, 1967.

"Keeping Sex Sacred." *Newsweek* (January 26, 1976):46–47.

Keith, A. N. *Three Came Home.* Boston: Little, Brown & Co., 1947.

Kelmer, Richard H. "Problems of Widowed, Divorced and Unmarried Women." *Medical Aspects of Human Sexuality* 3 (1969):6–11.

Kephart, William M. "Some Correlates of Romantic Love." *Journal of Marriage and the Family* 29 (1967):470–481.

Kephart, William M. "Sex and the Divorced Man." *Medical Aspects of Human Sexuality* 6 (1972):170–173.

Kephart, William M. "Evaluation of Romantic Love." *Medical Aspects of Human Sexuality* 7 (1973):92–94.

Kernodle, R. Wayne. "Some Implications of the Homogamy Complementary Needs Theories of Sociological Research." *Social Forces* 38 (1959):145–151.

Keyes, Ralph. "Singled Out." *Popular Psychology* 6 (1973):50–56.

King, Karl; Balswick, Jack O.; and Robinson, Ira E. "Continuing Premarital Sexual Revolution Among College Females." *Journal of Marriage and the Family* 39 (1977):455–459.

Kinsey, Alfred C.; Pomeroy, Wardell, B.; Martin, Clyde E.; and Gebhard, Paul H. *Sexual Behavior in the Human Female.* Philadelphia: W. B. Saunders Co., 1953.

Kinsey, Alfred C.; Pomeroy, Wardell, B.; Martin, Clyde E.; and Gebhard, Paul H. *Sexual Behavior in the Human Female.* Philadelphia: W. B. Saunders Co., 1953.

Kirkendall, Lester A. "Sex Drive." In *Encyclopedia of Sexual Behavior,* edited by Albert Ellis and Albert Abarbanel, pp. 939–948. New York: Jason Aronson, 1973.

Kirkpatrick, R. George. "Collective Consciousness and Mass Hysteria: Collective Behavior and Anti-Pornography Crusades in Durkheimian Perspective." *Human Relations* 28 (1974):42–49.

Kirschner, Betty F., and Walum, Laurel R. "Two-Location Families." *Alternative Lifestyles* 1 (1978):513–521.

Klapp, Orrin. *Models of Social Order.* Palo Alto: National Press, 1973.

Klauber, George T. "Circumcision and Phallic Fallacies, or The Case Against Routine Circumcision." *Connecticut Medicine* 37 (1973):445–448.

Klemer, Richard H., ed. *Counseling in Marital and Sexual Problems.* Baltimore: Williams and Wilkins, 1965.

Knapp, Jacquelyn J. "An Exploratory Study of Seventeen Sexually Open Marriages." *Journal of Sex Research* 12 (1976):206–219.

Koch, Joanne, and Koch, Lew. "The Urgent Drive to Make Good Marriages Better." *Psychology Today* (September, 1976):33–34.

Koedt, Anne. "The Myth of the Vaginal Orgasm." In *Writings from the Women's Liberation Movement: Liberation Now,* edited by Deborah Babcox and Madeline Belkin, pp. 308–309. New York: Dell Books, 1971.

Kogan, B. A. *Human Sexual Expression.* New York: Harcourt Brace Jovanovich, Inc., 1973.

Kohn, Melvin. *Class and Conformity.* Homewood, Illinois: Dorsey Press, 1969.

Kolodny, Robert; Masters, William; Hendrix, Julie; and Toro, Galson. "Plasma Testosterone and Semen Analysis in Male Homosexuals." *Journal of Medicine* 285 (1971):1170–1171.

Kolodny, R. C.; Masters, W. H.; and Johnson, V. E. *Textbook of Sexual Medicine.* Boston, Little, Brown & Co., 1979.

Komarovsky, Mirra. *Blue-Collar Marriage.* New York: Random House, 1962.

Kopkind, Andrew. "Gay Rock: The Boys in the Band." *Ramparts* 11 (1973):49–50.

Krafft-Ebing, Richard von. *Psychopathia Sexualis.* New York: Pioneer Publications, 1950.

Kremer, J. "Infertility: Male and Female." In *Handbook of Sexology,* Vol. 111, edited by John Money and Herman Musaph, *Procreation and Parenthood,* pp. 679–694. New York: Elsevier, 1977.

Kristol, Irving. "Pornography, Obscenity and the Case for Censorship." *New York Times Magazine* (March 28, 1971):24–25, 112, 115.

Kroger, William S. "Sexual Frustration." *Sexual Behavior* 2 (1972):41–44.

Lader, Lawrence. "A National Guide to Legal Abortion." *Ladies Home Journal* 73 (July, 1970):73.

Ladner, Joyce A. *Tomorrow's Tomorrow*. New York: Doubleday, 1971.

Lampe, David. "Cloning." *Science Digest* (June, 1978):9–14.

Laner, Mary R. "Prostitution as an Illegal Vocation: A Sociological Overview." In *Deviant Behavior: Occupational and Organizational Basis*, edited by Clifton D. Bryant. Chicago: Rand-McNally, 1974.

Laner, Mary R. "Personals Advertisements of Lesbian Women." *Journal of Homosexuality* 4 (1978):41–49.

Laner, Mary R. "Growing Older Female: Heterosexual and Homosexual." *Journal of Homosexuality* 4 (1979):267–272.

Laner, Mary R., and Kamel, G. W. Levi. "Newspaper Personals Ads of Homosexual Men. *Journal of Homosexuality* 3 (1977):149–162.

Langevin, R.; Paitich, D.; Ramsay, G.; Anderson, C.; Kamrad, J.; Pope, S.; Geller, G.; Pearl, L.; and Newman, S. "Experimental Studies in the Etiology of Genital Exhibitionism." *Archives of Sexual Behavior* 8 (1979):307–331.

Lanson, L. *From Woman to Woman. A Gynecologist Answers Questions About You and Your Body*. New York: Alfred A. Knopf, 1975.

Laslett, Barbara. "The Family as a Public and Private Institution: An Historical Perspective." *Journal of Marriage and the Family* 35 (August, 1973):480–492.

"Later Marriage, Fewer Babies, Less Illegitimacy." *Family Planning Digest* 2 (1973):3–4.

Laws, Judith Long. "A Feminist Review of Marital Adjustment Literature: The Rape of the Lock." *Journal of Marriage and the Family* 33 (1971):483.

Lazarus, Arnold A. "Psychological Causes of Impotence." In *Sexual Behavior*, edited by Leonard Gross, pp. 227–239. Flushing, New York: Spectrum Publications, 1974.

Lederer, William J., and Jackson, Don D. "False Assumptions: That Love Is Necessary for a Satisfactory Marriage." In *The Mirages of Marriage*. New York: W. W. Norton, 1968.

Lee, John Alan. "The Styles of Loving." *Psychology Today* 8 (1974):43–51.

Lee, John Alan. "Forbidden Colors of Love." *Journal of Homosexuality* 1 (1976):401–418.

Lee, John Alan. "Going Public." *Journal of Homosexuality* 3 (1977):49–78.

LeGare, Miriam. Unpublished communication on physiology of the menstrual cycle, 1974.

Le Masters, E. E. "Parenthood as Crisis." *Marriage and Family Living* 19 (1957):352–355.

Lenski, Gerhard, and Leggett, John C. "Caste, Class, and Deference in the Research Interview." *American Journal of Sociology* 65 (1960):463–467.

Leonard, George B. "Why We Need a New Sexuality." In *The Future of Sexual Relations*, edited by Robert T. Francoeur and Anna K. Francoeur. Englewood Cliffs, New Jersey: Prentice-Hall, 1974.

Leslie, Gerald R. "Sexual Behavior of College Men: Today vs 30 Years Ago." *Medical Aspects of Human Sexuality* (July, 1978):102–117.

Lessard, Suzannah. "Gay Is Good for Us All." *Washington Monthly* II (December, 1970):39–49.

Lester, David. "Incest." *Journal of Sex Research* 8 (1972):268–285.

Lester, David. "Rape and Social Structure." *Psychological Reports* 35 (1974):146.

Levin, Robert J. "The End of the Double Standard." *Redbook* 144 (October, 1975):38–44, 190, 192.

Levin, Robert J. "Thorarche—A Seasonal Influence but No Secular Trend." *Journal of Sex Research* 12 (1976):173–179.

Levin, Robert J., and Levin, Amy. "Sexual Pleasure: The Surprising Preferences of 100,000 Women." *Redbook* 144 (September, 1975):51–58.

Levitsky, Abraham, and Simkin, James S. "Gestalt Therapy." In *New Perspectives on Encounter Groups,* edited by Laurence N. Solomon and Betty Berzon, pp. 245–254. San Francisco: Jossey-Bass, 1972.

Lewinshon, Richard. *History of Sexual Customs.* New York: Harper & Row, 1958.

Lewis, Al. "Love and the Youth Culture." In *Love Today,* edited by Herbert A. Otto, pp. 197–210. New York: Dell Books, 1972.

Lewis, C. S. *The Four Loves.* London: Geoffrey Blas, 1960.

Lewis, Lionel S., and Brissett, Dennis. "Sex as Work: A Study of Avocational Counseling." *Social Problems* 15 (1967):8–18.

Lewis, Oscar. *La Vida.* New York: Random House, 1966.

Lewis, Robert A. "Parents and Peers: Socialization Agents in the Coital Behavior of Young Adults." *Journal of Sex Research* 9 (1973):156–162.

Lewis, Robert A., and Burr, Wesley R. "Premarital Coitus and Commitment Among College Students." *Archives of Sexual Behavior* 4 (1975):73–79.

Libby, Roger W.; Gray, Louis; and White, Mervin. "A Test and Reformulation of Reference Group and Role Correlates of Premarital Sexual Permissiveness Theory." *Journal of Marriage and the Family* 40 (1978):79–91.

Libby, Roger W., and Nass, Gilbert D. "Parental Views of Teenage Behavior." *Journal of Sex Research* 7 (1971):226–236.

Libby, Roger, and Whitehurst, Robert. *Renovating Marriage: Toward New Sexual Life Styles.* Danville, Calif.: Consensus Publishers, 1973.

Lieberman, E. James, and Jackson, Jean F. "Teenage Crushes." *Sexual Behavior* 3 (1973):45–49.

Liebow, Elliott. *Tally's Corner.* Boston: Little, Brown & Co., 1967.

Lindemann, Constance. "Factors Affecting the Use of Contraception in the Nonmarital Context." In *Progress in Sexology,* edited by Robert Gemme and Connie C. Wheeler. New York: Plenum Press, 1976.

Lindner, Robert. "Adultery — Kinds and Consequences." In *Sex Life of the American Woman and the Kinsey Report,* edited by Albert Ellis. New York: Greenberg Publishers, 1954.

Linton, Ralph. *The Study of Man.* New York: Appleton-Century-Crofts, 1936.

Lipton, Lawrence. *The Erotic Revolution.* Los Angeles: Sherbourne Press, 1965.

Lipton, Morris A. "Fact and Myth: The Work of the Presidential Commission on Obscenity and Pornography." Paper presented at the annual meeting of the American Psychopathological Association, 1971.

Liswood, Rebecca. "Bedroom Manners." *Sexual Behavior* 1 (1971):74.

Lobitz, W. Charles, and LoPiccolo, Joseph. "New Methods in the Behavioral Treatment of Sexual Dysfunction." *Journal of Behavior Therapy and Experimental Psychiatry* 3 (1972):265–271.

Lobsenz, Norman. "Sex and the Senior Citizen." *New York Times Magazine* (January 20, 1974):87–91.

Lopez, Enrique H. *Eros and Ethos.* Englewood Cliffs, New Jersey: Prentice-Hall, 1979.

LoPiccolo, Joseph, and Lobitz, U. C. "The Role of Masturbation in the Treatment of Primary Orgasmic Dysfunction." *Archives of Sexual Behavior* 2 (1972):163–172.

Loring, Rosalind. "Love and Women's Liberation." In *Love Today,* edited by Herbert A. Otto, pp. 73–85. New York: Dell Books, 1972.

Lowen, Alexander. "The Spiral of Growth: Love, Sex and Pleasure." In *Love Today,* edited by Herbert A. Otto, pp. 17–26. New York: Dell Books, 1972.

Lowry, T. Unpublished communication on vaginal biorhythms, 1973.

Lumby, Malcolm E. "Men Who Advertise for Sex." *Journal of Homosexuality* 4 (1978):63–72.

Maccoby, Eleanor E. *The Development of Sex Differences.* Stanford, California: Stanford University Press, 1966.

Macdonald, John M. *Rape Offenders and Their Victims.* Springfield, Illinois: Charles C Thomas, 1971.

Mace, David R. "Response to Inquiry." *Medical Aspects of Human Sexuality* 4 (1970):69.

Mace, David R. "The Alternative to the Alternatives." *Alternative Lifestyles* 2 (1979):273–293.

Maddux, Hilary C. *Menstruation.* The Women's Library. New Canaan, Connecticut: Tobey Publishing Company, 1975.

Mahoney, E. R. "Age Differences in Attitude Change Toward Premarital Coitus." *Archives of Sexual Behavior* 7 (1978):493–501.

Malthus, Thomas. "A Summary View of the Principle of Population." In *Three Essays on Population.* Introduction by Frank W. Notestein. New York: Mentor, 1958.

Mann, Jay. "The Effects of Erotica." *Sexual Behavior* 3 (1973):23–26.

Mannheim, Karl. *Ideology and Utopia.* New York: Harcourt, Brace and World, 1936.

Marcus, Steven. *Other Victorians.* New York: Basic Books, 1966.

Margold, Jane. "Bisexuality: The Newest Sex Stage." *Cosmopolitan* 176 (June, 1974):189–192.

Margolis, Herbert F., and Rubenstein, Paul M. *The Groupsex Tapes.* New York: Paperback Library, 1972.

Mark, I. M., and Gelder, M. C. "Transvestism and Fetishism: Clinical and Psychological Changes During Faradic Aversion." *British Journal of Psychiatry* 113 (1967):711–728.

Marmor, Judd. *Sexual Inversion: The Multiple Roots of Homosexuality.* New York: Basic Books, 1965.

Marmor, Judd. "Sex for Non-Sexual Reasons." *Medical Aspects of Human Sexuality* 3 (1969):8–21.

Martin, C. E. "Sexual Activity in the Aging Male." In *Handbook of Sexology IV: Selected Personal and Social Issues,* edited by John Money and Herman Musaph, pp. 813–824. New York: Elsevier, 1977.

Martinson, Floyd M. *Infant and Child Sexuality.* Privately published, 1973.

Martinson, Floyd M. "Eroticism in Infancy and Childhood." *Journal of Sex Research* 12 (November, 1976):251–262.

Maschhoff T. A.; Fanshier, W. E.; and Hansen, D. J. "Vasectomy: Its Effect upon Marital Stability." *Journal of Sex Research* 12 (1976):295–314.

Maslow, Abraham. *Toward a Psychology of Being,* 2nd ed. New York: D. Van Nostrand Co., 1968.

Maslow, Abraham. *The Farther Reaches of Human Nature.* New York: Viking Press, 1971.

Maslow, Abraham, and Mintz, N. "Effects of Esthetic Surroundings: 1. Initial Effects of Three Esthetic Conditions upon Perceiving 'Energy' and 'Well-being' in Faces." *Journal of Psychology* 41 (1956):247–254.

Masters, Robert E. L. *Patterns of Incest.* New York: Julian Press, 1963.

Masters, William H., and Johnson, Virginia E. *Human Sexual Response.* Boston: Little, Brown & Co., 1966.

Masters, William H., and Johnson, Virginia E. *Human Sexual Inadequacy.* Boston: Little, Brown & Co., 1970.

Masters, William H., and Johnson, Virginia E. "Current Status of the Research Programs." In *Contemporary Sexual Behavior: Critical Issues in the 1970's,* edited by Joseph Zubin and John Money, pp. 279–293. Baltimore: Johns Hopkins University Press, 1973.

Masters, William H., and Johnson, Virginia E. *Homosexuality in Perspective.* Boston: Little, Brown & Co., 1979.

Maxwell, Joseph W.; Sack, Alan R.; Frary, Robert B.; and Keller, James F. "Factors Influencing Contraceptive Behavior of Single College Students." *Journal of Sex and Marital Therapy* 3 (1977):265–273.

May, Rollo. *Man's Search for Himself.* New York: W. W. Norton, 1953.

Mazur, Ronald. *The New Intimacy.* Boston: Beacon Press, 1973a.

Mazur, Ronald. "Beyond Jealousy and Possessiveness." In *Renovating Marriage,* edited by Roger Libby and Robert Whitehurst. Danville, Calif.: Consensus Publishers, 1973b.

Mazur, Tom, and Money, John. "Prenatal Influences and Subsequent Sexuality." In *Handbook of Human Sexuality,* edited by Benjamin B. Wolman and John Money, pp. 3–14. Englewood Cliffs, New Jersey: Prentice-Hall, 1980.

McCaffrey, Joseph A. *The Homosexual Dialectic.* Englewood Cliffs, New Jersey: Prentice-Hall, 1972.

McCaghy, Charles H. "Child Molesting." *Sexual Behavior* 1 (1971):16.

McCall, George, and Simmons, J. L., eds. *Issues in Participant Observations: A Text and Reader.* Reading, Massachusetts: Addison-Wesley, 1969.

McCarthy, Barry W. "Strategies and Techniques for the Reduction of Sexual Anxiety." *Journal of Sex and Marital Therapy* 3 (1977):243–248.

McCary, James L. *Human Sexuality.* New York: D. Van Nostrand Co., 1973.

McLuhan, Marshall, and Leonard, George B. "The Future of Sex." In *The Future of Sexual Relations,* edited by Robert T. Francoeur and Anna K. Francoeur. Englewood Cliffs, New Jersey: Prentice-Hall, 1974.

McMurtry, John. "Monogamy: A Critique." In *Renovating Marriage,* edited by Robert W. Libby and Robert N. Whitehurst, pp. 48–58. Danville, Calif.: Consensus Publishers, 1973.

McPartland, John. "Our Changing Sex Codes." *Coronet* 38 (August, 1955):147–152.

McWhorter, William L. "Flashing and Dashing: Notes and Comments on the

Etiology of Exhibitionism." In *Sexual Deviancy in Social Context,* edited by Clifton Bryant, pp. 101–110. New York: New Viewpoints, 1977.

Mead, Margaret. *Sex and Temperament in Three Primitive Societies.* New York: William Morrow, 1935.

Mead, Margaret. *Coming of Age in Samoa.* New York: Dell Books, 1967.

Mears, Eleanor. *Handbook on Oral Contraception.* Boston: Little, Brown and Company, 1965.

Meiselman, Karin C. *Incest.* San Francisco: Jossey-Bass, 1978.

Merritt, Gary; Gerstl, Joel E.; and Lo Sciuto, Leonard A. "Age and Perceived Effects of Erotica-Pornography: A National Sample Study." *Archives of Sexual Behavior* 4 (1975):605–621.

Meyer, J. K.; Knorr, N. J.; and Blumer, D. "Characterization of a Self-Designated Transsexual Population." *Archives of Sexual Behavior* 1 (1971):219–222.

Meyer-Bahlburg, Heino F. L. Sex Hormones and Male Homosexuality in Comparative Perspective." *Archives of Sexual Behavior* 6 (1977):297–308.

Meyer-Bahlburg, Heino F. L. "Sex Hormones and Female Homosexuality." *Archives of Sexual Behavior* 8 (1979):101–118.

Middendorp, C. P.; Brinkman, W.; and Konnen, W. "Determinants of Premarital Sexual Permissiveness: A Secondary Analysis." *Journal of Marriage and the Family* 32 (1970):369–378.

Mikulas, William. "Criticisms of Behavior Therapy." *Canadian Psychologist* 13 (1972):83–104.

Miller, Brian. "Unpromised Paternity: The Life-Styles of Gay Fathers." In *Gay Men,* edited by Martin Levine, pp. 239–252. New York: Harper & Row, 1979.

Miller, Howard L., and Siegel, Paul S. *Loving.* New York: John Wiley & Sons, 1972.

Miller, Patricia Y., and Simon, William. "Adolescent Sexual Behavior: Context and Change." *Social Problems* 22 (1974):58–76.

Mills, C. Wright. "Situated Actions and Vocabularies of Motive." *American Sociological Review* (December, 1940):904–913.

Mischel, Walter. "A Social-Learning View of Sex Differences in Behavior." In *The Development of Sex Differences,* edited by Eleanor E. Maccoby, pp. 56–81. Stanford: Stanford University Press, 1966.

Mischell, D. R., Jr. "Assessing the Intrauterine Device." *Family Planning Perspectives* 7 (1975):103–111.

Modaressi, Taghi. "Personality Development and Sexuality." In *Handbook of Human Sexuality,* edited by Benjamin B. Wolman and John Money, pp. 147–161. Englewood Cliffs, New Jersey: Prentice-Hall, 1980.

Money, John. "Components of Eroticism in Man: Cognitional Rehearsals." In *Recent Advances in Biological Psychiatry.* New York: Grune & Stratton, Inc., 1961.

Money, John. "Influence of Hormones on Sexual Behavior." *Annual Review of Medicine* 16 (1965):67–82.

Money, John. "Psychosexual Differentiation." In *Sex Research, New Developments,* pp. 3–23. New York: Holt, Rinehart & Winston, 1965.

Money, John. "The Sex Instinct and Human Eroticism." *Journal of Sex Research* 1 (1965):3–16.

Money, John. *Sex Errors of the Body.* Baltimore: Johns Hopkins University Press, 1968.

Money, John. *Sexual Signatures.* Baltimore: Johns Hopkins University Press, 1975.

Money, John; Hampson, Joan G.; and Hampson, J. L. "Imprinting and the Establishment of Gender Role." *A.M.A. Archives of Neurology and Psychiatry* 77 (1957):333–336.

Monteflores, Carmen, and Schultz, Stephen J. "Coming Out: Similarities and Differences for Lesbians and Gay Men." *Journal of Social Issues* 34 (1978):59–72.

Moore, James E. "Problematic Sexual Behavior." In *The Individual, Sex, and Society,* edited by Carlfred B. Broderick and Jessie Bernard, pp. 343–372. Baltimore: Johns Hopkins University Press, 1969.

Morin, Stephen F. "Psychology and the Gay Community." *Journal of Social Issues* 34 (1978).1–6.

Morin, Stephen F., and Garfinkle, Ellen M. "Male Homophobia." *Journal of Social Issues* 34 (1978):29–47.

Morris, Jan. *Conundrum.* New York: Harcourt Brace Jovanovich, Inc., 1974.

Morrison, Peter. "Beyond the Baby Boom." *Futurist* (April, 1979):131–139.

Mosher, Donald L., and Greenberg, Irene. "Females' Affective Responses to Reading Erotic Literature." *Journal of Consulting and Clinical Psychology* 33 (1969):472–477.

Mowery, Jeni. "Systemic Requisites of Communal Groups." *Alternative Lifestyles* 2 (1979):235–253.

Moynihan, Daniel P. *The Negro Family: The Case for National Action.* Washington, D.C.: Office of Policy Planning and Research, U.S. Dept. of Labor, 1965.

Murdock, George P. *Social Structure.* New York: Macmillan Company, 1949.

Murstein, Bernard I. *Theories of Attraction and Love.* New York: Springer, 1971.

Myers, Lonny, and Leggitt, Rev. Hunter. "A New View of Adultery." *Sexual Behavior* 2 (1972):52.

Naeye, Richard L. "Sex In Late Pregnancy." *New England Journal of Medicine* (November 29, 1979).

Neiger, S. "Mate Swapping: Can It Save a Marriage?" *Sexology* (January, 1971):8–12.

Netter, Frank H. *The Ciba Collection of Medical Illustrations,* Volume 2. Summit, New Jersey: Ciba, 1965.

Neubeck, Gerhard. *Extramarital Relations.* Englewood Cliffs, New Jersey: Prentice-Hall, 1969.

Neubeck, Gerhard, and Schletzer, Vera M. "A Study of Extra-Marital Relationships." *Marriage and the Family Living* 24 (1963):279–281.

Newcomb, Paul R. "Cohabitation in America: An Assessment of Consequences." *Journal of Marriage and the Family* 41 (1979):597–602.

Newcomb, Theodore. "The Prediction of Interpersonal Attraction." *American Psychologist* 2 (1956):575.

Newman, Gustave, and Nichols, Claude R. "Sexual Activities and Attitudes in Older Persons." *Journal of American Medical Association* 173 (1960):33–35.

Newmark, Stephen R.; Rose, Leslie I.; Todd, Roberta; Birk, Lee; and Naftolin, Frederick. "Gonadotropin, Estradiol, and Testosterone Profiles in Homosexual Men." *American Journal of Psychiatry* 136 (1979):767–771.

Newton, Esther. *Mother Camp: Female Impersonators in America.* Englewood Cliffs, New Jersey: Prentice-Hall, 1972.

Newton, Miles. "Trebly Sensuous Women." *Psychology Today* 3 (1971):68.

Obler, Martin. "Systematic Desensitization in Sexual Disorders." *Journal of Behavioral Therapy and Experimental Psychiatry* 4 (1973):93.

Offir, Carole W. "Don't Take It Lying Down." *Psychology Today* (January, 1975):70–76.

O'Neill, George, and O'Neill, Nena. *Open Marriage: A New Lifestyle for Couples.* New York: M. Evans, 1972.

Opler, M. "Cross-Cultural Aspects of Kissing." *Medical Aspects of Human Sexuality* 3 (1969):11–21.

"Oral Contraceptives Found to Increase Sharply Risk of Heart Attacks, Especially Among Women 40 or Older and Smokers." *Family Planning Digest* 7 (1975):145–147.

Orlinsky, David F. "Love Relationships in the Life Cycle: A Developmental Interpersonal Perspective." In *Love Today,* edited by Herbert A. Otto, pp. 135–150. New York: Dell Books, 1972.

Orwell, George. *1984.* New York: New American Library, 1961. Originally published in 1949.

Osborn, Candice, and Pollack, Robert H. "The Effects of Two Types of Erotic Literature on Physiological and Verbal Measures of Female Sexual Arousal." *Journal of Sex Research* 13 (1977):250–256.

Otto, Herbert A., ed. *Love Today.* New York: Dell Books, 1972.

Otto, Herbert A. "Man-Woman Relationships in the Society of the Future." *Futurist* 7 (1973):55–61.

Packard, Vance. *The Hidden Persuaders.* New York: David McKay, 1957.

Paige, Karen E. "Women Learn to Sing the Menstrual Blues." *Psychology Today* 7 (1973):41–46.

Palson, Charles, and Palson, Rebecca. "Swinging in Wedlock." *Society* 9 (1972):43–48.

Panati, Charles. "Brain Breakthroughs: Your Body's Own Drugs for Pleasure and Pain." *Futurist* (February, 1980).

Parker, Tony. *The Twisting Lane* (British edition). London: Hutchinson and Co., 1969. *The Hidden World of Sex Offenders* (U.S. edition). Indianapolis, Ind.: Bobbs-Merrill, 1972.

Parron, Eugenia M., and Troll, Lillian E. "Golden Wedding Couples." *Alternative Lifestyles* 1 (1978):447–464.

Pearlman, Carl K. "Potency After Prostatectomy." *Medical Aspects of Human Sexuality* (March, 1978):119.

Peel, J., and Potts, M. *Textbook of Contraceptive Practice.* Cambridge: Harvard University Press, 1969.

Peele, Stanton, and Brodsky, Archie. "Stimulus/Response: Interpersonal Heroin: Love Can Be an Addiction." *Psychology Today* 8 (1974):22–28.

Peplau, Letitia A.; Rubin, Zick; and Hill, Charles T. "Sexual Intimacy in Dating Relationships." *Journal of Social Issues* 33 (1977):86–109.

Perls, Frederick S. *Gestalt Therapy Verbatim.* New York: Bantam Books, 1969.

Petersen, James R. "The Extended Male Orgasm." *Playboy* (May, 1977):90–92.

Pfeiffer, Eric. "Geriatric Sex Behavior." *Medical Aspects of Human Sexuality* 3 (1969):19–27.

Pfeiffer, Eric. "Sex and Aging." In *Sexual Issues in Marriage,* edited by Leonard

Gross, pp. 43–49. New York: Spectrum Publications, 1975.

Pfeiffer, Eric, and Davis, G. C. "Sexual Behavior in Aged Men and Women." *Archives of General Psychiatry* 19 (1968):753, 759.

Pfeiffer, Eric, and Davis, G. C. "Determinants of Sexual Behavior in Middle and Old Age." *Journal of American Geriatrics* 20 (1972):151–154.

Phillips, David Graham. "Restless Husband." *Cosmopolitan* 51 (August, 1971):419–423.

Pietropinto, Anthony, and Simenauer, Jacqueline. *Husbands and Wives.* New York: Times Books, 1979.

Pilder, Richard. "Encounter Groups for Married Couples." In *New Perspectives on Encounter Groups,* edited by Laurence N. Solomon and Betty Berzon, pp. 303–312. San Francisco: Jossey-Bass, 1972.

Piotrow, P. T., and Lee, C. M. "Oral Contraceptives — 50 Million Users." *Population Reports,* Ser. A, 1. April, 1974.

Pittman, David J. "The Male House of Prostitution." *Trans-action* 8 (1971):21–27.

Ploscowe, Morris. *Sex and the Law.* Englewood Cliffs, New Jersey: Prentice-Hall, 1951.

Polsky, Ned. *Hustlers, Beats and Others.* Chicago: Aldine Publishing Co., 1967.

Pomeroy, Wardell B. "Normal vs. Abnormal Sex." *Sexology* 32 (1966):436–439.

Ponse, Barbara. *Identities in the Lesbian World.* Unpublished Ph.D. dissertation, University of Southern California, 1976a.

Ponse, Barbara. "Secrecy in the Lesbian World." *Urban Life* Special Issue: *Sexuality: Encounters, Identities and Relationships,* edited by Carol A. B. Warren. Beverly Hills, Calif.; Sage Publications, 1976b.

Ponse, Barbara. *Identities in the Lesbian World.* Westport, Connecticut: Greenwood Press, 1978.

Potts, M., *et. al.* "Advantages of Orals Outweigh Disadvantages." *Population Reports,* Ser. A, 2. March, 1975.

Prescott, James W. "Abortion and the 'Right-to Life': Facts, Fallacies, and Fraud." *Humanist* (July/August, 1978):18–24.

Prescott, James W. "Alienation of Affection." *Psychology Today* (December, 1979);124.

Prescott, James W., and McKay, Cathy. "Human Affection, Violence and Sexuality: A Developmental and Cross-Cultural Perspective." Paper presented to the Society for Cross-Cultural Research, Philadelphia, February, 1973.

Prince, Virginia. "Homosexuality, Transvestism and Transsexualism." *American Journal of Psychotherapy* 11 (1957):80–85.

Prince, Virginia, and Betler, P. M. "Survey of 504 Cases of Transvestism." *Psychological Reports* 31 (1972):903–917.

Proulx, Cynthia. "Sex as Athletics in the Singles Complex." *Saturday Review/Society* (May, 1973):23–29.

Pumpian-Mindlin, Eugene. "Nymphomania and Satyriasis." In *Sexual Problems,* edited by Charles W. Wahl, pp. 163–171. New York: Free Press, 1967.

Rada, Richard. *Clinical Aspects of the Rapist.* New York: Grune and Stratton, Inc., 1978.

Rader, Dotson. "The Feminization of the American Male." In *The Future of Sexual Relations,* edited by Robert T. Francoeur and Anna K. Francoeur, pp. 118–121.

Englewood Cliffs, New Jersey: Prentice-Hall, 1974.

Rainwater, Lee. *Family Design.* Chicago: Aldine Publishing Co., 1965.

Rainwater, Lee. "Sex in the Culture of Poverty." In *The Individual, Sex, and Society,* edited by Carlfred B. Broderick and Jessie Bernard. Baltimore: Johns Hopkins University Press, 1969.

Rainwater, Lee. *Behind Ghetto Walls.* Chicago: Aldine Publishing Co., 1970.

Rainwater, Lee, and Yancey, William L. *The Moynihan Report and the Politics of Controversy.* Cambridge, Massachusetts: The M.I.T. Press, 1967.

Ramey, James W. "Emerging Patterns of Innovative Behavior in Marriage." *Family Coordinator* 21 (1972):435–456.

Ramey, James W. *Intimate Friendships.* Englewood Cliffs, New Jersey: Prentice-Hall, 1976.

Ramey, James W. "Dealing with the Last Taboo." *Siecus Report* 7 (May, 1979):1–7.

Rasmussen, Paul K., and Kuhn, Lauren H. "The New Masseuse: Play for Pay." *Urban Life* Special Issue: *Sexuality: Encounters, Identities and Relationships,* edited by Carol A. B. Warren. Beverly Hills, Calif.: Sage Publications, October, 1976.

Rechy, John. *City of Night.* New York: Grove Press, 1963.

Record, Jane Cassels. "Review Symposium." *Contemporary Sociology* 4 (1975):361–366.

Redekop, J. H. *The American Far Right.* Grand Rapids, Michigan: William Ferdmans, 1968.

Reed, John, and Robin, S. "P.R.U.D.E.S. (Pornographic Research Using Direct Erotic Stimuli)." *Journal of Sex Research* 8 (1972):237–241.

Reevy, William R. "Adolescent Sexuality." In *Encyclopedia of Sexual Behavior,* edited by Albert Ellis and Albert Abarbanal, pp. 52–68. New York: Jason Aronson, 1973.

Reich, Charles. *The Greening of America.* New York: Random House, 1970.

Reichelt, Paul A. "Coital and Contraceptive Behavior of Female Adolescents." *Archives of Sexual Behavior* 8 (June, 1979):159–171.

Reik, Theodor. *The Need to Be Loved.* New York: Bantam Books, 1963.

Reiss, Albert J. "The Social Integration of Queers and Peers." In *The Other Side,* edited by Howard S. Becker. New York: Free Press, 1964.

Reiss, Ira L. "Toward a Sociology of the Heterosexual Love Relationship." *Marriage and Family Living* 22 (1960):129–145.

Reiss, Ira L. "Consistency and the Sex Ethic." In *The Family and the Sexual Revolution,* edited by Edwin M. Shur, pp. 86–96. Bloomington: Indiana University Press, 1964.

Reiss, Ira L. *The Social Context of Premarital Sexual Permissiveness.* New York: Holt, Rinehart and Winston, 1967.

Reiss, Ira L. "How and Why America's Sex Standards Are Changing." *Transaction* 5 (1968):26–32.

Reiss, Ira L. *Heterosexual Relationships Inside and Outside of Marriage.* Morristown, New Jersey: General Learning Press, 1973.

Reither, Rosemary. "The Personality of Sexuality." In *The Future of Sexual Relations;* edited by Robert T. Francoeur and Anna K. Francoeur, pp. 42–49. Englewood Cliffs, New Jersey: Prentice-Hall, 1974.

Rene Guyon Society. *Bulletin.* September 1, 1975.

Resnik, H. L. P., and Wolfgang, Marvin E., eds. *Sexual Behavior: Social, Clinical and Legal Aspects.* Boston: Little, Brown & Co., 1972.

Restak, Richard M. "The Sex-Change Conspiracy." *Psychology Today* (December, 1979):20–25.

Ribal, Joseph E. *Learning Sex Roles.* San Francisco: Canfield Press, 1973.

Riddle, Dorothy I. "Relating to Children: Gays as Role Models." *Journal of Social Issues* 34 (1978):38–58.

Riess, Bernard R.; Safer, Jeanne; and Yotive, William. "Psychological Test Data on Female Homosexuality." *Journal of Homosexuality* 1 (1974):71–85.

Rimmer, Robert. *The Harrad Experiment.* New York: Bantam Books, 1967.

Rimmer, Robert. *Proposition 31.* New York: New American Library, 1968.

Rimmer, Robert. *Thursday, My Love.* New York: New American Library, 1972.

Rimmer, Robert. *The Premar Experiment.* New York: New American Library, 1975.

Robbins, Jhan, and Robbins, June. *Analysis of Human Sexual Inadequacy.* New York: Times Mirror, 1970.

Robbins, Mina B., and Jensen, Gordon D. "Multiple Orgasm in Males." In *Progress in Sexology,* edited by Robert Gemme and Connie C. Wheeler, pp. 323–327. New York: Plenum Press, 1976.

Roebuck, Julian, and McGee, Marsha G. "Attitudes Toward Premarital Sex and Sexual Behavior Among Black High School Girls." *Journal of Sex Research* 13 (1977):104–114.

Rogers, Carl R. *On Becoming a Person.* Boston: Houghton Mifflin, 1961.

Rogers, Carl R. *Becoming Partners: Marriage and Its Alternatives.* New York: Dell Books, 1972.

Roiphe, Anne R. *Up the Sandbox.* New York: Simon & Schuster, 1970.

Romano, Mary D.; Beigel, H. G.; Brecher, E. M.; and Kirkendall, L. A. "Sexual Counseling in Groups." *Journal of Sexual Research* 9 (1973):69–78.

Romano, Mary D., and O'Connor, John F. "Sexual Needs of the Physically Handicapped." *Medical Aspects of Human Sexuality* (September, 1978):82–97.

Rosen, H. S. "A Survey of the Sexual Attitudes and Behavior of Mate-Swappers in Houston, Texas." M.A. Thesis, University of Houston, 1971.

Ross, C., and Piotrow, P. T. "Periodic Abstinence: Birth Control Without Contraceptives." *Population Reports,* Series 1, No. 1 (June, 1974).

Ross, Michael W.; Rogers, Lesley J.; and McCulloch, Helen. "Stigma, Sex, and Society." *Journal of Homosexuality* 3 (1978):315–330.

Rossman, Parker. "The Pederasts." *Society* 10 (1973):29.

Roth, Gerald, "Exhibitionism Outside Europe and America." *Archives of Sexual Behavior* 2 (1973):351–363.

Roy, Rustum, and Roy, Della. *Honest Sex.* New York: Signet, 1968.

Roy, Rustum, and Roy, Della. "Is Monogamy Outdated?" *The Humanist* 19 (1970):19–26.

Rubin, Isadore. *Sexual Life After Sixty.* New York: Basic Books, 1965.

Rubin, Isadore. "Sex After Forty — and After Seventy." In *An Analysis of Human Sexual Response,* edited by Ruth Brecher and Edward Brecher. Boston: Little, Brown & Co., 1966.

Rubin, Isadore. "The 'Sexless Older Years' — A Socially Harmful Stereotype." *The Annals* 376 (1968):86–95.

Rubin, Isadore. "Concepts of Sexual Abnormality and Perversion in Marriage Counseling." In *Marital Therapy,* edited by Hirsch L. Silverman, pp. 214–226. Springfield, Illinois: Charles C Thomas, 1972.

Rubin, Lillian B. "The Marriage Bed." *Psychology Today* (August, 1976):44–50.

Rubin, Lillian B. *Worlds of Pain.* New York: Basic Books, 1976.

Rubin, R. D.; Brady, J. P.; and Henderson, J. G., eds. *Advances in Behavior Therapy,* Vol. 4. New York: Academic Press, 1973.

Rubin, Theodore I. *In the Life.* New York: Macmillan Company, 1961.

Ruitenbeek, Hendrick M. *Psychotherapy of Perversions.* New York: Citadel Press, 1967.

Ruitenbeek, Hendrick M. *The New Sexuality.* New York: New Viewpoints, 1974.

Rush, A. K. *Getting Clear. Body Work for Women.* New York: Random House, 1973.

Sagarin, Edward. "Language of the Homosexual Subculture." *Medical Aspects of Human Sexuality* 4 (1970):37.

Sagarin, Edward. "Cabbie, Where's the Action?" *Sexual Behavior* 1 (1971):56.

Sagarin, Edward. "Power to the Peephole." *Sexual Behavior* 3 (1973):2–7.

Sagarin, Edward, and MacNamara, Donald E. J. "The Problem of Entrapment." *Crime and Delinquency* 16 (1970):363–378.

Salisbury, Winifred W., and Salisbury, Frances F. "Sexual Ethics — New or Old? — A Debate." *Forum and Century* 94 (1936):65–69.

Salisbury, Winifred W., and Salisbury, Frances F. "Sex Freedom and Morals in the U.S." *Ladies Home Journal* 66 (1949):48–49.

Salisbury, Winifred W., and Salisbury, Frances F. "Youth and the Search for Intimacy." In *The New Sexual Revolution,* edited by Lester A. Kirkendall and Robert N. Whitehurst. New York: Donald W. Brown, 1971.

Salsberg, Sheldon. "Is Group Marriage Viable?" *Journal of Sex Research* 9 (1973):325–333.

Salzman, Leon. "Female Infidelity." *Medical Aspects of Human Sexuality* 6 (1972):118–122.

Schill, Thomas, and Chapin, James. "Sex Guilt and Males Preference for Reading Erotic Magazines." *Journal of Consulting and Clinical Psychology* 39 (1972):516–521.

Schimel, John L. "Sexual Conflicts in 'Young Marrieds.'" *Sexual Behavior* 1 (1971):30–38.

Schimel, John L. "Homosexual Fantasies in Heterosexual Males." *Medical Aspects of Human Sexuality* 6 (1972):144–148.

Schmidt, Gunter. "Male-Female Differences in Sexual Arousal and Behavior During and After Exposure to Sexually Explicit Stimuli." *Archives of Sexual Behavior* 4 (1975):353–366.

Schmidt, Gunther, and Sigusch, Volkimar. "Sex Differences in Response to Psychosexual Stimulation by Films and Slides." *Journal of Sex Research* 6 (1970):268–283.

Schofield, Michael. *Promiscuity.* London:Victor Gollancz, 1976.

Schultz, David A. *Coming Up Black.* Englewood Cliffs, New Jersey: Prentice-Hall, 1969.

See, Patricia. "The More, The Merrier?" In *Intimate Life Styles,* 2nd ed., edited by

B-30

Jack R. DeLora and Joann S. DeLora, pp. 320–328. Pacific Palisades, Calif.: Goodyear Publishing, 1975.

Selkin, James. "Rape." *Psychology Today* 8 (January, 1975):71–76.

Sex Information and Education Council. *Sexuality and Man.* New York: Charles Scribner's Sons, 1970.

Seyler, Lloyd E.; Canalis, Ernesto; Spare, Steven; and Reichlin, Seymour. "Abnormal Gonadotropin Secretory Responses to LRH in Transsexual Women After Diethylstilbestrol Priming." *Journal of Clinical Endocrinology and Metabolism* 47 (1978):176–183.

Shainess, Natalie. "How 'Sex Experts' Debase Sex." *World* (January 2, 1973):17–18.

Shainess, Natalie. "Sexual Problems of Women." *Journal of Sex and Marital Therapy* 1 (1974):110–123.

Sheehy, Gail. *Hustling: Prostitution in Our Wide Open Society.* New York: Delacorte Press, 1973.

Sherfey, Mary Jane. "The Evolution and Nature of Female Sexuality in Relation to Psychoanalytic Theory." *Journal of the American Psychoanalysis Association* 14 (January, 1966):28–127.

Sherfey, Mary Jane. *Nature and Evolution of Female Sexuality.* New York: Random House, 1972.

Sherfey, Mary Jane. "Some Biology of Sexuality." *Journal of Sex and Marital Therapy* 1 (1974):97–109.

Sherwin, Robert Veit, and Winick, Charles. "Debate: Should Prostitution Be Legalized?" *Sexual Behavior* 2 (1972):66–69.

Shettles, L. B. "Predetermining Children's Sex." *Medical Aspects of Human Sexuality* (June, 1972):172.

Shilts, Randy. "The Hazards of Sex." *The Advocate* (December 15, 1976):1–2.

Shope, David F. *Interpersonal Sexuality.* Philadelphia: W. B. Saunders Co., 1975.

Shostrom, Everett L. "Love, the Human Encounter." In *Love Today,* edited by Herbert A. Otto, pp. 185–196. New York: Dell Books, 1972.

Shusterman, Lisa Roseman. "The Treatment of Impotence by Behavior Modification Techniques." *Journal of Sex Research* 9 (1973):226–240.

Siegelman, Marvin. "Adjustment of Homosexual and Heterosexual Women: A Cross-National Replication." *Archives of Sexual Behavior* 8 (1979):121–136.

Silny, Ann J. "Sexuality and Aging." In *Handbook of Human Sexuality,* edited by Benjamin B. Wolman and John Money, pp. 123–145. Englewood Cliffs, New Jersey: Prentice-Hall, 1980.

Silverman, Hirsch L. *Marital Therapy: Moral, Sociological, and Psychological Factors.* Springfield, Illinois: Charles C. Thomas, 1972.

Simpson, Mary, and Schill, Thomas. "Patrons of Massage Parlors." *Archives of Sexual Behavior* 6 (1977):521–529.

Singer, Irving. *Goals of Human Sexuality.* New York: W. W. Norton, 1973.

Singer, Josephine, and Singer, Irving. "Types of Female Orgasm." *Journal of Sex Research* 8 (1972):255–267.

Skinner, B. F. *Walden Two.* New York: Macmillan Company, 1969.

Skipper, James K., Jr., and McCaghy, Charles H. "The Stripteaser." *Sexual Behavior* 1 (1971):78–79.

Skolnick, Arlene. *The Intimate Environment: Exploring Marriage and the Family.* Boston: Little, Brown & Co., 1973.

Slater, Philip. *Footholds.* New York, E. P. Dutton and Co., 1977.

Smith, James R., and Smith, Lynn G. "Co-Marital Sex and the Sexual Freedom Movement." *Journal of Sex Research* 6 (1970):131–142.

Smith, James R., and Smith, Lynn G. *Consenting Adults.* Baltimore: Johns Hopkins University Press, 1975.

Smith, Manuel. "Modification of Gynephobia by Photoelectric Penile Plethysmography." Paper presented to the Society for the Scientific Study of Sex, June 1–3, 1973.

Smith, R. Spencer. "Voyeurism: A Review of the Literature." *Archives of Sexual Behavior* 5 (1976):585–608.

Snyder, David P. "The Corporate Family." *Futurist* (December, 1976):323–331.

Solomon, Laurence N., and Berzon, Betty, eds. *New Perspectives on Encounter Groups.* San Francisco: Jossey-Bass, 1972.

Sonenschein, David. "Homosexual Humor." *Sexual Behavior* 3 (1973):25.

Sorensen, Robert C. *Adolescent Sexuality in Contemporary America.* New York: World Publishing Co., 1973.

Sorokin, Pitirim. *The Ways and Power of Love.* Chicago: Henry Regnery, 1967.

Southam, A. L. "Historical Review of Intrauterine Devices." In *Intrauterine Contraception: Proceedings of the 2nd International Conference,* pp. 3–5. Amsterdam, New York: Excerpta Medica Foundation, 1964.

Spanier, Graham B. "Romanticism and Marital Adjustments." *Journal of Marriage and the Family* 34 (1972):481–492.

Spanier, Graham B. "Sources of Sex Information and Premarital Sexual Behavior." *Journal of Sex Research* 13 (1977):73–88.

Spanier, Graham B., and Cole, Charles L. "Mate Swapping: Perceptions, Value Orientations, and Participation in a Midwestern Community." *Archives of Sexual Behavior* 4 (1975):143–159.

Sprey, Jetse. "On the Institutionalization of Sexuality." *Journal of Marriage and the Family* 31 (1969):432–440.

Sprey, Jetse. "Extramarital Relationships." *Sexual Behavior* 2 (1972):34–36.

Stall, Sylvanus. *What a Young Husband Ought to Know.* Philadelphia: VIR Publishing Co., 1897.

Stannard, Una. "The Mask of Beauty." *Sexuality Behavior* 1 (1971):27–29.

Staples, Robert. "Masculinity and Race: The Dual Dilemma of Black Men." *Journal of Social Issues* 34 (1978):169–178.

Staples, Robert. "Race, Liberalism-Conservatism and Premarital Sexual Permissiveness; A Bi-Racial Comparison." *Journal of Marriage and the Family* 40 (1978):733–741.

Stinnett, Nick, and Birdsong, Craig W. *The Family and Alternate Life Styles.* Chicago: Nelson-Hall, 1978.

Stoken, Dick. "What the Long-Term Cycle Tells Us About the 1980's." *Futurist* (February, 1980):14–19.

Stokes, Walter R. "Our Changing Sex Ethics." In *The Family and the Sexual Revolution,* edited by Edwin M. Shur. Bloomington: Indiana University Press, 1964.

Stoller, Frederick H. "The Intimate Network of Families." In *The Family in Search of a Future,* edited by Herbert A. Otto. New York: Appleton-Century-Crofts, 1970.

Stoller, Robert J. *Sex and Gender.* New York: Science House, 1968.

Stoller, Robert J. "Pornography and Perversion." *Archives of General Psychiatry* 22 (1970):490–497.

Stoller, Robert J. "The Term 'Transvestism.' " *Archives of General Psychiatry* 24 (1971):230–237.

Storaska, Frederic. *How to Say No to a Rapist and Survive.* New York: Random House, 1975.

Storms, Michael W. "Attitudes Toward Homosexuality and Femininity in Men." *Journal of Homosexuality* 3 (1978):257–283.

Story, Norman L. "Sexual Dysfunction Resulting from Drug Side Effects." *Journal of Sex Research* 10 (1974):132–149.

Strain, Frances B. *The Normal Sex Interests of Children.* New York: Appleton-Century-Crofts, 1948.

Strong, Leslie D. "Alternative Marital and Family Forms" *Journal of Marriage and the Family* 41 (1978):493–507.

Sue, David. "Erotic Fantasies of College Students During Coitus." *Journal of Sex Research* 15 (1979):299–305.

Sullivan, P. "What Is the Role of Fantasy in Sex?" *Medical Aspects of Human Sexuality* (1969):79–89.

Susann, Jacqueline. *Once Is Not Enough.* New York: Bantam Books, 1974.

Sussman, Marvin. "Non-Traditional Family Forms in the 1970's." *Family Coordinator* 21 (1972):132–149.

Svalastoga, Kaare. "Rape and Social Structure." *Pacific Sociological Review* 5 (1962):48–53.

Swensen, Clifford H. "The Behavior of Love." In *Love Today,* edited by Herbert A. Otto, pp. 86–101. New York: Dell Books, 1972.

Swerdlow, Hyman. "Trauma Caused by Anal Coitus." *Medical Aspects of Human Sexuality* (July, 1976):93–94.

Symonds, Carolyn. "Pilot Study of the Peripheral Behavior of Sexual Mate Swappers." M.A. Thesis, University of California at Riverside, 1968.

Szasz, Thomas. *Ceremonial Chemistry: The Ritual Persecution of Drugs, Addicts and Pushers.* New York: Doubleday/Anchor, 1975.

Talsimer, Isabel A.; Piotrow, P. T.; and Dumm, John J. "Condom — An Old Method Meets a New Social Need." *Population Reports,* H (1), (December, 1973).

Taylor, G. Rattray. *Sex in History.* New York: Harper & Row, 1970.

Temerlin, Maurice K. "My Daughter Lucy." *Psychology Today* 9 (1975):59–62.

Thomas, Elizabeth M. *The Harmless People.* New York: Vintage Books, 1959.

Thorpe, J.; Schmidt, E.; and Costell, D. "A Comparison of Positive and Negative Conditioning in the Treatment of Homosexuality." *Behavior Research and Therapy* 1 (1963):357–362.

Thorpe, Louis P.; Katz, Barney; and Lewis, Robert T. *Psychology of Abnormal Behavior.* New York: Ronald Press, 1961.

Tindall, Ralph H. "The Male Adolescent Involved with a Pederast Becomes an Adult." *Journal of Homosexuality* 3 (1978):373–382.

Toffler, Alvin. *Future Shock.* New York: Bantam Books, 1970.

Tolor, Alexander, and Di Grazia, Paul V. "Sexual Attitudes and Behavior Patterns During and Following Pregnancy." *Archives of Sexual Behavior* 5 (1976):539–551.

Topp, Darlys M. *Between Purple Cows and People.* M.A. Thesis, California State University, Sacramento, 1975.

Treas, J. "Aging and the Family." In *Aging,* edited by D. S. Woodruff and J. E. Birren, pp. 92–108. New York: D. Van Nostrand Co., 1975.

Tripp, C. A. *The Homosexual Matrix.* New York: McGraw-Hill, 1975.

Tuller, Neil R. "Couples: The Hidden Segment of the Gay World." *Journal of Homosexuality* 3 (1978):331–339.

Ullerstam, Lars. *The Erotic Minorities.* New York: Grove Press, 1966.

United Press International. "Woman Believed Pregnant 40 Years." *Davis Enterprise,* August 1, 1975.

U.S. Bureau of the Census. *Statistical Abstracts of the United States: 1973,* 94th ed. Washington, D.C.: U.S. Government Printing Office, 1973.

U.S. Department of Health, Education and Welfare. *Monthly Vital Statistics Report: Final Divorce Statistics.* HRA 76-1120 (Vol. 24, No. 4), July 7, 1975.

U.S. Department of Health, Education and Welfare. *Monthly Vital Statistics Report: Births, Marriages, Divorces and Deaths.* HRA 76-1120, (Vol. 24, No. 9), November 21, 1975.

Van den Haag, Ernest. "Love or Marriage." *Harper's Magazine* (May, 1962).

Vanderpool, John P., and White, Robert B. "Psychiatry and the Abortion Problem." *Texas Medicine* 64 (1968):48–51.

Van der Vlugt, Theresa, and Piotrow, P. T. "Menstrual Regulation — What Is It?" *Population Reports,* F (2), 1973, F-9 to F-23.

Van der Vlugt, Theresa, and Piotrow, P. T. "Menstrual Regulation Update," *Population Reports,* F (4), 1974, F-49 to F-64.

Van Deusen, Edmund L. *Contract Cohabitation.* New York: Grove Press, 1974.

Van de Velde, Theodore H. *Ideal Marriage, Its Physiology and Technique.* New York: Random House, 1968. Originally published in 1926.

Van Keep, Pieter A., and Gregory, Ann. "Sexual Relations in the Aging Female." In *Handbook of Sexology IV: Selected Personal and Social Issues,* edited by John Money and Herman Musaph, pp. 839–846. New York: Elsevier, 1977.

Varni, Charles A. "An Exploratory Study of Spouse-Swapping." *Pacific Sociological Review* 15 (1972):507–522.

Vener, Arthur M.; Stewart, Cyrus S.; and Hager, David L. "The Sexual Behavior of Adolescents in Middle America: Generational and American-British Comparisons." *Journal of Marriage and the Family* 34 (1972):696–704.

Verwoedt, Adriaan; Pfeiffer, Eric; and Hsioh-Shan, Wang. "Sexual Behavior in Senescence: I. Changes in Sexual Activity and Interest in Aging Men and Women." *Journal of Geriatric Psychiatry* 2 (1969):163.

Vessey, M. P., and Doll, R. "Investigation of Relation Between Use of Oral Contraceptives and Thromboembolic Disease." *British Medical Journal* 2 (1968):199–205.

Voigt, K. D., and Schmidt, H. "Sex and the Involution of the Genitals in the Aging Male." In *Handbook of Sexology IV: Selected Personal and Social Issues,* edited by John Money and Herman Musaph, pp. 825–838. New York: Elsevier, 1977.

Vreeland, Rebecca S. "Sex at Harvard." *Sexual Behavior* 2 (1972):72–77.

Wagner, Nathaniel. "Sexual Activity and the Cardiac Patient." In *Human Sexuality,* edited by Richard Green, pp. 173–180. Baltimore: Williams and Wilkins, 1975.

Wahl, Charles W., ed. *Sexual Problems: Diagnosis and Treatment in Medical Practice.* New York: Free Press, 1967.

Wake, F. R. "Attitudes of Parents Towards the Premarital Sex Behavior of Their Children and Themselves." *Journal of Sex Research* 5 (1969):170–171.

Walker, Edward L. *Conditioning and Instrumental Learning.* Belmont, Calif.: Brooks/Cole Publishing Co., 1969.

Walker, Marcia J., and Brodsky, Stanley L. *Sexual Assault.* Lexington, Massachusetts: D. C. Heath, 1976.

Wallace, Douglas, and Wehmer, Gerald. "Evaluation of Visual Erotica by Sexual Liberals and Conservatives." *Journal of Sex Research* 8 (1972):147.

Waller, Willard. *The Old Love and the New: Divorce and Readjustment.* Carbondale: Southern Illinois University Press, 1967.

Walshok, Mary L. "The Emergence of Middle Class Deviant Subcultures." *Social Problems* 18 (1971):82–89.

Walster, Elaine, and Berscheid, Ellen. "Adrenalin Makes the Heart Grow Fonder." *Psychology Today* 5 (1971):46–49.

Walster, Elaine; Traupmann, Jane; and Walster, G. William. "Equity and Extramarital Sexuality." *Archives of Sexual Behavior* 7 (1978):127–138.

Wanderer, Zev W. "Instrumentation and Motion Pictures of Behavior Therapy." Paper presented to the Society for the Scientific Study of Sex, November 3–5, 1972.

Ward, David A., and Kassebaum, Gene G. *Women's Prison: Sex and Social Structure.* Chicago: Aldine Publishing Co., 1965.

Warren, Carol A. B. *Identity and Community in the Gay World.* New York: John Wiley & Sons, 1974.

Warren, Carol A. B. "Women Among Men: Females in the Male Homosexual Community." *Archives of Sexual Behavior* 5 (1976):157–169.

Warren, Carol A. B., and Ponse, Barbara. "The Existential Self and the Gay World." In *Existential Sociology,* edited by Jack D. Douglas. Cambridge, Massachusetts: Harvard University Press, forthcoming.

Warwick, Donald P. "Tearoom Trade: Means and Ends in Social Research." *The Hastings Center Studies* 1(1), (1973):27–38.

Watson, John B. *Behaviorism.* Chicago: University of Chicago Press, 1958.

Weideger, Paula. "Diaphragms: A New Look at the Old Standby." *Ms. Magazine* 4 (2), (1975):101, 103–104.

Weinberg, Jack. "Sexuality in Later Life." *Medical Aspects of Human Sexuality* 5 (1971):216, 223, 226–227.

Weinberg, Samuel Kerson. *Incest Behavior.* New York: Citadel Press, 1955.

Welch, Gary J., and Granvold, Ronald K. "Seminars for Separated/Divorced: An Educational Approach to Postdivorce Adjustment." *Journal of Sex and Marital Therapy* 3 (1977):31–39.

Wells, John W. *Beyond Group Sex.* New York: Dell Books, 1972.

West, Donald J. *Homosexuality.* Chicago: Aldine Publishing Co., 1968.

West, Donald J. "Bisexual Chic: Anyone Goes." *Newsweek* (May 27, 1974).

Westoff, Charles F. "Recent Trends in Attitudes Toward Fertility Control and in the Practice of Contraception in the United States." In *Fertility and Family Planning: A World View,* edited by S. J. Behrman, Leslie Corsa, and Donald Freedman, pp. 48–57. Ann Arbor: University of Michigan Press, 1969.

Westoff, Charles F. "The Modernization of U.S. Contraceptive Practice." *Family Planning Perspectives* 4 (1972):9–12.

Westoff, Leslie A., and Westoff, Charles F. *From Now to Zero.* Boston: Little, Brown & Co., 1971.

White, Karol. "Undoing a Previous Commitment: Reversed Surgical Sterilization." *Science Digest* (May, 1980):26–29.

Whitehurst, Robert N. "Violence Potential in Extramarital Sexual Behavior." *Journal of Marriage and the Family* 33 (1971):683.

Whitehurst, Robert N. "The Monogamous Ideal and Sexual Realities." In *Renovating Marriage,* edited by Roger W. Libby and Robert N. Whitehurst, pp. 38–47. Danville, Calif.: Consensus Publishers, 1973.

Wilensky, Harold L. "Trends in Amount of Time Worked." *Social Problems* 9 (1961): 32–56.

Williams, Juanita H. "Sexuality in Marriage." In *Handbook of Human Sexuality,* edited by Benjamin B. Wolman and John Money, pp. 93–121. Englewood Cliffs, New Jersey: Prentice-Hall, 1980.

Willis, Stanley. "Sexual Promiscuity as a Symptom of Anxiety." In *Sexual Problems: Diagnosis and Treatment in Medical Practice,* edited by Charles W. Wahl, pp. 172–191. New York: Free Press, 1967.

Willis, Terry. "Birth Control in Colonial America." Unpublished paper prepared for History Master's Program. Sacramento: California State University, 1975a.

Willis, Terry. "Woman's Right to Choose." Unpublished paper prepared for History Master's Program. Sacramento: California State University, 1975b.

Willis, Terry, and Anderson, Marian. "The Flag and the Fetus." Mimeo discussion guide prepared to accompany slide-sound show on abortion, Sacramento City College, 1975.

Wills, Garry. "Measuring the Impact of Erotica." *Psychology Today* (August, 1977):30–34.

Wilson, J. B., and Meyers, Everett. *Wife Swapping: A Complete Eight-Year Survey of Morals of North America.* New York: Counterpoint, Inc., 1965.

Wilson, W. Cody. *Presidential Report of the Commission on Obscenity and Pornography.* San Diego, Calif.: Greenleaf Classics, 1970.

Wilson, W. Cody. "Facts vs. Fears: Why Should We Worry About Pornography?" *Annals of the American Academy of Political and Social Science* 397 (1971):105–117.

Wilson, W. Cody. "The 'Porn' Industry." *Medical Aspects of Human Sexuality* 7 (1971):92–97.

Wilson, W. Cody. "The Distribution of Selected Sexual Attitudes and Behaviors Among the Adult Population of the United States." *Journal of Sex Research* 11 (1975):46–64.

Winch, Robert S. "Permanence and Change in the History of the American Family and Some Speculations as to the Future." *Journal of Marriage and Family* 3 (1970):173–179.

Winick, Charles. "Prostitutes' Clients' Perception of the Prostitutes and of Themselves." *International Journal of Social Psychiatry* 8 (1962):289–297.

Winick, Charles. "A Neuter and Desexualized Society." In *The New Sexual Revolution,* edited by Lester A. Kirkendall and Robert N. Whitehurst. New York: Donald W. Brown, 1971.

Winick, Charles, and Kinsie, Paul M. "Prostitution." *Sexual Behavior* 3 (1973):33–39.

Winthrop, Henry. "Future of Sexual Revolution." *Diogenes* 70:42–47.

Wolfe, Linda. "The Question of Surrogates in Sex Therapy." *New York Magazine* (December 17, 1973):28–31.

Woody, Robert H. "Integrated Aversion Therapy and Psychotherapy: Two Sexual Deviation Case Studies." *Journal of Sex Research* 9 (1973):313–324.

Woolston, Howard B. *Prostitution in the United States.* Montclair, New Jersey: Patterson Smith, 1969.

Wortman, J. "Vasectomy — What Are the Problems?" *Population Reports,* Ser. D.1, January, 1975.

Wortman, J., and Piotrow, P. T. "Laparoscopic Sterilization — A New Technique." *Population Reports,* Ser. C. 1, January, 1973.

Wortman, J., and Piotrow, P. T. "Vasectomy — Old and New Techniques." *Population Reports,* Ser. D.1, December, 1973.

Wright, Barry. *Better Life Monthly.* Membership Form.

Wyden, Peter, and Wyden, Barbara. *Inside the Sex Clinic.* Cleveland: World Publishing Co., 1971.

Young, Wayland. "Prostitution." In *Observations of Deviance,* edited by Jack D. Douglas. New York: Random House, 1970.

Young, William C.; Goy, Robert W.; and Phoenix, Charles H. "Hormones and Sexual Behavior." *Science* 143 (1964):212–218.

Zalk, Sue R., and Bittman, Sam. *Expectant Fathers.* New York: Hawthorn Books, 1979.

Zelnick, Melvin, and Kantner, John F. "Sexual and Contraceptive Experience of Young Unmarried Women in the United States, 1976 and 1971." *Family Planning Perspectives* 9 (1977):55–71.

Zilbergeld, Bernie. "Group Treatment Program for Sexually Dysfunctional Men." Paper presented at Western Regional Meeting of the Society for the Scientific Study of Sex, September 19–21, 1975.

Zilbergeld, Bernie. *Male Sexuality.* Boston: Little, Brown & Co., 1978.

Zilbergeld, Bernie, and Ellison, Carol. "Social Skills Training as an Adjunct to Sex Therapy." *Journal of Sex and Marital Therapy* 5 (1979):340–350.

Zilbergeld, Bernie, and Ellison, Carol. "Desire Discrepancies and Arousal Problems in Sex Therapy." In *Principles and Practices of Sex Therapy,* edited by Sandra Leiblum and Lawrence Pervin, pp. 65–103. New York: Guilford Press, 1980.

Zilbergeld, Bernie, and Evans, Michael. "A Critical Review of Masters and Johnson's Outcome Research." *Psychology Today* (August, 1980).

Ziskin, Jay, and Ziskin, Mae. *The Extramarital Sex Contract.* Los Angeles: Nash Publishers, 1973.

Zubin, Joseph, and Money, John. *Contemporary Sexual Behavior: Critical Issues in the 1970's.* Baltimore: Johns Hopkins University Press, 1973.

Zurcher, Louis A., and Kirkpatrick, R. George. *Citizens for Decency.* Austin: University of Texas Press, 1976.

Zurcher, Louis A., and Kirkpatrick, R. George. "Youth Values and Adolescent Sexuality." *American Educator* (Winter, 1979):5.

Name Index

I-3

Subject Index

Hysterectomy, 225, 346
Hysteroscopic sterilization, 227–228
Hysterotomy, 239

Id, 43
Ideal
adult love, 525–526
search for, 521
Identity
bisexual, 409–410
sexual versus gender, 388
see also Gender identity
Ignorance, sexual, and poor communication, 139
Implants, contraceptive, 555
Impotence (erectile dysfunction), 139–140
treatment of, 150–151
Imprinting, 52–53
Incest, 479
incidence of, 481–483
offenders, convicted, 479–480
in other cultures, 483
taboo, 483
genetic inbreeding, 483–484
intrafamily rivalry, 484
types of, 480
Inclusion, 548
Individual values, sexuality and, 536–537
Individuation, mate swapping and, 379
Industrialization, 13–16
Industrial Revolution, 9, 12
Infancy
sensual-sexual development in, 273–274
sexual activities in childhood and, 279–288
Infatuation, love and, 513
In-home tests, to detect pregnancy, 175–176
Insertor-insertee roles, in homosexual fellatio, 397–398
Instinctive behavior, 53
Interfemoral intercourse, 397
International Committee for Contraception Research, 554–555
International Planned Parenthood Federation Central Medical Committee, 212
Interracial sex, 34–36
Intimacy
adolescent, 525
adult love and, 526–527
Intrauterine devices (IUDs), 184, 212, 213, 216

advantages of, 219
disadvantages of, 218–219
expulsion of, 218
failure rate of, 218
function of, 217
insertion of, 218
and pregnancy, 219
types of, 216

Jealousy
exclusion, 517–518
fear, 517
mate swapping and, 379
possessive, 517

Keeton v. *State of Texas,* 503
Kissing, 107
"French," 300
"soul," 300
Klismaphilia, 439

Labia majora, 63–64
Labia minora, 63–64
Labor, *see* Childbirth
Laboratory tests, to detect pregnancy, 175
Laminaria, 236
Laparoscopy, 227
Last Tango in Paris, 468
Learned behavior, 53–54
Legal nonconsent, 471
Leisure, trend toward, 544–545
Lesbianism, 400–401
bars, 406–407
and definition of self, 401–402
life style, 407–408
organizations and communities, 405–406
and prostitution, 447
relations between gay males and lesbians, 408
roles and activities, 403–404
social roles, 405
Leukorrhea, 220
Leydig (or interstitial) cells, 74, 75
Libido, 44, 50, 61
of adulthood, 47
autoerotic aspect of, 46
defined, 43
ego, 43, 47

I-14

Pornography *(cont.)*
  purpose of, 459
    masturbation, 459–460
    money making, 459
  Sexual Freedom League's position on obscenity and, 533–534
Positions, for coitus, 118–119
  man above, 119–120
  rear-entry, 121
  side-by-side, 121
  variations in, 121
  woman above, 120
Possessive love, 517–518
"Post-op" transsexuals, 418
Power struggles, in sexual relationships, 138–139
Pragma, 515, 516
Pregnancy, 173
  conception, 173–174
    breast changes, 174
    fatigue, 175
    frequency of urination, 174–175
    in-home tests, 175–176
    laboratory tests, 175
    nausea, 175
    pelvic exam, 176
  cultural attitudes toward, 164, 165
  ectopic, 175, 184
  and IUDs, 219
  and marital relationship, 179–180
    changes in sexual attitudes, 180–182
    intercourse during pregnancy, 182
    physical changes, 180
    potential hazards, 182–183
    sexual techniques, 183
    uterine contractions, 183–184
  Rh blood factor and, 185
  stages of, 176
    first trimester, 176
    second trimester, 176
    third trimester, 176–179
  surrogate, 551–552
Premarital sex
  attitudes toward, 306
  social class and, 24–25
Premature ejaculation, 128, 140–141
  treatment of, 147–149
Premenstrual syndrome, 171
"Pre-op" transsexuals, 416–417
Prepuce
  for clitoris, 64

of penis, 79
Priapism, 80, 81
Progestasert, 216
Progesterone, 75, 97
  discovery of, 200
  and menstruation, 169, 170
  production of, by ovaries, 70, 96
Progestin, 200–201, 341
  imbalance, 221
Projection, love and, 522
Promiscuity, 426
  defined, 426, 427
  psychological perspective on, 427
  sex drive and frequency of intercourse, 426–427
"Prophylactics," 208
Prostaglandins, 77, 217, 239
Prostate, 75, 77–78
Prostatectomy, 346
Prostitutes, prostitution, 443–444
  female, career of, 447–448
    customers, 451
    entry, 448
    income and expenses, 450
    pimps, 448–450
    sexuality, 451–452
    termination, 452
    training, 450–451
  female, and social class, 446
    lesbian, 447
    lower-class, 447
    middle-class, 447
  female, types of, 444
    in brothels, 445
    call girls, 446
    in massage parlors, 445–446
    streetwalkers, 444–445
  male heterosexual, 452–453
  male homosexual, 453
    gay hustlers, 454
    "heterosexual" hustlers, 453
  male homosexual organizations, 454
    masseur agencies, 454
    modeling agencies, 454
    steam baths, 454–456
  and sadomasochism, 500
  and society, 456
    adaptation to stigma, 458–459
    religious rituals, 456
    stigmatization, 457–458
    tolerance, 456